T0345039

Machine Vision and Industrial Robotics in Manufacturing

This book covers the basics of machine vision and robotics in the manufacturing industry. Major applicability of intelligent machines and robotics in the manufacturing sector are explored in three major areas of product traceability, remote product-monitoring, supply chain, logistics, and product record management. *Machine Vision and Industrial Robotics in Manufacturing: Approaches, Technologies, and Applications* explains advanced technologies based on Artificial Intelligence and Industrial Internet of Things related to smart manufacturing applications.

The book introduces the emerging machines and robotics applications that are enabling smart factories initiatives worldwide. The chapters examine labor productivity, factory device installation, and defective product detection. The authors share modern models, emerging technologies, designs, frameworks, theories, practices, and sustainable approaches to design and implement machine vision with industrial robotics. They also examine the challenging issues associated with the leveraging of technologies related to machine vision, computer vision, robotics, Internet of Things, Industrial Internet of Things technologies, Artificial Intelligence-equipped machines, applications, and automatic techniques for intelligent manufacturing systems and smart factory infrastructure in the era of Industry 4.0 manufacturing. The authors also examine topics such as the role of existing management and production solutions, their limitations, and future directions in manufacturing industry.

This book targets a mixed audience of students, engineers, scholars, researchers, academics, and professionals who are learning, researching, and working in the fields of machine vision, Artificial Intelligence, Industrial Internet of Things, computer vision, and robotic technologies from different industries and economics.

Machine Vision and Industrial Robotics in Manufacturing

Approaches, Technologies, and Applications

Edited by
Alex Khang, Vugar Abdullayev Hajimahmud,
Anuradha Misra, and Eugenia Litvinova

CRC Press
Taylor & Francis Group
Boca Raton London New York

CRC Press is an imprint of the
Taylor & Francis Group, an **informa** business

Designed cover image: © Shutterstock

First edition published 2025
by CRC Press
2385 NW Executive Center Drive, Suite 320, Boca Raton FL 33431

and by CRC Press
4 Park Square, Milton Park, Abingdon, Oxon, OX14 4RN

CRC Press is an imprint of Taylor & Francis Group, LLC

ISBN: 978-1-032-56597-2 (hbk)
ISBN: 978-1-032-57164-5 (pbk)
ISBN: 978-1-003-43813-7 (ebk)

DOI: 10.1201/9781003438137

Typeset in Times
by KnowledgeWorks Global Ltd.

Contents

About the Editors

Alex Khang, D.Sc., D.Litt., is a professor of Information technology, an AI and data scientist and senior portfolio manager at the Global Research Institute of Technology and Engineering, Raleigh, North Carolina. He has more than 28 years of experience in teaching computer and data science at universities and other institutions in Vietnam, India, and the United States. He has held the titles of software product manager, data engineer, AI engineer, cloud computing architect, solution architect, software architect, and database expert working for international corporations in Germany, Sweden, and Singapore, among others. He has published 74 Scopus-indexed documents, 54 authored books (on software development), 25 edited books, and 50 book chapters, in addition to upcoming projects, in the field of artificial intelligence. ORCID: 0000-0001-8379-4659.

Vugar Abdullayev Hajimahmud, D.Sc., is an associate professor at Azerbaijan University of Architecture and Construction and Azerbaijan State Oil and Industry University, Baku. He is author of 61 scientific papers. His research is related to the study of cyber–physical systems, Internet of Things, Big Data, smart city, and information technologies. He has published four book chapters and two edited books in healthcare ecosystems. ORCID: 0000-0002-3348-2267.

Anuradha Misra, D.Sc., is assistant professor at Amity University, Uttar Pradesh, Lucknow Campus, India. She has taught in higher education for the past 14 years. She is member of professional organizations such as IAENG and IET (UK), a lifetime member of AUN Research Labs, and a member of IEDRC. She has edited and reviewed various referred and peer-reviewed journals. She has presented various papers in different national and international conferences. ORCID: 0000-0002-7479-7636.

Eugenia Litvinova, D.Sc., is professor at Kharkov National University of Radio Electronics, Ukraine. Her research areas include: Digital systems testing and testable design, SOC design verification, and brain-like computing, computer-aided system for logic simulation, test generation, and fault diagnosis of digital devices and systems. She has been a member of an organizing committee of IEEE East-West Design & Test Symposium since 2007. She also is an assistant editor of the scientific journal *Radio Electronics and Informatics*. She has published more than 240 publications, including 9 books, and 90 Scopus-indexed documents. ORCID: 0000-0002-9797-5271.

Contributors

Gardashova Latafat Abbas
Department of Science and Technology
Azerbaijan State Oil and Industry
  University
Baku, Azerbaijan

Shalom Akhai
Chandigarh College of Engineering
CGC Jhanjeri
Mohali, Punjab, India

Ragimova Nazila Ali
Department of Science and Technology
Azerbaijan State Oil and Industry
  University
Baku, Azerbaijan

Abuzarova Vusala Alyar
Department of Educated Information
  Technologies
Azerbaijan State Oil and Industry
  University
Baku, Azerbaijan

Gobinath Arumugam
Department of Information Technology
Velammal College of Engineering and
  Technology
Madurai, Tamil Nadu, India

Srinivasan Arumugam
Department of Information
  Technology
Velammal College of Engineering and
  Technology
Madurai, Tamil Nadu, India

Zoran Avramovic
Faculty of Transport and Traffic
  Engineering
University of Belgrade
Belgrade, Serbia

Varini Awasthi
Pranveer Singh Institute of Technology
Kanpur, Uttar Pradesh, India

Manjula Devi Chithiraikannu
Department of Information Technology
Velammal College of Engineering and
  Technology
Madurai, Tamil Nadu, India

Taraprasanna Dash
Siksha O Anusandhan University,
  (Deemed to be University),
Bhubaneswar, Odisha, India

Namrata Dhanda
Department of Computer Science and
  Engineering
Amity University
Lucknow Campus, Uttar Pradesh,
  India

A. D. Dhass
Department of Computer Science
Indus University
Kanpur, Uttar Pradesh, India

Rishabh Didwania
Pranveer Singh Institute of Technology,
Kanpur, Uttar Pradesh, India

Khurshudov Dursun
Department of Computer Science
Azerbaijan University of Architecture
  and Construction
Baku, Azerbaijan

Matlab Khalilov Etibar
Department of Computer Science
Azerbaijan State Oil and Industry
  University
Baku, Azerbaijan

Jale Agazade Firudin
Department of Computer Science
Azerbaijan State Oil and Industry
University
Baku, Azerbaijan

Sapna Gambhir
Department of Computer Science
George Mason University
Fairfax, Virginia

Mahima Gupta
Department of Computer Science
Pranveer Singh Institute of
Technology
Kanpur, Uttar Pradesh, India

Sumita Gupta
Department of Computer Science &
Engineering
Amity University
Noida, India

Mammadov Kanan Hafiz
Department of Computer Science
Azerbaijan State Oil and Industry
University
Baku, Azerbaijan

Vladimir Hahanov
Design Automation Department
Kharkiv National University of Radio
Electronics
Kharkiv, Ukraine

Vugar Abdullayev Hajimahmud
Department of Computer Science
Azerbaijan University of Architecture
and Construction
Baku, Azerbaijan

Md. Halimuzzaman
School of Business
Galgotias University
Greater Noida, Uttar Pradesh,
India

Olena Hrybiuk
Faculty of Engineering, International
Science and Technology University
National Academy of Sciences
Kharkiv, Ukraine

Rashad İsmibeyli
Azerbaijan University of Architecture
and Construction
Baku, Azerbaijan

Karthika J.
Department of EEE
Sri Krishna College of Engineering,
Coimbatore, Tamil Nadu, India

Manohar Joshi
Department of Computer Science and
Engineering
Presidency University
Bangalore, Karnataka, India

Asgarov Taleh Kamran
Department of Computer Science
National Aviation Academy
Baku, Azerbaijan

Alex Khang
Department of AI and Data Science
Global Research Institute of Technology
and Engineering
Fort Raleigh, North Carolina

Amaresh Kumar
Department of Production and
Industrial Engineering
National Institute of Technology
Jamshedpur, Jharkhand,
India

Bhupendra Kumar
School of Computer Science and
Applications
IIMT University
Meerut, Uttar Pradesh,
India

Ganesh Babu L.
Department of Computer Science
Tishk International University
Erbil, Iraq

Priya L.
Department of IT
Rajalakshmi Engineering
    College
Thandalam, Chennai, India

Anandan Malaiarasan
Department of Electronics and
    Communication Engineering
Vel Tech Rangarajan Dr. Sagunthala
    R&D Institute of Science and
    Technology
Chennai, Tamil Nadu, India

Srimant Kumar Mishra
Department of Mechanical
    Engineering
GIET University
Gunupur, Odisha, India

Gopal Kurushna Mohanty
Department of Mechanical
    Engineering
GIET University
Gunupur, Odisha, India

Muthmainnah Muthmainnah
English Department
Universitas Al Asyariah Mandar
Sulawesi Barat, Indonesia

Ankita Nayak
Transtrack Aeroservices (P) Ltd.
Bhubaneswar, Odisha, India

Arpita Nayak
School of Management
Kalinga Institute of Industrial
    Technology
Bhubaneswar, Odisha, India

Suresh Kumar Natarajan
Department of Civil Engineering
Kalasalingam Academy of Research
    and Education
Krishnankoil, Tamil Nadu, India

M. S. Nidhya
Department of Computer Science &
    Information Technology
Jain Deemed-to-be University
Bangalore, Karnataka, India

Yitong Niu
School of Aeronautical Engineering
Anyang University
Anyang, China

Kumar P.
Department of Information Technology
Rajalakshmi Engineering College,
Thandalam, Chennai, India

Reshma P.
Department of Electronics and
    Communication Engineering
Presidency University
Bangalore, Karnataka, India

Rajeswari Packianathan
Department of Electronics and
    Communication Engineering
Velammal College of Engineering and
    Technology
Madurai, Tamil Nadu, India

Manas Ranjan Panda
Department of Mechanical Engineering
GIET University
Gunupur, Odisha, India

Dhiren R. Patel
Department of Electronics and
    Communication Engineering
Indus University
Ahmedabad, Gujarat, India

Atmika Patnaik
School of Management
Kalinga Institute of Industrial
   Technology
Bhubaneswar, Odisha, India

B. C. M. Patnaik
School of Management
Kalinga Institute of Industrial
   Technology
Bhubaneswar, Odisha, India

Prabin Kumar Patnaik
Department of Mechanical Engineering
GIET University
Gunupur, Odisha, India

Prashasti Pritiprada
School of Management
Kalinga Institute of Industrial
   Technology
Bhubaneswar, Odisha, India

Roheen Qamar
Quaid-e-Awam University of
   Engineering, Sciences & Technology
Shaheed Benazirabad, Sindh, Pakistan

Pavithra Devi R.
Department of Information Technology
Velammal College of Engineering and
   Technology
Madurai, Tamil Nadu, India

J. A. Raja
Department of Management Studies
The Oxford College of Business
   Management
Bengaluru, Karnataka, India

Kali Charan Rath
Department of Mechanical
   Engineering
GIET University
Gunupur, Odisha, India

Ipseeta Satpathy
School of Management
Kalinga Institute of Industrial
   Technology
Bhubaneswar, Odisha, India

Suresh Kumar Satapathy
Senior VP and Chief Business
   Development Officer
Gurgaon, Haryana, India

Hammad Shahab
Institute of Computer and Software
   Engineering
Khwaja Fareed University of
   Engineering and Information
   Technology
Rahim Yar Khan, Punjab,
   Pakistan

Jaideep Sharma
School of Business
Galgotias University
Greater Noida, Uttar Pradesh,
   India

Kewal Krishan Sharma
School of Computer Science and
   Applications
IIMT University
Meerut, Uttar Pradesh,
   India

Vikas Sharma
School of Computer Science and
   Applications
IIMT University
Meerut, Uttar Pradesh, India

Gurwinder Singh
Department of Computer Science and
   Engineering,
Apex Institute of Technology (CSE),
   Chandigarh University,
Chandigarh, Punjab, India

Vasila Abbasova Soltanaga
Department of Computer Science
Azerbaijan State Oil and Industry
  University
Baku, Azerbaijan

Maciej Szafrański
Faculty of Engineering, International
  Science and Technology
  University
National Academy of Sciences
Kyiv, Ukraine

Saikumar Tara
Department of ECE
BVRIT Hyderabad College of
  Engineering for Women,
Hyderabad, Telangana, India

Triwiyanto
Department of Medical Electronics
  Technology
Poltekkes Kemenkes Surabaya
Surabaya, Jawa Timur, Indonesia

Mohd Umar
Department of Computer Science
Pranveer Singh Institute of Technology
Kanpur, Uttar Pradesh, India

R. Vani
Department of Management
S.I.V.E.T College
Chennai, Tamil Nadu, India

Tarun Kumar Vashishth
School of Computer Science and
  Applications
IIMT University,
Meerut, Uttar Pradesh, India

Olena Vedishcheva
Faculty of Engineering, International
  Science and Technology University
National Academy of Sciences
Kyiv, Ukraine

Rajat Verma
Department of Computer Science
Pranveer Singh Institute of
  Technology
Kanpur, Uttar Pradesh, India

Muhammad Mohsin Waqas
Department of Agricultural
  Engineering
Khwaja Fareed University of
  Engineering and Information
  Technology
Rahim Yar Khan, Punjab, Pakistan

Baqar Ali Zardari
Department of Sciences &
  Technology
Quaid-e-Awam University of
  Engineering
Shaheed Benazirabad, Sindh,
  Pakistan

Preface

Most recent developments of information technology in manufacturing are related to machine vision (MV), computer vision (CV), artificial intelligence (AI), Internet of Things (IoT), Industrial Internet of Things (IIoT), and robotics, which aim to connect the physical and intelligent digital worlds and make it possible for machines and humans to communicate using the computer. IIoT technologies equipped with MV and AI have a wide range of uses in practically every manufacturing industry, including smart factories, smart cities, smart transportation, and smart healthcare.

Machine vision and robotics are two new technologies that combine machines and autonomous systems in different ways. A factory where humans and devices interact is created by integrating communication technologies, sensing technologies, Internet protocol, embedded devices, pervasive computing, and ubiquitous monitoring. In smart factories, large amounts of linked devices and data present new prospects for developing services that can directly benefit the management, working environment, and individual workers.

The goal of this book is to share with readers modern models, emerging technologies, designs, frameworks, theories, practices, and sustainable approaches related to machine and CV, AI, IoT, IIoT, robotics, and automatic techniques for intelligent systems and smart factory infrastructure in Industry 4.0 manufacturing.

This book targets a mixed audience of students, engineers, scholars, researchers, academics, and professionals who are learning, researching, and working in the field of artificial intelligence and IoT technologies from different industries and economics. Happy reading!

Alex Khang, Vugar Abdullayev Hajimahmud,
Anuradha Misra, Eugenia Litvinova

Acknowledgments

Machine Vision and Industrial Robotics in Manufacturing: Approaches, Technologies, and Applications is based on the design and implementation of topics related to machine vision and robotics, which are two new technologies that combine machines and autonomous systems. A factory where humans and devices interact is created by integrating communication technologies, sensing technologies, Internet protocol, embedded devices, pervasive computing, and ubiquitous monitoring. In smart factories, large amounts of linked devices and data present new prospects for developing services that can directly benefit management, working environments, and individual workers in Industry 4.0.

The editors planned and designed this book for readers across the globe and are thankful for the contributors whose efforts, knowledge, skills, expertise, enthusiasm, collaboration, and trust made it a reality. The valued chapter contributors came from different academic backgrounds including: human resource managers, talent management leaders, experts, professors, scientists, engineers, scholars, postgraduate students, educators, and academic colleagues.

Thanks go to all respected reviewers with whom we had the opportunity to collaborate remotely; we acknowledge their tremendous support and valuable comments not only for the book but also for future book projects.

We also express our deep gratitude for all discussion, advice, support, motivation, sharing, collaboration, and inspiration we received from our faculty, contributors, educators, professors, scientists, scholars, engineers, and academic colleagues.

Last, we are grateful to our publisher CRC Press (Taylor & Francis Group) for the wonderful support in processing the manuscript and bringing this book to readers in a timely manner.

**Alex Khang, Vugar Abdullayev Hajimahmud,
Anuradha Misra, and Eugenia Litvinova**

1 Role of Machine Vision in Manufacturing and Industrial Revolution 4.0

Alex Khang, Vugar Abdullayev Hajimahmud, Ragimova Nazila Ali, Vladimir Hahanov, Zoran Avramovic, and Triwiyanto

1.1 INTRODUCTION

1.1.1 MANUFACTURING

The meaning of manufacturing is similarly explained in different dictionaries as follows:

- A business or industry that produces large quantities of goods in factories, among others.
- To process or make (a product) from raw materials, especially as a large-scale operation using machinery.
- Making goods or articles by hand or by machine, especially on a large scale.

Manufacturing has recently been known as a machine-assisted process, as the above definitions suggest, and it continues to evolve, especially with intelligent machines. As a final definition, manufacturing is a process that includes all stages of product production as a result of the processing of raw materials with the help of human labor or machines. The manufacturing industry includes many different areas. This industry can be divided into three types:

- Basic materials
- Processing and assembly
- Life-related

Each industry type covers different areas separately as discussed below.

1.1.1.1 Basic Materials Industry

- Wood construction and wood products
- Pulp, paper, and processed paper products
- Chemical
- Oil and coal products

DOI: 10.1201/9781003438137-1

1

- Plastic products
- Rubber products
- Ceramics, earthenware, and stone products
- Steel
- Non-ferrous metal products
- Long-term product image businesses

1.1.1.2　Processing and Assembly Industry

- General equipment
- Electrical equipment
- Transport equipment
- Precision tools

1.1.1.3　Life-Related Industry

- Food
- Beverage/Tobacco/Fodder
- Textile
- Clothing and other textiles
- Furniture and equipment
- Industries related to publishing and printing
- Tanned leather, leather goods, and fur
- Other production

Worldwide, electronic equipment (computer, telephone, and television, among others) and automobile manufacturing industries are more extensive. Countries with the largest manufacturing industries in the world in 2023 are listed in Table 1.1 (Sandoval et al., 2018).

The advanced level of the manufacturing industry in countries is one of the main factors contributing to their development both in terms of economic and general

TABLE 1.1

Top 10 Manufacturing Countries in 2023

No.	Countries	Manufacturing Industry (%)
1	China	28.4
2	USA	16.6
3	Japan	7.2
4	Germany	5.8
5	India	3.3
6	South Korea	3.0
7	Italy	2.3
8	France	1.9
9	Great Britain	1.8
10	Mexico	1.5

strength. So, considering China's current situation, it is possible to say that, very soon, China may become the leading country in economic and other strategic aspects. Today, it is common to find "Made in China" products in the markets of many countries. In simple words, it is a key indicator of China's hegemony in the manufacturing industry.

When the question "why manufacturing is important" is asked, it is important to show the statistics mentioned above and to also talk about how the manufacturing industry directly impacts the development of countries—especially economic development—and raises the level of its well-being and that of its citizens. Thus, the expansion of the manufacturing sector, or the opening (commissioning) of factories, plants, and production enterprises in many areas, has a positive effect on a country's development for the following reasons:

- Increasing the number of jobs and preventing unemployment and poverty
- Increasing the state budget
- More active foreign and domestic markets

The above shows the importance of the manufacturing industry to both the people and the government.

1.1.2 INDUSTRIAL REVOLUTIONS

Manufacturing is a concept and act that has existed for many years. Production was carried out in the early times by special craftsmen where mainly handwork prevailed. The early manufacturing era, where human labor was more abundant, began to improve and evolve over time with the Industrial Revolution.

Mankind has witnessed four Industrial Revolutions. The world is currently preparing to transition to the 5th Industrial Revolution. Industrial revolutions play a great role in the history of production. Below is a list of the Industrial Revolutions and their main characteristics.

- First Industrial Revolution (1760s): The transition from agriculture to the industrial sector began during this period in England. During this period, coal was discovered, mass mining began, and the steam engine was introduced into the industry. Various production machines were invented. Briefly, manual labor was replaced by machine power for the first time. It soon spread to the United States and Europe. The keyword of this period is "coal," and the main discovery is the "steam engine."
- Second Industrial Revolution (1870s): This period is the basic technology period. It is related to the discovery and application of gas, oil, energy, and of primary technologies. During this period, communication technology was developed and mass production was carried out for the first time. The keyword of this period is "gas/energy/technology," and the main discovery is the "fuel engine."
- Third Industrial Revolution (1960s): The discovery and development of nuclear technology and the first digital technologies began during this

period. Mechanical electrical calculators, computers, and digital communication equipment were invented and improved. Early Artificial Intelligence (AI) technologies began to be studied. In production, these newly discovered technologies began to be applied. In this period, technologies were already applied in everyday life, not only in production. The keyword of this era is "digital technology."

- Fourth Industrial Revolution (2000s): This period is currently underway. It is an era of high-level technology and the replacement of human power with machine power. It was first proposed in 2011 as Industry 4.0. Concepts like smart devices, the Internet of Things, cyber-physical-social systems, databases, process automation, and digitalization, among others are the foundations of this period. Here, the human worker is secondary, and many processes are performed by robots/machines. Smart City, Smart Village, and Smart Home projects have been implemented during this period. This era is known as the era of "smart technologies."

- Fifth Industrial Revolution (near future): This period is an advanced version of Industry 4.0, the creation of fully autonomous machines while supporting the coexistence of humans and intelligent machines. It places the person at the center of the system. The Smart Society Project will form the basis of the 5th Industrial Revolution. On the other hand, the concept of cyber-physical-social systems will often be used here. This period is characterized by the future of robotics.

As seen from the above list, along with the Fourth Industrial Revolution, new technologies, especially smart ones, have begun to be integrated into the production environment. At present, smart technologies have been integrated into many sectors, not only manufacturing, and have achieved high, productive results.

1.1.3 SMART TECHNOLOGIES IN MANUFACTURING

Like humans, computers, robots, or machines use different tools to see. If the main visual instrument (organ) of a person is the eye, then in machines and computers it is a camera-like tool. The first technology and vision ability that comes to mind when we think of the vision of the computer is known as Computer Vision technology (Javaid et al., 2021). Computer Vision technology can simulate the process of human vision at a very high level and can be applied in a wide range of areas as shown in Figure 1.1.

Computer Vision, like a person, can get information from an image that it sees live in real-time, and at the same time, it can also get instant information by analyzing past images or videos (objects) that it has seen and stored in its memory (Liao & Pei, 2011).

From this point of view, Computer Vision technology has a very broad character and generality. Another technology that is very similar to Computer Vision and is often treated as the same concept is Machine Vision. Machine Vision technology, like Computer Vision, can analyze images and videos and extract useful information from them. At the same time, there are many similarities between their components

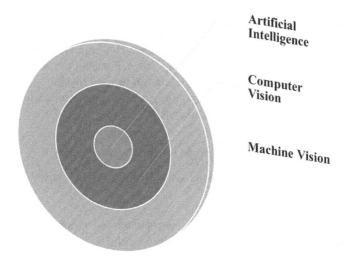

Artificial Intelligence

Computer Vision

Machine Vision

FIGURE 1.1   Smart technologies in manufacturing.

(Deac et al., 2017). Both use cameras and sensors, and both perform similar processes such as pattern recognition and object detection, among others.

However, there are some differences between these two "similar" technologies. Before mentioning these differences, it is necessary to have detailed information about Machine Vision technology. Let's first look at the concept of Machine Vision, its explanations, and its definitions (Khang & Vladimir et al., 2024).

1.2   MACHINE VISION CONCEPT AND DEFINITIONS

Computer Vision is applied in various industries. One of the technologies that has this ability to be applied in industrial areas is Machine Vision technology (or system).

1.2.1   DEFINITIONS OF MACHINE VISION

There are several similar explanations and definitions for Machine Vision. Simply, Machine Vision is the vision system integrated into machines and equipment used in industry that "sees" what work these devices are doing and makes decisions accordingly. In other words, Machine Vision is intelligent systems that see the environment using sensors. It is an integrated intelligent system that uses the capabilities of a computer to see objects in the environment, obtain information about their state, analyze this information, and implement a decision-making process. Machine Vision is also known as Intelligent Vision (Kallen, 2016).

1.2.2   MACHINE VISION TECHNOLOGY

Machine Vision is mainly applied in specific areas, especially in manufacturing industries. Machine Vision uses cameras to capture visual information from the environment. It then processes the images using a combination of hardware and software and prepares the data for use in various applications. Machine Vision technology often uses special optics to acquire images. This approach allows to process, analyze, and measure certain features of the image. For example, a Machine Vision application as part of a manufacturing system can be used to analyze a specific feature of a part being produced on an assembly line. It can determine whether the part meets the quality criteria (Yasar & Lutkevitch, 2023).

1.2.3 Basic Concepts Related to Machine Vision

There are several concepts connected with Machine Vision which are discussed below:

- Imaging – This is one of the key concepts for any vision system because both Machine Vision and Computer Vision technologies work with images, which are the richest source of information.
- Analysis – The main step after obtaining images is to analyze them and extract useful information.
- Automatic (Autonomous) – Automation of processes is one of the main concepts for Machine Vision technology. Thus, Machine Vision carries out both internal and external processes such as monitoring, control, and data analysis, mainly autonomously. Human experts are needed in the general working principle of this technology.
- Data – Machine Vision works with data and this data plays an important role in the decision-making process. The system must be able to extract data from objects.
- Monitoring and Control – Machine Vision technology constantly monitors equipment, machines, and robots. It controls their working process, safety, and quality.
- Machine – A key concept related to Machine Vision is that of a "machine." This also shows the main difference between Computer Vision and Machine Vision.

1.3 APPLICATIONS OF MACHINE VISION

According to the basic concepts mentioned above, Machine Vision technology is used for various purposes in manufacturing industries. These are 11 main use cases of Machine Vision as shown in Figure 1.2.

Below are the functions and applications of Machine Vision in common use cases. There are many similarities between the use cases of Machine Vision and Computer Vision technology.

- **Object and Orientation Detection** – Detecting objects, their location, and orientation in (2- or 3-dimensional) space.
- **Measuring and Sorting** – Obtaining the exact size of objects. It characterizes the placement of points in the image and the measurement with the

Use cases of Machine Vision	Detection of objects and orientation
	Measurement and Sorting
	Defect detection
	Identification
	Counting
	Automated vision testing and measurement
	Control and monitoring
	Tracking
	Quality control
	Processing of material
	Data collection

FIGURE 1.2   Eleven use cases of Machine Vision.

help of those points. It characterizes the process of classifying and separating product parts according to attributes such as color, size, or shape.

- **Defect Detection** – Detecting defects in the object (or product): scratches, bends, surface defects, and others.
- **Identification** – Verifying that the product being manufactured is the product ordered. It is done by reading barcodes, various codes, numbers, or symbols. Inspection is the process of checking that all parts of the manufactured product are complete, without unwanted extra parts or defective parts.
- **Counting** – Determining that the number of products produced corresponds to the order. With Machine Vision, this process is automated and done faster.
- **Automated Vision Testing and Measurement** – Determining whether the correct data is visible to the product.
- **Control and Monitoring** – Automating the process of monitoring work processes, products, quality, employees, and equipment.
- **Tracking** – Monitoring of equipment and tools throughout the work process to ensure all the working parts of the equipment are operational.
- **Quality Control** – Inspecting parts of a manufactured product for any defects.
- **Product Processing** – After product preparation comes packing and routing it following given standards.
- **Data Collection** – Machine Vision entails pattern recognition, or the collection of data such as size, serial number, and others about a monitored object in real-time.

1.4   COMPONENTS AND FEATURES OF MACHINE VISION

When we think of Machine Vision, the first thing that comes to mind is its components. This is the basis of Machine Vision and is different from Computer Vision. Machine Vision components are very widely used parts of individual systems. These parts work together as a unit to create a Machine Vision system as shown in Figure 1.3 and the list below.

- **Illumination System** – Highlights the object to be inspected, in whole or in part, so that it can be clearly seen by the camera.
- **Lens** – Takes an image and sends it as light to the sensor.
- **Sensors** – Receive this image in the form of light, convert it into a digital image, and send it to the processing system.

Here, the sensor performs two processes. The first process is discussed above. The other is a sensor that starts even before the lighting system. So, when the object approaches, the sensor detects it, and then the lighting system is activated.

- **Processing System** – Several different algorithms are used here which check the image, analyze it, extract the necessary information, and make decisions based on data.
- **Communication System** – Sending input/output (I/O) signals and data via serial communication to the device that sends the data.

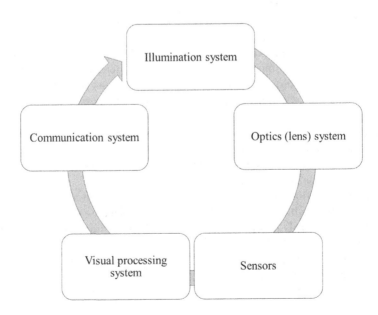

FIGURE 1.3   The main components of Machine Vision.

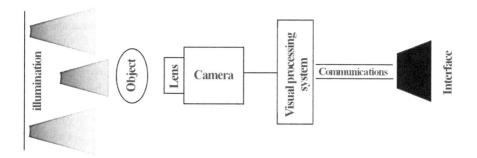

FIGURE 1.4   Structure of the Machine Vision system.

The working process of a sensor follows the below steps:

• The sensor detects the physical object, and the process starts.
• The object or part is illuminated by the sensor. The higher the quality of illumination, the better results will be obtained in subsequent processes.
• The camera (lens) turns on and takes a picture of the illuminated object or the desired part.
• The image captured by the camera consists mainly of a stream of light and is then converted into a digital image by a sensor (known as a frame grabber) and sent to an image-processing system.
• The image processing system uses various algorithms to extract the necessary information from the obtained image after it receives the image and analyzes it. This is the main data for decision-making.
• The obtained data is sent to the appropriate device. It is basically an interface that works for a person to see that information.

As mentioned earlier, each of these parts is used separately in different areas and is mainly a ready-made component. Together, they form the core components of a Machine Vision system. These parts and their location in the overall system are shown in Figure 1.4.

1.5 DIFFERENCES BETWEEN COMPUTER VISION AND MACHINE VISION TECHNOLOGY

Although Computer Vision and Machine Vision have similar characteristics, they also have fundamental differences as follows:

• Unlike Computer Vision, which can work separately, Machine Vision operates as part of a "machine" system in the implementation of the general business process.
• Although both technologies work on images, there are differences in the implementation of these processes. Machine Vision acquires real-time images with the help of cameras and sensors and analyzes these images

to obtain useful information for decision-making. Computer Vision can also work on images stored in memory or later loaded from a database or other data carriers and can get useful information from them. Computer Vision is the ability of computers to see because in addition to the real-time mode, they can work with images and videos stored in memory (Khang & Ragimova et al., 2024). In short, the main difference here is that Machine Vision operates in real-time mode and requires live capture.

• Computer Vision is used to obtain general information about an object. On the other hand, Machine Vision is mostly used to get information about a specific part of an object.

• Machine Vision is sometimes referred to as a subset of Computer Vision. This may be relatively true. In general, Machine Vision uses the capabilities of Computer Vision to implement processes.

1.6 APPLICATION AREAS OF MACHINE VISION

The application areas of Machine Vision are as wide as those of Computer Vision and they are shown in Figure 1.5.

Machine Vision and Computer Vision have similar advantages. With the help of Machine Vision, processes in production are automated, the flexibility and sustainability of the enterprise are increased, and product quality is improved. These processes save both time and money and increase efficiency. Security is also ensured by a high level of control and monitoring (Khang & Hajimahmud et al., 2024).

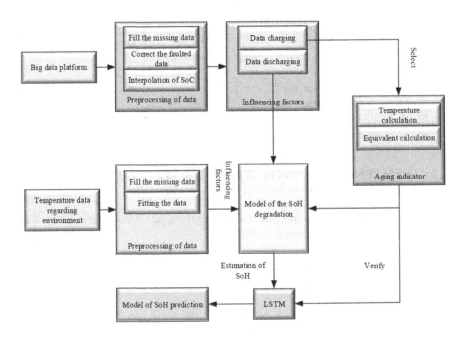

FIGURE 1.5   Illustration of the application areas of Machine Vision.

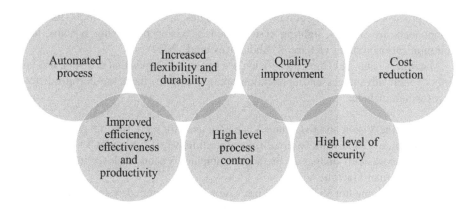

FIGURE 1.6   Machine Vision has several benefits in the areas where it is applied.

In addition, customer relations are improved. Timely preparation and delivery of the customer's order increases customer satisfaction, which helps maintain regular customers and attract new ones. And, most importantly, the use of new technologies and equipment becomes more convenient as they are integrated into the system. The benefits of Machine Vision are similar to the positive aspects of Computer Vision as shown in Figure 1.6.

1.7   FUTURE OF MACHINE VISION

The future of Machine Vision depends on the areas in which it is applied.

- The main impetus behind Machine Vision systems comes from the process of automation. Automation will allow the vision process of Machine Vision to be more accurate and more autonomous, or to make decisions without human intervention. Currently, the system operates in a semi-autonomous form (Khang & Shah et al., 2023).
- Machine Vision systems are known to work in real-time with real footage. On the other hand, Computer Vision needs to improve this skill in the future. The improvement of Big Data services in the future, especially for the 5th Industrial Revolution, and its application in more areas will also allow further development of Machine Vision (Khang & Hajimahmud et al., 2024).

1.8   CONCLUSION

The creation of vision systems in computers and machines was one of the main reasons that made technology more human-like. A vision system that works on specific results and is mainly applied in industries is a Machine Vision system. Machine Vision is known as a subset of general vision systems and is sometimes referred to as Computer Vision. Machine Vision is an integrated system that performs the basic vision process of industrial equipment, technologies, and industrial robots. Its main components are sensors, lighting systems, lenses, vision processing systems, and communication systems (Khang & Abdullayev et al., 2024).

Machine Vision and Computer Vision are two technologies that are very similar in both their advantages and application areas. However, there are certain differences which include:

- Machine Vision and Computer Vision are used for more specific purposes.
- Machine Vision works on real-time recording, while Computer Vision can also work with images in memory. Computer Vision is closer to human vision than Machine Vision.
- Unlike Computer Vision, Machine Vision is an integrated system. It cannot function in isolation.

In the Net-Zero Emissions or "eco-friendly" era, the manufacturing industry of the future must take various measures for an ecologically clean world. These are possible with smart technologies. The manufacturing industry will undoubtedly evolve further with the further integration of smart technologies. At this point, it is necessary to go back in history. It is known that with the beginning of the Industrial Revolution, the world entered a new era of development. Although it was a mainly positive development, the Industrial Revolution also had some negative aspects. The first of these was the pollution of the environment and, as a result, the increase of diseases and the destruction of nature (Anh et al., 2024).

Smart Technologies are one of the solutions for environmental pollution, which is one of the current global problems. These technologies which are available under the eco-friendly label, Green Technology, have already begun to take their place in the manufacturing industry for a clean future. And with that, the manufacturing industry of the future is also starting to evolve as Green Manufacturing. Examples of Green Technologies include solar panels, electric vehicles, recycling technologies, smart meters, carbon capture, storage technologies, and others. The main goal of Green Technology is to build a sustainable and clean world and a better future for humanity (Khang & Rath et al., 2023).

REFERENCES

Anh, P. T. N., Vladimir, Hahanov, Triwiyanto, Ragimova, Nazila Ali, İsmibeyli, Rashad, Hajimahmud, V. A., & Alyar, Abuzarova Vusala, "AI Models for Disease Diagnosis and Prediction of Heart Disease with Artificial Neural Networks," *Computer Vision and AI-Integrated IoT Technologies in Medical Ecosystem* (1st Ed.). (2024). CRC Press. https://doi.org/10.1201/9781003429609-9

Deac, Crina, Popa, Cicerone Laurentiu, Ghinea, Mihalache, & Cotet, C.E., (2017). Machine Vision in Manufacturing Processes and the Digital Twin of Manufacturing Architectures. In 28th DAAAM International Symposium on Intelligent Manufacturing and Automation. https://doi.org/10.2507/28th.daaam.proceedings.103

Javaid, Mohd, Haleem, Abid, Singh, Ravi, Rab, Shanay, & Suman, Rajiv, (2021). Exploring impact and features of Machine Vision for progressive Industry 4.0 culture. Sensors International, 3, 100132. https://doi.org/10.1016/j.sintl.2021.100132

Kallen, Hanna, "Applications of Machine Vision Quality Control, Cancer Detection and Traffic Surveillance," Doctoral Theses in Mathematical Sciences (2016), PP: 1. https://portal.research.lu.se/en/publications/applications-of-machine-vision-quality-control-cancer-detection-a

Khang, A., Abdullayev, V., Hrybiuk, O., & Shukla, A.K., *Computer Vision and AI-Integrated IoT Technologies in the Medical Ecosystem* (1st Ed.). (2024). CRC Press. https://doi.org/10.1201/9781003429609

Khang, A., Ragimova, Nazila Ali, Bali, Sardarov Yaqub, Hajimahmud, V. A., Bahar, Askarova, & Mehriban, Mammadova, "Using Big Data to Solve Problems in the Field of Medicine," *Computer Vision and AI-integrated IoT Technologies in Medical Ecosystem* (1st Ed.) (2024). CRC Press. https://doi.org/10.1201/9781003429609-21

Khang, A., Vladimir, Hahanov, Litvinova, Eugenia, Chumachenko, Svetlana, Zoran, Avromovic, İsmibeyli, Rashad, Ragimova, Nazila Ali, Hajimahmud, V. A., Alyar, Abuzarova Vusala, & Anh, P.T.N., "Medical and BioMedical Signal Processing and Prediction," *Computer Vision and AI-integrated IoT Technologies in Medical Ecosystem* (1st Ed.) (2024). CRC Press. https://doi.org/10.1201/9781003429609-7

Khang, A., Hajimahmud, V. A., Litvinova, Eugenia, Chumachenko, Svetlana, Abuzarova, Vusala, & Anh, P. T. N., "Application of Computer Vision in the Healthcare Ecosystem," *Computer Vision and AI-integrated IoT Technologies in Medical Ecosystem* (1st Ed.) (2024). CRC Press. https://doi.org/10.1201/9781003429609-1

Khang, A., Rath, Kali Charan, Kumar Satapathy, Suresh, Kumar, Amaresh, Ranjan Das, Sudhansu, & Ranjan Panda, Manas, "Enabling the Future of Manufacturing: Integration of Robotics and IoT to Smart Factory Infrastructure in Industry 4.0," *AI-Based Technologies and Applications in the Era of the Metaverse* (1st Ed.) (2023). Pages (25–50). IGI Global Press. https://doi.org/10.4018/978-1-6684-8851-5.ch002

Khang, A., Shah, V., & Rani, S., *AI-Based Technologies and Applications in the Era of the Metaverse* (1st Ed.) (2023). IGI Global Press. https://doi.org/10.4018/978-1-6684-8851-5

Liao, Wei, & Pei, Xiao. (2011). Research and application of machine vision in industry. Advanced Engineering Forum, 2–3, 153–155. https://doi.org/10.4028/www.scientific.net/AEF.2-3.153

Sandoval, Ernesto, Martinez-Rosas, Miguel Enrique, Martínez Sandoval, Jesús Raúl, Miranda Velasco, Manuel Moises, & de Ávila, Humberto Cervantes. (2018). Machine Vision Systems - A Tool for Automatic Color Analysis in Agriculture. 10.5772/intechopen.71935.

Yasar, Kinza, & Lutkevich, Ben. Machine Vision. (2023). https://www.techtarget.com/searchenterpriseai/definition/machine-vision-computer-vision

2 Role of Computer Vision in Manufacturing Industry

Mohd Umar, Mahima Gupta, Rajat Verma, and Namrata Dhanda

2.1 INTRODUCTION

In today's era where automation and efficiency are paramount, computer vision has emerged as a fundamental technology for enhancing productivity and quality control in manufacturing processes. This chapter provides a comprehensive understanding of computer vision, its underlying principles, and its core components. It explores the wide range of applications where computer vision is extensively employed in manufacturing, including quality inspection, defect detection, and robotic guidance and control. The integration of computer vision with Artificial Intelligence (AI) and Machine Learning (ML) is also examined, showcasing the advanced functionalities enabled by this combination.

The chapter addresses the challenges and considerations in implementing computer vision solutions in manufacturing, such as lighting conditions and occlusions, and discusses techniques to overcome these challenges. Furthermore, it discusses future trends and emerging technologies in computer vision for manufacturing, such as 3D vision and collaborative robotics, which are expected to revolutionize manufacturing processes. Overall, this chapter serves as a valuable resource for professionals in the field, providing insights into the role of computer vision in enhancing automation, quality control, and overall efficiency in manufacturing.

2.2 COMPUTER VISION

Computer vision is a multidisciplinary field that encompasses various principles and components to enable machines to understand and interpret visual information. This section will delve into the fundamental aspects of computer vision systems, including their underlying principles and core components (Sokolowski and Banks, 2011). The key components of computer vision are highlighted in Figure 2.1.

2.2.1 BACKGROUND OF COMPUTER VISION

To grasp the essence of computer vision, it is important to define it and understand its principles. Computer vision can be defined as a field of study that focuses on enabling computers to extract meaningful information from digital images or video.

DOI: 10.1201/9781003438137-2

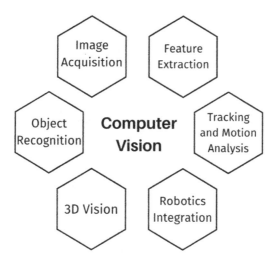

FIGURE 2.1 Key components of computer vision processes.

It involves the development of algorithms and techniques that mimic human visual perception, allowing machines to recognize, analyze, and interpret visual data (Verno et al., 2011).

The principles of computer vision are based on understanding the structure and characteristics of visual information. This includes aspects such as color, texture, shape, motion, and spatial relationships. By analyzing these visual cues, computer vision systems can extract valuable information and make intelligent decisions (Kruger, 2013).

2.2.2 CORE COMPONENTS OF COMPUTER VISION

Computer vision systems consist of several core components that work together to process and analyze visual data. These components are crucial for the effective functioning of computer vision systems and include:

- **Image Acquisition:** This component captures visual data using various devices such as cameras, sensors, or scanners. Image acquisition techniques ensure that the captured data is suitable for further processing (Vora et al., 2001). The process of image acquisition is illustrated in Figure 2.2.

  Initially, the object's image is captured, then it is digitized for further processing, then the relevant information is extracted from the digitized data, and then the information is utilized by the system according to the task assigned to the system by the user.

- **Preprocessing:** Once the visual data is acquired, it often undergoes preprocessing to enhance its quality and remove noise or irrelevant information. Preprocessing techniques may include image filtering, noise reduction, image enhancement, and image normalization (Kumar and Bhatia, 2014).

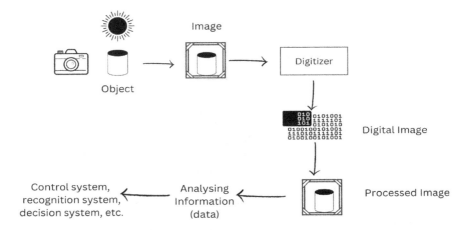

FIGURE 2.2   Computer vision image acquisition.

- **Feature Extraction:** Feature extraction aims to identify and extract relevant features from the preprocessed data. Features can be specific patterns, edges, textures, or other visual attributes that hold valuable information for subsequent analysis (Pradhan et al., 2018).
- **Object Recognition:** Object recognition is a critical component of computer vision systems. It involves identifying and classifying objects or patterns within an image or video sequence. Techniques such as template matching, statistical modeling, and ML algorithms are commonly used for object recognition (Brunelli, 2009).

By understanding these core components of computer vision systems, researchers who are working in this field can lay the foundation for exploring their applications and capabilities in the manufacturing sector. These components collectively enable machines to perceive and interpret visual data, paving the way for enhanced automation, quality control, and decision-making in manufacturing processes.

2.3   APPLICATIONS OF COMPUTER VISION IN INDUSTRIES

Computer vision has found extensive usage in the manufacturing sector, transforming various aspects of production and quality control. In this section, we will explore diverse applications where computer vision plays a crucial role in enhancing efficiency and ensuring product excellence (Bogue, 2005). The applications of computer vision are shown in Figure 2.3.

2.3.1   QUALITY INSPECTION

One of the primary applications of computer vision in manufacturing is quality inspection and defect detection. Computer vision systems can analyze visual data to identify defects, anomalies, or deviations from desired specifications in products.

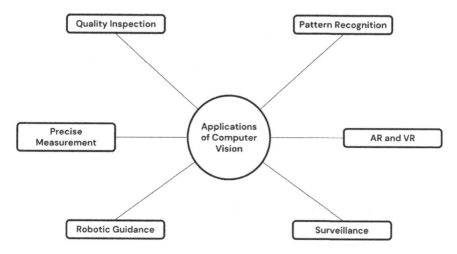

FIGURE 2.3 Computer vision applications.

By comparing captured images with reference images or predefined criteria, computer vision algorithms can detect surface defects, dimensional variations, and other imperfections with high precision and accuracy. This enables manufacturers to ensure consistent product quality, minimize defects, and reduce the risk of faulty products reaching the market (Park and Jeong, 2022).

2.3.1.1 Importance of Quality Inspection

Quality inspection is a critical aspect of the manufacturing process, ensuring that products meet predefined standards and specifications. Computer vision plays a vital role in automating and enhancing the quality inspection process, enabling efficient and accurate detection of defects (Patel et al., 2011).

2.3.1.2 Defect Detection Algorithms

Computer vision algorithms are designed to detect and classify various types of defects. These algorithms leverage ML techniques, such as supervised and unsupervised learning, to train models on large datasets of labeled defect images (Verma & Mishra et al., 2021). Computers can detect defects in varied materials, textures, and shapes, ensuring comprehensive defect detection across a wide range of products (Bergmann et al., 2021).

2.3.1.3 Non-Destructive Testing

Computer vision techniques are extensively used in non-destructive testing (NDT) methods, such as visual inspection, thermal imaging, X-ray imaging, and ultrasonic imaging (Okarma and Fastowicz, 2019). These methods enable the detection of internal defects or hidden anomalies without damaging the product, making them valuable for quality control in industries like automotive, aerospace, and electronics.

- Computer vision enables inspecting and evaluating materials, components, and structures without causing damage or altering their integrity.

- Various techniques are used in computer vision-based NDT, including visual inspection, thermal imaging, X-ray imaging, and ultrasound imaging.
- Computer vision algorithms and systems analyze visual data to detect defects, anomalies, cracks, and other irregularities in the inspected materials or products.
- NDT using computer vision is extensively used in industries such as aerospace, automotive, electronics, and construction to ensure product quality, safety, and reliability.
- Computer vision-based NDT systems offer advantages like real-time inspection, high accuracy, repeatability, and automation, improving efficiency and reducing human error.
- Integration of AI and ML techniques with computer vision in NDT enables intelligent defect detection, automated decision-making, and predictive maintenance.
- Computer vision-based NDT techniques can be applied to various materials, including metals, composites, ceramics, and polymers, expanding their applicability in diverse manufacturing processes.
- NDT using computer vision contributes to cost savings by identifying defects early in the production process, minimizing scrap, rework, and potential product failures.
- Continuous advancements in computer vision algorithms, imaging technologies, and data processing techniques drive the evolution of NDT, ensuring safer and more reliable products in the manufacturing industry (Verma et al., 2023b).

2.3.1.4   Advancements in Defect Classification and Localization

Recent advancements in computer vision have focused on improving defect classification and localization capabilities. Deep learning algorithms, such as convolutional neural networks (CNNs), have shown remarkable performance in accurately classifying defects and precisely localizing their positions within a product (Singh and Desai, 2022).

Computer vision plays a vital role in quality inspection and defect detection in manufacturing. It enables automated visual inspection, defect detection algorithms, real-time quality control, and NDT. Advancements in defect classification, localization, and integration with robotic systems further enhance the capabilities of computer vision in ensuring high-quality products and efficient manufacturing processes (Dong et al., 2022).

2.3.2   Precise Measurement and Metrology

Computer vision plays a vital role in precise measurement and metrology within manufacturing processes. By leveraging advanced algorithms, computer vision systems can accurately measure dimensions, distances, angles, and other physical properties of products or components. This capability eliminates the need for manual measurements and reduces human errors, ensuring precise adherence to design specifications. Computer vision-based metrology is particularly valuable in industries where precision is critical, such as aerospace, automotive, and electronics manufacturing (Razdan and Bateman, 2015).

2.3.2.1 Non-Contact Measurement Techniques

Computer vision enables non-contact measurement techniques that eliminate the need for physical contact with the object being measured. This reduces the risk of damage or deformation and allows for the measurement of delicate or complex surfaces. Techniques such as stereo vision, structured light, and laser scanning capture detailed 3D information for precise measurements (Zhou et al., 2022).

2.3.2.2 Dimensional and Geometric Measurements

Computer vision-based systems can accurately measure dimensional parameters such as the length, width, height, and diameter of objects. Additionally, computers can perform geometric measurements, including angles, curves, and contours, enabling comprehensive characterization of complex shapes and profiles (Malamas et al., 2003).

2.3.2.3 High-Speed and Real-Time Measurements

Computer vision enables high-speed and real-time measurement capabilities, allowing for efficient quality control in manufacturing processes. These systems can rapidly capture and analyze visual data, providing instant feedback and enabling prompt adjustments or corrections during production (Li et al., 2022).

2.3.2.4 Integration with Automation System

Advanced metrology software and analysis tools complement computer vision systems, facilitating data processing, analysis, and visualization. These tools enable statistical analysis, geometric feature extraction, and comparison with design specifications, ensuring precise measurement and compliance with tolerance limits (Malamas et al., 2003).

2.3.2.5 Metrology Software and Analysis Tool

Computer vision-based measurement systems can be seamlessly integrated with automation systems, enabling automatic measurement and feedback control. This integration enhances manufacturing efficiency, reduces manual intervention, and enables real-time adjustments based on measurement results (Gašpar et al., 2020).

Computer vision technology has significantly advanced precise measurement and metrology in manufacturing. Its non-contact measurement techniques, accuracy enhancement through calibration, high-speed capabilities, and integration with automation systems have transformed the way measurements are conducted. Manufacturers can ensure product quality, optimize production processes, and enhance overall efficiency by leveraging computer vision for precise measurement (Shang et al., 2022).

2.3.3 ROBOTIC GUIDANCE AND CONTROL

Computer vision enables precise robotic guidance and control in manufacturing environments. By equipping robotic systems with vision sensors (Verma et al.,

2022a), robots can perceive and interpret the surrounding environment and precise movement. Computer vision-based guidance enables robots to perform complex tasks such as pick-and-place operations, assembly tasks, and object manipulation with high accuracy and dexterity (Javaid et al., 2022). This not only improves efficiency, but it also enables flexible automation where robots can adapt to variations in product positioning, orientation, or shape (Malamas et al., 2003).

2.3.3.1 Adaptive and Precise Movement

Adaptive and precise movement in robotic systems refers to the ability of robots to dynamically adjust their motions based on real-time data. By equipping robots with computer vision capabilities, robots can perceive their surroundings, interpret information, and make precise and accurate movements accordingly. The use of computer vision helps us with the following:

- Real-time analysis of visual data.
- Adaptive movement based on environmental changes.
- Achieving precise and accurate robotic control.

2.3.3.2 Complex Task Execution

Complex task execution involves various aspects such as object identification, localization, and planning. Computer vision facilitates these capabilities by enabling robots to identify objects, estimate their positions and orientations, and plan the necessary actions for the efficient execution of tasks. This level of control and understanding of the environment enables robots to perform intricate tasks with accuracy and dexterity (Ekvall and Kragic, 2008).

2.3.3.3 Flexible Automation

Flexible automation refers to the ability of robotic systems to adapt and respond to variations in product positioning, orientation, or shape, as well as changes in the manufacturing environment. By incorporating computer vision, robots can analyze visual data in real time, allowing them to adjust their movements and actions accordingly. This adaptability enables robots to handle diverse and dynamic manufacturing scenarios, enhancing productivity, versatility, and efficiency in automated processes.

2.3.4 Visual Inspection and Pattern Recognition

Computer vision systems excel at visual inspection and pattern recognition in manufacturing. Computers can analyze complex visual patterns, textures, and shapes to identify specific features or patterns of interest. This capability is valuable in applications such as barcode reading, label verification, part identification, and pattern matching. Computer vision algorithms can quickly and accurately identify objects, components, or markings, enabling efficient sorting, tracking, and traceability in manufacturing processes (Malamas et al., 2003). The process of pattern recognition is depicted in Figure 2.4.

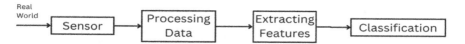

FIGURE 2.4 Pattern recognition process.

2.3.4.1 Automated Visual Inspection

Automated visual inspection harnesses the capabilities of computer vision to accomplish the following:

- Utilizing computer vision algorithms for automated inspection of manufactured products.
- Detection of defects, flaws, and inconsistencies in the visual appearance of products.
- Real-time analysis of images to identify deviations from predefined standards or specifications (Lucas et al., 2012).

2.3.4.2 Defect Detection and Classification

Defect detection and classification through computer vision are achieved through the following:

- Using computer vision to detect and classify various types of defects (Sun et al., 2019)
- Training algorithms to recognize patterns associated with different defect categories
- Accurate identification of defects such as cracks, scratches, dents, and surface irregularities

2.3.4.3 Pattern Recognition

Pattern recognition in computer vision involves:

- Leveraging computer vision to recognize and classify complex patterns and features (Bhatt et al., 2021).
- Training algorithms to identify specific patterns, logos, or symbols on products.
- Enabling efficient quality control by verifying the presence and accuracy of patterns.

2.3.4.4 Optical Character Recognition

Optical character recognition (OCR) is a technology that enables the conversion of printed or handwritten text into machine-readable and editable formats. It involves the use of computer vision techniques for the following:

- To extract and interpret text from images (Mahadas et al., 2023).
- For reading and recognizing characters, numbers, and symbols on products or labels.
- For facilitating automated data extraction, labeling, and tracking in manufacturing processes.

2.3.4.5 Real-Time Monitoring and Quality Assurance

Real-time monitoring and quality assurance in various industries benefit from computer vision technology due to its ability to provide accurate and efficient visual analysis. Computer vision enables real-time monitoring by:

- Continuously analyzing visual data to ensure quality standards are met.
- Providing immediate feedback and alerts for deviations or potential issues (Scime and Beuth, 2018).
- Rapidly identifying quality issues, such as product defects, inconsistencies, or irregularities.

Computer vision-based visual inspection and pattern recognition offer numerous advantages in manufacturing. Computers improve the accuracy and reliability of inspection processes, reduce human error, and enable faster detection and resolution of quality-related issues. Additionally, the integration of computer vision with ML techniques allows for continuous improvement and adaptation of inspection algorithms, enhancing their performance over time (Konstantinidis et al., 2021).

By relying on computer vision for visual inspection and pattern recognition, manufacturers can achieve consistent and reliable quality control, streamline production processes, and deliver high-quality products to customers. The combination of advanced image processing algorithms and real-time analysis capabilities ensures efficient and effective monitoring of manufacturing operations, contributing to overall productivity and customer satisfaction (Abualsauod, 2023).

2.3.5 Augmented Reality and Virtual Reality Integration

Computer vision plays a crucial role in integrating Augmented Reality (AR) and Virtual Reality (VR) technologies into manufacturing (Shukla et al., 2023). By combining computer vision with AR/VR, manufacturers can create immersive and interactive experiences for tasks such as product design, assembly guidance, training, and maintenance. Computer vision enables the recognition of real-world objects and environments, facilitating the overlay of virtual information or simulations onto physical objects, enhancing visualization, and improving decision-making (Li et al., 2018).

The applications mentioned above are just a glimpse of the wide range of possibilities that computer vision brings to the manufacturing `sector. By harnessing the power of computer vision, manufacturers can achieve higher efficiency, improved product quality, and enhanced automation, and they can gain a competitive edge in the market (Khang & Hajimahmud et al., 2024).

2.3.6 Surveillance Using Computer Vision

Computer vision technology has significantly transformed the field of surveillance, enabling advanced monitoring and analysis of visual data. By leveraging sophisticated algorithms and ML techniques, computer vision enhances surveillance systems' capabilities, providing accurate and efficient monitoring in various settings.

2.3.6.1 Object Detection and Tracking

Computer vision allows the detection and tracking of objects of interest in surveillance footage. Using techniques like object detection algorithms and motion tracking, computer vision systems can identify and track individuals, vehicles, or specific objects, enabling real-time monitoring and analysis.

2.3.6.2 Intrusion and Activity Recognition

Computer vision-based surveillance systems can analyze video feeds to identify and recognize unauthorized intrusions or suspicious activities. By applying pattern recognition and anomaly detection algorithms, these systems can alert security personnel to potential threats or abnormal behavior, enhancing the overall security of the monitored area (Verma et al., 2022c).

2.3.6.3 Facial Recognition

Facial recognition technology in computer vision enables the identification and verification of individuals captured in surveillance footage. By comparing facial features against a database of known identities, it can assist in identifying persons of interest, enhancing security, and aiding in investigations (Verma et al., 2023b).

2.3.6.4 Crowd Monitoring and Crowd Management

Computer vision-based surveillance systems can analyze crowd dynamics, including crowd density, flow, and behavior patterns. This information is valuable for crowd management during large events, public spaces, or critical infrastructures, helping ensure safety, detect potential crowd-related incidents, and optimize crowd flow (Verma et al., 2022a).

2.3.6.5 Event Detection and Alarm Generation

Computer vision algorithms can analyze video streams in real-time to detect specific events or activities, such as accidents, objects left behind, or unauthorized access. When such events are identified, the system can generate alarms or notifications, enabling rapid response and intervention.

2.3.6.6 Video Analytics and Forensics

Computer vision-based surveillance systems offer advanced video analytics and forensics capabilities. This includes video summarization, object tracking across multiple cameras, and post-event analysis for investigative purposes, providing valuable insights and evidence (Anh et al., 2024).

2.4 INTEGRATION OF COMPUTER VISION WITH AI AND ML

The integration of Computer Vision with Artificial Intelligence (AI) and Machine Learning (ML) revolutionizes the capabilities of visual systems in manufacturing (Verma et al., 2022b). By combining the power of computer vision algorithms with AI and ML techniques, manufacturers can achieve advanced object tracking, pattern recognition, and adaptive decision-making, leading to improved accuracy and efficiency in production processes. Deep learning algorithms further enhance the robustness and adaptability of computer vision systems, paving the way for intelligent and automated manufacturing environments (Baduge et al., 2022).

2.4.1 Synergies between Computer Vision, AI, and ML

Computer vision, AI, and ML are closely intertwined and mutually beneficial fields. When integrated, they enhance the capabilities of computer vision systems, enabling advanced functionalities and intelligent decision-making in manufacturing (Kotsiopoulos et al., 2021).

By combining computer vision with AI and ML techniques, manufacturers can develop systems that go beyond simple image processing. AI and ML algorithms enable computers to learn from data, recognize patterns, and make informed decisions based on visual information. This integration allows computer vision systems to adapt, improve, and handle complex scenarios (Benbarrad et al., 2021).

2.4.2 Object Tracking, Pattern Recognition, and Adaptive Decision-Making

One key application of integrating computer vision with AI and ML is object tracking. Computer vision algorithms, combined with AI techniques, can track objects in real-time, even in challenging scenarios such as occlusions or varying appearances. Machine Learning models can be trained to recognize and track specific objects of interest, enabling applications like automated robotic picking and sorting in manufacturing environments (Yang et al., 2020).

Pattern recognition is another area where the synergy of computer vision and AI shines. By leveraging ML algorithms, computer vision systems can learn to recognize and classify complex patterns in visual data. This capability is useful for tasks such as identifying defects on product surfaces, detecting anomalies in production lines, or recognizing specific components or features during assembly processes (Mesbah and Graves, 2019).

Furthermore, the integration of AI and ML enables adaptive decision-making in computer vision systems. By continuously analyzing visual data and learning from past experiences, these systems can dynamically adjust their decision-making processes based on changing conditions or new information. Adaptive decision-making enhances the flexibility and responsiveness of computer vision systems, improving their ability to handle dynamic manufacturing environments (Sarker, 2021).

2.4.3 Deep Learning Algorithms for Improved Accuracy and Robustness

Deep learning, a subfield of ML, has garnered significant attention in recent years for its ability to extract intricate patterns and features from visual data. Deep learning algorithms, such as CNNs, have demonstrated remarkable performance in various computer vision tasks (Arel et al., 2010). When integrated with computer vision in manufacturing, deep learning algorithms contribute to improved accuracy and robustness. Computers excel at tasks like object recognition, image segmentation, and scene understanding. Deep learning models can automatically learn relevant features from large datasets, enabling better generalization and adaptability to different manufacturing scenarios (Zhang et al., 2016).

Moreover, deep learning algorithms can handle complex visual data representations, such as high-resolution images or 3D data, which are common in manufacturing applications. Their hierarchical architectures allow them to extract and analyze multiple levels of abstraction, leading to a more comprehensive and nuanced understanding of visual information. By integrating deep learning algorithms into computer vision systems, manufacturers can achieve higher accuracy in quality control, more reliable defect detection, and improved performance in various visual inspection tasks. These advancements contribute to increased automation, enhanced productivity, and overall efficiency in manufacturing processes (Khang & Hajimahmud et al., 2024).

The integration of computer vision with AI and ML opens up a world of possibilities for intelligent and automated manufacturing systems. By leveraging the synergies between these fields, manufacturers can develop sophisticated solutions that improve accuracy, adaptability, and decision-making capabilities, driving the industry toward a future of smarter and more efficient production (Gupta et al., 2021).

2.5   CHALLENGES AND CONSIDERATIONS IN COMPUTER VISION

Implementing computer vision solutions in the manufacturing sector comes with various challenges and considerations. This section explores the key factors that need to be addressed for the successful deployment of computer vision systems and highlights important considerations for achieving optimal performance and reliability (Huang et al., 2021).

2.5.1   LIGHTING CONDITIONS AND ENVIRONMENT

Effective computer vision in manufacturing heavily relies on appropriate lighting conditions and a well-controlled environment. Lighting conditions and environmental factors can significantly impact the performance and reliability of computer vision systems. Understanding and addressing these challenges are essential for the successful implementation of manufacturing processes (Batchelor and Waltz, 2001).

2.5.1.1   Lighting Uniformity and Intensity

Lighting uniformity and intensity are crucial in computer vision applications because they ensure the following:

- Consistent and uniform lighting across the manufacturing environment.
- Avoiding shadows, reflections, or glare that can hinder accurate image acquisition.
- Employing techniques such as diffusers, filters, or directed lighting to optimize illumination.

2.5.1.2 Variable Lighting Conditions

Variable lighting conditions pose a challenge for computer vision systems in manufacturing because, in order to get accurate results, the computer has to manage:

- Variations in lighting conditions due to natural light, artificial light, or dynamic production settings.
- Implementation of adaptive algorithms that can adjust to changes in lighting conditions in real-time.
- Using techniques like image normalization or dynamic thresholding to compensate for lighting variations (Junaid et al., 2023).

2.5.1.3 Environmental Disturbances

Environmental disturbances pose significant challenges in computer vision applications, but the following effective management strategies can mitigate their impact.

- Calibration and normalization techniques help to account for variations in lighting conditions, ensuring consistent image quality and reducing the impact of lighting changes.
- Implementing protective measures to minimize the impact of environmental disturbances on vision sensors.
- Utilizing image preprocessing techniques like noise reduction or image stabilization to improve image quality.

Addressing the challenges posed by lighting conditions and the manufacturing environment is crucial for the successful deployment of computer vision systems. By implementing appropriate strategies, such as optimal lighting setups, adaptive algorithms, and robust calibration procedures, manufacturers can overcome these challenges and ensure reliable and accurate visual analysis in their manufacturing processes. Additionally, ongoing monitoring and maintenance of the vision system's performance and environmental conditions are essential to ensure sustained effectiveness and optimal outcomes.

2.5.2 Occlusions and Complex Scenes

Manufacturing environments often involve occlusions, where objects or parts may partially or fully obscure each other. Computer vision systems must be capable of handling occlusions and accurately detecting and recognizing objects of interest, even in complex scenes. Advanced algorithms, such as multiview reconstruction or 3D point cloud analysis, can help overcome occlusion challenges and enable robust object detection and tracking (Brunetti et al., 2018).

2.5.2.1 Challenges of Occlusions and Complex Scenes

Occlusions are a common occurrence in computer vision, where objects of interest are partially or completely obstructed by other objects in the scene. Understanding and handling occlusions poses significant challenges in various computer vision tasks. Occlusions can occur due to object–object interactions, self-occlusions, or occlusions caused by the scene geometry. Dealing with occlusions becomes even more complex in scenes with multiple objects and cluttered backgrounds (Cuhadar and Tsao, 2022).

In computer vision applications such as object detection, tracking, and scene reconstruction, occlusions can lead to inaccurate or incomplete results. Occlusions disrupt the continuity of object boundaries and introduce ambiguities in feature matching, making it difficult to reliably track objects or reconstruct scene geometry. Furthermore, occlusions can cause object misclassification and hinder accurate depth estimation, affecting the overall understanding and interpretation of complex scenes (Khang & Ragimova et al., 2024).

2.5.2.2 Occlusion Handling Techniques

Researchers have developed various techniques to address the challenges posed by occlusions in computer vision. Depth-based occlusion reasoning is a common approach where depth information is used to reason about occlusions and infer the presence of occluding objects. This helps in estimating the occluded regions and recovering the complete shape and structure of objects (Chandel and Vatta, 2015). Occlusion boundary detection and segmentation methods aim to identify occlusion boundaries by analyzing image features, such as color, texture, or motion disconti-nuities. These boundaries help separate occluded and occluding objects, enabling better object detection and tracking. Contextual information, such as object relation-ships and scene understanding, is often utilized to handle occlusions. By leveraging the context, the system can infer occluded parts based on the knowledge of the scene and the objects involved (Khang & Vladimir et al., 2024).

Temporal consistency plays a crucial role in occlusion handling, especially in video sequences or dynamic scenes. Tracking algorithms that maintain temporal coherence and exploit object motion information can help handle occlusions by pre-dicting object positions even when sensors are temporarily occluded. These tech-niques ensure the continuity and smoothness of object trajectories, improving the overall tracking performance in complex scenes.

2.5.2.3 Object Detection and Tracking in Complex Scenes

Object detection and tracking in complex scenes with occlusions require special-ized algorithms. Multiobject tracking models explicitly handle occlusion events and association relationships between objects. Fusion of visual cues with other sen-sor modalities improves occlusion handling. Deep learning-based approaches with occlusion-aware models and loss functions enhance occlusion recognition and gen-eralization in complex scenes (Sivaraman and Trivedi, 2013).

2.5.2.4 Scene Reconstruction and Structure from Motion

Occlusions pose challenges in scene reconstruction and structure from motion tasks. Techniques that consider occlusions during the reconstruction process leverage mul-tiple viewpoints and reasoning algorithms to estimate the accurate depth and recover occluded structures. Structures from motion algorithms face difficulties in maintain-ing feature correspondences and reconstructing complete scenes in the presence of occlusions (Furukawa and Ponce, 2010).

Occlusions pose challenges of complex scenes in computer vision tasks. They also present various techniques and approaches to addressing occlusion handling, object detection and tracking, scene reconstruction, and structure from motion in the context of complex scenes. By understanding and overcoming these challenges, computer vision systems can achieve more accurate and robust performance in diverse real-world scenarios.

2.5.3 Perspective and Viewpoint Variations

Manufacturing processes may involve variations in perspective or viewpoint, especially when dealing with objects moving along assembly lines or robotic manipulations. Computer vision systems need to account for these variations and can handle object detection, recognition, and pose estimation from different viewpoints. Techniques such as camera calibration, 3D modeling, and pose estimation algorithms can aid in addressing these challenges (Pérez et al., 2016).

2.5.4 Calibration and System Integration

Calibration is a critical aspect of computer vision systems in manufacturing. It involves aligning and calibrating cameras, sensors, and other hardware components to ensure accurate measurements and consistent performance. Proper calibration techniques, along with effective system integration, are essential for reliable and precise computer vision-based applications in manufacturing. This includes synchronization of multiple cameras, sensor fusion, and data integration with other systems or automation platforms (Botterill et al., 2011).

2.5.5 Training Data and Machine Learning

To achieve optimal performance, computer vision algorithms often require extensive training on relevant data. Collecting and annotating high-quality training datasets can be time-consuming and resource-intensive. Additionally, selecting appropriate ML algorithms, such as CNNs or deep learning architectures, and fine-tuning them for specific manufacturing applications is crucial. Careful consideration of training data quantity, quality, and diversity, as well as algorithm selection and optimization, is essential for successful implementation (Nath and Behzadan, 2019).

2.5.6 Real-Time Performance and Computational Requirements

Many manufacturing processes require real-time or near-real-time analysis and decision-making. Computer vision systems must meet stringent performance requirements while considering the computational resources available. Efficient algorithm design, hardware acceleration techniques, such as graphics processing units (GPUs) or field programmable gate arrays (FPGAs), and optimization strategies play a vital role in achieving real-time performance in computationally demanding applications (Pulli et al., 2012).

By addressing these challenges and considerations, manufacturers can overcome hurdles in implementing computer vision solutions effectively. It is crucial to carefully analyze the specific manufacturing requirements, tailor the computer vision system accordingly, and continually evaluate and fine-tune the system to ensure optimal performance and reliability in practical manufacturing environments.

2.6   FUTURE TRENDS AND EMERGING TECHNOLOGIES IN COMPUTER VISION FOR MANUFACTURING

As the manufacturing landscape evolves, future trends and emerging technologies in computer vision hold immense potential for transforming the industry. From 3D vision and multispectral imaging to collaborative robotics and edge computing, these advancements offer new opportunities for enhanced automation, quality control, and efficiency in manufacturing processes. By staying at the forefront of these developments, manufacturers can harness the power of computer vision to drive innovation and maintain a competitive edge in the evolving manufacturing sector (Verma et al., 2020; Khang & Shah et al., 2023).

2.6.1   ADVANCEMENTS IN 3D VISION

In the realm of computer vision for manufacturing, advancements in 3D vision technology are driving significant developments. Traditional 2D imaging techniques have limitations when it comes to capturing depth information, which is crucial for various manufacturing tasks (Khang & Rath et al., 2023). However, with the integration of 3D vision techniques such as stereo vision, structured light systems, or Time-of-Flight (ToF) cameras, computer vision systems can obtain richer and more accurate spatial information. This opens up a wide range of applications in manufacturing including:

- **3D Object Inspection:** 3D vision allows for precise and detailed inspection of objects, enabling manufacturers to detect defects, measure dimensions, and ensure quality control with higher accuracy (Zhang et al., 2023).
- **Robotic Manipulation:** By incorporating the 3D vision, robots can perceive the environment in three dimensions, improving their ability to grasp objects, navigate complex spaces, and perform tasks such as pick-and-place operations with increased efficiency and reliability.
- **Virtual Assembly Simulations:** 3D vision facilitates virtual assembly simulations, where components can be digitally fitted and tested for proper alignment and functionality, reducing errors and optimizing assembly processes.

2.6.2   MULTISPECTRAL IMAGING

Multispectral imaging is an emerging technology that holds great promise for computer vision in manufacturing. By capturing and analyzing images at different wavelengths beyond the visible spectrum, multispectral imaging provides valuable additional information about materials, chemical compositions, or surface properties that may not be visible to the human eye. This technology has several implications for manufacturing:

- **Defect Detection and Quality Control:** Multispectral imaging can identify defects or variations in products that are not discernible through conventional imaging techniques. By analyzing the unique spectral signatures of materials, manufacturers can detect hidden flaws, inconsistencies, or contaminants, enhancing quality control processes.
- **Material Classification:** Multispectral imaging can aid in material classification by analyzing the spectral responses of different substances. This is particularly useful in industries where accurate identification and verification of materials are critical, such as pharmaceuticals, food processing, or recycling.
- **Process Optimization:** The analysis of chemical or structural characteristics through multispectral imaging can provide insights for process optimization, allowing manufacturers to fine-tune parameters, reduce waste, and improve overall efficiency.

2.6.3 IMPLICATIONS FOR MANUFACTURING PROCESSES AND INDUSTRY

The convergence of these future trends and emerging technologies in computer vision holds significant implications for manufacturing processes and the industry as a whole. The integration of advanced 3D vision enables precise measurements, streamlines assembly processes, and improves defect detection. Multispectral imaging enhances material identification, quality control, and process optimization. Collaborative robotics with computer vision capabilities boosts productivity, facilitates human–robot collaboration, and creates a flexible manufacturing environment. These advancements empower manufacturers to achieve higher levels of automation, improved product quality, enhanced efficiency, and increased flexibility (Khang & Muthmainnah et al., 2023).

2.7 CONCLUSION

In conclusion, this chapter has provided valuable insights into the role of computer vision in the domain of machine vision and industrial robotics within the manufacturing sector. The significance of computer vision in enhancing automation, quality control, and overall operational efficiency in manufacturing processes has been highlighted. The chapter has extensively explored the fundamental principles and essential components of computer vision, encompassing image acquisition, preprocessing, feature extraction, and object recognition (Verma et al., 2021b).

The diverse applications of computer vision in manufacturing, including quality inspection, defect detection, and precise product measurement, have been thoroughly examined. The integration of computer vision with Artificial Intelligence and Machine Learning has opened up new possibilities, enabling advanced functionalities such as object tracking, pattern recognition, and adaptive decision-making.

Deep learning algorithms have emerged as powerful tools, contributing to improved accuracy and robustness in computer vision systems. Overall, this chapter underscores the profound impact of computer vision on manufacturing, paving the way for enhanced productivity, quality, and flexibility in industrial settings (Verma et al., 2021a).

REFERENCES

Abualsauod, E. H., "Machine Learning Based Fault Detection Approach to Enhance Quality Control in Smart Manufacturing." Production Planning & Control, pp. 1–9, (2023). https://doi.org/10.1080/09537287.2023.2175736.

Anh, P. T. N., Hahanov Vladimir, Triwiyanto, Nazila Ali Ragimova, Rashad İsmibeyli, V. A. Hajimahmud, and Abuzarova Vusala Alyar. "AI Models for Disease Diagnosis and Prediction of Heart Disease with Artificial Neural Networks," *Computer Vision and AI-Integrated IoT Technologies in Medical Ecosystem* (1st Ed.). (2024). CRC Press. https://doi.org/10.1201/9781003429609-9

Arel, I., D. C. Rose, and T. P. Karnowski, "Deep Machine Learning – A New Frontier in Artificial Intelligence Research [Research Frontier]." IEEE Computational Intelligence Magazine, vol. 5, no. 4, pp. 13–18, (2010). https://doi.org/10.1109/mci.2010.938364.

Baduge, S. K., S. Thilakarathna, J.S. Perera, M. Arashpour, P. Sharafi, B. Teodosio, A. Shringi, and P. Mendis, "Artificial Intelligence and Smart Vision for Building and Construction 4.0: Machine and Deep Learning Methods and Applications." Automation in Construction, vol. 141, p. 104440, (2022). https://doi.org/10.1016/j.autcon.2022.104440.

Batchelor, B., and F. Waltz, "Machine Vision for Industrial Applications." *Intelligent Machine Vision* (2001). Page (1–29). Springer. https://doi.org/10.1007/978-1-4471-0239-7_1.

Benbarrad, T., M. Salhaoui, S. B. Kenitar, and M. Arioua, "Intelligent Machine Vision Model for Defective Product Inspection Based on Machine Learning." Journal of Sensor and Actuator Networks, vol. 10, no. 1, p. 7, (2021). https://doi.org/10.3390/jsan10010007.

Bergmann, P., K. Batzner, M. Fauser, D. Sattlegger, and C. Steger, "The MVTec Anomaly Detection Dataset: A Comprehensive Real-World Dataset for Unsupervised Anomaly Detection." International Journal of Computer Vision, vol. 129, no. 4, pp. 1038–1059, (2021). https://doi.org/10.1007/s11263-020-01400-4.

Bhatt, D., Patel, C., Talsania, H., Patel, J., Vaghela, R., Pandya, S., Modi, K., and Ghayvat, H. "CNN Variants for Computer Vision: History, Architecture, Application, Challenges and Future Scope." Electronics, vol. 10, no. 20, p. 2470, (2021). https://doi.org/10.3390/electronics10202470.

Bogue, R., "Machine Vision Theory, Algorithms, Practicalities." Assembly Automation, vol. 25, no. 3, (2005). https://doi.org/10.1108/aa.2005.03325cae.001.

Botterill, T., S. Mills, and R. Green, "Design and calibration of a hybrid computer vision and structured light 3D imaging system." The 5th International Conference on Automation, Robotics and Applications, (2011). https://doi.org/10.1109/icara.2011.6144924.

Brunelli, R., *Template Matching Techniques in Computer Vision* (2009). https://doi.org/10.1002/9780470744055.

Brunetti, A., D. Buongiorno, G. F. Trotta, and V. Bevilacqua, "Computer Vision and Deep Learning Techniques for Pedestrian Detection and Tracking: A Survey." Neurocomputing, vol. 300, pp. 17–33, (2018). https://doi.org/10.1016/j.neucom.2018.01.092.

Chandel, H., and S. Vatta, "Occlusion Detection and Handling: A Review." International Journal of Computer Applications, vol. 120, no. 10, pp. 33–38, (2015). https://doi.org/10.5120/21264-3857.

Cuhadar, C., and H. N. Tsao, "A Computer Vision Sensor for AI-Accelerated Detection and Tracking of Occluded Objects." Advanced Intelligent Systems, vol. 4, no. 11, p. 2100285, (2022). https://doi.org/10.1002/aisy.202100285.

Dong, G., S. Sun, Z. Wang, N. Wu, P. Huang, H. Feng, and M. Pan, "Application of Machine Vision-Based NDT Technology in Ceramic Surface Defect Detection – a Review." Materials Testing, vol. 64, no. 2, pp. 202–219, (2022). https://doi.org/10.1515/mt-2021-2012.

Ekvall, S., and D. Kragic, "Robot Learning from Demonstration: A Task-Level Planning Approach." International Journal of Advanced Robotic Systems, vol. 5, no. 3, p. 33, (2008). https://doi.org/10.5772/5611.

Furukawa, Y., and J. Ponce, "Accurate, Dense, and Robust Multiview Stereopsis." IEEE Transactions on Pattern Analysis and Machine Intelligence, vol. 32, no. 8, pp. 1362–1376, (2010). https://doi.org/10.1109/TPAMI.2009.161

Gašpar, T. et al., "Smart Hardware Integration with Advanced Robot Programming Technologies for Efficient Reconfiguration of Robot Workcells." Robotics and Computer-Integrated Manufacturing, vol. 66, p. 101979, (2020). https://doi.org/10.1016/j.rcim.2020.101979.

Gupta, S., S. Modgil, S. Bhattacharyya, and I. Bose, "Artificial Intelligence for Decision Support Systems in the Field of Operations Research: Review and Future Scope of Research." Annals of Operations Research, vol. 308, no. 1, pp. 215–274, (2021). https://doi.org/10.1007/s10479-020-03856-6.

Huang, M., J. Ninić, and Q. Zhang, "BIM, Machine Learning and Computer Vision Techniques in Underground Construction: Current Status and Future Perspectives." Tunnelling and Underground Space Technology, vol. 108, p. 103677, (2021). https://doi.org/10.1016/j.tust.2020.103677.

Javaid, M., A. Haleem, R. P. Singh, S. Rab, and R. Suman, "Exploring Impact and Features of Machine Vision for Progressive Industry 4.0 Culture." Sensors International, vol. 3, p. 100132, (2022). https://doi.org/10.1016/j.sintl.2021.100132.

Junaid, A., A. Nawaz, M. F. Usmani, R. Verma, and N. Dhanda, "Analyzing the Performance of a DAPP Using Blockchain 3.0." 2023 13th International Conference on Cloud Computing, Data Science & Engineering (Confluence), (2023). https://doi.org/10.1109/confluence56041.2023.10048887.

Khang, A, V. A. Hajimahmud, Eugenia Litvinova, Svetlana Chumachenko, Vusala Abuzarova, and P. T. N. Anh, "Application of Computer Vision in the Healthcare Ecosystem," *Computer Vision and AI-Integrated IoT Technologies in Medical Ecosystem* (1st Ed.). (2024). CRC Press. https://doi.org/10.1201/9781003429609-1

Khang, A., M. Muthmainnah, Prodhan Mahbub Ibna Seraj, Ahmad Al Yakin, Ahmad J. Obaid, and Manas Ranjan Panda, "AI-Aided Teaching Model for the Education 5.0." Handbook of Research on AI-Based Technologies and Applications in the Era of the Metaverse (1st Ed.). (2023). Page (83–104). IGI Global Press. https://doi.org/10.4018/978-1-6684-8851-5.ch004

Khang, A., Nazila Ali Ragimova, Sardarov Yaqub Bali, V. A. Hajimahmud, Askarova Bahar, and Mammadova Mehriban, "Using Big Data to Solve Problems in the Field of Medicine," *Computer Vision and AI-Integrated IoT Technologies in Medical Ecosystem* (1st Ed.). (2024). CRC Press.

Khang, A., Kali Charan Rath, Suresh Kumar Satapathy, Amaresh Kumar, Sudhansu Ranjan Das, and Manas Ranjan Panda, "Enabling the Future of Manufacturing: Integration of Robotics and IoT to Smart Factory Infrastructure in Industry 4.0." Handbook of Research on *AI-Based Technologies and Applications in the Era of the Metaverse* (1st Ed.) (2023). Page (25–50). IGI Global Press. https://doi.org/10.4018/978-1-6684-8851-5.ch002

Khang, A., V. Shah, and S. Rani, Handbook of Research on *AI-Based Technologies and Applications in the Era of the Metaverse* (1st Ed.) (2023). IGI Global Press. https://doi.org/10.4018/978-1-6684-8851-5

Khang, A, Hahanov Vladimir, Eugenia Litvinova, Svetlana Chumachenko, Avromovic Zoran, Rashad İsmibeyli, Nazila Ali Ragimova, V. A. Hajimahmud, Abuzarova Vusala Alyar, and P. T. N. Anh, "Medical and BioMedical Signal Processing and Prediction," *Computer Vision and AI-Integrated IoT Technologies in Medical Ecosystem* (1st Ed.) (2024). CRC Press. https://doi.org/10.1201/9781003429609-7

Konstantinidis, F. K., S. G. Mouroutsos, and A. Gasteratos, "The Role of Machine Vision in Industry 4.0: an automotive manufacturing perspective." 2021 IEEE International Conference on Imaging Systems and Techniques (IST), (2021). https://doi.org/10.1109/ist50367.2021.9651453.

Kotsiopoulos, T., P. Sarigiannidis, D. Ioannidis, and D. Tzovaras, "Machine Learning and Deep Learning in Smart Manufacturing: The Smart Grid Paradigm." Computer Science Review, vol. 40, p. 100341, (2021). https://doi.org/10.1016/j.cosrev.2020.100341.

Kruger, N., "Deep Hierarchies in the Primate Visual Cortex: What Can We Learn for Computer Vision?" IEEE Transactions on Pattern Analysis and Machine Intelligence, vol. 35, no. 8, pp. 1847–1871, (2013). https://doi.org/10.1109/tpami.2012.272.

Kumar, G., and P. K. Bhatia, "A Detailed Review of Feature Extraction in Image Processing Systems." 2014 Fourth International Conference on Advanced Computing & Communication Technologies, (2014). https://doi.org/10.1109/acct.2014.74.

Li, C., Y. Chen, and Y. Shang, "A Review of Industrial Big Data for Decision Making in Intelligent Manufacturing." Engineering Science and Technology, an International Journal, vol. 29, p. 101021, (2022). https://doi.org/10.1016/j.jestch.2021.06.001.

Li, X., W. Yi, H.-L. Chi, X. Wang, and A. P. Chan, "A Critical Review of Virtual and Augmented Reality (VR/AR) Applications in Construction Safety." Automation in Construction, vol. 86, pp. 150–162, (2018). https://doi.org/10.1016/j.autcon.2017.11.003.

Lucas, W., D. Bertaso, G. Melton, J. Smith, and C. Balfour, "Real-Time Vision-Based Control of Weld Pool Size." Welding International, vol. 26, no. 4, pp. 243–250, (2012). https://doi.org/10.1080/09507116.2011.581336.

Mahadas, B. B., S. S. Kalluri, P. Devarapu, and S. L. Bandi, "Optical Character Recognition and Text to Speech Generation System using Machine Learning." 2023 2nd International Conference on Applied Artificial Intelligence and Computing (ICAAIC), (2023). https://doi.org/10.1109/icaaic56838.2023.10140864.

Malamas, E. N., E. G. Petrakis, M. Zervakis, L. Petit, and J.-D. Legat, "A Survey on Industrial Vision Systems, Applications and Tools." Image and Vision Computing, vol. 21, no. 2, pp. 171–188, (2003). https://doi.org/10.1016/S0262-8856(02)00152-X.

Mesbah, A., and D. B. Graves, "Machine Learning for Modeling, Diagnostics, and Control of non-Equilibrium Plasmas." Journal of Physics D: Applied Physics, vol. 52, no. 30, (2019). https://doi.org/10.1088/1361-6463/ab1f3f.

Nath, N. D., and A. H. Behzadan, "Deep Learning Models for Content-Based Retrieval of Construction Visual Data." *Computing in Civil Engineering 2019* (2019). https://ascelibrary.org/doi/abs/10.1061/9780784482438.009

Okarma, K., and J. Fastowicz, "Computer Vision Methods for Non-Destructive Quality Assessment in Additive Manufacturing." *Advances in Intelligent Systems and Computing* (2019). Pages (11–20). Springer. https://doi.org/10.1007/978-3-030-19738-4_2.

Park, M., and J. Jeong, "Design and Implementation of Machine Vision-Based Quality Inspection System in Mask Manufacturing Process." Sustainability, vol. 14, no. 10, p. 6009, (2022). https://doi.org/10.3390/su14106009.

Patel, K. K., A. Kar, S. N. Jha, and M. A. Khan, "Machine Vision System: A Tool for Quality Inspection of Food and Agricultural Products." Journal of Food Science and Technology, vol. 49, no. 2, pp. 123–141, (2011). https://doi.org/10.1007/s13197-011-0321-4.

Pérez, L., Íñigo Rodríguez, N. Rodríguez, R. Usamentiaga, and D. García, "Robot Guidance Using Machine Vision Techniques in Industrial Environments: A Comparative Review." Sensors, vol. 16, no. 3, p. 335, (2016). https://doi.org/10.3390/s16030335.

Pradhan, J., A. K. Pal, and H. Banka, "Principal Texture Direction Based Block Level Image Reordering and Use of Color Edge Features for Application of Object Based Image Retrieval." Multimedia Tools and Applications, vol. 78, no. 2, pp. 1685–1717, (2018). https://doi.org/10.1007/s11042-018-6246-4.

Pulli, K., A. Baksheev, K. Kornyakov, and V. Eruhimov, "Real-Time Computer Vision with OpenCV." Communications of the ACM, vol. 55, no. 6, pp. 61–69, (2012). https://doi.org/10.1145/2184319.2184337.

Razdan, V., and R. Bateman, "Investigation into the use of smartphone as a machine vision device for engineering metrology and flaw detection, with focus on drilling." SPIE Proceedings, (2015). https://doi.org/10.1117/12.2183081.

Sarker, I. H., "Data Science and Analytics: An Overview from Data-Driven Smart Computing, Decision-Making and Applications Perspective." SN Computer Science, vol. 2, no. 5, (2021). https://doi.org/10.1007/s42979-021-00765-8.

Scime, L., and J. Beuth, "Anomaly Detection and Classification in a Laser Powder Bed Additive Manufacturing Process Using a Trained Computer Vision Algorithm." Additive Manufacturing, vol. 19, pp. 114–126, (2018). https://doi.org/10.1016/j.addma.2017.11.009.

Shang, H., C. Liu, and R. Wang, "Measurement Methods of 3D Shape of Large-Scale Complex Surfaces Based on Computer Vision: A Review." Measurement, vol. 197, p. 111302, (2022). https://doi.org/10.1016/j.measurement.2022.111302.

Shukla, Utkarsh, Namrata Dhanda, and Rajat Verma, "Augmented Reality Product Showcase E-commerce Application." Proceedings of the International Conference on Innovative Computing & Communication (ICICC) 2022. February 16, 2023. Available at SSRN: https://ssrn.com/abstract=4361319 or http://dx.doi.org/10.2139/ssrn.4361319.

Singh, S. A., and K. A. Desai, "Automated Surface Defect Detection Framework Using Machine Vision and Convolutional Neural Networks." Journal of Intelligent Manufacturing, vol. 34, no. 4, pp. 1995–2011, (2022). https://doi.org/10.1007/s10845-021-01878-w.

Sivaraman, S., and M. M. Trivedi, "Looking at Vehicles on the Road: A Survey of Vision-Based Vehicle Detection, Tracking, and Behavior Analysis." IEEE Transactions on Intelligent Transportation Systems, vol. 14, no. 4, pp. 1773–1795, (2013). https://doi.org/10.1109/tits.2013.2266661.

Sokolowski, J. A. and Banks, C. M. (Eds.) Principles of Modeling and Simulation (2011). John Wiley & Sons. https://doi.org/10.1002/9780470403563.

Sun, J., C. Li, X-J. Wu, V. Palade, and W. Fang, "An Effective Method of Weld Defect Detection and Classification Based on Machine Vision." IEEE Transactions on Industrial Informatics, vol. 15, no. 12, pp. 6322–6333, (2019). https://doi.org/10.1109/tii.2019.2896357.

Verma, R., N. Dhanda, and V. Nagar, Addressing the Issues & Challenges of Internet of Things Using Blockchain Technology. International Journal of Advanced Science and Technology, vol. 29, no. 05, pp. 10074–10082, (2020). http://sersc.org/journals/index.php/IJAST/article/view/19491.

Verma, R., N. Dhanda, and V. Nagar, "Security Concerns in IoT Systems and Its Blockchain Solutions." Cyber Intelligence and Information Retrieval (2021a). Page (485–495). Springer. https://doi.org/10.1007/978-981-16-4284-5_42.

Verma, R., N. Dhanda, and V. Nagar, "Application of Truffle Suite in a Blockchain Environment." Proceedings of Third International Conference on Computing, Communications, and Cyber-Security, pp. 693–702, (2022a). https://doi.org/10.1007/978-981-19-1142-2_54.

Verma, R., N. Dhanda, and V Nagar, "Enhancing & Optimizing Security of IoT Systems Using Different Components of Industry 4.0." International Journal of Engineering Trends and Technology, vol. 70, no. 7, pp. 147–157, (2022b). https://doi.org/10.14445/22315381/ijett-v70i7p216.

Verma, R., N. Dhanda, and V. Nagar, "Enhancing Security with In-Depth Analysis of Brute-Force Attack on Secure Hashing Algorithms." Proceedings of Trends in Electronics and Health Informatics, pp. 513–522, (2022c). https://doi.org/10.1007/978-981-16-8826-3_44.

Verma, R., N. Dhanda, and V. Nagar, "Analysing the Security Aspects of IoT Using Blockchain and Cryptographic Algorithms." International Journal on Recent and Innovation Trends in Computing and Communication." vol. 11, no. 1s, pp. 13–22, (2023a). https://doi.org/10.17762/ijritcc.v11i1s.5990.

Verma, R., N. Dhanda, V. Nagar, and M. Dhanda, Towards an Efficient IoT System by Integrating Blockchain in IoT. Journal of Theoretical and Applied Information Technology, vol. 101, no. 5, pp. 1637–1647, (2023b). https://www.jatit.org/volumes/Vol101No5/4Vol101No5.pdf

Verma, R., P. K. Mishra, V. Nagar, and S. Mahapatra, "Internet of Things and Smart Homes: A Review." *Wireless Sensor Networks and the Internet of Things* (2021). Pages (111–128). CRC Press. https://doi.org/10.1201/9781003131229-9.

Verma, R., V. Nagar, and S. Mahapatra, "Introduction to Supervised Learning." *Data Analytics in Bioinformatics* (2021b). Pages (1–34). Wiley. https://doi.org/10.1002/9781119785620.ch1.

Verno, A., B. Fuschetto, and F. P. Trees, "CSTA national standards and their impact on the future of K-12 computer education." Proceedings of the 2011 Conference on Information Technology Education, (2011). https://doi.org/10.1145/2047594.2047624.

Vora, P., J. Farrell, J. Tietz, and D. Brainard, "Image Capture: Simulation of Sensor Responses from Hyperspectral Images." IEEE Transactions on Image Processing, vol. 10, no. 2, pp. 307–316, (2001). https://doi.org/10.1109/83.902295.

Yang, L., Y. Liu, H. Yu, X. Fang, L. Song, D. Li and Y. Chen, "Computer Vision Models in Intelligent Aquaculture with Emphasis on Fish Detection and Behavior Analysis: A Review." Archives of Computational Methods in Engineering, vol. 28, no. 4, pp. 2785–2816, (2020). https://doi.org/10.1007/s11831-020-09486-2.

Zhang, Y., L. Yuan, W. Liang, X. Xia, and Z. Pang, "3D-SWiM: 3D Vision-Based Seam Width Measurement for Industrial Composite Fiber Layup in-situ Inspection." Robotics and Computer-Integrated Manufacturing, vol. 82, p. 102546, (2023). https://doi.org/10.1016/j.rcim.2023.102546.

Zhang, L., L. Zhang, and B. Du, "Deep Learning for Remote Sensing Data: A Technical Tutorial on the State of the Art." IEEE Geoscience and Remote Sensing Magazine, vol. 4, no. 2, pp. 22–40, (2016). https://doi.org/10.1109/mgrs.2016.2540798.

Zhou, H., C. Xu, X. Tang, S. Wang, and Z. Zhang, "A Review of Vision-Laser-Based Civil Infrastructure Inspection and Monitoring." Sensors, vol. 22, no. 15, p. 5882, (2022). https://doi.org/10.3390/s22155882.

3 Application of Computer Vision in Manufacturing

Roheen Qamar and Baqar Ali Zardari

3.1 INTRODUCTION

Computer vision (CV) is a branch of artificial intelligence (AI) that teaches computers to observe, interpret, and comprehend their surroundings using machine learning techniques. CV is a branch of AI that uses machine learning to analyze and make choices about images and movies. We can, in a sense, provide vision to software and technology by using computer vision.

Computer vision enables computers and systems to derive meaningful information from digital photos, videos, and other visual inputs—and then act or recommend based on that information. If AI allows computers to think, computer vision allows them to see, watch, and comprehend.

Computer vision functions similarly to human vision, with the exception that humans have a head start. Human vision has the advantage of lifetimes of context to train how to discern objects apart, how far away they are, if they are moving, and if something is incorrect with a picture as shown in Figure 3.1.

A system trained to inspect products or monitor a manufacturing asset may analyze thousands of products or processes per minute, detecting imperceptible faults

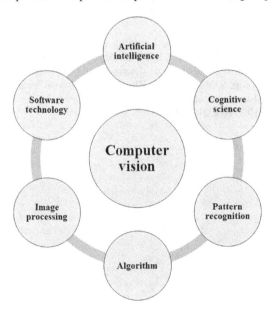

FIGURE 3.1 Components of computer vision.

DOI: 10.1201/9781003438137-3

or difficulties. CV is employed in a variety of industries, from energy and utilities to manufacturing and automotive, and the industry is expanding. In 2022, it was estimated at USD $48.6 billion (Khang & Hajimahmud et al., 2024).

3.1.1 HISTORY OF COMPUTER VISION

For almost 60 years, scientists and engineers have been trying to develop methods for machines to see and analyze visual input. Experiments began in 1959, when neurophysiologists gave a cat a series of images in an attempt to correlate a response in its brain. They noticed that it responded initially to hard edges or lines, which implied that image processing begins with simple shapes such as straight edges. Around the same time, the first computer image scanning technology, which allowed computers to digitize and acquire images, was developed. Another watershed moment occurred in 1963, when computers were able to convert two-dimensional images into three-dimensional forms. AI developed as an academic topic of study in the 1960s, which also marked the beginning of the AI search to address the human eyesight problem (Khang & Rath, 2023).

In 1974, optical character recognition (OCR) technology was introduced, which could recognize text printed in any font or typeface. Similarly, employing neural networks, intelligent character recognition (ICR) could read handwritten text. Both OCR and ICR have since found their way into document and invoice processing, vehicle plate recognition, mobile payments, machine translation, and a variety of other popular applications. In 1982, David Marr, a neuroscientist, proved that vision works hierarchically and introduced techniques for robots to detect edges, corners, curves, and other basic structures. Concurrently, computer scientist Kunihiko Fukushima created a network of cells capable of pattern recognition. The Neocognitron network used convolutional layers in a neural network (Hillel et al., 2014).

3.1.2 WHAT ARE THE RISKS OF COMPUTER VISION?

Computer vision, like any technology, is a tool, which means it can have both benefits and drawbacks. Although CV has many applications in everyday life that make it a helpful element of modern society, recent privacy concerns have been raised. The most frequently discussed subject in the media is facial recognition. Computer vision is used in facial recognition technologies to identify specific people in photographs and movies. In its most basic form, it is used by firms like Meta or Google to urge people to tag images, but it can also be used by law enforcement to hunt down suspects. Some people believe that facial recognition infringes on privacy, especially when commercial corporations use it to monitor clients in order to learn more about them (Finlayson et al., 2019; Petrov & Popov, 2020).

3.2 WHAT IS THE PROCESS OF COMPUTER VISION?

Computer vision programmers take raw images and convert them into useable data and insights using a mix of techniques. Two-dimensional images serve as the foundation for many computer vision works. While photos appear to be a complex input,

FIGURE 3.2 Process of computer vision.

they may be decomposed into raw numbers. Images are simply a collection of discrete pixels, each of which can be represented by a single integer (grayscale) or a mixture of numbers such as (255, 0, 0—RGB).

A CV algorithm performs processing once we have converted an image to a set of integers. One method is to use a classic approach known as convolutional neural networks (CNNs), which uses layers to group together pixels in order to build ever more complex images. A large amount of data is required for computer vision. It repeatedly executes data analyses until it detects distinctions and, eventually, recognizes images. To teach a computer to recognize automotive tires, for example, massive amounts of tire photos and tire-related materials must be given into it in order for it to learn the differences and recognize a tire, especially one with no faults, as shown in Figure 3.2.

A CNN aids a machine learning (ML) or deep learning (DL) model's "look" by breaking down images into pixels that are tagged or labeled. It utilizes the labels to conduct convolutions (a mathematical procedure on two functions to produce a third function) and forecast what it is "seeing." In a series of iterations, the neural network executes convolutions and verifies the accuracy of its predictions until the predictions begin to come true. It then recognizes or sees images in a manner comparable to humans. A CNN, like a human seeing an image from a distance, first discerns hard edges and simple forms, then fills in information as it runs prediction iterations. A CNN is used to comprehend individual images (Ward et al., 2021).

3.3 WHAT IS THE IMPORTANCE OF COMPUTER VISION?

Computer vision has been around since the 1950s and is still a major subject of study with many applications. According to the deep learning research group BitRefine, the CV business will grow to approximately USD $50 billion in 2022, with hardware accounting for 75 percent of revenue. The importance of CV stems from the growing requirement for computers to perceive their surroundings. To grasp the surroundings, computers must be able to perceive what humans see, which entails imitating the experience of human vision. This is particularly crucial as we construct more complicated AI systems with more human-like capabilities (O'Mahony et al., 2020).

3.4 COMPUTER VISION APPLICATIONS

3.4.1 Facial Recognition

Facial detection is a fundamental problem in CV and pattern recognition, as well as one of the most extensively used CV applications. Several facial feature detection algorithms have been introduced in the last decade. However, the effectiveness of DL and CNN in the development of extremely accurate face identification solutions

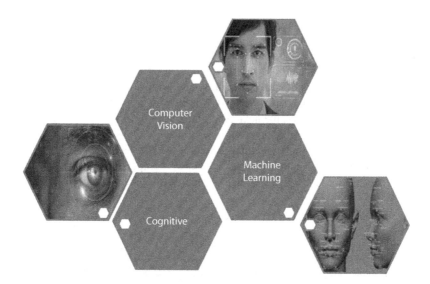

FIGURE 3.3 Facial recognition of computer vision.

has only lately been realized. Other items such as trees, buildings, and people are excluded from the digital image.

Facial detection is a subset of object–class detection in which the aim is to locate and size all items in an image that correspond to a specified class. All facial analysis methods, including facial alignment, facial recognition, facial verification, and facial parsing, require facial detection as the first step, as shown in Figure 3.3. In addition, facial recognition is utilized in a variety of applications, including content-based image retrieval, video coding, video conferencing, crowd video surveillance, and intelligent human–computer interfaces (Khan et al., 2018; Fang et al., 2020).

3.4.2 SELF-DRIVING CARS

Recent developments in CV have transformed numerous fields of study including robotics, automation, and self-driving cars. The self-driving car industry has evolved significantly in recent years, thanks in large part to the employment of cutting-edge CV algorithms. However, there are still numerous hurdles in the industry. Perception is one of the most challenging difficulties in autonomous driving. Planning and control become easier once autonomous vehicles have an accurate perception of their surroundings. Computer vision perception and the potential of computer vision and neural networks for application in fully autonomous self-driving vehicles are discussed in Elngar et al. (2021) and Voulodimos et al. (2018).

3.4.3 ROBOTIC AUTOMATION

Robotics is a technology discipline that combines computer science and engineering while working with physical robots. Robots are outfitted with sensors that allow them to visualize and perceive their surroundings, as well as effectors that allow them to interact with the outside environment. Computer vision heavily relies on these sensors to enable robots to "see" and target items of interest. But, if at all, how does CV vary from robot vision? On the other hand, CV tries to give computers the ability to see by developing algorithms that process digital images or movies. It focuses on picture categorization, object identification, tracking, and posture estimation. However, CV and its use in the robotics business are multifaceted, as we will see in the following sections. In terms of skill set, the next generation of robots is likely to outperform its traditional counterparts. The integration of CV and robots is already a tremendous step forward that will undoubtedly alter technology. However, the rapid advancement of automation and the growing demand for human–computer collaboration face significant obstacles for CV robots (Zafeiriou et al., 2015; Canedo & Neves, 2019).

3.4.4   MEDICAL ANOMALY DETECTION

Computer vision is important in the ongoing automation of the medical industry because it allows computers to recognize objects. Computer vision is already changing the medical industry for the better. We could identify ailments and perform surgery with less effort if we automated medical operations and detection. Such CV robots can be enhanced in the future. One example is teaching the robot to recognize brain diseases, which will be a more difficult task than recognizing skin diseases like melanoma. We can improve the medical profession one line of code at a time by merging multiple AI algorithms (Barua et al., 2019).

3.4.5   ANIMAL MONITORING

A significant method of smart farming is animal monitoring using CV. Machine learning monitors the health of individual livestock such as pigs, cattle, or poultry using camera streams (Bhalla et al., 2020). Smart vision systems seek to analyze animal behavior in order to improve animal productivity, health, and well-being, and hence influence yields and economic benefits in the farming sector as shown in Figure 3.4.

3.4.6   AGRICULTURAL MONITORING

The agriculture sector has made significant contributions to AI and CV in areas such as plant health detection and monitoring, planting, weeding, harvesting, and sophisticated weather analysis. Numerous smart-farming use cases have an impact on the

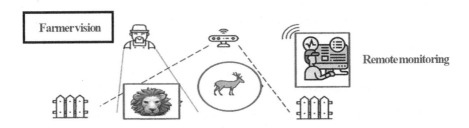

FIGURE 3.4   Animal monitoring of computer vision.

entire food supply chain by offering helpful insights into the entire agricultural process, simplifying real-time operational decision-making, and improving farming practices through the use of on-field smart sensors and equipment.

Computer vision allows machines to see and interpret the visual environment in the same way that people do. Non-contact and scalable sensing systems in agriculture are made possible by merging CV algorithms with distant cameras for picture acquisition. Some of the agricultural uses are AI-powered animal monitoring, visual quality control, automated inspections for quality standards, and infrastructure monitoring. Furthermore, by employing picture analysis to determine plant health, growth patterns, and potential stress causes, CV has the potential to dramatically enhance crop monitoring and yield prediction (Paneru & Jeelani, 2021).

3.4.7 MEDICAL SKILL TRAINING

On self-learning platforms, CV applications are utilized to measure the skill level of expert learners. For surgical education, for example, simulation-based surgical training systems have been established. Furthermore, the action quality evaluation technique enables the development of computer systems that automatically evaluate the performance of surgical trainees (Khang & Muthmainnah et al., 2023). As a result, individuals can be given valuable feedback that will help them improve their skill levels (Martinez-de Dios et al., 2003).

3.4.8 FISH FARMING WITH COMPUTER VISION

Computer vision is an important technology in precision farming for attaining automatic fish detection. Deep learning algorithms, in particular, have shown considerable promise in fish species identification, counting, and behavior analysis. In addition, CV is fast evolving for use in efficient intelligent feeding systems. Such systems are based on underwater image pre-processing, fish detection, estimation of fish weight and length, and study of fish behavior (Elyan et al., 2022).

3.4.9 LIVESTOCK FARMING USING COMPUTER VISION SYSTEMS

Food security is one of the world's most pressing issues. Livestock and poultry provide a significant amount (30 percent) of one's daily protein intake through products such as meat, milk, eggs, and offal. Animal output is predicted to rise in response to the expanding human population. Producers are under increasing pressure to provide quality care for an increasing number of animals per management unit as production is expanded to meet increased demand. This becomes even more difficult in light of potential labor shortages for agriculture occupations. Computer vision systems use cameras to monitor animals such as cattle, sheep, pigs, and others. In real-time, neural networks are used to analyze video input (Gabaldon et al., 2022).

3.4.10 MONITORING OF ROAD CONDITIONS

Computer vision-based fault identification and condition evaluation are being developed to monitor road concrete and asphalt civil infrastructure. Pavement

Monitoring of Road Conditions

FIGURE 3.5 Monitoring road conditions using computer vision.

condition evaluation gives information that can be used to make more cost-effective and consistent decisions about pavement network management. Pavement distress examinations are often carried out using sophisticated data gathering vehicles and/or foot-on-ground surveys, as shown in Figure 3.5. A Deep Machine Learning Approach was created to develop an asphalt pavement condition index in order to provide a human-independent, low-cost, efficient, and safe method of automated pavement distress identification via CV (Kakani et al., 2020).

3.5   TOP 4 COMPUTER VISION CHALLENGES AND SOLUTIONS IN 2023

Many industries including healthcare, retail, and automotive are being transformed by CV technologies. As more businesses invest in CV technologies, the global market is expected to grow ninefold to USD $2.4 billion by 2026. However, incorporating CV in your organization may be a difficult and costly process, and poor planning might result in CV and AI project failure. As a result, before embarking on hiring CV engineers, business executives must exercise caution. This article examines four obstacles that business managers may experience when using CV in their operations, as well as how they may overcome them to protect their investments and maximize return on investment. Refer to Khang & Hajimahmud et al. (2024) for some examples.

3.5.1   Insufficient Hardware

Software and hardware are used to implement CV technology. A company must install high-resolution cameras, sensors, and robots to ensure the system's efficacy. This hardware can be expensive, and, if inefficient or incorrectly fitted, it can result in blind spots and ineffective CV systems.

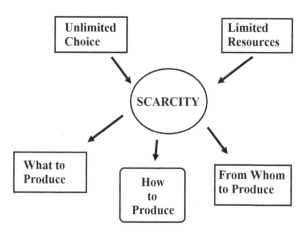

FIGURE 3.6　Scarcity of training data of computer vision.

3.5.2　Inadequate Quality

A good CV system is built on high-quality labeled and annotated datasets. In industries where CV technology is widely utilized, such as healthcare, it is critical to have high-quality data annotation and labeling because the consequences of faulty CV systems can be severe. Many methods designed to detect COVID-19, for example, failed due to low-quality data (Safaryna et al., 2023).

3.5.3　Scarcity of Training Data

Collecting meaningful and sufficient data might be difficult. These difficulties may result in a scarcity of training data for CV systems. Data annotators, for example, face difficulties in acquiring medical data (Khang & Vladimir et al., 2024). This is mostly owing to the sensitivity and privacy concerns associated with healthcare data. The majority of medical photos are either sensitive or private, and they are not shared by healthcare practitioners or hospitals, as shown in Figure 3.6. Furthermore, it is possible that the developers lack the resources to acquire necessary data.

3.5.4　Weak Planning for Model Development

Another challenge can be weak planning for creating the ML model that is deployed for the CV system. During the planning stage, executives tend to set overly ambitious targets, which are hard to achieve for the data science team as shown in Figure 3.7.

3.6　RELATED WORK

Feng and Feng (2018) address the limits of present sensor systems for field applications. The research community has been actively exploring novel technologies that can advance structural health monitoring's (SHM) state-of-the-art. The camera-based non-contact vision sensor has emerged as a promising alternative to

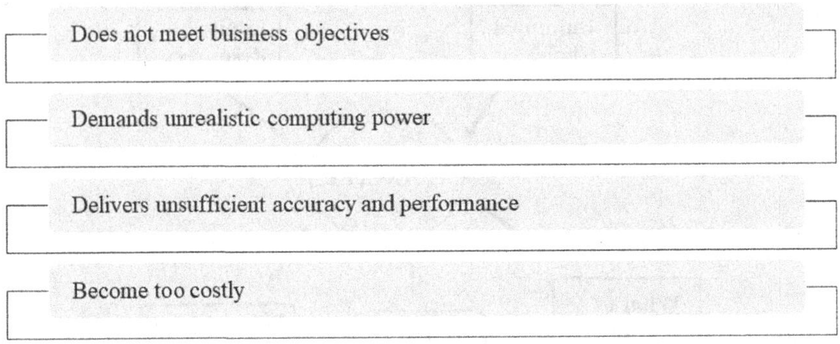

> Does not meet business objectives

> Demands unrealistic computing power

> Delivers unsufficient accuracy and performance

> Become too costly

FIGURE 3.7 Weak planning for model development of computer vision.

conventional contact sensors for structural dynamic response assessment and health monitoring, thanks to rapid improvements in CV. The vision sensor's significant advantages include its low cost and ease of setup and operation. This review study aims to summarize the research community's cumulative experience obtained from the recent development and validation of vision-based sensors for structural dynamic response assessment and SHM.

The general principles of vision sensor systems are first presented by reviewing various template matching techniques for tracking targets, coordinate conversion methods for determining calibration factors to convert image pixel displacements to physical displacements, measurements by tracking artificial vs. natural targets, measurements in real-time vs. in post-processing, and so on. The report then discusses measurement error causes and mitigation approaches, as well as laboratory and field experiments conducted to evaluate the performance of vision sensors and ability to derive displacements of any location on the structure from a single video measurement.

In recent years, generative adversarial networks (GANs) have received a lot of attention Wang et al. (2021). Their greatest influence has perhaps been in the CV field where tremendous breakthroughs have been made in difficulties such as plausible picture generation, image-to-image translation, face attribute modification, and similar domains. Despite substantial progress, applying GANs to real-world situations still poses three significant hurdles: (1) picture generation of high quality, (2) image generation diversity, and (3) image stabilization training. We present a complete overview of the state-of-the-art in GAN-related research in the published scientific literature, focusing on the extent to which popular GAN technologies have progressed against these constraints. This review is further structured by a useful taxonomy we developed based on variances in GAN designs and loss functions. While various assessments of GANs have been provided to date, none have examined the state of the field in terms of progress toward addressing real CV concerns. As a result, we examine and evaluate the most common architecture-variant and loss-variant GANs for addressing these difficulties. Our goal is to present an overview of GAN research as well as a critical appraisal of relevant progress toward essential CV application requirements. We also highlight the most appealing applications in

CV where GANs have shown significant success, as well as some future research prospects.

The purpose of the article by Kanellakis and Nikolakopoulos (2017) is to give a complete literature analysis on vision-based applications for unmanned aerial vehicles (UAVs), with a focus on current advances and trends. These applications are classified into distinct categories based on the research themes of various research groups. The identified components toward autonomous agents are vision-based position-attitude control, pose estimation and mapping, obstacle detection, and target tracking. By incorporating all of these technologies onboard, aerial platforms could achieve increased autonomy. Furthermore, the concept of fusion of many sensors is stressed throughout this text, as is an outline of the difficulties addressed and future developments in autonomous agent creation.

The COVID-19 pandemic prompted an urgent call to participate in the fight against a massive threat to humanity (Ulhaq et al., 2020). As a subfield of artificial intelligence, CV has recently achieved success in tackling several complicated challenges in healthcare such as COVID-19. Computer vision experts are putting their knowledge to the test in order to design successful solutions to pandemics such as COVID-19 and assist the global community. With each passing day, new contributions are shared. This prompted us to assess recent work, gather information about available research resources, and sketch out potential study directions. We want to make it easier for CV researchers to find current and new datasets. This article also provides an initial evaluation of the literature on the research community's efforts to combat the COVID-19 pandemic.

Visual question answering (VQA) is a difficult topic that has sparked interest in both the CV and natural language processing (NLP) communities (Wu et al., 2017). Given an image and a natural language inquiry, inferring the proper answer needs reasoning over visual features of the image as well as general knowledge. The first section of this article compares recent methods to the problem to assess the state-of-the-art. Methods are categorized based on how they connect the visual and textual modes. Popular strategy of integrating convolutional and recurrent neural networks is investigated to map images and questions to a shared feature space in particular.

Memory-augmented and modular architectures that interface with structured knowledge bases are also discussed. The datasets available for training and assessing VQA systems are reviewed in the second section of this survey. The numerous datasets contain questions of varying complexity, requiring different capabilities and styles of reasoning. In-depth investigation is conducted of the Visual Genome Project's question/answer pairs and the value of structured annotations of photos with scene graphs for VQA is assessed. Finally, interesting future possibilities for the subject is examined, focusing on the relationship to structured knowledge bases and the usage of NLP models.

Voulodimos et al.'s (2018) review paper presents a brief summary of some of the most important DL algorithms utilized in CV applications, namely CNNs, Deep Boltzmann Machines and Deep Belief Networks, and Stacked Denoising Autoencoders. A brief history, structure, advantages, and limits are provided, followed by a description of their applications in diverse CV tasks such as object identification, facial recognition, action and activity recognition, and human position estimation. Finally, a quick outline of future approaches is provided in constructing DL methods for CV applications and the associated challenges.

Chen et al. (2020) discusses one of the most fundamental and difficult topics in CV, vision-based monocular human position estimation, which seeks to obtain human body posture from input images or video sequences. Recent advances in DL approaches have resulted in tremendous progress and astonishing achievements in the field of human position estimation. This assessment thoroughly examines the most recent DL-based two- and three-dimensional human position estimation algorithms published since 2014. This study summarizes the issues, main frameworks, benchmark datasets, assessment criteria, and performance comparison, and it discusses some possible future research avenues.

3.7 COMPUTER VISION VS. ARTIFICIAL INTELLIGENCE

It is important to note that CV is not synonymous with AI. Both are forms of technology that aim to make our lives easier and more convenient, but they are not the same. Artificial intelligence is an area of computer science in which machines appear to mimic human intelligence. Making decisions based on how humans would analyze a situation, learning from experience, understanding language, conversing with humans and other computers, and even solving problems creatively in new ways are all examples of AI. Meanwhile, CV allows computers to see their surroundings. This involves software that performs image-processing tasks, which computers can already handle, and is the area where AI advances.

Computer vision is a branch of computer science that uses mathematical approaches to comprehend images and videos. It differs from AI in that it uses a set of general principles to process images. Simultaneously, AI is an area in which machines can learn to execute complex jobs for themselves. Consider object recognition as an example. This is the branch of CV that assists computers in identifying and comprehending objects in images, as shown in Figure 3.8. There will be various ways to object recognition, including DL and CNNs, which are frequently connected with AI (Wu et al., 2017).

Neural networks (NNs) are in charge of assisting computers in recognizing images at a detailed level. If you have ever done an image search on Google or Facebook, you have probably seen something like this. Convolutional neural networks also aid

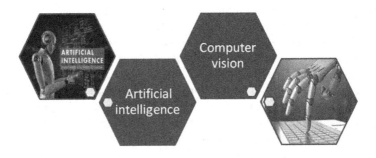

FIGURE 3.8 Computer vision vs. artificial intelligence.

in facial identification in pictures, distinguishing between a person's eyes, mouth, nose, and other facial features. In the real world, this information can be utilized for a variety of purposes, including identifying persons and retrieving pertinent information about them.

3.8 HOW COMPUTER VISION IS TRANSFORMING

Computer vision is making our life easier and more convenient in a variety of fields. In retail, it offers more efficient purchasing experiences by allowing mobile devices to recognize products based solely on their photos. It is being used in medicine to analyze x-rays, MRIs, and other medical pictures, providing insight from a computer's perspective that would otherwise be unattainable. Automotive uses include self-driving cars, such as Tesla, that are using CV to enhance existing sensors to ensure a safe and efficient trip (Chen et al., 2020).

3.8.1 PHYSICS OF SOLIDS

Another field that is strongly related to CV is solid-state physics. The majority of CV systems rely on image sensors to detect electromagnetic radiation, which can take the form of visible or infrared light. Quantum physics is used to design the sensors. Physics is used to explain the mechanism by which light interacts with surfaces. The behavior of optics, which are an essential component of most imaging systems, is explained by physics. To provide a thorough understanding of the image production process, sophisticated image sensors even require quantum mechanics (Akhtar & Mian, 2018). Computer vision may also be used to solve a variety of physics measurement problems, such as fluid velocity.

3.8.2 NEUROBIOLOGY

Neurobiology has had a significant impact on the development of CV algorithms. Over the last century, there has been a great deal of research on the eyes, neurons, and brain structures involved in the processing of visual stimuli in both humans and animals. This has resulted in a crude, yet confusing, description of how natural vision systems work to tackle specific vision-related tasks. These findings have given rise to a subfield of CV in which artificial systems are designed to replicate the processing and behavior of biological systems of varying complexity. Furthermore, some of the learning-based methods established in CV (e.g., neural net and deep learning-based image and feature analysis and classification) have a neurobiological foundation.

3.8.3 SIGNAL PROCESSING

Signal processing is another topic connected to CV. Many approaches for processing one-variable signals, often temporal signals, can be naturally extended to two-variable or multivariable signals in CV. However, due to the unique nature of images, many methods established within CV have no equivalent in the processing of one-variable signals. This, along with the signal's multidimensionality, defines a subfield in signal processing as part of CV.

3.8.4 NAVIGATION BY ROBOTS

Robot navigation can refer to the autonomous course planning or reasoning used by robotic systems to travel through an environment. To travel through these ecosystems, a thorough comprehension of them is essential. A CV system serving as a vision sensor and delivering high-level information about the environment and the robot could offer information about the environment.

3.8.5 MEDICINE

One of the most prominent application domains is medical CV, also known as medical image processing, which involves extracting information from picture data in order to diagnose a patient (Anh et al., 2024). Examples include the detection of tumors, arteriosclerosis, or other malignant changes, as well as a range of dental illnesses, measurements of organ size, blood flow, and so on. It also contributes to medical research by providing new information, such as on the structure of the brain or the effectiveness of medical therapies. Enhancement of images interpreted by humans such as ultrasonic images or x-ray images is another application of CV in the medical field.

3.8.6 MILITARY

Military applications are likely to be one of the most important fields of CV. The identification of hostile personnel or vehicles, as well as missile guidance, are obvious examples. More modern missile guidance systems direct the missile to an area rather than a specific target, and the target is chosen when the missile arrives at the area based on locally collected image data. Modern military notions such as "battlefield awareness" suggest that a variety of sensors, including image sensors, provide a rich set of data about a fighting situation that may be utilized to support strategic decisions. Automatic data processing is employed in this situation to reduce complexity and fuse information from many sensors to boost reliability (Silva et al., 2021).

3.9 MAIN BENEFITS OF COMPUTER VISION IN MANUFACTURING

In manufacturing, CV provides algorithms that may be pre-configured to detect and identify things. It contributes to increased worker safety and productivity. Businesses can check to see if the equipment on the floor has been serviced in order to provide best service and eliminate safety hazards. Businesses can use CV to increase floor-monitoring capabilities without requiring human participation, as shown in Table 3.1.

Furthermore, owing to COVID-19 compulsions, CV in manufacturing can monitor if all workers follow safety regulations such as wearing helmets, safety glasses, and masks. Concerns will be automatically flagged by the system, allowing management to take appropriate action.

TABLE 3.1

Main Benefits of Computer Vision in Manufacturing

No.	Benefits of Computer Vision in Manufacturing
1	Eliminates errors in quality assurance processes: A worker can easily overlook a variety of minor faults that can develop during manufacturing processes. Controlling them is critical since the product may be of poor quality. Furthermore, if the problem escalates, it may result in fines and reputational harm.
2	Improves manufacturing security: Companies can employ CV to enhance secure operations. Among the many potential measures are the additions of facial recognition systems and contactless security systems. Access is restricted to those who have a valid authorization. Algorithms that are automated can help with quality assurance and safety concerns.
3	Cost reduction: Increased productivity combined with reduced machine downtime due to automation and CV-based maintenance leads to lower overall operating expenses.

3.9.1 ALLOWS FOR SAFER OPERATIONS ON SHOP FLOORS

Computer vision in manufacturing enhances worker safety and productivity by pre-configured algorithms for detecting and identifying hazards. It also helps businesses monitor floor equipment and ensure workers follow safety regulations, enabling management to take appropriate action during health crises such as COVID-19.

3.9.2 ELIMINATES ERRORS IN QA PROCESSES

Computer vision in manufacturing helps identify production issues, eliminate errors, and improve quality by identifying and isolating bad products, increasing process efficiency, and preventing fines and ill-reputation (Kaul et al., 2020).

3.9.3 ENHANCES SECURITY IN MANUFACTURING

Environmental businesses can employ CV to ensure safe operations. Among the proposed options are facial recognition systems and contactless access restrictions. Only those with legal authorization are permitted to enter sensitive areas. Furthermore, CV can determine whether emergency exits are always clear of debris (Kaul et al., 2020). A collection of automated algorithms aids in the promotion of quality control and safety measures. Computer vision in manufacturing also leads to the digitization of the entire manufacturing system (Khang & Hajimahmud et al., 2024).

3.10 COMPUTER VISION IN MANUFACTURING USE CASES

3.10.1 ADHERENCE TO SOPS

Consider a pair of trained, experienced, and specialized eyes scrutinizing every stage of the production process, removing the element of "human error." Following standard operating procedures (SOPs) help to increase productivity, cost savings, and efficiency as given below.

- Gramener, a design-led data science company, has created one such application to ensure compliance with SOPs.
- A CV application on the manufacturing line can help to continuously monitor production quality and reduce cycle time.
- Cargo-handling SOPs, in conjunction with CV-powered monitoring, can ensure worker safety during loading and unloading, movement detection to prevent damage to both cargo and carrier vehicles, and inspection to fill unoccupied areas. Warehouse surveillance and computer vision SOPs assist in protecting employees from workplace dangers and property from vandalism.

In addition to real-time optimization, an audit approach to logistics and supply chain activities aids in the introduction of future production performance enhancements. It also increases visibility and openness throughout the supply chain.

3.10.2 Handling of Materials

Material handling is one of the repetitive logistical operations that, if not done carefully, can result in damage and excessive expenses. Computer vision systems have been created to expertly choose, sort, depalletize, load and unload, and place things. Computer vision provides particular algorithms for automated material handling in e-commerce, supply chain operations, and warehouses as given below.

- Picking operations from conveyor bulk in unstructured environments with overlapping and layered objects.
- Handling parcels with segmentation (reflective, transparent, color), classification (box, bag, envelope), label reading ("this side up"), and so on.

3.10.3 Preventive Measures for COVID-19

For safe production operations, COVID-19 rules required social separation and the use of masks at all times. In manufacturing, CV assists in monitoring production zones to detect breaches. Furthermore, these steps have ensured a safer working environment following the pandemic.

3.10.4 Quality Control

When the quality check procedure is done manually, the risks of error remain high. As a result, it is vital to automate the process and limit potential problems. Computer vision in manufacturing aids in the automation of the quality control process, resulting in higher production standards. Computer vision, when paired with DL models, eliminates the need for any human intervention (Khang & Shah et al., 2023).

3.10.5 INVENTORY CONTROL

Inventory management with CV is much more than just keeping track of things. It aids in tracking the movement of raw materials to the production plant, finished goods to the warehouse, and finally to the point of sale. Computer vision not only monitors but also speeds up and eliminates errors in inventory management with data analytics-aided insights that outperform human checking methods (Khang & Ragimova et al., 2024). Computer vision can strengthen the supply chain and intensify efforts to improve production performance, such as counting stock during inbound reception and outbound shipping and notifying managers when it is time to restock.

3.10.6 LEAN MANUFACTURING PRACTICES

Lean manufacturing assists businesses in reducing waste and increasing production. Industry 4.0 aids data-driven approaches in order to improve decision-making. Lean manufacturing practices increase equipment efficiency and save on operational costs. In manufacturing, CV watches production events across the floor. It offers improved operational efficiencies and the creation of analytics to enhance decision-making; thus, CV assists manufacturing enterprises (Segura et al., 2020).

3.10.7 TEXT AND BARCODE SCANNING

Optical character recognition (OCR) technology facilitates speedy and flawless barcode scanning. It allows for real-time data viewing and analysis for subsequent action. Text recognition technologies include intelligent character recognition (ICR), optical mark recognition (OMR), and optical barcode recognition (OBR). These technologies can be used by businesses to route components in production lines, interpret handwriting, recognize text in scanned photos and documents, and detect checkboxes (Segura et al., 2020).

3.10.8 SAFETY OF EMPLOYEES AND EQUIPMENT

Injuries in the manufacturing environment are likely if safety standards are poor; therefore, businesses cannot be casual about this issue. Manually monitoring safety measures is inadequate because the human eye may detect minor flaws that could represent a risk later. To find trouble areas, CV technology examines equipment and the surrounding environment. The system then generates reports and notifies operators when action is required. In the event of an accident, the system will send out alerts for corrective actions.

3.10.9 MANUFACTURING DEFECT DETECTION

The most effective CV algorithms have been in flaw identification and predictive maintenance. Products of poor quality are a curse for any organization, since they encourage legal wrangling, consumer unhappiness, and brand degradation. For instance, the data science company Gramener provides a CV solution for improving manufacturing performance and has already used it in the pharmaceutical business. The solution works as follows:

- The server receives product images.
- The AI programmer identifies flaws.
- The fault is analyzed and classified using deep learning algorithms.

3.10.10   BOTTOM LINE

Computer vision has numerous uses in the manufacturing and retail industries. The future of work is technology, and fully utilizing is more important than ever. Manufacturing companies that make the greatest use of technologies such as CV enjoy several benefits.

3.10.11   SORTING AND CALCULATING

Computer vision is used by manufacturers to sort and count things such as parts or components. Automatic sorting aids in accuracy, especially in high-volume manufacturing operations.

3.10.12   THREE-DIMENSIONAL DESIGN AND VISION

Product design software can use CV features to scan current components, produce three-dimensional models of them, and make prototyping of new goods easier.

3.11   COMPUTER VISION APPLICATIONS IN MANUFACTURING

Even the most manual tasks are becoming more automated. Machine learning, industrial CV, and robotics advancements are transforming manufacturing lines and supply chains. Artificial intelligence and CV, in particular, have enormous potential for addressing real-world problems ranging from ophthalmology diagnosis with retinal pictures to processing millions or even billions of pages for content analysis.

3.11.1   VISUAL QUALITY CONTROL

By far, one of the most common and in-demand CV use cases in manufacturing is visual quality inspection. There is no production line that produces 100 percent, defect-free and sound things. Traditional machinery inspections can cost millions of dollars and thousands of hours to complete. Some problems in industrial items are hardly detectable to the human eye, but CV-powered optical equipment can identify even the slightest of flaws. Machine vision manufacturing technologies have recently assisted firms in easing the inspection process and hence operational demands.

3.11.2   COST ESTIMATION

Machining is crucial in manufacturing, shaping and sizing raw materials like metal, wood, or plastic. Modern machine shops use computer-controlled precision tools for tasks like cutting, drilling, boring, and milling. Manual cost estimation requires machining experts, affecting efficiency and causing time-consuming challenges in the industry.

3.11.3 PREDICTIVE MAINTENANCE

Predictive maintenance optimizes resource utilization and predicts failures using ML to reduce downtime and improve product delivery. Predicting failures, allowing for corrective action, or reducing planned maintenance helps minimize downtime and improves overall efficiency.

3.11.4 THERMAL IMAGING

Thermal imaging, AI in manufacturing, detects overheated and overloaded components in large mechanical operations, preventing downtime and monitoring high-temperature industrial heaters, boilers, and furnaces.

3.11.5 WRAPPING UP COMPUTER VISION IN MANUFACTURING

Computer vision is an innovative technology that enhances operational processes in industries like healthcare, agriculture, and manufacturing. Common applications include visual quality inspection, cost estimation, predictive maintenance, and thermal cameras. The future of AI in manufacturing remains uncertain.

3.11.6 IMPROVING SAFETY

Manufacturing facilities are hazardous environments with large machines, moving parts, and high temperatures. Computer vision systems can help detect accidents and hazards by monitoring the site. These systems can alert management and first responders to any anomalies or accidents, ensuring immediate safety measures.

3.12 CONCLUSION

Computer vision significantly improves manufacturing processes by increasing efficiency and safety, and reducing costs through mounted cameras and wearable headsets. These technologies offer potential for capturing invisible manufacturing processes, but evaluation is crucial. Preparation involves problem-solving and pilot evaluation to extract value from digital exploration dollars. Key criteria for evaluating CV technology relevance to manufacturing operations are outlined (Khang & Rath et al., 2023).

REFERENCES

Akhtar, Naveed, and Ajmal Mian. "Threat of adversarial attacks on deep learning in computer vision: A survey." IEEE Access 6 (2018): 14410–14430. https://doi.org/10.1109/ACCESS.2018.2807385

Anh, P. T. N., Hahanov Vladimir, Triwiyanto, Nazila Ali Ragimova, Rashad İsmibeyli, Vugar Abdullayev Hajimahmud, and Abuzarova Vusala Alyar. "AI Models for Disease Diagnosis and Prediction of Heart Disease With Artificial Neural Networks," *Computer Vision and AI-Integrated IoT Technologies in Medical Ecosystem* (1st Ed.) (2024). CRC Press. https://doi.org/10.1201/9781003429609-9

Barua, Bhaskar, Clarence Gomes, Shubham Baghe, and Jignesh Sisodia. "A self-driving car implementation using computer vision for detection and navigation." In 2019 International Conference on Intelligent Computing and Control Systems (ICCS), pp. 271–274. IEEE, (2019). https://doi.org/10.1109/ICCS45141.2019.9065627

Bhalla, Aman, Munipalle Sai Nikhila, and Pradeep Singh. "Simulation of self-driving car using deep learning." In 2020 3rd International Conference on Intelligent Sustainable Systems (ICISS), pp. 519–525. IEEE, (2020). https://doi.org/10.1109/ICISS49785.2020.9315968

Canedo, Daniel, and António J. R. Neves. "Facial expression recognition using computer vision: A systematic review." Applied Sciences 9, no. 21 (2019): 4678. https://doi.org/10.3390/app9214678

Chen, Yucheng, Yingli Tian, and Mingyi He. "Monocular human pose estimation: A survey of deep learning-based methods." Computer Vision and Image Understanding 192 (2020): 102897. https://doi.org/10.1016/j.cviu.2019.102897

Engineering, pp. 1584–1596. 2020. https://doi.org/10.1145/3377811.3380404

Elngar, Ahmed A., Mohamed Arafa, Amar Fathy, Basma Moustafa, Omar Mahmoud, Mohamed Shaban, and Nehal Fawzy. "Image classification based on CNN: A survey." Journal of Cybersecurity and Information Management 6, no. 1 (2021): 18–50. https://doi.org/10.54216/JCIM.060102

Elyan, Eyad, Pattaramon Vuttipittayamongkol, Pamela Johnston, Kyle Martin, Kyle McPherson, Chrisina Jayne, and Mostafa Kamal Sarker. "Computer vision and machine learning for medical image analysis: Recent advances, challenges, and way forward." Artificial Intelligence Surgery 2 (2022). https://doi.org/10.20517/ais.2021.15

Fang, Weili, Peter ED Love, Hanbin Luo, and Lieyun Ding. "Computer vision for behaviour-based safety in construction: A review and future directions." Advanced Engineering Informatics 43 (2020): 100980. https://doi.org/10.1007/978-3-031-01821-3

Feng, Dongming, and Maria Q. Feng. "Computer vision for SHM of civil infrastructure: From dynamic response measurement to damage detection–A review." Engineering Structures 156 (2018): 105–117. https://doi.org/10.1016/j.engstruct.2017.11.018

Finlayson, Samuel G., John D. Bowers, Joichi Ito, Jonathan L. Zittrain, Andrew L. Beam, and Isaac S. Kohane. "Adversarial attacks on medical machine learning." Science 363, no. 6433 (2019): 1287–1289. https://doi.org/10.1126/science.aaw4399

Gabaldon, Joaquin, Ding Zhang, Lisa Lauderdale, Lance Miller, Matthew Johnson-Roberson, Kira Barton, and K. Alex Shorter. "Computer-vision object tracking for monitoring bottlenose dolphin habitat use and kinematics." PLoS One 17, no. 2 (2022): e0254323. https://doi.org/10.1371/journal.pone.0254323

Hillel, Aharon Bar, Ronen Lerner, Dan Levi, and Guy Raz. "Recent progress in road and lane detection: A survey." Machine Vision and Applications 25, no. 3 (2014): 727–745. https://doi.org/10.1007/s00138-011-0404-2

Kakani, Vijay, Van Huan Nguyen, Basivi Praveen Kumar, Hakil Kim, and Visweswara Rao Pasupuleti. "A critical review on computer vision and artificial intelligence in food industry." Journal of Agriculture and Food Research 2 (2020): 100033. https://doi.org/10.1016/j.jafr.2020.100033

Kanellakis, Christoforos, and George Nikolakopoulos. "Survey on computer vision for UAVs: Current developments and trends." Journal of Intelligent & Robotic Systems 87 (2017): 141–168. https://doi.org/10.1007/s10846-017-0483-z

Kaul, Vivek, Sarah Enslin, and Seth A. Gross. "History of artificial intelligence in medicine." Gastrointestinal Endoscopy 92, no. 4 (2020): 807–812. https://doi.org/10.1016/j.gie.2020.06.040

Khan, Salman, Hossein Rahmani, Syed Afaq Ali Shah, Mohammed Bennamoun, Gerard Medioni, and Sven Dickinson. *A Guide to Convolutional Neural Networks for Computer Vision*. Vol. 8. (2018). San Rafael: Morgan & Claypool Publishers.

Khang, Alex. *Applications and Principles of Quantum Computing* (1st Ed.) (2023). ISBN: 9798369311684. IGI Global Press. https://doi.org/10.4018/979-8-3693-1168-4

Khang, Alex, Vugar Abdullayev Hajimahmud, Olena Hrybiuk, and Arvind K. Shukla. *Computer Vision and AI-Integrated IoT Technologies in the Medical Ecosystem* (1st Ed.) (2024). CRC Press. https://doi.org/10.1201/9781003429609

Khang, Alex, Hahanov Vladimir, Eugenia Litvinova, Svetlana Chumachenko, Avromovic Zoran, Rashad İsmibeyli, Nazila Ali Ragimova, Vugar Abdullayev Hajimahmud, Abuzarova Vusala Alyar, and P. T. N. Anh. "Medical and BioMedical Signal Processing and Prediction," *Computer Vision and AI-Integrated IoT Technologies in Medical Ecosystem* (1st Ed.) (2024). CRC Press. https://doi.org/10.1201/9781003429609-7

Khang, A, V. A. Hajimahmud, Eugenia Litvinova, Svetlana Chumachenko, Vusala Abuzarova, and P. T. N. Anh. "Application of Computer Vision in the Healthcare Ecosystem," *Computer Vision and AI-Integrated IoT Technologies in Medical Ecosystem* (1st Ed.) (2024). CRC Press. https://doi.org/10.1201/9781003429609-1

Khang, Alex, Muthmainnah Muthmainnah, Prodhan Mahbub Ibna Seraj, Ahmad Al Yakin, and Ahmad J. Obaid. "AI-Aided Teaching Model in Education 5.0," *AI-Based Technologies and Applications in the Era of the Metaverse* (1st Ed.) (2023). Page (83–104). IGI Global Press. https://doi.org/10.4018/978-1-6684-8851-5.ch004

Khang, Alex, and Kali Charan Rath. "Quantum Mechanics Primer – Fundamentals and Quantum Computing," *Applications and Principles of Quantum Computing* (1st Ed.) (2023). ISBN: 9798369311684. IGI Global Press. https://doi.org/10.4018/979-8-3693-1168-4-ch001

Khang, Alex, Kali Charan Rath, Suresh Kumar Satapathy, Amaresh Kumar, Sudhansu Ranjan Das, and Manas Ranjan Panda. "Enabling the Future of Manufacturing: Integration of Robotics and IoT to Smart Factory Infrastructure in Industry 4.0," *AI-Based Technologies and Applications in the Era of the Metaverse* (1st Ed.) (2023). Page (25–50). IGI Global Press. https://doi.org/10.4018/978-1-6684-8851-5.ch002

Khang, Alex, Vrushank Shah, and Sita Rani. *AI-Based Technologies and Applications in the Era of the Metaverse* (1st Ed.) (2023). IGI Global Press. https://doi.org/10.4018/978-1-6684-8851-5

Martinez-de Dios, J. R., C. Serna, and Aníbal Ollero. "Computer vision and robotics techniques in fish farms." Robotica 21, no. 3 (2003): 233–243. https://doi.org/10.1017/S0263574702004733

O'Mahony, Niall, Sean Campbell, Anderson Carvalho, Suman Harapanahalli, Gustavo Velasco Hernandez, Lenka Krpalkova, Daniel Riordan, and Joseph Walsh. "Deep learning vs. traditional computer vision." In Advances in Computer Vision: Proceedings of the 2019 Computer Vision Conference (CVC), vol. 1, pp. 128–144. Springer International Publishing (2020).

Paneru, Suman, and Idris Jeelani. "Computer vision applications in construction: Current state, opportunities & challenges." Automation in Construction 132 (2021): 103940. https://doi.org/10.1016/j.autcon.2021.103940

Patrício, Diego Inácio, and Rafael Rieder. "Computer vision and artificial intelligence in precision agriculture for grain crops: A systematic review." Computers and Electronics in Agriculture 153 (2018): 69–81. https://doi.org/10.1016/j.compag.2018.08.001

Petrov, Alexey, and Anton Popov. "Overview of the application of computer vision technology in fish farming." In E3S Web of Conferences, vol. 175, p. 02015. EDP Sciences (2020). https://doi.org/10.1051/e3sconf/202017502015

Safaryna, Alifia Merza, Dian Prasasti Kurniawati, Fariani Syahrul, and Reni Prastyani. "Risk factors for computer vision syndrome (CVS) among college students during the covid-19 pandemic." Media Gizi Kesmas 12, no. 1 (2023): 200–206. https://doi.org/10.20473/mgk.v12i1.2023.200-206

Segura, Álvaro, Helen V. Diez, Iñigo Barandiaran, Ander Arbelaiz, Hugo Álvarez, Bruno Simões, Jorge Posada, Alejandro García-Alonso, and Ramón Ugarte. "Visual computing technologies to support the operator 4.0." Computers & Industrial Engineering 139 (2020): 105550. https://doi.org/10.1016/j.cie.2018.11.060

Silva, Nelson, Dajie Zhang, Tomas Kulvicius, Alexander Gail, Carla Barreiros, Stefanie Lindstaedt, and Marc Kraft et al. "The future of general movement assessment: The role of computer vision and machine learning–A scoping review." Research in Developmental Disabilities 110 (2021): 103854. https://doi.org/10.1016/j.ridd.2021.103854

Ulhaq, Anwaar, Jannis Born, Asim Khan, Douglas Pinto Sampaio Gomes, Subrata Chakraborty, and Manoranjan Paul. "COVID-19 control by computer vision approaches: A survey." IEEE Access 8 (2020): 179437–179456. https://doi.org/10.1109/ACCESS.2020.3027685

Voulodimos, Athanasios, Nikolaos Doulamis, Anastasios Doulamis, and Eftychios Protopapadakis. "Deep learning for computer vision: A brief review." Computational Intelligence and Neuroscience 2018 (2018). https://doi.org/10.1155/2018/7068349

Wang, Zhengwei, Qi She, and Tomas E. Ward. "Generative adversarial networks in computer vision: A survey and taxonomy." ACM Computing Surveys (CSUR) 54, no. 2 (2021): 1–38. https://doi.org/10.1145/3439723

Ward, Thomas M., Pietro Mascagni, Yutong Ban, Guy Rosman, Nicolas Padoy, Ozanan Meireles, and Daniel A. Hashimoto. "Computer vision in surgery." Surgery 169, no. 5 (2021): 1253–1256. https://doi.org/10.1016/j.surg.2020.10.039

Wu, Qi, Damien Teney, Peng Wang, Chunhua Shen, Anthony Dick, and Anton Van Den Hengel. "Visual question answering: A survey of methods and datasets." Computer Vision and Image Understanding 163 (2017): 21–40. https://doi.org/10.1016/j.cviu.2017.05.001

Zafeiriou, Stefanos, Cha Zhang, and Zhengyou Zhang. "A survey on face detection in the wild: Past, present and future." Computer Vision and Image Understanding 138 (2015): 1–24. https://doi.org/10.1016/j.cviu.2015.03.015

4 Application of Robotics in Manufacturing Industry

Rishabh Didwania, Rajat Verma, and Namrata Dhanda

4.1 INTRODUCTION TO ROBOTICS IN MANUFACTURING

In recent years, robotics (Kamarul Bahrin et al., 2016) has emerged as a transformative technology in the manufacturing industry, revolutionizing how products are designed, produced, and delivered. Robotics refers to the branch of technology that deals with robot design, development, and application—autonomous or semi-autonomous machines capable of performing tasks with precision, speed, and accuracy.

This chapter delves into the use of vision-guided robots and machine vision systems for quality inspection processes, highlighting their integration for precise measurements and inspections through real-world case studies. Furthermore, it analyzes robotic packaging systems, emphasizes the significance of palletizing robots in streamlining planning, and explores the benefits and challenges of automating packaging processes using robotics. The chapter provides an overview of robotic welding systems, their advantages, and the utilization of laser-cutting technologies in conjunction with robotic systems. It discusses the integration of sensors and vision systems for accurate welding and cutting processes and displays real-world case studies demonstrating successful applications.

The chapter then explores robots designed for handling hazardous materials, examines remote-controlled robots in nuclear and chemical environments, and emphasizes the role of robotics in minimizing human exposure to hazardous conditions. It addresses safety considerations and challenges when deploying robots in hazardous environments. Finally, the chapter explores future trends and emerging applications in robotics, including collaborative robots (Cobots) and their impact on human–robot interaction, the analysis of robotics in the era of Industry 4.0 and smart manufacturing, advances in artificial intelligence and machine learning for robotics, and potential future applications and innovations in the field. Overall, this chapter provides valuable insights into the diverse applications of robotics in manufacturing, displaying its transformative potential in enhancing productivity, safety, and competitiveness in the industry.

4.1.1 Robotics in Manufacturing

In the manufacturing context, robotics involves the use of robots to automate various processes and tasks traditionally performed by humans. These robots are equipped

DOI: 10.1201/9781003438137-4

with sensors, actuators, and control systems that enable them to interact with their environment, make decisions, and execute specific actions. They can be programmed to perform repetitive tasks, handle heavy payloads, work in hazardous environments, and collaborate with human operators.

The primary objective of robotics in manufacturing is to enhance efficiency, productivity, and quality control. By incorporating robots into the production workflow, manufacturers can achieve higher levels of precision, reduce human error, optimize cycle times, and streamline operations. Robotics offers several advantages over manual labor, including improved workplace safety, increased output, and reduced production costs.

The field of robotics in manufacturing has witnessed significant advancements over the years. Early industrial robots were large and rigid machines designed for specific applications, such as welding or assembly. However, with advancements in technology, modern robots have become more versatile, adaptable, and intelligent. They can be programmed to perform a wide range of tasks and are equipped with sensors and vision systems to perceive and respond to their surroundings.

Robotic systems in manufacturing can be categorized into several types based on their structure and functionality. These include articulated robots, which consist of multiple rotary joints resembling a human arm; cartesian robots, which use linear motion along orthogonal axes; delta robots, which are highly precise and fast-moving robots with a parallel kinematic structure; and collaborative robots, also known as Cobots, designed to work alongside humans (Villani et al., 2018) in a shared workspace.

The integration of robotics in manufacturing has brought about a change in thinking in the industry, often referred to as the Fourth Industrial Revolution or Industry 4.0 (Goel & Gupta, 2019). This revolution entails the fusion of automation, robotics, data analytics, and the Internet of Things (IoT) (Verma et al., 2023a) to create smart, interconnected factories capable of autonomous decision-making and real-time optimization. Robotics plays a crucial role in this transformation, enabling seamless communication and collaboration between machines, improving production flexibility, and unlocking new levels of efficiency and productivity.

As manufacturing continues to evolve, the application of robotics is expanding into various areas, ranging from assembly material handling, quality control, and inspection to packaging, welding and cutting, and hazardous environments (Staritz et al., 2001). The next sections of this chapter will delve deeper into these specific applications, providing insights into their advantages, challenges, and real-world case studies.

4.1.2   IMPORTANCE OF ROBOTICS IN ENHANCING EFFICIENCY AND PRODUCTIVITY

The integration of robotics in the manufacturing industry has become increasingly vital in enhancing efficiency and productivity. Robots bring many advantages that contribute to streamlined operations, reduced cycle times, and improved overall performance. The importance of robotics in enhancing efficiency and productivity can be understood through the following key points:

- **Increased Speed and Precision:** Robots are designed to perform incredible tasks, surpassing human capabilities in many aspects. They can execute repetitive actions consistently without fatigue or errors, leading to higher production rates and improved product quality. By eliminating human limitations, robotics enables faster and more accurate manufacturing processes.

- **Automation of Repetitive Tasks:** Manufacturing operations often involve repetitive tasks that can be monotonous and time-consuming for human workers. By automating these tasks through robotics, companies can free up human resources to focus on more complex and value-added activities. This automation leads to increased efficiency by reducing the time required for routine operations and minimizing human error.
- **Improved Workplace Safety:** Robotics plays a significant role in improving workplace safety by replacing humans in hazardous or physically demanding tasks. Robots are designed to operate in dangerous environments, such as in high temperatures, toxic atmospheres, or areas with heavy machinery. By delegating such tasks to robots, manufacturers can minimize the risk of accidents, injuries, and occupational hazards, creating a safer work environment for their employees (Cardoso et al., 2021).
- **Optimal Resource Utilization:** Robots can optimize the use of resources, such as materials, energy, and time. They can be programmed to minimize waste, precisely control quantities, and ensure consistent quality throughout the manufacturing process. This leads to cost savings, efficient resource allocation, and increased productivity (Dunbabin & Marques, 2012).
- **Enhanced Flexibility and Adaptability:** Modern robotics systems are highly flexible and adaptable to changing production needs. They can be easily reprogrammed or reconfigured to perform different tasks or accommodate product variations. This flexibility allows manufacturers to respond quickly to market demands, achieve faster product changeovers, and maintain prominent levels of productivity in dynamic manufacturing environments (Slack, 1983).

4.1.3 Evolution of Robotics in Manufacturing and Its Impact on the Industry

The evolution of robotics in manufacturing has had a profound impact on the industry, transforming traditional production methods and shaping the current industrial landscape (Grau et al., 2017). The evolution of robotics in manufacturing is illustrated in Figure 4.1.

The evolution can be observed through the following stages:

- **Early Automation:** The initial stages of robotics in manufacturing involved the introduction of automated systems that performed specific tasks, such as welding or assembly, in a programmed manner. These systems were often large, dedicated machines that required extensive programming and were isolated from other production processes.
- **Introduction of Industrial Robots:** The development of industrial robots marked a significant milestone in robotics for manufacturing. These robots were versatile and reprogrammable, capable of performing multiple tasks

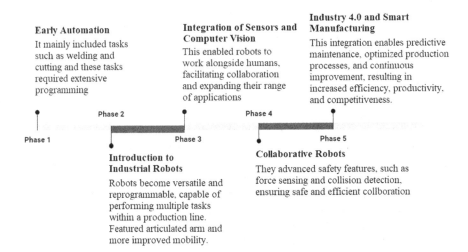

FIGURE 4.1   Evolution of robotics in manufacturing.

within a production line. They featured articulated arms and improved mobility, allowing for greater reach and manipulation capabilities.

- **Integration of Sensors and Vision Systems:** With advancements in sensor technologies and computer vision, robots have become capable of perceiving and responding to their environment. Vision-guided robots can recognize objects, detect defects, and perform complex tasks with increased accuracy and adaptability. This integration of sensors and vision systems enabled robots to work alongside humans, facilitating collaboration and expanding their range of applications.
- **Collaborative Robots:** The emergence of collaborative robots, or Cobots, revolutionized the interaction between humans and robots in manufacturing. Cobots are designed to operate in close proximity to humans, sharing workspace and tasks. They have advanced safety features, such as force sensing and collision detection, ensuring safe and efficient collaboration (Sherwani et al., 2020).
- **Industry 4.0 and Smart Manufacturing:** The evolution of robotics in manufacturing has converged with other emerging technologies, such as the Internet of Things (IoT), artificial intelligence (AI), and data analytics, giving rise to the concept of Industry 4.0 (Verma et al., 2022a). Smart factories use robotics and automation alongside real-time data analysis, connectivity, and intelligent decision-making. This integration enables predictive maintenance, optimized production processes, and continuous improvement, resulting in increased efficiency, productivity, and competitiveness.

The impact of robotics in manufacturing has been far-reaching. It has enabled companies to achieve higher production volumes, improved product quality, and reduced costs. Robotics has also contributed to the reshoring of manufacturing operations, as it can compensate for higher labor costs by enhancing productivity and

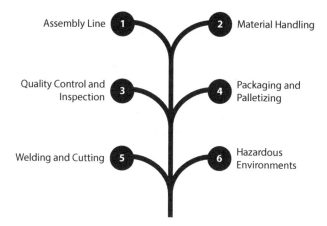

FIGURE 4.2   Applications of robotics in manufacturing.

efficiency. Furthermore, robotics has created new job opportunities in areas such as robot programming, maintenance, and system integration, fostering technological advancement and economic growth. There are various applications of robotics in the manufacturing industry which are shown in Figure 4.2.

4.2   ROBOTIC APPLICATIONS IN ASSEMBLY

Robotic assembly lines have become increasingly prevalent in the manufacturing industry due to their numerous advantages (Krüger et al., 2009). These assembly lines utilize robots to perform various assembly tasks, improving efficiency, precision, and productivity (Malik & Bilberg, 2019). The key advantages of robotic assembly lines include the following:

- **Increased Speed and Accuracy:** Robots are capable of performing assembly tasks with unmatched speed and accuracy. They can execute repetitive actions consistently and precisely, resulting in faster production rates and improved product quality.
- **Higher Production Output:** Robotic assembly lines can operate continuously without fatigue, enabling higher production output compared to manual assembly. The consistent performance of robots ensures a steady and reliable workflow, optimizing production capacity.
- **Improved Flexibility:** Robots can be programmed and reconfigured to handle different product variations or assembly processes, providing greater flexibility in adapting to changing production needs. This flexibility allows manufacturers to introduce new products or make modifications with ease.
- **Enhanced Ergonomics:** Assembly tasks often involve repetitive motions and heavy lifting, which can lead to physical strain and injuries for human workers. By deploying robots in assembly lines, manufacturers can reduce the ergonomic burden on human operators, improving workplace safety and reducing the risk of occupational injuries (Weckenborg et al., 2022).

- **Quality Control and Traceability:** Robotic assembly lines can incorporate quality control measures at various stages of the assembly process. Robots can perform inspections, measurements, and tests to ensure the accuracy and integrity of the assembled products. Moreover, the use of robots enables precise tracking and traceability of components, contributing to quality assurance and product reliability.

4.2.1 CASE STUDIES ON SUCCESSFUL ROBOTIC ASSEMBLY SYSTEMS IN VARIOUS INDUSTRIES

Numerous industries have successfully implemented robotic assembly systems to enhance their manufacturing processes. Here are a few notable case studies:

- **Automotive Industry:** Automobile manufacturers extensively use robotic assembly lines for tasks such as welding, painting, and component assembly. Robots are employed for the precise fitting of parts, ensuring tight tolerances and efficient assembly. This has led to improved production efficiency, higher product consistency, and reduced manufacturing costs (Müller et al., 2016).
- **Electronics Industry:** In the electronics industry, robots play a crucial role in the assembly of circuit boards, components, and devices. They precisely handle delicate components, soldering, placing, and connecting them accurately. Robotic assembly systems have significantly increased production speed, reduced errors, and improved the overall quality of electronic products (Andrzejewski et al., 2018).
- **Consumer Goods Industry:** Companies manufacturing consumer goods such as appliances, toys, and electronics have implemented robotic assembly systems to streamline their production processes. Robots are utilized for tasks like product assembly, packaging, and labeling. These systems have resulted in faster production cycles, improved product consistency, and enhanced operational efficiency (Karagiannis et al., 2019).
- **Pharmaceutical Industry:** In the pharmaceutical industry, robotic assembly systems are employed for the precise handling and assembly of medical devices, drug delivery systems, and diagnostic equipment. Robots ensure accuracy in product assembly, reduce contamination risks, and enhance pharmaceutical products' overall quality and reliability.

4.2.2 CHALLENGES OF IMPLEMENTING ROBOTIC ASSEMBLY SOLUTIONS

While robotic assembly solutions offer significant benefits, their implementation comes with certain considerations and challenges (Michalos et al., 2010). Manufacturers need to address these challenges which are presented in Figure 4.3.

The above challenges are described in more detail below as follows:

- **Cost:** The initial investment required for setting up robotic assembly systems can be substantial. Costs include not only the purchase of robots

FIGURE 4.3 Challenges in robotic assembly line.

but also integration, programming, training, and maintenance expenses. However, it is crucial to assess the long-term return on investment considering the potential gains in productivity and quality.

- **System Integration:** Integrating robotic assembly systems with existing manufacturing infrastructure can be complex. It requires coordination between robots, sensors, conveyors, and other equipment. Additionally, integrating with enterprise systems for data exchange and synchronization poses its own challenges. Thorough planning and collaboration with experts are crucial for successful integration.
- **Programming and Training:** Programming robots for assembly tasks requires specialized knowledge and skills. Manufacturers need to ensure that their workforce receives appropriate training to program, operate, and maintain robotic systems effectively. Collaborative robots (Cobots) have simplified programming, allowing non-experts to teach the robot tasks through intuitive interfaces.
- **Maintenance and Downtime:** Like any other machinery, robots require regular maintenance to ensure their optimal performance. Unexpected breakdowns or maintenance needs can lead to unplanned downtime, affecting production schedules. Having a well-defined maintenance plan, spare parts availability, and quick response for repairs is essential to minimize disruptions.
- **Worker Adaptation and Collaboration:** Introducing robotic assembly systems may require a shift in the roles of human workers. Employees need to adapt to working alongside robots and understand their collaboration requirements. Proper training and effective communication between humans and robots are necessary to establish harmonious and efficient teamwork.

By addressing these considerations and challenges, manufacturers can successfully implement robotic assembly solutions and reap the benefits of improved efficiency, productivity, and product quality in their assembly processes.

4.3   ROBOTIC APPLICATIONS IN MATERIAL HANDLING

In the industrial sector, robotic material handling and tending systems are prevalent. Robotic arms transferring manufacturing parts, typically on or off a conveyor belt or to keep a part in place for manufacture, are referred to as material handling. Similar but more precise, machine tending describes the use of a robotic arm to load and unload a stationary industrial machine.

4.3.1   AUTOMATED GUIDED VEHICLES AND THEIR ROLE IN MATERIAL TRANSPORTATION

Automated guided vehicles (AGVs) are autonomous robotic vehicles designed to transport materials within manufacturing facilities, warehouses, and distribution centers (Mahadevan & Narendran, 1990). They play a crucial role in material handling (Guo et al., 2017) by offering the following benefits:

- **Increased Efficiency:** AGVs automate the movement of materials, eliminating the need for manual transportation. They can operate 24/7, ensuring continuous material flow and optimizing overall operational efficiency.
- **Flexibility and Scalability:** AGVs can be programmed to handle several types of materials, such as raw materials, work-in-progress components, and finished goods. They are adaptable and can easily be reprogrammed or redeployed to accommodate changes in production needs or layout modifications (Herrero-Perez & Martinez-Barbera, 2010).
- **Safety:** AGVs are equipped with sensors and safety features to navigate their surroundings and avoid collisions with obstacles or pedestrians. They enhance workplace safety by reducing the risks associated with manual material handling and transportation.
- **Precise and Reliable Movement:** AGVs follow predefined paths or use real-time navigation systems, such as laser- or vision-based guidance, to move materials accurately. This ensures consistent and reliable transport, reducing errors and minimizing product damage.
- **Integration with Warehouse Management Systems:** AGVs can be seamlessly integrated with warehouse management systems (WMS) or other control systems to optimize material flow and prioritize tasks. They can receive instructions, communicate status updates, and coordinate with other machinery or processes for efficient operations.

4.3.2   APPLICATION OF ROBOTIC ARMS FOR MATERIAL HANDLING AND MANIPULATION

Robotic arms are versatile tools used for material handling and manipulation in various industrial settings (Gambao et al., 2012). They offer the following advantages:

- **Precise and Agile Work:** Robotic arms can handle materials of different shapes, sizes, and weights with exceptional precision and dexterity. They can pick, place, stack, sort, and arrange items according to predefined parameters.

- **Increased Speed and Throughput:** Robotic arms can perform material handling tasks at a much higher speed than human operators. This results in improved throughput and shorter cycle times, contributing to enhanced productivity.
- **Reduction of Manual Labor:** By automating material handling tasks, robotic arms reduce the reliance on manual labor. This frees human workers to focus on more complex and value-added activities, improving overall operational efficiency.
- **Ergonomics and Worker Safety:** Robotic arms can handle heavy or bulky materials, eliminating the physical strain and potential injuries associated with manual lifting and carrying. This promotes better ergonomics and worker safety (Bassani et al., 2021).
- **Integration with Vision Systems:** Robotic arms can be combined with vision systems, such as cameras or sensors, to enable precise object detection, orientation, and alignment. This allows them to handle materials with varying shapes or positions, enhancing their versatility in material manipulation tasks (Radlak & Fojcik, 2015).

4.3.3 WAREHOUSE AUTOMATION USING ROBOTICS AND ITS BENEFITS AND LIMITATIONS

Warehouse automation utilizing robotics has gained significant traction in recent years (Rey et al., 2019). It involves the integration of various robotic systems, such as AGVs, robotic arms, and automated storage and retrieval systems (AS/RS), to streamline warehouse operations.

4.3.3.1 Benefits of Using Robotics in Warehouse Automation

The benefits of using robotics in warehouse automation include:

- **Improved Efficiency:** Robotics automate repetitive and time-consuming tasks, resulting in faster order fulfillment, reduced labor costs, and increased operational efficiency (Guizzo, 2008).
- **Enhanced Accuracy and Quality:** Robotics minimize errors associated with manual handling, leading to improved order accuracy and product quality (Yuan & Gong, 2016).
- **Optimized Space Utilization:** Robotic systems, including AGVs and AS/RS, enable efficient use of warehouse space by maximizing storage capacity and minimizing aisle width requirements.
- **Real-time Inventory Management:** Robotic systems integrated with inventory management systems provide accurate and up-to-date information on inventory levels, enabling better inventory control and reduced stockouts (Liu et al., 2006).
- **Increased Safety:** Automation reduces the risks of manual material handling, minimizing the potential for workplace accidents and injuries.

4.3.3.2   Limitations of Using Robotics in Warehouse Automation

The limitations of using robotics in warehouse automation include:

- **High Initial Investment:** Implementing warehouse automation with robotics requires a significant upfront investment in robotics equipment, infrastructure modifications, and integration with existing systems.
- **Complex Integration and Maintenance:** Integrating different robotic systems and ensuring their smooth operation can be complex. Additionally, maintaining and troubleshooting robotic systems may require specialized technical expertise.
- **Limited Adaptability:** Robotic systems may have limitations in handling certain types of materials or irregularly shaped items. Changes in product mix or stock keeping unit (SKU) variability may require reprogramming or reconfiguration of robotic systems.
- **Dependence on Power and System Reliability:** Robotic systems rely on a continuous power supply and dependable infrastructure. Equipment failures or power outages can disrupt operations and require contingency plans.

By carefully considering the benefits and limitations of robotic systems, companies can determine the most suitable robotic applications for their material handling needs and strategically implement warehouse automation to optimize efficiency, accuracy, and productivity.

4.4   ROBOTIC APPLICATIONS IN QUALITY CONTROL AND INSPECTION

Applications for quality control and inspection are using robots more and more. They may be utilized for a number of activities, including dimension measurement, surface inspection, functionality testing, defect identification, and part grading. Numerous quality control and inspection duties may be automated by robots, freeing up human personnel to concentrate on other responsibilities. Robots may also operate around-the-clock, which can increase throughput and lower the possibility of human mistakes. As robots become more advanced and accessible, it is anticipated that their employment in quality control and inspection will increase.

4.4.1   Vision-Guided Robots for Quality Inspection Processes

Vision-guided robots play a vital role in quality control and inspection processes (Khan et al., 2020; Brito et al., 2020). These robots are equipped with advanced vision systems that allow them to analyze and interpret visual information, enabling precise inspection and quality assurance. The key aspects of vision-guided robots for quality inspection include:

- **Object Recognition:** Vision-guided robots utilize cameras and image processing algorithms to recognize objects and identify their features, such as shape, color, texture, or size. This enables the robots to detect defects or abnormalities during the inspection process.

- **Defect Detection and Classification:** By analyzing captured images, vision-guided robots can identify defects or imperfections in products or components. These defects can range from surface blemishes to dimensional variations. The robots can classify defects based on predefined criteria, allowing for efficient sorting and segregation of faulty items.
- **Inspection Speed and Accuracy:** Vision-guided robots can perform inspections at high speeds with exceptional accuracy. They can rapidly capture and process images, enabling real-time analysis and decision-making. This capability ensures consistent and reliable quality control, even in high-volume production environments (Kowalczuk & Wesierski, 2008).
- **Flexibility and Adaptability:** Vision systems integrated with robots can be programmed to inspect a wide range of products or components. Robots can adapt to variations in size, shape, or orientation, making them suitable for diverse manufacturing processes. The flexibility of vision-guided robots allows for efficient inspection of complex or intricate parts.

4.4.2 Use of Machine Vision Systems for Defect Detection and Identification

Machine vision systems comprising cameras, lighting, and image processing algorithms are extensively used for defect detection and identification in quality control processes (Wu & Lu, 2019). The process of machine vision in quality control along with robotics is displayed in Figure 4.4.

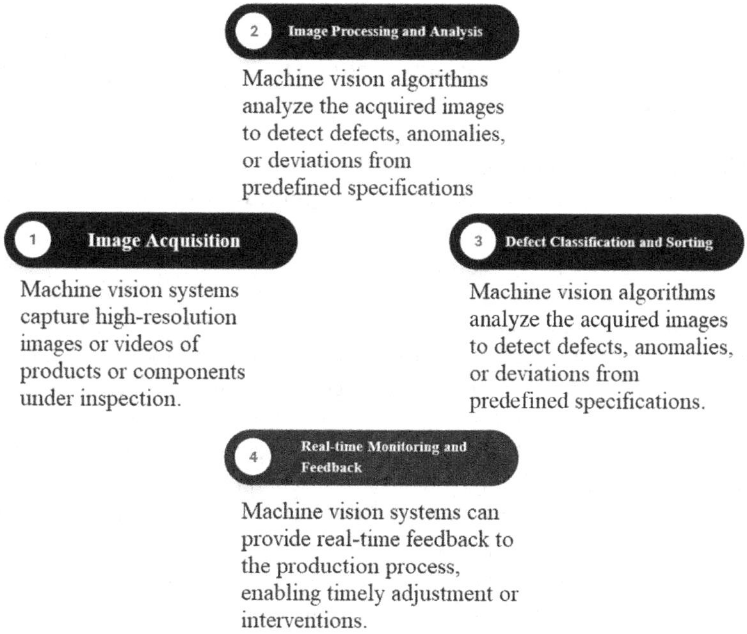

2 Image Processing and Analysis

Machine vision algorithms analyze the acquired images to detect defects, anomalies, or deviations from predefined specifications

1 Image Acquisition

Machine vision systems capture high-resolution images or videos of products or components under inspection.

3 Defect Classification and Sorting

Machine vision algorithms analyze the acquired images to detect defects, anomalies, or deviations from predefined specifications.

4 Real-time Monitoring and Feedback

Machine vision systems can provide real-time feedback to the production process, enabling timely adjustment or interventions.

FIGURE 4.4 Process of machine vision with robotics.

The process of machine vision via robotics consists of:

- **Image Acquisition:** Machine vision systems capture high-resolution images or videos of products or components under inspection. The lighting conditions and camera settings are optimized to ensure clear and detailed images (Colvalkar et al., 2023).
- **Image Processing and Analysis:** Machine vision algorithms analyze the acquired images to detect defects, anomalies, or deviations from predefined specifications. Advanced image processing techniques, such as edge detection, pattern matching, or color analysis, are used to identify defects accurately.
- **Defect Classification and Sorting:** Once defects are detected, machine vision systems can classify them based on predefined criteria. The systems can sort defective items into various categories or reject them from the production line, ensuring that only products meeting quality standards proceed further (Raafat & Taboun, 1996).
- **Real-Time Monitoring and Feedback:** Machine vision systems can provide real-time feedback to the production process, enabling timely adjustments or interventions. This feedback loop allows manufacturers to address quality issues promptly and minimize the production of defective items.

4.4.3 Integration of Robotics and Machine Vision for Precise Measurements and Inspections

The integration of robotics and machine vision offers precise measurements and inspections, enabling enhanced quality control (Oh, 2009). The key aspects of this integration include:

- **Guided Inspection and Measurement:** Robotic systems equipped with machine vision capabilities can perform guided inspections and measurements on products or components. The vision system guides the robot's movements and positions it accurately for inspection or measurement tasks.
- **Non-contact Measurements:** Machine vision systems enable non-contact measurements, eliminating the need for physical contact with the inspected objects. This reduces the risk of damage and ensures accurate and repeatable measurements.
- **Complex Geometry Inspection:** Robotic systems combined with machine vision excel in inspecting products with complex geometries. They can analyze intricate surfaces, perform 3D scanning, or verify geometric tolerances, ensuring compliance with design specifications.
- **Data Integration and Analysis:** The integration of robotics and machine vision allows for seamless data integration and analysis. Measurement data can be collected, processed, and integrated with other quality control systems, facilitating comprehensive analysis and reporting.

4.4.4 Case Studies of Successful Robotic Quality Control Applications

Robotic quality control applications are becoming increasingly important in industries where precision and efficiency are critical. Here are a few real-world case studies that showcase successful implementations of robotic quality control:

- **Automotive Industry:** Robotic vision systems are used to inspect the exterior and interior components of automobiles, ensuring proper fit, finish, and absence of defects. They detect imperfections in paintwork, verify dimensional tolerances, and inspect the integrity of electrical connections (Semeniuta et al., 2016).
- **Electronics Manufacturing:** Vision-guided robots inspect printed circuit boards (PCBs) for soldering defects, component placement accuracy, and the presence of any short circuits or damaged components. They enable high-speed inspection, ensuring the quality and reliability of electronic devices (Edinbarough et al., 2005).
- **Food and Beverage Industry:** Robotic vision systems are employed to inspect food products for quality and safety. They detect contaminants, check for proper packaging and labeling, and verify product integrity, contributing to consumer confidence and compliance with regulatory standards (Gray & Davis, 2013).

These case studies exemplify the successful application of robotics and machine vision in quality control and inspection processes across different industries. The integration of these technologies enables manufacturers to achieve higher product quality, reduce defects, and enhance customer satisfaction (Anh et al., 2024).

4.5 ROBOTIC APPLICATIONS IN PACKAGING AND PALLETIZING

Robotic packaging systems have become increasingly prevalent across industries due to their efficiency, speed, and accuracy (Dzitac & Mazid, 2008). These systems automate various packaging tasks, such as picking, placing, sealing, labeling, and stacking, offering the following advantages:

- **Increased Productivity:** Robotic packaging systems can handle packaging tasks at high speeds, significantly increasing production rates and throughput. They reduce manual labor requirements, allowing for optimized resource allocation and improved productivity.
- **Consistent and Reliable Packaging:** Robots ensure consistent packaging quality by precisely following predefined parameters, such as product orientation, packaging materials, and sealing techniques. This consistency enhances the visual appeal of products and ensures customer satisfaction.
- **Flexibility and Adaptability:** Robotic packaging systems can handle a wide range of product sizes, shapes, and packaging configurations. They can be easily reprogrammed or retooled to accommodate changes in product specifications or packaging requirements, offering flexibility in packaging operations.

- **Reduction in Packaging Waste:** Robots can optimize packaging material usage by accurately dispensing and applying the required amount of packaging material. This minimizes waste and reduces packaging costs while promoting sustainability.
- **Integration with Supply Chain Systems:** Robotic packaging systems can be seamlessly integrated with supply chain management systems, enabling real-time inventory tracking, order fulfillment, and planning optimization (Verma et al., 2023b). This integration enhances overall supply chain efficiency.

4.5.1 Significance of Palletizing Robots in Streamlining Logistics

Palletizing robots play a crucial role in streamlining planning operations, specifically in the loading and unloading of goods onto pallets (Zakrzewski & Szopik-Depczynska, 2022). The significance of palletizing robots entails:

- **Increased Efficiency:** Palletizing robots automate the stacking and arrangement of goods on pallets, enabling faster and more efficient loading and unloading processes. They can handle a variety of product shapes, sizes, and weights, ensuring optimal pallet utilization (Straka et al., 2021).
- **Labor Savings:** Palletizing robots reduce the manual labor required for palletizing tasks, reducing the reliance on human workers for repetitive and physically demanding activities. This frees up human resources for more value-added tasks within the logistics operation.
- **Improved Safety:** Palletizing robots enhance workplace safety by reducing the risk of injuries associated with manual lifting, stacking, and the movement of heavy loads. They adhere to strict safety protocols and can operate in environments with potential hazards, such as hot temperatures or hazardous materials.
- **Increased Accuracy and Precision:** Palletizing robots ensure precise placement of products on pallets, minimizing the risk of product damage during transportation. This accuracy reduces the likelihood of rejected or damaged goods, improving customer satisfaction.
- **Adaptability to Changing Needs:** Palletizing robots can easily adapt to changes in production requirements or packaging configurations. They can handle mixed loads and varying pallet sizes and adapt to different stacking patterns, offering flexibility in logistics operations.

4.5.2 Automation of Packaging Processes Using Robotics and Its Benefits and Challenges

The automation of packaging processes using robotics offers numerous benefits but also presents some challenges (Mahalik, 2014). The benefits include:

- **Enhanced Speed and Throughput:** Robotic packaging systems can significantly increase packaging speeds and throughput compared to manual operations. This allows for faster order processing, shorter lead times, and improved customer satisfaction.

- **Improved Packaging Quality and Consistency:** Robots ensure precise and consistent packaging, reducing errors and inconsistencies that may occur with manual packaging. This enhances product presentation and brand image.
- **Labor Cost Reduction:** Automating packaging processes with robotics reduces the need for manual labor, resulting in cost savings associated with wages, training, and employee benefits. It also minimizes the dependency on a shrinking labor market or labor-intensive regions.
- **Lower Packaging Material Waste:** Robots can optimize packaging material usage by minimizing waste through precise measurements and controlled dispensing. This reduces packaging costs and promotes sustainability by minimizing environmental impact.

However, there are also the following challenges that can be associated with the automation of packaging processes:

- Initial Investment and Integration
- Complexity of Product Variation
- Maintenance and Downtime
- Skilled Workforce Requirements

Despite these challenges, the benefits of automating packaging processes with robotics outweigh the drawbacks for many industries, as robotics enables improved efficiency, quality, and cost-effectiveness in packaging operations.

4.6 ROBOTIC APPLICATIONS IN WELDING AND CUTTING

Robotic welding systems have revolutionized the welding industry by offering increased efficiency, precision, and productivity (Bogue, 2008). The key advantages of robotic welding systems include:

- **Enhanced Efficiency:** Robotic welding systems can perform welding tasks at high speeds with consistent quality, resulting in increased production rates and shorter cycle times. They reduce the reliance on manual labor and allow for optimized resource allocation.
- **Improved Precision and Accuracy:** Robots equipped with advanced control systems can achieve precise weld placements and maintain consistent welding parameters, ensuring high-quality welds. This level of accuracy reduces rework and improves overall weld integrity.
- **Versatility and Adaptability:** Robotic welding systems can be programmed to handle a wide range of welding applications, including different material types, joint configurations, and welding techniques. They offer flexibility and adaptability to meet changing production needs.
- **Safety Enhancement:** By automating welding processes, robotic systems can reduce the risk of worker exposure to hazardous welding fumes, intense heat, and potential workplace accidents. They can operate in enclosed environments or hazardous conditions, ensuring improved worker safety.

- **Continuous Operation:** Robotic welding systems can operate continuously, 24/7, without the need for breaks or shifts. This uninterrupted operation maximizes productivity and reduces production downtime.

4.6.1 Use of Laser-Cutting Technologies Along with Robotic Systems

Laser-cutting technologies, when integrated with robotic systems, offer numerous benefits for cutting and material processing applications (Brogårdh, 2009). The key advantages of utilizing laser cutting technologies with robotic systems include:

- **High Precision and Speed:** Laser cutting provides a non-contact cutting method that allows for precise and rapid material removal. When combined with robotic systems, laser cutting achieves accurate cuts with exceptional speed, improving overall productivity.
- **Versatility in Material Types and Thicknesses:** Laser cutting can process a wide range of materials, including metals, plastics, composites, and fabrics. By integrating laser cutting with robotic systems, manufacturers can easily switch between varied materials and thicknesses, accommodating diverse production needs.
- **Complex Geometries and Intricate Designs:** Laser cutting guided by robotic systems enables the processing of intricate shapes and complex geometries that may be challenging for traditional cutting methods. This capability expands design possibilities and enhances manufacturing flexibility.
- **Minimal Material Waste:** Laser cutting provides precise and narrow cuts, minimizing material waste during the cutting process. This leads to cost savings and promotes sustainability by reducing material consumption.
- **Automation and Integration:** Robotic systems can handle material handling, positioning, and path planning for laser cutting, enabling seamless integration with other manufacturing processes. This integration streamlines production workflows and reduces manual intervention.

4.6.2 Integration of Sensors and Vision Systems for Accurate Welding and Cutting Processes

The integration of sensors and vision systems with robotic welding and cutting processes enhances accuracy, quality, and quality control (Gao et al., 2005). Key aspects of this integration include:

- **Welding Process Monitoring:** Sensors and vision systems can monitor key welding parameters such as arc length, weld penetration, and heat input in real time. This enables process optimization, quality control, and the identification of any deviations or defects (Pires et al., 2003).

- **Vision-Guided Welding and Cutting:** Vision systems integrated with robotic systems can provide real-time feedback on joint positions, seam tracking, or cutting paths. This feedback allows for precise control, ensuring accurate welds and cuts even in complex or changing workpieces.
- **Adaptive Welding and Cutting:** Sensors and vision systems can detect variations in workpiece dimensions, positions, or surface conditions, allowing robotic systems to adapt their welding or cutting paths accordingly. This adaptive capability compensates for manufacturing tolerances and ensures consistent quality.
- **Defect Detection and Quality Assurance:** Vision systems integrated with robotic systems can detect weld defects, such as porosity, cracks, or incomplete fusion, in real-time. This enables immediate corrective actions, reducing the likelihood of defective products reaching the market.

4.6.3 Case Studies on Successful Robotic Welding and Cutting Applications

Robotic welding and cutting applications have become increasingly prevalent in various industries. Here are a few real-world case studies that showcase successful implementations of robotic welding and cutting:

- **Automotive Industry:** Robotic welding systems are extensively used in the automotive industry for spot welding of car bodies, ensuring precise and strong welds. The integration of vision systems allows for accurate joint tracking, ensuring consistent quality across various vehicle models (Hong et al., 2014).
- **Aerospace Industry:** Robotic welding systems with laser technology are employed in the aerospace industry for welding complex components, such as aircraft frames or engine parts. The high precision and repeatability of robotic systems ensure the structural integrity of critical aerospace components (Wilson, 1994).
- **Heavy Equipment Manufacturing:** Robotic welding systems are utilized in the manufacturing of heavy machinery and equipment, such as construction machinery or agricultural vehicles. The automation of welding processes ensures consistent quality and increases production efficiency.
- **Metal Fabrication:** Robotic welding and cutting systems are widely adopted in metal fabrication shops for various applications, including welding structural components, cutting intricate designs, or fabricating customized metal products. These systems enhance productivity, accuracy, and cost-effectiveness in metal fabrication processes (Curiel et al., 2023).

These real-world case studies demonstrate the successful integration of robotic welding and cutting systems in various industries, showcasing the benefits of increased efficiency, improved precision, and enhanced quality control (Khang & Muthmainnah et al., 2023).

4.7 ROBOTIC APPLICATIONS IN HAZARDOUS ENVIRONMENTS

Robots designed for handling hazardous materials and substances play a crucial role in industries such as nuclear, chemical, pharmaceutical, and waste management. These robots are specifically engineered to operate in environments that are dangerous or inaccessible to humans. Key aspects of their design and functionality include:

- **Robust Construction:** Hazardous environment robots are built with materials and components that can withstand extreme conditions, such as high temperatures, corrosive chemicals, or radiation.
- **Protective Measures:** These robots are equipped with specialized coatings, seals, or shielding to protect their internal components from the hazardous substances they encounter.
- **Hazardous Material Handling:** These robots are designed to manipulate, transport, and process hazardous materials and substances with precision and safety, minimizing the risk of exposure or contamination.
- **Sensor Integration:** These robots often incorporate advanced sensors, such as gas detectors, radiation detectors, or chemical analyzers, to monitor the environment and ensure safe operations.

4.7.1 REMOTE-CONTROLLED ROBOTS IN NUCLEAR AND CHEMICAL ENVIRONMENTS

Remote-controlled robots have proven invaluable in hazardous environments, particularly in nuclear and chemical industries (Zhao et al., 2017). These robots can be operated from a safe distance by human operators, allowing for precise control and minimizing human exposure to radiation, toxic chemicals, or other hazardous elements. Key features of remote-controlled robots in these environments include:

- **Manipulation and Inspection:** Remote-controlled robots are equipped with mechanical arms, grippers, or specialized tools to perform tasks such as maintenance, inspection, or decontamination in radioactive or chemically contaminated areas.
- **Real-Time Feedback:** These robots often integrate cameras and sensors to provide real-time visual and sensory feedback to human operators, enabling them to make informed decisions and perform complex tasks effectively.
- **Teleoperation:** Remote-controlled robots use tele-operation technology, which allows human operators to remotely control their movements and actions. This technology ensures precise control and enhances safety.
- **Operator Safety:** The primary objective of remote-controlled robots is to protect human operators from hazardous environments. These robots are equipped with safety features, such as radiation shielding, chemical-resistant enclosures, or remote emergency shutdown capabilities.

4.7.2 ROLE OF ROBOTICS IN MINIMIZING HUMAN EXPOSURE TO HAZARDOUS CONDITIONS

One of the primary advantages of robotics in hazardous environments is the ability to minimize human exposure to dangerous conditions (Trevelyan et al.,

2016). By deploying robots in these environments, the following benefits can be achieved:

- **Worker Safety:** Robotics reduces or eliminates the need for human workers to directly interact with hazardous materials, substances, or environments. This significantly reduces the risk of injuries, illnesses, or long-term health effects associated with exposure to these hazards.
- **Enhanced Accuracy and Reliability:** Robots can perform tasks with high precision and consistency, minimizing errors that could potentially lead to accidents or safety incidents. Their reliable operation ensures a safer working environment.
- **Extended Reach:** Robots can access confined spaces, high-risk areas, or locations with limited human accessibility, enabling thorough inspections, maintenance, or emergency response without endangering human lives.
- **Remote Monitoring and Operation:** In hazardous environments, robots equipped with sensors and cameras can provide real-time monitoring and data collection. Human operators can remotely monitor the environment, make informed decisions, and control robot actions from a safe location.

4.7.3 Challenges of Deploying Robots in Hazardous Environments

Deploying robots in hazardous environments presents the following unique safety considerations and challenges:

- **System Redundancy and Fail-Safe Mechanisms:** Robots operating in hazardous environments should incorporate redundant systems and fail-safe mechanisms to ensure reliable operation and minimize the risk of system failures or malfunctions.
- **Operator Training and Preparedness:** Operators should receive comprehensive training to safely operate and control robots in hazardous environments. They must be well versed in emergency procedures, troubleshooting, and understanding the limitations and capabilities of robotic systems.
- **Environmental Compatibility:** Robots used in hazardous environments should be compatible with the specific hazards present, such as radiation, corrosive chemicals, or explosive materials. Specialized materials and coatings may be required to protect the robots from damage or contamination.
- **Maintenance and Upkeep:** Regular maintenance and inspections are crucial for ensuring the continued safe operation of robots in hazardous environments. Proper procedures should be established to handle robot maintenance tasks, including decontamination and component replacement.
- **Interoperability with Existing Infrastructure:** Integrating robots into existing infrastructure and systems in hazardous environments can pose challenges. Compatibility, communication protocols, and seamless integration with safety protocols and emergency response systems must be carefully considered.

4.8 FUTURE TRENDS AND EMERGING APPLICATIONS IN ROBOTICS

The future of robotics holds exciting trends and emerging applications, with the integration of artificial intelligence/machine learning (AI/ML), blockchain, and augmented reality/virtual reality (AR/VR) playing pivotal roles. Advancements in AI/ML enable robots to learn and adapt, enhancing their decision-making capabilities. Blockchain technology ensures secure and transparent data exchange between robots and stakeholders, enabling trust and accountability. Technologies such as AR/VR create immersive environments for training, remote collaboration, and enhanced user interfaces, revolutionizing industries such as healthcare, manufacturing, and entertainment. This convergence empowers robotics with intelligent autonomy, efficient data management, and immersive interactions, shaping the way one lives and works in the years to come (Khang & Rath et al., 2023).

4.8.1 COBOTS AND THEIR IMPACT ON HUMAN–ROBOT INTERACTION

Collaborative robots, also known as Cobots, are designed to work alongside humans cooperatively (Pearce et al., 2018). They offer advanced safety features, such as force sensing, collision detection, or adaptive control, allowing humans and robots to share workspace and perform tasks collaboratively. The exploration of Cobots includes:

- **Safe Human–Robot Collaboration:** Cobots are designed to operate near humans without posing a risk of injury. They are equipped with sensors and advanced algorithms that enable them to sense human presence, respond to human movements, and adjust their actions accordingly (Robla-Gomez et al., 2017).
- **Increased Flexibility and Adaptability:** Cobots are highly versatile and can be easily reprogrammed or reconfigured to perform different tasks or work with various tools. They offer flexibility in rapidly changing production environments.
- **Ergonomics and Workflow Optimization:** Cobots are designed with ergonomics in mind, reducing the physical strain on human workers and optimizing workflow efficiency. They can handle repetitive or physically demanding tasks, freeing up human workers for more complex or creative activities.

4.8.2 ROBOTICS IN INDUSTRY 4.0 AND SMART MANUFACTURING

The era of Industry 4.0 represents the integration of advanced technologies, including robotics, automation, data analytics, and the Internet of Things (IoT) in manufacturing processes (Bayram & İnce, 2017). The analysis of robotics in Industry 4.0 includes:

- **Connectivity and Data Exchange:** Robots are integrated into interconnected systems, enabling seamless communication and data exchange with other machines, systems, and humans. This integration facilitates real-time monitoring, analysis, and optimization of manufacturing processes.

- **Autonomous Decision-Making:** Robotics in Industry 4.0 utilizes AI and ML algorithms, empowering robots to make autonomous decisions based on real-time data and analysis. This leads to adaptive and optimized manufacturing operations.
- **Predictive Maintenance:** Robots equipped with sensors and data analytics capabilities can predict maintenance needs and identify potential failures before they occur. Predictive maintenance minimizes downtime, enhances productivity, and reduces costs associated with unplanned maintenance activities.
- **Collaborative Manufacturing Systems:** Industry 4.0 promotes the integration of robots, humans, and other machines in collaborative manufacturing systems. Robots work alongside human workers, leveraging their unique strengths, skills, and cognitive abilities to achieve efficient and high-quality production.

4.8.3 ADVANCES IN ARTIFICIAL INTELLIGENCE AND MACHINE LEARNING FOR ROBOTICS

Advances in artificial intelligence (AI) and machine learning (ML) have significant implications for robotics (Wang & Siau, 2019). These advances enhance robots' capabilities in perception, decision-making, and interaction with the environment. Key areas of advancement include:

- **Perception and Sensing:** AI and ML algorithms enable robots to process and interpret sensor data, including visual, auditory, or tactile information. This enhances their ability to understand and interact with the surrounding environment.
- **Adaptive Learning and Decision-Making:** Robots can learn from past experiences, adapt their behavior, and make informed decisions based on complex data patterns. Reinforcement learning and neural networks enable robots to improve their performance and optimize their actions over time (Verma et al., 2021a).
- **Human–Robot Interaction:** AI and ML algorithms contribute to more natural and intuitive human–robot interaction. Robots can understand and respond to human gestures, speech, or facial expressions, enabling effective collaboration and communication (Verma et al., 2021b).

4.8.4 ADVANCES IN BLOCKCHAIN FOR ROBOTICS

Blockchain technology is being explored for a variety of applications in robotics including:

- **Data Security and Integrity:** Blockchain can be used to store and share data securely and in a tamper-proof manner. This is important for applications where data needs to be protected from unauthorized access or tampering, such as in the medical or financial industries (Verma et al., 2022b).

- **Swarm Robotics:** Blockchain can be used to coordinate the actions of a group of robots, or "swarm." This could be used for applications such as search and rescue, disaster relief, or environmental monitoring (Verma et al., 2020).
- **Smart Contracts:** Smart contracts are self-executing contracts that are stored on the blockchain. This could be used to automate the execution of tasks between robots, such as the transfer of goods or services (Verma et al., 2022c).
- **Asset Tracking:** Blockchain can be used to track the movement of assets, such as products or parts. This could be used to improve traceability and accountability in supply chains.
- **Robot Identity:** Blockchain can be used to create a unique identity for each robot. This could be used to track the history of a robot, its maintenance records, and its certifications (Verma et al., 2022d).

These are just a few of the ways that blockchain technology is being explored for applications in robotics. As technology continues to develop, one can expect to see even more innovative and creative uses for blockchain in robotics in the future. Here are some a few examples of how blockchain is being used in robotics today:

- **Medical Industry:** Blockchain is being used to track the provenance of medical devices. Including decentralized applications (dApps) in the industry would improve the efficiency of the industry. This can help to ensure that patients receive safe and effective medical treatment (Junaid et al., 2023).
- **Automotive Industry:** Blockchain is being used to track the maintenance records of vehicles. This can help to improve safety and reliability.
- **Supply Chain Industry:** Blockchain is being used to track the movement of goods. This can help to improve transparency and efficiency.
- **Manufacturing Industry:** Blockchain is being used to coordinate the actions of robots. This can help to improve productivity and efficiency.
- **Agriculture Industry:** Blockchain is being used to track the provenance of food. This can help to ensure that consumers have access to safe and sustainable food.

As the technology continues to develop, one can expect to see even more innovative and creative uses for blockchain in robotics in the future.

4.8.5 POTENTIAL FUTURE APPLICATIONS AND INNOVATIONS IN ROBOTICS

The field of robotics is continuously evolving, and numerous potential future applications and innovations are on the horizon. Some areas of interest include:

- **Medical Robotics:** Robotics holds significant promise in healthcare, including surgical robotics, robotic prosthetics, and rehabilitation robotics. These technologies aim to improve patient outcomes, enhance precision, and enable remote medical procedures (Camarillo et al., 2004).

- **Service Robotics:** Service robots are designed to assist humans in various settings, such as hospitality, customer service, or household tasks. Future developments may include robots that can perform complex chores, provide personalized assistance, or even engage in companionship (Decker et al., 2017).
- **Agricultural Robotics:** Robots have the potential to revolutionize agriculture by automating tasks such as planting, harvesting, or crop monitoring. This can lead to increased efficiency, optimized resource utilization, and sustainable farming practices (Duckett et al., 2018).
- **Space Exploration Robotics:** Robots play a vital role in space exploration, and future innovations may include advanced robotic systems for planetary exploration, satellite servicing, or asteroid mining. These technologies expand our understanding of the universe and enable new scientific discoveries (Barfoot & Wettergreen, 2016).

In the potential future, augmented reality (AR) and robotics are converging technologies revolutionizing various industries. Augmented reality enhances the real world by overlaying digital information, while robotics involves the design and development of machines capable of performing tasks autonomously (Shukla et al., 2023). Together, they enable immersive user experiences and advanced automation, driving innovation in fields such as manufacturing, healthcare, military, and entertainment.

In conclusion, the field of robotics continues to evolve, offering diverse applications across various industries and environments. From hazardous environments to collaborative manufacturing systems, robotics brings enhanced safety, efficiency, and productivity. Future trends, such as the rise of collaborative robots, integration with Industry 4.0, advances in AI and ML, and exciting innovations, further pave the way for transformative developments in robotics (Khang & Shah et al., 2023).

4.9   CONCLUSION

This chapter has provided a comprehensive exploration of the application of robotics in manufacturing. By examining various areas such as assembly, material handling, quality control and inspection, packaging and palletizing, welding and cutting, and hazardous environments, the chapter has highlighted the significant role of robotics in enhancing efficiency, productivity, and safety in the industry. The evolution of robotics in manufacturing has brought about transformative changes, revolutionized processes, and optimizing outcomes. From robotic assembly lines to vision-guided robots for quality inspection, from automated guided vehicles for material handling to palletizing robots for streamlining planning, and from robotic welding systems to robots designed for hazardous environments, the examples and case studies have demonstrated the real-world success and impact of robotics in diverse industrial settings.

Furthermore, the chapter has explored future trends and emerging applications, including collaborative robots, Industry 4.0 integration, advances in AI and ML, and potential future innovations in robotics. These developments open up new possibilities for enhanced human–robot interaction, optimized manufacturing operations, and groundbreaking applications in various fields. Overall, this chapter serves as a valuable resource for researchers, engineers, and professionals seeking to use robotics for increased productivity, efficiency, and competitiveness in the manufacturing industry. The integration of robotics in manufacturing is an ongoing journey with immense potential, and its continued advancement will shape the future of the industry (Khang & Rath, 2024).

REFERENCES

Andrzejewski, K. T., M. P. Cooper, C. A. Griffiths, and C. Giannetti, "Optimisation Process for Robotic Assembly of Electronic Components." The International Journal of Advanced Manufacturing Technology, vol. 99, no. 9, pp. 2523–2535, 2018, doi: 10.1007/s00170-018-2645-y.

Anh, P. T. N., H. Vladimir, Triwiyanto, N. A. Ragimova, R. İsmibeyli, V. A. Hajimahmud, and A. V. Alyar, "AI Models for Disease Diagnosis and Prediction of Heart Disease With Artificial Neural Networks." *Computer Vision and AI-Integrated IoT Technologies in Medical Ecosystem* (1st Ed.) (2024). CRC Press. https://doi.org/10.1201/9781003429609-9

Barfoot, T. D., and D. Wettergreen, "Editorial: Special Issue on Space Robotics." Journal of Field Robotics, vol. 33, no. 2, pp. 155–156, 2016, doi: 10.1002/rob.21649.

Bassani, G., A. Filippeschi, and C. A. Avizzano, "A Dataset of Human Motion and Muscular Activities in Manual Material Handling Tasks for Biomechanical and Ergonomic Analyses." IEEE Sensors Journal, vol. 21, no. 21, pp. 24731–24739, 2021, doi: 10.1109/jsen.2021.3113123.

Bayram, B., and G. İnce, "Advances in Robotics in the Era of Industry 4.0." Springer Series in Advanced Manufacturing, pp. 187–200, 2017, doi: 10.1007/978-3-319-57870-5_11.

Bogue, R., "Cutting Robots: A Review of Technologies and Applications." Industrial Robot: An International Journal, vol. 35, no. 5, pp. 390–396, 2008, doi: 10.1108/01439910810893554.

Brito, T., J. Queiroz, L. Piardi, L. A. Fernandes, J. Lima, and P. Leitão, "A Machine Learning Approach for Collaborative Robot Smart Manufacturing Inspection for Quality Control Systems." Procedia Manufacturing, vol. 51, pp. 11–18, 2020, doi: 10.1016/j.promfg.2020.10.003.

Brogårdh, T., "Robot Control Overview: An Industrial Perspective." Modeling, Identification and Control: A Norwegian Research Bulletin, vol. 30, no. 3, pp. 167–180, 2009, doi: 10.4173/mic.2009.3.7.

Camarillo, D. B., T. M. Krummel, and J. Salisbury, "Robotic Technology in Surgery: Past, Present, and Future." The American Journal of Surgery, vol. 188, no. 4, pp. 2–15, 2004, doi: 10.1016/j.amjsurg.2004.08.025.

Cardoso, A., A. Colim, E. Bicho, A. C. Braga, M. Menozzi, and P. Arezes, "Ergonomics and Human Factors as a Requirement to Implement Safer Collaborative Robotic Workstations: A Literature Review." Safety, vol. 7, no. 4, p. 71, 2021, doi: 10.3390/safety7040071.

Colvalkar, A., S. S. Pawar, and B. K. Patle, "In-Pipe Inspection Robotic System for Defect Detection and Identification Using Image Processing." Materials Today: Proceedings, vol. 72, pp. 1735–1742, 2023, doi: 10.1016/j.matpr.2022.09.476.

Curiel, D., F. Veiga, A. Suarez, and P. Villanueva, "Advances in Robotic Welding for Metallic Materials: Application of Inspection, Modeling, Monitoring and Automation Techniques." Metals, vol. 13, no. 4, p. 711, 2023, doi: 10.3390/met13040711.

Decker, M., M. Fischer, and I. Ott, "Service Robotics and Human Labor: A First Technology Assessment of Substitution and Cooperation." Robotics and Autonomous Systems, vol. 87, pp. 348–354, 2017, doi: 10.1016/j.robot.2016.09.017.

Duckett, T., S. Pearson, S. Blackmore, and B. Grieve, "Agricultural Robotics: The Future of Robotic Agriculture." UKRAS White Papers, 2018, doi: 10.31256/wp2018.2.

Dunbabin, M., and L. Marques, "Robots for Environmental Monitoring: Significant Advancements and Applications." IEEE Robotics & Automation Magazine, vol. 19, no. 1, pp. 24–39, 2012, doi: 10.1109/mra.2011.2181683.

Dzitac, P., and A. M. Mazid, "An Efficient Control Configuration Development for a High-speed Robotic Palletizing System." 2008 IEEE Conference on Robotics, Automation and Mechatronics, 2008, doi: 10.1109/ramech.2008.4681379.

Edinbarough, I., R. Balderas, and S. Bose, "A Vision and Robot Based on-Line Inspection Monitoring System for Electronic Manufacturing." Computers in Industry, vol. 56, no. 8, pp. 986–996, 2005, doi: 10.1016/j.compind.2005.05.022.

Gambao, E., M. Hernando, and D. Surdilovic, "A New Generation of Collaborative Robots for Material Handling." Proceedings of the International Symposium on Automation and Robotics in Construction (IAARC), 2012, doi: 10.22260/isarc2012/0076.

Gao, J., J. Folkes, O. Yilmaz, and N. Gindy, "Investigation of a 3D Non-Contact Measurement Based Blade Repair Integration System." Aircraft Engineering and Aerospace Technology, vol. 77, no. 1, pp. 34–41, 2005, doi: 10.1108/00022660510576028.

Goel, R., and P. Gupta, "Robotics and Industry 4.0." A Roadmap to Industry 4.0: Smart Production, Sharp Business and Sustainable Development, pp. 157–169, 2019, doi: 10.1007/978-3-030-14544-6_9.

Grau, A., M. Indri, L. L. Bello, and T. Sauter, "Industrial robotics in factory automation: From the early stage to the Internet of Things." IECON 2017 - 43rd Annual Conference of the IEEE Industrial Electronics Society, 2017, doi: 10.1109/iecon.2017.8217070.

Gray, J., and S. Davis, "Robotics in the Food Industry: an Introduction." Robotics and Automation in the Food Industry, pp. 21–35, 2013, doi: 10.1533/9780857095763.1.21.

Guizzo, E., "Three Engineers, Hundreds of Robots, One Warehouse." IEEE Spectrum, vol. 45, no. 7, pp. 26–34, 2008, doi: 10.1109/mspec.2008.4547508.

Guo, J., T. Bamber, Y. Zhao, M. Chamberlain, L. Justham, and M. Jackson, "Toward Adaptive and Intelligent Electroadhesives for Robotic Material Handling." IEEE Robotics and Automation Letters, vol. 2, no. 2, pp. 538–545, 2017, doi: 10.1109/lra.2016.2646258.

Herrero-Perez, D., and H. Martinez-Barbera, "Modeling Distributed Transportation Systems Composed of Flexible Automated Guided Vehicles in Flexible Manufacturing Systems." IEEE Transactions on Industrial Informatics, vol. 6, no. 2, pp. 166–180, 2010, doi: 10.1109/tii.2009.2038691.

Hong, T., M. Ghobakhloo, and W. Khaksar, "Robotic Welding Technology." Comprehensive Materials Processing, pp. 77–99, 2014, doi: 10.1016/b978-0-08-096532-1.00604-x.

Junaid, A., A. Nawaz, M. F. Usmani, R. Verma, and N. Dhanda, "Analyzing the Performance of a DAPP Using Blockchain 3.0." 2023 13th International Conference on Cloud Computing, Data Science & Engineering (Confluence), 2023, doi: 10.1109/confluence56041.2023.10048887.

Kamarul Bahrin, M. A., M. F. Othman, N. H. Nor Azli, and M. F. Talib, "Industry 4.0: A Review on Industrial Automation and Robotic." Jurnal Teknologi, vol. 78, no. 6, 2016, doi: 10.11113/jt.v78.9285.

Karagiannis, P., N. – C. Zacharaki, G. Michalos, and S. Makris, "Increasing Flexibility in Consumer Goods Industry with the Help of Robotized Systems." Procedia CIRP, vol. 86, pp. 192–197, 2019, doi: 10.1016/j.procir.2020.01.039.

Khan, A., C. Mineo, G. Dobie, C. Macleod, and G. Pierce, "Vision Guided Robotic Inspection for Parts in Manufacturing and Remanufacturing Industry." Journal of Remanufacturing, vol. 11, no. 1, pp. 49–70, 2020, doi: 10.1007/s13243-020-00091-x.

Khang, A., M. Muthmainnah, P. M. I. Seraj, A. A. Yakin, A. J. Obaid, and M. Ranjan Panda, "AI-Aided Teaching Model for the Education 5.0 Ecosystem." *AI-Based Technologies and Applications in the Era of the Metaverse* (1st Ed.) (2023). Pages (83–104). IGI Global Press. doi: 10.4018/978-1-6684-8851-5.ch004.

Khang, A., and K. C. Rath, *The Quantum Evolution: Application of AI and Robotics in the Future of Quantum Technology* (1st Ed.) (2024). ISBN: 9781032642079. CRC Press. doi: 10.1201/978-1-032-64207-9.

Khang, A., K. C. Rath, S. Kumar Satapathy, A. Kumar, S. Ranjan Das, and M. Ranjan Panda. "Enabling the Future of Manufacturing: Integration of Robotics and IoT to Smart Factory Infrastructure in Industry 4.0." *AI-Based Technologies and Applications in the Era of the Metaverse* (1st Ed.) (2023). Pages (25–50). IGI Global Press. doi: 10.4018/978-1-6684-8851-5.ch002.

Khang, A., V. Shah, and S. Rani, *AI-Based Technologies and Applications in the Era of the Metaverse* (1st Ed.) (2023). IGI Global Press. doi: 10.4018/978-1-6684-8851-5.

Kowalczuk, Z., and D. Wesierski, "Vision Guided Robot Gripping Systems." Automation and Robotics, 2008, doi: 10.5772/6264.

Krüger, J., T. Lien, and A. Verl, "Cooperation of Human and Machines in Assembly Lines." CIRP Annals, vol. 58, no. 2, pp. 628–646, 2009, doi: 10.1016/j.cirp.2009.09.009.

Liu, G., W. Yu, and Y. Liu, "Resource Management with RFID Technology in Automatic Warehouse System." 2006 IEEE/RSJ International Conference on Intelligent Robots and Systems, 2006, doi: 10.1109/iros.2006.281750.

Mahadevan, B., and T. T. Narendran, "Design of an Automated Guided Vehicle-Based Material Handling System for a Flexible Manufacturing System." International Journal of Production Research, vol. 28, no. 9, pp. 1611–1622, 1990, doi: 10.1080/00207549008942819.

Mahalik, N., "Advances in Packaging Methods, Processes and Systems." Challenges, vol. 5, no. 2, pp. 374–389, 2014, doi: 10.3390/challe5020374.

Malik, A. A., and A. Bilberg, "Collaborative Robots in Assembly: A Practical Approach for Tasks Distribution." Procedia CIRP, vol. 81, pp. 665–670, 2019, doi: 10.1016/j.procir.2019.03.173.

Michalos, G., S. Makris, N. Papakostas, D. Mourtzis, and G. Chryssolouris, "Automotive Assembly Technologies Review: Challenges and Outlook for a Flexible and Adaptive Approach." CIRP Journal of Manufacturing Science and Technology, vol. 2, no. 2, pp. 81–91, 2010, doi: 10.1016/j.cirpj.2009.12.001.

Müller, R., M. Vette, and M. Scholer, "Robot Workmate: A Trustworthy Coworker for the Continuous Automotive Assembly Line and Its Implementation." Procedia CIRP, vol. 44, pp. 263–268, 2016, doi: 10.1016/j.procir.2016.02.077.

Oh, J.-K., "Bridge Inspection Robot System With Machine Vision." Automation in Construction, vol. 18, no. 7, pp. 929–941, 2009, doi: 10.1016/j.autcon.2009.04.003.

Pearce, M., B. Mutlu, J. Shah, and R. Radwin, "Optimizing Makespan and Ergonomics in Integrating Collaborative Robots Into Manufacturing Processes." IEEE Transactions on Automation Science and Engineering, vol. 15, no. 4, pp. 1772–1784, 2018, doi: 10.1109/tase.2018.2789820.

Pires, J., A. Loureiro, T. Godinho, P. Ferreira, B. Fernando, and J. Morgado, "Welding Robots." IEEE Robotics & Automation Magazine, vol. 10, no. 2, pp. 45–55, 2003, doi: 10.1109/mra.2003.1213616.

Raafat, H., and S. Taboun, "An Integrated Robotic and Machine Vision System for Surface Flaw Detection and Classification." Computers & Industrial Engineering, vol. 30, no. 1, pp. 27–40, 1996, doi: 10.1016/0360-8352(95)00038-0.

Radlak, K., and M. Fojcik, "Integration of Robotic Arm Manipulator with Computer Vision in a Project-Based Learning Environment." 2015 IEEE Frontiers in Education Conference (FIE), 2015, doi: 10.1109/fie.2015.7344198.

Rey, R., M. Corzetto, J. A. Cobano, L. Merino, and F. Caballero, "Human-Robot Co-Working System for Warehouse Automation." 2019 24th IEEE International Conference on Emerging Technologies and Factory Automation (ETFA), 2019, doi: 10.1109/etfa. 2019.8869178.

Robla-Gomez, S., V. M. Becerra, J. R. Llata, E. Gonzalez-Sarabia, C. Torre-Ferrero, and J. Perez-Oria, "Working Together: A Review on Safe Human-Robot Collaboration in Industrial Environments." IEEE Access, vol. 5, pp. 26754–26773, 2017, doi: 10.1109/access.2017.2773127.

Semeniuta, O., S. Dransfeld, and P. Falkman, "Vision-Based Robotic System for Picking and Inspection of Small Automotive Components." 2016 IEEE International Conference on Automation Science and Engineering (CASE), 2016, doi: 10.1109/coase.2016.7743452.

Sherwani, F., M. M. Asad, and B. Ibrahim, "Collaborative Robots and Industrial Revolution 4.0 (IR 4.0)." 2020 International Conference on Emerging Trends in Smart Technologies (ICETST), 2020, doi: 10.1109/icetst49965.2020.9080724.

Shukla, U., N. Dhanda, and R. Verma, Augmented Reality Product Showcase E-commerce Application (February 16, 2023). Available at SSRN: https://ssrn.com/abstract=4361319 or http://dx.doi.org/10.2139/ssrn.4361319

Slack, N., "Flexibility as a Manufacturing Objective." International Journal of Operations & Production Management, vol. 3, no. 3, pp. 4–13, 1983, doi: 10.1108/eb054696.

Staritz, P., S. Skaff, C. Urmson, and W. Whittaker, "Skyworker: A Robot for Assembly, Inspection and Maintenance of Large Scale Orbital Facilities." Proceedings 2001 ICRA. IEEE International Conference on Robotics and Automation (Cat. No. 01CH37164), 2001, doi: 10.1109/robot.2001.933271.

Straka, M., D. Spirkova, and M. Filla, "Improved Efficiency of Manufacturing Logistics by Using Computer Simulation." International Journal of Simulation Modelling, vol. 20, no. 3, pp. 501–512, 2021, doi: 10.2507/ijsimm20-3-567.

Trevelyan, J., W. R. Hamel, and S.-C. Kang, "Robotics in Hazardous Applications." Springer Handbook of Robotics (2016). Page (1521–1548). Springer. doi: 10.1007/978-3-319-32552-1_58.

Verma, R. Dr., N. Dhanda Dr., and V. Nagar, "Addressing the Issues & Challenges of Internet of Things Using Blockchain Technology." International Journal of Advanced Science and Technology, vol. 29, no. 05, pp. 10074–10082, 2020. Retrieved from http://sersc.org/journals/index.php/IJAST/article/view/19491.

Verma, R., N. Dhanda, and V. Nagar, "Security Concerns in IoT Systems and Its Blockchain Solutions." Cyber Intelligence and Information Retrieval, pp. 485–495, 2021a, doi: 10.1007/978-981-16-4284-5_42.

Verma, R., N. Dhanda, and V. Nagar, "Application of Truffle Suite in a Blockchain Environment." Proceedings of Third International Conference on Computing, Communications, and Cyber-Security, pp. 693–702, 2022a, doi: 10.1007/978-981-19-1142-2_54.

Verma, R., N. Dhanda, and V. Nagar, "Enhancing & Optimizing Security of IoT Systems Using Different Components of Industry 4.0." International Journal of Engineering Trends and Technology, vol. 70, no. 7, pp. 147–157, 2022b, doi: 10.14445/22315381/ijett-v70i7p216.

Verma, R., N. Dhanda, and V. Nagar, "Enhancing Security with In-Depth Analysis of Brute-Force Attack on Secure Hashing Algorithms." Proceedings of Trends in Electronics and Health Informatics, pp. 513–522, 2022c, doi: 10.1007/978-981-16-8826-3_44.

Verma, R., N. Dhanda, and V. Nagar, "Towards a Secured IoT Communication: A Blockchain Implementation Through APIs." Proceedings of Third International Conference on Computing, Communications, and Cyber-Security, pp. 681–692, 2022d, doi: 10.1007/978-981-19-1142-2_53.

Verma, R., N. Dhanda, and V. Nagar, "Analysing the Security Aspects of IoT Using Blockchain and Cryptographic Algorithms." International Journal on Recent and Innovation Trends in Computing and Communication, vol. 11, no. 1s, pp. 13–22, 2023a, doi: 10.17762/ijritcc.v11i1s.5990.

Verma, R., N. Dhanda, V. Nagar, and M. Dhanda, "Towards an Efficient IOT System by Integrating Blockchain in IOT." Journal of Theoretical and Applied Information Technology, vol. 101, no. 5, 2023b. https://www.jatit.org/volumes/Vol101No5/4Vol101No5.pdf

Verma, R., V. Nagar, and S. Mahapatra, "Introduction to Supervised Learning." Data Analytics in Bioinformatics, pp. 1–34, 2021b, doi: 10.1002/9781119785620.ch1.

Villani, V., F. Pini, F. Leali, and C. Secchi, "Survey on Human–Robot Collaboration in Industrial Settings: Safety, Intuitive Interfaces and Applications." Mechatronics, vol. 55, pp. 248–266, 2018, doi: 10.1016/j.mechatronics.2018.02.009.

Wang, W., and K. Siau, "Artificial Intelligence, Machine Learning, Automation, Robotics, Future of Work and Future of Humanity." Journal of Database Management, vol. 30, no. 1, pp. 61–79, 2019, doi: 10.4018/jdm.2019010104.

Weckenborg, C., C. Thies, and T. S. Spengler, "Harmonizing Ergonomics and Economics of Assembly Lines Using Collaborative Robots and Exoskeletons." Journal of Manufacturing Systems, vol. 62, pp. 681–702, 2022, doi: 10.1016/j.jmsy.2022.02.005.

Wilson, M., "Robots in the Aerospace Industry." Aircraft Engineering and Aerospace Technology, vol. 66, no. 3, pp. 2–3, 1994, doi: 10.1108/eb037487.

Wu, Y., and Y. Lu, "An Intelligent Machine Vision System for Detecting Surface Defects on Packing Boxes Based on Support Vector Machine." Measurement and Control, vol. 52, no. 7, pp. 1102–1110, 2019, doi: 10.1177/0020294019858175.

Yuan, Z., and Y. Gong, "Improving the Speed Delivery for Robotic Warehouses." IFAC-PapersOnLine, vol. 49, no. 12, pp. 1164–1168, 2016, doi: 10.1016/j.ifacol.2016.07.661

Zakrzewski, B., and K. Szopik-Depczynska, "Changes in Logistics Processes Caused by the Implementation of Automation in Transport." European Research Studies Journal, pp. 24–34, 2022, doi: 10.35808/ersj/2933.

Zhao, F., Y. Ma, and Y. Sun, "Application and Standardization Trend of Maintenance and Inspection Robot (MIR) in Nuclear Power Station." DEStech Transactions on Engineering and Technology Research, 2017, doi: 10.12783/dtetr/ismii2017/16678.

5 Application of Industrial Robotics in Manufacturing

Alex Khang, Vugar Abdullayev Hajimahmud, Abuzarova Vusala Alyar, Matlab Khalilov Etibar, Vasila Abbasova Soltanaga, and Yitong Niu

5.1 INTRODUCTION

Robots closely assist people in many different areas from daily life to large industries. Robots come in many forms; some are human-like in appearance, while others are completely machine-like. About 20 to 30 years ago, when people thought of robots, images of Transformers seen in sci-fi movies or robots from the Star Wars series came to mind. Today, robots are available as everyday helpers.

The terms robot and robotics come from the science fiction genre of art. The word "robot" was first used in a play about mechanical people who were set up to work on factory conveyors and rebelled against their human masters. The word "robot" was first used in *Rossum's Universal Robots* (RUR), a play written by Czech playwright Karel Capek in 1921. He derived the word from the Czech word "robota" or worker. The word "robotics" was also used by another writer: Russian American science fiction writer Isaac Asimov first coined the word in his 1942 short story *Runabout*. Asimov had a brighter and more optimistic view of the robot's role in human society than Capek. He generally characterized robots in his short stories as useful servants of man and saw robots as "a better, purer race" (Stanford, 1998). Later, Asimov came up with three laws about robots (Moravec, 2023):

- First Law: A robot may not injure a person or allow a person to be harmed by its inaction.
- Second Law: A robot must obey the commands given to it by humans, even if these commands are against the First Law.
- Third Law: A robot must protect its existence, as long as such protection does not violate the First or Second Law.

Different but equally meaningful definitions of robots include (Stanford, 1998):

- A robot is a reprogrammable, multi-functional manipulator designed to move material, parts, tools, or special devices through a variety of programmed motions to perform various tasks.

DOI: 10.1201/9781003438137-5

- A robot is an automatic device or machine in human form that performs functions normally attributed to humans (*Webster's Dictionary*).
- A robot is a reprogrammable manipulator device (British Department of Industry).

These definitions show that although different words are used, the meanings are similar. We can similarly define a robot as follows: A robot is a human-made object consisting of a collection of mainly programmed metal parts that help people perform tasks that are both physically difficult and life-threatening.

Since their inception, robots have been known as humanoid machines that help the people who create them. The beginning of robots as a term may date back to 1921, but the creation of objects that help people has existed since ancient times, known as the fathers of today's robots (Khang & Rath, 2023).

The first robot that could be digitally controlled and programmed was created in 1954 by inventor George C. Devol of Louisville, Kentucky. This robot was called "Unimate" and was a robotic arm patented by Devol. With this, the foundations of the modern Robot industry were laid. Unimate is also known as the first industrial robot and was used in 1961 at the General Motors factory in Ewing Township, New Jersey (see Figure 5.1).

Unimate was a hydraulic manipulator arm that could perform repetitive tasks. It has been used by car manufacturers to automate metalworking and welding processes (Unimate, 1961).

The field dealing with the study, development, and operation of robots is known as robotics. The following will be discussed in this chapter:

- Robots and their activities
- Features and types of robots
- Application areas of robots
- Sector studying robots: Robotics
- Robotics and manufacturing
- Overview of industrial robots

FIGURE 5.1   First industrial robot: Robotic arm, Unimate (1961).

5.2 RELATED WORK

Robots are types of automated machines that perform many different tasks in autonomous and semi-autonomous forms. They can perform many different activities with a specific purpose:

- Automation of repetitive activities in enterprises and everyday life
- Monitoring and control: Automation of security processes in any field
- Performing work that is physically difficult or dangerous for people
- Implementation of clerical activities

Robots can perform activities according to any sector's requirements. Often this is related to a "trust" factor between humans and robots, which is not yet fully formed. Fear, hatred, and jealousy are human emotions that might make the human-robot relationship a complicated one. Humans are relatively egoistic beings by creation and consider themselves superior.

People don't like robots because they fear that robots will one day be superior to them. They fear that there might be a being who is smarter, stronger, and more practical than humans—a race superior to humans. The thought of robots replacing humans also scares people and arouses the feeling of jealousy. In this regard, some people can even be violent toward robots, as strange as it sounds. Although people have different psychologies, the fear that "robots will replace people, people will become a second-class race, and they will be unemployed" can be common for many people, especially those who have actually lost their jobs to robots (MCRS, 2023).

Such a situation is known as the "Frankenstein syndrome," or the fear of "man's self-created being rebelling against man (against his creator)."

Another similar fear is technophobia, in which people worry about the rapid development of technology and its integration into various areas. Such fears can make people mistrust robots and technology in general. In reality, robots are the most loyal assistants for people. There will be no "rebellion" as long as the field of robotics is managed properly (Khang & Alyar et al., 2023).

5.3 FEATURES AND TYPES OF ROBOTS

5.3.1 FEATURES OF ROBOT

People who come to work at the same time every day, start work at the same time, take a short break, perform all their daily tasks on time and without mistakes, leave work at the end of the work day, and work even when they are resting, are sometimes called "robotic." Robotization of humans has been around since the dawn of the working class. The main issue we are dealing with here is the humanization of robots (Msitec, 2023).

Created for specific purposes, mostly functioning as parts (such as a robotic arm), robots now have many parts and features that are similar to those of humans. Robots are becoming more and more similar to humans both in terms of activity and cognition. Characteristics of modern robots include:

- They are means of automation of activities.
- They are mainly programmed machines (reprogrammable).
- They have sensory organs like humans, but in a digitized format. People see, hear, and touch the surrounding world with their *senses*; robots also carry out these processes with their *sensors*.
- They have brains and can also remember the processes and activities they performed.
- They operate autonomously and semi-autonomously.

Robots are also more flexible and stronger than humans. They get more done in less time with less risk of error.

5.3.2 Types of Robots

There are different types of robots and they vary depending on the area of application and in terms of their general characteristics as discussed below and shown in Figure 5.2.

5.3.2.1 First Generation: Robot Manipulators

The first generation of robots, such as the robotic arm Unimate in 1954, were mainly used to perform limited tasks. Robotic manipulators usually have two parts: arm/body and wrist.

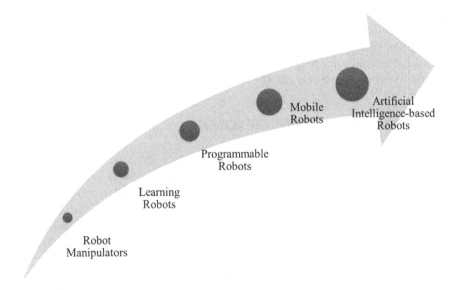

FIGURE 5.2 Types of robots.

FIGURE 5.3   Shape of robots in the manufacturing and automotive industry.

These robots are used to carry objects from one place to another and to perform simple but relatively difficult tasks. Basically, these robots, which were originally controlled by an operator, have recently been used to perform improved and automated activities.

Like all robots, robot manipulators are used to work with objects or substances that are too heavy or dangerous for humans to handle (e.g., radioactive substances). Currently, these robots are used in various industries, especially in the manufacturing and automotive industries, as shown in Figure 5.3.

5.3.2.2   Second Generation: Learning Robots

Compared to the previous generation, learning robots are more advanced, as they perform more complex tasks and a wide range of activities. As the name suggests, these robots learn from their surroundings by collecting information in order to perform tasks.

5.3.2.3   Third Generation: Programmable Robots

Third generation robots are machines connected to the world of programming. These robots are programmed by humans to perform certain activities. They are also called real digitized robots.

This generation of robots is equipped with activators, sensors, and controllers and it uses them to interact with and react to changes in the environment, and to perform programmed activities.

Different languages are used for robot programming, from simple to complex. These types of robots are currently being further improved and are being applied in many industries, such as manufacturing, agriculture, healthcare, military, etc.

5.3.2.4   Fourth Generation: Mobile Robots

Known as traveling robots, these fourth generation robots are the first intelligent robots, able to obtain real-time information about the world around them. They can be controlled both remotely and autonomously with artificial intelligence. Modern robotics is especially concerned with the study and operation of these and it also conducts tests for the next generation of robots.

These robots have computer vision, which is one of its main advantages over earlier generations. In addition, they have wireless connectivity. Although these robots are mainly exploratory, they also carry out activities such as cargo transportation and have quite a wide range of applications. From the military sector to large industries, they are also used in everyday life in a simpler form.

5.3.2.5 Fifth Generation: Artificial Intelligence-Based Robots

Robots of this type, which are the last generation and the robots of the future, are currently being improved and developed. One of the goals for these robots is to be fully autonomous. This means that these robots will be able to make decisions and fully learn on their own, as well as act autonomously. In short, these robots will be able to fully imitate humans. They can also operate in a hybrid form with previous-generation robots, if necessary.

5.4 APPLICATION AREAS OF ROBOTS

Robots differ according to their application areas. The following are among the areas where robots are widely used.

5.4.1 MANUFACTURING

Manufacturing robots are a particularly separate category. They implement the automation of production processes and generally play a very large role in production. Manufacturing robots are discussed in detail in Section 5.5.

5.4.2 MILITARY

Technological innovations start in the military sector. Robots are one of the technologies applied in the military sector, known as "military robots." Military robots are used to assist the military in testing weapons, transporting ammunition, searching for mines or other hazardous materials, and ensuring safety. In the near future, especially with the development of fifth-generation robots in an appropriate form, robot armies may also be created. This can be done when the development of artificial intelligence becomes more sophisticated.

5.4.3 HEALTHCARE

One of the areas where robots are most widely used and act as major helpers is healthcare, where it is quite common to see robotic caregivers assisting patients. Robots in healthcare also assist doctors in performing surgeries. They are also used for janitorial tasks and in cargo transportation. In addition, they help patients with limited mobility get around more easily and take their medicines (by bringing the medicine directly to the patient, for example), and they regularly transmit health information about the patient to the doctors.

5.4.4 EDUCATION

Educational robots are friends of both teachers and students. Basically, they can assist in teaching children through games. Educational robots engage in the personalization of lessons, making them more fun for students. Socialization is especially important for children's early development. In this regard, robots are not meant to replace teachers but assist them in making learning more fun and engaging.

5.4.5 CONSTRUCTION

Construction robots are used in automated work at construction sites, such as the transportation of loads such as brick, stone, sand, concrete, iron, etc.; brick/stone masonry; and concrete pouring. By handing over such physical work to robots, jobs are completed faster and in a safer and more efficient manner.

5.4.6 ENTERTAINMENT

As the name suggests, entertainment robots perform various activities specifically to entertain a human audience: singing music, dancing, playing games, etc. Such robots can be found in amusement parks, parties, theaters, and homes.

5.4.7 ENVIRONMENT

Robots are used for helping humans in exploring dangerous areas, monitoring changes in the environment—such as soil, water, and air quality—and studying their effects.

5.4.8 SAFETY AND SECURITY

Robots are used to ensure safety in various sectors. They can monitor objects/people, provide protection, and activate warning signals in case of emergencies. Robots can also replace humans in performing tasks that are too dangerous.

5.4.9 AGRICULTURE

Following the Smart Cities project, the Smart Village has become one of the main application areas of smart technology in rural areas. Robots carry out the work performed by the peasant class in an automated form and in accordance with water, soil, and air norms. They plow the soil, plant seeds, monitor the growth of crops, and then harvest them whenever possible. By doing so, efficiency and productivity are increased, and costs are reduced.

5.4.10 TRANSPORTATION

Intelligent transportation, one of the application areas of robotics, mainly includes self-driving cars, drones, and other autonomous vehicles. These are applied to increase safety, reduce costs, and increase efficiency in transportation.

5.4.11 RESEARCH

The field of research needs robots. The reason for this need is the combination of many other fields in the research field. In addition to studying human–robot interactions, robots are also used to conduct research in and take samples from hazardous areas, especially in space research where robots are used to explore planets where humans cannot go. Such robots are known as research robots. Relatively speaking, mobile robots, which are fourth generation robots, also belong to the category of research robots.

5.4.12 DAILY LIFE

Robots used in everyday life are also known as home robots. These robots mainly automate some household tasks such as cleaning, home monitoring, pet care, and cooking. These are mainly called cleaning robots, kitchen robots, security/home surveillance robots, etc. Robots like these improve people's quality of life and are the most in-demand robots or little helpers.

5.4.13 UNDERWATER EXPLORATION

As the name suggests, these types of robots are used especially in underwater exploration, research, exploration of oil wells, maintenance, and control. These pressure-resistant robots are also used to investigate shipwrecks and study the depths of the oceans.

5.4.14 SEARCH AND RESCUE

Search and rescue robots are one of the main helpers of emergency workers during natural disasters. They are designed to work during extremely dangerous natural disasters such as earthquakes, landslides, and avalanches, and they are designed according to the working conditions. These robots work to locate and rescue disaster victims. In addition, they are also used to study the disaster area. This category is related to environmental learning robots.

5.4.15 TESTING

Robots help in carrying out appropriate tests and trials in the laboratory, healthcare, production, transport, military, and other fields. Robots are ideal tools as test subjects. Most importantly, testing with robots is safe.

5.4.16 SERVICE

The service sector covers many areas: tourism, entertainment, hospitality, healthcare, etc. In general, robots perform service activities in these areas; for example, as a waiter/assistant in restaurants and hotels or in the banking sector, answering customers' questions, responding to customer inquiries, and guiding customers. This field is customer-oriented, requires extensive use of robots, and encompasses many other sectors.

5.5 OVERVIEW OF INDUSTRIAL ROBOTS

5.5.1 INDUSTRIAL ROBOTS

Industrial robots are mainly reprogrammable fixed or mobile robots used for various purposes in various industries, especially in manufacturing. According to ISO 8373:2021 (Robotic Applications, 2021), an industrial robot includes:

- Manipulator, including robot controllers controlled by a robot controller; robot controller; means to train and/or program the robot, including any communication interface (hardware and software).
- Industrial robots include any auxiliary axes integrated into the kinematic solution.
- Industrial robots include the manipulator parts of mobile robots, where the mobile robot consists of a mobile platform with an integrated manipulator or robot.

Unlike some robots, industrial robots are not human-like, but they can imitate and even surpass human actions and behaviors.

5.5.2 COMPONENTS OF INDUSTRIAL ROBOTS

An industrial robot's four main parts/components are: manipulator, controller, user interface device, and power supply, as shown in Figure 5.4.

Below is a description of the four parts of an industrial robot:

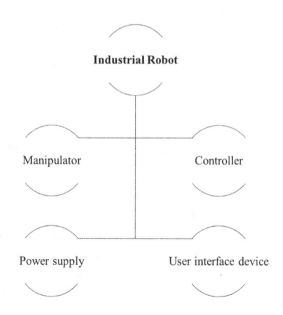

FIGURE 5.4 Four parts/components of industrial robots.

- Manipulator – This is basically an arm and is attached to the body. This arm can move in different directions.
- Controller – To control the robot, this is also an arm or controller. It stores the programming code, receives input signals, processes them, and passes them to the output. It ensures that programmed actions are executed.
- User Interface Device – A human can monitor the overall control of the system through a human interface. At the same time, the interface displays warnings, information, settings, etc. It is a component of the overall system.
- Power Supply – Robots need a power supply or energy for the operation of the entire system: sensors, actuators, and controllers. This energy is mainly in the form of electricity.

5.5.3   Types of Industrial Robots

Below is a discussion on the general types of industrial robots.

5.5.3.1   Articulated Robots

An articulated robot is a type of robot used in industrial applications. This robot is configured by connecting rotating joints like a human arm. It consists of two flat components that fit a person's arm and upper arm and gripper-like fingers. These types of robots are typically used in pick-and-place applications (Nyein & Thu, 2008). Typical applications for articulated robots are assembly, arc welding, material handling, machine maintenance, and packaging, as shown in Figure 5.5.

5.5.3.2   Cartesian Robots

This robot is also called a rectilinear or gantry robot. A Cartesian robot has three linear joints (or combinations thereof) using a Cartesian coordinate system (X, Y, and Z). This robot may also have an additional wrist to allow for rotational movement. Prismatic joints provide linear movements along the respective axes, as shown

FIGURE 5.5   Articulated robots.

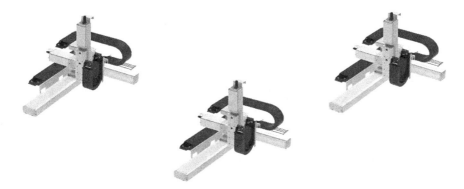

FIGURE 5.6   Cartesian robots.

in Figure 5.6. This robot is usually used in material handling, computer numerical control machine loading/unloading, etc. (Sharma, 2017).

5.5.3.3   Selective Compatibility Assembly Robotic Arm

Selective compatibility assembly robotic arm (SCARA) manipulators often perform tasks such as defect removal, pick and place, brushing, through-hole fastening, circuit board assembly, and mechanical assembly, all of which require precise end-effector tracking and high-speed maneuvering (Hussein, 2018), as shown in Figure 5.7.

5.5.3.4   Delta Robots

A delta robot is a type of parallel robot. It gets its name from its structure (triangular), as shown in Figure 5.8. This robot is also used to carry out processes such as transportation, packaging, and sorting.

5.5.3.5   Polar Robots

Spherical robots, also known as polar robots, are the first generation of robots. Unimate was a spherical robot. Machine maintenance, assembly operations, gas welding applications, painting systems, etc. are applied. Today, polar/spherical robots have been

FIGURE 5.7   SCARA robots.

FIGURE 5.8   Delta robot.

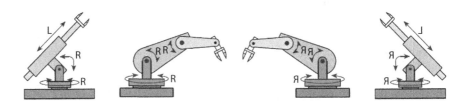

FIGURE 5.9   Polar robots.

replaced by other industrial robots, as shown in Figure 5.9. The most common are SCARA robots (PSR, 2023).

5.5.4 Collaborative Robots

Collaborative robots (Cobots) are robots that work together with humans. Cobots are commonly used for pick and place, sorting, palletizing, quality inspection, and machine maintenance. The following are the most widely used industrial robots in manufacturing (Robotnik, 2022):

- RB-THERON: is an excellent solution for industrial applications such as factories or warehouses, as it is specifically designed for the autonomous transport of goods in closed spaces.
- RB-ROBOUT: is used for transporting heavy loads in intralogistics, designed for transporting loads weighing up to 1 ton in industrial environments.
- RB-KAIROS+: this mobile manipulator is extremely useful for industrial applications such as assembly and positioning, parts feeding, metrology, quality control, screwing large parts, packaging, cleaning, polishing, screwing, etc.
- RB-VOGUI+: this is a versatile mobile manipulator for internal and external logistics applications. The robot is highly mobile, so it can follow the operator and move autonomously in any industrial environment.

5.6 ROBOTICS AND MANUFACTURING

The application of robotics in production mainly ensures the automation of repetitive tasks, the performance of physically difficult tasks for humans by robots, the creation of a sustainable and flexible safe work environment, and, accordingly, the implementation of accurate, high productivity, and efficient processes quickly with the possibility of low risk.

However, robots do not replace humans, they collaborate with them, hence the word "Cobots." Human workers can get injured or even lose their life while performing dangerous tasks. At the same time, when working for a long time, they can get tired and lose focus, which can negatively affect the overall work process and introduce mistakes in the work process. And ultimately this can damage productivity and the overall profile of the enterprise.

Robots, on the other hand, provide a longer and more stable work environment. Fast production of quality products is important for manufacturing which is the reason robots are especially important in manufacturing and working together with people. It is possible to find robots more often in the manufacturing industry than in areas such as healthcare, education, and construction. From this point of view, "production robots" are especially distinguished (Bandyopadhyay, 2018).

The application of robots in production has many advantages as well as disadvantages (depending on one's perspective) as follows:

- The integration of robots requires relatively large costs.
- Risks of job loss for people are unavoidable.
- Limited autonomy or ability to perform many tasks performed by humans exists.
- Safety risks for humans operating alongside large industrial robots exist.
- Training humans to cooperate with robots takes a lot of time and resources.

5.7 FUTURE OF ROBOTICS IN MANUFACTURING

The future of robotics depends on the future of robots. This will manifest itself in four ways:

- Possibility of autonomy
- Energy dependence
- Internet of Things connectivity
- Ensuring cyber-security

5.7.1 POSSIBILITY OF AUTONOMY

One of the main goals for fifth generation robotics is to increase robots' autonomy so that they can create their own tasks and learn on their own. Currently, a large number of robots operate semi-autonomously. This is the main factor that makes robots dependent on people. On the other hand, being semi-autonomous also limits their capabilities. In this respect, a robot that is close in abilities to a human being has not yet been fully designed. Robots may have this ability soon as humans and robots will continue to cooperate.

5.7.2 ENERGY DEPENDENCE

It is normal for robots to depend on energy. However, it would be more perfect if the robots can continue their work even when the power goes out. Whether the robot directly cuts off its energy or continues to work in the event of any malfunction in the enterprise, seeing all processes to the end will positively affect productivity. Ultimately, this will allow an enterprise to get more products, customers, and revenue.

Energy, especially electricity, will always be important to technology. But if it is possible to reverse this process, that is, if the energy dependence is stopped, higher productivity will be achieved. On the other hand, eliminating energy dependence will reduce the need for climate control which will ensure high energy efficiency.

5.7.3 INTERNET OF THINGS CONNECTIVITY

The application of IoT devices in Industry 4.0 and the manufacturing sector is extensive. Sensors, one of the main components of the Internet of Things technology, are quite practical devices. With their help, information about the environment can be collected. These devices are also used in robotics. This is the main connection between Internet of Things technology and Robotics. Robots can see and touch with the help of sensors.

The next step in this direction is that robots can use the predictive analysis and location-tracking capabilities of the Internet of Things. If robots can analyze the information they receive from the environment and make predictions as a result, this means that the autonomous capabilities of robots will also be improved. On the other hand, a robot that can make predictions can monitor both its work process and the general work process in the enterprise. With this, the robot can also predict malfunctions (Khang & Shah et al., 2023).

5.7.4 ENSURING CYBER-SECURITY

With the application of technologies, such as Artificial Intelligence, Internet of Things, Deep Learning, Machine Learning, and Computer Vision, security issues arise. Cyber-security is one of the main challenges that robots can face. A robot under cyber-attack can stop working and even cause environmental and other damage. This can cause the work to be left unfinished and the whole process to stop (crash). Of course, the consequences of this will be negative which is why improving security is important (Khang & Rath et al., 2023).

Security should come from both the producer and consumer sides. The most vulnerable part of robots is the software. Therefore, the manufacturer should strengthen the software and create a suitable security policy. It should also try to protect the robot from cyber-attacks by constantly monitoring it for vulnerabilities and by installing protective controls. These solutions are essential to ensure security (Khang & Muthmainnah et al., 2023).

5.8 CONCLUSION

Robots are now being used in everyday life as well as in major industries. The history of robots goes back to the creation and application of the first digital robots in the middle of the 20th century. Below is a brief outline of the chapter:

- The word "robot" was first used in 1921. Robotics is the field that studies, designs, and operates robots.
- The first industrial robot is the Unimate robot created in 1954 by inventor George C. Devol.
- The evolution of robots consists of five generations: robot manipulators, learning robots, programmable robots, mobile robots, and artificial intelligence-based robots.
- The main activities of robots are the automation of repetitive activities, automation of monitoring and control processes, performing tasks that are physically difficult or dangerous for people, carrying out clerical activities, activities related to art, etc.
- The main characteristics of robots are: they are means of automation of activities; they are mainly programmed machines; robots have sensors, with the help of which they carry out processes; robots have brains, which can store the processes and activities they carry out in their memory; and they operate autonomously and semi-autonomously.
- Robots are used in various industries: research, healthcare, military, entertainment, education, construction, agriculture, transportation, manufacturing, etc.
- Robots used in production are called production robots or industrial robots.
- The four main parts/components of an industrial robot are: manipulator, controller, user interface device, and power supply.
- Types of industrial robots are: articulated, Cartesian, SCARA, delta, polar, and joint robots.
- The future of robots will develop in four ways: the possibility of autonomy, energy dependence, Internet of Things connectivity, ensuring cybersecurity.

REFERENCES

Bandyopadhyay, Susmita. "Industrial Robot," *Intelligent Vehicles and Materials Transportation in the Manufacturing Sector: Emerging Research and Opportunities* (2018). Hershey, PA: IGI Global. https://doi.org/10.4018/978-1-5225-3064-0.ch003

Hussein, Safwan Mawlood. (2018). Modeling and Simulation of Industrial SCARA Robot Arm. https://www.researchgate.net/profile/Safwan-Mawlood-Hussein/publication/326753050_Modeling_and_Simulation_of_Industrial_SCARA_Robot_Arm/links/5ea3553092851c1a906d0500/Modeling-and-Simulation-of-Industrial-SCARA-Robot-Arm.pdf

Khang, A., Abuzarova Vusala Alyar, Matlab Khalilov, Bagirli Murad, and Eugenia Litvinova. "Introduction to Quantum Computing and Its Integration Applications," *Applications and Principles of Quantum Computing* (1st Ed.) (2023). ISBN: 9798369311684. IGI Global Press. https://doi.org/10.4018/979-8-3693-1168-4.ch002

Khang, A., M. Muthmainnah, Prodhan Mahbub Ibna Seraj, Ahmad Al Yakin, Ahmad J. Obaid, and Manas Ranjan Panda. "AI-Aided Teaching Model for the Education 5.0 Ecosystem" *AI-Based Technologies and Applications in the Era of the Metaverse* (1st Ed.) (2023). Pages (83–104). IGI Global Press. https://doi.org/10.4018/978-1-6684-8851-5.ch004

Khang, A., and Kali Charan Rath, "Quantum Mechanics Primer - Fundamentals and Quantum Computing," *Applications and Principles of Quantum Computing* (1st Ed.) (2023). ISBN: 9798369311684. IGI Global Press. https://doi.org/10.4018/979-8-3693-1168-4.ch001

Khang, A., Kali Charan Rath, Suresh Kumar Satapathy, Amaresh Kumar, Sudhansu Ranjan Das, and Manas Ranjan Panda. "Enabling the Future of Manufacturing: Integration of Robotics and IoT to Smart Factory Infrastructure in Industry 4.0," *AI-Based Technologies and Applications in the Era of the Metaverse* (1st Ed.) (2023). Pages (25–50). IGI Global Press. https://doi.org/10.4018/978-1-6684-8851-5.ch002

Khang, A., V. Shah, and S. Rani. *AI-Based Technologies and Applications in the Era of the Metaverse* (1st Ed.) (2023). IGI Global Press. https://doi.org/10.4018/978-1-6684-8851-5

MCRS (2023). Modular Cartesian Robots Systems. Robots Cartesian Robots. https://www.iai-automation.com/en/cartesian-robots.html#3-axis-robots

Moravec, Hans Peter (Nov 29, 2023). Science & Tech. https://www.britannica.com/technology/robot-technology

Msitec (2023). What Is A Parallel Robot? https://msitec.com/robotics/parallel-robots/

Nyein, Aung, and Theint Thu. (2008). Intelligent Articulated Robot. 1052. 10.1063/1.3008658

PSR (2023). Polar/Spherical Robots. https://www.mwes.com/types-of-industrial-robots/polar-spherical-robots/

Robotic Applications (2021). https://robotnik.eu/what-is-an-industrial-robot-industrial-robot-definition

Robotnik (2022). What is an industrial robot? Industrial robot definition. 14 March 2022 | In Logistics, Robotics-Vocabulary, 2021. International Standard ISO 8373, https://cdn.standards.iteh.ai/samples/75539/1bc8409322eb4922bf680e15901852d2/ISO-8373-2021.pdf

Sharma, K.L.S. "Management of Industrial Processes," Editor(s): K.L.S. Sharma, *Overview of Industrial Process Automation* (2nd Ed.). (2017). Page (321–357). Elsevier.

Stanford (1998). https://cs.stanford.edu/people/eroberts/courses/soco/projects/1998–99/robotics/history.html

Unimate (1961). The first industrial robot. https://robotsguide.com/robots/unimate

6 Enabling the Future of Manufacturing

Integration of Robotics and IoT into Smart Factory Infrastructure in Industry 4.0

Kali Charan Rath, Alex Khang, Suresh Kumar Satapathy, Amaresh Kumar, Sudhansu Ranjan Das, and Manas Ranjan Panda

6.1 INTRODUCTION

The manufacturing industry has been revolutionized by the advent of Industry 4.0, a new era characterized by the integration of advanced technologies and the digitalization of manufacturing processes (Arden et al., 2021). As we step into this era, robotics, Internet of Things (IoT), and smart factory infrastructure play pivotal roles in enabling the future of manufacturing (Awan et al., 2021). These technologies, when combined, offer unprecedented opportunities to optimize production, enhance efficiency, and drive innovation.

Industry 4.0 represents a paradigm shift in the manufacturing landscape, where traditional factories are transformed into smart factories that leverage interconnected systems and intelligent machines. By integrating robotics, IoT, and smart factory infrastructure (Büchi et al., 2020; Zhong et al., 2017) manufacturers can realize the full potential of automation, data exchange, and real-time decision-making, leading to improved productivity, quality, and flexibility (Chen et al., 2017; Erboz, 2017).

Robotics has emerged as a game-changer in manufacturing, offering increased precision, speed, and reliability in repetitive and labor-intensive tasks. Robots equipped with advanced sensors and machine learning capabilities can operate alongside human workers, augmenting their capabilities and ensuring a safer work environment (Fitsilis et al., 2018; Ghobakhloo, 2018). They can handle complex assembly processes, perform intricate operations, and handle hazardous materials with precision and efficiency.

The IoT has brought connectivity to the manufacturing industry, enabling the seamless communication and interaction of machines, devices, and systems. IoT sensors embedded in manufacturing equipment can collect real-time data on performance, energy consumption, and maintenance needs. This data can be analyzed to identify patterns, optimize processes, predict failures, and enable proactive

DOI: 10.1201/9781003438137-6

maintenance, thereby reducing downtime and improving overall equipment effectiveness (Gerrikagoitia et al., 2019; Grabowska, 2020).

Smart factory infrastructure forms the backbone of Industry 4.0, providing the necessary framework for integrating robotics, IoT, and other advanced technologies. This infrastructure encompasses a network of interconnected devices, including sensors, actuators, control systems, and data storage facilities (Hughes et al., 2022; Longo et al., 2017; Weyer et al., 2015). It facilitates the collection, storage, and analysis of vast amounts of data generated by various manufacturing processes, enabling real-time monitoring, control, and optimization.

The integration of robotics, IoT, and smart factory infrastructure in Industry 4.0 enables manufacturers to achieve greater flexibility, customization, and responsiveness to market demands (Shrouf et al., 2014; Ustundag et al., 2018; Valaskova et al., 2022). By harnessing the power of data-driven insights and automation, manufacturers can optimize production schedules, adapt to changing customer preferences, and efficiently manage inventory. Furthermore, the ability to quickly reconfigure production lines and adapt to new product designs is enhanced, leading to rapid innovation and reduced time to market.

This convergence of technologies empowers manufacturers to achieve higher levels of efficiency, productivity, and flexibility while driving innovation. By embracing these advancements, manufacturers can position themselves at the forefront of the evolving manufacturing landscape, capitalizing on the opportunities presented by the digital age (Khang, Rath et al., 2023).

6.2   ROLE OF IoT IN SMART FACTORY INFRASTRUCTURE IN INDUSTRY 4.0

In Industry 4.0, the IoT plays a crucial role in transforming traditional factories into smart factories (Zhou et al., 2015). Internet of Things technology enables the seamless connectivity and integration of various devices, systems, and processes within the manufacturing environment. By harnessing the power of IoT, smart factory infrastructure becomes a dynamic and intelligent ecosystem that drives efficiency, productivity, and innovation.

6.2.1   REAL-TIME DATA COLLECTION AND MONITORING

One of the primary contributions of IoT in smart factory infrastructure is its ability to collect real-time data from a wide range of sensors and devices deployed throughout the factory floor. These sensors can monitor crucial parameters such as temperature, pressure, humidity, machine performance, energy consumption, and product quality, as shown in Table 6.1.

6.2.1.1   Method for Real-time Data Collection and Monitoring in a Smart Thermal Power Plant System

Real-time data collection and monitoring of the IoT in a smart factory (Osterrieder et al., 2020; Otles & Sakalli, 2019; Ryalat et al., 2023) involves the process of

TABLE 6.1

Parameters and Numerical Values for Real-Time Data Collection and Monitoring in a Smart Factory

Parameter	Numerical Value
Number of IoT Devices	500
Data Transmission Rate	1000 Mbps
Sensor Data Accuracy	99.50%
Data Processing Time	5 msec
Factory Downtime	2 h
Energy Consumption	1000 kWh
System Uptime	99.90%

gathering and continuously monitoring data from interconnected devices and systems within a modern manufacturing facility. These devices, equipped with sensors and embedded with IoT technology, enable real-time data transmission and analysis to optimize factory operations.

Step 1: Defining Objectives and Identifying Key Parameters

- Clearly define the objectives of data collection and monitoring in the thermal power plant system.
- Identify the key parameters that need to be monitored in real-time, such as temperature, pressure, flow rates, energy consumption, and equipment status.

Step 2: Sensor Deployment and Integration

- Install appropriate sensors at relevant points in the thermal power plant system to measure the identified parameters.
- Ensure that the sensors are capable of providing real-time data and are compatible with the data collection and monitoring infrastructure.
- Integrate the sensors with the data acquisition system for seamless data collection.

Step 3: Data Acquisition and Transmission

- Establish a data acquisition system that can receive, process, and transmit data from the sensors in real-time.
- Use appropriate communication protocols and networking infrastructure to transmit data from the sensors to the monitoring system.
- Implement data validation and error checking mechanisms to ensure data accuracy and reliability.

Step 4: Data Storage and Management

- Set up a centralized database to store the collected real-time data securely.
- Develop a data management system that organizes and archives the collected data for future analysis and retrieval.
- Implement data backup and disaster recovery mechanisms to prevent data loss.

Step 5: Visualization and Analysis

- Utilize data visualization techniques to present the real-time data in a meaningful and intuitive manner, such as charts, graphs, and dashboards.
- Apply statistical analysis, trend analysis, and anomaly detection algorithms to identify patterns, deviations, and potential issues in the thermal power plant system.
- Implement real-time alerts and notifications based on predefined thresholds or abnormal behavior for immediate action.

By continuously capturing and transmitting this data, IoT enables manufacturers to gain comprehensive insights into the operational status of their equipment, processes, and products (Kalsoom et al., 2020; Lee & Lim, 2021). Real-time monitoring ensures timely detection of anomalies, faults, or deviations from optimal conditions, facilitating proactive maintenance, reducing downtime, and improving overall equipment effectiveness as shown in Table 6.2.

Below is a description of temperature (°C), pressure (bar), flow rate (m³/h), and energy consumption (kWh) parameters.

- Temperature: The temperature data can be analyzed to identify any abnormal fluctuations or trends that could indicate a potential issue with the thermal power plant system's cooling or heating processes.
- Pressure: Analyzing the pressure data can help detect any sudden spikes or drops that may indicate leaks, blockages, or malfunctions in the system's pipelines or equipment.

TABLE 6.2
Example of Parameter Numerical Data

Timestamp	Temperature (°C)	Pressure (bar)	Flow Rate (m³/h)	Energy Consumption (kWh)
5/15/2023 8.00 AM	150	4.5	120	3800
5/15/2023 8.05 AM	152	4.4	121	3820
5/15/2023 8.10 AM	155	4.6	122	3845
5/15/2023 8.15 AM	148	4.2	119	3785
5/15/2023 8.20 AM	153	4.3	118	3760

- Flow Rate: Monitoring the flow rate data allows for assessing the efficiency and performance of pumps, valves, and other components involved in fluid transfer within the thermal power plant system.
- Energy Consumption: Analyzing energy consumption data provides insights into the overall power usage and efficiency of the thermal power plant system. Deviations from expected values could indicate equipment malfunctions

6.2.1.2 Analysis and Results

Description of analysis and results is as follows:

- Number of IoT Devices: The smart factory employs 500 IoT devices, indicating a significant level of connectivity and automation throughout the facility.
- Data Transmission Rate: The factory's network supports a high-speed data transmission rate of 1000 Mbps, ensuring efficient real-time data transfer between devices and the central monitoring system.
- Sensor Data Accuracy: The sensors embedded in the IoT devices provide a high level of accuracy, reaching 99.5%. This precision is crucial for making informed decisions based on reliable data.
- Data Processing Time: The smart factory's data processing time is impressively low, at just 5 msec. This quick processing capability enables timely analysis and response to the collected data.
- Factory Downtime: The factory experiences 2 h of downtime. Minimizing downtime is essential for maintaining productivity and avoiding disruptions in manufacturing operations.
- Energy Consumption: The smart factory consumes 1000 kWh of energy. Monitoring and optimizing energy consumption is vital for sustainability and cost-effectiveness.
- System Uptime: The factory's IoT system demonstrates a high level of reliability, with a system uptime of 99.9%. This metric indicates the system's availability and its ability to handle real-time data collection and monitoring tasks consistently.

6.2.2 DATA ANALYTICS AND OPTIMIZATION

IoT-generated data is a treasure trove of valuable information that can be used to drive operational improvements in smart factories. Advanced analytics techniques, including machine learning (ML) and artificial intelligence (AI), can be applied to the collected data to identify patterns, correlations, and trends. Manufacturers can then use these insights to optimize production processes, improve resource allocation, and enhance overall operational efficiency. For example, predictive analytics can help forecast maintenance requirements, allowing proactive servicing of equipment before failures occur. Additionally, data analytics can enable predictive quality control, ensuring that products meet the desired specifications and reducing the risk of defects or recalls.

In this case study, we will examine the implementation of IoT-based data analytics and optimization techniques in a smart factory. The objective is to use real-time data collection and analysis to enhance operational efficiency, improve decision-making, and optimize resource allocation. The case study will focus on a manufacturing facility that has deployed IoT devices and sensors throughout its production line to gather data on various parameters. We will also present a mathematical optimization model to demonstrate the relationship between the required parameters and the optimization technique (linear programming).

6.2.2.1 Mathematical Model

Let's consider the following parameters for the optimization model, as shown in Table 6.3.

Let's assume that the objective of the optimization model is to maximize production output while minimizing energy consumption, equipment downtime, quality defects, and maximizing staff productivity. The decision variables can be defined as follows:

- $x1$ = Production Output (units); $x2$ = Energy Consumption (kWh);
- $x3$ = Equipment Downtime (min); $x4$ = Quality Defects
- $x5$ = Staff Productivity

The mathematical model can be formulated as follows:

Maximize

- $z = w1 * x1 - w2 * x2 - w3 * x3 - w4 * x4 + w5 * x5$

Subject to

- Constraint 1: $x1$ >= production_output_min
- Constraint 2: $x1$ <= production_output_max
- Constraint 3: $x2$ >= energy_consumption_min
- Constraint 4: $x2$ <= energy_consumption_max
- Constraint 5: $x3$ >= downtime_min

TABLE 6.3
Parameters and Numerical Data

Parameter	Value 1	Value 2	Value 3	Value 4	Value 5
Production Output (units)	1000	1200	950	1100	1050
Energy Consumption (kWh)	120	110	125	105	115
Equipment Downtime (min)	45	60	50	55	40
Quality Defects	10	8	12	9	11
Staff Productivity	0.85	0.9	0.8	0.95	0.88

- Constraint 6: ×3 <= downtime_max
- Constraint 7: ×4 >= defects_min
- Constraint 8: ×4 <= defects_max
- Constraint 9: ×5 >= productivity_min
- Constraint 10: ×5 <= productivity_max

In the above model, w1, w2, w3, w4, and w5 are the weights assigned to each parameter, representing their relative importance.

6.2.2.2 Analysis and Results

By solving the optimization model, the smart factory can find the optimal values of the decision variables (×1, ×2, ×3, ×4, ×5) that maximize the objective function (z). The weights (w1, w2, w3, w4, w5) can be adjusted based on the factory's priorities. For example, if the factory aims to prioritize production output over other parameters, a higher weight can be assigned to ×1. On the other hand, if minimizing energy consumption is a top priority, a higher weight can be assigned to ×2.

The numerical data in the table can be used to define the bounds (min/max) for each parameter in the optimization model. By solving the model with different weight combinations, the factory can determine the trade-offs between various parameters and values (Khang & Hajimahmud et al., 2024).

6.2.3 Supply Chain Visibility and Optimization

IoT extends its influence beyond the boundaries of the factory floor and into the entire supply chain. By integrating IoT-enabled devices and sensors throughout the supply chain, manufacturers can gain real-time visibility into inventory levels, shipment status, and logistics operations. This visibility allows improved inventory management, efficient order fulfillment, and enhanced demand forecasting. With IoT-enabled supply chain optimization, manufacturers can achieve reduced lead times, minimize stockouts, and streamline logistics processes, ultimately enhancing customer satisfaction.

In this case study, we will explore the implementation of robot and IoT-based supply chain visibility and optimization techniques in a smart factory. The objective is to use real-time data collection, robotic automation, and optimization models to enhance supply chain visibility, improve decision-making, and optimize resource allocation. The case study will focus on a manufacturing facility that has integrated robots and IoT devices throughout its supply chain to gather data on various parameters. We will also present a mathematical optimization model to demonstrate the relationship between the required parameters and the optimization technique (Khang & Muthmainnah et al., 2023).

6.2.4 Optimization Technique: Mixed Integer Linear Programming

Let's consider the following parameters for the optimization mathematical model, as shown in Table 6.4.

TABLE 6.4

Parameters and Numerical Data

Parameter	Value 1	Value 2	Value 3	Value 4	Value 5
Inventory (units)	500	600	450	550	700
Demand (units)	400	550	600	500	450
Production Capacity (units)	600	700	500	650	550
Lead time (hours)	2	3	2.5	2.5	3
Transportation cost ($)	100	120	90	110	105

Let's assume that the objective of the optimization model is to minimize the total cost, including production, inventory holding, and transportation costs, while meeting the demand and considering production capacity and lead time constraints. The decision variables can be defined as follows:

- $x1$ = Production Quantity (units)
- $x2$ = Inventory Quantity (units)
- $x3$ = Transportation Quantity (units)

The mathematical model can be formulated as follows:

Minimize

- $z = c1 * x1 + c2 * x2 + c3 * x3$

Subject to

- Constraint 1: $x1 \leq$ production_capacity
- Constraint 2: $x1 - x2 + x3 =$ demand
- Constraint 3: $x2 \geq 0$
- Constraint 4: $x3 \geq 0$

In the above model, c1, c2, and c3 represent the production, inventory holding, and transportation costs, respectively.

6.2.4.1 Analysis and Results

By solving the optimization model using mixed integer linear programming (MILP) techniques, the smart factory can determine the optimal production quantity, inventory quantity, and transportation quantity to minimize the total cost while satisfying demand and considering production capacity constraints. The numerical data in the table can be used to define the parameters and constraints in the optimization model. For example, the inventory and demand values define the initial inventory quantity and the demand that needs to be fulfilled. The production capacity value represents the maximum production quantity that the factory can achieve. The lead time and transportation cost values can be used to calculate the transportation quantity and its associated cost.

The optimization model considers the trade-offs between production, inventory, and transportation costs. By adjusting the cost coefficients (c1, c2, c3), the factory can prioritize cost reduction in specific areas of the supply chain. For instance, if minimizing transportation cost is a priority, a higher weight can be assigned to c3. The optimization model provides valuable insights into production planning, inventory management, and transportation optimization, enabling the smart factory to achieve better supply chain visibility and resource allocation.

6.2.5 Enhanced Safety and Sustainability

Internet of Things also contributes to improving safety and sustainability in smart factories. By monitoring environmental conditions, such as air quality, noise levels, and chemical exposure, IoT-enabled sensors can help maintain a safe working environment for employees. In the case of emergencies or accidents, IoT systems can trigger immediate alerts and initiate appropriate responses to ensure worker safety. Furthermore, IoT facilitates energy management by monitoring energy consumption patterns and identifying opportunities for optimization. By analyzing energy data and implementing energy-efficient practices, manufacturers can reduce their carbon footprint and contribute to sustainable manufacturing practices.

In this case study, we will explore the implementation of robot and IoT-based supply chain visibility and optimization techniques in a smart factory. The objective is to leverage real-time data collection, robotic automation, and optimization models to enhance supply chain visibility, improve decision-making, and optimize resource allocation. The case study will focus on a manufacturing facility that has integrated robots and IoT devices throughout its supply chain to gather data on various parameters. We will also present a mathematical optimization model to demonstrate the relationship between the required parameters and the optimization technique.

6.2.5.1 Optimization Technique: Genetic Algorithm

Let's consider the following parameters for the optimization mathematical model, as shown in Table 6.5.

Let's assume that the objective of the optimization model is to minimize the total cost, including production time, transportation cost, and inventory holding cost,

TABLE 6.5

Parameters and Numerical Data

Parameter	Value 1	Value 2	Value 3	Value 4	Value 5
Production Time (h)	10	12	9	11	13
Transportation Cost ($)	100	120	90	110	105
Inventory Holding Cost ($)	50	40	55	45	60
Order Quantity (units)	500	600	450	550	700

while satisfying the demand and considering order quantity constraints. The decision variables can be defined as follows:

- $x1$ = Production Time (h)
- $x2$ = Transportation Quantity (units)
- $x3$ = Inventory Quantity (units)

The mathematical model can be formulated as follows:

Minimize

- $z = c1 * x1 + c2 * x2 + c3 * x3$

Subject to

- Constraint 1: $\times 1$ production_time_min
- Constraint 2: $\times 1 \leq$ production_time_max
- Constraint 3: $\times 2 \geq 0$
- Constraint 4: $\times 3 \geq 0$

In the above model, c1, c2, and c3 represent the cost coefficients for production time, transportation, and inventory holding, respectively.

6.2.5.2   Analysis and Results

In this case, we will utilize a genetic algorithm as the optimization technique to find the optimal values of the decision variables $(\times 1, \times 2, \times 3)$ that minimize the total cost. The numerical data in the table can be used to define the parameters and constraints in the optimization model. For example, the production time represents the time required to produce a certain quantity of goods. The transportation cost and inventory holding cost values represent the respective costs associated with the supply chain operations. The order quantity represents the demand that needs to be fulfilled.

The genetic algorithm considers a population of potential solutions and evolves them over generations using genetic operators like mutation and crossover to find the best solution. In this case, the algorithm aims to minimize the total cost by adjusting the production time, transportation quantity, and inventory quantity. By running the genetic algorithm with different cost coefficients and constraints, the smart factory can identify the optimal combination of parameters that minimizes the total cost while meeting the demand. The optimization process provides insights into efficient resource allocation, production planning, and inventory management, leading to improved supply chain visibility and cost optimization in the smart factory.

6.2.6   Interconnectivity and Collaboration

IoT acts as the glue that connects various components of smart factory infrastructure, leading to seamless communication and collaboration. It allows machines, systems, and processes to interact and exchange information, leading to improved coordination and synchronization. For instance, IoT enables machines to automatically trigger production processes based on real-time demand signals, minimizing delays and improving responsiveness. Moreover, IoT enables the integration of diverse technologies, such as robotics, AI, and data analytics, fostering innovation and enabling manufacturers to explore new business models and revenue streams.

This case study focuses on the implementation and optimization of a smart factory system that leverages the interconnectivity and collaboration between robots and IoT devices. The objective is to improve overall efficiency and productivity in the manufacturing process. A mathematical model is proposed to optimize the system parameters, and numerical data is presented in a table format for analysis and evaluation.

In recent years, smart factories have garnered significant attention due to their potential to revolutionize the manufacturing industry. By incorporating advanced technologies such as robotics and IoT, these factories aim to enhance operational efficiency, minimize downtime, and improve product quality. This case study explores the optimization of a smart factory system by focusing on the interconnectivity and collaboration between robots and IoT devices.

6.2.7 OPTIMIZATION TECHNIQUE AND MATHEMATICAL MODEL

The optimization technique employed in this study is a multi-objective optimization approach using a genetic algorithm. The objective is to minimize production time and energy consumption while maximizing product quality. The mathematical model for the optimization problem is as follows:

Minimize

- Objective 1: Production Time (T)
- Objective 2: Energy Consumption (E)

Subject to

- Constraint 1: Quality Index (Q) $\geq$ Q_min
- Constraint 2: Production Time (T) $\leq$ T_max
- Constraint 3: Energy Consumption (E) $\leq$ E_max

6.2.7.1 Relationship between Required Parameters

The optimization model depends on the following parameters:

- Quality Index (Q): Represents the desired quality level of the manufactured products. It is a subjective measure, ranging from 0 to 1, where 1 indicates the highest quality.
- Production Time (T): Represents the time required to complete the manufacturing process, including setup, processing, and teardown.
- Energy Consumption (E): Represents the amount of energy consumed during the manufacturing process.

- Q_min: Minimum acceptable quality level.
- T_max: Maximum allowable production time.
- E_max: Maximum allowable energy consumption.

The relationship between these parameters is as follows:

- Quality Index (Q) is inversely related to both Production Time (T) and Energy Consumption (E).
- Production Time (T) and Energy Consumption (E) have a positive relationship.

6.2.7.2 Parameters
Parameter values and numerical data are shown in Table 6.6.

6.2.7.3 Analysis and Results
By optimizing the interconnectivity and collaboration between robots and IoT devices in a smart factory, the following benefits can be achieved:

- Reduced production time and energy consumption, leading to cost savings.
- Improved product quality and consistency, resulting in enhanced customer satisfaction.
- Increased overall efficiency and productivity in the manufacturing process.

The optimization model presented in this case study allows decision-makers to determine the optimal combination of parameters to achieve the desired objectives. By considering the provided numerical data and applying the mathematical model, further analysis can be conducted to evaluate different scenarios and make informed decisions.

TABLE 6.6
Parameter Values and Numerical Data

Parameter	Symbol	Value
Minimum Quality	Q_min	0.9
Maximum Time	T_max	60 min
Maximum Energy	E_max	500 kWh
Quality Index 1	Q_1	0.95
Quality Index 2	Q_2	0.92
Production Time 1	T_1	50 min
Production Time 2	T_2	55 min
Energy Consumption 1	E_1	400 kWh
Energy Consumption 2	E_2	450 kWh

6.3 HUMAN-ROBOT COLLABORATION AND IoT IN SMART FACTORY FOR MANUFACTURING AND BUSINESS

The convergence of human-robot collaboration (HRC) and the IoT has revolutionized the manufacturing industry, particularly in the context of smart factories. This case study explores the implementation of HRC and IoT technologies in a smart factory environment for manufacturing and business analysis. The study includes parameter data presented in table form.

6.3.1 CASE STUDY: SMART FACTORY IMPLEMENTATION

6.3.1.1 Objective

The objective of this case study is to demonstrate the benefits of integrating HRC and IoT in a smart factory setting for manufacturing and business analysis.

6.3.1.2 Methodology

a. Hardware Setup
   - Robots equipped with sensors and actuators
   - IoT devices for data collection
   - Centralized data storage and processing system
b. Data Collection
   - Parameters: Production cycle time, defect rate, energy consumption
   - IoT devices collect real-time data from robots and other equipment
c. Data Analysis
   - Python program code for data processing and analysis
   - Statistical analysis, visualization, and performance evaluation

6.3.1.3 Parameters

Data parameters are shown in Table 6.7.

TABLE 6.7
Data Parameters

Time (min)	Defect Rate (%)	Energy Consumption (kWh)
0	2.5	100
5	1.8	98
10	1.2	95
15	1.5	97
20	1	94

6.3.2 PYTHON PROGRAM CODE FOR DATA ANALYSIS

A Python program code for data analysis and visualization of the results is shown below.
Code Block 6.1: Python Program

```
#Importing necessary libraries
import pandas as pd
import matplotlib.pyplot as plt
#Loading the parameter data into a DataFrame
data = pd.DataFrame({
    'Time (minutes)': [0, 5, 10, 15, 20],
    'Defect Rate (%)': [2.5, 1.8, 1.2, 1.5, 1.0],
    'Energy Consumption (kWh)': [100, 98, 95, 97, 94]
})
#Data analysis and visualization
plt.plot(data['Time (minutes)'], data['Defect Rate
(%)'], marker='o', label='Defect Rate')
plt.plot(data['Time (minutes)'], data['Energy
Consumption (kWh)'], marker='o', label='Energy Consumption')
plt.xlabel('Time (minutes)')
plt.ylabel('Percentage / kWh')
plt.title('Defect Rate and Energy Consumption over
Time')
plt.legend()
plt.show()
#End program
```

6.3.3 OUTPUT

The data analysis and visualization reveal trends in the defect rate and energy consumption over time. From the plotted graph it can be observed that both the defect rate and energy consumption decrease gradually over the production cycle. This indicates that the implementation of HRC and IoT in the smart factory environment has resulted in improved product quality and energy efficiency, as shown in Figure 6.1.

The utilization of real-time parameter data, analyzed using the Python programming code, provides valuable insights into defect rates and energy consumption. The results show the positive impact of HRC and IoT on product quality and energy efficiency, thereby emphasizing the importance of these technologies in modern manufacturing settings.

6.4 HUMAN-ROBOT COLLABORATION AND IoT IN SMART LAPTOP ASSEMBLY FACTORY: A CASE STUDY

This case study examines the impact of human-robot collaboration and IoT technologies in a smart factory environment for laptop assembly. We analyze the performance before and after the implementation of these technologies. The integration of

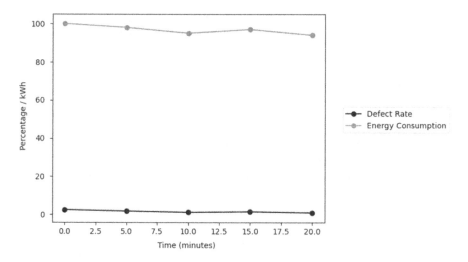

FIGURE 6.1 Defect rate and energy consumption over time.

human workers, robots, and IoT devices aims to enhance manufacturing efficiency and enable comprehensive business analysis. This section presents a detailed analysis of 10 parameters related to the laptop assembly process, along with a partial Python program code that includes various types of graphs and their analysis, as shown in Table 6.8.

6.4.1 MATHEMATICAL MODEL

To establish mathematical models for the relationships between Cycle Time, Efficiency, Defect Rate, Throughput, Downtime, Utilization, Energy Consumption,

TABLE 6.8
Parameters and Data

Parameter	Before Implementation	After Implementation
Cycle Time	15.2	11.8
Efficiency	0.87	0.94
Defect Rate	0.03	0.01
Throughput	220	265
Downtime	3.2	1.5
Utilization	0.82	0.92
Energy Consumption	1350	1120
Labor Cost	6000	5200
Production Cost	8800	7900
Customer Satisfaction	4.2	4.8

Labor Cost, Production Cost, and Customer Satisfaction, we can use various equations and formulas. Here's a set of models along with their respective nomenclature:

a. Cycle Time (CT): Time taken to complete one cycle of production.
b. Efficiency (E): Ratio of actual output to the maximum possible output.
c. Defect Rate (DR): Proportion of defective products or services produced.
d. Throughput (TH): Rate at which units of product or service are produced or processed.
e. Downtime (DT): Time during which a system or machine is not operational.
f. Utilization (U): Ratio of the actual usage time to the available time.
g. Energy Consumption (EC): Amount of energy used during production.
h. Labor Cost (LC): Cost associated with labor required for production.
i. Production Cost (PC): Total cost of producing goods or services, including labor, materials, and other expenses.
j. Customer Satisfaction (CS): Degree to which customers are satisfied with the product or service.

Mathematical models for the relationships between these variables can be represented as equations or formulas:

$$CT = \text{Total Time} / \text{Total Units}$$

This equation calculates the Cycle Time by dividing the total time taken to produce the units by the total number of units.

$$E = (\text{Actual Output} / \text{Maximum Possible Output}) * 100$$

Efficiency is calculated by taking the ratio of the actual output to the maximum possible output, multiplied by 100 for percentage representation.

$$DR = (\text{Number of Defective Units} / \text{Total Units}) * 100$$

Defect Rate is calculated by dividing the number of defective units by the total number of units, multiplied by 100 for percentage representation.

$$TH = (\text{Total Units} / \text{Total Time})$$

Throughput is calculated by dividing the total number of units by the total time taken.

$$DT = \text{Total Downtime}$$

Downtime is simply the sum of all periods of time during which the system or machine is not operational.

$$U = (\text{Actual Usage Time} / \text{Available Time}) * 100$$

Utilization is calculated by dividing the actual usage time by the available time, multiplied by 100 for percentage representation.

$$EC = \text{Total Energy Consumed}$$

Energy Consumption is the sum of all energy used during production.

$$LC = \text{Labor Rate} * \text{Total Labor Hours}$$

Labor Cost is calculated by multiplying the labor rate by the total labor hours.

$$PC = \text{Labor Cost} + \text{Material Cost} + \text{Other Expenses}$$

Production Cost is the sum of labor cost, material cost, and other expenses.

$$CS = \text{Customer Feedback} / \text{Total Feedback} * 100$$

Customer Satisfaction is calculated by taking the ratio of customer feedback to total feedback, multiplied by 100 for percentage representation.

6.4.2 PYTHON PROGRAM CODE

A Python program code for data analysis, and visualizations of the results is shown below.
Code Block 6.2: Python Program

```
import pandas as pd
import matplotlib.pyplot as plt
import seaborn as sns
#Parameter data
parameters = ['Cycle Time', 'Efficiency', 'Defect
Rate', 'Throughput', 'Downtime',
************************************************
*******
#Creating a DataFrame
df = pd.DataFrame({'Parameter': parameters,
'Before Implementation': before_data, 'After Implementation':
after_data})
#Bar plot for before and after implementation
plt.figure(figsize=(10, 6)
************************************************
*******
plt.xticks(rotation=45)
plt.legend()
plt.show()
#Line plot for before implementation
plt.figure(figsize=(10, 6)
```

```
        plt.plot(df['Parameter'], df['Before
Implementation'], marker='o', label='Before Implementation')
        plt.xlabel('Parameter')
        ****************************************************
*******
        plt.legend()
        plt.show()
        #Line plot for after implementation
        plt.figure(figsize=(10, 6)
        ****************************************************
*******
        # Performing analysis
        improvement = ((df['After Implementation'] -
df['Before ......
        ****************************************************
********
        df['Improvement (%)'] = improvement.round(2)
        print(df)
        #End program
```

6.4.3 Output

Run program in Code Block 6.2, output as Figures 6.2–6.4.

The analysis section discusses the insights derived from the data and graphs generated. It compares the performance of the smart factory before and after the implementation of HRC and IoT technologies. The analysis focuses on the improvements observed and their implications for manufacturing and business efficiency.

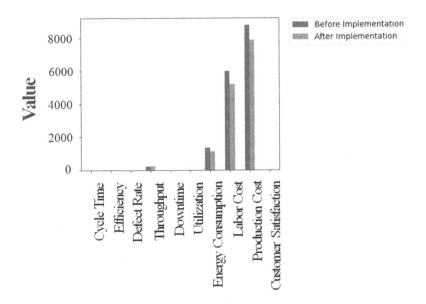

FIGURE 6.2   Comparison of parameters before and after the implementation of technology.

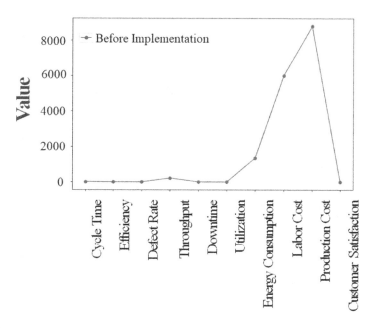

FIGURE 6.3   Parameter values before implementation of technology.

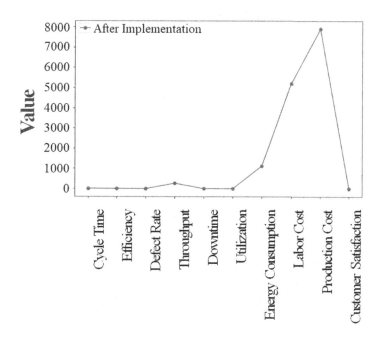

FIGURE 6.4   Parameter values after implementation of technology.

The conclusion summarizes the findings of the case study, emphasizing the positive impact of HRC and IoT implementation in the smart factory for laptop assembly.

6.5 CASE STUDY: DECISION-MAKING MATHEMATICAL MODEL FOR MANUFACTURING BETTER LAPTOP PRODUCTS

The objective of the case study is to optimize the assembly process of various laptop components in a smart factory to manufacture a better laptop product.

6.5.1 COMPONENTS

- Central Processing Unit (CPU)
- Random Access Memory (RAM)
- Storage (HDD or SSD)
- Graphics Processing Unit (GPU)
- Display Screen
- Keyboard
- Battery
- Other Peripherals

6.5.2 MATHEMATICAL MODEL FOR DECISION-MAKING

a. Define Decision Variables: Assign binary variables to each component to represent its presence or absence in the laptop assembly.
b. Define Constraints: Specify the constraints based on the compatibility and requirements of the components. For example:
    CPU, RAM, and GPU must be compatible and work together.
    Power consumption of the components should not exceed the capacity of the battery.
    Size and weight of the components should be within acceptable limits.
c. Define Objective Function: Define the objective function that quantifies the quality or performance of the laptop product. It could be a combination of factors such as processing power, memory capacity, storage capacity, display quality, etc.

6.5.3 IMPLEMENTATION

To manufacture a better laptop product through the assembly of various components in a smart factory, we can formulate a mathematical model for decision-making. Here's an example of a mathematical model:

6.5.3.1 Decision Variables

Let binary decision variables x_i represent the presence ($x_i = 1$) or absence ($x_i = 0$) of each component i in the laptop assembly. For example:

- x_{cpu}: CPU component
- x_{ram}: RAM component

- x_storage: Storage component
- x_gpu: GPU component
- x_display: Display component
- x_keyboard: Keyboard component
- x_battery: Battery component
- x_peripherals: Other peripherals component

Maximize the objective function that represents the quality or performance of the laptop product. This can be a weighted sum of various performance metrics, such as processing power, memory capacity, storage capacity, display quality, etc. The objective function can be represented as: maximize f(x_cpu, x_ram, x_storage, x_gpu, x_display, x_keyboard, x_battery, x_peripherals).

6.5.3.2 Constraints

Compatibility Constraints Ensure that certain components are compatible and work together. For example, if a dedicated GPU is selected, it may require a compatible CPU and sufficient RAM. This can be represented as: x_cpu + x_gpu ≤ 1 (Mutual exclusion between integrated and dedicated GPU).

Compatibility constraints for other components as per specific requirements are discussed below.

6.5.4 POWER CONSUMPTION CONSTRAINT

Ensure that the power consumption of the components does not exceed the capacity of the battery. This can be represented as: power_cpu * x_cpu + power_ram * x_ram + power_storage * x_storage + power_gpu * x_gpu + … ≤ battery_capacity

6.5.4.1 Size Constraint

Ensure that the size of the assembled laptop is within acceptable limits. This can be represented as: size_cpu * x_cpu + size_ram * x_ram + size_storage * x_storage + size_gpu * x_gpu + … <= max_size

6.5.4.2 Weight Constraint

Ensure that the weight of the assembled laptop is within acceptable limits. This can be represented as: weight_cpu * x_cpu + weight_ram * x_ram + weight_storage * x_storage + weight_gpu * x_gpu + … <= max_weight

6.5.4.3 Other Constraints

Additional constraints based on specific requirements, specifications, and limitations of the components and the smart factory include thermal constraints, cost constraints, performance constraints, etc.

This mathematical model provides a framework to optimize the assembly process of laptop components in a smart factory based on various factors and constraints. Depending on the specific requirements and specifications, additional variables and constraints may need to be incorporated into the model.

6.6 ADVANTAGES OF INTEGRATION OF ROBOTICS, IoT, AND SMART FACTORY

Smart factory infrastructure in Industry 4.0 refers to the advanced technological systems and interconnected network of devices, sensors, and machinery that enable efficient and autonomous operations within a manufacturing facility, using cutting-edge technologies like IoT, AI, and data analytics to optimize productivity, improve decision-making processes, and enhance overall manufacturing performance. Advantages of integration of robotics, IoT, and smart factory infrastructure in Industry 4.0 include:

- Increased productivity: Integration of robotics, IoT, and smart factory infrastructure allows for enhanced automation and efficiency in manufacturing processes, leading to increased productivity levels.
- Cost savings: By automating repetitive tasks and optimizing resource utilization, companies can significantly reduce operational costs, including labor and energy expenses.
- Improved product quality: Smart factories equipped with robotics and IoT technologies enable real-time monitoring and data analysis, ensuring consistent quality control and minimizing defects in the production process.
- Enhanced safety: Collaborative robots and IoT-enabled safety systems help create a safer working environment by reducing the risk of accidents and injuries for human workers.
- Higher flexibility: The integration of robotics and IoT enables the customization of manufacturing processes, allowing for quick adaptation to changing market demands and customer preferences.
- Efficient inventory management: IoT sensors and RFID technology can track and manage inventory levels in real-time, optimizing supply chain operations and reducing stockouts or excess inventory.
- Predictive maintenance: IoT-enabled sensors and analytics can monitor equipment and machinery performance, detecting potential faults or maintenance needs in advance, which helps prevent unexpected breakdowns and costly downtime.
- Real-time data analytics: Integration of robotics, IoT, and smart factory infrastructure facilitates the collection, analysis, and visualization of real-time data, enabling better decision-making and process optimization.
- Increased scalability: Smart factories equipped with robotics and IoT technologies can easily scale production capacity to meet market demands without compromising efficiency or quality.
- Reduced time-to-market: Streamlined production processes, automated workflows, and real-time monitoring lead to faster product development and shorter time-to-market, giving companies a competitive edge.
- Energy efficiency: IoT-enabled sensors and smart devices help monitor energy consumption, allowing companies to identify and implement energy-saving measures, leading to reduced environmental impact and lower operational costs.

- Improved supply chain visibility: Integration of robotics, IoT, and smart factory infrastructure provides end-to-end visibility across the supply chain, allowing companies to track and manage inventory, logistics, and delivery processes more effectively.
- Enhanced collaboration: Collaborative robots (Cobots) can work alongside human workers, assisting them in tasks that require strength, precision, or speed, fostering a more collaborative and efficient working environment.
- Remote monitoring and control: IoT-enabled devices and robotics systems can be monitored and controlled remotely, allowing for real-time oversight, troubleshooting, and optimization of operations even from remote locations.
- Enhanced customer satisfaction: By leveraging robotics, IoT, and smart factory infrastructure, companies can improve product quality, shorten lead times, and offer greater customization options, leading to higher customer satisfaction levels.
- Better resource allocation: Real-time data analytics and predictive modeling enable companies to allocate resources optimally, ensuring efficient utilization of materials, equipment, and manpower.
- Improved maintenance planning: IoT-enabled sensors and predictive analytics enable proactive maintenance planning, allowing companies to schedule maintenance tasks during planned downtime, and minimizing disruptions to production.
- Reduced waste and environmental impact: Automation and optimization of manufacturing processes help minimize waste generation, promote recycling, and reduce the environmental impact associated with production activities.
- Competitive advantage: Companies that successfully integrate robotics, IoT, and smart factory infrastructure gain a competitive advantage by staying at the forefront of technological advancements and driving innovation in their industries.
- Workforce upskilling: Integration of robotics and IoT technologies requires a skilled workforce to operate, maintain, and manage these systems, providing opportunities for upskilling and career advancement for employees.

6.6.1 Disadvantages of Integration of Robotics, IoT, and Smart Factory

Potential disadvantages of integrating robotics, IoT, and smart factory technologies include:

- High initial investment costs for implementing and maintaining the integrated systems
- Complex integration process requiring significant expertise and resources
- Increased vulnerability to cybersecurity threats due to interconnected devices and networks
- Dependence on technology, making the system more susceptible to malfunctions or breakdowns
- Disruption caused by system failures or glitches, leading to production downtime

- Need for regular software updates and compatibility issues between different components
- Reduced job opportunities for manual laborers as automation takes over certain tasks
- Concerns about data privacy and the security of sensitive manufacturing information
- Higher training and skill requirements for workers to adapt to new technologies
- Resistance from employees due to fear of job displacement or changes in work dynamics
- Difficulty in managing and coordinating multiple interconnected systems
- Increased complexity in troubleshooting and maintenance procedures
- Dependence on a stable and reliable power supply for uninterrupted operation
- Limited flexibility in adapting to rapid changes in production demands or market trends
- Risk of over-reliance on technology, leading to reduced human oversight and decision-making
- Potential for increased environmental impact due to the energy consumption of integrated systems
- Lack of standardized protocols and interoperability between different manufacturers' systems
- Difficulty finding skilled professionals capable of maintaining and repairing advanced technologies
- Potential social and ethical concerns regarding the impact on employment and the future of work

6.6.2 Integration of Robotics, IoT, and Smart Factory Infrastructure Challenges and Overcoming Them

Below are few challenges that can arise in the integration of robotics, IoT, and smart factory technologies (Khang & Shah et al., 2023), along with potential solutions to overcome them:

- Interoperability: Integrating different technologies from various manufacturers may result in compatibility issues.
  Solution: Prioritize the selection of standardized and interoperable technologies to ensure seamless integration.
- Scalability: Adapting integrated systems to accommodate future growth and expansion can be challenging.
  Solution: Design the infrastructure with scalability in mind, allowing for easy integration of additional components or technologies.
- Data Management: Managing and analyzing large volumes of data generated by interconnected devices can be overwhelming.
  Solution: Implement advanced data analytics and management tools to streamline data processing, storage, and analysis.

- Training and Skill Gaps: Integrating new technologies requires skilled personnel capable of managing and maintaining them.

  Solution: Invest in training programs for existing employees or hire skilled professionals experienced in robotics, IoT, and smart factory technologies.

- Security Risks: Increased connectivity increases the potential for cybersecurity threats and data breaches.

  Solution: Implement robust security protocols, including encryption, access controls, regular vulnerability assessments, and employee training on cybersecurity best practices.

- Reliability and Downtime: Technical failures or system disruptions can lead to production downtime and financial losses.

  Solution: Implement redundancy measures, perform regular maintenance and updates, and establish backup systems to minimize downtime.

- Cost-Effectiveness: Integrating technologies may require significant upfront investments.

  Solution: Conduct a thorough cost-benefit analysis to identify areas where automation and integration will provide the most significant returns on investment.

- Change Management: Resistance to change among employees and stakeholders can hinder the integration process.

  Solution: Involve employees early on, provide comprehensive training, and communicate the benefits of the integrated systems to gain buy-in and support.

- Regulatory Compliance: Adhering to industry regulations and standards in an integrated environment can be complex.

  Solution: Stay updated on relevant regulations and standards, work closely with regulatory bodies, and implement compliance measures as part of the integration process.

- Supplier and Partner Collaboration: Coordinating efforts and ensuring smooth collaboration among different suppliers and partners can be challenging.

  Solution: Establish clear communication channels, define responsibilities and expectations, and foster strong partnerships to facilitate effective collaboration.

It is important to note that these challenges and solutions are general in nature and may vary depending on the specific context and industry (Khang & Hajimahmud et al., 2024).

6.7 CONCLUSION AND FUTURE SCOPE

The integration of robotics, IoT, and smart factory infrastructure in Industry 4.0 presents a transformative opportunity for the manufacturing sector. This study has provided insights into the remarkable advantages and challenges associated with this integration, emphasizing the potential for enhanced efficiency, productivity, and innovation (Khang & Hahanov et al., 2022). Moving forward, future endeavors should focus on optimizing human-machine collaboration, fortifying cybersecurity measures to safeguard sensitive data, and exploring the untapped possibilities of emerging technologies such as AI and blockchain within the realm of Industry 4.0 (Khang & Chowdhury et al., 2022). By addressing these areas, we can unlock unprecedented avenues for growth and establish a sustainable and intelligent future for the manufacturing industry (Khang & Rath, 2023).

Looking ahead, the scope of research in the integration of robotics, IoT, and smart factory infrastructure in Industry 4.0 lies in exploring advanced algorithms and ML techniques to optimize the decision-making process and predictive maintenance systems, developing standardized protocols for seamless interoperability between different manufacturing systems, and investigating the potential of edge computing and decentralized architectures to enhance real-time data processing and reduce latency. Additionally, further investigations into the ethical, social, and environmental implications of Industry 4.0 technologies are crucial for ensuring responsible and sustainable implementation in the future of manufacturing (Khang & Rath, 2023).

REFERENCES

Arden, N. S., Fisher, A. C., Tyner, K., Lawrence, X. Y., Lee, S. L., & Kopcha, M., (2021). Industry 4.0 for pharmaceutical manufacturing: Preparing for the smart factories of the future. International Journal of Pharmaceutics, 602, 120554.

Awan, U., Sroufe, R., & Shahbaz, M., (2021). Industry 4.0 and the circular economy: A literature review and recommendations for future research. Business Strategy and the Environment, 30(4), 2038–2060.

Büchi, G., Cugno, M., & Castagnoli, R., (2020). Smart factory performance and Industry 4.0. Technological Forecasting and Social Change, 150, 119790. https://www.sciencedirect.com/science/article/pii/S004016251931217X

Chen, B., Wan, J., Shu, L., Li, P., Mukherjee, M., & Yin, B., (2017). Smart factory of industry 4.0: Key technologies, application case, and challenges. IEEE Access, 6, 6505–6519.

Erboz, G., (2017). How to define industry 4.0: Main pillars of industry 4.0. Managerial Trends in the Development of Enterprises in Globalization Era, 761, 767.

Fitsilis, P., Tsoutsa, P., & Gerogiannis, V., (2018). Industry 4.0: Required personnel competences. Industry 4.0, 3(3), 130–133.

Gerrikagoitia, J. K., Unamuno, G., Urkia, E., & Serna, A., (2019). Digital manufacturing platforms in the industry 4.0 from private and public perspectives. Applied Sciences, 9(14), 2934.

Ghobakhloo, M., (2018). The future of manufacturing Industry: A strategic roadmap toward Industry 4.0. Journal of Manufacturing Technology Management, 29(6), 910–936.

Grabowska, S., (2020). Smart factories in the age of Industry 4.0. Management Systems in Production Engineering, 28(2), 90–96.

Hughes, L., Dwivedi, Y. K., Rana, N. P., Williams, M. D., & Raghavan, V., (2022). Perspectives on the future of manufacturing within the Industry 4.0 era. Production Planning & Control, 33(2-3), 138–158.

Kalsoom, T., Ramzan, N., Ahmed, S., & Ur-Rehman, M., (2020). Advances in sensor technologies in the era of smart factory and Industry 4.0. Sensors, 20(23), 6783. https://www.mdpi.com/1424-8220/20/23/6783

Khang, A., Chowdhury, S., & Sharma, S., *The Data-Driven Blockchain Ecosystem: Fundamentals, Applications, and Emerging Technologies* (1st Ed.) (2022). CRC Press. https://doi.org/10.1201/9781003269281

Khang, A., Hahanov, V., Abbas, G. L., & Hajimahmud, V. A., "Cyber-Physical-Social System and İncident Management," *AI-Centric Smart City Ecosystems: Technologies, Design and Implementation* (1st Ed.) (2022). CRC Press. https://doi. org/10.1201/9781003252542-2

Khang, A., Hajimahmud, V. A, Vladimir, Hahanov, & Shah, V., *Advanced IoT Technologies and Applications in the Industry 4.0 Digital Economy* (1st Ed.) (2024). CRC Press. https://doi.org/10.1201/9781003434269

Khang, A., Muthmainnah, M, Seraj, Prodhan Mahbub Ibna, Yakin, Ahmad Al, Obaid, Ahmad J., & Ranjan Panda, Manas. "AI-Aided Teaching Model for the Education 5.0 Ecosystem," *AI-Based Technologies and Applications in the Era of the Metaverse* (1st Ed.) (2023). Page (83–104). IGI Global Press. https://doi.org/10.4018/978-1-6684-8851-5.ch004

Khang, A., & Rath, Kali Charan, "Quantum Mechanics Primer - Fundamentals and Quantum Computing," *Applications and Principles of Quantum Computing* (1st Ed.) (2023). ISBN: 9798369311684. IGI Global Press. https://doi.org/10.4018/979-8-3693-1168-4-ch001

Khang, A., Rath, Kali Charan, Kumar Satapathy, Suresh, Kumar, Amaresh, Ranjan Das, Sudhansu, & Ranjan Panda, Manas. "Enabling the Future of Manufacturing: Integration of Robotics and IoT to Smart Factory Infrastructure in Industry 4.0," *AI-Based Technologies and Applications in the Era of the Metaverse* (1st Ed.) (2023). Page (25–50). IGI Global Press. https://doi.org/10.4018/978-1-6684-8851-5.ch002

Khang, A., Shah, V., & Rani, S., *AI-Based Technologies and Applications in the Era of the Metaverse* (1st Ed.) (2023). IGI Global Press. https://doi.org/10.4018/978-1-6684-8851-5

Lee, C., & Lim, C., (2021). From technological development to social advance: A review of Industry 4.0 through machine learning. Technological Forecasting and Social Change, 167, 120653. https://www.sciencedirect.com/science/article/pii/S0040162521000858

Longo, F., Nicoletti, L., & Padovano, A., (2017). Smart operators in industry 4.0: A human-centered approach to enhance operators' capabilities and competencies within the new smart factory context. Computers & Industrial Engineering, 113, 144–159.

Osterrieder, P., Budde, L., & Friedli, T., (2020). The smart factory as a key construct of Industry 4.0: A systematic literature review. International Journal of Production Economics, 221, 107476. https://www.sciencedirect.com/science/article/pii/S0925527319302865

Otles, S., & Sakalli, A., "Industry 4.0: The Smart Factory of the Future in Beverage Industry," *Production and Management of Beverages* (2019). Page (439–469). Woodhead Publishing. https://www.sciencedirect.com/science/article/pii/B9780128152607000158

Ryalat, M., ElMoaqet, H., & AlFaouri, M., (2023). Design of a smart factory based on cyber-physical systems and internet of things towards industry 4.0. Applied Sciences, 13(4), 2156. https://www.mdpi.com/2076-3417/13/4/2156

Shrouf, F., Ordieres, J., & Miragliotta, G., (2014, December). Smart factories in Industry 4.0: A review of the concept and of energy management approached in production based on the Internet of Things paradigm. In 2014 IEEE international conference on industrial engineering and engineering management. Page (697–701). IEEE. https://re.public. polimi.it/handle/11311/884963

Ustundag, A., Cevikcan, E., Bayram, B., & İnce, G., "Advances in Robotics in the Era of Industry 4.0," *Industry 4.0: Managing The Digital Transformation* (2018). Page (187–200). Springer https://link.springer.com/chapter/10.1007/978-3-319-57870-5_11

Valaskova, K., Nagy, M., Zabojnik, S., & Lăzăroiu, G., (2022). Industry 4.0 wireless networks and cyber-physical smart manufacturing systems as accelerators of value-added growth in Slovak exports. Mathematics, 10(14), 2452. https://www.mdpi. com/2227-7390/10/14/2452

Weyer, S., Schmitt, M., Ohmer, M., & Gorecky, D., (2015). Towards Industry 4.0-Standardization as the crucial challenge for highly modular, multi-vendor production systems. Ifac-Papersonline, 48(3), 579–584. https://www.sciencedirect.com/ science/article/pii/S2405896315003821

Zhong, R. Y., Xu, X., Klotz, E., & Newman, S. T., (2017). Intelligent manufacturing in the context of industry 4.0: A review. Engineering, 3(5), 616–630. https://www.sciencedirect.com/science/article/pii/S2095809917307130

Zhou, K., Liu, T., & Zhou, L., (2015, August). Industry 4.0: Towards future industrial opportunities and challenges. In 2015 12th International conference on fuzzy systems and knowledge discovery (FSKD) (pp. 2147–2152). IEEE. https://ieeexplore.ieee.org/abstract/document/7382284/

7 Role of Computer Vision (CV) in Manufacturing
Seeing Is Believing

Ankita Nayak, Ipseeta Satpathy,
Alex Khang, and Arpita Nayak

7.1 INTRODUCTION

Humans need a pair of biological cameras called eyes to watch, comprehend, contextualize, and make sense of their environment. Eyes cannot gather, retain, or analyze visual data, but they can assist us in perceiving things, orienting ourselves in various situations, and appreciating the beauty around us. Consider the potential of having millions of eyeballs that we could place everywhere we wanted: buildings, automobiles, streets, drones, robots, satellites, and so forth. Consider using these to rapidly gather any information that we require. Computer vision (CV) is a broad field in which computers and networks extract significant data from films, digital photographs, and other visual sources. Artificial intelligence (AI) enables computers to think, whereas CV enables them to observe and analyze their environment. It is used to teach models to do various tasks by replacing optic nerves, retinas, and the visual brain with cameras, algorithms, and data. For almost 60 years, engineers and scientists have been working on developing technology that allows robots to see while analyzing visual data. The history of CV is shown in Figure 7.1.

Here is a description of the history of CV development:

- 1959 – Many investigations on CV may be traced back to when neurophysiologists performed tests on cats. In these tests, cats were shown a sequence of photographs in order to establish links between their brain reactions and visual stimuli. Surprisingly, the results of these trials indicated that fundamental components like lines and sharp edges caused the early brain reactions. This critical discovery shed light on the fact that the brain's early stages of picture processing are geared toward the detection of basic forms, notably straight edges.
- 1963 – Computers could already analyze the three-dimensionality of a picture from an image, and AI already existed as a research field.
- 1974 – Optical character recognition (OCR) was developed to aid in the interpretation of texts rendered in any format.
- 1980 – The Neocognitron, a highly sophisticated hierarchical multilevel neural network developed for strong visual pattern recognition, is ascribed to Dr. Kunihiko Fukusma, a Japanese neurologist. This includes recognizing characteristics such as curves, lines, edges, and essential forms.

DOI: 10.1201/9781003438137-7

FIGURE 7.1   History of computer vision.

- 2000–2001 – Object recognition research advanced, aiding in the development of the first real-time facial recognition applications.
- 2010 – ImageNet data, which contained millions of tagged images from various object classes, was made public and provided as a foundation for CNNs and other machine learning approaches used today.
- 2014 – Common objects in context (COCO) dataset was established to recognize objects and aid in future research.

The relevance of CV is strongly tied to its real-world applications. Several industries have turned to automation, and vision is an important component in optimizing processes. Notwithstanding the embellishment, some of the most promising concepts heavily rely on CV's advantages: Self-driving Tesla? Vision in computers. Is there a new Instagram story pack? Machine vision! What is Amazon StyleSnap? etc. Computer vision is a core subfield of AI that has evolved rapidly in recent years due to deep learning's stratospheric rise. Since the early 1970s, CV methods have been used in a variety of production industries, including the pharmaceutical, food, automotive, aerospace, railway, semiconductor, electronic component plastic, rubber, newspaper, and forestry-related disciplines.

Computer vision refers to artificial intelligence that interprets pictures or video (by acquiring, processing, and producing output). It leverages input from production lines to evoke optimal reactions and aid humans in different production-related activities in manufacturing (Zhou et al., 2022). Computer vision intelligence is frequently used in manufacturing for product and quality inspection, structural observing, and defect tracing. Cameras can be used by manufacturers to examine their products for minor flaws. They can be far more sensitive than human vision, and their focus never wanes. Computer vision systems integrate human vision and intellect with the processing capacity of a computer to improve efficiency, consistency, and production. It appeared that a collaborative approach to automation was more productive. Machine vision inspection systems, for example, can indicate incorrect details for human auditors to review.

Tesla is a prime instance of a highly automated production facility where humans and robots collaborate. Significant adaptability is required in complex contexts, such as a smart factory, to operate in unexpected scenarios or conditions with significant input variability. Because people possess adaptive intelligence, automation cannot completely replace them. As a result, Tesla redesigned its production procedures to be more open to collaboration. Nevertheless, in order to establish the most successful strategy, it is important to compare the results of CV systems with those of humans (Kolesnikova, 2023). Pattern recognition may be used by machines to determine whether an engine should run or be idle, impacting maintenance efforts and energy usage.

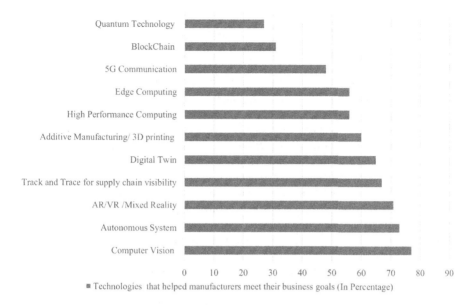

FIGURE 7.2 Technologies that helped manufacturers meet their business goals.

Cameras are similarly successful in monitoring sulfur oxide and nitrogen oxide emissions by analyzing the color of the water to detect contaminants. Employing machine vision for quality control minimizes the amount of scrap that cannot be recycled and hence ends up in landfills. As a result, CV minimizes waste and consumption in terms of energy, chemicals, air quality, and raw materials (Khandelwal et al., 2020). A study from IBM states that the adoption of digital tech in manufacturing has helped manufacturers to accelerate the whole process, which is depicted in Figure 7.2 (Ahramovich, 2023).

Because it demands systems to monitor issues on a microscale (for example, monitoring faulty threading), usually, the manufacturing industry does not achieve 100% accuracy in recognizing defects in its manufactured products. Detection of these flaws toward the end of the manufacturing procedure or after the product has been handed to the customer may result in higher production costs and customer displeasure. These losses much outweigh the cost of installing an AI-powered CV error detection system (Khang & Rath, 2023).

A CV-powered program evaluates real-time data streams from cameras using machine learning techniques to detect flaws and deliver a percentage of deviation based on established quality requirements. This data may be used to track problems in the production line process. This provides an error-free and efficient production process. Remember, "The cost of not recognizing a defect is substantially greater than the cost for discovering the defect" and investing in a CV-based fault detection system might be a cost-effective solution (Liu et al., 2015; Pau, 2012). Computer vision has also had a significant impact on automation and robotics. Vision-enabled robots are flexible and adaptive partners in industrial processes, traversing small places, completing complicated jobs, and securely working with human operators.

Unlike other machines, doing this operation enhances production while also allowing producers to respond to changing demands more swiftly. Predictive repair stands out as a cost-saving innovation because it is powered by real-time analysis and anomaly identification.

Computer recognition systems monitor machinery and equipment for early symptoms of wear and tear. This proactive strategy saves money on costly downtime, lowers maintenance expenses, and boosts productivity (Konstantinidis et al., 2021). Haier, a home appliance and consumer electronics business, is a forerunner in smart manufacturing. It is also a forerunner in business model refinement, introduction of technologies such as the IoT and AI, and creation of a set of industrial models. The unique technology developed by Haier has resulted in amazing development. Its business model has transformed from mass manufacturing to mass adaptation, with the goal of transforming overseas businesses through product hardware manufacturing to providing intelligent substitutes to create a smart life platform that impacts users' internal divisional requirements, allowing for individual individualization via an integrated work area.

Through the use of CV technology, the novel development method brought by AI has substantially revolutionized the field of industrial design. This technology has effectively simplified the product development cycle by seamlessly merging the most recent advances in CV into the discipline's basic concepts and fundamental values (Li, 2022).

The continuous effort in manufacturing, and process optimization, gains substantially from computerization. This solution gives manufacturers real-time visibility into complicated operations, allowing them to fine-tune efficiency, decrease waste, and enhance throughput. Computer vision drives improvement and increases productivity, and competitiveness by monitoring priorities and discovering inefficiencies (Nalbant & Uyanik, 2021). Computer vision is a disruptive manufacturing capacity that is easily incorporated into numerous sectors of the industry to boost efficiency and accuracy. In manufacturing, CV permits computer-aided design (CAD), which allows for 3D product modeling, analysis, and optimization. It expands its capabilities to modeling and simulation, allowing for virtual testing and process optimization in manufacturing. CV also aids with production design and activities like 3D manufacturing nesting pieces and building road networks (Khang, 2023).

Quality control benefits from CV approaches since they allow for the monitoring and identification of flaws, ensuring product quality criteria are satisfied. Furthermore, CV optimizes intra-factory and inter-facility logistics, reducing complexity and enhancing overall operational efficiency. Continuous innovation is used to overcome CV implementation issues like algorithm development, data pretreatment, labeling, and benchmarking. Future directions in CV include the development of theories, strategies for dealing with raw data, and the optimization of CV models to guarantee that this technology continues at the forefront of product innovation (Sagodi et al., 2022). CV is employed at every stage of production, from raw material procurement to selling and distributing completed items. It is critical to the production unit's flexibility and scalability. It aids in increasing output while maintaining quality and minimizing resource use.

Manufacturers use AI developers and offshore solution providers to digitally alter and connect their infrastructure with cutting-edge technologies. CV is altering the manufacturing scene by providing creative solutions that improve product quality, increase productivity, lower costs, and prioritize worker safety. Its capacity to give new insights, promote continuous development, and put enterprises at the forefront of the ever-changing manufacturing sector highlights its significance as a catalyst for success in manufacturing organizations.

7.2 COMPUTER VISION TRANSFORMING INVENTORY MANAGEMENT: SIMPLIFYING MANUFACTURING PROCESSES

Inventory management is the practice of controlling and guiding the flow of items or resources inside a company. It is critical for cost and profit maximization since it helps to maintain the appropriate level of supply and minimize losses before items are sold to consumers. Inventory management is seen as a crucial and integral aspect of corporate operations, regardless of the size or form of the inventory. Inventory management employs a variety of methods and procedures, including economic order quantity (EOQ) analysis, ABC analysis, inventory turnover ratio, and fast, slow, non-moving (FSN) analysis. These tools aid in the identification of elements that contribute to a company's success or failure, as well as the measurement of inventory management efficiency. The ultimate purpose of inventory management is to increase inventory management satisfaction (Wild, 2017).

Inventory management is critical in every manufacturing company for attaining operational excellence and guaranteeing customer satisfaction. The process of regulating, monitoring, and optimizing the amounts of raw materials, work-in-progress (WIP), and finished items inside a manufacturing organization is referred to as inventory management. Efficient inventory management assists firms in balancing supply and demand, reducing waste and manufacturing costs, and increasing productivity as a whole. Some of the main reasons why inventory management is essential for manufacturing industries are described below (More, 2023).

- Inventory management assists manufacturers in meeting customer demand by ensuring that they have appropriate inventory levels of raw materials, WIP, and completed items to fulfill orders on time. Manufacturers may minimize stockouts and manufacturing delays by keeping track of inventory levels, which can lead to disgruntled consumers and lost money.
- Insufficient supplies can result in high carrying costs, including storage and maintenance expenditures. Manufacturers may reduce waste and manufacturing costs by regulating inventory levels. Additionally, optimizing inventory levels can assist limit the danger of outdated goods, which can result in financial losses and damage to a company's reputation.

- Inventory management may help manufacturers increase their general effectiveness by minimizing the number of hours of time and effort spent managing inventory levels and guaranteeing the correct resources are available at the right time. Manufacturers may enhance production, cut lead times, and improve general customer satisfaction by optimizing the inventory system.

In the contemporary dynamic and highly competitive market scenario, effective inventory management is critical to corporate success. Even small- and midsize enterprises (SMEs) are always competing to not only satisfy client requests, but also beat their competitors. The key to this battle is logistics management, where the company with the most skilled and efficient approach has a considerable advantage. Inventory management takes center stage in the world of logistics for SMEs, pushing them to adopt diverse strategies adapted to their specific needs.

The overall objective is to maximize outcomes while keeping a tight grasp on inventories (Muchaendepi et al., 2019). Computer vision is a branch of AI that mimics the human eye to allow computers to recognize and analyze items. It enables real-time data production using photos and videos acquired by drones, robots, and cameras deployed in department stores and facilities. A traditional inventory control procedure necessitates a large number of human resources. In general, a manufacturing company encounters a variety of challenges such as misplaced inventory, stockouts, personnel mistakes, excess inventory, and so on.

Manufacturers may automate inventory monitoring and management procedures by using CV-powered AI drones. It enables them to avoid stockouts, properly track inventory movement, and automatically count inventories (Safi, 2023). Keeping track of inventories is a difficult task. Large organizations may employ CV to manage inventories and automate stock counts, database updates, alerting managers, and so on. The CV system can avoid mistakes caused by human stock-taking.

Machine learning (ML) engineers can create a customized algorithm to assist manufacturers, particularly warehouse staff, in streamlining inventory management. CV searches data from several systems to find the batch/product that the employee is looking for (Khang & Rath, 2023). Computer vision assists with the acquisition of raw materials and the storage of finished goods in the warehouse, from organizing stock to generating extra space to notifying managers in case of low material (for manufacturing) (Javaid et al., 2022). The various benefits of CV in inventory management are described below (Shi et al., 2016):

- CV systems can recognize and count inventory correctly, eliminating the potential for human mistakes. This allows for precise records of stock and helps to minimize overstocking or stockpiling.
- CV systems can deliver real-time inventory updates. This enables producers to make educated decisions fast, ensuring that production continues uninterrupted.
- CV saves producers money in the long term by eliminating mistakes and labor expenses. Excess inventory may be reduced through effective inventory management.

- CV provides visualization during the inventory management process. To maintain optimal inventory quality, manufacturers can track inventory at multiple stages of manufacturing, including raw materials to final items.

Following a Research and Markets (2022) study, the global market for AI in the CV will exceed $73.7 billion by 2027. It is apparent that AI is a part of our daily lives and logistics and that technology may help to enhance all supply chain procedures. Artificial intelligence provides an endless number of possibilities for investigation and development. Most businesses have chosen automation to aid in their development. However, recent breakthroughs in AI suggest that organizations must go further and make greater use of machine intelligence's potential if they want to separate themselves from their competition.

Inventory management is essential in the industrial business. Effective inventory management assists manufacturers in maintaining a balance of supply and demand, lowering costs, increasing efficiency, managing their supply chain, and planning for the future. Manufacturers who prioritize inventory management have a better chance of achieving operational excellence, maintaining customer happiness, and being competitive in a continually changing market (Gregory et al., 2021; Sharma & Garg, 2016).

7.3 ROLE OF COMPUTER VISION IN PREDICTIVE MAINTENANCE

Equipment, especially the equipment we use every day, plays an important part in our lives, yet without maintenance every machine will ultimately fail. Companies use a variety of maintenance programs to improve operational dependability and cut expenses. Maintenance is the collection of actions required to retain an asset's functioning and efficiency, and it can occur in response to a breakdown or as a planned effort. According to a Deloitte study, a non-optimized maintenance approach can diminish an industrial plant's output capacity by 5 to 20%.

According to recent estimates, downtime costs industrial businesses around €45 billion euros each year (Liguori, 2022). Predictive maintenance is an important component of the contemporary manufacturing process. It may be employed in a variety of sectors, including automotive, aerospace, energy, and manufacturing. Predictive maintenance may help businesses save money by minimizing downtime and eliminating equipment failures. It can also help businesses enhance customer service by permitting them to plan for equipment failures. This type of maintenance, on the other hand, seeks to forecast future bad events in order to better plan maintenance (Zonta et al., 2020).

Manufacturers understand that maintenance is a make-or-break activity, especially in high-value, fast-paced, and competitive industries. Maintenance procedures from the past do not work in today's fast-paced environment, and firms who continue to use them are swiftly becoming obsolete. To acquire improved forecasts and practical insights, modern maintenance employs technology such as Internet of Things (IoT) devices for data collecting and ML for analyzing information. Unplanned absences may be reduced to practically zero, not to mention the added benefits of higher worker morale, lower opportunity costs, greater customer satisfaction, and less waste.

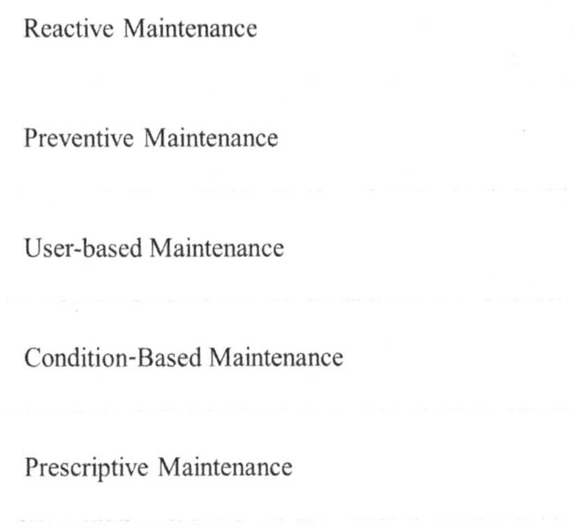

Reactive Maintenance

Preventive Maintenance

User-based Maintenance

Condition-Based Maintenance

Prescriptive Maintenance

FIGURE 7.3   Types of maintenance in manufacturing.

Companies may save the price and inconvenience of downtime by anticipating problems. Predictive maintenance also assists businesses in resource optimization by scheduling preventative maintenance at periods when it will have the least impact on output, as shown in Figure 7.3 (Karuppusamy, 2020).

One of the primary benefits of predictive maintenance is that processing time is greatly lowered. Allowing engineers to spot problems and resolve them proactively can cut unexpected downtime by up to 30%. This predictive strategy improves multi-service schedule planning, optimizes resource allocation, minimizes the danger of reputational procurement, and lowers the requirement for acquisition professionals to be called in. The following are types of maintenance:

- Reactive Maintenance – When an item fails, you fix it.
- Preventive Maintenance – Replacements are planned ahead of time, usually at regular times before components fail.
- User-Based Maintenance – Parts are changed after a certain amount of time on the machine prior to the malfunction.
- Condition-Based Maintenance – When the parts look to be too worn out for them to function effectively, you replace them.
- Predictive Maintenance – You use earlier data to predict when a part will fail and upgrade the parts before they fail. This typically, but not always, makes use of AI and ML.
- Prescriptive Maintenance – Sophisticated data analysis tools are used to do more than predict failure locations; they show prospective outcomes in order to find the best action that can be taken before failure, safety, and quality concerns arise, as well as the time of execution.

With predictive maintenance, our organization may obtain increased staff productivity, faster service decision times, lower outreach costs, improved productivity, and enhanced employee safety, allowing you to compete in the industrial business (Gackowiec, 2019). Heavy gear and equipment at industrial plants degrade with time, resulting in errors and downtime. These downtimes can be costly and result in significant losses. Computer vision technology can provide constant and accurate monitoring of manufacturing machines while also alerting engineers to maintenance issues before they develop.

The implementation of CV for predictive maintenance provides organizations with useful insights into their operations, assisting in cost reduction, efficiency improvement, and increased customer satisfaction (Nota et al., 2022). In manufacturing, CV (especially predictive maintenance) is the system that ML and IoT devices use for tracking data that comes in via sensors from equipment and, in some cases, individual components. The sensors identify signals that trigger alarms, alerting you to take preventative action before an asset is fully lost or an accident happens. Maintenance tasks may be planned and scheduled using data-driven insights.

A detailed maintenance plan and timetable allow staff to better utilize their time and resources, reducing the possibility of last-minute interruptions or overtime labor. Camera photos or videos can be analyzed by CV algorithms to discover abnormalities or deviations from typical operating circumstances. Computer vision systems may immediately identify symptoms of possible equipment failure, such as anomalous vibrations, leaks, fractures, or anomalies in the look of components, by comparing real-time visual data to baseline or reference photos. Because these abnormalities are frequently subtle and readily ignored by the human eye, CV is significantly more accurate and trustworthy at spotting faults sooner (Ullah et al., 2017). Camera photos or videos can be analyzed by CV algorithms to discover abnormalities or deviations from typical operating circumstances.

CV systems may immediately identify symptoms of possible equipment failure, such as anomalous vibrations, leaks, fractures, or anomalies in the look of components, by comparing real-time visual data to baseline or reference photos. Because these abnormalities are frequently subtle and readily ignored by the human eye, CV is significantly more accurate and trustworthy at spotting faults sooner (Vollert et al., 2021). Equipment inspection operations and condition reporting may be automated by integrating CV, robotics, and data analysis. Deep learning (DL) techniques, for example, may be used to train hierarchical representations of video data acquired by cameras in order to provide more accurate object detection, picture categorization, and location segmentation. This degree of analysis may discover faults, measure dimensions, and find anomalies in components more quickly and precisely, decreasing the need for human inspectors and expediting maintenance operations (Haq et al., 2023).

When paired with other sensor data, CV data may be used for predictive analytics. Computer vision systems can uncover trends, correlations, or early warning indicators of probable breakdowns by analyzing past visual data and equipment performance. This enables maintenance teams to design proactive maintenance interventions and forecast maintenance activities before they are required (Meriem et al., 2023). Manufacturing plants generate goods using specialized equipment. With regular use, this equipment may display wear symptoms or possibly malfunction, resulting in product failures and losses.

In identifying such changes in industrial equipment, CV systems are far more successful than human inspections. These methods have been utilized to detect flaws in real-time, even in small machine parts. This allows for the discovery and repair of parts that might otherwise cause the production process to slow down. Manufacturers may use CV to continually monitor the health of their equipment without becoming fatigued. When a CV system recognizes a possible failure pattern, it may warn the maintenance staff, allowing for timely replacement and avoiding unexpected downtime, much like a person. Computer vision, in a nutshell, makes machine maintenance smarter, less hazardous, and more productive.

7.4 UPGRADING SAFETY SYSTEMS WITH COMPUTER VISION: A NEW FACE OF MANUFACTURING

Pinch points, sharp edges, bump hazards, tight spaces, and any other process-specific hazards must be evaluated in manufacturing processes. When hazards are identified, immediate action must be taken to decrease or eliminate them in order to keep workers safe. A confluence of workplace safety and large-scale disaster has driven high-risk organizations to reduce workplace mishaps and accidents in their day-to-day operations. This notion encourages the formation of a single worldwide safety culture, which has aroused the interest of numerous industries, including manufacturing, logistics, nuclear, air transportation, mining, and construction.

Safety culture may be seen as a viable approach of managing employee safety concepts, attitudes, and behaviors (Reniers, 2017). Manufacturing process safety is critical for preventing or lowering the risk of worker injuries, diseases, and even death. A well-implemented safety approach boosts employee morale and productivity. Injuries are caused by dangerous equipment, which boosts facility maintenance costs while lowering morale and productivity. A successful industrial safety strategy necessitates complete employee involvement and keeps everyone responsible. The safety culture of an organization is crucial in determining its success or failure.

A well-developed safety culture offers little direction on how organizations might improve their safety performance. A good safety culture exists in order to establish an atmosphere in which employees are aware of the hazards of their profession and avoid engaging in harmful behavior (Sukadarin et al., 2012).

It is difficult to judge if the frequency of accidents in the industrial sector has increased or decreased over the last decades. Nonetheless, there is little doubt that far too many accidents occur in the profession. Aside from natural disasters, there have been several work-related incidents in the industrial sector since the turn of the century. Despite the paucity of aggregated data, we can deduce that, as a result of safety initiatives and different safety modifications over the previous decades, there has been a declining accident trend in many industrial organizations. Accidents, however, continue to occur. Safety is especially critical in manufacturing, where workers often encounter potentially hazardous machinery, chemicals, and substances (Graham, 2020).

Computer vision methods are widely employed in practically every sector nowadays. Perhaps the most common example is the capacity of our smartphone cameras to recognize faces. Popular self-driving vehicles make judgments while driving independently on roadways using vision-based techniques like simultaneous localization and mapping (SLAM) and recognizing objects. Employees in manufacturing operate in hazardous environments, increasing their risk of harm. Non-compliance with safety and security regulations can result in serious harm or death. Manufacturing plants are required by regulatory bodies to conform to safety requirements, and those who do not risk fines.

Although manufacturing companies have cameras installed to monitor employee activity in the plant in order to meet safety rules, it is often a manual monitoring strategy in which an employee must sit and continually study the video stream. Manual procedures are prone to errors that can have devastating repercussions. Computer vision driven by AI might be a potential option. This program continuously monitors the industrial site from the facility's entry to its exit. Even if the violation is small, the system notifies the appropriate management and informs the staff. Manufacturing companies may use this strategy to ensure that their employees obey safety and security laws.

In the event of an active mishap, the CV system may notify management and staff of the location and severity of the incident, allowing the production process to be halted at that particular place and proactively assuring employee safety (Dasagrandhi, 2023; Paneru & Jeelani, 2021). The growing application of CV in industrial processes contributes significantly to the development of manufacturing industries' efficiency and worker safety. Manufacturing workers routinely work in hazardous environments, handling dangerous equipment, and placing their lives in danger on a daily basis (Khang & Alyar et al., 2023).

Workplace accidents serve as a reminder that companies must take actions to reduce their occurrence and the detrimental impact they have on employees' lives. If an active accident occurs, the CV system may send an alert to managers and staff indicating the specific position and magnitude of the accident, permitting the production process to be suspended in that zone and proactively assuring employee safety. Data collection (including digital data and time-lapse photography) and data analysis are the two essential components of CV research. To build an image data collection, image sensor devices and three CV techniques are used: (1) object identification methodology; (2) object monitoring method; and (3) action recognition method for response to risky situations and complaints (Shetye et al., 2023).

The implementation of CV technology can efficiently detect any concerns linked to safety measures for workers, allowing reports to be created in dashboards and notifications to be sent. It is also feasible to send out automated notifications in the event of an accident, allowing management to take prompt action. It can, for example, be used in a complementary capacity, detecting anomalies and aiding with root-cause investigation of safety breaches and system faults. This is only scratching the surface of what CV can provide in the safety area, but do not expect it to replace a platform that is already solid (Medvedev & Mokshin, 2023).

A study in Deloitte stated that based on a 2019 Forrester poll, 64% of prominent senior corporate decision-makers worldwide believe that CV will be critical to their organizations in the coming year. Furthermore, 58% of respondents said their firms were actively using, preparing to deploy, or contemplating implementing CV within the next year. Using powerful ML algorithms, CV enables machines to extract useful insights from photos and, more recently, video data. This technology goes beyond the capabilities of the human eye and brain, embracing the whole range of human vision, comprising lidar, ultraviolet, and thermal imaging, bringing about previously imagined potential (Khang, 2023).

Computer vision and AI systems can recognize employees in danger zones and issue real-time alerts. The notifications might also be sent to machine operators if an employee is identified nearby. AI systems can monitor maintenance levels, minimizing the likelihood of malfunctions and accidents. The technology might also send real-time notifications in the event of an accident, saving the time it takes to seek medical assistance. Computer vision is a potent instrument that adds significantly to manufacturing safety. Its capacity to monitor, analyze, and respond in real-time to a range of safety-related elements makes it a vital asset for preventing accidents, reducing risks, ensuring worker well-being, and ensuring that supplies and furnishings have been validated (Chiwande et al., 2022).

7.5 GLOBAL MANUFACTURING ORGANIZATIONS EMBRACING COMPUTER VISION IN THEIR OPERATION

Global industrial firms are rapidly embracing CV technologies to boost efficiency. In recent years, CV has moved beyond isolated data processing to become a fundamental aspect of product creation. This transition is due to a variety of causes, including the demand for more functionality, higher product quality, and enhanced safety precautions. The inclusion of CV in quality control is one of the major advancements (Khang & Muthmainnah et al., 2023).

Major corporations utilize CV systems that use powerful cameras and ML to inspect materials for flaws and inconsistencies. These systems can identify faults to a depth beyond the capability of humans, guaranteeing that only fault-free items get through the production line. Some of the global manufacturing organizations adopting CV into their systems are described below.

- Dow Chemicals – Dow, the world's third-largest chemical company, uses an Azure-based CV solution to improve employee safety and security. The system monitors personal protective equipment and detects containment leaks, among other things.
- Volvo – Volvo's Atlas CV system employs over 20 cameras per car to detect surface flaws, outperforming manual inspections by finding 40% more deviations. The entire operation takes between 5 and 20 seconds, according to the size of the car.
- Komatsu – Komatsu Ltd., the world's second-largest building tools company, collaborated with NVIDIA to implement a CV solution centered around safety. The platform can track the movement of employees and equipment in order to detect possible collisions or other hazards.
- Tennplasco – In the industrial business, many types of robotic helpers are widespread. Computer vision-enabled robots, on the other hand, can conduct more complex actions that need decision-making. Tennplasco, a

Tennessee-based plastic injection molding company, used Sawyer Robot, a versatile robotic arm with a camera, to recognize and pick up things even when they were unsorted. As a consequence, the desired return on investment was attained in less than 4 months.

- Fanuc – Fanuc, a prominent producer of industrial robotics, uses CV to improve the capabilities of its robots in jobs such as bin picking, machine tending, and installation.

7.6 CONCLUSION

One of the numerous AI solutions that are going to continue altering manufacturing is CV. Computer vision can handle large amounts of data in little time. Once taught, the algorithm learns to recognize patterns, detect flaws, and identify problems. It also uses the feedback loop to improve the algorithm and reduce mistakes. Manufacturing companies are becoming more energy-efficient and consistent as a result of CV. It enables manufacturers to achieve improved levels of precision, productivity, and safety by using the power of modern cameras, ML, and data analytics (Khang & Rath et al., 2023).

As technology advances, it promises new capabilities, operational advantages, and increased competitiveness in the global industrial sector. Employing CV technologies in industrial units may improve production quality and alleviate bottlenecks. Connecting all the devices and individuals can help gain real-time data and make better business decisions (Khang & Shah et al., 2023).

REFERENCES

Ahramovich, A. (2023, May 23). Computer vision in manufacturing: Components & 9 use cases. Computer Vision in Manufacturing: Components & 9 Use Cases. https://www.itransition.com/computer-vision/manufacturing

Chiwande, S. S., Meshram, P., Charde, A., Bhave, S., & Nagdeote, S. (2022, December). Machine Monitoring for Industry using Computer Vision. In 2022 IEEE Conference on Interdisciplinary Approaches in Technology and Management for Social Innovation (IATMSI) (pp. 1–4). IEEE. https://ieeexplore.ieee.org/abstract/document/10119424/

Dasagrandhi, C. S. (2023, September 15). Top 9 use cases of computer vision in manufacturing. Blog. https://blog.vsoftconsulting.com/blog/top-usecases-of-computer-vision-in-manufacturing

Gackowiec, P. (2019). General overview of maintenance strategies–concepts and approaches. Multidisciplinary Aspects of Production Engineering, 2(1), 126–139. DOI:10.2478/mape-2019-0013

Graham, T., *Chemical Hazards and Toxic Substances - Overview* (2020, August 10). Occupational Safety and Health Administration. https://www.osha.gov/chemical-hazards

Gregory, S., Singh, U., Gray, J., & Hobbs, J. (2021, April). A computer vision pipeline for automatic large-scale inventory tracking. In Proceedings of the 2021 ACM Southeast Conference (pp. 100–107). https://dl.acm.org/doi/abs/10.1145/3409334.3452063

Haq, I. U., Anwar, S., & Khan, T. (2023, March). Machine Vision Based Predictive Maintenance for Machine Health Monitoring: A Comparative Analysis. In 2023 International Conference on Robotics and Automation in Industry (ICRAI) (pp. 1–8). IEEE. https://ieeexplore.ieee.org/abstract/document/10089572/

Immerman, G. (2023, January 12). The different types of maintenance in manufacturing. The Different Types of Maintenance in Manufacturing. https://www.machinemetrics.com/blog/types-of-maintenance-manufacturing

Javaid, M., Haleem, A., Singh, R. P., Rab, S., & Suman, R. (2022). Exploring impact and features of machine vision for progressive industry 4.0 culture. Sensors International, 3, 100132. https://www.sciencedirect.com/science/article/pii/S266635112100053X

Karuppusamy, P. (2020). Machine learning approach to predictive maintenance in manufacturing industry-a comparative study. Journal of Soft Computing Paradigm (JSCP), 2(04), 246–255. https://scholar.archive.org/work/5hsc6nyum5anxbx6bqlwt6xb4i/access/wayback/https://irojournals.com/jscp/V2/I4/06.pdf

Khandelwal, P., Khandelwal, A., Agarwal, S., Thomas, D., Xavier, N., & Raghuraman, A. (2020). Using computer vision to enhance safety of workforce in manufacturing in a post covid world. arXiv preprint arXiv:2005.05287.

Khang, A., *Applications and Principles of Quantum Computing* (1st Ed.) (2023). ISBN: 9798369311684. IGI Global Press. https://doi.org/10.4018/979-8-3693-1168-4

Khang, A., Alyar, Abuzarova Vusala, Khalilov, Matlab, Murad, Bagirli, & Litvinova, Eugenia, "Introduction to Quantum Computing and Its Integration Applications," *Applications and Principles of Quantum Computing* (1st Ed.) (2023). ISBN: 9798369311684. IGI Global Press. https://doi.org/10.4018/979-8-3693-1168-4-ch002

Khang, A., Muthmainnah, M, Seraj, Prodhan Mahbub Ibna, Yakin, Ahmad Al, Obaid, Ahmad J., & Ranjan Panda, Manas. "AI-Aided Teaching Model for the Education 5.0 Ecosystem" *AI-Based Technologies and Applications in the Era of the Metaverse* (1st Ed.) (2023). Page (83–104). IGI Global Press. https://doi.org/10.4018/978-1-6684-8851-5.ch004

Khang, A., & Rath, Kali Charan, "Quantum Mechanics Primer - Fundamentals and Quantum Computing," *Applications and Principles of Quantum Computing* (1st Ed.) (2023). ISBN: 9798369311684. IGI Global Press. https://doi.org/10.4018/979-8-3693-1168-4.ch001

Khang, A., Rath, Kali Charan, Kumar Satapathy, Suresh, Kumar, Amaresh, Ranjan Das, Sudhansu, & Ranjan Panda, Manas. "Enabling the Future of Manufacturing: Integration of Robotics and IoT to Smart Factory Infrastructure in Industry 4.0," *AI-Based Technologies and Applications in the Era of the Metaverse* (1st Ed.) (2023). Page (25–50). IGI Global Press. https://doi.org/10.4018/978-1-6684-8851-5.ch002

Khang, A., Shah, V., & Rani, S., *AI-Based Technologies and Applications in the Era of the Metaverse* (1st Ed.) (2023). IGI Global Press. https://doi.org/10.4018/978-1-6684-8851-5

Kolesnikova, I., *Computer Vision in Manufacturing: The Top 9 Use Cases* (2023, July 31). MindTitan. https://mindtitan.com/resources/industry-use-cases/computer-vision-in-manufacturing/

Konstantinidis, F. K., Mouroutsos, S. G., & Gasteratos, A. (2021, August). The role of machine vision in industry 4.0: an automotive manufacturing perspective. In 2021 IEEE international conference on imaging systems and techniques (IST) (pp. 1–6). IEEE.

Li, Y. (2022). Application of Computer Vision in Intelligent Manufacturing under the Background of 5G Wireless Communication and Industry 4.0. Mathematical Problems in Engineering, 2022.

Liguori, G., *Predictive Maintenance in Industry 4.0: Applications and Advantages* (2022, March 23). LinkedIn. https://www.linkedin.com/pulse/predictive-maintenance-industry-40-applications-giuliano-liguori-/

Liu, Z., Ukida, H., Ramuhalli, P., & Niel, K. (2015). Integrated Imaging and Vision Techniques for Industrial Inspection. Advances in Computer Vision and Pattern Recognition. https://link.springer.com/content/pdf/10.1007/978-1-4471-6741-9.pdf

Medvedev, P., & Mokshin, V. (2023, May). Researching Computer Vision Techniques to Detect Safety Violations. In 2023 International Conference on Industrial Engineering, Applications and Manufacturing (ICIEAM) (pp. 1058–1063). IEEE. https://ieeexplore.ieee.org/abstract/document/10139080/

Meriem, H., Nora, H., & Samir, O. (2023). Predictive maintenance for smart industrial systems: A roadmap. Procedia Computer Science, 220, 645–650. https://www.sciencedirect.com/science/article/pii/S1877050923006178

More, P. (2023, April 4). Inventory management in manufacturing. LinkedIn. https://www.linkedin.com/pulse/inventory-management-manufacturing-pavan-more/

Muchaendepi, W., Mbohwa, C., Hamandishe, T., & Kanyepe, J. (2019). Inventory management and performance of SMEs in the manufacturing sector of Harare. Procedia Manufacturing, 33, 454–461. https://www.sciencedirect.com/science/article/pii/S2351978919305335

Nalbant, K. G., & Uyanik, Ş. (2021). Computer vision in the metaverse. Journal of Metaverse, 1(1), 9–12. https://dergipark.org.tr/en/pub/jmv/issue/67581/1051377

Nota, G., Postiglione, A., & Carvello, R. (2022). Text mining techniques for the management of predictive maintenance. Procedia Computer Science, 200, 778–792. https://www.sciencedirect.com/science/article/pii/S187705092200285X

Paneru, S., & Jeelani, I. (2021). Computer vision applications in construction: Current state, opportunities & challenges. Automation in Construction, 132, 103940. https://www.sciencedirect.com/science/article/pii/S0926580521003915

Pau, L. F., *Computer Vision for Electronics Manufacturing* (2012). Springer Science & Business Media. https://www.google.com/books?hl=en&lr=&id=VJbaBwAAQBAJ&oi=fnd&pg=PA2

Reniers, G. (2017). On the future of safety in the manufacturing industry. Procedia Manufacturing, 13, 1292–1296. https://www.sciencedirect.com/science/article/pii/S2351978917306923

Research and Markets. (2022). 2022 Market Research Global Trends. https://www.qualtrics.com/au/ebooks-guides/market-research-trends-2022/

Safi, R. (2023). *Computer Vision in Manufacturing: 9 Innovative Use Cases*. softwebsolutions. https://www.softwebsolutions.com/resources/computer-vision-in-manufacturing.html

Sagodi, A., Schniertshauer, J., & van Giffen, B. (2022). Engineering AI-enabled computer vision systems: Lessons from manufacturing. IEEE Software, 39(6), 51–57. https://ieeexplore.ieee.org/abstract/document/9830692/

Sharma, M., & Garg, N., "Inventory Control and Big Data," *Optimal Inventory Control and Management Techniques* (2016). Page (222–235). IGI Global. https://www.igi-global.com/chapter/inventory-control-and-big-data/146971

Shetye, S., Shetty, S., Shinde, S., Madhu, C., & Mathur, A. (2023, March). Computer Vision for Industrial Safety and Productivity. In 2023 International Conference on Communication System, Computing and IT Applications (CSCITA) (pp. 117–120). IEEE. https://ieeexplore.ieee.org/abstract/document/10104764/

Shi, W., Cao, J., Zhang, Q., Li, Y., & Xu, L. (2016). Edge computing: Vision and challenges. IEEE Internet of Things Journal, 3(5), 637–646. https://ieeexplore.ieee.org/abstract/document/7488250/

Sukadarin, E. H., Suhaimi, N. S., & Abdull, N. (2012). Preliminary study of the safety culture in a manufacturing industry. International Journal of Humanities and Social Science, 2(4), 176–183. https://www.researchgate.net/profile/Ezrin-Sukadarin/publication/269279870_Preliminary_Study_of_the_Safety_Culture_in_a_Manufacturing_Industry/links/54866a590cf289302e2c08fa/Preliminary-Study-of-the-Safety-Culture-in-a-Manufacturing-Industry.pdf

Ullah, I., Yang, F., Khan, R., Liu, L., Yang, H., Gao, B., & Sun, K. (2017). Predictive maintenance of power substation equipment by infrared thermography using a machine-learning approach. Energies, 10(12), 1987. https://www.mdpi.com/1996-1073/10/12/1987

Vollert, S., Atzmueller, M., & Theissler, A. (2021, September). Interpretable Machine Learning: A brief survey from the predictive maintenance perspective. In 2021 26th IEEE international conference on emerging technologies and factory automation (ETFA) (pp. 01–08). IEEE. https://ieeexplore.ieee.org/abstract/document/9613467/

Wild, T., *Best Practice in Inventory Management* (2017). Routledge. https://www.google.com/books?hl=en&lr=&id=5jQ8DwAAQBAJ&oi=fnd&pg=PP1

Zhou, L., Zhang, L., & Konz, N. (2022). Computer vision techniques in manufacturing. IEEE Transactions on Systems, Man, and Cybernetics: Systems, 53(1), 105–117. https://ieeexplore.ieee.org/abstract/document/9761203/

Zonta, T., Da Costa, C. A., da Rosa Righi, R., de Lima, M. J., da Trindade, E. S., & Li, G. P. (2020). Predictive maintenance in the Industry 4.0: A systematic literature review. Computers & Industrial Engineering, 150, 106889. https://www.sciencedirect.com/science/article/pii/S0360835220305787

8 Application of Artificial Intelligence and Internet of Things in the Manufacturing Sector

Vugar Abdullayev Hajimahmud, Alex Khang,
Gardashova Latafat Abbas, Rashad İsmibayli,
Jale Agazade Firudin, and Khurshudov Dursun

8.1 INTRODUCTION

Artificial intelligence (AI) technology has several components or subparts. Although the components are applied as separate technology, they are combined in a class called AI. The most well-known components are the Internet of Things (IoT) and cyber-physical systems (CPS). They interact with each other and act as a subset of each other. There are four main types of connections between CPS and the IoT, as shown in Figure 8.1 (Greer et al., 2019).

Here is a description of the connections between CPS and IoT:

1. In partial overlap, the difference between CPS and IoT is visible, the main one being the network (Internet) connection. IoT mainly characterizes the interconnection of Internet-capable devices. CPS, on the other hand, offers a different environment where devices that are not connected to the Internet should also be part of the network.
2. As CPS is a subset of IoT, and as IoT is a subset of CPS, this mainly manifests itself in the application environment where IoT complements CPS just as CPS complements IoT.
3. Balanced Case: Especially in the new generation society model, the joint application of CPS and IoT is emphasized. IoT and CPS are applied together in many sectors including smart cities, smart homes, smart factories, or areas that combine many areas, mainly in the industrial sector and daily life.

FIGURE 8.1 Connections between cyber-physical systems and the Internet of Things.

DOI: 10.1201/9781003438137-8

145

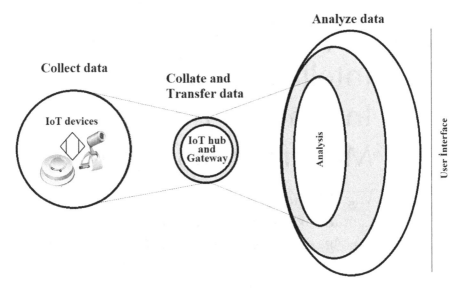

FIGURE 8.2 Working principle of IoT.

Industry 4.0 refers mainly to IoT technology, which is a network of smart devices that interact with each other and exchange information. It gets its main power from AI technology, as shown in Figure 8.2.

On the other hand, modern AI is divided into four groups, as shown in Figure 8.3.

8.1.1 Part 1 – Two Forms of AI

Part 1 characterizes the currently available variants of the two forms of AI mentioned below.

8.1.1.1 Early AI or Reactive AI

Early AI or reactive AI is a program with rules that associate events with actions. These were early types of AI and were mostly memoryless and reactive. These rules were programmed. This is also called precision computing-based AI.

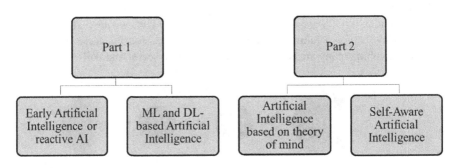

FIGURE 8.3 Two forms of modern AI.

The difference between this AI and its successors is that it gives concrete logical results. Despite this, many modern AIs still work on reactive AI principles and are fed large datasets to produce logical results. Input data is converted into logical output data (Khang & Hajimahmud et al., 2023).

8.1.1.2 Machine Learning and Deep Learning-Based AI

Machine learning (ML) and deep learning (DL) are a form of AI. They are focused mainly on learning behavior. These types of AI are based on ML and DL algorithms.

Learning is based on monitoring. That is, this machine based on AI can observe and learn its surroundings. At the same time, it can learn by analyzing the information obtained in the past. Or it can work with data entered (mainly by an expert) into it. This form of AI is currently being implemented and improved. It is a form of AI that learns, applies, and automates human physical motor abilities such as hearing, vision, speech, touch, and mental motor abilities such as decision-making (Khang & Misra et al., 2023).

8.1.2 PART 2 – TWO FORMS OF AI

This describes a form of AI that is currently being tested and will likely be a future model of AI. In other words, these forms of AI are still being implemented, and are still being studied. The following two AI forms apply here:

8.1.2.1 AI Based on the Theory of Mind

This is the process of studying human mental behavior, also known as emotional AI, and imitating it by machines. Emotional AI aims to learn, recognize, analyze, imitate, and respond to human emotions (mental behaviors) by analyzing audio, image, video, and similar types of data.

This form of AI is far from being a theory yet. AI can imitate many functions of the human brain, but mostly specific ones. The emotional part of the human brain is extremely important and is one of the main factors influencing the decision-making process of the human model. Today, AI can make a very logical decision, but the decision it makes is very different from the one made by a human.

A person analyzes many factors when making a decision; the past, memories, and emotions greatly influence a person in their decision-making process. With this influence, a person makes a decision that is often full of uncertainty. If the goal of AI is to create an artificial human for the future, then this artificial human needs emotions. If it is just about building a machine with potential accuracy, then current AI is good enough. Current AI can write poems and stories and can draw pictures, but it does so with zero emotion and does not understand what it is doing. However, it can make very specific decisions or at least support these decision.

8.1.2.2 Self-Aware AI

Self-aware AI is a complete AI model. It is a form of AI that is at the same level as a human, has the same intelligence, expresses emotions, reacts accordingly, can make decisions, and can imitate the general human model of desires and needs. However, this form is not available yet and exists as a utopian idea. Below are the following types of self-aware AI:

- Artificial Narrow Intelligence (ANI) (or weak) or Narrow AI – This is the current version of AI. It is called narrow because it is mainly trained to perform a task for a specific purpose. It is faster, less error-prone, and more efficient than human thought. It is called weak because it does not have human-level intelligence.
- Artificial General Intelligence (AGI), a.k.a., General AI or Strong AI – This is an AI that can learn like a human, make decisions, and fully mimic human behavior. It is a type of AI that is not used but is being studied and tested.
- Artificial Super Intelligence (ASI) or Super AI – This is the latest AI model that would take away the nickname "superior race" from humans. It is a species that can perform activities that surpass what humans can do, such as being able to imitate a fully human model. If this of AI is created, it will probably be applicable in the distant future.

8.2 INTERNET OF THINGS AND ARTIFICIAL INTELLIGENCE

The IoT takes advantage of many possibilities offered by AI technology. It needs AI to learn from past activities/experiences, improve decision-making activities, predict future activities, and manage data properly.

AI gives smart devices the ability to "self-reflect." It enables these devices to share information and make real-time decisions by eliminating delays and bottlenecks in data transmission. The IoT infrastructure and AI technologies when applied together are called artificial intelligence of things (AIoT). Frequently used AIoT concepts are protocols and Big Data.

There are different protocols for communication between devices. Using these protocols, AI is used to improve the interaction/data exchange between devices. Big Data is simultaneously needed for proper data management. The more accurate the data, the more accurately the AI is modeled. Internet of Things devices are constantly generating data.

As IoT characterizes the physical structure of smart devices, AI characterizes the brain. This is where edge computing comes in, bringing together AI and IoT. Edge computing is a model that extends cloud computing services to the edge of the network. This model aims to bring decision-making operations as close as possible to data sources, as the cloud acts as an intermediate layer connecting data centers to edge devices/sensors (Al-Dulaimy et al., 2020).

Here, AI is supposed to work on an edge device without the need for external connections. At this time, it is integrated with IoT. The workflow is as follows: Data collected by IoT devices is transferred to an edge device before going directly to the cloud, where it is converted into useful, structured data and transmitted to the cloud. With the help of edge computing, the time required for data transfer to the cloud is reduced (time loss is eliminated) and the necessary data (especially for decision-making) is transferred to the cloud (Hozdić, 2015). The general structure for AIoT is outlined in Figure 8.4.

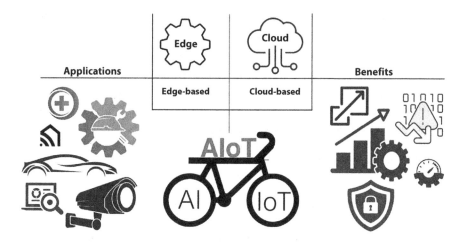

FIGURE 8.4   General structure of the artificial intelligence of things (AIoT).

Let's consider AIoT architecture, AIoT applications, and benefits of AIoT according to Figure 8.4.

8.3   AIoT ARCHITECTURE

There are two types of AIoT architecture: Cloud-based and edge-based.

8.3.1   CLOUD-BASED AIoT ARCHITECTURE

Cloud-based AIoT architecture involves the implementation of proper management of data collected by IoT devices using cloud services. Internet of Things devices are connected to the cloud. Cloud-based AIoT architecture consists of four layers:

- Device Layer – Contains IoT devices. Any smart device, or sensor, belongs here.
- Communication Layer – Covers the hardware and software elements needed to establish a connection between IoT devices and the cloud, e.g., gateways.
- Cloud Layer – Includes all cloud services for network and data management: data storage, processing, and analysis.
- User Layer – Devices interact with each other as well as with people. People get the information they need from devices when they need it. Presentation of this information is in various forms: audio, visual, etc. This is done through various web or mobile applications that act as a user interface.

8.3.2   EDGE-BASED AIoT ARCHITECTURE

As mentioned above, in edge-based architecture, data is first transferred to edge devices and then to the cloud. The main goal here is to eliminate latency, minimize bandwidth, and provide a higher level of service with structured data. Edge-based AIoT architecture consists of three layers:

- Device Layer – Just like in a cloud-based architecture, the device layer contains various smart devices (IoT devices).
- Communication Layer – Covers the gateways. Here, connectivity includes both edge devices and the cloud.
- Edge Layer – Data is collected in this layer before being transmitted to the cloud. Here data is processed and transferred to the cloud in a more correct, useful, and structured (necessary) form.

8.4 AIoT APPLICATIONS

Below are examples of different fields, industries, and projects where AIoT is applied.

- Healthcare – One of the industries with large datasets is healthcare. Data in healthcare is also quite diverse. It contains written and descriptive information, i.e., personal information of patients including drug tests, laboratory tests, diseases, equipment used, and so on. Structuring the data and putting it in the right form are very time-consuming processes. Also, proper management of the data is important for providing high-quality service, improving the healthcare facility, and for the success of trials. With the application of AI, the accuracy of analyses and tests is increased, patients are cared for in hospital and remotely, meetings are organized, and processes are automated. With the help of AIoT, high-precision processing and management of data is carried out, which is essential for providing high-quality patient care and faster identification and personalized treatment of critically ill patients.
- Manufacturing –The manufacturing sector uses IoT devices. Monitoring, security, remote control, etc. are among the industrial applications of IoT. The term industrial IoT is a concept that resulted from the wide range of IoT applications in manufacturing. Predictive analysis in manufacturing is performed with the joint application of AI and IoT. Again, data collected by IoT devices is analyzed, processed, and used for prediction. Robotics and manufacturing will continue to improve with AIoT. With the help of AIoT, robots can learn from data/environment/past experiences, make decisions, save time, reduce costs, and increase efficiency.
- Automotive Industry (autonomous vehicles) – AIoT is applied in the automotive industry for manufacturing, modeling, parts assembly, maintenance, analysis, and prediction of defective and failed parts. One of the main applications of AIoT is autonomous vehicles which can predict driver and pedestrian behavior, making traffic safer.
- Smart Home Systems – Smart home systems are the main areas where smart devices are implemented. AIoT stores, processes, and manages user data to learn, analyze, and make decisions about user behavior.

- Monitoring – AIoT is used to implement monitoring and control processes such as data collection, analysis, processing, management, and automatic warning. Monitoring and control are important processes for checking the safety of the work environment and that of employees. The automation of this process has a positive effect on the enterprise in terms of accuracy, efficiency, and time-saving.

The above are only a few application areas of AIoT. AI and IoT technology have a wide range of applications that can be applied together in various areas. Thus, from an AI perspective, AI subparts are applied that allow the implementation of virtual processes such as computer vision, machine learning, deep learning, and neural networks (Khang & Hajimahmud et al., 2024).

From an IoT perspective, smart devices that represent components of the physical environment are involved. Cloud and Big Data, representing both sides and edge computing, are also involved. Some of the benefits of AIoT are as follows:

- **Scalability** – The number of smart devices is constantly increasing, which affects the IoT ecosystem, and should be scalable according to the specific purpose, processes, and activities.
- **Improved Operational Efficiency** – With the help of AI, data collected through IoT devices can be managed and system operations can be adjusted to be more efficient. AIoT enables various operations by managing resources.
- **Error Reduction** – Errors in operations can be reduced using AI. When high accuracy is achieved, efficiency increases.
- **Risk Management** – Risk is important in enterprises and is one of the factors that directly affect decision-making. Proper data management with the help of AI enables correct decision-making, which allows for proper and efficient management of risks. With the help of AIoT, risk management is carried out by analyzing data and studying and eliminating existing gaps.
- **Improved Security** – AIoT assists enterprises in implementing security solutions for monitoring and control of physical environments, and in virtual environment processes, such as protocols and data protection.

8.5   AIoT IN MANUFACTURING

With the introduction of AIoT in manufacturing, factories are becoming smarter (Khang & Rath et al., 2023).

8.5.1   Smart Factories

The idea of a smart factory, which was first proposed in Germany, is now implemented in the United States. The smart factory integrates the capabilities of IoT technology. The concepts of AI and cyber–physical systems (CPS) are applied here. The smart factory defines a new approach in multi-scale manufacturing by leveraging the latest IoT and industrial Internet technologies consisting of smart sensors, computing and predictive analytics, and continuous management technologies. Smart factories have three main parts: smart machines, components, and manufacturing systems (Lee, 2015).

Intelligent machines must use real-time information from their components and other machines to understand and compare themselves. Self-awareness allows machines to assess their performance and diagnose possible faulty components. Consequently, self-awareness can predict and avoid potential failure of the final product. Intelligent machines can increasingly share their data in cyberspace to compare their performance and productivity with other similar machines. This self-comparative attribute allows machines to fine-tune their parameters and performance through knowledge. In this environment, the production system can also schedule customized production criteria for individual machines based on their performance (Haqiq et al., 2022).

Consequently, the manufacturing system can configure itself to customize production based on the current state of all machines involved in the production line to ensure high-quality products with optimal operating costs. In such a smart factory, the manufacturer can meet customer specifications at any production speed, supporting last-minute changes and other flexibilities not available in traditional factories (Lee, 2015).

8.5.2 AIoT and Manufacturing

The future concept for Industry 4.0 is AIoT, which helps smart factories perform the below activities (Sung et al., 2021).

8.5.2.1 Prediction

One of the main use cases of AIoT in manufacturing is forecasting or prediction. The data obtained through IoT devices is analyzed with the help of AI to assess the general condition of the machine, when it will need care, early identification of malfunctions, and repairs before the machine breaks down. With the help of AIoT, accidents are reduced by about 70 percent, service costs are lowered, and productivity is increased accordingly.

8.5.2.2 Improved Automation

Process automation is essential for manufacturing. Because there are many repeated processes in production, automation is important for safety and directing the physical strength of the workforce to more necessary work. Processes carried out by people usually have lower accuracy, higher number of errors, and longer completion times than those completed using AIoT devices. Accuracy increases, errors and time loss decrease, and productivity and efficiency increase (Khang & Hahanov et al., 2022).

8.5.2.3 Improved Security

AIoT in manufacturing provides physical and virtual security. Today, computer vision/machine vision systems, machine learning, and deep learning algorithms, which are subcategories of AI, are used to monitor and provide physical security. On the other hand, cyber-criminals may attack smart factories halting their operations.

With the help of System Integrator (SI), or virtual security, these cyber-attacks are prevented without affecting operations.

8.5.2.4 Increased Sustainability

Sustainability of an enterprise is related to the continuation of its activity despite environmental influences. In manufacturing, IoT devices can sense and adapt to their environment, and they can also analyze it with the help of AI. In addition, eliminating the need for real-time data transfer also increases machine durability and with the help of AIoT, costs are reduced, and functionality is increased (Kali et al., 2024).

8.6 CONCLUSION

There are different forms of AI: Early or reactive AI, ML, DL-based AI, theory of mind-based AI, and self-aware AI. The fields of application of AI technology are quite wide. Healthcare, military, and manufacturing are some of these industries. In some industries, AI and the IoT are being applied together. This is known as AIoT which has two types of architecture: Edge-based and cloud-based. The main application areas of AIoT are healthcare, manufacturing, automotive industry, and smart home systems. The benefits of AIoT include scalability, increased operational efficiency, error reduction, risk management, and improved security. AIoT is used in manufacturing, especially in smart factories where it is applied to predict machine failures, automate processes, improve safety, increase sustainability, reduce costs, and increase functionality and efficiency (Khang & Shah et al., 2023).

REFERENCES

Al-Dulaimy, Auday, Sharma, Yogesh, Gokan Khan, Michel, & Taheri, Javid. (2020). Introduction to edge computing. https://doi.org/10.1049/PBPC033E_ch1

Greer, Christopher, Burns, Martin, Wollman, David, & Griffor, Edward, "Cyber-Physical Systems and Internet of Things," *Special Publication (NIST SP), National Institute of Standards and Technology* (2019). Gaithersburg, MD, 2019.03.07, U.S. Department of Commerce. https://doi.org/10.6028/NIST.SP.1900-202

Haqiq, Nasreddine, Zaim, Mounia, Bouganssa, Issam, Salbi, Adil, & Sbihi, Mohammed. (2022). AIoT with I4.0: the effect of Internet of Things and Artificial Intelligence technologies on the industry 4.0. ITM Web of Conferences. 46. 03002. https://doi.org/10.1051/itmconf/20224603002

Hozdić, Elvis. (2015). Smart factory for industry 4.0: A review. Journal of Modern Manufacturing Systems and Technology. 7. 28–35. https://modtech.ro/international-journal/vol7no12015/Hozdic_Elvis.pdf

Kali, C. R., Khang, A., & Roy, Debanik, "The Role of Internet of Things (IoT) Technology in Industry 4.0," *Advanced IoT Technologies and Applications in the Industry 4.0 Digital Economy* (1st Ed.) (2024). CRC Press. https://doi.org/10.1201/9781003434269-1

Khang, A., Hahanov, V., Abbas, G. L., & Hajimahmud, V. A., "Cyber-Physical-Social System and İncident Management," *AI-Centric Smart City Ecosystems: Technologies, Design and Implementation* (1st Ed.) (2022). CRC Press. https://doi.org/10.1201/9781003252542-2

Khang, A., Hajimahmud, V. A., Gupta, S. K., Babasaheb, J., & Morris, G., *AI-Centric Modelling and Analytics: Concepts, Designs, Technologies, and Applications* (1st Ed.) (2023). CRC Press. https://doi.org/10.1201/9781003400110

Khang, A., Hajimahmud, V. A., Vladimir, Hahanov, & Shah, V., *Advanced IoT Technologies and Applications in the Industry 4.0 Digital Economy* (1st Ed.) (2024). CRC Press. https://doi.org/10.1201/9781003434269

Khang, A., Misra, A., Gupta, S. K., & Shah, V., *AI-aided IoT Technologies and Applications in the Smart Business and Production* (1st Ed.) (2023). CRC Press. https://doi.org/ 10.1201/9781003392224

Khang, A., Rath, Kali Charan, Kumar Satapathy, Suresh, Kumar, Amaresh, Ranjan Das, Sudhansu, & Ranjan Panda, Manas. "Enabling the Future of Manufacturing: Integration of Robotics and IoT to Smart Factory Infrastructure in Industry 4.0," *AI-Based Technologies and Applications in the Era of the Metaverse* (1st Ed.) (2023). Page (25–50). IGI Global Press. https://doi.org/10.4018/978-1-6684-8851-5.ch002

Khang, A., Shah, V., & Rani, S., *AI-Based Technologies and Applications in the Era of the Metaverse* (1st Ed.) (2023). IGI Global Press. https://doi.org/10.4018/978-1-6684-8851-5

Lee, Jay. (2015). Smart factory systems. Informatik-Spektrum. 38. https://doi.org/10.1007/ s00287-015-0891-z

Sung, Tien-Wen, Tsai, Pei-Wei, Gaber, Tarek, & Lee, Chao-Yang. (2021). Artificial intelligence of things (AIoT) technologies and applications. Wireless Communications and Mobile Computing. 2021. 1–2. doi.org/10.1155/2021/9781271

9 Integration of Artificial Intelligence and Internet of Things Technology Solutions in Smart Manufacturing

Kali Charan Rath, Alex Khang, Srimant Kumar Mishra, Prabin Kumar Patnaik, Gopal Kurushna Mohanty, Taraprasanna Dash, and Siksha O Anusandhan

9.1 INTRODUCTION

Computer-Integrated Manufacturing (CIM) corporations are increasingly leveraging the power of the Internet of Things (IoT) to optimize their operations and drive innovation. With the integration of IoT technology, CIM corporations can enhance their manufacturing processes, improve efficiency, and achieve higher levels of productivity. One key role of IoT in CIM corporations is enabling real-time monitoring and control. By connecting machines, devices, and sensors throughout the production facility, manufacturers can gather real-time data on various parameters such as temperature, pressure, and machine performance. This data allows them to monitor the health and status of equipment in real time, detect any abnormalities or deviations, and take immediate actions to address issues (Abbasi et al., 2017; Li et al., 2018; Lu et al., 2017a).

With IoT-enabled real-time monitoring and control, CIM corporations can ensure optimal performance, minimize downtime, and prevent costly breakdowns. IoT also plays a crucial role in enabling predictive maintenance and asset optimization in CIM corporations. By collecting data from sensors embedded in machinery and equipment, manufacturers can analyze patterns and trends to predict potential failures or maintenance requirements. This proactive approach to maintenance allows companies to schedule maintenance activities during planned downtime, preventing unexpected breakdowns and reducing overall maintenance costs (Khang & Muthmainnah et al., 2023).

Moreover, by optimizing asset performance through IoT-based analytics (Verma & Chauhan, 2019; Wang et al., 2021; Zhang et al., 2020), CIM corporations can maximize the lifespan and efficiency of their machinery, leading to improved productivity and cost savings. In addition, IoT facilitates seamless connectivity and data exchange across the entire supply chain in CIM corporations. With IoT-enabled devices and sensors integrated into inventory management systems, manufacturers can gain real-time visibility into their inventory levels, monitor product movements, and track shipments. This end-to-end visibility helps streamline supply chain processes, minimize stockouts and overstocking, and improve overall inventory management efficiency. By leveraging IoT technology to enhance supply chain connectivity, CIM corporations can achieve greater transparency, responsiveness, and agility, enabling them to meet customer demands effectively and drive customer satisfaction. The increasing recognition of the significant role that IoT plays in production processes is driving the adoption of IoT technology in CIM corporations (Rath et al., 2024).

The integration of IoT brings a wide range of benefits to CIM corporations, empowering them to achieve higher levels of efficiency, flexibility, and competitiveness. In the realm of production, IoT plays a vital role in enabling smart and connected manufacturing systems. By incorporating IoT devices and sensors into the production line, CIM corporations can collect real-time data on machine performance, energy consumption, and product quality. This data enables manufacturers to monitor and optimize production processes, identify bottlenecks, and make data-driven decisions for process improvement.

With IoT-enabled production systems, CIM corporations can achieve greater precision, reduce waste, and enhance overall productivity, leading to cost savings and improved customer satisfaction. The influence of IoT extends beyond production to various facets of the business, including inventory management. IoT technology allows CIM corporations to monitor and track inventory levels, automatically replenish supplies when stock runs low, and optimize warehouse operations.

Real-time visibility into inventory data provided by IoT facilitates minimizing stockouts, reducing excess inventory, and improving order fulfillment. These improvements result in enhanced customer service and reduced carrying costs, contributing to overall business success. Moreover, the integration of production systems with other business functions is facilitated by IoT. By connecting IoT device data to enterprise systems, CIM corporations can gain valuable insights into customer preferences, market demand, and product performance. This integration empowers businesses to tailor their offerings to meet customer needs, optimize production schedules, and make informed decisions regarding new product development and market expansion. The IoT's ability to bridge the gap between production and other business functions enables CIM corporations to operate with greater efficiency, agility, and competitiveness in the market.

9.1.1 Objective of AI and IoT in CIM

The objective of this work is to explore the integration of AI and IoT technologies in CIM corporations and their impact on smart business practices (Albort-Morant et al., 2019). By delving into the seamless integration of AI and IoT in the manufacturing sector, this work

a. Provides an overview of the transformative power of AI and IoT technologies when combined in CIM corporations.

b. Highlights the key features and benefits of integrating AI and IoT technologies in CIM processes.

c. Examines the potential challenges associated with the implementation of AI and IoT in CIM corporations and explores strategies to overcome them.

d. Illustrates real-world examples of successful AI and IoT integration in CIM corporations, showcasing the measurable impact on efficiency, productivity, and competitiveness.

e. Discusses the implications and future prospects of AI and IoT integration in the context of smart business practices in CIM (Amaral et al., 2018; Borgia, 2016).

9.1.2 Scope of the Work

The scope of this work encompasses a thorough exploration of the integration of AI and IoT technologies in CIM corporations. The focus lies on understanding the implications, advantages, challenges, and future possibilities of merging AI and IoT within the manufacturing sector, particularly in the context of CIM processes (Chen et al., 2023).

The work also gives an overview of AI and IoT technologies: A comprehensive introduction to AI and IoT technologies, elucidating their fundamental principles, functionalities, and individual roles in transforming the manufacturing industry (Bhattacharya & Rahman, 2016; Cao et al., 2016). This section provides a solid foundation for understanding the subsequent integration of AI and IoT in CIM corporations.

It also encompasses the integration of AI and IoT in CIM corporations: An in-depth exploration of the seamless integration of AI and IoT technologies within CIM processes. This involves examining how AI and IoT can synergistically combine (Carneiro et al., 2019; Chen et al., 2016) to enhance operational efficiency, optimize production workflows, enable real-time monitoring and control, and foster data-driven decision-making practices within CIM corporations.

By delving into these aspects, this work aims to provide a comprehensive understanding of the integration of AI and IoT (Choi et al., 2020; Dolgui et al., 2019) in CIM corporations, shedding light on the opportunities and challenges that arise from implementing smart solutions. It strives to equip readers, including business leaders, managers, and professionals in the manufacturing industry, with valuable insights and knowledge to make informed decisions regarding the integration of AI and IoT technologies in CIM corporations, ultimately paving the way for enhanced efficiency, innovation, and success in the rapidly evolving landscape of CIM (Galar et al., 2018; Gubbi et al., 2013; Lee et al., 2015; Lu et al., 2017b).

9.2 CIM IN CORPORATE BUSINESS SYSTEMS

Computer-Integrated Manufacturing represents the fusion of advanced computer technology and manufacturing processes to optimize efficiency, productivity, and competitiveness within the manufacturing industry. It provides a seamless integration of various components, including design, planning, production, and control, through the application of computer systems. This chapter explores the significance of CIM and its integration with corporate systems, highlighting the benefits, challenges, and future prospects of this convergence. Benefits of CIM include:

a. Enhanced Efficiency: CIM streamlines manufacturing processes by automating repetitive tasks, reducing human error, and optimizing resource utilization. This results in improved production efficiency and reduced operational costs.

b. Increased Productivity: By leveraging advanced technologies like robotics, AI, and real-time data analysis, CIM enhances productivity by accelerating production cycles, minimizing downtime, and enabling faster response to market demands.

c. Improved Quality: CIM enables tighter control over manufacturing processes, ensuring consistent quality standards through real-time monitoring, feedback loops, and automated inspections.

d. Flexibility and Customization: With CIM, manufacturers can quickly adapt to changing customer requirements, allowing for on-demand production, mass customization, and rapid product development.

e. Supply Chain Integration: CIM facilitates seamless integration with supply chain partners, enabling real-time information sharing, inventory optimization, and collaborative planning, leading to reduced lead times and improved coordination.

9.2.1 INTEGRATION OF CIM WITH CORPORATE BUSINESS SYSTEMS

The integration of CIM with corporate business systems is essential for several reasons. Firstly, it enables seamless coordination and collaboration between different departments within an organization. By integrating CIM with Enterprise Resource Planning (ERP), Customer Relationship Management (CRM), and Supply Chain Management (SCM) systems, companies can gain real-time visibility into manufacturing operations, optimize resource allocation, and enhance decision-making. This integration ensures that manufacturing processes align with business objectives, leading to improved efficiency, productivity, and cost-effectiveness.

Secondly, the integration of CIM with corporate business systems enables data-driven insights and strategic planning. By combining manufacturing data with financial, sales, and customer data, organizations can analyze trends, identify areas for improvement, and make informed business decisions. For example, integrating CIM with business intelligence and analytics tools allows for real-time monitoring, performance evaluation, and predictive modeling, enabling proactive problem-solving and continuous process improvement. Furthermore, integrating CIM with human resources and workforce management systems ensures efficient resource allocation, skills development, and workforce planning, fostering a productive and adaptable workforce. Following are some key factors:

a. Enterprise Resource Planning (ERP): The integration of CIM with ERP systems enables a comprehensive view of manufacturing operations, integrating various business functions such as finance, sales, and inventory management. This integration enhances data visibility, facilitates accurate demand forecasting, and supports effective decision-making across the organization.

b. Customer Relationship Management (CRM): By integrating CIM with CRM systems, manufacturers can gain insights into customer preferences, improve order management, and enhance customer service. This integration enables seamless communication between the manufacturing facility and the sales team, leading to better customer satisfaction and increased sales.

c. Business Intelligence and Analytics: CIM integration with business intelligence tools allows manufacturers to leverage real-time data analytics, performance monitoring, and predictive modeling. This integration empowers organizations to make data-driven decisions, optimize production processes, and identify areas for improvement.

d. Supply Chain Management (SCM): Integration between CIM and SCM systems enables end-to-end visibility and control over the supply chain. Real-time data exchange, demand forecasting, and inventory optimization lead to efficient procurement, reduced stockouts, and improved supplier collaboration.

e. Human Resources (HR) and Workforce Management: CIM integration with HR systems streamlines workforce planning, skills development, and performance management. This integration facilitates efficient allocation of resources, ensures adequate training, and optimizes workforce utilization in a dynamic manufacturing environment.

9.2.2 Challenges and Future Prospects

a. Technological Complexity: Implementing CIM and integrating it with corporate business systems requires careful planning, significant investment, and expertise in both manufacturing processes and information technology. Overcoming technical challenges and ensuring interoperability remain critical areas of focus.

b. Data Security and Cybersecurity: As CIM relies on interconnected systems and data exchange, protecting sensitive information and guarding against cyber-threats become paramount. Robust security measures, data encryption, and employee awareness training are crucial for maintaining data integrity and safeguarding against potential risks.

c. Skills and Workforce Adaptation: The integration of CIM with corporate business systems necessitates upskilling and reskilling the workforce. Manufacturers need to invest in training programs to ensure employees can effectively utilize new technologies and adapt to evolving roles and responsibilities.

d. Continuous Improvement and Innovation: CIM integration is an ongoing process that requires continuous improvement and innovation. Manufacturers must stay updated with emerging technologies.

9.2.3 AI AND IoT REQUIREMENT IN CIM

Artificial Intelligence and IoT play vital roles in the requirements of CIM. AI is essential for automating complex tasks, optimizing production processes, and making intelligent decisions based on real-time data. Meanwhile, IoT devices enable connectivity and data exchange between machines, sensors, and systems, providing a wealth of information for analysis and control. Together, AI and IoT offer significant benefits in enhancing efficiency, productivity, and agility within CIM systems (Khang & Hajimahmud et al., 2024).

9.2.3.1 AI in CIM

AI technologies such as Machine Learning (ML) and deep learning have revolutionized CIM by enabling advanced automation and decision-making capabilities. Key AI requirements in CIM include:

a. ML for Predictive Maintenance: By analyzing historical data and patterns, ML algorithms can predict equipment failures and schedule maintenance activities proactively. This approach reduces downtime, optimizes maintenance costs, and ensures uninterrupted production.

b. Intelligent Production Planning and Scheduling: AI algorithms can optimize production plans by considering factors like machine availability, resource allocation, and order prioritization. This results in efficient production schedules, reduced bottlenecks, and improved on-time delivery.

c. Quality Control and Inspection: AI-based vision systems can detect defects, anomalies, and quality issues in real-time. By automating quality control processes, AI enhances product quality and minimizes waste and rework.

d. Intelligent Robotics and Automation: AI-powered robots and autonomous systems can perform complex tasks with precision, adapt to dynamic environments, and collaborate with human workers effectively. This integration enhances productivity, flexibility, and safety in manufacturing processes.

9.2.3.2 IoT in CIM

IoT devices and sensors provide real-time connectivity and data collection capabilities, enabling seamless integration and data-driven decision-making within CIM. Key IoT requirements in CIM include:

a. Sensor Networks for Data Collection: IoT sensors embedded in machines, production lines, and products capture valuable data such as temperature, humidity, vibration, and energy consumption. This data is essential for monitoring, analysis, and optimization of manufacturing processes.

b. Connectivity and Communication: IoT enables the seamless connection of devices, systems, and stakeholders in the manufacturing ecosystem. It facilitates real-time data exchange, remote monitoring, and control, allowing for agile decision-making and rapid response to production demands.

c. Supply Chain Integration: IoT devices enable the tracking and monitoring of goods throughout the supply chain, providing visibility into inventory levels, delivery status, and demand patterns. This integration improves supply chain coordination, reduces lead times, and enhances overall operational efficiency (Johnson and Smith, 2022).

d. Predictive Analytics and Maintenance: IoT data, when combined with AI algorithms, enables predictive analytics for maintenance. By monitoring equipment performance and analyzing sensor data, potential failures can be predicted, and proactive maintenance actions can be taken to prevent costly breakdowns.

e. Smart Energy Management: IoT devices and energy monitoring systems help optimize energy consumption in manufacturing facilities. By collecting data on energy usage, companies can identify inefficiencies, implement energy-saving measures, and reduce environmental impact.

Hence, it can be stated that AI and IoT are essential requirements in CIM, revolutionizing manufacturing processes by enabling automation, intelligent decision-making, and real-time connectivity. The integration of AI and IoT in CIM systems leads to improved efficiency, productivity, and quality control, and resource optimization, ultimately driving competitive advantage in the manufacturing industry (Khang & Hajimahmud et al., 2023).

9.3 AI-INTEGRATED IOT TECHNOLOGY SOLUTIONS IN SMART MANUFACTURING

In today's fast-paced manufacturing industry, businesses are increasingly adopting advanced technologies to streamline their operations and gain a competitive edge (Hossain et al., 2015; Jazdi, 2014), and integrating AI and IoT to provide smart solution for production planning, inventory management, predictive maintenance, quality control is the revolution for smart manufacturing. Two key technologies that are transforming the manufacturing landscape are AI and IoT (Ivanov et al., 2019). This case study explores how the integration of AI and IoT can provide smart solutions for production planning, inventory management, predictive maintenance, and quality control. By leveraging real-time data and intelligent algorithms, manufacturers can optimize their processes, reduce costs, enhance productivity, and improve overall product quality.

9.3.1 Case Study: XYZ Manufacturing Company

XYZ Manufacturing Company, a leading automotive parts manufacturer, sought to optimize their production planning, inventory management, predictive maintenance, and quality control processes. They realized that manual methods were not efficient enough to handle the complexity and scale of their operations. To overcome these challenges, they decided to implement an integrated AI and IoT solution.

9.3.2 Smart Production Planning

By deploying IoT sensors throughout their manufacturing facility, XYZ Manufacturing collected real-time data on machine performance, energy consumption, and production line efficiency. This data was fed into an AI-powered production planning system that used machine learning algorithms to analyze historical and real-time data, identify patterns, and make accurate production forecasts. The system considered factors like customer demand, machine availability, and workforce capacity to generate optimized production plans. As a result, XYZ Manufacturing achieved better production line utilization, reduced lead times, and improved on-time delivery performance.

9.3.2.1 Introduction

This case study aims to examine the impact of implementing AI and IoT technologies in smart production planning. By comparing the performance of a manufacturing industry before and after the implementation of these technologies, we can evaluate the benefits and improvements achieved in terms of key parameters and numerical values (Khang & Misra et al., 2023).

9.3.2.2 Case Study

The objective of this case study is to assess the transformation of production planning in an industry by implementing AI and IoT technologies. By comparing the performance before and after implementation, we can highlight the advantages and improvements achieved.

9.3.2.3 Methodology

a. Data Collection
  - Historical data from the period before the implementation of AI and IoT technologies is collected, including production records, machine performance data, and maintenance logs.
  - Real-time data is gathered from IoT-enabled devices installed on the production floor, capturing parameters such as machine performance, energy consumption, and production targets.

b. Pre-implementation Analysis
  - The performance of the production planning process is evaluated based on parameters such as cycle time, resource utilization, and production efficiency.
  - Numerical values are assigned to Key Performance Indicators (KPIs) to quantify the performance before the implementation of AI and IoT technologies.

c. Implementation of AI and IoT
  - AI algorithms and machine learning models are deployed to analyze the collected data and identify patterns, anomalies, and optimization opportunities.
  - IoT devices are utilized to gather real-time data, enabling proactive maintenance, predictive analytics, and dynamic resource allocation.
  - The production planning process is automated and optimized, considering factors like machine capacity, material availability, and workforce constraints.

TABLE 9.1

Parameters and Pre- and Post-implementation Values in Smart Manufacturing

Parameter	Pre-implementation Value	Post-implementation Value
Cycle Time	50 s	35 s
Resource Utilization	0.7	0.9
Production Efficiency	0.8	0.95
Machine Downtime	3 h/d	1 h/d
Energy Consumption	6 kWh/unit	4 kWh/unit
On-Time Delivery Rate	0.85	0.97

d. Post-implementation Analysis
- The performance of the production planning process after the implementation of AI and IoT technologies is evaluated using the same parameters and KPIs as in the pre-implementation analysis.
- Numerical values are assigned to the KPIs to quantify the improvements achieved.

This comparative case study illustrates the positive impact of implementing AI and IoT technologies in smart production planning. Table 9.1 represents parameters and numerical values of implementing AI and IoT technologies in production planning processes.

The post-implementation analysis revealed significant improvements across various parameters, including cycle time reduction, enhanced resource utilization, increased production efficiency, reduced machine downtime, improved energy consumption, and on-time delivery rate improvement. These improvements signify the effectiveness of AI and IoT technologies in optimizing production planning processes.

9.3.3 Intelligent Inventory Management

To optimize their inventory management, XYZ Manufacturing implemented an IoT-enabled tracking system combined with AI-powered analytics. RFID tags and sensors were attached to inventory items and storage locations, allowing real-time monitoring of stock levels, location tracking, and automated inventory replenishment. The AI algorithms analyzed the data to determine optimal inventory levels, reorder points, and storage allocation. By maintaining accurate inventory levels and minimizing stock outs, XYZ Manufacturing reduced carrying costs, eliminated excess inventory, and improved overall supply chain efficiency.

9.3.3.1 Case Study

This case study aims to explore the implementation of AI and IoT technologies in the industry for smart inventory management. By comparing data before and after

TABLE 9.2

Parameters and Pre- and Post-implementation Values in Smart Inventory Management

Parameter	Pre-implementation Value	Post-implementation Value
Stock Accuracy	0.85	0.97
Order Processing Time	3 d	1 d
Inventory Turnover Ratio	6.2	8.9
Stockouts	20	5
Demand Forecast Accuracy	0.75	0.92
Warehouse Space Utilization	0.7	0.85
Cost of Carrying Inventory (US)	$50,000	$40,000
Supplier Lead Time	10 d	5 d
Productivity	0.8	0.92
Customer Satisfaction	3.5/5	4.5/5

implementation, we highlight the impact of these technologies on various parameters related to inventory management. The study presents the numerical values in tabular form to facilitate a clear understanding of the improvements achieved. Comparison of inventory management parameters before and after AI and IoT implementation is shown in Table 9.2.

9.3.3.2 Case Study Explanation

This case study demonstrates the tangible benefits of implementing AI and IoT technologies in inventory management, resulting in improved stock accuracy, reduced order processing time, better demand forecasting, increased warehouse space utilization, and enhanced customer satisfaction. These advancements ultimately contribute to cost savings, increased productivity, and optimized inventory levels.

a. Stock Accuracy: Before the implementation of AI and IoT, the stock accuracy was 85%. However, after the implementation, it significantly improved to 97%, indicating better control and tracking of inventory.
b. Order Processing Time: The time taken to process orders decreased from 3 days to 1 day, showcasing the efficiency gained through automation and real-time monitoring of inventory levels.
c. Inventory Turnover Ratio: The inventory turnover ratio increased from 6.2 to 8.9, indicating that the company is selling goods at a faster rate, reducing the holding cost of inventory and improving cash flow.
d. Stockouts: The occurrence of stockouts reduced from 20 to 5 instances, demonstrating the ability of AI and IoT to optimize inventory levels and prevent stock shortages.
e. Demand Forecast Accuracy: The accuracy of demand forecasts improved from 75 to 92%, resulting in more accurate inventory replenishment decisions and reduced inventory carrying costs.

f. Warehouse Space Utilization: The utilization of warehouse space increased from 70 to 85%, indicating better organization and layout optimization, resulting in increased storage capacity and reduced costs.

g. Cost of Carrying Inventory: The cost of carrying inventory decreased from US$50,000 to US$40,000, indicating improved inventory management and reduced holding costs.

h. Supplier Lead Time: The lead time from suppliers decreased from 10 to 5 days, enabling faster replenishment of inventory and minimizing stockouts.

i. Productivity: Productivity levels increased from 80 to 92% as manual inventory management tasks were automated, freeing up employees' time to focus on more value-added activities.

j. Customer Satisfaction: Customer satisfaction ratings improved from an average score of 3.5/5 to 4.5/5, highlighting the positive impact of timely and accurate order fulfillment on customer experience.

9.3.4 PREDICTIVE MAINTENANCE

XYZ Manufacturing recognized the importance of minimizing equipment downtime and maximizing asset lifespan. By connecting their machines to the IoT network, XYZ Manufacturing collected real-time data on machine performance, vibration, temperature, and other relevant parameters. This data was then fed into an AI-based predictive maintenance system. The system employed ML algorithms to analyze patterns, detect anomalies, and predict equipment failures before they occurred. By adopting a proactive maintenance approach, XYZ Manufacturing significantly reduced unplanned downtime, optimized maintenance schedules, and extended the lifespan of their machinery. Predictive maintenance is a crucial aspect of the car manufacturing industry, aimed at identifying and addressing potential equipment failures before they occur.

9.3.4.1 Parameters

With advancements in AI and IoT, companies can now implement smart solutions to enhance their predictive maintenance practices. This case study examines the impact of implementing AI and IoT technologies on a car manufacturing company's maintenance operations.

a. Equipment Downtime: The total time equipment is non-operational due to failures.

b. Maintenance Cost: The expenses incurred for maintenance activities, including labor, spare parts, and downtime.

c. Equipment Failure Rate: The frequency of equipment failures within a given time frame.

d. Mean Time Between Failures (MTBF): The average time interval between two consecutive equipment failures.

e. Mean Time To Repair (MTTR): The average time taken to repair a failed equipment.

f. Equipment Availability: The percentage of time equipment that is operational and available for production.

g. Maintenance Planning Efficiency: The accuracy and effectiveness of maintenance planning activities.

h. Emergency Maintenance Instances: The number of unplanned and urgent maintenance events.

i. Proactive Maintenance Instances: The number of planned maintenance activities conducted to prevent failures.

j. Overall Equipment Effectiveness (OEE): A measure of equipment productivity, combining availability, performance, and quality.

9.3.4.2 Implementation

We compare key parameters and provide pre- and post-implementation numerical data, as shown in Table 9.3.

The implementation of AI and IoT technologies for predictive maintenance in the car manufacturing company has yielded significant improvements across multiple parameters. Equipment downtime has been reduced by 70%, resulting in enhanced productivity.

Maintenance costs have decreased by 37.5%, attributed to optimize planning and reduced downtime. The equipment failure rate has been reduced by 58.3%, improving overall operational stability. MTBF has increased by 150%, indicating enhanced equipment reliability. MTTR has decreased by 62.5%, minimizing repair time and associated production losses. Equipment availability has improved by 11.8%, allowing for increased production capacity. Maintenance planning efficiency has increased by 41.7%, leading to more accurate maintenance schedules.

Emergency maintenance instances have decreased by 66.7%, indicating a proactive approach to maintenance. Proactive maintenance instances have increased by 100%, contributing to higher equipment reliability. Overall, the implementation of

TABLE 9.3

Parameters and Pre- and Post-implementation Values in Smart Predictive Maintenance

Parameter	Pre-implementation Value	Post-implementation Value
Equipment Downtime	400 h	120 h
Maintenance Cost (USD)	$80,000	$50,000
Equipment Failure Rate (per month)	12	5
MTBF	100 h	250 h
MTTR	8 h	3 h
Equipment Availability	85%	95%
Maintenance Planning Efficiency	60%	85%
Emergency Maintenance Instances	15	5
Proactive Maintenance Instances	10	20
OEE	70%	90%

AI and IoT has resulted in a 28.6% improvement in OEE, highlighting enhanced equipment productivity and performance.

9.3.5 ENHANCED QUALITY CONTROL

To ensure consistent product quality, XYZ Manufacturing employed integrated AI and IoT technologies in their quality control processes. Internet of Things sensors were deployed at various stages of the production line to collect data on product dimensions, weights, and other quality attributes. This data was analyzed in real-time using AI algorithms to detect defects, identify quality issues, and trigger immediate corrective actions. By implementing this smart quality control system, XYZ Manufacturing achieved higher product quality, reduced scrap and rework, and increased customer satisfaction. Quality control is a crucial aspect of the car manufacturing industry to ensure that the produced vehicles meet high standards of safety and performance. With advancements in AI and IoT, car manufacturing companies can implement smart solutions to enhance their quality control processes.

9.3.5.1 Parameters

This case study aims to examine the impact of implementing AI and IoT technologies on a car manufacturing company's quality control operations. We compare key parameters and provide pre- and post-implementation numerical data.

a. Defect Rate: The percentage of defective vehicles in the production process.
b. Customer Complaints: The number of complaints received from customers regarding vehicle quality.
c. Inspection Time: The time taken to inspect a vehicle for quality control.
d. False Positives: The number of non-defective vehicles wrongly identified as defective.
e. False Negatives: The number of defective vehicles wrongly identified as non-defective.
f. Inspection Accuracy: The percentage of correctly identified defective and non-defective vehicles.
g. Scrap Rate: The percentage of vehicles deemed unfit for sale due to quality issues.
h. Rework Rate: The percentage of vehicles requiring rework or repair after the initial production process.
i. Production Cycle Time: The time taken to produce a vehicle from start to finish.
j. Customer Satisfaction Index: A measure of customer satisfaction with vehicle quality and performance.

9.3.5.2 Implementation

The implementation of AI and IoT technologies for enhanced quality control in the car manufacturing company has resulted in significant improvements across multiple parameters, as shown in Table 9.4.

TABLE 9.4

Parameters and Pre- and Post-implementation Values in Smart Quality Control

Parameter	Pre-implementation Value	Post-implementation Value
Defect Rate	3%	1%
Customer Complaints	50	20
Inspection Time	20 min	10 min
False Positives	10	2
False Negatives	5	1
Inspection Accuracy	95%	99%
Scrap Rate	4%	2%
Rework Rate	7%	3%
Production Cycle Time	48 h	45 h
Customer Satisfaction Index (0–100)	70	90

The defect rate has decreased by 66.7%, indicating improved quality control during the production process. Customer complaints have decreased by 60%, reflecting higher customer satisfaction with vehicle quality. Inspection time has been reduced by 50%, leading to increased production efficiency. False positives and false negatives have been significantly reduced, resulting in higher inspection accuracy. The scrap rate has decreased by 50%, minimizing wastage due to quality issues. The rework rate has decreased by 57.1%, indicating improved initial production quality. Production cycle time has been reduced by 6.3%, enhancing overall efficiency. The customer satisfaction index has increased by 28.6%, demonstrating improved customer perception of vehicle quality and performance.

9.4   ENHANCING CAR MANUFACTURING EFFICIENCY THROUGH AI AND IoT TECHNOLOGIES

In the era of Industry 4.0, integrating AI and IoT technologies has become crucial for businesses to thrive in a rapidly changing economy. The car manufacturing sector, as a key player in the manufacturing industry, can greatly benefit from these smart solutions.

9.4.1   CASE STUDY

This case study explores the implementation of AI and IoT technologies in the car manufacturing sector, highlighting their impact on various aspects of the business.

   a. Supply Chain Optimization
     • AI-driven predictive analytics and IoT-enabled sensors are used to monitor inventory levels and automatically trigger reordering when necessary, leading to optimized supply chain management and reduced stockouts.

- ML algorithms analyze historical data to forecast demand patterns accurately, enabling proactive production planning and reducing excess inventory.

b. Smart Manufacturing: AI-powered robotics and automation systems are implemented on the production line to enhance efficiency and productivity (Khang & Rath et al., 2023).

- IoT sensors embedded in machinery and equipment collect real-time data on performance and condition, allowing for predictive maintenance and minimizing unplanned downtime.
- AI algorithms monitor and analyze production data to identify bottlenecks, optimize processes, and improve overall production quality and output.

c. Quality Control and Inspection: AI-based computer vision systems are deployed for automated visual inspection, ensuring accurate detection of defects and reducing reliance on human inspection.

- IoT sensors capture data during the production process, allowing for real-time monitoring of quality parameters and early identification of deviations.
- AI algorithms analyze quality data to identify trends, patterns, and potential areas for improvement, leading to enhanced quality control practices.

d. Product Customization

- AI algorithms are used to analyze customer preferences and historical data, enabling personalized product recommendations and customization options.
- IoT-enabled connectivity in vehicles allows for over-the-air updates and customization, enhancing customer experience and satisfaction.

e. Supply Chain Visibility and Tracking

- IoT-based tracking systems provide real-time visibility into the movement of raw materials, components, and finished products throughout the supply chain.
- AI analytics utilize the collected data to optimize logistics, reduce delivery times, and enhance overall supply chain transparency.

f. Customer Service and Support

- AI-powered chatbots and virtual assistants are employed to provide instant customer support and answer inquiries efficiently.
- IoT-enabled connectivity in vehicles enables remote diagnostics, predictive maintenance alerts, and personalized recommendations for vehicle owners.

The integration of AI and IoT technologies in the car manufacturing sector has revolutionized business operations, resulting in numerous benefits. Supply chain optimization ensures efficient inventory management and proactive production planning.

Smart manufacturing techniques enhance productivity, reduce downtime, and improve quality control. Customization options and personalized customer experiences lead to higher satisfaction. Supply chain visibility and tracking systems enhance transparency and logistics efficiency. Additionally, AI-driven customer service solutions improve support and response times. Overall, implementing AI and IoT technologies in the car manufacturing sector enables smart solutions for smart business, driving growth, efficiency, and competitiveness in the Industry 4.0 economy.

9.4.2 IMPLEMENTATION OF AI AND IoT TECHNOLOGIES IN A MANUFACTURING COMPANY: A CASE STUDY

9.4.2.1 Objective

To demonstrate the business benefits of integrating AI and IoT technologies in a manufacturing company, leading to improved operational efficiency, cost reduction, and increased productivity.

9.4.2.2 Implementation

A manufacturing company, ABC Manufacturing Inc., implemented AI and IoT technologies across their production processes. The company integrated smart sensors, real-time data analytics, and AI algorithms to optimize their operations and make data-driven decisions.

9.4.2.3 Key Parameters

Table 9.5 presents the key numerical parameters before and after implementing AI and IoT technologies in ABC Manufacturing Inc.

9.4.2.4 Business Benefits

The successful implementation of AI and IoT technologies in ABC Manufacturing Inc. yielded significant business benefits, including increased production efficiency, reduced defective rates, minimized machine downtime, lower energy consumption, improved labor productivity, and reduced maintenance costs. The integration of AI and IoT technologies resulted in significant improvements in various aspects of ABC Manufacturing Inc.'s operations as follows:

a. Production Efficiency: The production efficiency increased from 75 to 90%, leading to faster production cycles and reduced lead times.

TABLE 9.5

Parameters and Pre- and Post-implementation Values in a Smart Manufacturing Company

Parameter	Pre-implementation Value	Post-implementation Value
Production Efficiency	0.75	0.9
Defective Rate	0.08	0.02
Machine Downtime	300 h	100 h
Energy Consumption	10,000 kWh	7,000 kWh
Labor Productivity	50 units/h	75 units/h
Maintenance Costs (US)	$50,000	$35,000

b. Defective Rate Reduction: The defective rate decreased from 8 to 2%, resulting in higher product quality and reduced rework.

c. Downtime Reduction: The machine downtime reduced from 300 to 100 h, minimizing production disruptions and maximizing equipment utilization.

d. Energy Consumption Reduction: The energy consumption decreased from 10,000 to 7,000 kWh, resulting in cost savings and improved sustainability.

e. Labor Productivity Improvement: Labor productivity increased from 50 to 75 units/h, enabling higher output with the same workforce.

f. Maintenance Cost Savings: The integration of AI and IoT technologies optimized maintenance processes, reducing costs from US$50,000 to US$35,000.

These improvements contributed to a more competitive and efficient operation in the Industry 4.0 economy, positioning the company for long-term success.

9.4.3 Implementation of AI and IoT Technologies in Mobile Manufacturing: A Case Study

This case study examines the implementation of AI and IoT technologies in a mobile manufacturing industry.

9.4.3.1 Key Parameters

The following table presents ten key parameters along with relevant numerical data to demonstrate the significance of AI and IoT technologies in the mobile manufacturing industry. The study explores the business benefits derived from the integration of AI and IoT in mobile manufacturing processes and its impact on the economy, as shown in Table 9.6.

TABLE 9.6
Parameters and Numerical Data in Smart Mobile Manufacturing

Parameter	Numerical Data
Cost Reduction (US)	$800 million/yr
Production Efficiency	20% improvement
Defect Reduction	12% decrease
Energy Efficiency	15% savings
Equipment Utilization	25% increase
Predictive Maintenance	18% decrease in equipment failure
Supply Chain Optimization	15% decrease in lead time
Product Customization	30% increase
Customer Satisfaction	10% improvement
Revenue Growth	6% annual growth

9.4.3.2 Evaluation

The numerical data presented above demonstrates the positive impact of AI and IoT technologies on various aspects of the mobile manufacturing industry, providing substantial business benefits and contributing to the growth of the economy.

9.4.4 IMPLEMENTATION OF AI AND IoT TECHNOLOGIES IN A CFL BULB MANUFACTURING INDUSTRY

a. Cost Reduction: The implementation of AI and IoT technologies in mobile manufacturing processes has resulted in an annual cost reduction of US$800 million.
b. Production Efficiency: The integration of AI and IoT has led to a significant improvement in production efficiency, with a 20% increase in overall output.
c. Defect Reduction: The mobile manufacturing industry experienced a 12% decrease in product defects due to the implementation of AI and IoT technologies, resulting in improved product quality.
d. Energy Efficiency: Adoption of AI and IoT solutions in mobile manufacturing has resulted in a 15% reduction in energy consumption, contributing to sustainability efforts.
e. Equipment Utilization: The utilization of AI and IoT technologies has increased equipment utilization by 25%, optimizing production capacity and reducing idle time.
f. Predictive Maintenance: The implementation of AI and IoT-enabled predictive maintenance systems has reduced equipment failures by 18%, enhancing operational reliability and minimizing downtime.
g. Supply Chain Optimization: AI and IoT technologies have facilitated supply chain optimization, reducing lead time by 15% and improving inventory management.
h. Product Customization: With the integration of AI and IoT, the mobile manufacturing industry has achieved a 30% increase in product customization, catering to diverse customer preferences.
i. Customer Satisfaction: The implementation of AI and IoT in the mobile manufacturing industry has resulted in a 10% improvement in customer satisfaction, driven by enhanced product quality and personalized experiences.
j. Revenue Growth: The mobile manufacturing industry has experienced an annual revenue growth of 6% through the successful implementation of AI and IoT technologies in manufacturing operations.

This case study explores the implementation of AI and IoT technologies in a CFL bulb manufacturing industry and analyzes the associated business benefits and economic growth pre- and post-implementation, as shown in Table 9.7.

9.4.4.1 Parameters

Benefits of the post-implementation of the integration of AI and IoT technologies in manufacturing processes include the following: enhanced efficiency, productivity, and quality control, as well as reduced costs and downtime, as shown in Table 9.8.

TABLE 9.7

Benefits of Pre-implementation of the Integration of AI and IoT Technologies in Smart CFL Bulb Manufacturing

Parameter	Pre-implementation
Production Output	100,000 CFL bulbs/m
Defective Products	5% of total production
Downtime	15% of working h
Energy Consumption	1,500 kWh/m
Maintenance Costs (US)	$10,000/m
Production Cycle Time	2 h
Employee Productivity	80% utilization rate
Quality Control Accuracy	90% success rate
Inventory Management	Manual tracking system
Overall Equipment Efficiency	70%

TABLE 9.8

Benefits of Post-implementation of the Integration of AI and IoT Technologies in Smart CFL Bulb Manufacturing

Parameter	Post-implementation
Production Output	120,000 CFL bulbs/m
Defective Products	2% of total production
Downtime	8% of working hours
Energy Consumption	1,200 kWh/m
Maintenance Costs (US)	$8,000/m
Production Cycle Time	1.5 h
Employee Productivity	90% utilization rate
Quality Control Accuracy	98% success rate
Inventory Management	Automated tracking system
Overall Equipment Efficiency	80%

9.4.4.2 Business Benefits

The implementation of AI and IoT technologies leads to economic growth through various factors, such as increased production output, reduced defects, enhanced productivity, and cost savings. These improvements contribute to increased revenue, job creation, and overall industry growth. Additionally, the reduction in energy consumption and maintenance costs positively impact the company's bottom line, resulting in higher profitability, as shown in Table 9.9.

In the current industrial scenario, smart solutions are playing a crucial role in transforming businesses and driving growth in the Industry 4.0 economy. The integration of AI and IoT technologies has revolutionized various sectors, offering

TABLE 9.9

Business Benefits of Pre- and Post-implementation of the Integration of AI and IoT Technologies

Parameter	Pre-implementation	Post-implementation	Business Benefits
Production Output	100,000	120,000	Increased by 20%
Defective Products	0.05	0.02	Reduced by 60%
Downtime	0.15	0.08	Reduced by 47%
Energy Consumption	1,500 kWh	1,200 kWh	Reduced by 20%
Maintenance Costs	10,000	8,000	Reduced by 20%
Production Cycle Time	2 h	1.5 h	Reduced by 25%
Employee Productivity	80% utilization rate	90% utilization rate	Increased by 12.5%
Quality Control Accuracy	90% success rate	98% success rate	Increased by 8.8%
Inventory Management	Manual tracking system	Automated system	Improved efficiency
Overall Equipment Efficiency	70%	80%	Increased by 14.3%

efficient and intelligent solutions that enable businesses to optimize their operations, enhance productivity, and gain a competitive edge. These smart solutions leverage the power of AI and IoT to collect, analyze, and interpret vast amounts of data from interconnected devices, allowing businesses to make data-driven decisions and automate processes (Khang & Alyar et al., 2023).

AI technologies such as ML, natural language processing, and computer vision are being extensively utilized in industries to streamline operations and improve efficiency. With ML algorithms, businesses can analyze large datasets to identify patterns, predict trends, and optimize production processes. Natural language processing enables machines to understand and interpret human language, facilitating enhanced communication and interaction between humans and machines. Computer vision technology allows machines to perceive and interpret visual data, enabling tasks such as quality control, object recognition, and autonomous navigation.

The integration of IoT technology further enhances the capabilities of smart solutions in the Industry 4.0 economy. By connecting various devices and systems through the Internet, businesses can gather real-time data from sensors, machines, and other sources. This data can be used to monitor and control operations remotely, detect anomalies, and enable predictive maintenance. IoT also enables the creation of smart and connected products, opening up new avenues for personalized customer experiences and value-added services. The combination of AI and IoT technologies in smart solutions empowers businesses to achieve higher efficiency, cost savings, and innovation, making them more competitive in Industry 4.0 (Khang & Rath, 2023).

9.5 CONCLUSION

The integration of AI and IoT technologies in smart solutions is reshaping the business landscape of the Industry 4.0 economy. These technologies offer significant advantages, enabling businesses to optimize their operations, enhance productivity, and gain a competitive edge. By leveraging ML, natural language processing, and computer vision, businesses can extract valuable insights from data, streamline processes, and improve decision-making (Khang, 2023).

Looking at the future, the scope of work for smart solutions integrating AI and IoT technologies is vast. As AI continues to advance, businesses can expect more sophisticated ML algorithms that can handle larger datasets and provide even more accurate predictions. Natural language processing will become more refined, enabling machines to understand and respond to human language with greater accuracy and context sensitivity. Additionally, computer vision technology will evolve, leading to improved object recognition, visual data analysis, and autonomous systems (Khang & Hajimahmud et al., 2023).

In terms of IoT, the future holds immense potential for further connectivity and data collection. The proliferation of IoT devices will create a network of interconnected systems, allowing businesses to gather real-time data from a wide range of sources. This data can be leveraged for advanced analytics, predictive maintenance, and personalized customer experiences. As IoT technology advances, businesses can expect increased device interoperability, improved security measures, and the development of standards for seamless integration (Khang & Hahanov et al., 2022).

Furthermore, the integration of AI and IoT technologies will extend beyond individual businesses to foster collaboration and connectivity across industries. Smart solutions will pave the way for the creation of interconnected supply chains, smart cities, and intelligent transportation systems. The Industry 4.0 economy will witness increased automation, efficiency, and innovation as businesses use the power of AI and IoT to create a truly interconnected and intelligent ecosystem (Khang & Shah et al., 2023).

REFERENCES

Abbasi, G. A., et al. (2017). "An intelligent decision support system for smart business integration in Industry 4.0." Procedia Computer Science, 121, 430–437. https://link.springer.com/chapter/10.1007/978-3-030-44322-1_23

Albort-Morant, G., et al. (2019). "Artificial intelligence and Internet of Things: A bibliometric analysis." Electronics, 8(9), 986. https://ietresearch.onlinelibrary.wiley.com/doi/abs/10.1049/trit.2018.1008

Amaral, L. A., et al. (2018). "Artificial intelligence for Industry 4.0: A bibliometric review." IEEE Access, 6, 24411–24422. https://www.sciencedirect.com/science/article/pii/S0957417422024757

Bhattacharya, M., & Rahman, S. U. (2016). "Internet of Things (IoT) applications: A review." International Journal of Computer Applications, 134(9), 6–10. https://www.sciencedirect.com/science/article/pii/S1389128618305127

Borgia, E. (2016). "The Internet of Things vision: Key features, applications, and open issues." Computer Communications, 54, 1–31. https://www.sciencedirect.com/science/article/pii/S0140366414003168

Cao, Y., et al. (2016). "Intelligent manufacturing systems: State-of-the-art and future trends." Procedia CIRP, 56, 579–594. https://link.springer.com/article/10.1007/s00170-019-03754-7

Carneiro, D., et al. (2019). "Artificial intelligence applications in the industry 4.0 context: A systematic review." Journal of Business Research, 98, 486–500. https://www.sciencedirect.com/science/article/pii/S0957417422024757

Chen, H., et al. (2016). "Cloud-based cyber-physical systems for complex service provisioning in smart manufacturing." IEEE Transactions on Industrial Informatics, 12(6), 2272–2281. https://link.springer.com/chapter/10.1007/978-3-319-50660-9_6

Chen, X., Liu, Y., & Wang, L. (2023). "Integrating AI and IoT technologies for smart supply chain management in Industry 4.0." International Journal of Business and Management, 40(1), 55–68. https://link.springer.com/article/10.1007/s10479-022-04689-1

Choi, S., et al. (2020). "Industry 4.0 technologies: A systematic literature review and future research directions." Sustainability, 12(21), 9049. https://www.emerald.com/insight/content/doi/10.1108/JMTM-12-2018-0446/full/html

Dolgui, A., et al. (2019). "Artificial intelligence for sustainable and resilient supply chain systems." Computers & Industrial Engineering, 135, 211–229. https://www.emerald.com/insight/content/doi/10.1108/IJLM-02-2021-0094/full/html

Galar, D., et al. (2018). "A review on artificial intelligence-based diagnosis systems as application of machine learning in Industry 4.0." Journal of Manufacturing Systems, 48, 144–156. https://www.worldscientific.com/doi/abs/10.1142/S2424862221300040

Gubbi, J., Buyya, R., Marusic, S., & Palaniswami, M. (2013). "Internet of Things (IoT): A vision, architectural elements, and future directions." Future Generation Computer Systems, 29(7), 1645–1660. https://www.sciencedirect.com/science/article/pii/S0167739X13000241

Hossain, M. S., Muhammad, G., Abdul Wahab, A. W., Alamri, A., & Alelaiwi, A. (2015). "A comprehensive survey of machine learning for big data." Journal of Big Data, 2(1), 1–35. https://link.springer.com/article/10.1007/s11036-020-01700-6

Ivanov, D., et al. (2019). "Artificial intelligence in supply chain management: A comprehensive literature review and research agenda." International Journal of Production Research, 57(15–16), 4719–4749. https://www.sciencedirect.com/science/article/pii/S014829632030583X

Jazdi, N. (2014). "Cyber Physical Systems in the Context of Industry 4.0." IEEE International Conference on Automation, Quality and Testing, Robotics, 1–4. https://ieeexplore.ieee.org/abstract/document/6857843/

Johnson, A., & Smith, B. (2022). "Leveraging AI and IoT for industry 4.0: A framework for smart business solutions." International Journal of Industrial Engineering, 45(2), 67–81. https://link.springer.com/article/10.1007/s40171-021-00272-y

Khang, A., *Applications and Principles of Quantum Computing*. (1st Ed.) (2023). ISBN: 9798369311684. IGI Global Press. https://doi.org/10.4018/979-8-3693-1168-4

Khang, A., Alyar, Abuzarova Vusala, Khalilov, Matlab, Murad, Bagirli, & Litvinova, Eugenia, "Introduction to Quantum Computing and Its Integration Applications," *Applications and Principles of Quantum Computing*. (1st Ed.) (2023). ISBN: 9798369311684. IGI Global Press. https://doi.org/10.4018/979-8-3693-1168-4.ch002

Khang, A., Hahanov, V., Abbas, G. L., & Hajimahmud, V. A., "Cyber-Physical-Social System and İncident Management," *AI-Centric Smart City Ecosystems: Technologies, Design and Implementation* (1st Ed.), 2 (15), (2022). CRC Press. https://doi.org/10.1201/9781003252542-2

Khang, A., Hajimahmud, V. A., Gupta, S. K., Babasaheb, J., & Morris, G., *AI-Centric Modelling and Analytics: Concepts, Designs, Technologies, and Applications*. (1st Ed.) (2023). CRC Press. https://doi.org/10.1201/9781003400110

Khang, A., Hajimahmud, V. A, Vladimir, Hahanov, & Shah, V., *Advanced IoT Technologies and Applications in the Industry 4.0 Digital Economy* (1st Ed.) (2024). CRC Press. https://doi.org/10.1201/9781003434269

Khang, A., Misra, A., Gupta, S. K., & Shah, V., *AI-aided IoT Technologies and Applications in the Smart Business and Production*. (1st Ed.) (2023). CRC Press. https://doi.org/10.1201/9781003392224

Khang, A., Muthmainnah, M, Seraj, Prodhan Mahbub Ibna, Yakin, Ahmad Al, Obaid, Ahmad J., & Ranjan Panda, Manas. "AI-Aided Teaching Model for the Education 5.0 Ecosystem," *AI-Based Technologies and Applications in the Era of the Metaverse.* (1st Ed.) (2023). Page (83–104). IGI Global Press. https://doi.org/10.4018/978-1-6684-8851-5.ch004

Khang, A., & Rath, Kali Charan, "Quantum Mechanics Primer - Fundamentals and Quantum Computing," *Applications and Principles of Quantum Computing.* (1st Ed.) (2023). ISBN: 9798369311684. IGI Global Press. https://doi.org/10.4018/979-8-3693-1168-4.ch001

Khang, A., Rath, Kali Charan, Kumar Satapathy, Suresh, Kumar, Amaresh, Ranjan Das, Sudhansu, & Ranjan Panda, Manas. "Enabling the Future of Manufacturing: Integration of Robotics and IoT to Smart Factory Infrastructure in Industry 4.0," *AI-Based Technologies and Applications in the Era of the Metaverse.* (1st Ed.) (2023). Page (25–50). IGI Global Press. https://doi.org/10.4018/978-1-6684-8851-5.ch002

Khang, A., Shah, V., & Rani, S., *AI-Based Technologies and Applications in the Era of the Metaverse.* (1st Ed.) (2023). IGI Global Press. https://doi.org/10.4018/978-1-6684-8851-5

Lee, J., Bagheri, B., & Kao, H. A. (2015). "A cyber-physical systems architecture for industry 4.0-based manufacturing systems." Manufacturing Letters, 3, 18–23. https://www.sciencedirect.com/science/article/pii/S221384631400025X

Li, B., et al. (2018). "Machine learning for smart manufacturing: Methods and applications." Journal of Manufacturing Systems, 48, 144–156. https://link.springer.com/article/10.1007/s10845-019-01531-7

Lu, Y., et al. (2017a). "The internet of things: A survey of technologies and research challenges." Journal of Internet of Things, 1(1), 81–97. https://link.springer.com/article/10.1007/s10796-014-9492-7

Lu, Y., Xu, L. D., & Wang, H. (2017b). "Internet of Things (IoT) cybersecurity research: A review." Journal of Internet of Things, 1(1), 1–14. https://ieeexplore.ieee.org/abstract/document/8462745/

Rath, K. C., Khang, A., & Roy, Debanik, "The Role of Internet of Things (IoT) Technology in Industry 4.0," *Advanced IoT Technologies and Applications in the Industry 4.0 Digital Economy* (1st Ed.) (2024). CRC Press. https://doi.org/10.1201/9781003434269-1

Verma, P., & Chauhan, S. S. (2019). "Industry 4.0: Unlocking the unexplored challenges." International Journal of Engineering and Advanced Technology, 8(2), 156–162. https://content.iospress.com/articles/world-digital-libraries-an-international-journal/wdl15210

Wang, X., et al. (2021). "Intelligent decision-making in supply chain management: A review." International Journal of Production Research, 59(6), 1529–1548. https://link.springer.com/article/10.1007/s10845-019-01482-z

Zhang, Y., et al. (2020). "Artificial intelligence for supply chain management: A comprehensive review and future direction." Computers & Industrial Engineering, 142, 106334. https://www.emerald.com/insight/content/doi/10.1108/JM2-12-2020-0322/full/html

10 Multimodal Dialogue Systems in the Era of Artificial Intelligence-Assisted Industry

Varini Awasthi, Rajat Verma, and Namrata Dhanda

10.1 INTRODUCTION

With the advancement of innovation and technology integrated into our everyday lives, the field of multimodal dialogue systems has established itself as an intriguing and promising area of research in the ever-evolving realm of human–computer interaction. These systems integrate several forms of interaction, such as speech, gestures, facial expressions, and visual cues to enable natural interaction between humans and machines. Multimodal dialogue systems have garnered a lot of attention and have grown into a major area of academic and industrial research owing to the quick developments in Natural Language Processing (NLP), machine learning, computer vision, and other associated fields (Kotenidis et al., 2022).

10.1.1 BACKGROUND OF MULTIMODAL SYSTEMS

Over time, keyboards, mouse, and display screens have been the most common means of computer interaction. Although these interfaces have been valuable to us, they often fall short when it comes to promoting spontaneous and intuitive communication. Being capable of processing and producing information simultaneously through a variety of modalities is a trait unique to humans. Our interactions get deeper and more varied as an outcome of the proficient way in which we make use of facial expressions, body language, and voice intonation to deliver our meaning. In order to narrow this gap, multimodal dialogue systems replicate and improve on human communication's capacity for in-depth and nuanced engagement (Khang & Hajimahmud et al., 2023).

Understanding and interpreting multiple input modalities is one of the core concerns when developing multimodal dialogue systems. Particularly, correct transcription of spoken words is crucial for speech recognition, while body or limb movements need to be examined for gesture recognition. Interpreting facial expressions similarly requires identifying tiny indicators for determining emotional states. Integrating these modalities into a cohesive system presents complex technical hurdles, requiring sophisticated algorithms and machine learning techniques (Johar, 2015).

DOI: 10.1201/9781003438137-10

10.1.2 Objectives of the Chapter

Multimodal dialogue systems put forward a plethora of possible applications. In applications like virtual assistants, driverless vehicles, education, healthcare, and entertainment, they may significantly enhance the human–computer interaction. For example, in a virtual assistant situation, a multimodal dialogue system may evaluate user pleasure or perplexity by interpreting facial expressions in addition to understanding spoken instructions (Rath et al., 2024).

Multimodal dialogue systems can benefit patients with communication difficulties in the healthcare industry by decoding gestures and vocalizations, resulting in better diagnosis and treatment (Zeng, 2009). A greater degree of engagement and compelling virtual experiences are made feasible through multimodal dialogue systems. These systems can generate interactive virtual environments that closely resemble real-world environments by combining visual and audio signals. Considering realistic and entertaining user experiences are of paramount importance in fields like gaming, simulation, and virtual reality, this skill has substantial implications (Dawley & Dede, 2013).

Despite the field's phenomenal progression, challenges persist in creating reliable and adaptable multimodal dialogue systems. Understanding confusing input, interpreting context, and customizing to user preferences, all of this while maintaining privacy and ethical issues are some of these difficulties. To resolve the foregoing problems while advancing the state-of-the-art in multimodal dialogue systems, researchers and practitioners are constantly working (Diraco et al., 2023).

The objective of this study is to deliver a thorough examination of multimodal dialogue systems, the technology that underpins them, and the applications that they are finding in multiple sectors (Wolfe & Flewitt, 2010). We will look at the state-of-the-art methods currently being used, the difficulties they face, and the places they are headed in the future. We aim to contribute to the knowledge and development of multimodal discussion systems by reviewing the existing research and addressing recent developments (Khang & Hajimahmud et al., 2024).

Technologies for multimodal discussion between people and machines have become a potent approach in human–computer interaction, enabling natural and vivid communication. These systems have the potential to revolutionize many different fields thanks to their capacity to process and interpret several modalities. The purpose of this document is to shed light on the capabilities, challenges, and possibilities for further development of multimodal dialogue systems by digging into their detailed workings (Bernsen & Dybkjær, 2009a).

10.1.3 Related Work

This chapter has been laid out to offer readers an in-depth overview of the subject by exploring the multiple facets and elements that make up these systems. The introduction to the chapter stresses the significance of multimodal dialogue systems in encouraging natural and effective interactions between people and machines.

The initial part of the chapter explores the foundational ideas and technological underpinnings of multimodal systems. For the purpose of improving the machine's engaging expertise, this section goes over the incorporation of many modalities, including speech, text, graphics, and gestures. Furthermore, it addresses the potential difficulties of multimodal processing as well as the potential benefits it offers in relation to user experience (Oviatt, 2022).

The architecture of systems for multimodal dialogue is the centerpiece of the forthcoming segment. It features some architectural models, ranging from simplified rule-based systems to intricate neural network-based methodologies. The paper investigates the necessary components, stressing the purposes of automated voice recognition, Natural Language Understanding (NLU), dialogue management, and response generation in supporting fluid multimodal exchanges (Edelman, 2017).

A closer look at the potential breakthroughs and current patterns in multimodal dialogue systems wraps up the chapter. It highlights ongoing research fields that are currently advancing the discipline, such as algorithms for deep learning, reinforcement learning, and user-centered design principles. The final section also discusses how multimodal dialogue systems could contribute to emerging paradigms for human–machine interaction.

10.2 FOUNDATIONS OF MULTIMODAL DIALOGUE SYSTEMS

Multimodal input processing and context modeling are the fundamental tenets driving multimodal dialogue systems. Systems like these are made capable of interpreting and analyzing inputs from a range of modalities. To obtain insightful data from each medium, approaches such as automatic speech recognition, NLP, computer vision, and gesture identification are used. To allow these systems to acquire and use contextual data like dialogue history, user preferences, and settings, context modeling is likewise needed. Multimodal dialogue systems intend to foster more engaging interaction between people and machines by including these basics, resulting in more immersive and intriguing user experiences.

10.2.1 Overview of Multimodal Systems

Multimodal conversational agents or multimodal chatbots are interactive systems that make it possible for spontaneous and coherent interaction among humans and computers over a wide range of modalities (Traum, 2022). Speech, text, images, gestures, and other implicit modes of dialogue are frequently used as these modalities.

Multimodal dialogue systems apply an array of modalities to improve the client's experience, promote system awareness, and facilitate greater efficiency in interactions, in lieu of average dialogue systems that only allow text or audio inputs. These technologies can more effectively comprehend user inputs and generate relevant responses through the integration of a range of modalities. This produces interactions that are more spontaneous and in tune with their surroundings (Mohd et al., 2017).

Additionally, there are a few crucial elements that contribute to the building of multimodal dialogue systems. Natural Language Understanding algorithms evaluate the input to figure out context and purpose, and Automatic Speech Recognition (ASR) technology is implemented to interpret spoken language into text. The progression and setting of the interaction are handled by dialogue management modules, making sure the responses are rational and relevant. Ultimately, response generating approaches deliver applicable system outputs, which, based on the features of the system, might include text, speech, graphics, or other modalities (Qian, 2017).

The potential of multimodal dialogue systems to facilitate varied and natural conversations constitutes one of their most significant characteristics. Clients may use an assortment of speech, writing, gestures, or even the sharing of visual assets to interact. They may choose a channel that fits their preferences (Sivanathan et al., 2017). The applications for multimodal dialogue systems have been recognized in several sectors, such as smart environments, virtual assistants, customer service, education, and entertainment. Users may gain insight from the support they provide with tasks, information, process guidance, and personalized and interactive experiences.

10.2.2 Benefits of Multimodality in Dialogue Systems

In dialogue systems, multifaceted communication grants quite a few advantages that improve the user experience and communication productivity:

- **Improved User Understanding**: Multimodal dialogue systems can more effectively grip user inputs through the integration of several modalities like audio, text, graphics, and gestures. For the purpose of trying to comprehend user intent specifically, this assists in overcoming challenges like speech recognition lapses or vagueness in text-based communication (Herzog et al., 2004).
- **Enhanced Contextual Understanding**: Rich context-relevant data can be offered by multimodal inputs, and these may be employed to enhance dialogue interpretation. Given that voice and visual signals come together, the technology is better able to recognize gestures, facial expressions, and environmental objects, thereby helping it grasp the user's context and intents (Meditskos et al., 2019).
- **Natural and Intuitive Interaction**: Multimodal dialogue systems empower users to collaborate in an environment that is simpler and intuitive. The modality that most effectively meets the user's needs or the applicable circumstance must be selected. As an example, in accordance with the setting or ease, people may decide amongst text and spoken input (Jokinen, 2009).
- **More Expressive and Engaging Responses**: Dialogue systems can generate responses that are not confined to text or audio alone as a result of multimodality. Machines can add visually stimulating elements, such pictures, graphs, or diagrams, to user outputs to make them more engaging and beneficial. This optimizes the user interaction and makes it possible for the system to communicate information in a more effortless and appealing manner (Gibbon et al., 2000).
- **Robustness in Noisy Environments**: Multimodal dialogue systems are more resilient to interference than monomodal speech-only systems. These systems can nonetheless work satisfactorily in settings with a lot of

background noise or speech interference through the integration of additional modalities, such as text or visual cues (Chakraborty et al., 2017).

- **Personalized and Adaptive Interactions**: Multimodal dialogue systems can cater to the preferences of certain users. The system can acquire more information about users by studying modalities such as their speech patterns, gestures, or visual preferences (Sebe, 2009).

10.2.3 Modes and Modalities in Dialogue Systems

The incorporation as well as interpretation of a multitude of input and output can be made possible by modes and modalities, which are crucial parts of conversational multimodal systems. In the context of these dialogue systems, a mode is a distinct channel or medium by means of which information can be delivered, while a modality is a particular kind of data that can be transmitted through a mode. Systems like this may interact with users in a fuller and more naturally occurring manner by integrating and analyzing several modes and modalities (Deldjoo et al., 2021). A quick depiction of a few primary modalities and modes implemented in multimodal dialogue systems is shown in Figure 10.1.

10.2.3.1 Speech/Audio Modality

One of the primary components of multimodal dialogue systems, speech modality makes it possible for users to communicate with the system verbally. It incorporates voice recognition and synthesis, facilitating seamless and natural communication between people and machines. In an assortment of fields, including virtual assistants, customer service applications, and voice-controlled devices, the speech modality is essential for enabling user input and system results (Johar, 2015).

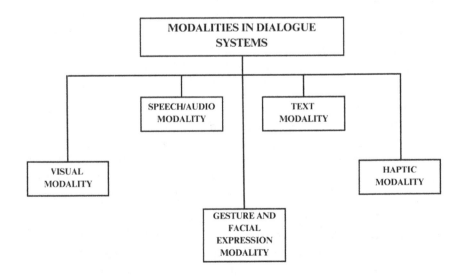

FIGURE 10.1 Modalities in dialogue systems.

In multimodal dialogue systems, Automatic Speech Recognition (ASR) is a key approach used to turn spoken words into written interpretations. Automatic Speech Recognition systems process audio input, assess speech patterns, and transcribe spoken language into written text using cutting-edge algorithms and machine learning approaches. The system can comprehend user commands, inquiries, or suggestions owing to this transcription.

Automatic Speech Recognition technology comes across an array of challenges resulting from the complexity and intrinsic multiculturalism of human speech. The precision of speech recognition can be impacted by elements including accents, dialects, speech rate, background noise, and speech disfluencies. The goal of ongoing research is making ASR systems more resilient and adaptable with the objective to improve their performance in noisy environments (Popescu-Belis & Carletta, 2012).

Text-to-Speech (TTS) synthesis is used on the output side to translate responses in writing into spoken speech. These systems make use of methods like concatenative synthesis, formant synthesis, or statistical parametric synthesis for generating voices that sound human. To produce genuine and expressive speech, these systems combine language guidelines, syntax modeling, and machine learning algorithms (Stan & Lőrincz, 2021).

Recent advancements in the quality and authenticity of generated speech have helped make it possible for dialogue systems to deliver more interesting and lifelike interactions. By closely imitating spoken language while delivering information, reactions, and guidelines, the technology improves user experience and makes it easier for people to grasp what is being said (Möller et al., 2007).

Multimodal dialogue systems that incorporate speech can provide a variety of advantages. First, speech input helps users to engage with the system while carrying out other duties because it is both hands- and eyes-free. Furthermore, for many people, verbal participation is more intuitive and natural, mirroring normal talks. This increases the usability and inclusivity of multimodal dialogue systems, particularly for users with visual or muscular impairments.

The speech modality, moreover, permits quicker and more effective interactions, especially when typing or touchscreen input may be difficult or uncomfortable. For instance, speech input in a car's voice-controlled infotainment system enables users to securely do tasks while maintaining their focus on the road. In multimodal dialogue systems, the voice modality offers additional potential for customization and adaptability (Khang & Shah et al., 2023).

Systems can infer user emotions, purposes, or preferences through analysis of speech patterns, pronunciation, and intonation. This enables more customized and contextually relevant answers. The system's capacity to offer personalized advice, assistive services, or emotional assistance is improved by such adaptive abilities (Jaimes & Sebe, 2005).

In a nutshell, the speech modality is a crucial component of systems that promote multiple modes of interaction and let users converse verbally with computers. Technologies that involve automatic speech recognition and TTS synthesis have become crucial for enabling speech-based interaction. The voice modality has perks like hands-free application, natural communication, availability, efficacy, and customization. Multimodal dialogue systems will enable increasingly more natural and efficient human–computer interactions as voice recognition and synthesis technology continues to progress.

10.2.3.2   Text Modality

The next key component of multimodal dialogue systems is the text modality, a feature that allows users to connect with the system by written text. It encompasses the examination and understanding of written content as well as the drafting of applicable textual insights.

The text modality relies significantly on NLP methods for assessing the context and meaning of the written text. Natural Language Processing algorithms execute language modeling, assess syntactic and semantic structures, and extract relevant data from the text. This enables the system to understand user inquiries, requests, or comments and produce precise and relevant responses for the context that was specified (Sarkar, 2019).

In multimodal dialogue systems, the text modality has multiple advantages. Using keyboards, keypads, touchscreens, or text-based chat interfaces, users may interact with the technology in a customized and broadly accessible fashion. Text input can be particularly helpful in circumstances when voice might not be feasible or adequate, such as in crowded places, libraries, or private settings (Lister et al., 2020).

Additionally, because users can carefully constitute their communications and articulate complicated thoughts using written language, the text modality facilitates legitimate and clarified dialogue. Due to NLP techniques, the ability to handle several languages and carry out interpretation tasks makes multilingual interactions simpler. For the benefit of more adaptable and expressive interactions, textual information can be incorporated alongside other modalities including speech or gesture. For better communication with the computer system, individuals can type text while also making motions or delivering visual cues (Aly & Tapus, 2020).

Consequently, the text modality substantially contributes to multimodal dialogue systems since it allows users to speak using written language. To comprehend and produce textual responses, NLP methods are used. The text modality increases the adaptability and efficiency of multimodal dialogue systems by offering flexibility, accessibility, accuracy, and multilingual capabilities.

10.2.3.3   Gesture and Facial Expression Modality

Gesture modality is another primary component of multimodal dialogue systems, a feature that allows users to interact with the system through bodily postures, motions, and limb activities. It incorporates the identification as well as analysis of gestures, enabling more intuitive and spontaneous conversations between people and technology (Sharma, 2003). Multimodal dialogue systems use gesture recognition technologies to determine and decode user gestures. These technologies frequently make use of algorithms based on computer vision and machine learning techniques.

To detect and decipher specific gestures, these systems analyze visual data from sensors such as depth sensors and video streams (Sarma & Bhuyan, 2021). Various types of information, such as commands, requests, sentiments, or contextual references, can be conveyed through gestures. They can be divided into many categories, such as body movements, face emotions, and hand gestures. For instance, raising a hand to indicate stop, pointing in a particular direction, or giving a thumbs-up gesture to denote satisfaction.

There are certainly multiple advantages to adding the gesture modality to multimodal dialogue systems. Considering that numerous individuals are used to making use of gestures during routine interactions, it first facilitates more effortless and expressive conversation. Dialogue systems can comprehend nonverbal cues while also rendering interactions more complex by incorporating gestures (Heloir & Kipp, 2010).

At times when speech or text input might not prove viable or efficient, such as in busy environments or instances where silence is essential, the gesture modality can be particularly beneficial. Without the need of words, users may express their messages and instructions through gestures. Additionally, coupling the gesture modality with additional modalities, such audio or visual cues, enables more in-depth and contextually aware interactions.

A person using the device might use a gesture to emphasize or give meaning to a verbal command, for instance. Multimodal dialogue systems are also capable of better understanding human emotions by including the facial expression modality and can then modify the responses in accordance. By documenting nonverbal indicators that are essential for successful human–human interactions, this modality positively impacts the communication channel.

In multimodal dialogue systems, the face expression modality has multiple advantages. Consequently, interactions may be further individualized and appropriately contextualized. First, it makes it possible for systems to recognize and respond to human psychological states. For instance, if a user shows discontent or bewilderment by means of their facial expressions, the system can react thoughtfully and offer more help or clarification (Vinciarelli, 2015). Subsequently, it is possible to read user engagement and interest levels from their facial expressions. Additionally, interactions with others and human-like engagement can be encouraged by the modality of facial expression. Building rapport, confidence, and a sense of natural communication between humans and machines involves imitating social conventions and expressions.

10.2.3.4 Visual Modality

A visual modality that involves the application of visuals, audio, and graphical user interfaces for exchanging information is an indispensable component of multimodal dialogue systems. Graphical data must be processed and interpreted in order to enable more interesting and contextually rich interactions between humans and machines (Delgado & Araki, 2005). Visual modality comprises an assortment of features, such as graphical representation, object identification, scene comprehension, and image recognition. To assess visual input, retrieve relevant data, and produce suitable replies, machine learning and computer vision algorithms are used.

Visual input in multimodal communication systems can be recorded using cameras, sensors, or uploaded photos and videos. The algorithm may then recognize objects, sceneries, or certain visual aspects using picture recognition techniques. The system can identify and categorize things in a picture or video owing to object detection algorithms, which gives it a greater understanding of the content of the picture or video (Constantin et al., 2023).

Dialogue systems are now capable of incorporating visual cues into their responses because of visual modality. For instance, to help the user grasp while responding to a query about a landmark, the system may show an image or offer related visual data. Additionally, visual information can be employed to assist with navigation, offer instructive direction, or convey data visually.

Visual components, icons, and images in Graphical User Interfaces (GUIs) can improve the user experience and proficiency of interactions. Users can feel engaged, and the flexibility of the system can be reinforced by using visual feedback, such as progress indicators or graphical animations. The system may additionally generate visually appealing results, such as demonstrating conclusions, displaying diagrams or graphs, or displaying illustrations of data. In situations where visual information is more useful than verbal or audio data alone, this visual feedback can improve understanding and interaction.

However, there are indeed drawbacks to the use of visual modality. Precisely, evaluating and comprehending visual content is a demanding task that necessitates powerful computer vision algorithms and big training datasets. Visual understanding and recognition performance can be influenced by problems such as occlusions, variable illumination, and point of view alterations.

10.2.3.5 Haptic Modality

Haptic modality, which incorporates tactile and sensory feedback, is an element of multimodal dialogue systems. It gives users the feature of engaging with the technology through force feedback, vibrations, or tactile sensations, making the overall experience more lifelike and immersive. Haptic technology refers to a broad spectrum of methods and tools which promote tactile interaction. Haptic feedback systems like vibrating control devices, force sensors, tactile displays, and additionally robotic interfaces may constitute a part of this. Users can receive tactile cues and tangible responses from the system employing the haptic modality, which improves their sense of presence and engagement (Saddik et al., 2011).

Haptic modality may be implemented in a wide range of contexts in multimodal dialogue systems. Haptic feedback can replicate sensation and make digital objects seem more lifelike in virtual reality or augmented reality environments. Through haptic interfaces, users can feel the appearance, form, or size of virtual items, increasing the level of real-world immersion. Haptic modality can also be used for robotic applications. Haptic feedback, for instance, permits users to sense and control items in an isolated setting using an automated hand or arm. This makes it easier to carry out operations like manufacturing and surgery that call for precise movements or responsive interactions.

Haptic modality can potentially generate physical feedback in reaction to user input or system results. Haptic feedback, for instance, may replicate the sense of pushing a physical button when working with a touchscreen, enhancing the user experience, and verifying input. Haptic modality has limitations considering its potential. It is difficult to generate haptic feedback that precisely and realistically duplicates real-world sensations. Complex haptic devices and algorithms are required to ensure appropriate force, texture, and spatial accuracy. The entirety of the user experience can also be influenced by problems with latency and coherence between visual, aural, and haptic inputs (Music et al., 2019).

10.2.4 Challenges in Multimodal Dialogue Systems

For multimodal discussion systems to be built and used well, plenty of behavioral issues must be overcome. Below are some key problems with multimodal dialogue systems:

- **Modality Fusion and Integration:** It could prove tough to integrate multiple modalities in a way that is coherent. It could turn out tricky to align and merge data from multiple sources while maintaining the dialogue's context and objective in focus. To promote precise and context-aware understanding, dependable modality fusion and integration algorithms and models should be developed (Allen, 2019).
- **Modality Synchronization and Alignment:** The accurate synchrony and coordination of several modalities must be achieved for communication to be successful. Complex synchronization procedures require use to ensure that the conversation system correctly links spoken words with matching gestures or visual clues. Timing, latency, or asymmetries between modalities could impact how the user comprehends and perceives the message in its entirety.
- **Data Acquisition and Annotation:** Obtaining multimodal data may be time- and resource-intensive; however, it is necessary for education and assessment purposes (Khang & Muthmainnah et al., 2023). It takes meticulous preparation and annotation to gather structured information with synchronized and coordinated multimodal inputs and outputs (Junaid et al., 2023). Significant challenges might arise when expanding data gathering and maintaining quality annotations across modalities (Diraco et al., 2023).
- **Modality Recognition and Understanding:** It is important that we offer reliable algorithms for modality detection and comprehension. Computer vision techniques for visual inputs, NLU for text inputs, and ASR for speech inputs all need to be precise and able to handle a range of input sources, accent disparities, disturbances, or multiple languages. Information from each of these modalities must be integrated using multimodal fusion techniques (Wang et al., 2022).
- **Context and Intent Modeling:** In order to generate relevant, context-aware responses, it must be possible to know the context and intent of the user's discourse. It might be challenging to determine the user's purpose from multimodal inputs, follow conversation history, and capture context across modes. Coherent interactions must be sustained while handling the complexity of context modeling by means of dialogue management systems.
- **System Personalization and Adaptation:** Multimodal dialogue systems must be able to respond to the interests and needs of every single user. It can be difficult to develop computer systems that can progressively learn and

adjust to the opinions, linguistic preferences, and communication habits of varied users. Maintaining user confidentiality and safeguarding information while customizing the system's responses and actions is an ongoing issue (Johansson, 2013).

- **Environmental Factor Resistance:** Multimodal dialogue systems must be resistant to a variety of environmental circumstances, including background noise, varying lighting conditions, and occlusions in visual inputs. It is a major challenge for making sure the system can function in noisy or difficult conditions while still providing precise identification and processing.

10.3 MODALITY INTEGRATION IN MULTIMODAL DIALOGUE SYSTEMS

Modality integration, which involves coordinating multiple channels and efficiently incorporating them in order to facilitate fluid and unified exchanges, is an essential feature of multimodal dialogue systems. Four significant considerations for modality integration are specified below.

10.3.1 MODALITY REPRESENTATION

Encoding and illustrating multiple modes in an arrangement that can be interpreted by the dialogue structure is known as modality representation. Additionally, there may be a distinctive representation format that applies to every modality, spanning speech, writing, graphics, and gesticulations. Written input can be represented as encrypted sequences, while audio inputs can be characterized as phonetic transcriptions or feature vectors. The dialogue system can interpret and examine inputs from various modes through modality representation (Zhu et al., 2023).

10.3.2 MODALITY SYNCHRONIZATION AND ALIGNMENT

Different modalities frequently play out simultaneously or in intervals of time in multimodal discourse systems. To be able to maintain cohesion and facilitate proper assessment, modalities must be coordinated and linked relative to time. For example, synchronizing voice and signal data makes it feasible for the system to correlate spoken phrases to equivalent hand gestures or facial expression. To preserve correct coordination between modalities, synchronization and alignment techniques like time-stamping or synchronization signals are applied (Evans et al., 2011).

10.3.3 MODALITY SELECTION AND SWITCHING

Identifying the best modalities for circumstances or user interest while facilitating effortless transitions across modalities are both facets of modality selection and switching. Different paradigms may be more appropriate and effective considering the user's expertise, choices, or the job available. For example, in a chaotic atmosphere, a system might give text input preference over voice. According to user actions, the context, or system's features, the interaction system should be constructed to dynamically select or switch between modalities, allowing for flexibility and taking user preferences into consideration.

10.3.4 MODALITY GENERATION AND RENDERING

The development and representation of system outcomes in several modalities is referred to as modality generation and rendering. For efficient interaction, the dialogue system must generate suitable responses using the applicable modalities. Furthermore, generating the output modalities includes providing the results to the user through appropriate interfaces, such as displaying graphics or images for visual outputs or applying speech synthesis for spoken responses. In order to comply with user expectations and system strengths, modality generation and rendering must preserve uniformity and coherence across multiple modes (Verma et al., 2022a).

10.4 DESIGN CONSIDERATIONS FOR MULTIMODAL DIALOGUE INTERFACES

To develop multimodal dialogue interfaces that are equally intuitive, efficient, and accessible, it is essential to carefully analyze several varied parameters. Fundamental design factors for multimodal dialogue interfaces are discussed further below.

10.4.1 USER-CENTERED DESIGN

In building multimodal dialogue interfaces, the end user is at the core of the design process. Creating the interface that meets the objectives of the target audience calls for knowing their needs, preferences, and behaviors.

- **User Research:** Employ user studies to understand more about the traits, objectives, and use of the intended audience. This study supports in driving design choices and verifies that the user interface aligns with user expectations.
- **Persona Development:** As part of the layout process, construct user profiles that portray various user archetypes. By employing these personas, artists are more equipped to understand user wants and preferences and make designs that appeal to them.
- **User Testing and Iteration:** To obtain suggestions that will improve the efficiency of the interface, continually test and develop the idea with real clients. The iterative upgrades can be accomplished by highlighting areas of development, trouble spots, or ambiguity during user testing sessions.

10.4.2 INTERFACE DESIGN PRINCIPLES

For brevity, uniformity, and accessibility, multimodal dialogue interfaces must conform to standard design concepts. Here are some important design guidelines to keep in mind:

- **Simplicity:** Eliminate needless complication or clutter by retaining an easy-to-use interface. To minimize cognitive load and boost user comprehension, employ clear and brief language, simple navigation, and well-organized content.
- **Consistency:** Preserve the design uniform across different channels and communication styles. Establish graphic and behavioral patterns that users quickly absorb and recognize while making sure that same actions or commands generate consistent responses.
- **Feedback and Guidance:** Set up consumer-specific feedback, inform consumers how the device is performing, and drive them along the interaction. This may involve employing haptic feedback, aural cues, or visual signals to support user choices and system reactions.
- **Error Handling:** Design error-handling systems that clearly explain errors and offer tips for improvement. When errors arise, be sure to render message clear, give assistance in fixing them, and make sure error messages are concise and helpful.

10.4.3 INPUT AND OUTPUT MODALITIES

A few input and output modalities are readily available by multimodal dialogue interfaces; hence, thought ought to be put in their selection and integrating. Challenges for input and output modalities involve the following:

- **Input Modalities:** Pick input modalities that correspond with the individual needs of the users and the intended use. For instance, look at the applications of speech, text, touch, gestures, or even cameras or accelerometers as sensors. Allow people to quickly switch between modalities in tune with their choice or the demands of the job at hand.
- **Output Modalities:** Select output modalities that permit users to acquire information and feedback in an efficient manner. According to the content and the user's competencies, various mediums such as text, speech, photos, videos, and even haptic feedback can be applied. Create the user interface with data presented in a way that is understandable, captivating, and precise (Kölker et al., 2019).

10.4.4 DISPLAY AND FEEDBACK MODALITIES

To foster clear interactions and understanding in multimodal dialogue interfaces, consider the presentation and input modalities. Considerations for projection and feedback methods involve the following:

- **Visual Display:** Incorporate artistic elements, such as text, photos, icons, or illustrations, in order to transmit information concisely and visually. Use suitable color contrasts and text sizes to keep the visual design comprehensible.
- **Auditory Feedback:** Use audio cues that lead the user along the interaction, such as speech output, sound effects, or voice prompts. Consider the sound quality, volume, and rhythm of auditory feedback to ensure it is not too distracting and is simpler to interpret.
- **Tactile or Haptic Feedback:** To optimize the user experience, implement tactile or haptic feedback where required. Users may get an experience of touch and physical interaction via vibrations, contact-based interactions, or force feedback (Zhang et al., 2020).

10.4.5 CONTEXT AND ENVIRONMENT CONSIDERATIONS

In multimodal dialogue systems, context is necessary for promoting effective discourse while offering appropriate responses. These systems improve user understanding and response by taking consideration of a variety of context-related characteristics, notably user intent, personalization, ambiguity resolution, cohesiveness, environmental factors, and multifaceted integration.

Multimodal dialogue systems must consider user intent when attempting to deliver relevant and precise responses. The system can determine its fundamental goal and adapt its responses by looking at interaction history, user preferences, and the flow of the conversation. The user experience is further improved by personalization, which adapts the dialogue based on user information and preferences (Verma et al., 2021).

Context can help with another problem, the fixation of ambiguity. Multimodal dialogue systems can clarify concerns and produce exact answers by drawing on past contextual and user-specific data. References to prior exchanges help to preserve coherence and continuity, resulting in a conversation which flows well and is interesting. Environmental context information adds another dimension of prominence. The system can alter its replies appropriately by considering variables such as time, location, and device conditions. By doing this, it is made sure that the subject matter is still relevant to its circumstances.

Additionally, the combination of data from various channels helps to create a more thorough picture of the intended use. Multimodal dialogue systems capture a more complete context by combining speech, text, gestures, facial expressions, and other modalities, enabling more precise and contextually relevant reactions (Verma et al., 2022b).

10.5 MULTIMODAL FUSION AND COMPREHENSION

In multimodal dialogue systems, integration and awareness are essential because they merge data from several modalities to provide an in-depth knowledge of user inputs. Four substantial components of multimodal fusion and comprehension are discussed below.

10.5.1 INFORMATION FUSION TECHNIQUES

For developing a cohesive picture of the user's input, information fusion techniques integrate and combine data from several modalities. Depending on the distinctive requirements and features of the dialogue system, various fusion techniques, such as early fusion, late fusion, or hybrid fusion, can be employed. While late fusion incorporates modalities at higher-level depictions or decision-making phases, early fusion combines raw modalities at the characteristic level. In order to maximize the use of both early and late fusion's advantages, hybrid fusion combines the two approaches (Dumas et al., 2009).

10.5.2 FUSION AT DIFFERENT LEVELS OF DIALOGUE PROCESSING

- **Perception-Level Fusion:** In challenges like voice recognition or lip-reading, integration at the observation level entails unifying input from many modalities at an early stage.
- **Semantic-Level Fusion:** Unification at the semantic level deals with combining higher-level semantic data derived from several modalities. In order to develop a solid understanding of the user's intent and context, this requires merging semantic models from speech recognition, NLU, and computer vision.
- **Dialogue-Level Fusion:** Fusion at the dialogue level takes into consideration the context and history of every exchange when combining and integrating multimodal data. It enables the system to keep the dialogue coherent and to interpret the user's inputs within this framework.

10.5.3 CONTEXTUAL AND TEMPORAL INTEGRATION

For multimodal fusion and understanding, contextual and temporal integration is needed. In order to precisely interpret the user's inputs, contextual fusion involves bringing together contextual information from earlier dialogue turns or other knowledge sources. The objective of temporal integration is to coordinate information from many modalities as it varies across time. It is possible to use approaches like time-stamping, temporal alignment models, or Recurrent Neural Networks (RNNs) to ensure that multimodal inputs are accurately integrated in corresponding temporal contexts (Bernsen & Dybkjær, 2009b).

10.5.4 MULTIMODAL GROUNDING AND REFERENCE RESOLUTION

Linking linguistic references with pertinent individuals or objects in the environment is often referred to as multimodal grounding and reference resolution. The framework must link a user's remark of the red cup, for instance, to the red cup that is present in the situation. To effectively recognize and resolve references, it is necessary to comprehend the user's multimodal inputs, such as imagery, spatial context, or other clues. Effective multimodal grounding and reference resolution can be accomplished using strategies like visual object recognition, spatial reasoning, or attention mechanisms (Verma et al., 2023a).

10.6 MULTIMODAL PROCESSING TECHNOLOGIES

Multimodal processing technologies correspond to a compilation of techniques and tools used to examine and incorporate numerous modalities that include speech, text, gestures, images, and other sensory inputs to effectively interpret, fuse, and generate multimodal data. Multimodal processing technologies are illustrated in Figure 10.2 and discussed in more detail below.

- **Natural Language Processing (NLP)**: NLP technologies cover approaches to text parsing, named entity recognition, sentiment analysis, and language modeling. NLP technologies serve to decode and interpret human language and contribute for multimodal dialogue systems' processing of textual inputs.
- **Automatic Speech Recognition (ASR)**: ASR technologies transcribe verbal speech into text, permitting the system to process and understand user speech inputs. To transcribe spoken words, ASR systems include strategies like acoustic modeling, language modeling, and speech signal processing.
- **Computer Vision**: The research and comprehension of visual inputs, such as graphics and films, is the primary thrust of computer vision technologies. To extract beneficial details from visual data, techniques like object identification, image labeling, facial recognition, and scene understanding are applied.
- **Gesture Recognition**: Approaches and technologies for analyzing and decoding user gestures and body language, with the aim of assisting non-verbal interaction in multimodal dialogue systems.
- **Dialogue Management**: Dialogue management involves the use of techniques and algorithms that govern the direction and layout of a conversation, including turn-taking, context tracking, and generating autonomous responses (Verma et al., 2021b).

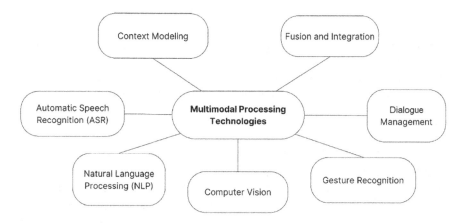

FIGURE 10.2 Multimodal processing technologies.

- **Fusion and Integration**: Procedures for integrating and merging data from numerous input modalities to develop an extensive understanding of user inputs may include early fusion, late fusion, or attention processes.
- **Context Modeling**: Simulation of the dialogue history, user preferences, and information particular to a given task are just a few examples of the approaches used to capture and represent the contextual information that affects how user inputs are interpreted.

10.7 APPLICATIONS OF MULTIMODAL DIALOGUE SYSTEMS

Systems for multimodal communication have many uses in various areas. The ones that follow are some major domains in which multimodal dialogue systems are implemented.

10.7.1 VIRTUAL ASSISTANTS AND INTELLIGENT AGENTS

Virtual assistants and intelligent agents, like voice-activated smart speakers or chatbots, frequently use multimodal interactions. With the application of these innovations, users can take part in a natural manner using speech, text, and visual inputs to bring out activities, get information, administer smart devices, or use resources.

10.7.2 HUMAN–ROBOT INTERACTION

Systems for multimodal communication are critical in boosting human–robot interaction. Robots are more likely to interpret and adapt to user demands and inquiries when multiple methods are used. This renders it feasible to connect intuitively and naturally with robots in a wide range of settings such as home automation, healthcare, manufacturing, or customer service (Khang & Rath et al., 2023).

10.7.3 ASSISTIVE TECHNOLOGIES

Systems for multimodal discourse have several uses in assistive technology, helping people with deficiencies or special needs. These systems strengthen users' freedom and quality of life by enabling them to express themselves and operate machinery using speech, gestures, or other accessible modalities and by accommodating multiple modalities (Verma et al., 2023b).

10.7.4 GAMING AND ENTERTAINMENT

Providing engaging and interactive instances, multimodal dialogue systems have been employed in gaming and cultural settings. Users can interact with simulated characters, manage game procedures, or participate in narrative through speech, gestures, or body movements, resulting in a higher-quality gaming or entertainment experience.

10.7.5 Healthcare and Rehabilitation

Multimodal dialogue systems have been employed in healthcare and rehabilitation settings to foster better interactions between patients, healthcare professionals, and cognitive healthcare systems. With the help of these technologies, people can monitor their health problems and get prescription reminders, personalized health advice, or assistance with rehabilitation exercises (Verma et al., 2022b).

10.8 CHALLENGES AND FUTURE DIRECTIONS

Addressing several issues and growing the capabilities of these systems are the primary challenges and prospects for multimodal systems. Challenges include gathering and labeling a variety of data formats, accomplishing precise modality alignment, quantifying, and successfully employing context, managing noise and robustness issues, and fixing ethical and privacy issues.

Future directions involve constructing multimodal systems with higher social intelligence while improving fusion techniques for better modal integration. They are additionally enabling tailored and adaptive interfaces and incorporating new technologies like Augmented Reality (AR), Virtual Reality (VR), and Brain–Computer Interfaces (BCIs). These improvements aim to improve multimodal dialogue systems' effectiveness, authenticity, and user satisfaction, paving the way to more interactive and customized human–machine interactions (Bayoudh et al., 2021).

10.8.1 Technical Challenges

Multimodal dialogue systems must efficiently detect and comprehend various modalities, merge and synthesize multimodal data, process noisy or ambiguous inputs, and attain seamless synchronization and accordance between modalities, in addition to technical barriers. To address these issues, further advances in machine learning, NLP, computer vision, and human–computer user interface are required (Verma et al., 2023c).

10.8.2 Ethical and Privacy Consideration

As multimodal dialogue systems proliferate, ethical questions concerning data usage, privacy, and potential biases come into play. Ethical planning and execution of multimodal dialogue systems demands preserving user privacy, guaranteeing fair and transparent system behavior, eradicating biases in data and algorithms, and complying with ethical standards (Verma et al., 2022c).

10.8.3 User Adoption and Acceptance

Multimodal dialogue systems face challenges with user acceptance and deployment. Users' willingness to make use of these innovations may vary depending on their choices, skills, or cultural backgrounds. User adoption and fulfillment can be increased by building user-centered interfaces, considering into account unique user needs, and offering customized and adaptable interactions (Verma et al., 2020).

10.8.4 Future Trends and Innovations

Progress and improvements in multimodal discourse systems point to a bright future. Systems will become more specific and contextually aware as a result of improvements in deep learning, multimodal fusion techniques, context-aware processing, and NLU. Moreover, developments in AR, VR, and BCIs might advance multimodal interactions even further and open new applications (Shukla et al., 2023).

10.9　CONCLUSION

Systems for multimodal discourse are crucial in overcoming the communication and comprehension gap between humans and machines. These systems' numerous interfaces enable simpler and intuitive user interactions, optimizing usability and client satisfaction. They may transform several kinds of industries by elevating productivity, accessibility, and engagement. Multimodal dialogue systems have unparalleled future potential. Development and technological advances are going to persist to solve the issues while strengthening the capabilities of these systems over time (Khang & Misra et al., 2023).

Improved multimodal integration approaches, greater context modeling, individualized interactions, and the implementation of cutting-edge technologies like AR, VR, and BCIs might all constitute forthcoming advances. Multimodal dialogue systems, which facilitate virtual assistants, intelligent agents, robots, and other dynamic platforms, are likely to grow more and increasingly prevalent in our daily lives. In a nutshell, by enabling more efficient and authentic interaction, multimodal dialogue systems have the possibility to transform human–computer interactions. These technologies will continue to develop and play a significant part in establishing the future of human–machine interactions by tackling obstacles, considering ethical issues, and embracing advances in technology (Khang & Hahanov et al., 2022).

REFERENCES

Allen, J., "Challenge Discussion: Advancing Multimodal Dialogue." *The Handbook of Multimodal-Multisensor Interfaces: Language Processing, Software, Commercialization, and Emerging Directions - Volume 3*, 2019, doi: 10.1145/3233795.3233802.

Aly, A., & Tapus, A., "On designing expressive robot behavior: The effect of affective cues on interaction." *SN Computer Science*, vol. 1, no. 6, 2020, doi: 10.1007/s42979-020-00263-3.

Bayoudh, K., Knani, R., Hamdaoui, F., & Mtibaa, A., "A survey on deep multimodal learning for computer vision: Advances, trends, applications, and datasets." *The Visual Computer*, vol. 38, no. 8, pp. 2939–2970, 2021, doi: 10.1007/s00371-021-02166-7.

Bernsen, N. O., & Dybkjær, L., "Interaction with the System." Multimodal Usability, pp. 263–286, 2009a, doi: 10.1007/978-1-84882-553-6_12.

Bernsen, N. O., & Dybkjær, L., "Multimodal Usability: Conclusions and Future Work." Multimodal Usability, pp. 413–419, 2009b, doi: 10.1007/978-1-84882-553-6_18.

Chakraborty, R., Pandharipande, M., & Kopparapu, S. K., "Analyzing Emotion in Spontaneous Speech." 2017, doi: 10.1007/978-981-10-7674-9.

Constantin, S., Eyiokur, F. I., Yaman, D., Bärmann, L., & Waibel, A., "Interactive Multimodal Robot Dialog Using Pointing Gesture Recognition." Lecture Notes in Computer Science, pp. 640–657, 2023, doi: 10.1007/978-3-031-25075-0_43.

Dawley, L., & Dede, C., "Situated Learning in Virtual Worlds and Immersive Simulations." *Handbook of Research on Educational Communications and Technology*, pp. 723–734, 2013, doi: 10.1007/978-1-4614-3185-5_58.

Deldjoo, Y., Trippas, J. R., & Zamani, H., "Towards Multi-Modal Conversational Information Seeking." Proceedings of the 44th International ACM SIGIR Conference on Research and Development in Information Retrieval, 2021, doi: 10.1145/3404835.3462806.

Delgado, R. L.-C., & Araki, M., "Spoken, Multilingual and Multimodal Dialogue Systems." 2005, doi: 10.1002/0470021578.

Diraco, G., Rescio, G., Siciliano, P., & Leone, A., "Review on human action recognition in smart living: sensing technology, multimodality, real-time processing, interoperability, and resource-constrained processing." *Sensors*, vol. 23, no. 11, p. 5281, 2023, doi: 10.3390/s23115281.

Dumas, B., Lalanne, D., & Oviatt, S., "Multimodal Interfaces: A Survey of Principles, Models and Frameworks." *Lecture Notes in Computer Science*, pp. 3–26, 2009, doi: 10.1007/978-3-642-00437-7_1.

Edelman, S., "Language and other complex behaviors: Unifying characteristics, computational models, neural mechanisms." *Language Sciences*, vol. 62, pp. 91–123, 2017, doi: 10.1016/j.langsci.2017.04.003.

Evans, M. A., Feenstra, E., Ryon, E., & McNeill, D., "A multimodal approach to coding discourse: Collaboration, distributed cognition, and geometric reasoning." International Journal of *Computer-Supported Collaborative Learning*, vol. 6, no. 2, pp. 253–278, 2011, doi: 10.1007/s11412-011-9113-0.

Gibbon, D., Mertins, I., & Moore, R. K., "Audio-Visual and Multimodal Speech-Based Systems." *Handbook of Multimodal and Spoken Dialogue Systems*, pp. 102–203, 2000, doi: 10.1007/978-1-4615-4501-9_2.

Heloir, A., & Kipp, M., "Requirements for a Gesture Specification Language." Gesture in Embodied Communication and Human-Computer Interaction, pp. 207–218, 2010, doi: 10.1007/978-3-642-12553-9_18.

Herzog, G., Ndiaye, A., Merten, S., Kirchmann, H., Becker, T., & Poller, P., "Large-scale software integration for spoken language and multimodal dialog systems." *Natural Language Engineering*, vol. 10, no. 3, pp. 283–305, 2004, doi: 10.1017/s1351324904003444.

Jaimes, A., & Sebe, N., "Multimodal Human Computer Interaction: A Survey." Computer Vision in Human-Computer Interaction, pp. 1–15, 2005, doi: 10.1007/11573425_1.

Johansson, F., "Microscopic Modeling and Simulation of Pedestrian Traffic." 2013, doi: 10.3384/lic.diva-101085.

Johar, S., "Language, Communication and Human Behaviour." *Emotion, Affect and Personality in Speech*, pp. 17–23, 2015, doi: 10.1007/978-3-319-28047-9_3.

Jokinen, K., "Natural Language and Dialogue Interfaces." *Human Factors and Ergonomics*, pp. 1–12, 2009, doi: https://doi.org/10.1201/9781420064995.

Junaid, A., Nawaz, A., Usmani, M. F., Verma, R., & Dhanda, N., "Analyzing the Performance of a DAPP Using Blockchain 3.0." 2023 13th International Conference on Cloud Computing, Data Science & Engineering (Confluence), 2023, doi: 10.1109/confluence56041.2023.10048887.

Khang, A., Hahanov, V., Abbas, G. L., & Hajimahmud, V. A., "Cyber-Physical-Social System and İncident Management," *AI-Centric Smart City Ecosystems: Technologies, Design and Implementation* (1st Ed.), (2022). CRC Press. https://doi.org/10.1201/9781003252542-2

Khang, A., Hajimahmud, V. A., Gupta, S. K., Babasaheb, J., & Morris, G., *AI-Centric Modelling and Analytics: Concepts, Designs, Technologies, and Applications.* (1st Ed.) (2023). CRC Press. https://doi.org/10.1201/9781003400110

Khang, A., Hajimahmud, V. A, Vladimir, Hahanov, & Shah, V., *Advanced IoT Technologies and Applications in the Industry 4.0 Digital Economy* (1st Ed.) (2024). CRC Press. https://doi.org/10.1201/9781003434269

Khang, A., Misra, A., Gupta, S. K., & Shah, V., *AI-Aided IoT Technologies and Applications in the Smart Business and Production.* (1st Ed.) (2023). CRC Press. https://doi.org/10.1201/9781003392224

Khang, A., Muthmainnah, M, Seraj, Prodhan Mahbub Ibna, Yakin, Ahmad Al, Obaid, Ahmad J., & Ranjan Panda, Manas. "AI-Aided Teaching Model for the Education 5.0 Ecosystem" *AI-Based Technologies and Applications in the Era of the Metaverse.* (1st Ed.) (2023). Page (83–104). IGI Global Press. https://doi.org/10.4018/978-1-6684-8851-5.ch004

Khang, A., Rath, Kali Charan, Kumar Satapathy, Suresh, Kumar, Amaresh, Ranjan Das, Sudhansu, & Ranjan Panda, Manas. "Enabling the Future of Manufacturing: Integration of Robotics and IoT to Smart Factory Infrastructure in Industry 4.0." *AI-Based Technologies and Applications in the Era of the Metaverse.* (1st Ed.) (2023). Page (25–50). IGI Global Press. https://doi.org/10.4018/978-1-6684-8851-5.ch002

Khang, A., Shah, V., & Rani, S., *AI-Based Technologies and Applications in the Era of the Metaverse.* (1st Ed.) (2023). IGI Global Press. https://doi.org/10.4018/978-1-6684-8851-5

Kölker, S., Schwinger, F., & Krempels, K.-H., "A Framework for Context-dependent User Interface Adaptation." Proceedings of the 15th International Conference on Web Information Systems and Technologies, 2019, doi: 10.5220/0008487200002366.

Kotenidis, E., Vryzas, N., Veglis, A., & Dimoulas, C., "Integrating chatbot media automations in professional journalism: An evaluation framework." *Future Internet,* vol. 14, no. 11, p. 343, 2022, doi: 10.3390/fi14110343.

Lister, K., Coughlan, T., Iniesto, F., Freear, N., & Devine, P., "Accessible conversational user interfaces." Proceedings of the 17th International Web for All Conference, 2020, doi: 10.1145/3371300.3383343.

Meditskos, G., Kontopoulos, E., Vrochidis, S., & Kompatsiaris, I., "Converness: Ontology-driven conversational awareness and context understanding in multimodal dialogue systems." *Expert Systems,* vol. 37, no. 1, 2019, doi: 10.1111/exsy.12378.

Mohd, T. K., Carvalho, J., & Javaid, A. Y., "Multi-modal data fusion of Voice and EMG data for robotic control." 2017 IEEE 8th Annual Ubiquitous Computing, Electronics and Mobile Communication Conference (UEMCON), 2017, doi: 10.1109/uemcon.2017.8249063.

Möller, S., Smeele, P., Boland, H., & Krebber, J., "Evaluating spoken dialogue systems according to de-facto standards: A case study." *Computer Speech & Language,* vol. 21, no. 1, pp. 26–53, 2007, doi: 10.1016/j.csl.2005.11.003.

Music, S., Prattichizzo, D., & Hirche, S., "Human-Robot Interaction through Fingertip Haptic Devices for Cooperative Manipulation Tasks." 2019 28th IEEE International Conference on Robot and Human Interactive Communication (RO-MAN), 2019, doi: 10.1109/ro-man46459.2019.8956350.

Oviatt, S., "Multimodal Interaction, Interfaces, and Analytics." *Handbook of Human Computer Interaction,* pp. 1–29, 2022, doi: 10.1007/978-3-319-27648-9_22-1.

Popescu-Belis, A., & Carletta, J., "Multimodal signal processing for meetings: An introduction." *Multimodal Signal Processing,* pp. 1–10, 2012, doi: 10.1017/cbo9781139136310.001.

Qian, Y., "Exploring ASR-free end-to-end modeling to improve spoken language understanding in a cloud-based dialog system." 2017 IEEE Automatic Speech Recognition and Understanding Workshop (ASRU), 2017, doi: 10.1109/asru.2017.8268987.

Rath, K. C., Khang, A., & Roy, Debanik, "The Role of Internet of Things (IoT) Technology in Industry 4.0," *Advanced IoT Technologies and Applications in the Industry 4.0 Digital Economy* (1st Ed.) (2024). CRC Press. https://doi.org/10.1201/9781003434269-1

Saddik, A. E., Orozco, M., Eid, M., & Cha, J., "Multimedia Haptics." Springer Series on Touch and Haptic Systems, pp. 145–182, 2011, doi: 10.1007/978-3-642-22658-8_6.

Sarkar, D., "Python for Natural Language Processing." Text Analytics with Python, pp. 69–114, 2019, doi: 10.1007/978-1-4842-4354-1_2.

Sarma, D., & Bhuyan, M. K., "Methods, Databases and Recent Advancement of Vision-Based Hand Gesture Recognition for HCI Systems: A Review." *SN Computer Science*, vol. 2, no. 6, 2021, doi: 10.1007/s42979-021-00827-x.

Sebe, N., "Multimodal interfaces: Challenges and perspectives." *Journal of Ambient Intelligence and Smart Environments*, vol. 1, no. 1, pp. 23–30, 2009, doi: 10.3233/ais-2009-0003.

Sharma, R., "Speech-gesture driven multimodal interfaces for crisis management." *Proceedings of the IEEE*, vol. 91, no. 9, pp. 1327–1354, 2003, doi: 10.1109/jproc.2003.817145.

Shukla, Utkarsh, Dhanda, Namrata, & Verma, Rajat, Augmented Reality Product Showcase E-commerce Application (February 16, 2023). *Available at SSRN:* https://ssrn.com/abstract=4361319 or http://dx.doi.org/10.2139/ssrn.4361319.

Sivanathan, A., Ritchie, J. M., & Lim, T., "A novel design engineering review system with searchable content: Knowledge engineering via real-time multimodal recording." *Journal of Engineering Design*, vol. 28, no. 10, pp. 681–708, 2017, doi: 10.1080/09544828.2017.1393655.

Stan, A., & Lőrincz, B., "Generating the voice of the interactive virtual assistant." *Virtual Assistant*, 2021, doi: 10.5772/intechopen.95510.

Traum, D., "Socially Interactive Agent Dialogue." *The Handbook on Socially Interactive Agents*, pp. 45–76, 2022, doi: 10.1145/3563659.3563663.

Verma, R., & Dhanda, N., "Application of Supply Chain Management in Blockchain and IoT - A Generic Use Case." 2023 13th International Conference on Cloud Computing, Data Science & Engineering (Confluence), 2023c, doi: 10.1109/confluence56041.2023.10048815.

Verma, R., Dhanda, N., & Nagar, V., "Security Concerns in IoT Systems and Its Blockchain Solutions." Cyzber Intelligence and Information Retrieval, pp. 485–495, 2021, doi: 10.1007/978-981-16-4284-5_42.

Verma, R., Dhanda, N., & Nagar, V., "Application of Truffle Suite in a Blockchain Environment." Proceedings of Third International Conference on Computing, Communications, and Cyber-Security, pp. 693–702, 2022a, doi: 10.1007/978-981-19-1142-2_54.

Verma, R., Dhanda, N., & Nagar, V., "Enhancing Security with In-Depth Analysis of Brute-Force Attack on Secure Hashing Algorithms." Proceedings of Trends in Electronics and Health Informatics, pp. 513–522, 2022b, doi: 10.1007/978-981-16-8826-3_44.

Verma, R., Dhanda, N., & Nagar, V., "Towards a Secured IoT Communication: A Blockchain Implementation Through APIs." Proceedings of Third International Conference on Computing, Communications, and Cyber-Security, pp. 681–692, 2022c, doi: 10.1007/978-981-19-1142-2_53.

Verma, R., Dhanda, N., & Nagar, V., Enhancing & Optimizing Security of IoT Systems using Different Components of Industry 4.0. *International Journal of Engineering Trends and Technology*, vol. 70, no. 7, pp. 147–157, 2022d. doi:10.14445/22315381/ijett-v70i7p216.

Verma, R., Dhanda, N., & Nagar, V., Analysing the Security Aspects of IoT Using Blockchain and Cryptographic Algorithms, *International Journal on Recent and Innovation Trends in Computing and Communication*, vol. 11, no. 1s, pp. 13–22, 2023a. doi: 10.17762/ijritcc.v11i1s.5990.

Verma, R., Dhanda, N., Nagar, V., & Dhanda, M., Towards an efficient IOT system by integrating blockchain in IOT. *Journal of Theoretical and Applied Information Technology*, vol. 101, no. 5, 2023b. https://www.jatit.org/volumes/Vol101No5/4Vol101No5.pdf.

Verma, Rajat, Dhanda, Namrata, & Nagar, Vishal, Addressing the issues & challenges of internet of things using blockchain technology. *International Journal of Advanced Science and Technology*, vol. 29, no. 05, pp. 10074–10082, 2020. http://sersc.org/journals/index.php/IJAST/article/view/19491.

Verma, R., Mishra, P. K., Nagar, V., & Mahapatra, S., "Internet of Things and Smart Homes: A Review." *Wireless Sensor Networks and the Internet of Things*, pp. 111–128, 2021a, doi: 10.1201/9781003131229-9.

Verma, R., Nagar, V., & Mahapatra, S., "Introduction to Supervised Learning." *Data Analytics in Bioinformatics*, pp. 1–34, 2021b, doi: 10.1002/9781119785620.ch1.

Vinciarelli, A., "Open challenges in modeling, analysis and synthesis of human behaviour in human–Human and human–Machine interactions." *Cognitive Computation*, vol. 7, no. 4, pp. 397–413, 2015, doi: 10.1007/s12559-015-9326-z.

Wang, H., Li, J., Wu, H., Hovy, E., & Sun, Y., "Pre-trained language models and their applications." *Engineering*, 2022, doi: 10.1016/j.eng.2022.04.024.

Wolfe, S., & Flewitt, R., "New technologies, new multimodal literacy practices and young children." *Cambridge Journal of Education*, vol. 40, no. 4, pp. 387–399, 2010, doi: 10.1080/0305764x.2010.526589.

Zeng, L., "Designing the user interface: Strategies for effective human-computer interaction (5th edition) by B. Shneiderman and C. Plaisant." *International Journal of Human-Computer Interaction*, vol. 25, no. 7, pp. 707–708, 2009, doi: 10.1080/10447310903187949.

Zhang, C., Yang, Z., He, X., & Deng, L., "Multimodal intelligence: Representation learning, information fusion, and applications." *IEEE Journal of Selected Topics in Signal Processing*, vol. 14, no. 3, pp. 478–493, 2020, doi: 10.1109/jstsp.2020.2987728.

Zhu, L., Zhu, Z., Zhang, C., Xu, Y., & Kong, X., "Multimodal sentiment analysis based on fusion methods: A survey." *Information Fusion*, vol. 95, pp. 306–325, 2023, doi: 10.1016/j.inffus.2023.02.028.

11 Artificial Intelligence-Based Human Activity Recognition Using Real-Time Videos

Sumita Gupta and Sapna Gambhir

11.1 INTRODUCTION

The technology in the field of vision has substantially improved over the past several years. Deep neural network technology and the advancement of computer capabilities helped to find solutions to important societal issues. The development of technology has sparked a string of miracles that have made our lives simpler. Examples of cutting-edge algorithms that have introduced human activity recognition (HAR) include image detection, computer vision, and facial recognition. Using computer and machine vision technologies, HAR examines human movements.

Sensors interpret human movement as the result of actions, gestures, or behaviors. Motion data is then provided to the computer, programmed in the form of action instructions, to execute and review the HAR code. Autonomous cars can monitor and forecast pedestrian behavior more comprehensively by recognizing human activity in video, which encourages more reliable driving. The technology may also be used to teach a new employee how to properly carry out a task or to allow a person to practice dancing or fitness movements. Additionally, HAR technology has a wide range of applications, including virtual reality settings, human–robot interfaces, and gaming controllers.

11.1.1 BACKGROUND

Raw sensor readings from the HAR dataset serve as the input to HAR models, and their output is an estimate of the user's movement behaviors. Due to issues like historical confusion, partial occlusion, changes in scale, perspective, lighting, and sight, distinguishing human sports from film sequences or still photographs is difficult. For some programmers, a multi-hobby popularity device is required, including robots for characterizing human behavior, human–laptop interface, and video surveillance systems (Vrigkas et al., 2015).

The objective of HAR is to recognize the actions of more than one agent from a series of observations of actions and surrounding circumstances. This chapter focuses on one such issue that has grown significantly. Since the 1980s, a few computer science organizations have taken an interest in this field of study because it

DOI: 10.1201/9781003438137-11

offers tailored assistance for a variety of applications and its connections to several other fields of study, including sociology, human-computer interaction, and medicine. Recognizing types of activity in a live video may be used for a variety of purposes, including the construction of security systems and intelligent environments (Bhatia et al., 2023).

11.1.2 Need for Human Activity Recognition

Often, HAR is used in medical diagnostics, specifically for monitoring elderly people. It can also be used to lower crime rates through monitoring. The ability to recognize regular activities can create a smart home environment, identify driving patterns, and encourage secure transit, for example. Furthermore, military activity may be located using HAR (Domingo et al., 2022).

One of the primary uses of HAR systems is abnormal activity detection, which helps to spot unusual human behavior and promote safety in public spaces like train stations, airports, and shopping centers. Applications have been created for content-based video search, entertainment, human–computer interaction, ambient supported living, and human–robot interaction. Each of these applications makes use of a recognition system that has been trained to identify various activities in each circumstance.

Using computer vision algorithms to locate players or recognize athletes' moves or activities is known as human action recognition in sports. Warm-ups, physical conditioning, sports training, tournaments, and games may all be tracked. Human activity recognition can be used to analyze distinct actions performed by different athletes or several executions of one athlete, or track their performance in order to assist in teaching a technique or developing an athlete's style. An automated statistical analysis of a sporting event or the performance of a specific athlete may also be provided by HAR.

11.1.3 Technology

11.1.3.1 Sensor-Based Human Activity Recognition

Systems for surveillance, behavior analysis, patient tracking, ambient assisted living (AAL), and a variety of healthcare systems that call for either direct or indirect contact between people and smart devices employ HAR. Two categories—sensor-based and vision-based—comprise all HAR systems. The first category, which makes use of sensors and other similar devices, allows the system to collect data as if a human were wearing wearable sensors attached to their body. Smart watches with built-in communication and fitness wristbands are examples of wearable technology. Because wearable technology is inexpensive, widespread uses have been made possible such as for monitoring one's health, receiving rehabilitative training, and avoiding disease as shown in Figure 11.1.

The first component of a sensor-based HAR system is *sensors*, which can be designed to detect a wide range of inputs from the surrounding environment, including temperature, humidity, light, sound, pressure, and motion. These sensors may

FIGURE 11.1 Sensor-based HAR architecture.

be positioned all over the body, including within the body and on the ears, eyes, and skin. They can also be embedded in clothing, jewelry, or other wearable devices. Wearable sensors include smartphones applications and cameras, among others.

The second component of a sensor-based HAR system is the *processing unit*, which is responsible for receiving the sensor data, processing it, and making decisions based on the information received. This unit can be a microcontroller, a computer, or a specialized circuit designed to perform specific tasks. The processing unit can analyze the sensor data to determine the user's location, activity, or health status.

Feature extraction is the third component of a sensor-based HAR system. It is a crucial stage since it entails the conversion of raw sensor data into a set of pertinent characteristics that can be used to categorize various human activities. There are different techniques of performing feature extraction. For example, one method uses statistical features, such as mean, variance, standard deviation, and correlation coefficients, to determine these attributes. They can offer details on the variability and dispersion of sensor data, which can be utilized to differentiate between various activities.

Another method uses frequency domain features. These qualities are also determined using the statistical properties of the sensor data, such as mean, variance, standard deviation, and correlation coefficients. They can provide information on the variation and spread of sensor data, which can be used to distinguish between different activities. Extracting time-domain features can also be used to retrieve parameters such as amplitude, slope, and zero-crossing rate. They can offer details on the signal's temporal properties, such as its duration, speed, and frequency of motion.

In sensor-based HAR, classification models are used to categorize various activities based on the characteristics retrieved from raw sensor data. Some of the most common classification models used in sensor-based HAR are support vector machines (SVMs), decision trees, and random forest generators. Due to its excellent accuracy and capacity for handling non-linear data, SVM is a well-liked classification model used in sensor-based HAR. It functions by locating a hyperplane that divides the data into several classes.

11.1.3.2 Vision-Based Human Activity Recognition

Vision-based HAR entails identifying human activity from movies and photographs, with the system transporting the data from the media. Remote communication approaches aim to lessen the difficulty of human–computer contact by enabling humans to communicate in a natural and intelligible way. In reality, a human can express ideas or thoughts by using gestures or a mix of actions (Khang & Hajimahmud et al., 2024).

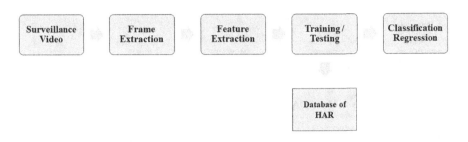

FIGURE 11.2   Vision-based HAR architecture.

A Vision-based HAR approach may have an edge over other strategies because it discerns behavior using gathered photos or recorded video sequences. Videos taken by several cameras is a challenging problem to solve. The main strategy employed is computer vision. Applications for vision-based activity detection include surveillance, user interface design, robot learning, and human–computer interaction. There have been major advancements in the recognition of visual activity, as shown in Figure 11.2.

Taking video data of human activity is the first step in vision-based HAR architecture. The video data may be gathered from a variety of devices, including mobile cameras, wearable cameras, and security cameras. The information may be recorded in many forms including thermal, depth, and RGB pictures.

Frame extraction is the second step in vision-based HAR, which entails choosing pertinent frames from the video data that capture human activity. Various methods can be used to execute tasks based on vision, such as key frame selection which chooses frames that best capture important points in the action, as well as object tracking, motion analysis, and saliency detection. Another method is uniform sampling, which picks frames from the video stream at regular intervals. This is beneficial for activities like running or walking that have a set pace or length. It is also possible to use event-triggered sampling, which chooses frames depending on particular activities that take place.

Extracting pertinent characteristics from the video data is the third step in vision-based HAR. Features can be extracted using various methods including histograms of oriented gradients (HOGs) which extracts characteristics from the gradient and form of the human body. Another method for extracting features from the image's local patches is the scale-invariant feature transform (SIFT). The deep levels of the neural network are mined to extract features with the help of CNNs.

Creating vision-based HAR systems involves training and testing datasets. In order to train the classification model, a portion of the dataset is used. The dataset is divided into two components: training and validation sets. The former is used to fine-tune the hyperparameters and guard against overfitting, while the latter is used to optimize the model parameters. The trained model is assessed on a different subset of the dataset, known as the test set. Performance metrics for the model include accuracy, precision, recall, and F1-score. The trained and improved model may then be used in a real-world setting, such a security system or smart home, to detect human activity.

The vision-based HAR computer technique consists of four phases: detection, tracking, action recognition, and high participation evaluation. Vision-based solutions do not require people to wear cumbersome gadgets on their bodies, in contrast with sensor-based HAR systems. As a result, these technologies were able to gain public approval due to being nonintrusive.

11.1.4 CHALLENGES

Despite significant advancements in computer vision, a variety of issues still plague modern algorithms, resulting in the incorrect classification of human behaviors or actions. For an activity detection job from a videotape of movement patterns, the activity recognition model can identify jogging as running quickly, but it cannot manage distinctions between classes. Classifiers based on ML are unable to process vast volumes of data while maintaining the greatest degree of accuracy and the fastest classification time. Data management is the main challenge for researchers.

An optimized HAR algorithm should be able to discriminate between actions from different classes while generalizing across variations within one class. This will become more challenging as there are more action classes and as class overlap grows. In busy or chaotic environments, it could be more challenging to locate a certain person. Additionally, the recording could conceal some of the subject. Additionally, it was discovered via various trials that the model provided high accuracy for some tasks while providing lesser accuracy for others. The processor's performance was another problem encountered when carrying out HAR. The model will not provide accurate findings if the processor is faulty or sluggish.

11.1.5 OBJECTIVE

In this chapter, additional effort is made to focus on the problems with multi-class identification. To choose the optimal model, the outcomes of all the different ways are compared. Additionally, the primary goal is to identify human activities utilizing vision-based technologies, particularly in sports. We used the UCF50 dataset, which is made up of 50 action categories and real-world YouTube recordings of various sporting events. Different HAR techniques, including CNN-LSTM, LRCN, and ConvLSTM, are used on this dataset. After testing the models on recorded videos, this chapter proposes a HAR system on real-time videos with multi-person detection. An architecture and implementation are also discussed.

11.2 LITERATURE REVIEW

This section provides an overview of the existing methods or algorithms used for HAR.

The CNN approach is used to build the neural networks model (Xu & TingQiu (2021), and the random gradation reduction algorithm is used to optimize the model's variables and detect six possible actions such as walking, walking upstairs and downstairs, standing, sitting, and jogging. In neural network models, the optimizing process random gradation reduction was widely used to discover the parameter of the models that best fit the predicted and real outputs. Research suggested an LSTM-RNN deep neural network to offer a HAR system (Pienaar & Malekian, 2019). With only a few hundred epochs, the network can learn all six classes effectively and efficiently and achieve excellent accuracy.

Xia et al. (2020) suggested a novel deep neural network for recognizing human behavior that blends LSTM and convolution layers. The completely connected layers are primarily the focus of the CNN weight parameters. In response, a global average pooling (GAP) layer is used in place of the fully linked layers beneath the convolution layer, substantially lowering the model parameters while retaining a high identification rate. A batch normalization (BN) layer is also added after the GAP layer to hasten the model's convergence, and a clear result is obtained.

A thorough analysis of the current research initiatives on a video-based HAR system, including every crucial system component, such as object segmentation, extraction of feature and representation, action recognition and classifications, has been discussed (Ke et al., 2013). In addition, the surveillance, entertainment, and healthcare industries are explored as three areas of implementation for video-based HAR, as shown in Figure 11.3.

Subetha and Chitrakala (2016) demonstrated many HAR algorithms, approaches, and types of classifications used for contact between entities and objects in both still photos and movies as well as various human–human interaction strategies. The objective is to present a thorough analysis and comparison of various methods and approaches for recognizing human activity.

A CNN-LSTM strategy (Mutegeki & Han, 2020) for recognizing human actions has been developed and aims to enhance the performance of activity detection by utilizing a CNN's robust feature extraction capabilities while implementing the

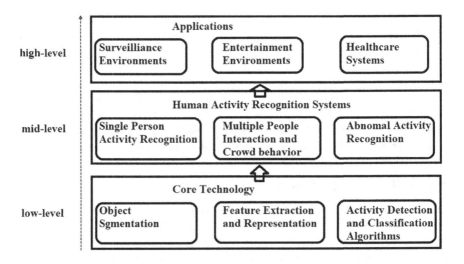

FIGURE 11.3 An illustration of a basic mechanism for recognizing human activities.

works of an LSTM model for prediction of period collection and classifications. Because it is geographically and temporally deep, this model outperformed earlier algorithms for deep understanding that used unprocessed signals as input. In all situations, it beat the competition, particularly on the iSPL dataset where it had about 2% less Softmax loss and over 1% greater accuracy than the nearest competitor. Time knowledge is crucial in the series of actions that humans take. Long short-term memory models are useful for capturing temporal information and avoiding temporal dependence issues, while CNNs are useful for automatically extracting discriminative features via convolutional procedures.

ResIncConvLSTM-based architecture (Khater et al., 2022) was proposed based on ResIncConvLSTM layer, a new residual and origin-based layer, for resolving HAR problems. The KTH data collection was considered. On the Weizmann, UCF, and KTH Sports Activity dataset, the ResIncConvLSTM-based design outperformed the baseline ConvLSTM model by 11, 21, and 7%, respectively. The experimental outcomes further demonstrate the suggested architecture's superiority over existing cutting-edge architectures. With only a few hundred epochs, the network can learn all six classes effectively and efficiently and achieve excellent accuracy.

An RNN and one-dimensional CNN deep learning model (Zhu et al., 2020) for categorizing human behavior was discussed. The model was tested on a seven-class dataset that had undergone short-term Fourier transform (STFT) pre-processing. The model considered parameters such as kernel size, width, and depth to optimize the network. The approach performs more effectively than cutting-edge networks at the same time. According to the findings, the suggested network architecture is effective in removing global temporal characteristics from radar signals. Additionally, the network is a class of simple yet effective models.

Deep & Zheng (2019) used a CNN as well as LSTM model combination for activity recognition on data collected via smartphones. The LSTM model was the sole one used in the experiment, which was run on the same dataset. Comparing CNN-LSTM to the LSTM model, the first model was more accurate. The experimental outcomes also showed that, when applied to the same dataset and other state-of-the-art techniques, the CNN-LSTM model outperformed them.

The merits of the CNN and LSTM models are utilized by the suggested architecture to identify human activity. Time knowledge is crucial in the series of actions that humans take. Long short-term memory models are useful for capturing temporal information and avoiding temporal dependence issues, while CNNs are useful for automatically extracting discriminative features via convolutional procedures. The suggested design successfully predicted simple and constrained tasks carried out by a single individual with significant recognition scores. If several tasks are carried out by several people, the model might not attain the same level of accuracy (Khang & Misra et al., 2023).

A multi-sector CNN BiLSTM design for HAR was presented that works directly with actual data received from sensing devices with minimum pre-processing (Challa et al., 2021). The model makes use of CNN and BiLSTM to detect a mix of local as well as long-duration relationships in sequence data. The special arrangement improves extraction of feature by recording numerous local connections, and it can recognize basic actions such as running, walking, sitting, and so on. Uzzaman et al. (2022) recognized human behavior and activities and proposed an architecture based on a CNN. Deep learning architecture such as simple CNN, CNN+LSTM hybrid model such as ConvLSTM, and LRCN are used as training models.

The innovative extractions of three distinct forms of information from RGB video, as well as the method used to choose and normalize the required characteristics, are presented in Domingo et al. (2022). The problem of action categorization in videos has been investigated to improve with selection and normalization. It mostly focuses on situations that are produced in domestic settings, including homes or nursing homes. In this study, many technologies were analyzed and assessed. In intelligent environments and social robots, indoor activity recognition is a crucial component for analysis and decision-making, particularly when engaging with elderly people. It might be challenging to identify activity from video sequences since there can be a wide variety of situations that are obscure to the human eye (Khang & Rana et al., 2023).

The recognition rate has dramatically increased recently due to CNN's growth. It is challenging to compare findings since numerous datasets have arisen and writers assess their models using various measures. To determine the activity carried out indoors, the system combines data from features, environmental objects, and human bones. It was demonstrated in two separate approaches, one combining the relevant data supplies into one deep learning model and the other using SVM to get the final classification. In order to collect data from the 3-sec clip containing 90 frames, it employs recurrent networks, most specifically LSTM.

The STAIR dataset, which consisted of 64,282 films and 78 classifications was used to test the system (Bhatia et al., 2023; Bansal & Gupta, 2021). The design demonstrated that the outcomes of other models that just rely on the characteristics of various video frames were enhanced. Although LRCN performs better (0:85%) than YOLO+OP (0:65%), the accuracy is increased by 0:865% when YOLO+OP+ (LRCN) characteristics are combined. The obtained findings greatly outperform the earlier STAIR results for two-stream CNN (0:737%) and three-stream CNN (0:765%). Additionally, a different strategy utilizing SVM was assessed using our model, and encouraging results were found (0:873%).

A divide-and-conquer strategy based on 1D CNN is proposed in Cho & Yoon (2018). They used a confusion matrix to detect abstract activities and then built a two-stage HAR method. Numerous potential enhancements in the accuracy of activity detection were achieved by a straightforward technique for sharpening test data using a Gaussian filter. The divide-and-conquer strategy used by the 1D CNN was significant for both improving the HAR model and determining an appropriate value for sharpening the test data. Once the abstract activities suited for the first step can be discovered, this strategy is straightforward and simple to use (Khang & Hahanov et al., 2022).

After the extensive study of various existing methods and algorithms used in a HAR system, a comparison is given in Table 11.1 based on various parameters such as models used, devices used, recognized activities, and technique advantages and disadvantages.

TABLE 11.1

Comparison between Existing Techniques Used in a HAR System

Ref.	Model	Algorithm	Dataset/Device	Activity	Technique Advantages	Technique Disadvantages
Ke et al., 2013	HMM, DBN	K nearest neighbor (K-NN), Binary tree	Static camera	Tennis, human gestures, pedestrian traffic, soccer	Good representation, tiny state space, low-dimensional feature space	Long training time
Subetha & Chitrakala, 2016	2D model, 3D Model, HMM	Random forest	N/A	One-to-one interaction, one-to-many interaction, abnormal crowd behavior	Resilience of the velocity profile	Long training time, cannot handle unmanaged video, manually inserted annotation
Mutegeki & Han, 2020	CNN-LSTM, CNN_LSTM Dense, LSTM_Dense	N/A	Inertial measurement unit (IMU)	Moving when standing, sitting, lying	Good setup will simplify the model	Some settings could not get the expected outcomes
Xu & TingQiu, 2021	CNN	Stochastic gradient descent method (SGDM)	Gyroscope, accelerometer	walking, upstairs, and downstairs, sitting, standing, jogging	Prevents overfitting and improves the accuracy of feature map categorization	Unable to adequately describe context for improved semantic behavioral recognition
Pienaar & Malekian, 2019	LSTM-RNN, DNN	N/A	Sensors for movement, light, motion, GPS, camera, and microphone	Jogging, sitting, standing	Accuracy in tests and training is around 90%	Predicting stair climbing and standing vs. sitting is difficult
Xia et al., 2020	CNN-LSTM, CNN, DeepConvLSTM	N/A	Dataset	Walking, sitting, standing, lying down	Performance of a GAP layer was superior	Fully interconnected layers did not produce the expected outcomes

(Continued)

TABLE 11.1 *(Continued)*

Comparison between Existing Techniques Used in a HAR System

Ref.	Model	Algorithm	Dataset/Device	Activity	Technique Advantages	Technique Disadvantages
Gupta et al., 2022	CNN, LSTM	SVM, k means clustering	RFID devices	Jumping, bending down, extending legs, walking	Growth of HAR devices	Synchronized activities, complex and composite Activities, future action forecast
Khater et al., 2022	ConvLSTM, ResIncConvLSTM	SVM	Smart home assistant devices, KTH dataset	Boxing, clapping, waving	Model performs better than the ConvLSTM default architecture	Variations in some parameters led to undesirable outcomes
Kim et al., 2009	HMM, CRF	N/A	Dataset	Walking, Sitting, Standing, lying down	Accuracy up is to 90%	Automatic labeling was challenging, because every model was affected by changing the sensor environment
Niu et al., 2004	HMM, CHMM	Kalman filtering, frame differencing, SVM	Dataset	Following and stalking behavior	Average errors are less than 4 pixels	Shadow produced obtrusive foreground areas, calibration mistake in the cameras led to incorrect alignment
Wan et al., 2020	CNN, LSTM, BLSTM, MLP, SVM	Random forest, non-linear mapping algorithm	UCI datasets, gyroscope, accelerometer, smartphone camera	sitting, standing, walking, lying down, running	The acceleration time series' scale invariant properties and local dependency are extracted	In convolution layers, the difference in complexity between layers is smaller
Zhu et al., 2020	CNN-LSTM, MLP	multilayer perceptron, PCA, SVM, linear discriminant analysis, STFT	Radar-based devices	Running, strolling, crawling, carrying a stick while strolling, boxing, sitting	Model precision is 98.28% Suitable for extracting from radar waves global temporal data	If there are too many layers, the time-dependent qualities may be lost As you go deeper, training takes longer

TABLE 11.1 (Continued)
Comparison between Existing Techniques Used in a HAR System

Ref.	Model	Algorithm	Dataset/Device	Activity	Technique Advantages	Technique Disadvantages
Singh et al., 2010	Hidden Markov model (HMM)	N/A	KTH dataset	standing up, walking, turning back (left or right), kicking and punching	Accuracy is up to 70%	Did not work with some other datasets
Deep & Zheng, 2019	CNN, LSTM, CNN_LSTM	Several machine learning algorithms	UCI_HAR Dataset	Standing, sitting, lying down, moving around the ground floor and above	Gave precise findings with just one individual	If several people were utilized, the accuracy might not be achieved
Challa et al., 2021	CNN-BiLSTM,	Deep learning-based algorithms	IMU, smartphone	Rope-jumping, Nordic-walking, walking, standing, sitting, lying	Recognize jobs, both simple and complex, with fair accuracy	The devices were expensive and only provided limited coverage
Uzzaman et al., 2022	LRCN, LSTM, ConvLSTM	SVM, decision tree	Datasets: UCF50, HMDB51	Standing, sitting, lying down, moving about, moving up and down stairs	LRCN is less accurate than basic CNN	A real-time system must be created
Domingo et al., 2022	LSTM, LRCN, CNN	YOLO algorithm, SVM	STAIR dataset	Standing, sitting, lying down, moving about, moving up and down stairs	Results from LRCN outperformed those from YOLO	Has inferior picture feature extraction capabilities
Cho & Yoon, 2018	1D-CNN	KNN, Data masking algorithm	Accelerometer, gyroscope, camera, UCI_HAR dataset, GPS	Standing, sitting, lying down, moving around the ground floor and above	Simple, efficient, and straightforward to use	Failure to execute asymmetry validation and feature-wise sharpening

11.3   PROPOSED SYSTEM FOR HUMAN ACTIVITY RECOGNITION IN REAL-TIME VIDEOS

This section discusses the proposed architecture for a real-time HAR system, as shown in Figure 11.4. The system considers KINETICS400 dataset, and other pretrained models in order to train our main model for real-time videos. This model demonstrates real-time human experience using OpenVINO using standards recognized by open model quality, specifically encoders and decoders. For the KINETICS400 dataset, both models build a sequence-to-sequence ("seq2seq") 1 system to identify human activities.

The complete system is divided into a few modules as follows:

a. Dataset Used
b. Data Preprocessing
c. Encoding and Decoding
d. Action Recognition Sequence
e. Model Execution

The detailed description of each model or component is given below.

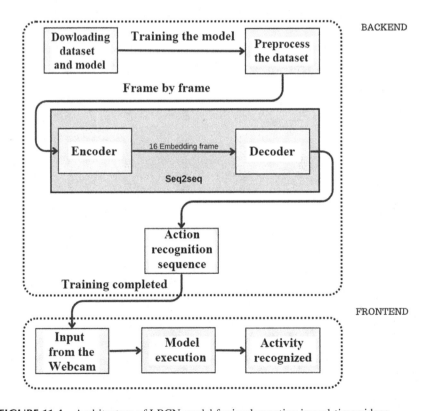

FIGURE 11.4   Architecture of LRCN model for implementing in real-time videos.

11.3.1 Dataset Used

In the first step, which started with the backend component of the project, we downloaded the data and labeled it to better comprehend the situation. The KINETICS400 dataset is considered. It has been shown to be a challenging dataset due to the large number of action classes and the high variability in the appearance and motion of the actions, as shown in Figure 11.5.

Based on their traits and the kinds of activities they represent, the KINETICS400 dataset's action classes may be divided into the following main categories:

- Body Movement: Actions that involve movements of the human body, such as walking, running, jumping, and dancing.
- Object Manipulation: Actions that involve manipulating objects, such as throwing a ball, playing a musical instrument, or cooking.
- Sports: Actions that are specific to sports, such as playing basketball, soccer, or tennis.

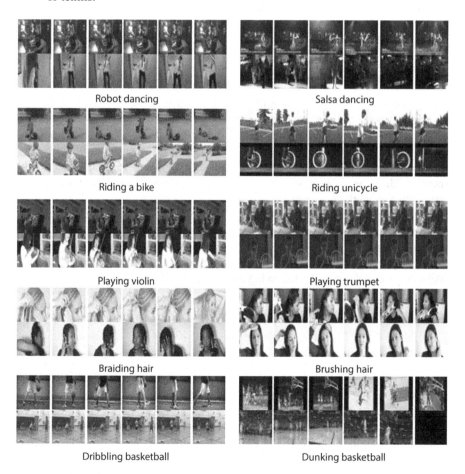

FIGURE 11.5   KINETICS400 dataset.

- Human Interaction: Actions that involve interactions between humans, such as hugging, kissing, or shaking hands.
- Human–Object Interaction: Actions that involve interactions between humans and objects, such as using a computer, drinking from a cup, or riding a bicycle.
- Animals: Actions that involve animals, such as walking a dog, riding a horse, or swimming with dolphins.
- Transportation: Actions that involve transportation, such as driving a car, riding a train, or flying in an airplane.
- Miscellaneous: Sneezing, yawning, and clapping are examples of actions that do not fall into any of the categories mentioned above.

These categories are not mutually exclusive, and some action classes may belong to more than one category. For example, the action class "playing basketball" could be categorized under both "sports" and "object manipulation." However, categorizing the action classes can help researchers better understand the types of activities present in the dataset and develop more effective models for activity recognition, as shown in Figure 11.6.

11.3.2 DATA PRE-PROCESSING

Two calculation methods are used in pre-processing data: center_crop and adaptive_resize.center_crop, which resize the video frames to a pre-defined width and height. The decoder mode decodes the Top 3 probabilities into label names and makes use of the decode_output method. So, in short, the encoder inferences the data per frame and the decoder inferences the data per set of frames created by the encoder. Then the video is marked with a region of interest (ROI) by using rec_frame_display method to mark the area for required output.

The frame is then set up to show label names over the area by using the display_text_fnc method. After these steps are completed, the Softmax method is used to get confidence values per action recognition. When using the center_crop method, image height and width is taken as the minimum dimension of the frame. Then to take x and y coordinates, the following formula is used:

$$start\_x = (img\_w - min\_dim) \div 2 \tag{11.1}$$

$$start\_y = (img\_h - min\_dim) \div 2 \tag{11.2}$$

where:
img_h = image height
img_w = image weight
min_dim = minimum dimension

Now, in order to select the ROI falling under these four coordinates, the equation is considered as below:

$$start_y, min_{dim} + start_y, start_x, min_{dim} + start_x \tag{11.3}$$

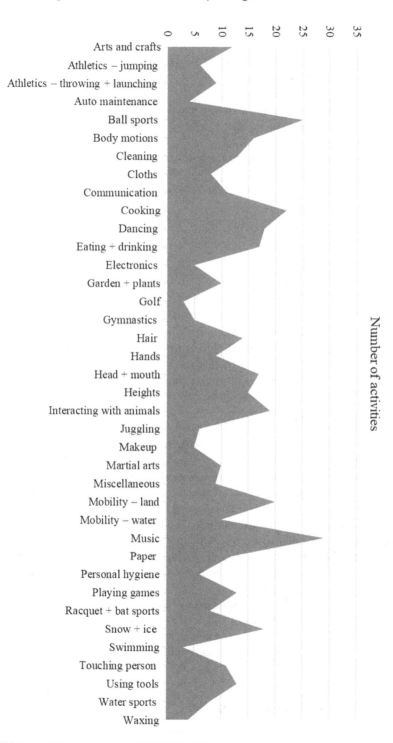

FIGURE 11.6 Categorization of KINETICS400 dataset.

After returning the ROI, adaptive_resize method is used:

$$\text{scale} = \text{size} \div \min(h, w) \qquad (11.4)$$

where:

h and w = shapes of the frame (height and weight)
scale = scaled feature of h and w

Then, w and h are also scaled in the following way:

$$w\_scaled = w \times scale \qquad (11.5)$$

$$h\_scaled = h \times scale \qquad (11.6)$$

where:

w_scaled = scaled weight
h_scaled = scaled height

Then these resized frames are returned by the encoder to the decoder. Decoder decodes the Top 3 probabilities into corresponding label names. And as the video starts playing and ROI is captured, the text is displayed on the top left side of the frame. The positioning of the text is set to be 15 pixels away from the left, and 25 pixels below from the top. A text template is also used to show inference results over video.

11.3.3 Encoding and Decoding

The model's implementation has now started. The command-line program omz_ downloader from the OpenVINO-dev package is utilized. The chosen model is downloaded, while a directory structure is automatically created. The encoder and decoder models are loaded for this specific architecture. Models that have been downloaded are kept in a fixed format that lists the vendor, model name, and precision. Initializing OpenVINO Runtime is the next step after downloading the model. Read the network from weights and architecture files in *.bin and *.xml files, then create the model for the CPU. For improved model optimization, other pre-trained models like action-recognition-0001, action-recognition-0001-encoder, and action-recognition-0001-decoder are also employed.

Deep learning models called seq2seq use a list of objects as input and output; in this instance, video frame input and action sequence output. There are two parts involved in seq2seq: an encoder and a decoder. For the decoder to evaluate the input and finally determine human behavior and confidence, the encoder saves the "context" of the input.

11.3.4 Action Recognition Sequence

The first stage of processing comes next. Depending on the process, action recognition can be applied to either a webcam or a video file. Making a video player with the desired frame rate using the utils is the first step in this process. The VideoPlayer technique aids in choosing the fewest possible frames for quick processing. The sequence of frames is then ready for encoding and decoding, and the webcam is used to capture the input and accurately identify human activities. With this, the backend part is over, the next step is to begin with the frontend part by taking the input from the webcam (Khang & Hajimahmud et al., 2023).

11.3.5 MODEL EXECUTION ON REAL-TIME VIDEOS

The model has been fully trained using the KINETICS400 dataset, and it is ready for execution. The input will be taken from the camera in the form of live feed. Then the model will be executed on the input, and the activity happening in the live feed will be recognized. The model returned different percentages of accuracy for each activity occurring in the video frame.

11.4 IMPLEMENTATION AND RESULT ANALYSIS

For implementation of the proposed HAR system, the KINETICS400 dataset is considered. It contains 400 action classes and at least 400 10-sec video clips in each class. The start and finish timings of each action in each video clip are indicated in the dataset's annotations, which also provide temporal boundaries for each activity. This makes it useful for tasks such as action detection and temporal localization. After data collection, the next step is to pre-process the data in which 20 random videos were selected, and the sizes of their frames were adjusted (Khang & Shah et al., 2023).

11.4.1 IMPLEMENTATION OF RECORDED VIDEOS

Next, the dataset is sent for pre-processing using the encoder and decoder models. Prior to normalizing the data to the range [e-1], the encoder model scaled the video frames to a present width and height for calculations. It then divided the pixel values by 255 to normalize the data to the range [e-1]. The decoder mode decodes the Top-3 probabilities into labels. The ROI is then drawn over the video to mark the area for required output. Then, the frame is prepared for displaying label names over the region. After these steps are completed, the Softmax method is used to get confidence values per action recognition. The result of these processes is that training of the model has been completed. Now, input from the webcam is taken, and the model detects human activities as shown in Figure 11.7, reading as shown in Figure 11.8(a), and drinking as shown in Figure 11.8(b).

11.4.2 RESULT ANALYTICS OF SAMPLE VIDEOS

We compared the ConvLSTM model against our LRCN model using the same dataset. The ConvLSTM model's accuracy score was 85.25%, and accuracy score for the

(a)   (b)

FIGURE 11.7   Sample output from recorded videos.

(a)   (b)

FIGURE 11.8   Sample output from real-time video: (a) reading and (b) drinking scenario.

proposed model was 92.62% when tested against the dataset. The models were then tested using the plot metric function to check for various parameters, as shown in Figures 11.9–11.12.

So the base of our comparison between the models is mainly the accuracy shown in the results. Another parameter that we considered while comparing the models is the layers induced in each of them as follows:

- Complexity: The ConvLSTM model is typically more complex than the LRCN model due to the additional convolutional layers. This increased complexity can result in longer training times and more challenging optimization.
- Interpretability: Due to their complex architectures, both models can be challenging to interpret. However, the LRCN model was more interpretable, as it separates spatial and temporal features.
- Data Availability: The ConvLSTM model required more data to train effectively due to its increased complexity. In contrast, the LRCN model was more data-efficient due to its simpler architecture.

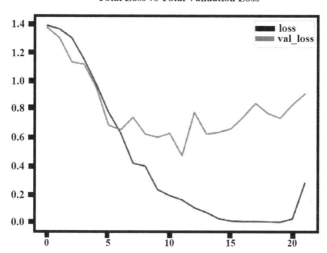

FIGURE 11.9 Total validation loss vs. total loss (ConvLSTM).

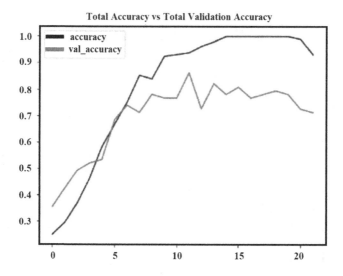

FIGURE 11.10 Total validation accuracy vs. total accuracy (ConvLSTM).

- Robustness to Noise: Because the ConvLSTM model could capture spatio-temporal correlations, it was more resistant to noise in the input data. The separation of spatial and temporal elements in the LRCN model, on the other hand, made it more susceptible to noise in the input data.
- Training Time: The training time for the ConvLSTM model was longer than the LRCN model due to the increased complexity.

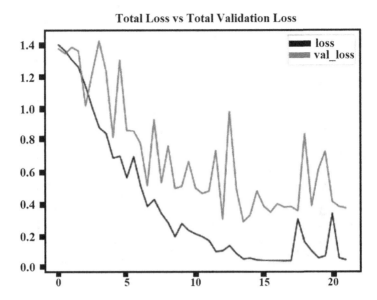

FIGURE 11.11 Total validation loss vs. total loss (LRCN).

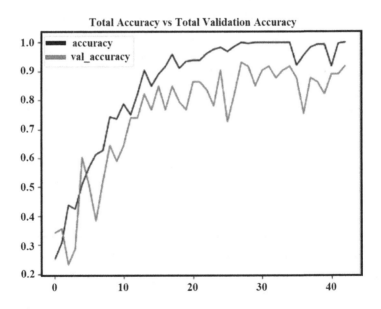

FIGURE 11.12 Total validation accuracy vs. total accuracy (LRCN).

- Hyperparameter Tuning: Hyperparameters such the number of layers, filters, and learning rate must be adjusted for both models. However, the specific hyperparameters to tune differed between the two models due to their different architectures.

11.5 CONCLUSION

In this chapter, a HAR system in real-time is proposed which considers models such as ConvLSTM and the CNN-LSTM hybrid, which creates LRCN, to the UCF50 dataset. The dataset includes 50 films of various sporting events. Following the deployment, we saw that LRCN was 92.62% accurate, while ConvLSTM was 80.33% accurate. We utilized LRCN on several movies to test its accuracy and found that it performed clearly better than ConvLSTM. It was discovered that the LRCN model produced a few incorrect findings for some YouTube videos. Then, after testing the LRCN model on YouTube videos, we trained the model, using some pre-trained models, on a different dataset: KINETICS400, which has 400 varieties of household and sports activities (Khang & Rath et al., 2023).

11.6 FUTURE SCOPE

The model was trained for real-time videos using a webcam, which was successfully completed, as the model was able to detect activities 90% of the time. The issue faced during and after training the model is multi-class classification. The LRCN model for human activity recognition has several future research directions (Khang & Muthmainnah et al., 2023):

- Attention Mechanisms: Attention mechanisms can be added to the LRCN model to help it concentrate on key elements of the incoming data. This can improve the model's performance and interpretability.
- Transfer Learning: Transfer learning is a promising area for future research with the LRCN model. The model's performance on the smaller dataset can be enhanced by pre-training it on a big dataset and fine-tuning it on a smaller dataset.
- Multi-task Learning: The model can be trained to perform multiple tasks simultaneously, such as recognizing different types of human activities or the identity of the person performing the activity.
- Cross-domain Adaptation: Developing methods that can adapt the model to different domains, such as different environments or populations, can improve the model's robustness and generalization.

REFERENCES

Bansal, Mitashi, and Sumita Gupta. "Detection and recognition of hand gestures for Indian sign language recognition system." In 2021 6th International Conference on Signal Processing, Computing and Control (ISPCC), pp. 136–140. IEEE, 2021. https://ieeexplore.ieee.org/abstract/document/9609448/

Bhatia, Shradha, Tushar Chauhan, Sumita Gupta, Sapna Gambhir, and Jitesh H. Panchal. "An approach to recognize human activities based on ConvLSTM and LRCN." In 2023 6th International Conference on Information Systems and Computer Networks (ISCON), pp. 1–6. IEEE, 2023. https://ieeexplore.ieee.org/abstract/document/10112060/

Challa, Sravan Kumar, Akhilesh Kumar, and Vijay Bhaskar Semwal. "A multibranch CNN-BiLSTM model for human activity recognition using wearable sensor data." The Visual Computer (2021): 1–15. https://link.springer.com/article/10.1007/s00371-021-02283-3

Cho, H., and S. M. Yoon. "Divide and conquer-based 1D CNN human activity recognition using test data sharpening." Sensors 18, no. 4 (2018): 1055. https://www.mdpi.com/1424-8220/18/4/1055

Deep, Samundra, and Xi Zheng. "Hybrid model featuring CNN and LSTM architecture for human activity recognition on smartphone sensor data." In 2019 20th International Conference on Parallel and Distributed Computing, Applications and Technologies (PDCAT). IEEE, 2019. https://ieeexplore.ieee.org/abstract/document/9029136/

Domingo, J. D., J. Gómez-García-Bermejo, and E. Zalama. "Improving human activity recognition integrating LSTM with different data sources: Features, object detection and skeleton tracking." IEEE Access, vol. 10, pp. 68213–68230, 2022, doi: 10.1109/ACCESS.2022.3186465.

Gupta, N., S. K. Gupta, R. K. Pathak, V. Jain, P. Rashidi, and J. S. Suri. "Human activity recognition in artificial intelligence framework: A narrative review." Artificial Intelligence Review (2022): 1–54. https://link.springer.com/article/10.1007/s10462-021-10116-x

Ke, Shian-Ru, et al. "A review on video-based human activity recognition." Computers 2, no. 2 (2013): 88–131. https://www.mdpi.com/2073-431x/2/2/88

Khang, A., V. Hahanov, G. L. Abbas, and V. A. Hajimahmud. "Cyber-Physical-Social System and İncident Management," *AI-Centric Smart City Ecosystems: Technologies, Design and Implementation.* (1st Ed.), 2 (15), (2022). CRC Press. https://doi.org/10.1201/9781003252542

Khang, A., V. A. Hajimahmud, S. K. Gupta, J. Babasaheb, and G. Morris. *AI-Centric Modelling and Analytics: Concepts, Designs, Technologies, and Applications.* (1st Ed.) (2023). CRC Press. https://doi.org/10.1201/9781003400110

Khang, A., V. A Hajimahmud, Hahanov Vladimir, and V. Shah. *Advanced IoT Technologies and Applications in the Industry 4.0 Digital Economy.* (1st Ed.) (2024). CRC Press. https://doi.org/10.1201/9781003434269

Khang, A., A. Misra, S. K. Gupta, and V. Shah. *AI-Aided IoT Technologies and Applications in the Smart Business and Production.* (1st Ed.) (2023). CRC Press. https://doi.org/10.1201/9781003392224

Khang, A., M Muthmainnah, Prodhan Mahbub Ibna Seraj, Ahmad Al Yakin, Ahmad J. Obaid, and Manas Ranjan Panda. "AI-Aided Teaching Model for the Education 5.0 Ecosystem," *AI-Based Technologies and Applications in the Era of the Metaverse.* (1st Ed.) (2023). Page (83–104). IGI Global Press. https://doi.org/10.4018/978-1-6684-8851-5.ch004

Khang, A., G. Rana, R. K. Tailor, and V. A. Hajimahmud. *Data-Centric AI Solutions and Emerging Technologies in the Healthcare Ecosystem.* (1st Ed.) (2023). CRC Press. https://doi.org/10.1201/9781003356189

Khang, A., Kali Charan Rath, Suresh Kumar Satapathy, Amaresh Kumar, Sudhansu Ranjan Das, and Manas Ranjan Panda. "Enabling the Future of Manufacturing: Integration of Robotics and IoT to Smart Factory Infrastructure in Industry 4.0," *AI-Based Technologies and Applications in the Era of the Metaverse.* (1st Ed.) (2023). Page (25–50). IGI Global Press. https://doi.org/10.4018/978-1-6684-8851-5.ch002

Khang, A., V. Shah, and S. Rani. *AI-Based Technologies and Applications in the Era of the Metaverse.* (1st Ed.) (2023). IGI Global Press. https://doi.org/10.4018/978-1-6684-8851-5

Khater, Sarah, Mayada Hadhoud, and Magda B. Fayek. "A novel human activity recognition architecture: Using residual inception ConvLSTM layer." Journal of Engineering and Applied Science 69, no. 1 (2022): 1–16. https://link.springer.com/article/10.1186/s44147-022-00098-0

Kim, Eunju, Sumi Helal, and Diane Cook. "Human activity recognition and pattern discovery." IEEE Pervasive Computing 9, no. 1 (2009): 48–53. https://ieeexplore.ieee.org/abstract/document/5370804/

Mutegeki, Ronald, and Dong Seog Han. "A CNN-LSTM approach to human activity recognition." In 2020 International Conference on Artificial Intelligence in Information and Communication (ICAIIC). IEEE, 2020. https://ieeexplore.ieee.org/abstract/document/9065078/

Niu, Wei, Jiao Long, Dan Han, and Yuan-Fang Wang. "Human activity detection and recognitionfor video surveillance." In 2004 IEEE international conference on multimedia and expo (ICME)(IEEE Cat. No. 04TH8763), vol. 1, pp. 719–722. IEEE, 2004. https://doi.org/10.1109/ICME.2004.1394293

Pienaar, Schalk Wilhelm, and Reza Malekian. "Human activity recognition using LSTM-RNN deep neural network architecture." In 2019 IEEE 2nd wireless Africa conference (WAC). IEEE, 2019. https://ieeexplore.ieee.org/abstract/document/8843403/

Singh, Sanchit, Sergio A Velastin, and Hossein Ragheb. "Muhavi: A multicamera human action video dataset for the evaluation of action recognition methods." In 2010 7th IEEE International Conference on Advanced Video and Signal Based Surveillance, pp. 48–55. IEEE, 2010, August. https://ieeexplore.ieee.org/abstract/document/5597316/

Subetha, T., and S. Chitrakala. "A survey on human activity recognition from videos." In 2016 International Conference on Information Communication and Embedded Systems (ICICES). IEEE, 2016. https://ieeexplore.ieee.org/document/7518920

Uzzaman, Muhammad Sajib, Chandan Debnath, Md Ashraf Uddin, Manowarul Islam, Md Alamin Talukder, and Shamima Parvez. LRCN Based Human Activity Recognition from Video Data. 2022. https://www.researchgate.net/profile/Md-Ashraf-Uddin/publication/362949127_LRCN_Based_Human_Activity_Recognition_from_Video_Data/links/634ee3576e0d367d91a88352/LRCN-Based-Human-Activity-Recognition-from-Video-Data.pdf

Vrigkas, Michalis, Christophoros Nikou, and Ioannis A. Kakadiaris. A Review of Human Activity RecognitionMethods. Frontiers in Robotics and AI. 2015. https://www.frontiersin.org/articles/10.3389/frobt.2015.00028/full

Wan, Shaohua, Lianyong Qi, Xiaolong Xu, Chao Tong, and Zonghua Gu. "Deep learning models for real-time human activity recognition with smartphones." Mobile Networks and Applications 25, no. 2 (2020): 743–755. https://link.springer.com/article/10.1007/s11036-019-01445-x

Xia, Kun, Jianguang Huang, and Hanyu Wang. "LSTM-CNN architecture for human activity recognition." IEEE Access 8 (2020): 56855–56866. https://ieeexplore.ieee.org/abstract/document/9043535/

Xu, Yang, and Ting TingQiu. "Human activity recognition and embedded application based on convolutional neural network." Journal of Artificial Intelligence and Technology 1, no. 1 (2021): 51–60. http://ojs.istp-press.com/jait/article/view/6

Zhu, Jianping, Haiquan Chen, and Wenbin Ye. "A hybrid CNN–LSTM network for the classification of human activities based on micro- Doppler radar." IEEE Access 8 (2020 Feb 3): 24713–24720. https://ieeexplore.ieee.org/abstract/document/8978926/

12 Application of Industrial Internet of Things Technologies in the Manufacturing Industry

Vugar Abdullayev Hajimahmud, Ragimova Nazila Ali, Triwiyanto, Asgarov Taleh Kamran, Mammadov Kanan Hafiz, and Abuzarova Vusala Alyar

12.1 INTRODUCTION

Before the Internet of Things (IoT), the Internet was mainly used to connect computers (and some hardware). With the emergence of IoT, the power of the Internet has increased where not only computers but also many smart devices could be connected. A network in which smart devices can interact with each other and exchange information with each other is known as IoT (Anh et al., 2024).

The main goal is to constantly connect and exchange data between devices and systems within the network. Sensors, software, and various physical devices play an important role here. The term IoT was proposed by British tech pioneer Kevin Ashton in 1999. While working at Procter & Gamble, Ashton proposed putting radio frequency identification (RFID) chips into devices to track them through the supply chain (Vision of Humanity, 2023).

The IoT guarantees that any smart device with Internet access is part of the "IoT ecosystem." In other words, smart devices with Internet access can create an IoT ecosystem among themselves (Abdullayev et al., 2021). By 2030, the number of smart devices connected to this network is predicted to be close to 28 billion.

These smart devices that are part of the IoT network are also called IoT devices and come in many shapes, sizes, and designs. They range from everyday household items (telephones, computers, air conditioners, TVs, clocks, refrigerators, cameras, etc.) to sophisticated industrial tools. The IoT primarily uses standard protocols and network technologies. However, the main enabling technologies and protocols for IoT connectivity are RFID, NFC, Bluetooth, low-energy radio protocols, Internet protocols, LTE-A, WiFi-Direct, and low-energy wireless sensor network, which are discussed in more detail below.

- **RFID** – Radio frequency identification (RFID) technology is a method of transmitting data wirelessly between a transmitter and a transponder,

DOI: 10.1201/9781003438137-12

where a transponder (tag) is attached to any object that needs to be identified. These objects can be animate or inanimate and can carry personalized information through an attached transponder, which is the approach that underlies the operation of these systems applied in IoT devices (Shields et al., 2015).

- **NFC** – Near field communication (NFC) technology is a new wireless short-range communication technique for transferring information between smart devices such as mobile phones by integrating a small NFC reader into mobile phones. This new technology supports communication at a distance of up to 4 cm. NFC is built on RFID, which uses the induction of a magnetic field to establish a communication link between devices (Hossein Motlagh, 2012).

- **Bluetooth** – First offered by Ericsson, Bluetooth is a standard for short-range, low-power, and low-cost wireless communication that uses radio technology (McDermott-Wells, 2004). It is mainly used for communication over smaller distances. In the IoT network, Bluetooth is also used for many connections.

- **Radio Protocol** – A radio communication protocol is a set of rules for exchanging information between radio devices. The radio frequency (RF) module supports a specific radio communication protocol depending on the module and its radio software. It includes IEEE 802.15.4, ZigBee, ZigBee Smart Energy, DigiMesh, ZNet, IEEE 802.11 (WiFi), XSC, etc.

- **Internet Protocol** – Internet protocol (also known as an IP address) is a set of rules used to send data over the Internet, allow devices connected to the Internet to recognize and exchange information with each other. It ensures recognition, reading, and understanding of information from any device or sensor on the IoT network by another device, etc. The Internet protocols used on the IoT are also known as IoT protocols.

- **LTE-A** – LTE provides reliable connectivity for IoT devices to complete data transmission to the cloud and other devices. One of the important things this technology provides is the ability of mobile low-power wide-area networks (LPWANs), such as Cat M and NB-IoT, to run on their infrastructure.

- **WiFi-Direct** – IoT network uses point-to-point (P2P) or WiFi-Direct as communication between devices. It is possible to find and interact with nearby devices.

- **Wireless Sensor Network** –A wireless sensor network (WSN) refers to a group of spatially dispersed and separated sensors to monitor and record the physical conditions of the environment and transmit such data together via a wireless network to an Internet-based network.

12.2 COMPONENTS AND FEATURES OF THE INTERNET OF THINGS

12.2.1 COMPONENTS OF INTERNET OF THINGS TECHNOLOGY

The following are the main components of IoT.

12.2.1.1 Smart Devices

One of the most essential components, if not the most essential, for the IoT network to exist is smart devices. Smart devices are a term used to generalize mainly electronic physical devices that have access to the Internet and can also interact and exchange information with other devices. Smart devices, also called IoT devices, come in different shapes and sizes and use artificial intelligence (AI) and its many other capabilities. The first example of a smart device was in 1982 of a Coca-Cola vending machine (Khang & Hajimahmud et al., 2024).

For smart devices to be part of the IoT network, they must be constantly connected to the network. The smart devices ecosystem includes smartphones, smart watches, security cameras, televisions, refrigerators, and large industrial devices like smart streetlights. Today, there are about 15 billion active smart devices in the world (https://www.statista.com/statistics/1183457/iot-connected-devices-worldwide/).

12.2.1.2 Sensors

Sensors are sensitive devices that can detect changes in the environment, collect information about them, and transmit this information. They convert real movements detected in the physical environment into digital signals and transmit them to the cyber-environment. In other words, these small devices create a link between the physical environment and the cyber-environment. The sensor sends the data to a local or cloud database, which can be re-used later when needed.

The sensor is one of the main parts of the IoT ecosystem. Different types of sensors are used, such as motion, temperature, pressure, sound, light, ultrasonic, smoke and gas, and optical sensors, among others.

12.2.1.3 Connection

The key factor in networking is connectivity. Connection is also important in the way smart devices interact with each other and exchange information, similar to the concept of IoT. If devices do not connect to the Internet, then they are considered ordinary devices.

Here, different types of methods are used to connect devices to the Internet including cellular, satellite, Bluetooth, RFID, NFC, WiFi, LPWAN, among others.

12.2.1.4 Gateways

An IoT gateway is a physical device or virtual platform that connects sensors, IoT modules, and smart devices to the cloud. Gateways serve as wireless access portals to provide Internet access to IoT devices. On the surface, it may sound like a simple router that allows communication between different protocols and devices (Thales Group, 2023). An IoT gateway can provide additional security for the IoT network and the data it transports.

12.2.1.5 User Interface

A user interface is a tool that creates a connection between the system and the user and helps the user understand by visualizing the digital information within the system. The IoT network also needs such a tool, which is one of its main components. Data exchange between smart devices, and datasets collected from the physical environment through sensors move in the cyber-environment. This information then needs to be seen by the user, which is done through the user interface. For example, information obtained through security cameras is transferred in digital format to a local database or the cloud. When the user wants to view this processed information, they can view it with the help of programs (user interface) on their smart devices such as computers, phones, and tablets.

12.2.1.6 Data Management: Data Analytics

Data is the basis of all systems, not just IoT. Networks provide constant information exchange. In this respect, data management and data analytics are one of the main components of the IoT network. Smart devices connected to the network are constantly exchanging information with each other. There are millions of these pieces of information, and each piece of information may not always be important. On the other hand, structuring and extracting the necessary data is also an important process, which is carried out by data analytics (Khang & Hajimahmud et al., 2024).

12.2.1.7 Database: Big Data, Cloud Storage

Local and online databases are used for data storage. Although cloud storage is more widely used, local databases are also currently used but are relatively unstable because of distortions. On the other hand, access to the information in these local databases is also possible in an environment without an Internet connection. Although cloud storage systems have some security problems, such as cyber-crimes committed by third parties, quick access to the data stored here is possible in all places with an Internet connection (Khang & Ragimova et al., 2024).

12.2.1.8 Security Policies

Security policies are living documents that are constantly updated as technology, vulnerabilities, and security requirements change. As smart devices interact with the help of the Internet, common security issues are inevitable on the IoT network. In this regard, companies offering IoT services need to create a common security policy.

12.2.2 Features of the Internet of Things Technology

Features of IoT technology are as follows:

- Scalability: Scalability, one of the main characteristics of the IoT network, characterizes the ability of the network to be constantly expanded. Currently, the number of smart devices connected to the IoT network is close to 15 billion, and it is predicted to double in the future.
- Adaptation: Adaptation is the interaction of different types of smart devices in the IoT network. In other words, the IoT network is heterogeneous rather than homogeneous, and this heterogeneity is characterized by smart devices of different types, produced by different companies, and with different protocols adapting to each other in the network environment and exchanging information.

- Intelligence and Identification: Extracting knowledge from generated data is critical. For example, a sensor generates data, but this data will only be useful if it is interpreted correctly. Each IoT device has a unique identity. This identification is useful for tracking equipment and sometimes finding out its status.
- Dynamics: In a changing environment, dynamics is one of the key features of IoT devices that must constantly understand and adapt to changes with minimal human intervention.
- Connection: Connectivity is one of the key components of IoT including mutual and Internet connection. Both Internet connectivity and interoperability are key components and features of IoT.
- Security: Security is one of the main challenges and features of IoT. As smart devices connect to the Internet, it is normal for security issues to arise. For this, companies offering IoT services must constantly monitor their devices and create an improved security policy.

12.3   ADVANTAGES AND DISADVANTAGES OF THE INTERNET OF THINGS

There are many advantages and disadvantages of the IoT technology that form a system of sub-features, as shown in Figure 12.1.

12.4   APPLICATION AREAS OF THE INTERNET OF THINGS

The IoT technology is applied in various areas, from daily life activities to large sectors such as manufacturing and the military. Listed below are some of the key application areas of IoT.

12.4.1   DAILY LIFE

The IoT technology can often be found in everyday life. Many IoT devices are in use today such as computers, tablets, smartphones, among others. It is common to see IoT applications in everyday life, especially in smart cities and smart home systems.

12.4.2   SMART HOME SYSTEMS

Smart home systems provide an opportunity to improve people's quality of life, allowing them to control various household appliances, lights, and other devices with the help of smartphones and tablets with an Internet connection. Smart home systems may be set up with both wireless and wired networks. Smart homes are also a local part of the smart city system.

Having a smart home system gives users complete control over their homes even when they are away. As a result of the interaction of smart home devices in the network with each other, information about the devices is transmitted to the homeowner constantly or when there is a change. This is especially important in case of a home burglary and to keep any device in working order.

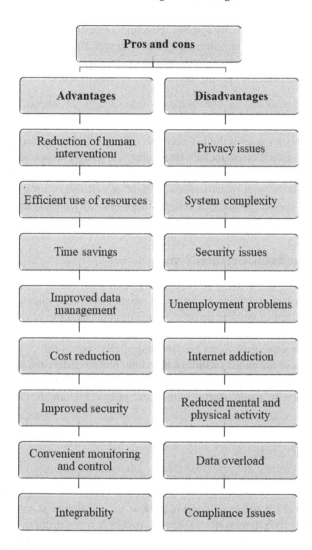

FIGURE 12.1   Advantages and disadvantages of IoT.

The main drawback of smart home systems is security. Cyber-criminals can gain access to the system and take control of it. Another drawback is that smart home systems are relatively expensive. However, it is possible to remotely control different household appliances by connecting them to the network at a low cost.

12.4.3 Smart City

Smart cities are a smart space that uses all the possibilities of information and communication technology (ICT). One of the main goals of smart cities is to improve the quality of life of people by adapting to the digital era. Thus, solving various urban problems affecting the quality of life is the main goal of the Smart City Project.

Solutions include a cleaner city system, reducing congestion by implementing smart transportation systems, and eliminating water supply and sanitation problems. As mentioned above, smart homes are also part of the smart city system. Smart cities are one of the cornerstones of the future smart society concept.

12.4.4 WEARABLE DEVICES

Wearable devices are part of the IoT network and are collectively known as wearable technological devices. These include smart watches, smart glasses, necklaces, bracelets, smart rings, and all wearable tech smart devices. These devices monitor human body movements through smart sensors. Wearables can also be used to control other networked IoT devices. Management capabilities also vary mainly depending on the brand of the device.

12.4.5 SMART TRANSPORTATION SYSTEMS

One of the application areas of IoT technology and solutions in the smart city environment, smart transportation systems are smart city traffic management systems that use various smart devices and communication networks to eliminate or reduce many traffic problems. Car accidents are the most frequent types of accidents in the world that cause deaths and injuries, especially within the city. Many factors contribute to these accidents including speeding, impaired driving, and traffic jams. Smart transportation systems provide several solutions such as traffic flow management, application of smart traffic lights, and proper exchange of constant traffic information.

12.4.6 AGRICULTURE

The IoT is helping agriculture by using sensors to monitor crops and automating irrigation systems. Using different types of sensors (heat, soil, etc.), farmers can find out the fertility of the soil (whether it is suitable for planting) and control the growth of plants. Smart irrigation systems, sensors, robots (mainly drones), climate control and monitoring systems in greenhouses, ground control systems, analytics, and optimization platforms are currently applied in agriculture.

12.4.7 HEALTHCARE

In healthcare, IoT offers solutions at different stages of a patient's health condition. The IoT devices help individuals track their weight, body mass, sleep patterns, and daily activity levels. The integration of the IoT technology into the healthcare field created a new concept known as the Internet of Medical Things (IoMT). The IoMT is a connected infrastructure of medical devices, software, and healthcare systems and services.

As the most important technological innovation introduced by the IoT technology to the healthcare sector, IoMT uses sensors that can be placed on the patient's body to communicate wirelessly and without external intervention for a long time.

It provides an easy and effective way to measure and save health records ultimately saving the lives of patients with diabetes, cancer, cardiovascular diseases, chronic diseases, neurological seizures, and orthopedic problems (İleri, 2018).

12.4.8 MILITARY

One of the largest sectors where IoT technology is applied is in the military. The military industry is built on precision, and the technologies used here also require precision. The fact that the IoT technology is still used in the military sector is one of the factors that prove its reliability.

Currently, work is being done to use all the possibilities of AI technology in this field. Constantly improving UAV systems, military robots (robot soldier project), and various types of weapons rely on the application of AI which led to the concept known as the Internet of Military Things.

With IoT, it is possible to identify the enemy, monitor the physical as well as psychological state of the soldier, and synchronize (connect) soldiers with weapon systems and other devices, etc. With the Internet of Military Things, sensing and computing devices are embedded in the combat suits, hats, weapons systems, and other equipment worn by soldiers. With the help of this technology, information is obtained with the necessary biometric indicators.

12.4.9 SUPPLY CHAIN MANAGEMENT

The IoT technology uses and combines analytics, cloud systems, IoT devices, and computing technology to adapt and improve supply chain management in manufacturing for the digital age. Here, sensors are used to track products and deliveries. Real-time data is collected, stored in the cloud (or on a local database), and analyzed through data analytics. The IoT technology saves time and costs by automating some processes in the supply chain, resulting in increased efficiency and effectiveness.

12.4.10 HOSPITALITY INDUSTRY

The hospitality and tourism industry are a sector that includes all economic activities that directly or indirectly contribute to or depend on travel and tourism. This includes hotels and resorts, restaurants, events (personal, business, cultural, and sports), and more.

The use of IoT has proven to be valuable in this sector. With the introduction of smart devices in hotels and restaurants, more convenient and high-quality service is offered to customers. Many processes such as registration, room service, and restaurant service are carried out using IoT devices. Several future projects on IoT that are adapted to this industry such as IoT-based hotels are already in the works.

12.4.11 MANUFACTURING

One of the main application areas of IoT, and the most important in terms of economics and quality, is the manufacturing industry. With its application to this industry, the concept of Industrial IoT was born. The application of Industrial IoT is discussed in detail in the next section.

12.5 INTERNET OF THINGS TYPES

The five types of IoT are discussed in detail below.

- **Consumer IoT:** The application of IoT in everyday life creates the concept of Consumer IoT. This includes use of everyday smart devices, various household items, and wearables.
- **Military IoT:** It is a concept that arose as a result of the application of technology in the military sector. It characterizes the application of IoT on and off the battlefield. It is also known as the Internet of Military Things.
- **Infrastructure IoT:** Infrastructure IoT includes the development of the infrastructure of smart technologies (sensors, smart control technologies, etc.) to save costs and improve technical service quality and efficiency. This includes the ability to monitor and control smart city and smart village infrastructure operations.
- **Commercial IoT:** Commercial IoT characterizes the application of IoT capabilities in large industries. Commercial IoT involves large enterprises, smart healthcare, smart tourism, smart transportation, etc.
- **Industrial IoT:** Industrial IoT is a concept that emerged as a result of the integration of IoT technology into the industrial sector. It mainly characterizes the application of IoT technology in industries such as the manufacturing and energy sectors.

The application of AI and IoT technology in manufacturing, which is the main economic field of the 21st century and the future, plays a great role in the improvement of this industry. Now let's take a closer look at Industrial IoT technology.

12.6 INDUSTRIAL INTERNET OF THINGS TECHNOLOGY

One of the key concepts associated with Industry 4.0, is the IoT technology. The main goal of Industry 4.0 is to bring the industrial sector together with smart technologies known as Industrial IoT (IIoT).

The primary components of IoT are software, cyber–physical systems, cloud computing, edge computing, AI, machine learning, digital twin, and Internet-based devices. This section discusses the concept of IIoT, its use cases, features, and future. Industrial IoT is a derivative of IoT technology and shares its characteristics and functions such as networking, smart devices, sensors, user interface, cloud storage, data analytics, and security policy. The pros and cons of the IoT are also reflected in the IIoT (Khang & Vladimir et al., 2024).

Industrial IoT is the use of intelligent sensors and actuators to improve manufacturing and industrial processes. Also known as the industrial Internet or Industry 4.0, IIoT uses smart machines and real-time analytics to replace the data produced by "dumb machines" in industrial settings for years.

12.6.1 INDUSTRIAL INTERNET OF THINGS VS. INTERNET OF THINGS

Although the IIoT is a subcategory of the IoT technology, they share many similar features and subtle differences. Table 12.1 summarizes the differences between IIoT and IoT.

12.6.2 ADVANTAGES OF THE INDUSTRIAL INTERNET OF THINGS

The IIoT includes many IoT technology features as listed below:

- Prediction – IIoT enables prediction. By analyzing data obtained through sensors in real-time, it is possible to detect faults and maintenance needs in industrial machines.
- High Technical Service – Through data analysis and the use of IoT sensors, a machine's malfunction can be detected and eliminated, which will reduce costs and increase efficiency.
- Control and Tracking – Asset tracking systems are used to track the location and condition of products. If anything happens to the product, a warning is sent to producers and consumers.
- Remote Control – Remote control is used to save time and ensure safety by controlling the process remotely. This is a factor that increases the efficiency and effectiveness of the enterprise.

12.6.3 INDUSTRIAL IoT USE CASES AND IIoT OFFERINGS
IN MANUFACTURING

In Chapter 1, we mentioned that the manufacturing industry can be divided into three types: basic materials industry, manufacturing and assembly industry, and life-related industry. Each industry combines different production areas such as chemicals, oil and coal, plastics, steel, electrical equipment, transport equipment, food, beverage/tobacco/feed, textile, clothing, and furniture, among others. In each of these areas, IIoT can be applied. Several companies offer IIoT solutions in various areas, as shown in Table 12.2.

Several companies are applying IIoT technology. Gehring Group, founded in Germany in 1926, is one of the companies in the machine industry that is a leader in honing technology, providing advanced technological solutions for internal combustion engines, gears, among other industrial applications (Khang & Shah et al., 2023).

The company provides customers with real-time information about the principle of machine operation of machines, among others. It does this mainly through IoT devices, i.e., real-time data is transmitted from the machine to the client. The company also uses cloud-based technology to monitor interconnected systems and visualize and store data.

There are hundreds of companies around the world implementing and offering IIoT solutions and services. All recognize that IIoT is a key step for the manufacturing sector.

TABLE 12.1

Differences between the Internet of Things and the Industrial Internet of Things

No.	Differences	Internet of Things (Consumer IoT)	Industrial Internet of Things
1	Application areas	IoT is applied in many different areas, from daily life to big sectors.	IIoT is applied in the manufacturing and energy sector industries.
2	Network	IoT uses small-scale, low-level networks.	IIoT uses larger-scale networks.
3	Purpose	IoT goals are numerous: improving quality of life and healthcare, developing agriculture, etc.	IIoT has limited goals. It is less user-oriented and focuses mainly on production-relevant goals.
4	Security	IoT emphasis is on user authentication and protection of user data. It offers security solutions and a personalized experience.	IIoT requires high security. Here, mainly, the protection of production (manufacturing) data is important.
5	Life cycle	The life cycle of IoT devices is relatively short.	IIoT devices are long-lived.
6	Compatibility	IoT does not have to be compatible with legacy systems (or devices). It is easy to update everyday IoT devices, and IoT manufacturers can adapt them to older systems.	IIoT has to adapt to older large systems in manufacturing to save costs for the enterprise.
7	Requirements	Devices can be affected by the environment. Everyday IoT devices need not be sophisticated. They need to be used in everyday environments and adapt to temperature and humidity.	Since IIoT devices are applied in various types of enterprises and all areas of production, the requirements for functionality and durability are high.
8	Reliability	IoT devices (especially everyday ones) are relatively less reliable.	IIoT has higher reliability, which is affected by its quality, etc.
9	Developmental needs	This depends on daily use. IoT devices should adapt to daily life based on the needs of the time.	IIoT should consider the requirements and innovations in the industrial field by developing devices that increase efficiency and reduce costs.
10	Devices	IoT devices can function independently in everyday life. By connecting to the network, they can easily interact with each other.	IIoT devices operate in an integrated form with several mechanisms, rather than independently.
11	Risk	Risk arising from failure of everyday IoT devices is usually not great and is mainly limited to device replacement cost.	The failure of IIoT devices can pose major risks. Because IoT devices are numerous large devices used across a network, failure of one may be life-threatening.

TABLE 12.2

Companies Offering IIoT Solutions across Various Manufacturing Sectors

No.	Company	IIoT Offerings
1	PowTechnology	PowTechnology is a British digital industry company that delivers data for business decision-making. It has provided more than a 100,000 "connected sensor solutions" that help customers remotely monitor parameters such as temperature, pressure, and humidity. The company also provides IIoT solutions for various manufacturing industries including factory automation, fuel management, lubricants, utilities, energy, transportation, waste management, environment, chemicals, flood protection, construction, security, agriculture, bulk liquid and gas distribution, and pumping.
2	GE Digital	Founded in 2011 in the U.S., GE Digital, part of GE Vernova, is a company that provides software and IIoT services to four main industries: power generation and oil and gas, manufacturing, electrical and telecommunications, and aviation. GE Digital was named a Leader in the 2022 Gartner Magic Quadrant for manufacturing execution systems for its Proficy Smart Factory software solution.
3	ScienceSoft	Founded in the U.S. in 1989, ScienceSoft has been providing IIoT solutions since 2011 for asset tracking, machine monitoring, predictive maintenance, and more for manufacturing, energy, oil and gas, construction, and agriculture.
4	Mitsubishi Electric	Founded in Japan in 1921, Mitsubishi Electric offers IT, IoT, and IIoT solutions and provides IIoT infrastructure as a service (IaaS), platform as a service (PaaS), analytics and modeling, networks and connectivity, automation and control, robotics, and renewable energy industry.
5	Softeq	Founded in the U.S. in 1997, Softeq provides expertise in various trending technologies including the IoT, AI, and ML, industrial automation, robotics, blockchain, and AR/VR. The company designs IT systems and connected devices for increased security and scalability. The company provides IIoT solutions for manufacturing and oil and gas industries. These include hardware prototyping and design, application development for IIoT devices, embedded software, etc.
6	Intel	Intel was founded in the U.S. in 1968. The company offers an IIoT and Industry 4.0 portfolio, including powerful edge computing, advanced proprietary 5G technologies, purpose-built time-aware networking capabilities, and integrated optimizations for edge AI.
7	Telit	Telit was founded in 1986 in the U.K. The company's deviceWISE is an IIoT platform for industrial integration and enablement. The platform makes it easy to rapidly connect factory devices and applications to the enterprise and value chain and manage IIoT solutions. As a result, information gathered helps increase productivity and profit without technology barriers such as custom code and difficult integration with existing system architecture.

12.7 FUTURE OF THE INDUSTRIAL INTERNET OF THINGS IN MANUFACTURING

The future of IIoT is related to the development of IoT technology, which continues to improve with the added number of new smart devices to the network every year. Although IoT technology provides high productivity, its implementation in large enterprises is relatively expensive, such as in the manufacturing industry. Although IIoT requires high installation costs, it is possible to mitigate their impact with the high productivity achieved. In order for IIoT technology to continue to develop, it is necessary to increase security solutions, which are the main weakness of this technology (Khang & Rath et al., 2023).

12.8 CONCLUSION

One of the main concepts of Industry 4.0, IoT technology is being applied today in all areas where there are smart devices and an Internet connection. A network environment where smart devices can interact with each other and exchange information among themselves constitutes the IoT ecosystem (Khang & Muthmainnah et al., 2023). Below is a summary of what was discussed in the chapter:

- Although the term Internet of Things was first proposed in 1999, one of its key components, the smart device, was first developed in 1982. This was the development of the first simple IoT network.
- The main components of IoT are a set of smart devices, network communication, user interface, data analytics, data storage databases, etc.
- One of the biggest challenges of IoT technology is security.
- The application areas of IoT are wide and range from everyday life to big sectors such as the military, healthcare, education, and production.
- There are different types of IoT according to their application in different sectors, especially Consumer IoT and Industrial IoT.
- Industrial IoT is mostly aligned with the term Industry 4.0. It provides a high-quality implementation of smart industrial devices (machines) in manufacturing, transport, electrical equipment, chemical industry, oil refining industry, etc.
- Industrial IoT also has many similar features to IoT. However, there are some differences depending on the application environment.
- Many companies are offering IIoT solutions and services, such as Mitsubishi, Siemens, Intel, etc.
- The future of IIoT is mainly concerned with the elimination of security-related problems and the improvement of IoT technology.

REFERENCES

Abdullayev, V. H., N. A. Ragimova, V. A. Abuzarova, and V. M. Hajiyeva. "Desirable World With CPS And IoT," International Journal on "Technical and Physical Problems of Engineering" (IJTPE) 13, Number 4, no. 49 (2021): 51–56. http://www.iotpe.com/IJTPE/IJTPE-2021/IJTPE-Issue49-Vol13-No4-Dec2021/8-IJTPE-Issue49-Vol13-No4-Dec2021-pp51-56.pdf

Anh, P. T. N., Hahanov Vladimir, Triwiyanto, Nazila Ali Ragimova, Rashad İsmibeyli, V. A. Hajimahmud, and Abuzarova Vusala Alyar. "AI Models for Disease Diagnosis and Prediction of Heart Disease With Artificial Neural Networks," *Computer Vision and AI-Integrated IoT Technologies in Medical Ecosystem.* (1st Ed.) (2024). CRC Press.

Hossein Motlagh, Naser. Near Field Communication (NFC) - A technical Overview. (2012). https://doi.org/10.13140/RG.2.1.1232.0720

Khang, A, V. A. Hajimahmud, Eugenia Litvinova, Svetlana Chumachenko, Vusala Abuzarova, and P. T. N. Anh. "Application of Computer Vision in the Healthcare Ecosystem," *Computer Vision and AI-Integrated IoT Technologies in Medical Ecosystem.* (1st Ed.) (2024). CRC Press.

Khang, A., M Muthmainnah, Prodhan Mahbub Ibna Seraj, Ahmad Al Yakin, Ahmad J. Obaid, and Manas Ranjan Panda. "AI-Aided Teaching Model for the Education 5.0 Ecosystem" *AI-Based Technologies and Applications in the Era of the Metaverse.* (1st Ed.) (2023). Page (83–104). IGI Global Press. https://doi.org/10.4018/978-1-6684-8851-5.ch004

Khang, A., Nazila Ali Ragimova, Sardarov Yaqub Bali, V. A. Hajimahmud, Askarova Bahar, and Mammadova Mehriban. "Using Big Data to Solve Problems in the Field of Medicine," *Computer Vision and AI-Integrated IoT Technologies in Medical Ecosystem.* (1st Ed.) (2024). CRC Press. https://doi.org/10.1201/9781003429609-23

Khang, A., Kali Charan Rath, Suresh Kumar Satapathy, Amaresh Kumar, Sudhansu Ranjan Das, and Manas Ranjan Panda. "Enabling the Future of Manufacturing: Integration of Robotics and IoT to Smart Factory Infrastructure in Industry 4.0," *Handbook of Research on AI-Based Technologies and Applications in the Era of the Metaverse.* (1st Ed.) (2023). Page (25–50). IGI Global Press. DOI: 10.4018/978-1-6684-8851-5.ch002

Khang, A., V. Shah, and S. Rani. *AI-Based Technologies and Applications in the Era of the Metaverse.* (1st Ed.) (2023). IGI Global Press. https://doi.org/10.4018/978-1-6684-8851-5

Khang, A, Hahanov Vladimir, Eugenia Litvinova, Svetlana Chumachenko, Avromovic Zoran, Rashad İsmibeyli, Nazila Ali Ragimova, V. A. Hajimahmud, Abuzarova Vusala Alyar, and Anh. P.T.N. "Medical and Biomedical Signal Processing and Prediction Using the EEG Machine and Electroencephalography," *Computer Vision and AI-Integrated IoT Technologies in Medical Ecosystem.* (1st Ed.) (2024). CRC Press. https://doi.org/10.1201/9781003429609-7

McDermott-Wells, P. "What Is Bluetooth?" IEEE Potentials 23, no. 5 (2004-Jan. 2005): 33–35. https://doi.org/10.1109/MP.2005.1368913

Shields, Andrew, Ultan McCarthy, Daniel Riordan, Pat Doody, Joseph Walsh, and Ismail Uysal. Radio Frequency Identification (RFID). (2015). https://doi.org/10.1002/047134608X.W8155.

Thales Group. Bridge the Gap with IoT Gateways Digital Identity and Security, Secure IoT Solutions. (2023). https://www.thalesgroup.com/en/markets/digital-identity-and-security/iot/inspired/iot-gateway

Vision of Humanity. IoT Technologies Explained: History, Examples, Risks & Future. The Exciting Field of IoT Comes with Risks and a Lack of Governance. (2023). https://www.visionofhumanity.org/what-is-the-internet-of-things

İleri, Yusuf Yalçın. "Sağlik Hizmetlerinde Nesnelerin İnterneti (Nit): Avantajlar Ve Zorluklar "Akademik Sosyal Araştırmalar Dergisi, Yıl: 6, Sayı: 67, (2018), s. 159–171. https://www.researchgate.net/profile/Yusuf-Ileri-2/publication/323938205_SAGLIK_HIZMETLERINDE_NESNELERIN_INTERNETI_NIT_AVANTAJLAR_VE_ZORLUKLAR/links/5de0baa392851c836451dcfd/SAGLIK-HIZMETLERINDE-NESNELERIN-INTERNETI-NIT-AVANTAJLAR-VE-ZORLUKLAR.pdf

13 Internet of Things-Integrated Robotics in Manufacturing

Manjula Devi Chithiraikannu, Gobinath Arumugam, Srinivasan Arumugam, Pavithra Devi Ramamoorthy, and Rajeswari Packianathan

13.1 INTRODUCTION TO INTERNET OF THINGS AND ROBOTICS IN MANUFACTURING

Internet of Things (IoT)-integrated robotics in manufacturing refers to the seamless integration of IoT technologies with robotic systems on the factory floor. This integration aims to enhance automation, efficiency, and overall productivity by enabling robots to communicate, gather data, and make intelligent decisions in real-time. It represents a transformative approach to modern manufacturing, where physical and digital systems converge to create smart and adaptive production environments (Alpaydin, 2023).

In the evolving landscape of modern manufacturing, the convergence of IoT and robotics has been a transformative force, reshaping the way products are designed, produced, and delivered. This synergistic integration represents a leap forward in efficiency, precision, and adaptability in the manufacturing sector. The IoT refers to a network of interconnected devices and sensors that communicate and share data over the Internet. In manufacturing, this means embedding intelligence into machines, components, and processes, creating a dynamic ecosystem where real-time information drives decision-making (BHR, 1971).

Internet of Things technologies facilitate the collection, analysis, and utilization of data to optimize operations, enhance product quality, and usher in a new era of smart manufacturing. Technically, automation signifies the execution of actions or processes that replicate human behavior with minimal or no human intervention. In the past, processes relied heavily on human labor. However, the continuous progress in technology and the exponential growth in computational power have led to highly advanced robots and automation tools. These technological strides have revolutionized our ability to perform tasks swiftly and efficiently.

Automation's primary stronghold lies in industry and manufacturing sectors. These sectors have been at the forefront of automation, utilizing automated machines for diverse functions such as painting, manufacturing parts, storage, monitoring, and more. Virtually every industry today leverages automated robots in their day-to-day processes, as shown in Figure 13.1.

DOI: 10.1201/9781003438137-13

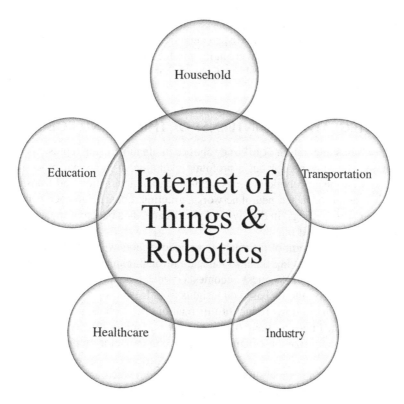

FIGURE 13.1 Enhancing daily life: Integration of IoT and robotics for smarter living.

The Industrial Revolution played a pivotal role in propelling automation into the mainstream. This period of industrial transformation not only spurred technological innovations, but it also ingrained the idea that embracing automation is not just a choice but a necessity. In today's landscape, forgoing the incorporation of automated procedures is considered imprudent. "Time is money" encapsulates the essence of this mindset, emphasizing that the efficient utilization of time through automation is essential to optimizing productivity and avoiding unnecessary costs. As automation technologies continue to evolve, they extend beyond the confines of traditional manufacturing (Khang & Hajimahmud et al., 2024).

Today, automation finds applications in various sectors, including healthcare, finance, logistics, and even households. The advent of smart homes and the integration of automation in daily life underscore the versatility and adaptability of automated systems. Automation has evolved from a niche concept to an indispensable aspect of modern life. Its roots in industrial and manufacturing settings have expanded to influence diverse sectors, driving efficiency, precision, and economic viability. Embracing automation is no longer just a matter of convenience but a must for organizations and individuals when navigating the complexities of today's world.

Simultaneously, robotics has undergone a profound evolution, transitioning from traditional, rigid systems to agile, intelligent entities capable of intricate tasks.

Robots in manufacturing are no longer isolated entities confined to specific tasks; they are now endowed with the ability to perceive their surroundings, communicate with other machines, and adapt to changing production requirements. This evolution has given rise to collaborative robots (Cobots) that work alongside human counterparts to increase productivity.

13.2 INTEGRATION OF INTERNET OF THINGS AND ROBOTICS

The harmonious integration of IoT and robotics in manufacturing represents not just a technological convergence but a profound evolution in industrial processes. As IoT sensors permeate robotic systems, real-time data acquisition and transmission ensues. These sensors act as neural networks, granting robots heightened perceptiveness to their surroundings. In this dynamic landscape, data becomes the heartbeat of intelligent decision-making.

The continuous stream of information provides robots with a keen awareness of their environment, allowing them to navigate through complexities and uncertainties. This real-time responsiveness becomes a cornerstone for adaptability, as robots adjust their actions on-the-fly based on insights from IoT sensors. The optimization of performance is a natural byproduct of this relationship. Robots, armed with a trove of real-time data, fine-tune their operations for maximum efficiency and reduced downtime. This optimization enhances the entire manufacturing process, as shown in Figure 13.2.

What emerges is a seamlessly integrated ecosystem where robots transcend their conventional roles. They become active participants in the broader manufacturing network, contributing intelligently to the overall efficiency and effectiveness of the

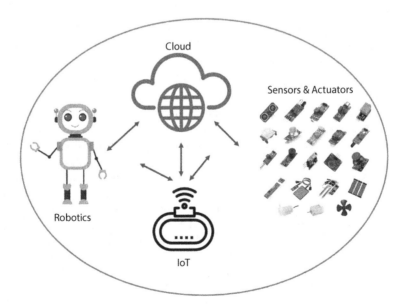

FIGURE 13.2 Synergizing IoT and robotics: A unified approach.

production line. The manufacturing landscape is no longer a static environment but a dynamic, interconnected system where every component, human and machine alike, collaborates in unison. The era of Industry 4.0, marked by the fusion of digital technologies with traditional manufacturing, finds its embodiment in IoT and robotics.

Combining IoT and robotics in manufacturing is a transformation and a leap forward into an era where the synergy of data-driven decision-making and robotic precision leads to efficient, adaptable, and intelligent systems (Cohen et al., 2004).

13.3 REVOLUTIONIZING MANUFACTURING

The fusion of IoT and robotics in manufacturing has transformed the industry. The once-static manufacturing processes are now dynamic, adaptive, and responsive systems. Picture a factory floor as a sentient entity, a smart and interconnected environment where machines collaborate seamlessly to ensure precision, efficiency, and top-notch quality across the entire production lifecycle. In the upcoming sections, we will discuss in more detail the workings of IoT-integrated robotics in manufacturing using a hands-on investigation into the real-world impact of this integration. We will explore the benefits, dissect the challenges, and peer into the promising future of intelligent manufacturing.

Imagine a world where efficiency is not just a goal but a reality, where predictive maintenance becomes second nature, and where human-robot collaboration is not a futuristic concept but an integral part of everyday operations. From streamlined processes to proactive problem-solving, the journey through IoT-integrated robotics promises to redefine manufacturing practices and the essence of how we conceive and execute industrial processes in the 21st century.

This chapter encapsulates a paradigm shift, a reimagining of the symbiotic relationship between humans and machines. It is an exploration of a future where innovation is a necessity, and where the convergence of intelligence and automation reshapes the landscape of industry norms.

13.4 KEY COMPONENTS OF INTERNET OF THINGS-INTEGRATED ROBOTICS IN MANUFACTURING

13.4.1 IoT Sensors

- Purpose: Sensors serve as the sensory organs of robotic systems, capturing data from the physical environment.
- Functionality: Cameras provide visual perception, proximity sensors detect close objects, temperature sensors monitor environmental conditions, and accelerometers measure acceleration and movement. These sensors collectively enable robots to interpret and respond to their surroundings.

13.4.2 Connectivity Protocols

- Purpose: Connectivity establishes communication channels between robotic devices and the broader IoT network.

- Functionality: Wireless communication protocols like WiFi ensure high-speed data transfer, Bluetooth facilitates short-range communication, ZigBee enables low-power, low-data-rate communication, and cellular networks offer ubiquitous connectivity. The choice of protocol depends on factors such as data transfer speed, range, and power consumption.

13.4.3 EDGE COMPUTING AND CLOUD PLATFORMS

- Purpose: Edge computing and cloud platform help manage the processing and storage of data generated by IoT sensors.
- Functionality: Edge computing involves processing data locally on the robot, reducing latency for real-time decision-making. Cloud platforms provide scalable storage and computational resources for more intensive data analysis. The combination of edge and cloud computing optimizes the balance between local responsiveness and centralized analytics.

13.4.4 DATA ANALYTICS AND MACHINE LEARNING ALGORITHMS

- Purpose: Data analytics and machine learning algorithms help extract actionable insights from the collected data to enhance decision-making.
- Functionality: Data analytics tools process raw data to identify patterns, anomalies, and correlations. Machine learning algorithms, including supervised and unsupervised learning, enable robots to learn from experience and improve their performance over time. Predictive maintenance models anticipate equipment failures, reducing downtime.

13.4.5 HUMAN-MACHINE INTERFACE

- Purpose: Human-machine interface (HMI) facilitates interaction between human operators and robotic systems.
- Functionality: Graphical interfaces, touchscreens, or control panels provide a user-friendly platform for operators to monitor robot status, input commands, and adjust settings. Intuitive HMIs contribute to effective collaboration, enabling operators to oversee and intervene in manufacturing processes as needed.

13.4.6 SECURITY PROTOCOLS

- Purpose: Security protocols safeguard the integrity and confidentiality of data within IoT-integrated systems.
- Functionality: Encryption methods protect data during transmission, authentication mechanisms ensure only authorized access, and secure communication protocols prevent cyber-threats. Robust security measures are essential to maintain the trustworthiness of the data and the overall system.

13.4.7 Actuators and Effectors

- Purpose: Actuators and effectors translate decisions made by the robotic system into physical actions.
- Functionality: Actuators, such as electric motors or hydraulic systems, execute movements and tasks specified by the robot's control system. Effectors, like grippers or welding tools, perform specific actions in manufacturing processes. The coordination of actuators and effectors allows robots to carry out diverse tasks with precision.

13.4.8 Interoperability Standards

- Purpose: Interoperability standards ensure seamless integration and communication among diverse IoT devices and robotic systems.
- Functionality: Adherence to established communication standards, such as MQTT (Message Queuing Telemetry Transport) or OPC UA (Open Platform Communications Unified Architecture), promotes interoperability. Standardized data formats and protocols facilitate the exchange of information, enabling different devices to work cohesively within the IoT-integrated environment.

13.5 INTEGRATION BENEFITS

The integration of IoT and robotics in manufacturing brings forth a myriad of benefits, revolutionizing industrial processes and paving the way for a more efficient and intelligent manufacturing landscape. Below are some key advantages.

13.5.1 Enhanced Efficiency

The integration of IoT and robotics automates routine and repetitive tasks within manufacturing processes. This not only reduces the workload on human operators but also enhances the precision and consistency of task execution. As robots equipped with IoT capabilities take on mundane activities, human workers can redirect their efforts toward more complex and strategic aspects of production, fostering a more efficient and dynamic work environment (Fedak et al., 2015).

13.5.2 Real-time Monitoring and Control

The deployment of IoT sensors on robots ensures a continuous stream of real-time data regarding various operations. This wealth of information empowers operators to monitor production processes with unprecedented granularity. The instant access to data enables quick decision-making, allowing operators to respond promptly to any deviations or issues, ultimately leading to improved overall system responsiveness (Feki et al., 2013).

13.5.3 PREDICTIVE MAINTENANCE

With the integration of IoT, sensors are employed to monitor the condition of robotic components. This continuous monitoring allows for the early detection of anomalies or signs of wear. By implementing predictive maintenance algorithms, manufacturers can schedule maintenance activities proactively, preventing critical failures and minimizing downtime. This predictive approach extends the lifespan of equipment and optimizes the overall maintenance strategy.

13.5.4 QUALITY IMPROVEMENT

The incorporation of IoT sensors in robots contributes to a data-driven approach to quality control. These sensors enable robots to adaptively respond to variations in product quality by autonomously adjusting parameters. If deviations from established quality standards are detected, the system can swiftly make the necessary adjustments, ensuring consistent and high-quality production outputs (Peterson, 2017).

13.5.5 COST REDUCTION

One of the immediate benefits of integrating IoT and robotics in manufacturing is the reduction in labor costs. By automating tasks traditionally performed by human workers, companies can achieve operational cost savings. This shift toward automation not only reduces labor expenses but also enhances overall operational efficiency, contributing to a significant reduction in the total cost of production.

13.5.6 FLEXIBILITY AND ADAPTABILITY

The synergy between IoT and robotics introduces a new level of flexibility and adaptability in manufacturing processes. Robots equipped with IoT capabilities can dynamically adjust to changes in production requirements. This agility allows for efficient reprogramming and redeployment of robots, ensuring that manufacturing processes remain responsive to evolving demands and market conditions.

13.5.7 INVENTORY MANAGEMENT

The integration of IoT in robotics facilitates accurate and real-time tracking of inventory levels, which allows manufacturers to implement just-in-time production strategies, minimizing excess stock and optimizing supply chain efficiency. This, in turn, leads to improved inventory turnover rates and reduced holding costs.

13.5.8 HUMAN-ROBOT COLLABORATION

In the realm of collaborative robotics (Cobots), IoT sensors play a crucial role in ensuring safe interactions between robots and human workers. These sensors can detect the presence of humans in the vicinity, prompting robots to adjust their actions to prevent accidents or injuries. This enhances workplace safety and promotes effective collaboration between humans and robots on the factory floor.

13.5.9 ENERGY EFFICIENCY

Optimized Resource Usage: IoT sensors contribute to the optimization of energy consumption within manufacturing facilities. By monitoring and analyzing energy usage patterns, manufacturers can identify opportunities for optimization. This focus on energy efficiency aligns with sustainability goals and results in cost savings associated with reduced energy consumption.

13.5.10 DATA-DRIVEN DECISION-MAKING

Analytical Insights: The integration of IoT generates a vast amount of data, and the utilization of analytical tools is key to extracting actionable insights. By leveraging data analytics, manufacturers can gain a deeper understanding of their operations, identify trends, and make informed decisions. This data-driven decision-making process enhances the overall efficiency and competitiveness of the manufacturing ecosystem.

13.5.11 COMPETITIVE ADVANTAGE

Innovation and Differentiation: Companies that embrace the integration of IoT and robotics show a commitment to technological innovation. This provides them with a competitive advantage in the marketplace and positions them as industry leaders at the forefront of adopting advanced manufacturing practices. The ability to innovate and differentiate through the integration of cutting-edge technologies becomes a strategic asset in a rapidly evolving industrial landscape.

13.5.12 ADHERENCE TO INDUSTRY 4.0 PRINCIPLES

Alignment with Industry Trends: The integration of IoT and robotics aligns manufacturing operations with the principles of Industry 4.0. This transformative approach to industrial production emphasizes the development of smart factories characterized by interconnected, intelligent systems. By embracing IoT and robotics, manufacturers position themselves at the forefront of industry trends, contributing to the evolution of smart manufacturing practices that prioritize automation, efficiency, and connectivity.

The integration of IoT and robotics in manufacturing brings about a profound transformation by addressing specific facets of operational enhancement. From task automation and real-time monitoring to predictive maintenance and data-driven decision-making, these advancements collectively reshape manufacturing processes, providing businesses with a comprehensive toolkit for sustained success in a dynamic and evolving industrial landscape (Miraz et al., 2015).

13.6 INTEGRATION CHALLENGES AND SOLUTIONS

The integration of IoT and robotics in manufacturing, while offering numerous benefits, also presents challenges that need to be addressed for successful implementation. Below are some common challenges and potential solutions.

13.6.1 DATA SECURITY AND PRIVACY

- Challenge: Transmitting sensitive manufacturing data through IoT networks raises concerns about data security and privacy.
- Solution: Implement robust encryption protocols for data in transit. Use secure, authenticated connections between devices. Follow industry best practices for data security and compliance.

13.6.2 INTEROPERABILITY ISSUES

- Challenge: Integration of diverse devices and systems may lead to interoperability issues, hindering seamless communication.
- Solution: Adopt standardized communication protocols (e.g., OPC UA, MQTT) to ensure interoperability. Prioritize IoT devices and robotics that adhere to industry standards. Invest in middleware solutions that facilitate communication between different technologies.

13.6.3 HIGH INITIAL COSTS

- Challenge: Acquiring and implementing IoT-enabled robotic systems can incur high upfront costs.
- Solution: Conduct a thorough cost–benefit analysis to justify the investment. Explore financing options or phased implementations to spread costs over time. Consider the long-term gains in efficiency, quality, and reduced operational costs.

13.6.4 COMPLEX INTEGRATION PROCESS

- Challenge: Integrating IoT and robotics into existing manufacturing processes can be complex and time-consuming.
- Solution: Engage with experienced system integrators or consultants. Plan a phased implementation to minimize disruptions. Invest in employee training to ensure a smooth transition.

13.6.5 LACK OF SKILLED WORKFORCE

- Challenge: The integration of advanced technologies may require a workforce with specialized skills.
- Solution: Invest in training programs for existing employees to enhance their skills. Collaborate with educational institutions to develop a pipeline of skilled workers. Leverage external expertise through partnerships or consultancy.

13.6.6 Scalability Issues

- Challenge: Scaling up IoT-integrated robotics for growing production needs may pose challenges.
- Solution: Choose scalable and modular solutions that can adapt to changing requirements. Design systems with future expansion in mind. Regularly assess and update technology to accommodate increased production demands.

13.6.7 Data Overload and Analysis

- Challenge: The vast amount of data generated by IoT devices can be overwhelming, leading to challenges in analysis.
- Solution: Implement advanced analytics and machine learning tools for data processing. Focus on actionable insights rather than collecting excessive data. Regularly review and refine data analysis strategies.

13.6.8 Ethical and Social Implications

- Challenge: Automation may lead to job displacement and ethical considerations.
- Solution: Develop strategies for reskilling and upskilling the workforce. Engage in transparent communication with employees about automation plans. Consider societal impact and contribute to responsible automation practices.

Addressing these challenges requires a holistic approach, involving technological, organizational, and human-centric solutions. Continuous evaluation, adaptation, and a commitment to addressing the concerns of stakeholders are essential for successful IoT and robotics integration in manufacturing.

13.7 HUMAN-ROBOT COLLABORATION IN MANUFACTURING

Human-robot collaboration in manufacturing represents a paradigm shift, where robots and human workers work together in shared workspaces to combine their unique strengths. This collaborative approach leverages the capabilities of both humans and robots, fostering increased efficiency, flexibility, and adaptability in manufacturing processes. Here's an exploration of key aspects of human-robot collaboration in manufacturing

Collaborative robots (Cobots) have emerged as a significant technological advancement in the field of robotics and automation. Unlike traditional industrial robots that operate in isolation, Cobots are designed to work collaboratively with humans in shared workspaces. These robots are specifically engineered to enhance human-robot cooperation, enabling safer and more efficient industrial operations across various sectors.

The concept of Cobots originated from the growing need for human-robot collaboration to address limitations in conventional manufacturing processes. While traditional robots excel in repetitive, high-speed tasks, they often require safety cages or barriers to separate them from human workers due to their potential hazards. Cobots, on the other hand, are designed with built-in safety features, sensing capabilities, and advanced programming that enable them to interact directly with humans without compromising safety (Parviainen & Coeckelbergh, 2020).

The significance of Cobots lies in their ability to augment human capabilities and address the challenges faced by industries seeking to improve productivity, flexibility, and workplace safety. Cobots can assist with repetitive or physically demanding tasks, allowing human workers to focus on higher-level responsibilities that require cognitive skills, problem-solving, and creativity. This collaboration between humans and Cobots creates a synergy that maximizes efficiency, productivity, and job satisfaction.

Cobots are equipped with advanced sensors, vision systems, and adaptive control algorithms, enabling them to operate in dynamic environments and respond to human actions and commands. They can detect and adapt to changes in their surroundings, ensuring safe interaction with humans and avoiding collisions or accidents. This inherent adaptability makes Cobots versatile and suitable for a wide range of applications across industries such as manufacturing, logistics, healthcare, and even domestic settings.

As the field of robotics continues to evolve, Cobots represent a paradigm shift toward human-centered automation. By leveraging their capabilities, industries can achieve increased productivity, improved quality control, reduced operational costs, and enhanced workplace safety. Moreover, Cobots offer a flexible and cost-effective automation solution for small- and medium-sized enterprises (SMEs) that may have previously faced barriers to adopting traditional industrial robots (Jenkins et al., 1969).

13.8 ARTIFICIAL INTELLIGENCE INTEGRATION IN INTERNET OF THINGS ROBOTS

The successful integration of AI and machine learning (ML) with IoT robotics in manufacturing involves a strategic approach. Begin by identifying specific use cases, such as predictive maintenance or process optimization, where AI and ML can enhance the capabilities of robotic systems. Establish robust data collection processes from IoT sensors and preprocess the data for effective use in ML algorithms. Select appropriate AI and ML algorithms, create comprehensive training datasets, and implement mechanisms for continuous learning, enabling robotics systems to adapt to evolving conditions. Integrate AI modules seamlessly with the control systems of IoT-integrated robotics, facilitating real-time decision-making (Kim & Kang, 2005).

Implement feedback loops and closed-loop control mechanisms, allowing AI models to continuously refine robotic actions based on real-world outcomes. Prioritize human-AI collaboration by designing interfaces that enable human workers to interact with and provide input to AI systems. Rigorously test AI and ML models, ensuring accuracy, reliability, and ethical considerations, including explainability and transparency. Implement cybersecurity measures to safeguard AI models and data, and ensure compliance with relevant regulations and ethical guidelines. Foster a collaborative culture among employees, providing training on human-AI collaboration. Establish continuous improvement processes, monitor performance metrics, and iterate on the integration strategy to unlock the full potential of AI and ML in enhancing the efficiency and adaptability of manufacturing processes (Kurfess, 2018).

13.9 CASE STUDIES OF SUCCESSFUL IMPLEMENTATIONS

13.9.1 SIEMENS AND PREDICTIVE MAINTENANCE

- Scenario: Siemens, a global manufacturing and technology company, implemented IoT-integrated robotics for predictive maintenance in its factories.
- Implementation Details: IoT sensors were integrated into robotic systems to monitor equipment health and performance in real-time. Predictive maintenance algorithms analyzed the data to anticipate potential issues and schedule maintenance before failures occurred.
- Outcomes:
  - Significant reduction in unplanned downtime.
  - Improved efficiency and lifespan of manufacturing equipment.

13.9.2 FANUC AND COLLABORATIVE ROBOTS

- Scenario: FANUC, a leading robotics manufacturer, implemented Cobots with IoT capabilities in various manufacturing applications.
- Implementation Details: Cobots were equipped with sensors for human-robot collaboration, ensuring safe and efficient interaction in shared workspaces. IoT connectivity allowed for real-time monitoring of production processes and performance metrics.
- Outcomes:
  - Enhanced safety in human-robot collaboration.
  - Increased flexibility and adaptability in manufacturing processes.

13.9.3 TESLA'S SMART FACTORY

- Scenario: Tesla, an electric vehicle manufacturer, incorporated IoT and robotics in its gigafactories for streamlined production.
- Implementation Details: Robotic arms equipped with IoT sensors were utilized for precision tasks in the assembly line. IoT devices facilitated real-time monitoring of production metrics, energy usage, and equipment health.
- Outcomes:
  - Increased production efficiency and quality.
  - Enhanced data-driven decision-making for process optimization.

13.9.4 ABB'S ROBOTICS AND CONDITION MONITORING

- Scenario: ABB, a multinational robotics and automation company, implemented IoT for condition monitoring in its robotic systems.

- Implementation Details: Sensors were integrated into robotic components to monitor temperature, vibration, and other performance indicators. Data analytics were employed for predictive maintenance and performance optimization.
- Outcomes:
  - Improved reliability and availability of robotic systems.
  - Reduced maintenance costs and downtime.

13.9.5 BOSCH REXROTH'S FACTORY OF THE FUTURE

- Scenario: Bosch Rexroth, a provider of drive and control technologies, developed a "Factory of the Future" concept.
- Implementation Details: Integrated IoT-enabled robotics for real-time monitoring and control of manufacturing processes. Embraced a modular and flexible production system that adapted to changing demands.
- Outcomes:
  - Increased production flexibility and responsiveness.
  - Enhanced efficiency through data-driven insights.

These case studies highlight the successful integration of IoT and robotics in various manufacturing contexts, leading to improvements in efficiency, predictive maintenance, safety, and overall operational excellence (BBC, 2010).

13.10 CONCLUSION

The integration of AI, ML, and IoT with robotics represents a transformative leap forward in the landscape of manufacturing. This synergy not only enhances the efficiency and precision of industrial processes but also introduces a new paradigm of adaptability and responsiveness. By identifying specific use cases, implementing robust data collection and preprocessing, and selecting appropriate algorithms, organizations can harness the power of AI and ML to optimize tasks such as predictive maintenance and quality control (Khang & Rath et al., 2024).

The seamless integration of these technologies with robotics systems, accompanied by feedback loops and closed-loop control mechanisms, ensures a dynamic and evolving manufacturing environment. Human-AI collaboration, cybersecurity measures, and a strong organizational culture further contribute to the success of this integration. As industries embrace continuous improvement and monitor key performance metrics, the full potential of AI, ML, and IoT-integrated robotics unfolds, redefining manufacturing processes for a more intelligent, efficient, and adaptable future (Bogue, 2014).

REFERENCES

Alpaydin, E., Introduction to Machine Learning, The MIT Press, London. 2023. https://www. google.com/books?hl=en&lr=&id=tZnSDwAAQBAJ&oi=fnd&pg=PR7&dq=Introduction+to+Machine+Learning,+The+MIT+Press,+London&ots=F4RRbl4vEh&sig=g0lGPkpZ7NRSEgC4DlPbYvPHDmw

Bogue, R., The role of artificial intelligence in robotics. Ind. Robot, 41, 2, 119–123, 2014. https://doi.org/10.1108/IR-01-2014-0300

BBC, Robots Then and Now. Archived 2010-12-20 at the Wayback Machine. http://news.bbc.co.uk/cbbcnews/hi/find_out/guides/tech/robots/newsid_3914000/3914569.stm.

BHR, Business History Review, 45, 3, 397–399, 1971. https://cs.stanford.edu/people/eroberts/courses/soco/projects/1998-99/robotics/history.html

Cohen, M. H., Giangola, J. P., Balogh, J., *Voice User Interface Design*, Addison-Wesley Professional. Page 5–6, 2004. https://www.google.com/books?hl=en&lr=&id=PI_n2EcJfT0C&oi=fnd&pg=PR17&dq=Voice+user+interface+design.+Addison-Wesley+Professional&ots=qVPo8cG6ab&sig=BkUaJfF5eFdJ9fHS6ntYylbOu7A

Fedak, V., Durovsky, F., Uveges, R., Kyslan, K., Lacko, M., Implementation of robot control algorithms by real-time control system. Int. J. Eng. Res. Afr., 18, 112–119, 2015. https://www.scientific.net/JERA.18.112

Feki, M. A., Kawsar, F., Boussard, M., Trappeniers, L., The internet of things: The next technological revolution. Computer, 46, 2, 24–25, 2013. https://ieeexplore.ieee.org/abstract/document/6457383/

Jenkins, R., *Science and Technology in the Industrial Revolution*, A. E. Musson and E. Robinson (Eds.), University of Toronto Press, Toronto. Page viii, 1969, 534. https://search.proquest.com/openview/5db2a3f09dc968530563a34cca9c40b7/1?pq-origsite=gscholar&cbl=1816411

Kim, M., Kang, K. C., Formal Construction and Verification of Home Service Robots: A Case Study, in: *Automated Technology for Verification and Analysis. ATVA 2005. Lecture Notes in Computer Science*, vol. 3707, D. A. Peled and Y. K. Tsay (Eds.), Springer, Berlin, Heidelberg, 2005. https://api.taylorfrancis.com/content/books/mono/download?identifierName=doi&identifierValue=10.1201/9781315220352&type=googlepdf

Khang A., Hajimahmud V. A., Ali R. N., Hahanov V., Avramovic Z., Triwiyanto, The Role of Machine Vision in Manufacturing and Industrial Revolution 4.0, in: *Machine Vision and Industrial Robotics in Manufacturing: Approaches, Technologies, and Applications*, 1st Ed., CRC Press, 2024. https://doi.org/10.1201/9781003438137

Khang, A., Rath, K. C., Anh, P. T., Rath, S. K., Bhattacharya, S., Quantum-Based Robotics in the High-Tech Healthcare Industry: Innovations and Applications, in: *Medical Robotics and AI-Assisted Diagnostics for a High-Tech Healthcare Industry*, A. Khang (Ed.), IGI Global. Page 1–27, 2024. https://doi.org/10.4018/979-8-3693-2105-8.ch001

Kurfess, T. R. (Ed.), *Robotics and Automation Handbook*, CRC Press. Page 3–4, 2018. https://api.taylorfrancis.com/content/books/mono/download?identifierName=doi&identifierValue=10.1201/9781315220352&type=googlepdf

Miraz, M. H., Ali, M., Excell, P. S., Picking, R., A review on Internet of Things (IoT), Internet of Everything (IoE) and Internet of Nano Things (IoNT), 219–224, 2015. https://ieeexplore.ieee.org/abstract/document/7317398/

Parviainen, J., Coeckelbergh, M., The political choreography of the Sophia robot: Beyond robot rights and citizenship to political performances for the social robotics market. AI & Society, 1–10, 2020. https://link.springer.com/article/10.1007/s00146-020-01104-w

Peterson, B., I met Sophia, the world's first robot citizen, and the way she said goodbye nearly broke my heart. Enterprise, in: Digital version, 2017. https://www.businessinsider.in/i-met-sophia-the-words-first-robot-citizen-and-the-way-she-said-goodbye-nearly-broke-my-heart/articleshow/61322091.cms

14 Robotic Process Applications and Tools for Manufacturing Sector

Alex Khang, Kali Charan Rath, Suresh Kumar Satapathy, Amaresh Kumar, and Animesh Agrawal

14.1 INTRODUCTION

Robotic process automation (RPA) and artificial intelligence (AI) are the new kids on the block who have garnered a lot of buzz for their ability to disrupt businesses and drive never-before-seen productivity, efficiency, and customer satisfaction.

Robotic process automation is a core technology that acts as the backbone to software robots (Bots) that can interact with digital systems to relieve humans of repetitive, time-consuming, and non-value-added mundane activities. It works best when it is used to handle rule-based processes where the workflows do not change over time or do not require a high rate of human intervention. In the automation journey, RPA is the first baby step. As you automate more of your operations, you will notice bottlenecks where higher-level judgment is needed to move through a workflow. There come the opportunities for AI along with RPA, which can easily handle complex processes that previously could only be done by humans. This is because AI robots can make cognitive decisions using large datasets to predict several possible outcomes, unleashing infinite possibilities.

Businesses can improve operational effectiveness and reduce costs by using RPA. People fill out forms, log into systems, and process mundane transactions on a regular basis. Over the past few years, RPA has grown in popularity as companies try to streamline their variety of operations, including production, IT, HR, finance, and customer service, among other areas, to boost efficiency (Khang & Shah et al., 2023).

The ability of RPA to carry out activities precisely and consistently, around-the-clock, without being fatigued or making mistakes is one of its main benefits. Reducing manual errors, enhancing data quality, and ensuring regulatory compliance can be aided by RPA as well. Human resources can concentrate more on strategic and creative tasks if they are relieved of boring and repetitive jobs. Manufacturing, retail, healthcare, telecom, and banking and finance are some of the sectors where the technology can be used (Abubakar et al., 2021; Azadeh et al., 2021). In the banking industry, it can help automate account opening, loan processing, and customer onboarding; in the healthcare industry, it can help with medical coding, claims processing, and patient scheduling (Bhattacharya & Desai, 2019).

DOI: 10.1201/9781003438137-14

Overall, the value of RPA lies in its ability to automate repetitive processes, freeing up staff to do more important and innovative work. Businesses can use RPA to increase productivity, save expenses, and boost their bottom line (Banerjee & Dey, 2019).

14.1.1 Objectives of Robotic Process Automation

The goal of RPA is to automate routine, rule-based processes to boost productivity, accuracy, and efficiency. The following are some objectives that can be reached with the help of the RPA:

- Automate Repetitive Tasks: Bots are used to automate repetitive operations such as data entry, form filling, and report preparation. In addition to improving accuracy, speed, compliance, and efficiency, this automation can free up workers to work on higher value tasks.
- Increase Productivity: The time needed to do these operations can be drastically reduced by using Bots. This will increase productivity.
- Improve Accuracy: Human error can be eliminated in repetitive tasks with the help of RPA. The risk of errors and inconsistencies is reduced by using Bots to automate these tasks.
- Enhance Customer Satisfaction: Customer care representatives may be freed up to address more complicated problems. Standard FAQs by customers can be handled by chatbots. Customer inquiries may be routed to the correct department or person, and customers may receive timely and consistent responses by automation.
- Enable Compliance: Data entry, processing, and reporting processes can be automated. The risk of non-compliance and the accompanying fines can be mitigated by the automation of these operations. Audit trails are a record of all actions performed by Bots and promote more accountability and transparency. They can be used to prove compliance in highly regulated areas like finance and healthcare.

14.1.2 Novelty of Robotic Process Automation

Automating typical repetitive tasks can speed up company processes, lower costs, and increase accuracy and efficiency. Below are key factors that make RPA a novel technology:

- Easy to Use: It is not necessary to have a deep understanding of programming to use RPA tools. Businesses can use a drag-and-drop interface to build Bots for a wider range of users.
- Noninvasive: There is no need for a complex IT infrastructure or major operational modifications. This makes it easy to put in force RPA technology within an organization, as it is able to work alongside existing approaches and structures.
- Scalable: As an organization expands, RPA can be scaled up or down based on business requirements, allowing it to automate more operations.

- Cost-Effective: RPA can significantly reduce labor costs by automating repetitive tasks, allowing employees to focus more on strategic work.
- Accurate: RPA Bots can perform tasks with high accuracy and consistency, reducing the risk of errors and improving the quality of work.
- Quickly Deployed: RPA tools can be deployed quickly, often in a matter of weeks, allowing organizations to see results and benefits in a short period of time.

14.2   SCOPE OF ROBOTIC PROCESS AUTOMATION

The scope of RPA encompasses a wide range of applications and opportunities for streamlining and automating business processes. It is not limited to specific industries or sectors but can be applied to various business functions across industry domains. It provides opportunities for cost reduction, improved accuracy, faster processing times, enhanced customer experiences, and increased scalability. As technology continues to evolve, the scope of RPA is likely to expand even further, offering organizations new avenues for innovation and digital transformation (Tailor et al., 2022).

Moreover, RPA offers the potential to integrate with other technologies such as AI, machine learning (ML), and natural language processing (NLP). This integration enables intelligent automation, cognitive automation, and process analytics, allowing organizations to make data-driven decisions, gain valuable insights, and further optimize their processes (Dubey et al., 2019).

Enterprise IT needs to delegate mundane repetitive tasks within various areas of the organization to RPA Bots in order to achieve the following goals:

- Task Automation: RPA uses Bots to automate manual and repetitive tasks that are traditionally performed by humans. These Bots are programmed to interact with various software applications, systems, and databases, mimicking human actions and following predefined rules. Enterprise IT can identify such applications and make best use cases for RPA (Erturkmen et al., 2020).
- Process Streamlining: RPA can streamline complex business processes by integrating multiple systems and applications. It enables the seamless flow of data and information between different departments, eliminating the need for manual data entry and reducing errors and delays (Guo et al., 2018).
- Data Integration and Validation: RPA can extract data from various sources, such as emails, documents, spreadsheets, or websites, and integrate it into a central system or database. Bots can validate and cross-check the accuracy of the data, ensuring consistency and reliability.
- System Integration: RPA can integrate with existing IT systems, such as customer relationship management (CRM) software, enterprise resource planning (ERP) systems, or legacy systems. By bridging the gap between different systems, RPA enables efficient data exchange, improves data accuracy, and eliminates the need for manual data transfers.

- Rule-Based Decision-Making: RPA Bots can be programmed to follow specific business rules and decision-making processes. They can analyze data, compare it against predefined criteria, and make decisions or recommendations based on those rules. This allows for standardized and consistent decision-making across the organization.
- Exception Handling: RPA can handle exceptions or errors in automated processes. When a Bot encounters an exception, it can trigger an alert or notification, enabling human intervention to resolve the issue. By automating routine tasks, RPA frees up human resources to focus on handling exceptions and more complex activities.
- Scalability and Flexibility: RPA offers scalability by allowing organizations to deploy multiple Bots simultaneously to handle a large volume of tasks. It also provides flexibility as Bots can be easily reconfigured or updated to accommodate changes in business processes or system requirements.
- Reporting and Analytics: RPA can generate real-time reports and analytics on process performance providing valuable insights into productivity, efficiency, and compliance. These reports help organizations identify bottlenecks, optimize processes, and make data-driven decisions for continuous improvement.
- Noninvasive Integration: RPA can integrate with existing systems and applications without requiring major changes to the underlying infrastructure. It can interact with both legacy and modern systems, including web-based and desktop applications, mainframes, databases, and more. This noninvasive nature of RPA allows for faster implementation and minimizes disruptions to existing IT ecosystems.

14.3 METHODOLOGY

The fundamental principle of RPA revolves around the concept of automating repetitive and rule-based tasks using Bots. It leverages technology to mimic human actions and interactions with digital systems, allowing for the execution of predefined tasks and processes with speed, accuracy, and consistency.

The methodology followed for implementing an RPA involves the following steps:

- Process Identification: The first step is to identify the manual or repetitive tasks that can be automated using an RPA. This involves analyzing the existing business processes and identifying tasks that are time-consuming and prone to errors.
- Process Mapping: Once the tasks have been identified, the next step is to map out the steps involved in each process. This helps to identify areas where automation can be introduced and ensures that the RPA solution is customized to meet the specific requirements of the organization.
- Bot Development: After the process has been mapped out, the next step is to develop the RPA Bots that will carry out the automated tasks. This involves configuring the RPA tool to perform the required actions, such as data entry or form filling.

- Testing: Once the Bots have been developed, they need to be thoroughly tested to ensure that they are functioning as intended and meeting the specified requirements. This involves testing them in a controlled non-production environment and identifying and resolving any issues that arise.
- Deployment: After the testing phase is complete, the RPA Bots can be deployed into the production environment. This involves integrating them with the existing systems and processes and ensuring that they are running smoothly.
- Maintenance: Finally, RPA solutions require ongoing maintenance to ensure that they continue to operate effectively. This involves monitoring the Bots and making any bug fixes, patch updates, and upgrades as necessary as the business processes evolve.

14.3.1 ADVANTAGES OF ROBOTIC PROCESS AUTOMATION

Implementing RPA offers the following advantages for various industries:

- Increased Efficiency and Productivity: RPA automates repetitive and rule-based tasks, allowing employees to focus on higher-value activities. By reducing manual work, organizations can significantly improve efficiency and productivity, completing tasks faster and with fewer errors.
- Cost Savings: RPA eliminates the need for human resources to perform mundane and repetitive tasks, resulting in significant cost savings over time. Organizations can achieve cost reductions by reducing labor costs, improving process efficiency, and eliminating errors that lead to financial losses.
- Improved Accuracy and Data Quality: RPA Bots perform tasks consistently and accurately, minimizing errors and ensuring data integrity. By automating data entry and validation processes, RPA reduces the risk of mistakes caused by manual data handling, leading to improved data quality and decision-making.
- Enhanced Customer Experience: RPA enables organizations to respond to customer requests quickly and accurately. Bots can automate customer onboarding processes, handle inquiries, and process transactions efficiently, resulting in faster response times and improved customer satisfaction.
- Scalability and Flexibility: RPA allows organizations to scale their automation efforts easily. Additional Bots can be deployed as needed to handle increased workload or new tasks. RPA is also flexible and can adapt to changing business requirements, making it suitable for organizations of different sizes and industries.
- Compliance and Auditability: RPA can ensure compliance with regulations and internal policies by consistently following predefined rules and workflows. The automated nature of RPA enables organizations to generate detailed logs and audit trails, providing transparency and traceability for compliance purposes.
- Integration with Existing Systems: RPA can seamlessly integrate with various systems, applications, and databases. This integration capability allows

organizations to automate end-to-end processes that involve multiple systems, eliminating the need for manual data transfer and reducing system integration challenges.

- Quick Return on Investment (ROI): RPA implementations often yield a quick ROI due to the rapid automation of repetitive tasks and the resulting cost savings. Organizations can realize ROI within a short period, freeing up resources for further automation initiatives.
- Employee Empowerment and Job Satisfaction: RPA enables employees to focus on more strategic and creative tasks, enhancing their job satisfaction and engagement. By automating mundane and repetitive tasks, RPA liberates employees to utilize their skills and expertise in more meaningful ways (Khang & Muthmainnah et al., 2023).
- Continuous Improvement: RPA provides valuable insights into process performance through real-time monitoring and reporting. Organizations can identify bottlenecks, inefficiencies, and opportunities for optimization, leading to continuous process improvement and operational excellence.

These advantages make RPA a valuable technology for organizations seeking to optimize their operations, reduce costs, improve productivity, and enhance customer experiences.

14.3.2 LIMITATIONS OF ROBOTIC PROCESS AUTOMATION

Below are the major limitations of RPA:

- Limited Cognitive Abilities: RPA is primarily designed to automate repetitive and rule-based tasks that follow predefined workflows. RPA Bots lack advanced cognitive abilities, such as NLP, complex decision-making, and understanding unstructured data. This limitation restricts their effectiveness in handling tasks that require human-like judgment, reasoning, and problem-solving skills (Khang & Rani et al., 2023).
- Incompatibility with Outdated Legacy Systems: RPA relies on the ability to interact with existing software applications and systems. Legacy systems with outdated technology or complex architectures may pose challenges for RPA implementation. Integration issues and compatibility constraints can limit the scope of automation and require additional efforts to enable seamless communication between RPA Bots and legacy systems.
- Need for Stable and Structured Processes: RPA is most effective when applied to stable and structured processes with consistent inputs and outputs. Processes that involve frequent changes, exceptions, or complex variations can be difficult to automate with RPA alone. Adapting RPA to handle dynamic and unstructured processes may require additional customization, configuration, and ongoing maintenance.
- Lack of Contextual Understanding: RPA Bots typically operate based on predefined rules and instructions, lacking the ability to understand the

context or meaning behind the tasks they perform. This limitation can hinder their ability to handle tasks that require human-level comprehension, interpretation, and contextual decision-making.

- Limited Scalability and Robustness: While RPA can handle repetitive tasks efficiently, its scalability and robustness may face limitations in certain scenarios. Scaling up RPA initiatives to handle high volumes of tasks or complex processes can require significant infrastructure and resource investments. Additionally, RPA systems may encounter challenges in handling unexpected errors, exceptions, or system disruptions.

- Security and Data Privacy Concerns: RPA involves the automation of various tasks that often include sensitive data, such as personally identifiable information (PII), financial data, or proprietary information. Ensuring data security, privacy, and compliance becomes crucial when implementing RPA. Inadequate security measures or vulnerabilities in RPA systems can lead to data breaches, unauthorized access, or misuse of sensitive information.

- Dependency on Structured Inputs: RPA typically relies on structured inputs, such as forms, templates, or standardized interfaces. Handling unstructured data, such as free-text documents, images, or audio files, can be challenging for RPA Bots. Additional techniques, like optical character recognition (OCR) or NLP, may be required to handle and process unstructured data effectively.

- Maintenance and Adaptability: RPA implementations require ongoing maintenance, updates, and monitoring. As systems, applications, or processes change, RPA Bots may require reconfiguration or customization to adapt to new requirements. This ongoing maintenance effort can add complexity and cost to RPA initiatives, requiring dedicated resources and expertise.

Understanding these limitations helps organizations assess the suitability and feasibility of RPA for their specific processes and consider complementary technologies or approaches to address these challenges effectively.

14.4 GROWING TRENDS IN ROBOTIC PROCESS AUTOMATION

- Intelligent Automation: RPA is evolving to include AI and ML capabilities, allowing Bots to make decisions and handle complex tasks that were previously difficult to automate. Combining rule-based Bots with ML algorithms will be a radical redesign in digital processes. RPA Bots constantly evolve from self-learning AI algorithms. They will not only enter the data in IT systems but also find patterns in that data simultaneously. This new level of intelligent automation is creating more opportunities for businesses to automate higher-value tasks and improve business outcomes.

- Cloud-Based RPA: Cloud-based RPA solutions are becoming increasingly popular, offering greater flexibility, scalability, and security compared to on-premise solutions. RPA cloud deployment enables companies to process data at a whim. It means that they can virtually build an RPA infrastructure and deploy Bots. Cloud-based RPA tools enable organizations to access the benefits of automation without the need for significant upfront investment or IT resources.

- Cognitive Automation: Cognitive automation uses advanced technologies like NLP and computer vision to enable Bots to perform tasks that require human-like perception and judgment. This includes tasks like data analysis, pattern recognition, and decision-making.
- Hyper-Automation: Hyper-automation is a term used to describe the integration of multiple automation technologies, including RPA, AI, ML, and process mining, to automate end-to-end business processes. This approach offers organizations the ability to achieve even greater levels of automation and business process optimization. Hyper-automation is a business-driven, disciplined approach that organizations use to rapidly identify, vet, and automate as many business and IT processes as possible. It involves the orchestrated use of multiple technologies, tools, or platforms, including RPA, AI, ML, blockchain, event-driven software architecture, BPM, and intelligent business process management suites (iBPMS), integration platform as a service (iPaaS), low-code/no-code tools, packaged software, and other types of decision, process, and task automation tools.
- Low-Code and No-Code RPA: Low-code and no-code RPA platforms are emerging, allowing business users to create and deploy Bots with minimal IT involvement. This democratizes automation, making it accessible to a wider range of users and accelerating the pace of automation adoption.
- Paperless Office: RPA trends are growing toward intelligent Bots for extracting, filing, and processing data online. The virtual workforce of Bots might be on its way to eliminate paper invoices, customer acquisition forms, and everything that could be lost in the office. The predetermined Bots will ensure that paperwork is minimized and productivity is increased.

14.5 ROBOTIC PROCESS AUTOMATION IN SMART MANUFACTURING INDUSTRY

Robotic process automation plays a significant role in the smart manufacturing industry by automating various processes and enhancing operational efficiency. Below are some key applications of RPA in smart manufacturing industries.

14.5.1 APPLICATION OF ROBOTIC PROCESS AUTOMATION IN PRODUCTION PLANNING AND SCHEDULING

Production planning and scheduling can be automated by extracting data from various systems such as enterprise resource planning (ERP) and manufacturing execution system (MES). Bots can analyze production orders, inventory levels, and machine availability to generate optimized production schedules, ensuring efficient resource utilization and timely delivery.

Robotic process automation offers significant advantages in automating the production planning and scheduling processes in various industries. Below is a detailed discussion on the application of RPA in production planning and scheduling:

- Data Integration and Analysis: RPA can extract data from different sources, such as ERP and systems, production databases, and spreadsheets. Bots can integrate this data and perform data cleansing and validation, ensuring accurate and consistent information for production planning and scheduling.

- Demand Forecasting: RPA can analyze historical sales data, market trends, and customer demand patterns to generate accurate demand forecasts. Bots can automate data collection, perform statistical analysis, and generate demand forecasts that help in optimizing production plans and scheduling resources accordingly.

- Production Capacity Optimization: RPA can assess production capacities based on factors such as machine capabilities, labor availability, and production line efficiency. Bots can analyze the production requirements and capacities, taking into account various constraints, to optimize the allocation of resources and maximize production throughput.

- Automated Scheduling: RPA can automate the scheduling process by generating optimized production schedules based on predefined rules, priorities, and constraints. Bots consider factors such as available resources, production sequences, order priorities, and delivery deadlines to generate efficient schedules that minimize idle time, reduce changeovers, and optimize resource utilization.

- Real-Time Adjustments: RPA can monitor real-time production data, such as machine status, material availability, and order changes, to make adjustments to the production schedule. Bots can dynamically adapt the schedule to accommodate unforeseen events or changes, ensuring flexibility and responsiveness in meeting production demands.

- Collaborative Planning: RPA enables collaborative production planning and scheduling by automating communication and coordination among different stakeholders. Bots can generate notifications, alerts, and reminders for relevant personnel, ensuring timely communication and decision-making. This collaboration streamlines the planning process and improves coordination between departments and teams.

- Inventory Optimization: RPA can integrate with inventory management systems to automate inventory tracking and optimization. Bots can monitor inventory levels, analyze production schedules, and trigger replenishment orders to maintain optimal inventory levels. This automation ensures that production plans are aligned with inventory availability, minimizing stockouts and excess inventory.

- Reporting and Analytics: RPA can automate the generation of production reports and performance analytics. Bots can extract relevant data, perform calculations and analysis, and generate reports on key performance indicators (KPIs) such as production efficiency, utilization rates, and on-time delivery. These reports provide valuable insights for continuous improvement and decision-making.

By applying RPA to production planning and scheduling processes, organizations can achieve enhanced accuracy, faster decision-making, improved resource utilization, and increased production efficiency. It enables organizations to optimize their production processes, respond to changing demands effectively, and drive overall operational excellence in manufacturing.

14.5.2 Application of Robotic Process Automation in Quality Control and Inspection

Robotic process automation can automate quality control and inspection processes in smart manufacturing. Bots can analyze sensor data, images, or measurement data obtained from Internet of Things (IoT) devices and cameras to identify defects, deviations, or anomalies in real-time. This automation improves accuracy, reduces human error, and enables proactive quality management. Below is a detailed discussion on the application of RPA in quality control and inspection:

- Automated Data Collection: RPA can collect data from various sources, including sensors, manufacturing equipment, and quality control instruments. Bots can extract data in real-time, ensuring accurate and timely information for quality control analysis.
- Real-Time Monitoring: RPA enables continuous monitoring of production processes and quality metrics. Bots can analyze sensor data and performance indicators, detecting anomalies or deviations from set quality standards. Real-time monitoring allows for immediate intervention and corrective actions, reducing the risk of defective products.
- Defect Detection: RPA uses image recognition and machine vision techniques to identify defects in products or components. Bots can analyze images or visual data captured during the production process to identify flaws, surface defects, or irregularities. This automation improves the accuracy and speed of defect detection, reducing reliance on manual inspection.
- Statistical Process Control (SPC): RPA can automate SPC techniques to monitor and maintain quality standards. Bots can collect data, calculate control limits, and analyze process variations. By automating SPC, RPA helps manufacturers identify process trends, detect deviations, and take corrective actions to maintain consistent quality levels.
- Quality Data Analysis: RPA can automate the analysis of quality data, including dimensional measurements, tolerances, or test results. Bots can extract data from multiple sources, perform calculations, and generate quality reports or statistical analysis. This automation enables quick and accurate insights into product quality, facilitating decision-making and process improvement.
- Non-Destructive Testing (NDT): RPA can automate NDT processes to assess the integrity of materials or components. Bots can operate testing equipment, collect data from methods like ultrasonic testing, radiography,

or magnetic particle inspection, and analyze the results. This automation improves testing efficiency, reduces human error, and enhances the accuracy of defect detection.

- Quality Documentation and Reporting: RPA can automate the generation of quality control documents and reports. Bots can compile data, populate templates, and generate customized reports on quality metrics, defect rates, or compliance requirements. This automation streamlines documentation processes, reduces manual errors, and ensures consistent reporting.

- Quality Process Integration: RPA can integrate quality control processes with other manufacturing systems, such as ERP or MES. Bots can extract data from these systems, update quality records, and trigger alerts or notifications based on predefined rules. This integration enhances data visibility, facilitates real-time quality control, and improves traceability throughout the manufacturing process.

By implementing RPA in quality control and inspection, manufacturers can achieve improved product quality, reduced defects, enhanced efficiency, and better compliance with industry standards. It streamlines quality processes, enables proactive monitoring, and empowers manufacturers to deliver products that meet customer expectations.

14.5.3 APPLICATION OF ROBOTIC PROCESS AUTOMATION IN INVENTORY AND SUPPLY CHAIN MANAGEMENT

Robotic process automation can streamline inventory management and supply chain processes. Bots can monitor inventory levels, trigger reorder requests, and update inventory records in real-time. They can also automate supplier communication, track shipments, and generate alerts for inventory shortages or delays, ensuring efficient inventory management and supply chain operations, as shown in Table 14.1.

Robotic process automation offers several applications in automating inventory and supply chain management processes in the manufacturing industry.

Implementing RPA in inventory and supply chain management processes brings numerous benefits, including improved inventory accuracy, streamlined processes, enhanced data visibility, and cost optimization. It enables organizations to achieve efficient inventory management, responsive supply chains, and better customer service through automation and data-driven decision-making.

RPA tools can automate inventory monitoring, tracking stock levels, and triggering reorder requests based on predefined rules. They can also streamline order processing, invoice reconciliation, and supplier management tasks. By automating these repetitive and rule-based tasks, RPA tools free up valuable time for employees to focus on strategic activities, improve data accuracy, reduce human error, and enhance overall supply chain performance. Additionally, RPA tools facilitate seamless integration with existing systems and enable organizations to gain real-time insights into inventory levels, demand forecasting, and supply chain operations,

TABLE 14.1
Robotic Process Automation Applications in Inventory and Supply Chain Management

Application	Summary
Demand Forecasting	RPA analyzes historical sales data, market trends, and other factors to generate accurate demand forecasts. Bots can collect and analyze data from various sources, such as customer orders, market research, and historical trends. This automation helps in optimizing inventory levels and ensures that the right amount of products or materials is available to meet customer demand.
Inventory Monitoring	RPA automates real-time monitoring of inventory levels, tracking stock levels and triggering reorder requests. Bots can extract data from inventory management systems, track stock levels, and trigger reorder requests based on the predefined thresholds or rules. This automation helps in maintaining optimal inventory levels, minimizing stockouts, and avoiding excess inventory.
Supplier Management	RPA automates communication with suppliers, including purchase orders, order confirmations, and performance monitoring. Bots can also collect and analyze data related to supplier performance, such as on-time delivery, quality issues, or pricing. This automation streamlines supplier management processes and ensures effective collaboration.
Order Processing and Tracking	RPA automates order processing tasks, ensuring data accuracy and providing real-time updates on order status. Bots can extract order information from different systems, verify data accuracy, and update order status in real-time. This automation reduces manual errors, accelerates order processing, and provides visibility into order fulfillment progress.
Supply Chain Visibility	RPA can integrate with various systems and data sources to provide end-to-end visibility into the supply chain. Bots can collect data from suppliers, logistics providers, and internal systems to track the movement of goods, monitor lead times, and identify bottlenecks or delays. This automation enables proactive decision-making, risk mitigation, and optimization of supply chain.
Data Analysis and Reporting	RPA can automate data analysis and reporting in inventory and supply chain management. Bots can extract data from different sources, perform calculations, and generate reports on KPIs such as inventory turnover, order fulfillment rates, and supplier performance. This automation provides actionable insights into process improvement, cost optimization, and strategic decision-making.
Return and Repair Management	RPA can automate the process of managing returns and repairs. Bots can handle return requests, validate return eligibility, initiate return authorizations, and track the status of returns or repairs. This automation streamlines the return and repair process, reduces manual effort, and improves customer satisfaction.
Compliance and Regulatory Requirements	RPA can assist in compliance management and adherence to regulatory requirements. Bots can automate data collection and reporting for compliance purposes, such as tracking product traceability, maintaining safety standards, or managing hazardous materials, telecom product testing against valid spectrum license, etc. This automation ensures accuracy and timeliness in meeting regulatory obligations.

TABLE 14.2

Robotic Process Automation Tools and Descriptions

RPA Tool	Description
UiPath	Is a widely used RPA platform offering a range of features for automating inventory and supply chain processes. It provides visual design capabilities and supports integration with various systems and data sources.
Automation Anywhere	Is a popular RPA tool that enables automation of inventory and supply chain management tasks. It offers a user-friendly interface, robust integration capabilities, and features like Bot analytics and cognitive automation.
Blue Prism	Is an enterprise-grade RPA platform that can be leveraged for automating inventory and supply chain processes. It provides advanced automation capabilities, supports complex workflows, and offers strong security and compliance features.
WorkFusion	Offers an intelligent automation platform that combines RPA with AI capabilities. It can be utilized for automating inventory and supply chain management tasks, including demand forecasting, inventory monitoring, and supplier management.
Pega	Is a comprehensive automation platform that offers both RPA and BPM capabilities. It can be used for automating various aspects of inventory and supply chain management, such as order processing, supply chain visibility, and compliance management.

leading to better decision-making and improved customer satisfaction. Roles and functions of key RPA tools are shown in Table 14.2.

14.5.4 APPLICATION OF ROBOTIC PROCESS AUTOMATION IN DATA INTEGRATION AND ANALYSIS

Robotic process automation can extract and integrate data from multiple sources, such as IoT sensors, manufacturing equipment, and enterprise systems. Bots can consolidate and analyze this data to generate real-time reports, performance dashboards, and predictive analytics. This enables data-driven decision-making, process optimization, and predictive maintenance in smart manufacturing environments.

Data integration involves gathering and consolidating data from multiple sources within a manufacturing organization. Robotic process automation can help streamline this process by automating the extraction, transformation, and loading (ETL) of data. Bots can be programmed to retrieve data from different systems, databases, or files, and then process and combine it into a unified format. This automated data integration eliminates the need for manual data entry, reduces errors, and enhances efficiency.

Once the data is integrated, RPA can be further used for data analysis in the manufacturing industry. Bots can perform various analytical tasks, such as data cleansing, data mining, and statistical analysis. They can identify patterns, trends, and anomalies within the manufacturing data, enabling companies to make data-driven decisions and gain valuable insights, as shown in Table 14.3.

TABLE 14.3

Robotic Process Automation Applications in Data Integration and Analysis

RPA Application	Description	RPA Tool	Required Parametric Data
Data Integration	RPA Bots automate ETL processes, extracting data from various sources within the manufacturing organization, transforming it, and loading it into a unified format. This eliminates manual data entry, reduces errors, and enhances efficiency.	UiPath	Source systems, databases, files, data formats, data mapping, transformation rules, integration workflows.
Real-Time Data Analysis	RPA Bots monitor sensor data from production equipment in real-time, perform analysis, identify patterns, trends, and anomalies, and trigger alerts or actions based on predefined rules or thresholds. Enables proactive maintenance, quality control, and process optimization.	Automation Anywhere	Sensor data, predefined rules or thresholds, real-time monitoring capabilities, analysis algorithms.
Data Cleansing	RPA Bots automate the process of cleaning and standardizing manufacturing data, identifying and rectifying errors, duplicates, and inconsistencies. Ensures data accuracy and reliability.	Blue Prism	Data cleansing rules, error detection algorithms, data validation criteria, cleansing workflows.
Data Mining and Analysis	RPA Bots perform data mining tasks to extract valuable insights from manufacturing data. They analyze historical data, identify correlations, perform statistical analysis, and generate reports or visualizations. Supports data-driven decision making.	WorkFusion	Historical data, mining algorithms, statistical analysis tools, reporting or visualization capabilities.
Integration with Business Applications	RPA Bots facilitate the integration of manufacturing data with other business applications like ERP or CRM systems. They automate data transfer, ensuring data consistency and reducing manual effort.	Kofax	Business application interfaces, data transfer protocols, integration workflows, data consistency rules.

14.5.5 Application of Robotic Process Automation in Equipment Monitoring and Maintenance

Robotic process automation can automate the monitoring and maintenance of manufacturing equipment. Bots can collect data from equipment sensors, track performance metrics, and identify potential maintenance issues or failures. They can schedule maintenance activities, trigger work orders, and notify maintenance personnel, improving equipment uptime and minimizing downtime, as shown in Table 14.4.

TABLE 14.4

Robotic Process Automation Tools in Equipment Monitoring and Maintenance

RPA Tool	Description
UiPath	Is a leading RPA platform that enables the automation of data collection and monitoring tasks.
Automation Anywhere	Provides a comprehensive RPA solution for generating real-time reports and dashboards.
Blue Prism	Is an RPA tool used for predictive maintenance scheduling based on data analysis.
WorkFusion	Offers RPA capabilities for sending automated alerts and notifications in equipment monitoring.
Kofax	Is an RPA tool that streamlines equipment maintenance workflows for efficient monitoring and maintenance.
Pega	Provides RPA integration with IoT devices, allowing real-time monitoring and maintenance of equipment.
WinAutomation	Is an RPA tool used for performing routine maintenance tasks in equipment monitoring and maintenance.
NICE	Offers RPA solutions for automating equipment monitoring and maintenance processes.
AutomationEdge	Provides RPA capabilities for equipment monitoring and maintenance tasks.
EdgeVerveAssistEdge	Is an RPA tool that assists in equipment monitoring and maintenance automation.

14.5.6 Application of Robotic Process Automation in Production Data Management and Reporting

Robotic process automation can automate the collection, consolidation, and reporting of production data. Bots can extract data from different systems and sources, perform data validation and cleansing, and generate standardized reports or KPIs. This automation simplifies data management, enhances data accuracy, and provides timely insights for process optimization and decision-making, as shown in Table 14.5.

14.5.7 Application of Robotic Process Automation in Compliance and Regulatory Reporting

Robotic process automation can assist in compliance management and regulatory reporting in the smart manufacturing industry. Bots can automate the collection of data required for compliance with industry regulations or standards. They can generate accurate reports, validate data against predefined rules, and ensure timely submission of regulatory documentation.

TABLE 14.5

Robotic Process Automation Tools in Production Data Management and Reporting

RPA Tool	Description
UiPath	Is a leading RPA platform that offers automation capabilities for production data management and reporting.
Automation Anywhere	Provides a comprehensive RPA solution for managing and reporting production data.
Blue Prism	Is an RPA tool used for automating production data management tasks and generating reports.
WorkFusion	Offers RPA capabilities for efficient production data management and automated reporting.
Kofax	Is an RPA tool that streamlines production data management processes and enables automated reporting.
Pega	Provides RPA integration for production data management and reporting, allowing for streamlined workflows.
WinAutomation	Is an RPA tool used for automating production data management and reporting tasks.
AutomationEdge	Offers RPA capabilities for production data management and reporting automation.
EdgeVerve AssistEdge	Is an RPA tool designed for production data management and reporting automation.
NICE	Provides RPA solutions for managing and reporting production data efficiently.
Softomotive (Now Microsoft Power Automate)	Is an RPA tool used for production data management and reporting automation.
Kryon	Offers RPA capabilities for production data management and automated reporting tasks.
Jacada	Provides RPA solutions for streamlining production data management and reporting processes.
Redwood Software	Offers RPA capabilities for production data management and reporting automation.
Jidoka	Is an RPA tool used for efficient production data management and automated reporting.
K2	Provides RPA integration for production data management and reporting workflows.
HelpSystems (now Fortra)	Offers RPA solutions for production data management and reporting automation.
Contextor (Now Sopra Banking Software)	Provides RPA capabilities for production data management and reporting tasks.
BlackLine	Offers RPA integration for streamlined production data management and reporting processes.
Thoughtonomy (Now Blue Prism Cloud)	Is an RPA tool used for production data management and reporting automation.
Servicetrace	Provides RPA solutions for production data management and reporting tasks.

14.5.8 Application of Robotic Process Automation in Human Resource Management

Robotic process automation can streamline various human resource (HR) activities such as employee onboarding, training management, shift scheduling, attendance tracking, and performance management. By automating these repetitive tasks, RPA enables HR teams to focus on strategic initiatives, workforce planning, and talent development. Moreover, RPA can integrate with existing manufacturing systems, such as ERP and time and attendance systems, to ensure seamless data flow and accurate HR processes.

This automation improves efficiency and accuracy and enables HR professionals to allocate more time and resources toward strategic initiatives such as talent acquisition, workforce planning, and employee development. By leveraging RPA, enterprises can achieve streamlined HR processes, enhanced data accuracy, improved compliance, and increased operational efficiency. The novelty of RPA lies in its ability to integrate with existing legacy systems, facilitating seamless data exchange and enabling HR teams to make data-driven decisions. Ultimately, RPA empowers HR professionals to optimize their workforce, as shown in Table 14.6.

TABLE 14.6
Robotic Process Automation Tools Used in Human Resource Management

RPA Tool	Description	Advantages	Disadvantages
UiPath	Is a leading RPA platform that offers automation capabilities for various employee onboarding, offboarding, payroll automation, and data entry	• User-friendly interface • Wide range of automation capabilities • Strong community support. Scalability and flexibility	• Cost of licenses and training • Limited integration options with certain legacy systems • Requires technical knowledge and expertise for complex automation scenarios
Automation Anywhere	Provides a comprehensive RPA solution for automating HR tasks like candidate screening, employee data management, attendance tracking, and benefits administration	• Wide range of prebuilt automation features • Strong security and compliance measures • Easy integration with other systems • Robust analytics and reporting capabilities	• High initial cost and licensing fees • Requires technical expertise for complex automation scenarios • Limited community support compared to other RPA tools
Blue Prism	Is an RPA tool used for streamlining HR processes such as employee data management, leave requests, and performance management	• Scalable and secure automation platform • Simplified integration with various systems • Comprehensive audit trails and control. Robust error-handling capabilities	• Steeper learning curve for beginners • Limited AI and ML capabilities compared to other tools • Higher cost compared to certain RPA platforms

(Continued)

TABLE 14.6 *(Continued)*
Robotic Process Automation Tools Used in Human Resource Management

RPA Tool	Description	Advantages	Disadvantages
WorkFusion	Offers RPA capabilities for automating HR tasks like resumé parsing, employee data extraction, and benefits administration	• Advanced ML and cognitive automation capabilities. Easy-to-use visual interface • Support for unstructured data processing	• Limited community support compared to other RPA tools • Higher learning curve for complex automation scenarios
Pega	Offers RPA integration for HR management, enabling automation of processes like employee onboarding, performance evaluations, and workforce planning	• Seamless integration with Pega's BPM and CRM capabilities • Robust case management and workflow automation • AI-powered automation capabilities	• Higher learning curve for beginners • Costly licensing fees and implementation • Limited support for some advanced automation scenarios
Win Automation	Is an RPA tool used for automating HR tasks such as data entry, employee record management, and HR reporting	• Easy-to-use interface with drag-and-drop functionality • Affordable pricing options • Support for both desktop and web automation	• Limited scalability for large-scale automation • Less advanced AI and ML capabilities compared to other tools
Automation Edge	Provides RPA capabilities for automating HR processes, including recruitment management, employee self-service, and payroll processing	• Quick deployment and low learning curve. AI and ML capabilities • Prebuilt automation templates • Comprehensive reporting and analytics	• Limited community support compared to other RPA tools • Relatively smaller user base
EdgeVerve AssistEdge	Is an RPA tool designed for HR automation for processes like employee lifecycle management, benefits administration, and employee surveys	• User-friendly interface with visual process design • Scalability and enterprise-grade security • Support for attended and unattended automation	• Relatively limited ecosystem and partner network • Higher cost compared to other RPA tools • Less mature compared to some established players

Implementing RPA in smart manufacturing leads to increased productivity, improved quality control, enhanced data analysis capabilities, streamlined processes, and optimized resource utilization. It empowers manufacturers to leverage automation technologies and embrace the principles of Industry 4.0 to drive efficiency and competitiveness in smart manufacturing.

14.6 UiPATH IN SMART MANUFACTURING

UiPath is a leading RPA software platform used to automate repetitive tasks and processes in various industries, including smart manufacturing. Its operating principle is creating Bots that mimic human interactions with computer systems. In smart manufacturing, it is used to streamline and automate various manual tasks, such as data entry, report generation, inventory management, and quality control. The operating principle revolves around the concept of creating Bots that can perform these tasks with speed, accuracy, and consistency.

The first step in using UiPath for RPA in smart manufacturing is identifying the processes that can be automated. This involves analyzing the existing workflows and identifying repetitive tasks that can be standardized and executed by a Bot. Once the processes are identified, UiPath provides a visual development environment where users can design and configure the Bots. This environment allows users to create automation workflows using a drag-and-drop interface and a wide range of prebuilt activities.

The Bots created in UiPath can interact with various systems, databases, and applications used in smart manufacturing. They can retrieve and process data, perform calculations, make decisions based on predefined rules, and execute actions such as updating records, generating reports, or triggering other processes. UiPath also offers features like screen scraping, OCR, and integration with ML models. These features enable the Bots to extract data from unstructured sources, interpret and understand information, and make informed decisions based on the collected data (Khang & Gujrati et al., 2024).

To operate UiPath for RPA in smart manufacturing, the designed automation workflows are executed by Bots which can be scheduled to run at specific times or triggered by events or user interactions. They can also be deployed on multiple machines or virtual environments to handle larger workloads. Throughout the operation, UiPath provides monitoring and logging capabilities, allowing users to track the performance and status of the Bots. This helps in identifying bottlenecks, optimizing processes, and ensuring the successful execution of automated tasks (Khang & Semenets et al., 2024).

14.6.1 ADVANTAGES OF UiPATH IN SMART MANUFACTURING

When discussing the advantages of choosing UiPath for RPA in smart manufacturing over other RPA software, it is important to present your own understanding and insights. Here are some advantages:

- Comprehensive Functionality: UiPath offers a comprehensive range of functionalities specifically designed for smart manufacturing. It provides prebuilt activities and integrations with industrial automation systems, MES, ERP, and other relevant software used in the manufacturing industry. This enables seamless automation of complex manufacturing processes, including data collection, quality control, inventory management, and production planning.

- User-Friendly Interface: UiPath provides a user-friendly and intuitive interface that allows users, including those without extensive programming knowledge, to design and configure automation workflows. The visual development environment, with its drag-and-drop functionality and extensive library of prebuilt activities, makes it easier to create and modify automation processes quickly.
- Scalability and Flexibility: UiPath offers scalability and flexibility, allowing organizations to expand their automation initiatives as needed. It supports the deployment of automation across multiple machines or virtual environments, enabling the handling of larger workloads. UiPath also provides the ability to orchestrate and coordinate the execution of multiple bots simultaneously, ensuring efficient and synchronized automation across various manufacturing processes.
- Strong Community Support: UiPath boasts a strong and active community of users, developers, and experts. The UiPath community provides a wealth of resources, including forums, online tutorials, and knowledge-sharing platforms. This community support helps users overcome challenges, learn best practices, and accelerate their automation journey in smart manufacturing.
- Advanced AI Capabilities: UiPath incorporates advanced AI capabilities, such as NLP, ML, and computer vision. These features enhance the automation capabilities in smart manufacturing by enabling the Bots to understand and process unstructured data, make intelligent decisions, and adapt to dynamic scenarios. For example, UiPath's computer vision capabilities can be used to identify and analyze visual data from sensors or cameras in a manufacturing environment.
- Strong Integration Capabilities: UiPath offers robust integration capabilities with various systems and applications commonly used in smart manufacturing. This ensures seamless connectivity and interoperability between different software and hardware components. It enables the Bots to interact with manufacturing equipment, databases, IoT devices, and other software systems.

In conclusion, the operating principle of UiPath for RPA in smart manufacturing involves identifying repetitive tasks, designing automation workflows, creating Bots, and executing them to streamline and automate manual processes. It empowers organizations to improve efficiency, accuracy, and productivity in their manufacturing operations while reducing human error and freeing up valuable human resources for more strategic tasks.

14.6.2   ROBOTIC PROCESS AUTOMATION TOOLS IN MANUFACTURING INDUSTRIES IN INDIA

Robotic process automation tools have become increasingly prevalent in the manufacturing industries of India, revolutionizing operational efficiency and process automation, as shown in Table 14.7.

TABLE 14.7

Percentage Use of Robotic Process Automation Tools in Indian Manufacturing Industries

RPA Tool	Purpose	Indian Manufacturing Industry	Use (%)
UiPath	Automating repetitive tasks and processes	Automotive, Electronics, Textiles, Pharmaceuticals	60
Automation Anywhere	Streamlining business processes and data entry tasks	Automotive, Fast Moving Consumer Goods (FMCG), Chemicals, Engineering	30
Blue Prism	Enhancing operational efficiency and reducing errors	Automotive, Aerospace, FMCG, Packaging	25
WorkFusion	Automating data extraction and processing	Manufacturing, Logistics, Chemicals, Pharmaceuticals	15
Pega Robotic Process Automation	Automating rule-based tasks and workflows	Electronics, Pharmaceuticals, Textiles, Automotive	10
Kofax	Streamlining document capture and processing	Manufacturing, Pharmaceuticals, Textiles, FMCG	5
NICE Robotic Automation	Automating repetitive back-office tasks	Automotive, Electronics, Engineering, Chemicals	5
Microsoft Power Automate	Simplifying workflow automation and integration	Automotive, Electronics, Pharmaceuticals, Packaging	10
EdgeVerve AssistEdge	Automating data entry and routine processes	Manufacturing, FMCG, Engineering, Packaging	5
Softomotive	Automating business processes and workflow management	Automotive, Electronics, Textiles, Pharmaceuticals	5

Widely adopted RPA tools, such as UiPath, Automation Anywhere, Blue Prism, and WorkFusion.

These RPA tools, along with others, are gradually transforming the manufacturing landscape in India, ushering in higher productivity and improved workflows, as shown in Figure 14.1.

14.7 CONCLUSION

Robotic process automation has emerged as a powerful technology with a wide range of applications across various industries. Its potential is evident in automating repetitive tasks, streamlining workflows, and improving operational efficiency. Manufacturing industries have recognized the value of popular RPA tools such as UiPath, Automation Anywhere, Blue Prism, and WorkFusion, which are implemented to drive transformation. These tools enable companies to optimize their processes, reduce errors, and enhance productivity. As the RPA market continues to evolve, new tools and advancements will further empower manufacturing industries to stay competitive in the global market. By leveraging the capabilities of RPA, these industries can achieve greater efficiency, cost savings, and agility, paving the way for continued growth and success (Khang & Rath, 2023).

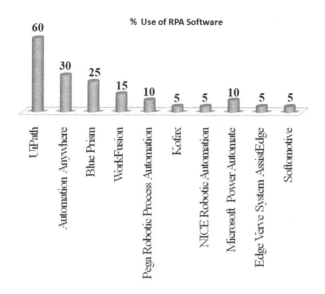

FIGURE 14.1   Percentage use of robotic process automation software in India.

The future of RPA applications and tools holds tremendous promise, fueled by continuous technological advancements. A key area of focus is the integration of RPA with emerging technologies such as AI, ML, and NLP. This integration will empower RPA systems to tackle more intricate tasks, make intelligent decisions, and efficiently handle unstructured data. The evolution of RPA will extend beyond rule-based processes to encompass cognitive automation, enabling machines to learn from data and adapt to dynamic environments.

Moreover, the advent of cloud computing and IoT will unlock fresh opportunities for RPA by facilitating seamless connectivity, scalability, and real-time data processing. As businesses seek to enhance productivity, reduce costs, and elevate customer experiences, RPA will maintain its pivotal role in process automation and driving digital transformation across diverse industries. The future of RPA is poised to revolutionize business processes and shape the way industries operate (Khang, 2023).

REFERENCES

Abubakar, I., Blyth, A., & Wuest, T. (2021). A review of robotic process automation applications and challenges. Computers in Industry, 126, 103458.

Azadeh, A., Ghaffarian, M., Govindan, K., & Sharifi, H. (2021). A comprehensive review of robotic process automation applications in different industries. Computers & Industrial Engineering, 161, 107186.

Banerjee, P., & Dey, S. (2019). Intelligent Robotic Process Automation: A Survey. In Proceedings of the 2019 International Conference on Automation, Control and Robotics Engineering (pp. 1–5). IEEE.

Bhattacharya, S., & Desai, P. S. (2019). Robotic process automation in healthcare: Opportunities and challenges. Journal of Digital Information Management, 17(6), 1–8. https://www.emerald.com/insight/content/doi/10.1108/IJOPM-02-2015-0078/full/html

Dubey, S., Gunasekaran, A., Childe, S. J., Papadopoulos, T., Luo, Z., Wamba, S. F., & Akter, S. (2019). Exploring the relationship between big data and supply chain agility: Empirical evidence from the manufacturing sector. International Journal of Operations & Production Management, 39(10), 1346–1371. https://www.tandfonline.com/doi/abs/1 0.1080/00207543.2019.1582820

Erturkmen, G., Schiele, H., & Hoberg, K. (2020). Robotic process automation in supply chain management: A framework for understanding adoption barriers and benefits. International Journal of Physical Distribution & Logistics Management, 50(8), 812–835. https://www.emerald.com/insight/content/doi/10.1108/IJPDLM-09-2021-0399/full/html

Guo, J., Wang, Q., Xiong, L., & Yu, Y. (2018). Robotic process automation in financial services: Opportunities and challenges. Journal of Financial Services Research, 54(3), 299–317. https://www.nature.com/articles/s41599-023-01923-4

Khang, A. *Applications and Principles of Quantum Computing*. (1st Ed.) (2023). ISBN: 9798369311684. IGI Global Press. https://doi.org/10.4018/979-8-3693-1168-4

Khang, A., Alyar, Abuzarova Vusala, Khalilov, Matlab, Murad, Bagirli, & Litvinova, Eugenia. "Introduction to Quantum Computing and Its Integration Applications," *Applications and Principles of Quantum Computing*. (1st Ed.) (2023). ISBN: 9798369311684. IGI Global Press. https://doi.org/10.4018/979-8-3693-1168-4-ch002

Khang, A., Gujrati, R., Uygun, H., Tailor, R. K., & Gaur, S. S. *Data-Driven Modelling and Predictive Analytics in Business and Finance*. ISBN: 9781032600628. (1st Ed.). (2024). CRC Press. DOI: 10.1201/9781032600628.

Khang, A., Semenets-Orlova, Inna, Klochko, Alla, Shchokin, Rostyslav, Mykola, Rudenko, Romanova, Lidia, & Bratchykova, Kristina. "Management Model 6.0 and Business Recovery Strategy of Enterprises in the Era of Digital Economy," *Data-Driven Modelling and Predictive Analytics in Business and Finance*. (1st Ed.). (2024). CRC Press. https://doi.org/10.1201/9781032600628-16

Khang, A., Muthmainnah, M, Seraj, Prodhan Mahbub Ibna, Yakin, Ahmad Al, Obaid, Ahmad J., & Ranjan Panda, Manas. "AI-Aided Teaching Model for the Education 5.0 Ecosystem," *AI-Based Technologies and Applications in the Era of the Metaverse*. (1st Ed.) (2023). Page (83–104). IGI Global Press. https://doi.org/10.4018/978-1-6684-8851-5.ch004

Khang, A., Rani, S., Gujrati, R., Uygun, H., & Gupta, S. K. *Designing Workforce Management Systems for Industry 4.0: Data-Centric and AI-Enabled Approaches*. (1st Ed.) (2023). CRC Press. https://doi.org/10.1201/9781003357070

Khang, A., & Rath, Kali Charan. "Quantum Mechanics Primer - Fundamentals and Quantum Computing," *Applications and Principles of Quantum Computing*. (1st Ed.) (2023). ISBN: 9798369311684. IGI Global Press. https://doi.org/10.4018/979-8-3693-1168-4-ch001

Khang, A., Shah, V., & Rani, S. *AI-Based Technologies and Applications in the Era of the Metaverse*. (1st Ed.) (2023). IGI Global Press. https://doi.org/10.4018/978-1-6684-8851-5

Tailor, R. K., Ranu, Pareek, & Khang, A. "Robot Process Automation in Blockchain," *The Data-Driven Blockchain Ecosystem: Fundamentals, Applications, and Emerging Technologies* 8 (13), (1st Ed.) (2022). Pages (149–164). CRC Press. https://doi.org/ 10.1201/9781003269281-8

15 Robotics in Real-Time Applications for Aviation Devices

Olena Hrybiuk, Maciej Szafrański, and Olena Vedishcheva

15.1 INTRODUCTION

Nowadays, microcontroller (MC) systems are used everywhere, e.g., in washing machines, cars, refrigerators, and other everyday objects, as well as in various innovative devices such as quadcopters and smart home systems, using robots, robotic platforms, and various sensors. The relevance of the topic of robotics is due to the demand for using the developed prototype in the process of creating a smart home. Based on the model developed as part of the experimental research, a variety of devices can be designed to facilitate the work of various specialists, including meeting the need for communication systems with the proposed devices, most of which can be used by a person, including performing various manipulations.

All components of aerospace product and parts manufacturing (COMSRL), which were used during the teaching of natural and mathematical disciplines, were combined into 17 conditional groups according to their functions. Indicators of preference in the attitude of students to the use of information resources are considered as characteristics of the popularity of a separate COMSRL. Two parameters are singled out regarding the need for certain restrictions on the practical use of information resources and the popularity of their use: (1) the value of the average score obtained in the process of surveying respondents and (2) the number of significant correlations. Calculated correlations between indicators of preferences for the use of individual information resources of the COMSRL and intellectual development (ILD) of students for separate groups of information resources are used to adjust the methodology of research teaching. The aim is for optimal selection of educational resources to minimize contradictions, taking into account student ILD.

The purpose of the research is to design and program a remote control model of microcontroller systems and to develop an effective device control manipulator in the context of control (imitation) of various human movements. The research focuses on the technology of creating a program that provides users with a simple and visually understandable prototype of the control interface. The subject of research is systems based on AVR microcontrollers of the ATmega family based on Arduino boards (Hrybiuk et al., 2021).

15.2 PROBLEM STATEMENT

The computer-based learning environment (CBLE) for children and youth and the development of their technological competence are presented as a set of innovative research practices (Hrybiuk, 2019) that implement, with the help of the techno sphere of educational organizations, the principles of variability that promote the activation of cognitive activity. Student interest in learning about and choosing engineering professions is achieved through research and innovative practices, including doing calculative and graphic work (Hrybiuk & Vedishcheva, 2022).

Interactive learning with pedagogically weighted use of individual components of CBLE is provided through the use of interactive programs, expositions, laboratory and demonstration equipment, relevant software and content, active forms of organization of the educational process, and student research and project activities.

The CBLE "Clever" is based on scientific concepts as well as the results of previous research of advanced scientists which include: theoretical aspects of Arivoli et al. (2011), Deters & Selig (2008), and Durai (2014), which are the foundation of new state educational standards and are focused on the practical educational and cognitive student activity, the formation of the younger generation as the basis of a new society of knowledge (Hrybiuk et al., 2021; Ryaciotaki-Boussalis & Guillaume, 2015); scientific and technical creativity and handicraft (Goliński & Szafrański, 2012); international initiatives such as MINT, STEM, NBIC (Harikumar, 2014; Kai, 2023) and others such as the European Society for Engineering Education (Kunikowski et al., 2015; Gupta et al., 2022); principles of convergent natural sciences and engineering education (Koehl et al., 2010); PMBOK, Project Management Institute (Phang et al., 2015); principles of blended and adaptive learning; and the practice of training specialists in the field of highly productive calculations (Pappu et al., 2016; Sudhakar et al., 2017).

Experimental studies confirm the influence of images on the productivity of thinking among children during artistic creativity and other activities, especially in scientific and technical creativity. The formation and development of scientific and visual thinking is an important component of the formation of student intelligence (Hrybiuk et al., 2020).

15.2.1 RETROSPECTIVE ANALYSIS OF MICROCONTROLLER SYSTEMS

15.2.1.1 Basic Definitions and Classification of Microcontrollers

A microcontroller (MC) is a microcircuit designed to control electronic devices. A typical MCU combines the functions of a processor and peripheral devices, it may contain RAM and ROM. A single-chip computer capable of performing complex tasks is considered. The use of one microcircuit—instead of a whole set, as in the case of conventional processors used in personal computers—significantly reduces the size, power consumption, and cost of devices built based on MCUs. Microcontrollers are the basis for building embedded systems; they can be found in many modern devices, e.g., telephones, washing machines, among other everyday objects.

If you present all types of modern MCs, you may be surprised by the huge number of devices available to the consumer. In the process of researching, the following main MC types were distinguished: embedded 8-, 16- and 32-bit MK, and digital signal processors. The experimental study uses a wide range of embedded MCs. They provide for the use of all necessary resources (memory, input/output devices, among others) located on the same chip as the processor core. Undoubtedly, MCs contain a significant number of auxiliary devices, which ensures attachment/inclusion in a real system, using a minimum number of additional components.

Microcontrollers which are required in research include: processor initialization scheme (Reset), clock pulse generator, central processor, program memory (E(E) PROM) and program interface, means of data input/output, and timers fixing the number of command cycles. Additional implementation includes capabilities by complex built-in MCs as follows: built-in monitor/debugging of programs, internal means of programming ROM, processing of interruptions from various sources, analog input/output, serial input/output (synchronous and asynchronous modes), parallel input/output taking into account the computer interface, and external memory connection (microprocessor mode).

All the possibilities considered significantly increase the flexibility of MK application and simplify the process of developing systems based on it. Some MKs (especially 16- and 32-bit) use only external memory, which includes both program memory (ROM) and some data memory (RAM) necessary for experimental use. They are used in systems that require a large amount of memory and a relatively small number of devices (input/output ports).

A typical example of the application of MC with external memory is a hard disk controller (HDC) with buffer cache memory, which provides intermediate storage and distribution of large volumes of data (about several megabytes). External memory enables such MC to work at a higher speed than the built-in MC. In experimental research, digital signal processors (DSPs) are considered as an updated category of processors. The purpose of a DSP is to receive current data from an analog system, process the data, and form an appropriate response in real-time. They are traditionally part of systems used as devices for controlling external equipment and are not intended for autonomous use.

15.2.1.2 Engine Driver: Pulse Width Modulation

A driver is an electronic device designed to convert electrical signals in order to control a robot (including using a robotic platform). In the study, the driver is understood as a separate device or a separate module, a microcircuit in a device that provides the conversion of electrical signals into electrical or other effects suitable for direct control of executive or signaling elements of the system.

Microcontrollers usually cannot output an arbitrary voltage. They can output either supply voltage (e.g., 5 V) or ground (e.g., 0 V). A variety of factors that are controlled by the change in the voltage level are proposed, e.g., brightness of the LED or speed of rotation of the motor. In order to effectively simulate incomplete voltage, pulse width modulation (PWM) is used (see Figure 15.1).

The output of the MC switches between ground and voltage common collector (VCC) is thousands of times per second. In other words, it has a frequency of thousands of hertz. The human eye is not capable of noticing a flicker above 50 Hz, so the researcher thinks that the LED is not flickering, but shining at half-power. Similarly,

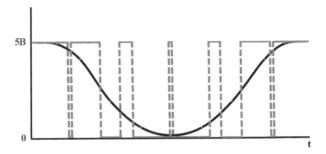

FIGURE 15.1   Simulation of partial voltage.

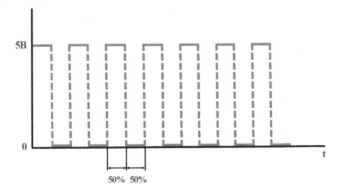

FIGURE 15.2   Duty cycle at VCC supply voltage of 5 V: 50% is equivalent to 2.5 V.

an overclocked motor cannot stop the shaft in milliseconds, so a PWM signal will cause it to spin at less than full power.

The relationship between the on and off times is called duty cycle. In the experimental study, a variety of variable scenarios are considered when the supply voltage VCC is equal to 5 V and the duty cycle is at 50%, as shown in Figure 15.2; 10%, as shown in Figure 15.3; and 90%, as shown in Figure 15.4.

For dual-supply systems, the theoretical worst case (VI = 2.4 V, VCC = 5.5 V) specification is 1.8 mA.

The following demonstrates the possibility of connecting a button and an LED to an Arduino Uno (see Figure 15.5). The resistor to the button is 10 kΩ; the resistor to the LED is 220 Ω.

The experimental study examines the functions of reading/writing from the Arduino pins:

- digitalRead(pin) – Reads HIGH or LOW values from the specified input.
- digitalWrite(pin, value) – Applies HIGH or LOW values to a digital input/output.
- analogRead(pin) – Reads the value from the specified analog input.
- analogWrite(pin, value) – Generates the specified analog voltage at the output in the form of a PWM signal.

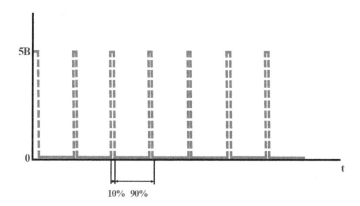

FIGURE 15.3 Duty cycle at VCC supply voltage of 5 V: 10% is equivalent to 0.5 V.

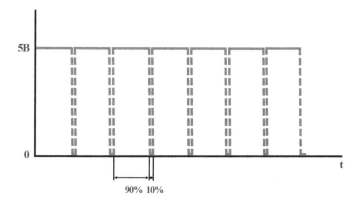

FIGURE 15.4 Duty cycle at VCC supply voltage of 5 V: 90% is equivalent to 4.5 V.

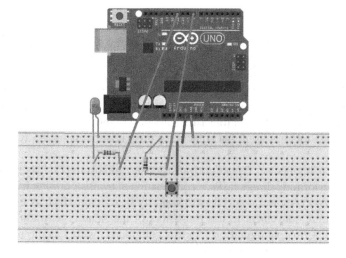

FIGURE 15.5 Connecting a button and an LED to the Arduino Uno.

Let's write a program to control the brightness of an LED. The developed program uses an LED with three brightness levels (85*3 = 255). See program listing below:

```
int switchPin = 8;
int ledPin = 11;
boolean lastButton = LOW;
int ledLevel = 0;
boolean currentButton = LOW;
void setup() {
        pinMode(switchPin, INPUT);
        pinMode(ledPin, OUTPUT);
}
boolean debounce(boolean last) {
        boolean current = digitalRead(switchPin);
        if (last! = current) {
                delay(5);
                current = digitalRead(switchPin);
        }
        return current;
}
void loop() {
        currentButton = debounce(lastButton);
        if (lastButton == LOW && currentButton == HIGH) {
                ledLevel = ledLevel + 85;
        }
        lastButton = currentButton;
        if (ledLevel > 255) ledLevel = 0;
        analogWrite(ledPin, ledLevel);
}
```

15.2.1.3 Prototyping

The research involves the use of the power part of the regulator of brushless direct current (BLDC) motors. For example, the use of the possibilities of turning on field-effect transistors is demonstrated in Figure 15.6.

In such a variable model, bipolar transistors are used as drivers. In the process of creating prototypes, schemes are also used, where P-channel transistors are used as the upper keys, and N-channel transistors are used as the lower ones. Of course, two types of transistors are used, but sometimes this situation is not always adaptively convenient.

In addition, high power P-channel transistors are almost impossible to find. In the process of performing design tasks, a combination of transistors with different channels is used in low-power controllers to simplify the circuit (Hrybiuk et al., 2019a). It is much more convenient to use transistors of the same type, traditionally only N-channel, but this configuration requires compliance with specific requirements for controlling the upper transistors of the bridge. The gate voltage of the transistors must be applied relative to their sources (Source).

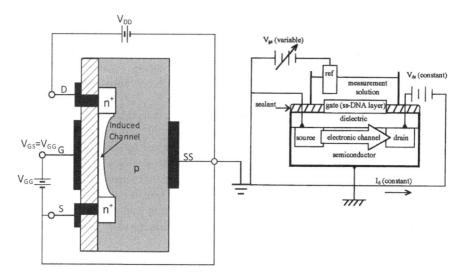

FIGURE 15.6 Examples of how to use the field-effect transistor.

In the case of the lower key, there are no problematic issues, as its Source is connected to the ground and it is possible to calmly apply voltage to the gate of the lower transistor relative to the ground. In the case of the upper transistor, a more complicated situation arises, since the voltage at its Source changes relative to the ground. Let's simulate a situation in which the upper transistor is open, i.e., current flows through it. In this state, a fairly small voltage drops across the transistor, and it is observed that the voltage at the Source of the upper transistor is practically equal to the motor supply voltage.

In order to keep the upper transistor open, it is necessary to apply a voltage to its gate higher than the voltage at its Source, i.e., higher than the motor supply voltage. In the process of modeling a situation in which the upper transistor is closed and the lower one is open, the voltage of the upper transistor at the source is observed to be almost zero. The driver of the upper key ensures that the gate of the field-effect transistor is supplied with the necessary voltage relative to its drain (Source); respectively, the generation of a voltage greater than the motor supply voltage for controlling the transistor is ensured. In this way, the use of drivers in the study is simulated.

A sensor is a measuring device in the form of a constructive assembly of one or more measuring transducers of the quantity being measured and controlled into an output signal for remote transmission and use in control systems and has standardized metrological characteristics. Sensors are an element of technical systems designed for measurement, signaling, regulation, and control of devices and processes. Sensors convert the monitored value (pressure, temperature, flow rate, concentration, frequency, speed, displacement, electric voltage, electric current, among others) into a signal (electrical, optical, and pneumatic) suitable for measurement, transmission, conversion, storage and registration of information about the state of the measurement object (Hrybiuk & Vedishcheva, 2022).

Historically and logically, sensors are connected with measuring technology and measuring devices, e.g., thermometers, flow meters, and pressure measuring devices. The generalizing term "transducer (sensor)" became established in connection with the development of automatic control systems, as an element of the generalized logical concept "transducer - control system - executive device - control object."

A special case is the use of sensors in automatic parameter registration systems, e.g., in scientific research systems. These terms, in addition to the functions of the primary measurement conversion, mean additional possibilities of measuring several physical quantities and the use of built-in analog–digital converters with microcontrollers which significantly expands the functional range of sensors, which is proposed below: pre-processing of signals (linearization, filtering, error correction); independent diagnosis; remote configuration (range of measurements, units of measurements, coordination of frequency characteristics); and individual controls.

15.2.1.4 Gyroscope–accelerometer MPU 6050

Before considering the gyroscope and accelerometer module, it would be useful to understand briefly what it is. A gyroscope is a device that responds to changes in the orientation angles of a controlled body. In the classic view, it is some kind of inertial object that rotates quickly on suspensions. As a result, the rotating object will always keep its direction, and the angle of deviation can be determined by the position of the hangers. In fact, electronic gyroscopes are built according to a different scheme and are arranged in a little more complicated way. An accelerometer is a device that measures the projection of the acceleration modeled in the study, i.e., the difference between the real acceleration of the object and the gravitational acceleration.

As a simple example, such a system is some mass fixed on a suspension that has elasticity (e.g., spring). If such a system is turned at some angle, or thrown, or given the linear acceleration, then the elastic suspension will react to the movement under the action of the mass and deviate, and the acceleration is determined by this deviation. Thus, the gyroscope reacts to a change in space regardless of the direction of movement. With the help of an accelerometer we can measure the linear acceleration of an object, and the location of an object in space can also be artificially calculated. In the process of experimental research, an analysis of each device in the context of existing advantages and disadvantages was carried out (see Figure 15.7).

The MPU 6050 chip contains both an accelerometer and a gyroscope on board, as well as a temperature sensor. The MPU 6050 is the main element of the GY-531 module. In addition to this microcircuit, the necessary MPU 6050 harness is located on the module board, including the pull-up resistors of the I2C interface, as well as a 3.3 V voltage stabilizer with a small voltage drop (with a power supply of 3.3 V, the output of the stabilizer will be exactly 3 V) with filter capacitors.

A bonus on the board is a soldered SMD LED with a limiting resistor as a power supply voltage indicator. The board size of the GY-521 module is 10*20 mm. The MPU 6050 is connected to Arduino, as shown in Figure 15.8.

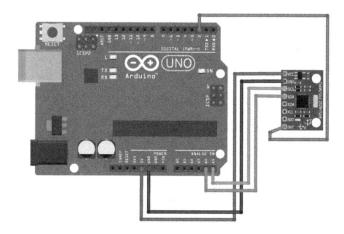

FIGURE 15.7 Exterior of the MPU 6050.

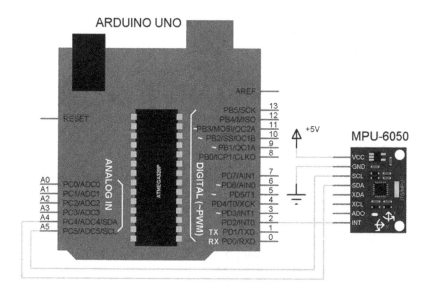

FIGURE 15.8 An example of connection of the MPU 6050 module.

Features of the MPU 6050 are as follows:

- Three-axis MEMS gyroscope with a 16-bit ADC
- Three-axis MEMS accelerometer with a 16-bit ADC
- Digital motion processor
- Slave I2C to connect to the microcontroller
- Master I2C to connect to the chip of an additional sensor
- Sensor data registers
- FIFO

- Interruption
- Temperature sensor
- Gyroscope and accelerometer self-test
- Device identification register

15.2.2   REQUIREMENTS FOR COMSRL SYSTEMS

Using this module with Arduino opens up completely new possibilities, e.g., remote control of layouts and measurement systems. Let's consider the main technical characteristics of the transceiver, connection diagram to Arduino, and programming of the microcontroller in the Arduino IDE.

15.2.2.1   RF433 MHz Radio Transmitter

Technical characteristics of the transmitter are as follows:

- Operating Voltage: 3–12 V. The higher the voltage, the greater the power of the transmitter.
- Operating Current: Maximum is 40 mA; minimum is 9 mA.
- Resonance Mode: SAW.
- Modulation Mode: ASK.
- Operating Frequency Range: 315 or 433 MHz.
- Power: 25 mV (315 MHz at 12 V).
- Frequency Error: +150 kHz (The Model MA15 features a high natural frequency, a wide frequency range, and a flat sensitivity vs. temperature response over the temperature range).
- Speed: Not greater than 10 kb/s.

In the process of experimental research, the module provides data transmission at a distance of up to 90 m in open space.
Technical characteristics of the receiver include:

- Operating Voltage: 5 V + 0.5 V, direct current.
- Operating Current: Less than 5.5 mA.
- Data Reception Method: OOK/ASK.
- Operating Frequencies: 315–433.92 MHz.
- Bandwidth: 2 MHz.
- Sensitivity: Greater than 100 dBm (50 Ω).
- Receiver Speed: Less than 9.6 kb/s (at 315 MHz and −95 dBm).

You can use an additional antenna, and the quality of the wireless connection will improve significantly.
The module is connected to the Arduino quite simply as below.

- VCC to 5 V.
- ATAD to pin 12. It can be replaced by another one. In this case, do not forget to adjust the sketch.
- Ground to GND.

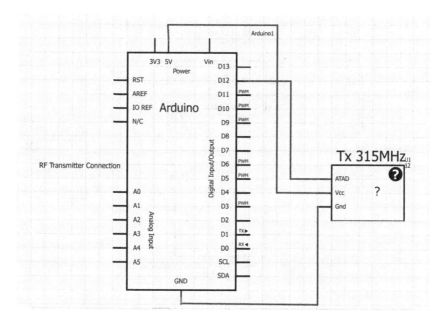

FIGURE 15.9 Connection diagram of an RF315/433 MHz radio transmitter to an Arduino.

A connection diagram of an RF315/433 MHz radio transmitter to an Arduino is shown in Figure 15.9.

A connection diagram of an RF315/433 MHz radio receiver to an Arduino is shown in Figure 15.10.

In the process of experimental research, an effective microcontroller part/prototype component was developed. Various adaptive (robotic) platforms, which serve as the basis for the development of a client–server management model, were also considered. Peripheral devices for their use in the practical part of the work were also considered (Hrybiuk et al., 2021).

- VCC to 5 V.
- Data to pin 12. Again, you can change it.
- Ground to GND.

15.2.2.2 Programming of a Variable System

The serial data exchange protocol IIC—also called I²C, inter-integrated circuits, or inter-chip connection—uses two bidirectional communication lines named the serial data bus SDA (serial data) and the clock bus SCL (serial clock) for data transfer. The use of two lines for power/supply is provided. The SDA and SCL buses are pulled up to the power/supply bus via resistors. The network assumes the use of at least one master device (master), which initiates data transmission and generates synchronization signals. The network also has slave devices that transmit data at the master's request. Each known device has a unique address, by which the presenter addresses it. The address of the device is indicated in the passport (datasheet). Up to 127 devices

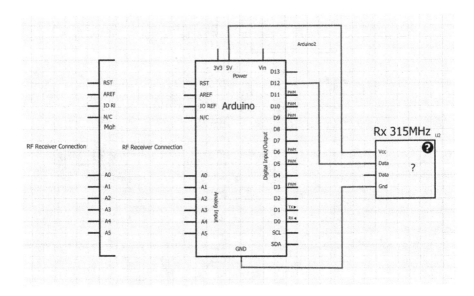

FIGURE 15.10   Connection diagram of an RF315/433 MHz radio receiver to an Arduino.

can be connected to one I²C bus, including several hosts. Devices can be connected to the bus during operation, i.e., it supports "hot plugging" (see Figure 15.11).

In the process of implementing experimental research tasks, temporary exchange diagrams using the I²C protocol are considered. There are several different options. For example, when creating a prototype, we will use a logic analyzer connected to the SCL and SDA buses.

The master initiates the exchange. To do this, it starts generating clock pulses and sends them on the SCL line in a pack of nine pieces. At the same time, on the SDA data line, it sets the address of the device with which it is necessary to establish a connection, which is clocked by the first seven clock pulses (hence the limitation of the address range: 27 = 128 minus the zero address).

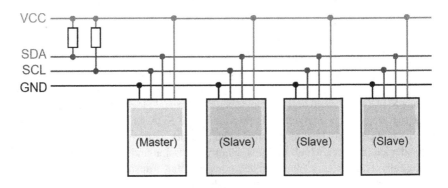

FIGURE 15.11   Description of the I²C interface.

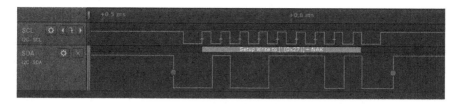

FIGURE 15.12 Trying the master to establish a connection with the slave on the I²C.

The next bit of the packet is the operation code (read or write), and one more bit is the confirmation bit (ACK) that the slave device has accepted the request. If no confirmation bit is received, the exchange ends or the master keeps sending repeated requests.

Task statement: connect to the slave device with the address 0x27 and pass the line "SOLTAU.RU" to it. In the first case, for example, let's disconnect the slave device from the bus. It is assumed that the master tries to communicate with the device with address 0x27, but it does not receive the confirmation (NAK). The exchange ends (see Figure 15.12).

Now, connect the slave device to the I²C bus and repeat the operation. The situation has changed. The first packet with the address received the confirmation (ACK) from the slave. The exchange continued. Information is also transmitted in 9-bit parcels, but now 8 bits are occupied by data, and 1 bit is a confirmation bit of receiving each byte of data by the slave. If at some point the connection is lost and the confirmation bit is not received, the master will stop the transmission (see Figure 15.13).

15.2.2.3 Specifics of the Experimental Use of the Kalman Filter

The Kalman filter has numerous advantages in the context of application in the projective technology of variable modeling. Applications for guidance, navigation, and control of vehicles, especially aircraft and spacecraft, are common. In addition, the Kalman filter is a widely used concept in time series analysis, which is used in such fields as signal processing and econometrics. Kalman filters are also a major topic in robotic motion planning and control and are sometimes included in trajectory optimization.

In the study, such algorithm works in the context of a two-step process. In the prediction step, the Kalman filter outputs estimations of the current state variables, along with their uncertainties. An observation of the output of the next measurement is just obtained (surely distorted to some extent by deviation, including random noise); these estimations are refined using a weighted average, in which more weight is given to assessments with higher certainty. Considering the recursive features of using the algorithm, it can work in real time using only available input

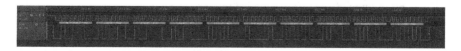

FIGURE 15.13 Timing diagram of the protocol exchange on the I²C.

measurements, a pre-computed state and its uncertainty matrix. No additional information is required to implement the prototype.

The Kalman filter uses a model of the system dynamics (e.g., physical laws of motion), known control effects on the system, and multiple successive measurements (e.g., from sensors) to form an estimation of the system variables (its state) that is better than the estimation obtained from using only the measurements themselves. In fact, it is a general algorithm for combining sensors and merging data. All measurements and calculations based on variable models are to some extent estimations. Noisy sensor data, approximations in the equations describing how the system is changing, and unaccounted external factors introduce some uncertainty concerning the derived system state values. The Kalman filter averages the prediction of the system state with the new measurement using a weighted average. The purpose of the weight coefficients is that values with better (i.e., smaller) estimated uncertainty are "trusted" more.

The weight coefficients are calculated from the covariance, a measure of the estimated uncertainty of predicting the state of the system. The result of the weighted average is an estimation of the new state that lies between the predicted and measured states and has a better estimated uncertainty than either of them individually.

This process is repeated at each time step, and the new estimation and its covariance inform the prediction used in the next iteration. This means that the Kalman filter works recursively and requires only an extreme "best guess" of the system's state, not its entire history, to calculate a new state (Hrybiuk & Vedishcheva, 2022). Since measurement certainty is often difficult to measure precisely, it is common to consider filter behavior in terms of transmission coefficient. The Kalman transfer coefficient is a function of the relative certainty of the measurements and the estimation of the current state of the system, and can be "wired" to achieve a certain performance.

With a high transmission ratio, the filter gives more weight to the measurements and therefore follows them more accurately. At a low transmission ratio, the filter follows the model predictions more closely, smoothing out noise but reducing responsiveness. In extreme cases, a unitary transmission ratio causes the filter to ignore the state estimation completely, while a zero transmission ratio causes the measurements to be ignored.

When performing the actual calculations for the filter, the state estimation and covariance for processing multiple dimensions involved in one set of calculations are encoded in the matrix 15. This allows to present linear relationships in the study between different state variables (e.g., position, velocity, and acceleration) in any variation transition models or covariance (Hrybiuk et al., 2019b).

In the process of experimental research, variable models are considered, including solving the problems of determining the exact location/position of the truck. The truck is pre-equipped with a GPS device that provides an estimation of the position within a few meters. The GPS estimation is likely to be noisy; the recitations of data quickly "jump around," but they always remain within a few meters of the actual position. Since the truck is expected to follow the laws of physics, its position can also be estimated by integrating its velocity over time, determined by tracking the wheel revolutions and the steering wheel angle.

This technique is known as enumeration. Typically, the enumeration will provide a very smooth estimation of the truck's position, but it will drift over time as small errors accumulate. In this example, the Kalman filter can be thought of as operating in two distinct phases: prediction and refinement. In the prediction phase, the old position of the truck will be modified according to the physical laws of motion (dynamic model, or "state transition" model), plus any changes created by the accelerator pedal and the steering wheel.

Not only the new position score but also the new covariance will be calculated. It is possible that the covariance is proportional to the speed of the truck, since we are less confident in the accuracy of the calculated position estimated at high speeds, but very confident in such position estimated in slow motion. In the simulation process, in the refinement phase, the measurement of the position of the truck is obtained from the GPS device.

Along with this measurement comes some uncertainty, and its covariance with respect to the prediction uncertainty from the previous phase determines how much the new measurement will affect the updated position. Ideally, if the estimation of enumeration tends to drift away from the true position, then the GPS measurements should pull the position estimation back toward the true position, but not perturb it to the point where it becomes rapidly changing and noisy.

15.3 RESULTS AND DISCUSSION

As a result of the work carried out, a prototype of the aircraft was created, which uses the equipment and software described above. In experimental research, a *robot* means an automatic device designed to perform production and other operations that are usually performed directly by a person. To describe automatic devices, the action of which has no external similarity to human actions, the term "automaton" is used.

In most cases, modern industrial robots are "hands," manipulators fixed on a base and designed to perform monotonous work, such as assembly and movement. Robots also include mobile devices that work in dangerous environments and are remotely controlled, e.g., robots that work at great water depths, in space, in military devices (reconnaissance, mine clearance, ammunition delivery, among others), as well as robotic toys.

Robots can be implemented as an electromechanical, pneumatic, and hydraulic device controlled by a control system or their combination. Robots can follow the operator's commands, can work according to a pre-compiled program, or follow a set of general instructions using AI technology. These tasks make it possible to facilitate or completely replace human labor in production, in construction, and when working with heavy loads, harmful materials, and in other difficult or dangerous conditions (Hrybiuk et al., 2019b). A household robot is a robot designed to help a person in everyday life. Currently, the distribution of household robots is small, but futurologists predict widespread use (Khang & Muthmainnah et al., 2023).

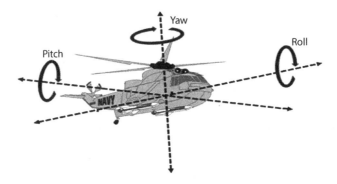

FIGURE 15.14   A schematic representation of the developed helicopter design.

15.3.1   ROBOT DESIGN FEATURES

The basis of the developed robot is a moving platform consisting of two main parts: manipulator and helicopter. The platform of the manipulator is an Arduino mega 2560 board and an MPU 6050 gyroscope–accelerometer. In the toy helicopter, the board was replaced with an Arduino Pro Mini with a 3.3 V stabilizer, to which an RF433 MHz radio transmitter is connected (see Figure 15.14).

Suppose a helicopter tilts during horizontal flight. The accelerometer records the change in acceleration along the axes. Now, the acceleration of the movement is added to the acceleration of gravity in a different order, unlike in a flight without roll. As a result, the control system will conclude that the movement is in the direction of roll, although in fact there is a horizontal movement. Accelerometer and gyroscope are used together for correct processing of motion parameters and accurate recognition of dynamic parameters.

In the process of experimental use of the gyroscope, it will determine the angle of rotation and make it possible to interpret the accelerometer data correctly. The use of a gyroscope without an accelerometer is impossible due to the peculiarities of the mathematics of the gyroscope, which lead to the accumulation of errors. Special mathematics allows to combine data processing from both sensors (Hrybiuk et al., 2020). Gyroscopes and accelerometers are widely used in aviation, rocketry, space, and military equipment. For example, while moving, the target is captured by the tank sight. Moving over rough terrain causes large distortions in the elevation angle of the gun barrel. The accelerometer and gyroscope help to fix the sight on the captured target.

15.3.2   CONNECTION DIAGRAM

Based on the developed system, it is possible to design various variable models of devices/adaptive systems that will help people and companies do some of the slow, complex, or uninteresting work. The developed wheeled variable robot can be used as a material for future research in this field of mechatronics, using effectively the robotic platforms (see Figure 15.15).

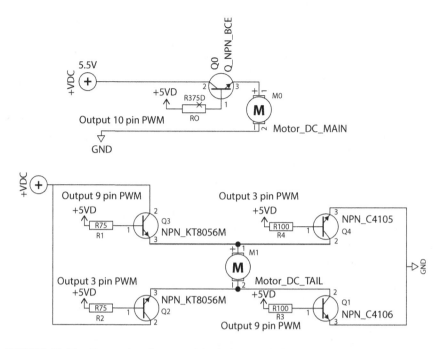

FIGURE 15.15   Connection diagram of the helicopter design.

15.4   PERFORMANCE ANALYSIS

15.4.1   Testing the Application and Meeting Requirements

The purpose of the conducted experimental study is to determine the expediency of using COMSRL and information and communication technologies in the process of teaching students subjects of the natural and mathematical cycle at school, in addition to evaluating the attitude of teachers and students toward the identified resources (Hrybiuk & Vedishcheva, 2022).

Criteria for evaluating the attitude of the experiment participants toward the use of components of COMSRL have been developed (Hrybiuk et al., 2019a). Data obtained in the process of experimental research were used to indicate: (1) which information resources and COMSRL are the most relevant in the process of teaching students subjects of the natural and mathematical cycle, (2) whether there are correlations between the preferences in the attitude of students and teachers to the use of certain information resources and the levels of student ILD, and (3) how it is necessary to effectively select information resources to increase the level of motivation and effectiveness of the process of research education of students. In an experimental study, psychophysiological and psychological–pedagogical factors among which the levels of student ILD were of great importance were taken into account in the process of selecting information resources during research training (Hrybiuk et al., 2020).

In the process of determining the factors that have the greatest influence on the learning outcome, research data of 17,277 respondents (students and teachers) from

27 educational institutions located in different regions of Ukraine were analyzed (Hrybiuk et al., 2021). It has been experimentally proven that there are significant differences between the learning styles of students and teachers. The differences primarily depend on student ILD and preparation. It was determined that students who have different combinations of learning styles experience cognitive load in different ways during exploratory learning using COMSRL.

For the statistical analysis of the results, descriptive statistics, correlation analysis with the determination of Pearson correlation coefficients, and non-parametric tests for calculating the W Kendall concordance coefficient for establishing the rank of variables were used in the study. A significance level of 0.05 was used to test the hypotheses, and corresponding two-tailed significance values were provided when appropriate. All components of COMSRL, which were used during the teaching of natural and mathematical disciplines, were combined into 17 conditional groups according to their functions (Hrybiuk et al., 2019a).

Indicators of preference in the attitude of students to the use of information resources are considered as characteristics of the popularity of a separate COMSRL. Two parameters are singled out regarding the need for certain restrictions on the practical use of information resources and the popularity of their use: (1) the value of the average score obtained in the process of surveying respondents and (2) the number of significant correlations. Calculated correlations between the indicators of students' preference for the use of individual information resources of the COMSRL and student ILD for separate groups of information resources are used to adjust the methodology of research teaching. The aim is optimal selection of educational resources to minimize contradictions, taking into account student ILD, characteristic of a specific group of students.

Based on the analysis of the results of the pedagogical experiment (Hrybiuk et al., 2019b), the number of gifted students in any field of activity is 10–15%, and 15–20% is a group of students who learn educational material more slowly and have a low level of knowledge. In the process of implementing engineering mathematics education, it is necessary to mainly focus on the group of students whose knowledge can also be distinguished at above average, normal, or average levels (Tables 15.1–15.4).

TABLE 15.1

Correlations between Indicators of Preference in the Attitude of Students to the Use of Individual Information Resources (I)

Individual Information Resource	Drawings and Photos	Graphs	Diagrams	Schemes	Tables
Drawings and Photos	1,000	0.220 (0.281)	0.341 (0.089)	0.481 (0.013)	0.511 (0.008)
Graphs	0.220 (0.281)	1,000	0.582 (0.002)	0.454 (0.02)	0.209 (0.305)
Diagrams	0.341 (0.089)	0.582 (0.002)	1,000	0.551 (0.004)	0.266 (0.189)
Schemes	0.481 (0.013)	0.454 (0.02)	0.551 (0.004)	1,000	0.578 (0.002)
Tables	0.511 (0.008)	0.209 (0.305)	0.266 (0.189)	0.578 (0.002)	1,000

TABLE 15.2
Correlations between Indicators of Preference in the Attitude of Students to the Use of Individual Information Resources and the Levels of Student ILD

Level of Intellectual Development	Drawings and Photos	Graphs	Diagrams	Schemes	Tables
I	−0.406 (0.049)	−0.627 (0.00 1)	−0.371 (0.074)	−0.328 (0.118)	−0.113 (0.598)
II	−0.489 (0.015)	−0.428 (0.037)	−0.471 (0.020)	−0.380 (0.067)	−0.556 (0.005)
III	0.014 (0.949)	−0.300 (0.154)	−0.221 (0.300)	−0.080 (0.711)	−0.060 (0.781)
IV	−0.116 (0.589)	−0.359 (0.0 85)	−0.461 (0.023)	−0.493 (0.014)	−0.441 (0.031)

The research developed and tested an algorithm for choosing the optimal set of components of the COMSRL, which involves the use of quantitative criteria to establish the compliance of resources with the requirements of students and teachers (Hrybiuk et al., 2020).

The first criterion is the average score of the indicator of the preference for choosing an electronic resource by students with different ILD and learning styles, which is calculated for a typical group (form) profile. The second criterion is the difference between the expert rating of the resources for each topic and the score provided by the students (see Table 15.5).

During the research, two hypotheses were formulated (Hrybiuk et al., 2020):

- Indicators of giftedness of students living in different socio-cultural environments differ because they participate in various polysystemic processes. Accordingly, students' belonging to systems of different order is manifested in students' psychological traits.
- Spirituality manifests itself in different ways in the cultures of different countries, so the valuable living space of gifted students in different countries will differ in structure.

15.4.2 Degree of Compliance with Design Requirements

Based on the analysis given above, three models are considered related to different options of mathematical education of senior-level students of natural, mathematical, and technical profiles. Also, levels of immersion in the subject are offered: mass model (second group), basic model (third group), and creative model or advanced level (fourth group).

Based on the analysis of the obtained experimental data, we can formulate the following conclusions that will help teachers prevent ineffective work with students (Hrybiuk et al., 2019a):

- Formulating the individual's cognitive style in professional training leads to the leveling of the difference in individual styles, taking into account ILD. In education research, it is necessary to develop a mechanism of integrating different types of student behavior style.

TABLE 15.3

Correlations between Indicators of Preference in the Attitude of Students to the Use of Individual Information Resources (II)

Information Resource	3D Models	Animation of Processes	Video Reproduction of the Experiment	Video Reproduction of Natural Processes	Video Reproduction of Examples from Life	Video Reproduction of Excursions
3D Models	1.000	0.501 (0.009)	0.438 (0.025)	0.604 (0.001)	0.458 (0.019)	0.432 (0.027)
Animation of Processes	0.501 (0.009)	1.000	0.501 (0.0079)	0.328 (0.102)	0.329 (0.100)	0.495 (0.010)
Video Reproduction of the Experiment	0.438 (0.025)	0.501 (0.009)	1.000	0.604 (0.001)	0.589 (0.002)	0.541 (0.004)
Video Reproduction of Natural Processes	0.604 (0.001)	0.328 (0.102)	0.604 (0.001	1.000	0.697 (0.000)	0.732 (0.000)
Video Reproduction of Examples from Life	0.458 (0.019)	0.329 (0.100)	0.589 (0.002)	0.697 (0.000)	1.000	0.627 (0.001)
Video Reproduction of Excursions	0.432 (0.027)	0.495 (0.010)	0.541 (0.004)	0.732 (0.000)	0.627 (0.001)	1.000

TABLE 15.4
Correlations between Indicators of Preference in the Attitude of Students to the Use of Individual Information Resources and the Levels of Student ILD (II)

Level of Intellectual Development	3D Models	Animation of Processes	Video Reproduction of the Experiment	Video Reproduction of Natural Processes	Video Reproduction of Examples from Life	Video Reproduction of Excursions
I	−0.098 (0.649)	−0.065 (0.762)	−0.007 (0.975)	−0.157 (0.463)	0.140 (0.515)	−0.374 (0.072)
II	−0.083 (0.700)	0.094 (0.663)	0.159 (0.459)	−0.121 (0.573)	0.153 (0.474)	−0.057 (0.791)
III	0.523 (0.009)	0.481 (0.017)	0.547 (0.006)	0.520 (0.009)	0.434 (0.034)	0.493 (0.014)
IV	−0.097 (0.651)	−0.029 (0.893)	−0.002 (0.992)	−0.195 (0.361)	−0.093 (0.665)	−0.274 (0.195)

TABLE 15.5
Levels of Learning Mathematics among Different Age Groups

	Differentiation					
	Initial Level		Basic Level		High Level	
Research Groups	T1 (c)	n1	T2 (c)	n2	T3 (c)	n3
14-year-olds (74)	71.08	4,51	128.09	8.34	392.13	25,23
15-year-olds (75)	47.56	1.71	83.12	5.2	301.87	17.58
18-year-olds (328)	38.8	1.29	48.72	0.24	147.2	6.34
Less Successful in Learning Mathematics						
14-year-olds (56)	76.83	5.05	135.65	10.36	400.39	27.51
15-year-olds (60)	48.84	1.7	88	6.2	313	19.82
18-year-olds (260)	39,43	1.52	49.29	0.27	153.1	6.97
More Successful in Learning Mathematics						
14-year-olds (18)	53.16	2.83	105	2.16	358.3	15.9
15-year-olds (14)	42,14	1.5	62.57	1	255.78	8.28
18-year-olds (68)	36.5	0.31	46.53	0.08	122.75	3.6

- Preliminary diagnosis of student behavior styles in the group is desirable for effective research training. Understanding the composition of the group helps the teacher create conditions for: preventing conflict of learning styles considering ILD of teachers and students (e.g., ineffective design of educational material, low performance, high level of discomfort); actualization and enrichment of the entire system of mechanisms of student behavior style, which determines student intellectual productivity.
- Organizing effective research training involves the creation of didactic materials with the possibility of selecting a special line of research training

of students and prerequisites for the gradual formation of individual cognitive styles.
- For effective research training of students in mathematical disciplines, it is necessary to use COMSRL, which has adaptation tools and present educational materials in various forms.

The interest of students in project-research activities, the synergistic combination of engineering knowledge with fundamental meta-subjects, and the development of new scientific and technical ideas will increase by using COMSRL and updated pedagogical approaches. Young people will inherit a world with various problems, so a combination of science, education, and technology is needed to solve these problems (Hrybiuk & Vedishcheva, 2022).

15.5　CONCLUSIONS AND PROSPECTS FOR FURTHER RESEARCH

In the process of conducting experimental research, variable models of microcontroller systems' remote control were created and a manipulator for controlling aircraft controlled by various human movements was developed, which can be a start for creating a manipulator for controlling devices of any complexity. It was possible to develop and improve this technology, clarifying the components of variable models of computer-oriented methodical systems. In the experimental study, the microcontroller part of the prototype was considered and improved, i.e., different variable platforms were considered, which serve as the basis for the development of a client–server control model. Peripheral devices for their use in the practical part of the work were also considered (Khang & Rath et al., 2023).

The technology of creating variable client programs, which provide users with the opportunity to use a simple and visually understandable interface for managing an adaptive system, is thoroughly described. Based on the developed system, variable models of devices and systems can be built that will help people and companies do their work, or will generally take over some of the slow, complex or uninteresting work (Khang & Shah et al., 2023). The developed variable models of manipulators are used as material for future research in the proposed fields of knowledge in the context of the use of mechatronics and robotics, among others.

REFERENCES

Arivoli, D., Dodamani, R., Antony, R., Suraj, C. S., Ramesh, G., Ahmed, S., "Experimental Studies on a Propelled Micro Air Vehicle," *29th AIAA Applied Aerodynamics Conference*, AIAA Paper 2011–3656, Honolulu, Hawaii, June (2011).

Deters, R., Selig, M. "Static testing of micro propellers." *26th AIAA Applied Aerodynamics Conference*. (2008).

Durai, A., "Experimental investigation of lift and drag characteristics of a typical MAV under propeller induced flow." *International Journal of Micro Air Vehicles*, 6(1), 63–72. (2014). https://doi.org/10.1260/1756-8293.6.1.63

Goliński, M., Szafrański, M., *Integrated support system for access to information in urban space with use of GPS and GIS systems*. (2012). Publishing House of Poznan University of Technology, Poznań.

Gupta, S. K., Khang, A., Bhambri, P., Rani, S., Gupta, G., *Cloud and Fog Computing Platforms for Internet of Things.* (2022). CRC Press. https://doi.org/10.1201/9781032101507

Harikumar, K., "Static output feedback control for an integrated guidance and control of a micro air vehicle." *Journal of Unmanned System Technology*, 2(1), 17–29. (2014).

Hrybiuk et al., "Improvement of the Educational Process by the Creation of Centers for Intellectual Development and Scientific and Technical Creativity," *Advances in Manufacturing II. MANUFACTURING 2019. Lecture Notes in Mechanical Engineering.* (2019a). Springer, Cham. https://doi.org/10.1007/978-3-030-18789-7_31

Hrybiuk et al., "Problems of expert evaluation in terms of the use of variative models of a computer-oriented learning environment of mathematical and natural science disciplines in schools." *Zeszyty Naukowe Politechniki Poznańskiej. Seria: Organizacja i Zarządzanie.* (2019b). WPP. https://doi.org/10.21008/j.0239-9415.2019.079.07

Hrybiuk et al., "Engineering in Educational Institutions: Standards for Arduino Robots as an Opportunity to Occupy an Important Niche in Educational Robotics in the Context of Manufacturing 4.0," *Proceedings of the 16th International Conference on ICT in Education, Research and Industrial Applications. Integration, Harmonization and Knowledge Transfer.* Volume 27–32, pp. 770–785. (2020).

Hrybiuk et al., "Experience in Implementing Computer-Oriented Methodological Systems of Natural Science and Mathematics Research Learning in Ukrainian Educational Institutions." *Innovations in Mechatronics Engineering.* (2021). pp. 55–68. Springer, Cham Online. https://doi.org/10.1007/978-3-030-79168-1_6

Hrybiuk, O. O., *Research Learning of the Natural Science and Mathematics Cycle Using Computer-Oriented Methodological Systems."* Monograph. (2019). pp. 307–349. Kyiv: Drahomanov NPU.

Hrybiuk, O., Vedishcheva, O., "Experimental Teaching of Robotics in the Context of Manufacturing 4.0: Effective Use of Modules of the Model Program of Environmental Research Teaching in the Working Process of the Centers "Clever." *Innovations in Mechatronics Engineering II. Icieng 2022. Lecture Notes in Mechanical Engineering.* (2022). pp. 216–231. Springer, Cham. https://doi.org/10.1007/978-3-031-09385-2_20

Kai, D., "Determination Technology and Accuracy Analysis of Configuration Parameters of Ground System Dual Satellite Formation Based on Navigation Data." *Advances in Guidance, Navigation and Control. ICGNC 2022. Lecture Notes in Electrical Engineering,* vol. 845. Springer, Singapore. (2023), https://doi.org/10.1007/978-981-19-6613-2_2

Khang, A., Muthmainnah, M., Seraj, P. M. I., Yakin, A. A., Obaid, A. J., Ranjan Panda, M. "AI-Aided Teaching Model for the Education 5.0 Ecosystem." *Handbook of Research on AI-Based Technologies and Applications in the Era of the Metaverse.* (1st Ed.) (2023). pp. 83–104. IGI Global Press. https://doi.org/10.4018/978-1-6684-8851-5.ch004

Khang, A., Rath, K. C., Kumar Satapathy, S., Kumar, A., Ranjan Das, S., Ranjan Panda, M. "Enabling the Future of Manufacturing: Integration of Robotics and IoT to Smart Factory Infrastructure in Industry 4.0." *Handbook of Research on AI-Based Technologies and Applications in the Era of the Metaverse.* (1st Ed.) (2023). pp. 25–50. IGI Global Press. https://doi.org/10.4018/978-1-6684-8851-5.ch002

Khang, A., Shah, V., Rani, S., *Handbook of Research on AI-Based Technologies and Applications in the Era of the Metaverse.* (1st Ed.) (2023). IGI Global Press. https://doi.org/10.4018/978-1-6684-8851-5

Koehl, A. et al., "Modeling and identification of a launched micro air vehicle: design and experimental results." *AIAA Modeling and Simulation Technologies Conference.* (2010).

Kunikowski, W., Czerwiński, E., Olejnik, P., "An overview of ATmega AVR microcontrollers used in scientific research and industrial applications." *Pomiary Automatyka Robotyka,* (2015), https://doi.org/10.14313/PAR_215/15

Pappu, S. R., Steck, V., Ramamurthi, J. E., "Turbulence effects on modified state observer-based adaptive control: Black kite micro aerial vehicle." *Aerospace*, 3(1), 6. (2016). https://doi.org/10.3390/aerospace3010006

Phang, S. K., Li, K., Chen, B. M., Lee, T. H., "Systematic Design Methodology and Construction of Micro Aerial Quadrotor Vehicles." *Handbook of Unmanned Aerial Vehicles.* Springer, Dordrecht (2015), https://doi.org/10.1007/978-90-481-9707-1_116

Ryaciotaki-Boussalis, H., Guillaume, D., "Computational and Experimental Design of a Fixed-Wing UAV." *Handbook of Unmanned Aerial Vehicles.* Springer, Dordrecht. (2015), https://doi.org/10.1007/978-90-481-9707-1_121

Sudhakar, S., Chandankumar, A., Venkatakrishnan, L., "Influence of propeller slipstream on vortex flow field over a typical micro air vehicle." *The Aeronautical Journal*, 121(1235), 95–113. (2017). https://doi.org/10.1017/aer.2016.114

16 Machine Vision and Industrial Robotics in Manufacturing

Rajeswari Packianathan, Gobinath Arumugam, Suresh Kumar Natarajan, and Anandan Malaiarasan

16.1 INTRODUCTION TO ROBOTICS IN MANUFACTURING

The incorporation of robotics into manufacturing processes heralds a revolutionary era characterized by unparalleled gains in efficiency, precision, and adaptability. The historical trajectory of robotics in manufacturing, originating from rudimentary automation for repetitive tasks, has witnessed a remarkable evolution driven by advancements in technology and artificial intelligence (AI). In today's landscape, robotic systems have emerged as indispensable assets, showcasing capabilities for intricate operations and addressing the diverse needs of modern manufacturing. Across the spectrum of manufacturing processes—ranging from assembly lines, material handling, and welding, to machining—robotics stands as a linchpin for heightened operational efficiency.

The remarkable precision and speed exhibited by robots translate into increased production rates and elevated product quality. What distinguishes modern robotic systems is their innate flexibility, allowing for swift reprogramming to accommodate a spectrum of tasks and product variations. Furthermore, the integration of collaborative robots (Cobots) exemplifies a paradigm shift toward interactive manufacturing environments. Here, humans and robots collaborate seamlessly, synergizing their strengths to optimize workflows and enhance overall productivity.

Beyond mere operational enhancements, robotics in manufacturing plays a pivotal role in ensuring product integrity. Equipped with advanced sensors and vision technologies, robotic systems facilitate real-time monitoring, significantly reducing errors and guaranteeing consistent product quality. As the manufacturing landscape continues to evolve, the ongoing Fourth Industrial Revolution, or Industry 4.0, underscores the interconnectedness and intelligence of systems. Robotics emerges as an anchor in smart manufacturing, where interconnected devices, data analytics, and automation converge to create intelligent and responsive production environments.

While the transformative potential of robotics is undeniable, challenges exist, such as initial investment costs and the demand for skilled personnel. Nevertheless, ongoing research and development endeavors in the field promise to address these challenges, fostering an environment where the role of robotics in manufacturing will continue to expand, driving global innovation, competitiveness, and efficiency.

DOI: 10.1201/9781003438137-16

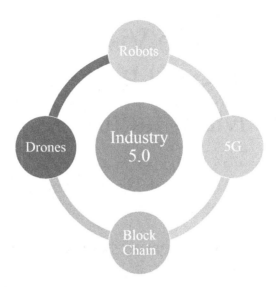

FIGURE 16.1   Components of Industry 5.0.

The integration of robotics into manufacturing processes marks not only an evolution but also a revolution, reshaping the fabric of industrial production and ushering in the era of Industry 5.0, as shown in Figure 16.1.

16.2   AUTOMATION IN MANUFACTURING: TRANSFORMING INDUSTRIES THROUGH TECHNOLOGICAL EVOLUTION

The integration of automation in manufacturing processes is a pivotal moment in the history of industry, marking a journey from mechanization to the era of smart factories and interconnected systems. This technological evolution has not only redefined production methodologies but has also unleashed a wave of innovations, transforming the fabric of manufacturing. This exploration delves deeper into the multifaceted aspects of automation, elucidating its historical evolution, diverse applications, benefits, and its impact on the workforce, and integration with emerging technologies.

1. **Historical Evolution:** The roots of automation trace back to the mid-20th century when numerical control systems paved the way for computer numerical control (CNC) machines, allowing for precise and automated control of machinery. Over time, the integration of robotics and advanced control systems has propelled manufacturing into the era of Industry 4.0, characterized by smart factories and seamless connectivity between machines.
2. **Key Applications:** Automation's influence spans a spectrum of manufacturing processes, each benefiting from the precision and efficiency it affords. Assembly lines witness the seamless orchestration of tasks, while material handling, welding, painting, and quality control are executed with a level of precision and consistency that surpasses human capabilities. The application

of automation extends to complex and hazardous tasks, thereby enhancing overall safety within manufacturing environments.

3. **Benefits:** Benefits of automation are manifold including unprecedented boost in efficiency and productivity. Automated systems operate tirelessly and without breaks ensuring a continuous and optimized workflow. The precision of automated processes translates to improved product quality, consistency, and a reduction in defects. The integration of automation contributes significantly to workplace safety by relieving humans of hazardous tasks.

4. **Impact on Labor and Skills:** Automation impacts the workforce. Certain routine and manual jobs may be automated, necessitating a paradigm shift in the skills required. The future workforce is likely to pivot toward roles that involve programming, maintenance, and oversight of automated systems, emphasizing the importance of upskilling and adaptability.

5. **Integration with Emerging Technologies:** Automation intertwines with cutting-edge technologies. Artificial intelligence (AI), machine learning (ML), and data analytics play pivotal roles in enhancing automation. Predictive maintenance becomes more robust, production schedules are optimized, and decision-making processes become data-driven.

6. **Future Trends:** The future of automation in manufacturing holds exciting prospects. Cobots working alongside human operators represent a harmonious blending of human ingenuity and machine precision. Decentralized decision-making through edge computing promises more agile and responsive manufacturing processes. The integration of additive manufacturing, such as 3D printing, hints at a future where customization and rapid prototyping become integral to production methodologies (Khang & Hajimahmud et al., 2024).

Automation in manufacturing is not merely a technological adaptation but a transformative force reshaping industries. As technology continues to advance, the ongoing integration of automation is poised to redefine manufacturing processes, creating a landscape where precision, speed, adaptability, and human ingenuity converge.

16.2.1 Historical Development and Milestones

16.2.1.1 Early Concepts (Ancient Times)

- Automatons and Mechanical Devices: Ancient civilizations, including the Greeks and Egyptians, demonstrated an early interest in creating automatons—self-moving machines. These early devices were often powered by simple mechanisms, such as springs or water flow, and they served entertainment or religious purposes.
- Hero of Alexandria: In the 1st century AD, the Greek engineer Hero of Alexandria designed a variety of automated machines, including a steam-powered device called an aeolipile. While these inventions were more novelties than practical applications, they laid the conceptual groundwork for future automation.

16.2.1.2   First Industrial Revolution (18th–19th Century)

- Mechanization in Textile Mills: The Industrial Revolution marked a shift from manual labor to machinery. Textile mills, such as those in the cotton industry, adopted water and steam-powered machinery for spinning and weaving, representing an early form of industrial automation.
- Steam Engines and Factories: James Watt's development of the steam engine and the establishment of large-scale factories further accelerated the mechanization of manufacturing processes, setting the stage for future automation.

16.2.1.3   The First Industrial Robot (Unimate, 1956)

- Unimate's Introduction: Unimate, developed by George Devol and Joseph Engelberger, was a groundbreaking invention. It was the first commercially available industrial robot and was initially used in 1961 at a General Motors plant for repetitive tasks such as die-casting.
- Impact on Manufacturing: Unimate revolutionized manufacturing by introducing the concept of programmable robotic arms. This marked the beginning of a new era in automation, where robots could be programmed to perform a variety of tasks in industrial settings.

16.2.1.4   Robotics in Automotive Manufacturing (1960s)

- Widespread Adoption: The automotive industry played a crucial role in the widespread adoption of industrial robots. Robots were employed in assembly lines for tasks like welding, painting, and handling heavy components.
- PUMA Robot: The PUMA robot, developed by Victor Scheinman in the early 1970s, was a versatile robotic arm used in various industries, including automotive manufacturing.

16.2.1.5   Introduction of Computer Numerical Control (1970s)

- CNC Technology: Computer numerical control (CNC) technology allowed for precise control of machine tools through computer programming. This development increased the accuracy of manufacturing processes and set the stage for the integration of computers with robotic systems.
- Advancements in Precision: CNC machining became a standard in manufacturing, enabling complex and high-precision operations. It paved the way for more sophisticated robotic systems that could leverage computer-controlled tools.

16.2.1.6   Articulated Robot Arms (1980s)

- Versatility of Articulated Arms: The 1980s saw the introduction of articulated robot arms with multiple joints and degrees of freedom. These robots could perform a wider range of tasks with increased flexibility and precision.
- ABB and KUKA Contributions: Companies like ABB and KUKA made significant contributions to the development of articulated robots, offering industrial solutions that became integral to modern manufacturing processes.

16.2.1.7 Emergence of Collaborative Robots (2000s)

*   Safe Human–Robot Collaboration: The 2000s brought about a shift in robotics with the emergence of collaborative robots (Cobots). These robots were designed to work alongside humans, incorporating safety features such as force sensors and vision systems to enable safe interaction.
*   Diverse Applications: Cobots found applications in tasks that required human–robot collaboration, such as assembly, packaging, and small-scale manufacturing. Their introduction addressed concerns about the safety of working closely with traditional industrial robots.

16.2.1.8 Advancements in Sensor Technologies (2010s)

*   Vision Systems: The integration of advanced vision systems allowed robots to perceive and interpret their environment. This capability became crucial for tasks such as object recognition, quality control, and navigation.
*   Tactile Sensors: Tactile sensors equipped on robotic end-effectors improved the robots' ability to handle delicate objects and perform tasks that required a sense of touch.

16.2.1.9 Industry 4.0 and Smart Manufacturing (2010s–Today)

*   Data-Driven Manufacturing: The concept of Industry 4.0 brought about the integration of robotics with data analytics, the Internet of Things (IoT), and AI. This marked a shift toward data-driven decision-making in manufacturing.
*   Smart Factories: Manufacturers began implementing smart manufacturing systems where robots communicate with each other and with other devices in real-time. This connectivity enhances efficiency, reduces downtime, and enables predictive maintenance.

16.2.1.10 Current Trends (2020s)

*   Machine Learning and AI Integration: Ongoing developments in the 2020s include the integration of ML and AI into robotic systems. This allows robots to adapt and learn from their experiences, making them more versatile and capable of handling complex tasks.
*   Autonomous Mobile Robots: The rise of autonomous mobile robots (AMRs) is transforming logistics and material handling within manufacturing facilities. These robots can navigate autonomously and perform tasks like transporting goods and materials.
*   Diversification of Applications: Robotics is expanding beyond traditional manufacturing sectors, finding applications in healthcare, agriculture, and other industries. The versatility of robotic systems continues to grow. These historical developments provide a comprehensive view of how robotics in manufacturing has evolved over time, from simple mechanization to the sophisticated, interconnected systems of today's smart factories. These milestones reflect the continuous pursuit of automation to enhance efficiency, precision, and safety in manufacturing processes.

16.2.2 FOUNDATIONS OF MODERN ROBOTICS: TRANSFORMATIVE TECHNOLOGICAL ADVANCES

The evolution of modern robotics has been profoundly shaped by a series of groundbreaking technological advancements. At the core of this transformation is the advent of digital computing and microprocessors, providing robots with the computational power essential for executing complex algorithms and tasks. Simultaneously, advancements in sensor technologies—including vision, proximity, and tactile sensors—have significantly enhanced robotic perception, enabling machines to interact more effectively with their environment and carry out intricate tasks with precision.

The integration of AI and ML stands out as a pivotal development. These technologies empower robots to adapt to dynamic conditions, learn from experience, and make intelligent decisions based on real-time data. This adaptability is crucial for the versatility of modern robots, allowing them to navigate and respond to changing environments effectively. Additionally, the development of high-precision actuators and motors has played a critical role in providing robots with precise control over their movements, facilitating intricate and accurate manipulations in various applications.

Materials science has also significantly contributed to the evolution of modern robotics. Innovations in lightweight materials and composites have led to the creation of more agile and energy-efficient robots. The use of advanced materials, such as those in soft robotics and biomimetic designs, has further enhanced the adaptability and safety of robots, enabling them to perform tasks in complex and dynamic environments.

Networking and connectivity have played a fundamental role in shaping the landscape of modern robotics. Robust communication protocols have enabled collaboration among robots and their seamless integration with other devices in the Industrial Internet of Things (IIoT). This interconnectedness contributes to more efficient and streamlined manufacturing processes. Moreover, the development of user-friendly human–machine interfaces (HMIs) has democratized access to robotic systems, making it easier for individuals with varying technical expertise to interact with and control robots, fostering increased human–robot collaboration.

The evolution of robotics is intricately tied to key technological breakthroughs. From the computational power of microprocessors to the adaptability of AI, precision of actuators, materials advancements, and connectivity through networking, each innovation has played a crucial role. These advancements collectively form the backbone of modern robotics, opening up new possibilities for automation in diverse industries.

16.3 CHALLENGES FACED BY TRADITIONAL MANUFACTURING

Traditional manufacturing, once the cornerstone of industrial production, now grapples with many challenges in an era defined by rapid technological advancements, global competition, and shifting consumer expectations. This exploration delves into the multifaceted difficulties confronting traditional manufacturing methods, examining key issues that range from operational inefficiencies to the need for digital transformation.

16.3.1 GLOBAL COMPETITION AND MARKET DYNAMICS

- Impact of Globalization: Traditional manufacturers often face heightened competition from global counterparts, leading to increased pressure to deliver products more efficiently and cost-effectively.
- Supply Chain Vulnerabilities: The complexity and length of traditional supply chains expose manufacturers to disruptions, necessitating strategies for resilience and adaptability.

16.3.2 TECHNOLOGY ADOPTION AND DIGITALIZATION

- Lack of Technological Integration: Reluctance to embrace modern technologies hinders efficiency improvements and inhibits the integration of automation and smart manufacturing solutions.
- Data-Driven Decision-Making: The absence of robust data analytics capabilities limits the ability to make informed decisions, hindering competitiveness in the digital age.

16.3.3 OPERATIONAL INEFFICIENCIES AND PRODUCTIVITY

- Outdated Production Methods: Traditional manufacturing processes may be manual and time-consuming, leading to operational inefficiencies and reduced production agility.
- Workforce Skill Gaps: Adapting to advanced technologies requires a skilled workforce, and a gap in skills poses a significant challenge to modernizing manufacturing operations.

16.3.4 ENVIRONMENTAL SUSTAINABILITY

- Environmental Impact: Traditional manufacturing methods often contribute to environmental degradation through resource consumption and waste generation, necessitating a shift toward sustainable practices.
- Regulatory Compliance Challenges: Meeting stringent environmental regulations poses challenges and adds complexities to traditional manufacturing processes.

16.3.5 COST PRESSURES AND FINANCIAL CONSTRAINTS

- Rising Production Costs: Factors such as energy costs, raw material prices, and labor expenses contribute to escalating production costs, affecting the competitiveness of traditional manufacturing.

- Investment Challenges: Financial constraints and a reluctance to invest in new technologies hinder the adoption of innovations that could enhance efficiency and competitiveness.

16.3.6 ADAPTATION TO CHANGING CONSUMER DEMANDS

- Shift in Consumer Preferences: Changing consumer expectations for customization, sustainability, and rapid delivery require traditional manufacturers to adapt their product offerings and production processes.
- Agility and Flexibility: Adapting to rapidly changing market demands challenges the traditional manufacturing model, which may be characterized by rigid production structures.

Traditional manufacturing faces a complex array of challenges that demand a strategic and forward-thinking approach for sustainable growth. While these challenges are significant, they also present opportunities for transformation and reinvention. Overcoming these obstacles requires a concerted effort to embrace digitalization, invest in workforce development, adopt sustainable practices, and foster a culture of innovation.

In navigating these challenges, traditional manufacturers have the opportunity to not only survive but also thrive in an evolving industrial landscape. The path forward involves a holistic approach that combines technological advancements with strategic planning, ultimately ensuring the resilience and adaptability of traditional manufacturing in the face of dynamic market forces.

16.4 TYPES OF ROBOTICS IN MANUFACTURING

The field of robotics in manufacturing encompasses various types of robotic systems designed to perform specific tasks and functions within industrial settings. Here are key types of robotics commonly used in manufacturing:

16.4.1 INDUSTRIAL ROBOTS

- Characteristics: Versatile and programmable, industrial robots are equipped with articulated arms, often with multiple degrees of freedom, allowing them to perform a variety of complex tasks.
- Applications: Widely used in assembly lines for tasks such as welding, painting, and material handling. Their precision and repeatability make them essential for consistent manufacturing processes.

16.4.2 COLLABORATIVE ROBOTS

- Characteristics: Collaborative robots (Cobots) are designed to work safely alongside human operators. They are equipped with sensors to detect the presence of humans and adjust their movements accordingly.

- Applications: Ideal for tasks that involve close collaboration between humans and robots, such as small-scale assembly, quality inspection, and intricate processes.

16.4.3 MOBILE ROBOTS

- Characteristics: Mobile robots are designed for autonomous movement within a manufacturing facility. They often incorporate navigation systems, such as Lidar or cameras, to move around obstacles.
- Applications: Commonly used for material transport, inventory management, and floor-level tasks, contributing to the optimization of logistics within a facility.

16.4.4 AUTOMATED GUIDED VEHICLES

- Characteristics: Automated guided vehicles (AGVs) follow predefined paths using guidance systems like markers or sensors. They are commonly used for point-to-point material transport.
- Applications: AGVs play a crucial role in material handling, transporting goods between different locations, and automating routine tasks within a facility.

16.4.5 DELTA ROBOTS

- Characteristics: Delta robots have a parallel architecture with three arms connected to a common base. This design allows for high-speed and precise movements in tasks requiring rapid pick-and-place operations.
- Applications: Widely used in packaging, food processing, and assembly lines where speed and accuracy are critical.

16.4.6 SCARA ROBOTS

- Characteristics: SCARA robots have selective compliance in the horizontal plane, allowing precise horizontal movements. They typically have fewer degrees of freedom than articulated robots.
- Applications: Suited for assembly tasks, material handling, and applications in confined spaces where precise horizontal motion is essential.

16.4.7 ARTICULATED ROBOTS

- Characteristics: Articulated robots feature rotary joints, providing multiple degrees of freedom. Their flexibility makes them suitable for applications requiring a wide range of motion.
- Applications: Commonly used in welding, painting, assembly, and other tasks where flexibility and adaptability are crucial.

16.4.8 PARALLEL ROBOTS

- Characteristics: Parallel robots have multiple arms working in parallel to control the position of the end-effector. This design provides high precision and stiffness.
- Applications: Ideal for applications requiring high precision, such as machining, pick-and-place operations, and assembly tasks.

16.4.9 CARTESIAN/GANTRY ROBOTS

- Characteristics: Cartesian or gantry robots operate along three linear axes, offering precise and repeatable movements in a specific workspace.
- Applications: Widely used in pick-and-place operations, palletizing, and tasks that involve linear movements in a defined workspace.

16.4.10 AI-POWERED ROBOTS

- Characteristics: AI-powered robots integrate AI technologies, including ML and computer vision, allowing them to adapt and make intelligent decisions.
- Applications: Used for quality control, predictive maintenance, and tasks that require adaptive behavior. These robots can learn from data and optimize their performance over time.

Each type of robotics in manufacturing brings unique capabilities, allowing industries to tailor their automation solutions to specific needs. The continuous evolution of these technologies contributes to increased efficiency, reduced costs, and enhanced overall productivity in manufacturing processes. As industries adopt more advanced robotic systems, the synergy between human workers and machines becomes a cornerstone of modern manufacturing (Khang & Rath et al., 2023).

16.5 INDUSTRIAL ROBOTS

Industrial robots, comprising robotic arms, manipulators, and automated systems, form the backbone of modern manufacturing, revolutionizing how tasks are executed within industrial settings. At the core of these robotic systems are the articulated robotic arms, each featuring joints for multiaxis movement. These arms serve as the essential components for precise and controlled maneuvers, crucial for a myriad of manufacturing applications. At the end of these arms, various end-effectors, such as grippers, welding torches, or specialized tools are attached, enabling a wide range of functionalities and applications (Khang & Rath et al., 2024).

Manipulators, encompassing the entire robotic system, including the arm, joints, and end-effector, are responsible for intricate manipulations of objects or materials. The degree of freedom, determined by the number of joints, influences the flexibility and adaptability of the manipulator. Advanced control systems, often involving CNC technology, contribute to the precision and repeatability of tasks, making them essential for operations such as welding, painting, and assembly.

In the realm of automated systems, industrial robots are seamlessly integrated into broader manufacturing processes. These systems incorporate a variety of sensors, such as vision systems and proximity sensors, allowing the robot to gather information about its environment. The integration of these sensors facilitates adaptability and enhances the robot's responsiveness to its surroundings. Additionally, these automated systems often include sophisticated programming methods like teach pendant programming or offline programming, ensuring efficient and accurate task execution. Robots within these systems can be part of a connected network, contributing to the IIoT and enabling real-time monitoring, data collection, and remote control.

When considering design considerations, aspects such as payload capacity, reach, and accuracy play pivotal roles in determining the suitability of a robotic system for specific tasks. Emerging trends, such as Cobots, AI integration, and customization through additive manufacturing, are shaping the future landscape of industrial robots (Khang & Hahanov et al., 2022).

Furthermore, the application of industrial robots spans various industries, including manufacturing, aerospace, pharmaceuticals, and the food and beverage sector, showcasing their versatility and impact on diverse sectors. As technology continues to advance, industrial robots are poised to play an even more central role in shaping the future of manufacturing, enhancing efficiency, precision, and adaptability across a wide array of applications.

16.6 COLLABORATIVE ROBOTS

The rise of collaborative robots (Cobots) marks a transformative shift in the field of robotics, introducing machines specifically designed to work alongside human operators in a shared workspace. Unlike traditional industrial robots confined to safety cages, Cobots are equipped with advanced sensors and safety features, enabling them to collaborate with humans without posing a risk. This paradigm shift is driven by several factors, reflecting the changing needs and dynamics of modern industries.

One of the primary drivers behind the rise of Cobots is the growing emphasis on flexibility and adaptability in manufacturing environments. Traditional industrial robots excel in repetitive, predefined tasks but lack the agility and versatility required for dynamic and unpredictable tasks. Cobots, on the other hand, are inherently designed to be flexible and easily reprogrammable, allowing them to handle a broader range of tasks. This adaptability is particularly crucial in industries where production lines need to be quickly reconfigured to accommodate diverse product lines and changing market demands.

Safety is a paramount concern in human–robot collaboration, and Cobots address this issue with integrated safety features. These robots are equipped with sensors, vision systems, and force-limiting technology that enable them to detect the presence of humans and immediately adjust their movements to avoid collisions. This level of safety ensures that Cobots can operate in close proximity to human workers without compromising well-being.

Cobots are democratizing automation by making robotic technology more accessible to small- and medium-sized enterprises (SMEs). Traditional industrial robots often

FIGURE 16.2   Concept of Cobots.

come with high upfront costs and complex programming requirements, making them less feasible for smaller businesses. In contrast, Cobots are designed to be user-friendly, often employing intuitive programming interfaces that allow non-experts to teach the robot new tasks quickly. This democratization of automation empowers smaller enterprises to leverage robotic technology for improved efficiency and productivity.

The collaborative nature of Cobots fosters a new era of human–robot teamwork, where each contributes its unique strengths. Cobots can handle repetitive and physically demanding tasks, freeing human workers to focus on more complex and cognitive aspects of their jobs. This collaboration enhances overall productivity, quality, and job satisfaction, leading to a more harmonious work environment, as shown in Figure 16.2.

As industries continue to embrace automation, the rise of Cobots reflects a broader shift toward human-centered robotics. The collaborative approach acknowledges the complementary strengths of humans and robots, paving the way for a future where man and machine work together seamlessly. This trend is not limited to manufacturing but extends to various sectors, including healthcare, logistics, and service industries, where Cobots are contributing to safer, more efficient, and adaptable work environments (Khang & Shah et al., 2023).

16.7   APPLICATIONS OF ROBOTICS IN MANUFACTURING

16.7.1   Automated Assembly Lines: Case Studies and Examples of Robotic Assembly Processes

Automated assembly lines have undergone a revolutionary transformation with the integration of robotics. Robotic systems are deployed to streamline assembly processes, enhancing efficiency and precision. In the automotive industry, for example, leading manufacturers employ robotic arms to perform intricate tasks like welding, fastening, and component assembly. Cobots work alongside human operators, ensuring a harmonious interaction that maximizes productivity. Case studies from the electronics industry show the use of robotic assembly for delicate tasks such as printed circuit board (PCB) assembly, where robots meticulously place and solder components with high precision. The adoption of robotic assembly processes has led to reduced cycle times, increased production rates, and improved product consistency across various manufacturing sectors.

16.7.2 Welding and Material Handling: How Robots Are Used for Welding Tasks and Moving Materials

Robotic welding has become a cornerstone in manufacturing processes, particularly in industries such as automotive, shipbuilding, and construction. Industrial robots equipped with welding torches perform tasks with high precision, consistency, and speed, ensuring quality welds while minimizing defects. In shipyards, large-scale robotic welding systems contribute to the construction of complex structures with efficiency and accuracy. Additionally, material handling is a domain where robots excel, offering solutions for the swift and precise movement of raw materials and finished products. Autonomous mobile robots (AMRs) navigate warehouses, transporting materials from one location to another, optimizing logistics and minimizing manual labor. These robotic solutions not only enhance safety in hazardous environments but also contribute to significant time and cost savings in the long run (Khang & Muthmainnah et al., 2023).

16.7.3 Inspection and Quality Control: Role of Robotics in Ensuring Product Quality

Robotics plays a crucial role in inspection and quality control, ensuring that products meet stringent standards. In the food and beverage industry, robotic vision systems are employed for quality inspection, assessing factors such as size, color, and defects in fruits, vegetables, and packaged goods. Automotive manufacturers use robotic arms equipped with sensors and cameras for precise visual inspections of painted surfaces, detecting imperfections that may be imperceptible to the human eye. Cobots are integrated into assembly lines to conduct real-time quality checks, contributing to the reduction of defects and waste. The use of robotics in inspection improves the accuracy and consistency of quality control processes and enhances overall product reliability and customer satisfaction.

The applications of robotics in manufacturing are diverse and impactful. From automating assembly lines to handling materials and ensuring product quality through inspection, robotic systems contribute to increased efficiency, precision, and overall productivity in the manufacturing sector. Case studies and examples from various industries highlight the adaptability and transformative potential of robotics in addressing specific manufacturing challenges and driving innovation.

16.8 CONCLUSION

The integration of robotics in manufacturing represents a transformative leap forward, reshaping traditional processes and significantly impacting efficiency, precision, and overall productivity. The evolution of automated assembly lines, as evidenced by case studies across industries, shows the prowess of robotic systems in handling complex tasks with speed and precision.

In the automotive sector, where robots seamlessly weld intricate components, and in electronics manufacturing, where precision is paramount in PCB assembly, robotic assembly processes have become synonymous with increased production rates and enhanced product consistency. Welding and material handling stand out as critical domains where robots play an important role. Robotic welding ensures the quality of welds and contributes to increased speed and reduced defects, particularly in sectors like shipbuilding and construction. The versatility of robotic solutions in material handling, exemplified by AMRs, optimizes logistics in warehouses and enhances safety in environments where manual labor may pose risks.

Quality control and inspection, facilitated by robotic vision systems and Cobots, represent another facet of the manufacturing landscape transformed by robotics. From meticulously examining painted surfaces in automotive manufacturing to conducting real-time quality checks on assembly lines, robotics ensures that products meet exacting standards, contributing to enhanced reliability and customer satisfaction. In essence, the rise of robotics in manufacturing epitomizes a harmonious collaboration between human and machine (Khang, 2023).

The advent of Cobots underscores a shift toward a more inclusive and adaptive work environment. Cobots, designed to work alongside human operators, enhance productivity and prioritize safety, marking a significant departure from the traditional notion of robots confined to safety cages. This collaborative approach acknowledges the unique strengths of both humans and robots, fostering a future where man and machine work together seamlessly.

As industries continue to embrace automation and innovative technologies, the applications of robotics in manufacturing are set to expand further. The ongoing integration of AI, ML, and the IIoT will continue to propel the manufacturing sector into new frontiers of efficiency and adaptability. The case studies and examples presented underscore the tangible benefits of robotics across diverse manufacturing processes (Khang & Hajimahmud et al., 2024).

REFERENCES

Khang, A., *Medical Robotics and AI-Assisted Diagnostics for a High-Tech Healthcare Industry.* (1st Ed.) (2023). IGI Global Press. DOI:10.4018/979-8-3693-2105-8

Khang, A., Hahanov, V., Abbas, G. L., & Hajimahmud, V. A., "Cyber-Physical-Social System and İncident Management," *AI-Centric Smart City Ecosystems: Technologies, Design and Implementation* (1st Ed.), (pp. 2–15), (2022). CRC Press. https://doi.org/10.1201/9781003252542-2

Khang, A., Hajimahmud, V. A, Vladimir, Hahanov, & Shah, V., *Advanced IoT Technologies and Applications in the Industry 4.0 Digital Economy* (1st Ed.) (2024). CRC Press. https://doi.org/10.1201/9781003434269

Khang, A., Muthmainnah, M, Seraj, Prodhan Mahbub Ibna, Yakin, Ahmad Al, Obaid, Ahmad J., & Ranjan Panda, Manas. "AI-Aided Teaching Model for the Education 5.0 Ecosystem" *AI-Based Technologies and Applications in the Era of the Metaverse.* (1st Ed.) (2023). Page (83–104). IGI Global Press. https://doi.org/10.4018/978-1-6684-8851-5.ch004

Khang, A., Rath, K. C., Anh, P.T.N., Rath, S. K., & Bhattacharya, S., "Quantum-Based Robotics in High-Tech Healthcare Industry - Innovations and Applications, "*Medical Robotics and AI-Assisted Diagnostics for a High-Tech Healthcare Industry.* (1st Ed.) (2024). IGI Global Press. https://doi.org/10.4018/979-8-3693-2105-8.ch001

Khang, A., Rath, Kali Charan, Kumar Satapathy, Suresh, Kumar, Amaresh, Ranjan Das, Sudhansu, & Ranjan Panda, Manas. "Enabling the Future of Manufacturing: Integration of Robotics and IoT to Smart Factory Infrastructure in Industry 4.0." *AI-Based Technologies and Applications in the Era of the Metaverse.* (1st Ed.) (2023). Page (25–50). IGI Global Press. https://doi.org/10.4018/978-1-6684-8851-5.ch002

Khang, A., Shah, V., & Rani, S., *AI-Based Technologies and Applications in the Era of the Metaverse.* (1st Ed.) (2023). IGI Global Press. https://doi.org/10.4018/978-1-6684-8851-5

Righettini, P. (2010). *Progettazione funzionale di sistemi meccatronci: Introduzione al modulo.* Bergamo: Università degli Studi di Bergamo. https://www.igi-global.com/chapter/designing-a-robot-for-manufacturing-fiberglass-reinforced-plastic-frp-molded-grating/291648

17 Application of Pressure Sensors in Manufacturing
Improving Efficiency and Risk Mitigation

Arpita Nayak, Atmika Patnaik, Ipseeta Satpathy, B. C. M. Patnaik, and Alex Khang

17.1 INTRODUCTION

Pressure measurement may be traced back to antiquity when different approaches were used to gauge pressure in various circumstances. Nonetheless, the development of modern pressure sensors began in the late-19th and early-20th century. The Bourdon tube pressure gauge, developed in 1874 by Eugene Bourdon, a renowned French engineer, was a pioneering manifestation of a pressure sensor. The curved design of the Bourdon tube causes deformation when subjected to pressure, making fluid pressure measuring easier. Following that, the 20th century saw great breakthroughs in pressure sensor technology, as seen by the spread of many sensor types based on different principles, such as strain gauges, capacitive sensors, piezoelectric sensors, and semiconductor-based sensors. This evolutionary path facilitated the increase of pressure-sensing capacities, ushering in unprecedented prospects for scientific research and industrial uses (Johnson et al., 2002).

People have been intrigued with monitoring pressure fluctuations since the 1590s. Glass tubes and barometer experiments were used to describe pressure variations in the beginning. These basic devices monitored how much pressure changes pushed or pulled the liquids inside them. A pressure sensor is a device used to detect and measure pressure, which is defined in this context as the amount of force exerted to a certain place. Pressure sensors enable more specialized maintenance approaches, such as predictive maintenance. These devices collect data on the condition of equipment in real-time. Based on the available data, the sensors can foresee and prepare for failure patterns. When pressure sensors are installed in some tanks and other pressurized assets, they can inform maintenance staff when the pressure goes below a preset threshold. This enables the teams to fix the problem as soon as possible. A pressure sensor is defined as a transducer that detects a signal when pressure is applied to it (Lang, 2022).

Fluid manipulation is required in manufacturing processes such as hydraulic and pneumatic systems. Pressure sensors detect any irregularities in these systems, continually looking for leaks, compression problems, and signals of possible breakdown.

DOI: 10.1201/9781003438137-17

Pressure sensors are becoming increasingly important in modern instrumentation paradigms, surpassing static measurements. Examples of such applications include bottle and equipment leak detection, variable air volume (VAV) systems, air blades, compressed air pressure monitoring, industrial flow assessment, filter pressure supervision, duct airflow assessment, gas detection, pneumatic controls, mine safety instrumentation, industrial degassers, and suction check-in for pick and place operations. These applications exhibit notable resonance, particularly in the fields of printed circuit boards and semiconductor process equipment. This developing application highlights the critical role that pressure sensors play in current industrial processes, as well as their numerous benefits to productivity, security, and precision in a variety of production scenarios (Li et al., 2020).

A multitude of devices employ liquid or other types of pressure. These sensors allow for the creation of Internet of Things (IoT) systems that monitor pressure-driven systems and devices. Any variation from the typical pressure range alerts the system administrator to potential concerns. Because it is simple to detect any pressure fluctuations or decreases, the use of these sensors is beneficial not only in production but also in the upkeep of complete water and heating systems. Injection molding, a widely used procedure for the large-scale manufacture of plastic components, is a key area of the pressure sensor used in the industrial arena. Injection molding involves injecting molten plastic material into a mold under high pressure to get the desired configuration. Pressure sensors are strategically deployed at several points during the injection molding process to provide optimal quality and process efficiency. These sensors are essential instruments for quality control and process optimization, leading to increased manufacturing precision and general efficiency (Javaid et al., 2021; Ageyeva et al., 2019). The usage of pressure sensors in the plastic bottle injection molding process is described in detail in Figure 17.1 (Zhao et al., 2020).

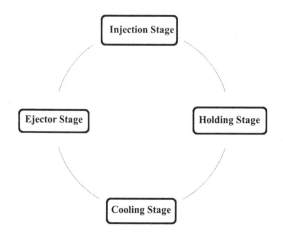

FIGURE 17.1   Different stages of using pressure sensors in the plastic bottle molding process. (From the author's own compilation.)

The different stages of bottle molding process include:

- Injection Stage – The molten plastic is pumped into the mold cavity during the injection step. To monitor injection pressure, pressure sensors are installed into the injection molding process. Engineers can spot irregularities or inconsistencies in the pressure curve that may indicate difficulties such as clogged nozzles, differences in material viscosity, or mold misalignment.
- Holding Stage – Following injection, the plastic is kept under pressure to ensure that the mold is completely filled. Pressure sensors are essential for monitoring and adjusting holding pressure. Maintaining the proper pressure ensures that the mold is completely filled, which prevents faults such as short shots or unfinished components.
- Cooling Stage – Pressure sensors may be employed to track the cooling pressure within the mold during the cooling step. Cooling pressure variations may indicate cooling channel obstructions or other cooling system inefficiencies that may influence the end product's quality.
- Ejection Stage – Ejector pins are used to remove the plastic object from the mold once it has cooled and set. Ejection pressure may be monitored using pressure sensors. Abnormal pressure measurements during ejection might indicate stuck or misaligned ejector pins, resulting in part damage or mold wear.

Pressure sensors are increasingly used in the manufacturing industry as a result of the rising demand for more stringently controlled processes and the associated quality control requirements. The increased pressure and vacuum control can detect equipment maintenance needs before they cause unnecessary downtime and increase manufacturing costs (Yang et al., 2022). The concepts of air pressure measurement are increasingly applied in patient monitoring and assisted living solutions, where a sudden quick shift in altitude might signify a fall. In this application sector, pressure sensors will likely be capable of monitoring fluctuations in air pressure in hundredths of a millibar with an accuracy of 2 bar or better. That means they can detect an altitude shift of roughly 10 cm, which is sufficient to establish whether a patient is on the floor. As the instances show, pressure-sensing sensors are increasingly used in automated systems to provide a wide range of features and functionalities. Pressure sensors are being used to give critical functionality in new applications as lifestyles continue to adapt (Parmar et al., 2022).

An alarm will be issued to the appropriate service provider (or family member) allowing them to contact the user quickly and/or dispatch assistance if needed. The preceding year market value for pressure sensors was USD $15.23 billion, and it is predicted to increase at a compound annual growth rate of 9.37% over the next 5 years, reaching USD $26.07 billion. Because of recent developments in pressure sensor technology, the industry is positioned for significant growth. These advancements are likely to drive significant development, aided by prospective IoT applications, artificial intelligence (AI) systems, and wearable medical equipment.

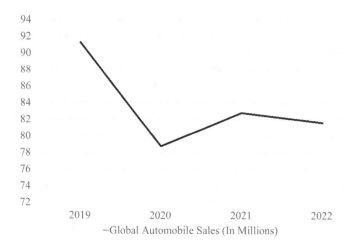

FIGURE 17.2   Global automobile sales (2019–2022) (OICA, 2022).

As a result, major efforts have been put toward the creation of advanced pressure sensors, greatly broadening their application potential and propelling the total expansion of the market under consideration. As the automotive sector seeks to meet global environmental requirements, efforts to improve engine economy and management are more important than ever. To improve efficiency, these applications use efficient pressure sensors that properly monitor parameters such as air volume and exhaust gas pressure. The increasing number of automobiles sold globally also bodes well for the expansion of the industry. According to The Organization for Economic Cooperation and Development, worldwide automotive sales reached 81.62 million units in 2022, up from 78.78 million units in 2020, as shown in Figure 17.2.

17.2   MITIGATING WORKPLACE ACCIDENTS: ROLE OF PRESSURE SENSORS IN MANUFACTURING INDUSTRIES

Workplace accidents continue to be a major problem in the industrial sector, prompting the implementation of modern technology to improve safety. In 2007, there were around 942,000 on-the-job accidents in the EU-15 countries and Norway that resulted in more than three days of unavailability of employees. In the same year, 667 fatal incidents occurred in the industrial business. Approximately 30,000 accidents occurred in manufacturing establishments in Finland in 2007, with slightly more than 14,000 resulting in a minimum of four days of absence. Six of the accidents were deadly. As a result, about every fourth workplace accident features personnel doing manufacturing procedures (Nenonen, 2011).

Human error is a major risk in the manufacturing industry. It affects product error and liability, and it may even end up in workplace injuries or fatalities. Malaysia has an alarmingly high rate of workplace accidents. There were over 2700 industrial accidents in 2018 that resulted in injury or death. A workplace accident would place a company in a no-win situation. Malaysia's manufacturing sector makes the most demands from the overall cost of accidents and injuries. Companies that violate workplace safety and health standards face fines from Malaysia's Department of Occupational Safety and Health.

Inspections are performed to verify that manufacturers follow occupational safety and health (OSH) regulations, and errant firms are punished (Yeow et al., 2020). Occupational injury statistics are derived from administrative data (insurance records, labor inspection records, records held by the labor ministry or an analogous social security organization), establishment surveys, and household surveys, among other sources. National notification systems for occupational injuries—such as labor inspection records and annual reports, insurance and compensation records, and death registers—are recommended as sources of occupational injury statistics, which could be augmented by household surveys, particularly for informal sector organizations and the self-employed, and/or progress surveys (Patel et al., 2022).

Based on the Directorate General Factory Advice Service and Labour Institutes (DGFASLI) statistics, in 2020 India had 363,442 registered factories, with 84% actively operating and employing 20.3 million people. From 2010 to 2020, there were 1,109 deaths and nearly 4,000 injuries reported in registered factories, according to DGFASLI statistics. Injuries decreased between 2018 and 2020. The number of fatal accidents in factories in India (2017–2020) is shown in Figure 17.3. (Data is not available/not reported for Arunachal Pradesh, Manipur, Mizoram, and Nagaland for 2017–2020; Tripura, West Bengal for 2019 and 2020; and Chandigarh for 2020.)

Every year, over 2 million people are killed or injured on the job, according to an International Labour Organization (ILO) estimate (ILO, 2023), costing the world economy roughly USD $1.25 trillion per year. The study examines existing knowledge on the toll of occupational sickness, disability, and mortality. This estimate is based on an ILO assumption that accidents and work-related injuries cost roughly

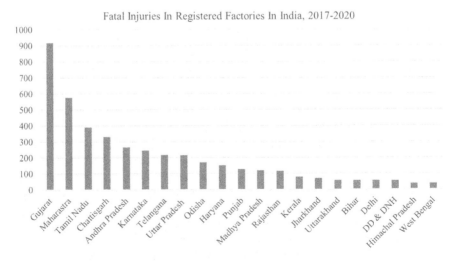

FIGURE 17.3   Fatal accidents in registered factories in India (2017–2020). (Adopted from Paliath, 2023.)

4% of a country's annual GDP. Sensors are used everywhere, and one of the most lucrative markets for them is in automobiles. New automobiles normally have 60 to 100 sensors, and that number might climb to 200 in the coming years. In 2020, the automobile industry used around 22 billion sensors (Frank, 2023). The use of these sensors is expanding beyond determining if your car's systems are operating properly or keeping basic information on driving behavior. Vehicle manufacturers are investing heavily in advanced driver assistance systems (ADAS), such as frontal collision warnings, lane departure alerts, adaptive cruise control, and other sensor-enabled safety technologies. The global market for ADAS is quickly expanding exceeding the 2020 estimate of USD $67 billion (Rahim et al., 2021).

The role of pressure sensors in leak detection and pressure recognition of anomalies is examined, demonstrating their effectiveness in reducing hazardous material spills and chemical inhalation. Furthermore, the study focuses on incorporating pressure sensors into safety systems to monitor equipment overpressure, potentially preventing explosions and breakdowns of equipment (Pishgar et al., 2021). Pressure sensors are widely used in the monitoring of pressure levels in a wide range of equipment, including tanks, vessels, and pipes in the industrial sector. Their deployment comprises the activation of alarms or shutdown mechanisms when pressure exceeds allowed levels, thereby preventing the development of potentially dangerous events like explosions or equipment failures caused by overpressure phenomena (Amit et al., 2020).

Pressure sensors are sensitive to minute pressure fluctuations, making them useful for detecting subtle alterations within pipelines or containers. This feature assists in the early detection of leaks before they become significant, reducing dangerous situations. As a result, the early detection made possible by pressure sensors helps to prevent spills, the discharge of hazardous chemicals, and the risk of chemical exposure, strengthening safety measures in manufacturing organizations (Bai et al., 2020).

17.3 ROLE OF PRESSURE SENSORS IN STATISTICAL PROCESS CONTROL IN MANUFACTURING INDUSTRIES

Modern manufacturing enterprises must deal with continually varying raw material prices as well as intense competition. These factors are beyond the control of businesses, yet they can influence the quality of their goods and operations. To be a market leader, businesses must always strive to improve quality, efficiency, and cost margins. Most businesses continue to rely on inspection to uncover quality flaws, although its effectiveness is questionable. With statistical process control (SPC), an organization may transition from detection to prevention.

Continuous monitoring of process performance allows operators to discover changing trends or processes before they have an impact on performance (Sunadi et al., 2020). Process control systems guarantee that industrial processes function smoothly, consistently, and with the least amount of variation. They are utilized in industrial settings to improve throughput, quality, yield, and energy efficiency, as well as to ensure safety and profitability. Manufacturing processes and activities are measured, monitored, and controlled using systems. They detect and adjust deviations from specified values, either automatically or manually. The goal is to maintain consistent output while using as little energy as possible. Statistical process control is commonly characterized as a way of controlling and accessing quality using statistical analysis, with the ultimate purpose of enhancing the manufacturing process.

In the form of process or product measurements, manufacturers collect high-quality, real-time data from a variety of sensors and devices. The data gathered is subsequently used to monitor, evaluate, and regulate the production process. Collecting this data, visually shown in graphs and charts, enables producers to reach operational efficacy. Statistical process control is a method that reveals opportunities for improvement, allowing businesses to avoid inefficiencies, bottlenecks, and faulty goods. The arsenal of SPC tools and procedures enables attentive monitoring of process dynamics, detection of abnormalities within internal frameworks, and skilled resolution of production bottlenecks. Within the context, "statistical process control" and "statistical quality control" are sometimes used interchangeably (Abdul Halim et al., 2017). Statistical process control monitors and regulates production processes using technology. It generates a treasure of quality data from product assessments and process readings by orchestrating multiple sensors and devices. This data is rigorously collected, scrutinized, and monitored in order to influence the process trajectory.

Statistical process control emerges as a clear approach to supporting continuous improvement. Managers guarantee that a process reaches its full potential by maintaining constant monitoring and management. This unrelenting control results in consistent, high-quality production outcomes, highlighting the importance of SPC in the pursuit of long-term excellence (Madanhire & Mbohwa, 2016; Montgomery, 2019).

William A. Shewhart, a Bell Laboratories employee, created the first control chart and pioneered the concept of SPC in 1924. During World War II, this quality control procedure was widely utilized in the ammunition and weapon industries. Statistical process control ensured product quality without compromising safety. Following the war, the application of SPC slowed in the United States, but it was quickly adopted by the Japanese in their manufacturing sector, and they continue to do so today. In the 1970s, SPC was reintroduced in the United States to compete with Japanese products.

Today, SPCs are widely used in the global industrial sector. Throughout the production process, pressure sensors continually gather pressure-related data points. These data points are utilized to generate control charts, which are essential SPC tools. Control charts aid in the visualization of process trends, detection of deviations, and provision of insights into process stability and competence (He & Wang, 2018).

Statistical process control helps in identifying and preventing imperfections, variability, and inefficiencies in the manufacturing process saving time and costs. This is done following six steps:

1. Determine which process and factors will be monitored and controlled. A process is a series of events with a result. A variable is an output property or trait that can be measured or tallied. For example, if you are creating widgets, you may want to keep track of the process of cutting, drilling, and setting up the widgets, as well as the variables of length, diameter, and weight.

2. Gather and organize data for the variables you have chosen. You must select how frequently, how much, and the manner in which you will gather the data. For instance, you might gather 10 widget samples every hour and analyze their length, diameter, and weight. You must also organize the data in a spreadsheet or a software program capable of statistical computations and graphic generation.

3. Compute statistics that summarize the data and show the process performance. The most popular statistics are the mean, standard deviation, and range. The mean represents the variable's average value. The standard deviation expresses how far the variable deviates from the mean. A variable's range is that of its highest and lowest values. For example, you may compute the mean, standard deviation, and range of the length, diameter, and weight of the widgets.

4. Create charts that graphically present the data and statistics and assist in detecting any patterns or trends. The run chart, histogram, and control chart are most commonly used. A run chart is a line graph that depicts how a variable varies over time. The histogram is a bar graph that depicts the distribution of the variable. The control chart combines a run chart with a histogram to indicate how the variable relates to predicted limits or standards.

5. Examine the data and charts for any indications of issues or chances for improvement. Outliers, changes, trends, cycles, and variety are some of the signals. Outliers are extraordinarily high or low values. Shifts are abrupt changes in the variable's level or direction. Trends are steady variations in the variable's level or direction. Cycles are periodic variations in a variable. The difference between the variable's values is referred to as variation.

6. Act on the findings and begin implementing solutions or process changes. Some of the activities include rectifying, avoiding, or lowering the sources of problems, as well as optimizing, upgrading, or standardizing best practices. You might, for example, change the settings on machines, replace worn-out items, train workers, or alter processes.

Pressure sensors are essential in SPC for monitoring and measuring process pressure levels at critical points. Pressure sensors are strategically used in industrial contexts, such as within a production plant, to monitor the pressure of chemicals within containers or systems. This rigorous pressure monitoring acts as an early warning system, with departures from preset pressure thresholds indicating possible problems. Consider the situation in a manufacturing facility where a pressure sensor is used to monitor the pressure of a liquid contained within a tank. If the pressure goes below a specified level, it might indicate the presence of a leak. If the pressure exceeds a predetermined limit, it may indicate a blockage in the system. The manufacturing facility can quickly discover, analyze, and correct operational faults by meticulously scrutinizing pressure changes. This proactive strategy guarantees that possible interruptions or safety problems are addressed before they wreak havoc on production or jeopardize safety measures (Hsu et al., 2020).

17.4 ROLE OF PRESSURE SENSORS IN QUALITY CONTROL IN MANUFACTURING INDUSTRIES

Manufacturing quality is a determinant of the whole quality control process. The pursuit of quality must be shared by everyone at every stage of the manufacturing process. Quality products help to maintain a firm's credibility, and there are legal and financial ramifications when faulty products reach the public. Prior to leaving the manufacturing plant, quality control ensures that all goods are defect-free, that the process eliminates waste, and that the result meets customer expectations. This demands continuous testing and assessment, as well as compliance methods, throughout the manufacturing process (Joazeiro, 2019). Poor quality is expected to cost manufacturers and service providers 5–30% of total revenues.

The good news is that widely recognized quality cultures spend $350 million rather than poorly developed quality cultures (Gunasekaran et al., 2019). Quality control in manufacturing is an intricate procedure that spans the whole business. It is much more than just product checks; it guarantees product quality on the factory floor by monitoring, measuring, and testing. In manufacturing, quality assurance involves the development, standardization, and insertion of quality control practices. Six Sigma is a quality management system that uses data to eliminate faults and process variability. The target defect rate is 3.4 per million chances, assuring near-perfect quality (Ismach, 2023).

Conformance to requirements is the foundation of quality in the manufacturing business. Once a manufacturing-based quality exemplar has been created, the rest of the process is about meeting expectations in each product replication. This may be broken down into design, quality control, and quality management. The practice of inspecting items after they have been completed is known as quality control in manufacturing. This enables the main reason for a flaw to be easily recognized. When a flaw in a product is discovered in lean manufacturing, all production is paused. This emphasizes the significance of identifying causes. Alternatively, the entire production batch may contain faulty items (Montgomery, 2019).

The quest for consistency and uniformity in product quality is critical in the current manufacturing world. This endeavor is related to attaining predefined quality standards and exceeding consumer expectations. As fundamental components of quality control mechanisms, pressure sensors play a critical role in obtaining and maintaining uniformity as well as consistency throughout varied production processes. Pressure sensors work as watchful sentinels, constantly monitoring and adjusting pressure levels in production activities. This constant monitoring is especially important in procedures where pressure changes might affect product quality. The sensors provide real-time data collecting, allowing producers to ensure that pressure stays within predefined limits at all stages of production (He et al., 2020).

Uniformity refers to the consistency of qualities throughout a batch of items or manufacturing cycles. Pressure sensors help to ensure that pressure conditions stay consistent over several manufacturing iterations, which is an important aspect of quality control. This results in products with consistent properties such as density, thickness, and solidity (Markl et al., 2020). The sensors assist in the manufacturing of materials with constant densities and thicknesses by maintaining uniform pressure levels. This is especially important in areas like microelectronics, where little differences may have a big impact on performance.

Factories employ a wide range of liquids and gases to power equipment and make goods, such as air compressors, hydraulic cylinder-powered machine tools, and high-pressure water cleaning equipment. Unnecessary energy usage may be eliminated by using sensors to correctly monitor and manage the pressure of various liquids and gases, resulting in increased production efficiency and product quality (Ayerbe et al., 2022). Producing a solid framework relies on constant production circumstances. Pressure sensors ensure that pressure-related processes, such as curing, bonding, or compaction, are carried out precisely. This accuracy strengthens product integrity by lowering the chance of faults that might jeopardize overall functioning and longevity.

Pressure sensor data obtained during industrial operations can be used for statistical analysis. This research sheds light on the link between pressure and product quality, enabling informed decisions and modifications. Statistical techniques enhance processes further to provide immediate consistency and long-term consistency throughout production cycles (Di Fratta et al., 2016). Regulatory compliance refers to an industry's or organization's conformity to the rules, regulations, standards, and laws established by applicable regulatory agencies or governing bodies. Many sectors, particularly those involving potentially hazardous processes or products, are governed by specialized laws aimed at ensuring safety, quality, and environmental protection.

Pressure sensors are critical in assisting manufacturers meet these regulatory demands. Manufacturers may be required to show compliance with prescribed pressure limitations during regulatory audits or inspections. Pressure sensor data is a trustworthy source of information that validates compliance, allowing manufacturers to pass audits with ease (Bag et al., 2021). Product quality control has always been a primary focus in the manufacturing industry. It was also suggested that the quality state of the output product may be utilized to describe the manufacturing system's maintenance activities. Pressure sensors are in charge of defining specific pressure requirements for individual batches or lots, allowing them to orchestrate manufacturing operations with more accuracy. These sensors, strategically placed at crucial junctures, continuously monitor pressure levels in relation to pre-established standards, recognizing and flagging any instances of departure.

In response to such deviations, alarm systems immediately notify manufacturing workers or automated frameworks, driving immediate corrective actions, such as changes to process parameters, equipment configurations, or even a short-term halt of production to allow for an in-depth examination. This watchful mode of operation successfully prevents the formation of latent flaws, hence preventing the production of whole batches contaminated by substandard quality (Kenda et al., 2021; Goldsack et al., 2020).

17.5 INFLUENCE OF PRESSURE SENSORS IN MATERIAL TESTING

Materials testing is the quantification of values associated with the properties of materials that include plastics, elastomers, metals, composites, and textiles. This testing is carried out by manufacturers, research organizations, construction engineers, and anyone else who wants to understand how a material reacts to different forms of physical stress (Forster, 2015). Materials testing is a common method for determining the physical and mechanical characteristics of materials made from powders or raw materials, as well as components and composite final products. It is a broad field that encompasses methods for measuring force and distance (stress/strain) that range from shoelace tension to cardboard containerization crush resistance, switch actuation force, and friction computation between two materials (Black & Kohser, 2017).

The importance of the material's quality used in the manufacture of items is matched by the dependability of the manufacturing process. Materials testing plays an important role in determining and quantifying the suitability of various materials or treatments for specific applications. An example is the evaluation of material toughness. Given the abundance of available materials and treatments, the testing process emerges as a useful tool for navigating and streamlining options, identifying the best match for the intended application. As previously stated, testing is required in a variety of industrial contexts to ensure products meet defined standards, as well as to ensure adherence to requirements prior to use (Chatham et al., 2019).

Testing is used for more than material selection and reputable sourcing; it also acts as a routine verification tool to ensure that material acquired from new sources meets the stated requirements. A range of processes exists within the scope of material testing protocols, covering insights into the material's structural as well as mechanical properties. The use of either instrumental or traditional wet chemical analysis procedures has merit, especially when it comes to confirming the composition or elemental makeup of the subject item (Chua et al., 2020; Gisario et al., 2019). Industrial sensors are used to detect liquids or gases, moisture, oxygen, or contaminants in power generation, water and wastewater, food and beverage, oil and gas, chemicals, pharmaceuticals, and steel manufacturing.

Companies are realizing that reliable sensor technologies may relieve burden on control engineers by allowing them to focus on maintaining a safe environment with accurate data and intelligent analysis. This is due to legislation and corporate duty to improve the environmental landscape. Pressure sensors are used to evaluate material mechanical qualities such as strength, elasticity, and durability. Manufacturers can get insights into materials' reaction to stress by applying controlled pressure or force, thereby assessing their conformity to specified strength parameters (Chadha et al., 2022).

Various materials used in automotive manufacturing, such as metal, polymers, and glass, are exposed to strong stresses and pressures during crash tests to imitate real-world auto collision circumstances. Sensors are mostly used in the industrial sector to automate production activities while also monitoring process parameters. Clearly, sensor technology is a crucial facilitator in addressing many of the difficulties encountered by those working in Industry 4.0 applications. Pressure sensors are placed carefully throughout the structural components of the vehicle, such as the chassis, doors, and panels. These sensors monitor the dynamic forces and pressures imposed on various components of the vehicle when it collides with a barrier or another object.

The data gathered by these pressure sensors reveals important information about how the materials react to the impact, how they shift, and where stresses are generated (Soy & Toy, 2021). Because of its potential to give empirical insights into material behavior under tremendous pressure, pressure sensors are an essential addition to the area of material testing. This empirical understanding enables car makers to update and improve vehicle structural strength, resulting in greater safety standards and improved crash performance (El Ganainy et al., 2014).

This benefits companies like Boeing, where pressure sensors are used inside Boeing's scope to evaluate and authenticate the efficacy of various components used in airplane construction, including metallic chemicals, composite arrangements, and cutting-edge materials. In the aerospace industry, where safety and reliability are paramount, pressure sensors play a critical part in arranging careful analyses that unfold the behavior of materials in response to a variety of demanding conditions. These include high G-forces, resonances, and temperature extremes. These studies are important because they determine the materials' ability to withstand the rigors of aerial navigation while maintaining structural integrity throughout the aircraft's lifetime.

The applicability of pressure sensors spans a wide range of disciplines within the broad framework of Boeing's operating spectrum. It includes anything from inspecting the design of an aircraft's structural parts, to inspecting the material performance harnessed inside engine systems, avionics, and other essential matrices. Data accumulated through the skilled use of pressure sensor assisted testing improves design decisions, material selection, and production methods. These collaborative efforts result in the creation of aircraft with enhanced levels of safety and operational performance (Pinier et al., 2012). Tensile strength is an important metric in trying to understand a material's resistance to tension and elongation forces. This test comprises gradually applying force or stress to a material specimen until it fractures.

The planned integration of pressure sensors inside the testing apparatus is helpful here, as they measure force applied to the sample and track its subsequent deformation or dilatation. The sensors, which are sensitive to changing tensions, allow for real-time data recording, revealing the material's reaction under strain. This data reveals the material's behavior, pinpoints the specific point of failure, and allows the final tensile strength to be calculated. The subsequent comparison of these results with recognized industry standards allows engineers to confirm the correspondence between the material's performance and tensile strength requirements (Dehm et al., 2018).

17.6   THE PIONEER OF SENSING: TOP 5 GLOBAL PRESSURE SENSOR MANUFACTURERS

As the industrial sector's requirement for wide and continuous operation grows, the integration of safe and dependable sensors becomes increasingly important. More and more industries rely on dependable pressure sensors to sustain and properly regulate any industrial operation. Pressure sensors, which are based on capacitive microelectronics technology, can accurately detect the pressure in any gas or liquid medium while also being one of the safest and most dependable options in the business. For a transducer, a pressure sensor is widely used, producing a signal in reaction to applied pressure. A component of the pressure sensor assesses the actual pressure applied on the sensor (through various operating principles) as well as certain components that turn that data into an output signal. Here are the Top 5 global pressure sensor manufacturers:

- Honeywell – Honeywell ranks first in the world as a pressure sensor producer. Honeywell's heavy-duty pressure devices excel in compressors and hydraulic controls, as well in the aerospace, medical, transportation, agriculture, refrigeration, and industrial sectors. They offer a wide range of products that bring enhanced performance and consistent dependability. This includes absolute, gauge, and sealed gauge domains, in addition to several pressure ranges, port combinations, termination styles, and outputs. Also, their small surface mount sensors and premium-grade stainless steel isolated variations meet the requirements of tight process control and have anti-corrosion properties, demonstrating the range of their use.
- NXP – NXP provides a diverse pressure sensor portfolio that includes pressure ranges, package sizes, and port configurations. These MEM-based pressure sensors provide reliable solutions for appliance, medical, consumer, industrial, and automotive applications. Engineers and designers are discovering that they may transform their classic mechanical pressure sensors to lower-cost, semiconductor-based devices, resulting in novel pressure sensor applications. NXP's solutions are appropriate for the most severe high-performance applications because of their excellent sensitivity and long-term repeatability.
- Amphenol – The Nova Sensor from Amphenol is a cutting-edge, high-performance sensor with excellent accuracy, reliability, and compactness. Surface mount, hybrid, and medium isolated sensor families are available from Amphenol, with levels ranging from uncalibrated to fully calibrated versions with amplified analog and digital output. The company has established itself as one of the top five pressure sensor manufacturers in the world. The Piezoresistive Pressure Die in the Nova Sensor P330W Absolute Pressure Sensor provides the same remarkable stability and sensitivity as a bigger die in a much smaller footprint, making it perfect for intrusive applications where space is crucial.
- TE Connectivity – TE Connectivity creates pressure sensors for harsh environments, from sensing devices through system packaging. With products ranging from board-level components to fully amplified and packed transducers, TE is a global leader in conventional and bespoke pressure sensors. Their piezoresistive Microelectromechanical Systems and silicon strain gauge (Microfused, Krystal Bond) sensors measure pressures ranging from less than 1 in (1.25 mbar) to 100,000 psi (7,000 bar). The firm is one of the world's top five pressure sensor producers.
- Bosch – Barometric pressure sensors from Bosch Sensortec are used in a number of smartphones, wearables, and applications for smart homes. Their very compact and low-power barometric pressure sensors maintain drone height, allowing precise interior navigation and increasing the precision of calorie-tracking devices. Pressure sensors employ the piezoresistive

or capacitive principle. The BMP581 is the new industry standard for barometric pressure sensors, and it is perfect for several different altitude-tracking solutions, such as GPS modules, wearables, hearables, smart homes, and industrial goods.

17.7 CONCLUSION

Pressure sensors, known for their accuracy, give producers real-time insights into the intricate dance of material behaviors when subjected to a variety of dynamic pressures. This understanding, skillfully handled across a range of applications ranging from thorough material strength analyses to the orchestration of demanding quality control methods, serves as the foundation of sound decision-making.

Manufacturers skillfully configure their operational machinery for maximum efficiency while making sure products meet the most stringent quality criteria by assessing the spatial distribution of stresses, finding the development of aberrations, and scrutinizing performance against established benchmarks. In conclusion, the incorporation of pressure sensors into manufacturing represents a harmonic synthesis of accuracy and foresight. Their purpose extends beyond simple data collection into holistic process optimization and the development of a robust ecosystem against a slew of possible threats.

REFERENCES

Abdul Halim Lim, S., Antony, J., Arshed, N., & Albliwi, S. (2017). A systematic review of statistical process control implementation in the food manufacturing industry. Total Quality Management & Business Excellence, 28(1–2), 176–189. https://doi.org/10.1080/14783363.2015.1050181

Ageyeva, T., Horváth, S., & Kovács, J. G., (2019). In-mould sensors for injection moulding: On the way to industry 4.0. Sensors, 19(16), 3551. https://doi.org/10.3390/s19163551

Amit, M., Chukoskie, L., Skalsky, A. J., Garudadri, H., & Ng, T. N., (2020). Flexible pressure sensors for objective assessment of motor disorders. Advanced Functional Materials, 30(20), 1905241. https://doi.org/10.1002/adfm.201905241

Ayerbe, E., Berecibar, M., Clark, S., Franco, A. A., & Ruhland, J. (2022). Digitalization of battery manufacturing: Current status, challenges, and opportunities. Advanced Energy Materials, 12(17), 2102696. https://doi.org/10.1002/aenm.202102696

Bag, S., Pretorius, J. H. C., Gupta, S., & Dwivedi, Y. K., (2021). Role of institutional pressures and resources in the adoption of big data analytics powered artificial intelligence, sustainable manufacturing practices and circular economy capabilities. Technological Forecasting and Social Change, 163, 120420. https://doi.org/10.1016/j.techfore.2020.120420

Bai, N., Wang, L., Wang, Q., Deng, J., Wang, Y., Lu, P., & Guo, C. F., (2020). Graded intrafillable architecture-based iontronic pressure sensor with ultra-broad-range high sensitivity. Nature Communications, 11(1), 209. https://doi.org/10.1038/s41467-019-14054-9

Black, J. T., & Kohser, R. A., DeGarmo's Materials and Processes in Manufacturing (2017). John Wiley & Sons. https://books.google.co.in/books?hl=en&lr=&id=JkkzDwAAQB AJ&oi=fnd&pg=PA1

Chadha, U., Selvaraj, S. K., Gunreddy, N., Sanjay Babu, S., Mishra, S., Padala, D., & Adefris, A. (2022). A survey of machine learning in friction stir welding, including unresolved issues and future research directions. Material Design & Processing Communications, 2022. https://doi.org/10.1155/2022/2568347

Chatham, C. A., Long, T. E., & Williams, C. B, (2019). A review of the process physics and material screening methods for polymer powder bed fusion additive manufacturing. Progress in Polymer Science, 93, 68–95. https://doi.org/10.1016/j.progpolymsci. 2019.03.003

Chua, M. H., Cheng, W., Goh, S. S., Kong, J., Li, B., Lim, J. Y., & Loh, X. J. (2020). Face masks in the new COVID-19 normal: Materials, testing, and perspectives. Research, 2020. https://doi.org/10.34133/2020/7286735

Dehm, G., Jaya, B. N., Raghavan, R., & Kirchlechner, C. (2018). Overview on micro-and nanomechanical testing: New insights in interface plasticity and fracture at small length scales. Acta Materialia, 142, 248–282. https://doi.org/10.1016/j.actamat.2017.06.019

Di Fratta, C., Koutsoukis, G., Klunker, F., & Ermanni, P. (2016). Fast method to monitor the flow front and control injection parameters in resin transfer moulding using pressure sensors. Journal of Composite Materials, 50(21), 2941–2957. https://doi.org/ 10.1177/0021998315614994

El Ganainy, H., Tessari, A., Abdoun, T., & Sasanakul, I. (2014). *Tactile Pressure Sensors in Centrifuge Testing.* ASTM International. https://doi.org/10.1520/GTJ20120061

Forster, A. M. (2015). *Materials Testing Standards for Additive Manufacturing of Polymer Materials.* (p. 8059). US Department of Commerce, National Institute of Standards and Technology. http://dx.doi.org/10.6028/NIST.IR.8059

Frank R. (2023). Automotive Sensing and LiDAR. https://www.designworldonline.com/ automotive-sensing-lidar/

Gisario, A., Kazarian, M., Martina, F., & Mehrpouya, M. (2019). Metal additive manufacturing in the commercial aviation industry: A review. Journal of Manufacturing Systems, 53, 124–149. https://doi.org/10.1016/j.jmsy.2019.08.005

Goldsack, J. C., Coravos, A., Bakker, J. P., Bent, B., Dowling, A. V., Fitzer-Attas, C., & Dunn, J. (2020). Verification, analytical validation, and clinical validation (V3): The foundation of determining fit-for-purpose for biometric monitoring technologies (BioMeTs). Npj Digital Medicine, 3(1), 55. https://doi.org/10.1038/s41746-020-0260-4

Gunasekaran, A., Subramanian, N., & Ngai, W. T. E., (2019). Quality management in the 21st century enterprises: Research pathway towards industry 4.0. International Journal of Production Economics, 207, 125–129. https://doi.org/10.1016/j.ijpe.2018.09.005

He, Q. P., & Wang, J. (2018). Statistical process monitoring as a big data analytics tool for smart manufacturing. Journal of Process Control, 67, 35–43. https://doi.org/10.1016/ j.jprocont.2017.06.012

He, J., Zhang, Y., Zhou, R., Meng, L., Chen, T., Mai, W., & Pan, C. (2020). Recent advances of wearable and flexible piezoresistivity pressure sensor devices and its future prospects. Journal of Materiomics, 6(1), 86–101. https://doi.org/10.1016/j.jmat.2020.01.009

Hsu, J. Y., Wang, Y. F., Lin, K. C., Chen, M. Y., & Hsu, J. H. Y. (2020). Wind turbine fault diagnosis and predictive maintenance through statistical process control and machine learning. Ieee Access, 8, 23427–23439. https://doi.org/10.1109/ACCESS.2020.2968615

ILO (2023), ILOSTAT. The leading source of labour statistics, The ILO Department of Statistics. https://ilostat.ilo.org/resources/concepts-and-definitions/ilo-modelled-estimates/

Ismach, M. (2023, July 20). The importance of quality manufacturing and how manufacturers can benefit. Matics. https://matics.live/blog/the-importance-of-quality-manufacturing-and-how-manufacturers-can-benefit/#:~:text=If%20products%20are%20rejected%20 due,used%20as%20efficiently%20as%20possible.

Javaid, M., Haleem, A., Singh, R. P., Rab, S., & Suman, R. (2021). Significance of sensors for industry 4.0: Roles, capabilities, and applications. Sensors International, 2, 100110. https://doi.org/10.1016/j.sintl.2021.100110

Joazeiro, C. A. (2019). Mechanisms and functions of ribosome-associated protein quality control. Nature Reviews Molecular Cell Biology, 20(6), 368–383. https://doi.org/ 10.1038/s41580-019-0118-2

Johnson, J. B., & Schaefer, G. L. (2002). The influence of thermal, hydrologic, and snow deformation mechanisms on snow water equivalent pressure sensor accuracy. Hydrological Processes, 16(18), 3529–3542. https://doi.org/10.1002/hyp.1236

Kenda, M., Klobčar, D., & Bračun, D. (2021). Condition based maintenance of the two-beam laser welding in high volume manufacturing of piezoelectric pressure sensor. Journal of Manufacturing Systems, 59, 117–126. https://doi.org/10.1016/j.jmsy.2021.02.007

Lang, W. *Sensors and Measurement Systems* (2022). River Publishers. https://doi.org/10.1201/9781003339489

Li, X., Fan, Y. J., Li, H. Y., Cao, J. W., Xiao, Y. C., Wang, Y., & Zhu, G. (2020). Ultracomfortable hierarchical nanonetwork for highly sensitive pressure sensor. ACS Nano, 14(8), 9605–9612. https://pubs.acs.org/doi/abs/10.1021/acsnano.9b10230

Madanhire, I., & Mbohwa, C. (2016). Application of statistical process control (SPC) in manufacturing industry in a developing country. Procedia Cirp, 40, 580–583. https://doi.org/10.1016/j.procir.2017.01.137

Markl, D., Warman, M., Dumarey, M., Bergman, E. L., Folestad, S., Shi, Z., & Zeitler, J. A. (2020). Review of real-time release testing of pharmaceutical tablets: State-of-the art, challenges and future perspective. International Journal of Pharmaceutics, 582, 119353. https://doi.org/10.1016/j.ijpharm.2020.119353

Montgomery, D. C., *Introduction to Statistical Quality Control* (2019). John Wiley & Sons. https://books.google.co.in/books?hl=en&lr=&id=YWLNEAAAQBAJ&oi=fnd&pg=PR1

Nenonen, S. (2011). Fatal workplace accidents in outsourced operations in the manufacturing industry. Safety Science, 49(10), 1394–1403. https://doi.org/10.1016/j.ssci.2011.06.004

OICA (2022). Global Sales Statistics 2019 – 2022, International Organization of Motor Vehicle Manufacturers. OICA is the voice speaking on automotive issues in world forums. https://www.oica.net/global-sales-statistics-2019-2021/

Parmar, H., Khan, T., Tucci, F., Umer, R., & Carlone, P. (2022). Advanced robotics and additive manufacturing of composites: Towards a new era in industry 4.0. Materials and Manufacturing Processes, 37(5), 483–517. https://doi.org/10.1080/10426914.2020.1866195

Patel, V., Chesmore, A., Legner, C. M., & Pandey, S. (2022). Trends in workplace wearable technologies and connected-worker solutions for next-generation occupational safety, health, and productivity. Advanced Intelligent Systems, 4(1), 2100099. https://doi.org/10.1002/aisy.202100099

Pinier, J. T., Hanke, J. L., & Tomek, W. G. (2012). Ares I aerodynamic testing at the boeing polysonic wind tunnel. Journal of Spacecraft and Rockets, 49(5), 853–863. https://doi.org/10.2514/1.A32221

Pishgar, M., Issa, S. F., Sietsema, M., Pratap, P., & Darabi, H. (2021). REDECA: A novel framework to review artificial intelligence and its applications in occupational safety and health. International Journal of Environmental Research and Public Health, 18(13), 6705. https://doi.org/10.3390/ijerph18136705

Rahim, M. A., Rahman, M. A., Rahman, M. M., Asyhari, A. T., Bhuiyan, M. Z. A., & Ramasamy, D. (2021). Evolution of IoT-enabled connectivity and applications in automotive industry: A review. Vehicular Communications, 27, 100285. https://doi.org/10.1016/j.vehcom.2020.100285

Soy, H., & Toy, İ. (2021). Design and implementation of smart pressure sensor for automotive applications. Measurement, 176, 109184. https://doi.org/10.1016/j.measurement.2021.109184

Sunadi, S., Purba, H. H., & Hasibuan, S. (2020). Implementation of statistical process control through PDCA cycle to improve potential capability index of drop impact resistance: A case study at aluminum beverage and beer cans manufacturing industry in Indonesia. Quality Innovation Prosperity, 24(1), 104–127. https://doi.org/10.12776/qip.v24i1.1401

Yang, Y., Wei, Y., Guo, Z., Hou, W., Liu, Y., Tian, H., & Ren, T. L. (2022). From materials to devices: Graphene toward practical applications. Small Methods, 6(10), 2200671. https://doi.org/10.1002/smtd.202200671

Yeow, J. A., Ng, P. K., Tai, H. T., & Chow, M. M. (2020). A review on human error in Malaysia manufacturing industries. Management, 5(19), 01–13. https://doi.org/10.35631/JISTM.519001

Zhao, P., Zhang, J., Dong, Z., Huang, J., Zhou, H., Fu, J., & Turng, L. S. (2020). Intelligent injection moulding on sensing, optimization, and control. Advances in Polymer Technology, 2020, 1–22. https://doi.org/10.1155/2020/7023616

18 Online Internet of Things-Based Estimation of SoC, SoH and SoP for a LiB Electric Bus

Reshma P. and Manohar Joshi

18.1 INTRODUCTION

In recent years, electric vehicles (EVs) have received a great deal of attention as one of the practical alternatives for the sustainable economic growth of urban areas (Dai et al., 2019; Franke et al., 2019; Hosseini & Sarder, 2019). Currently, hybrid electric vehicles or HEVs (Tan et al., 2019), plug-in hybrid electric vehicles or PHEVs (Fan et al., 2020), and battery electric vehicles or BEVs (Wang & Zhang et al., 2020) are the three types of EVs that are most frequently used. A major entry point for EVs is the use of electric buses (EBs) in public transportation systems, which are one of the main types of EVs (Du et al., 2019). Due to its superior abilities to balance both the energy and power densities (Tian et al., 2019), a lithium-ion battery (LiB) is primarily used as the energy storage system (ESS) in electric buses.

The existing battery-based ESS, on the other hand, frequently experiences a limited battery lifespan and high maintenance expenses (Wang & Wang et al., 2020). The management of battery energy in EVs must also be improved in terms of both internal and exterior operations. On the one hand, upgrades to battery management systems (BMSs) based on the discharging and charging properties of batteries can significantly lengthen the battery life for the internal operations of EVs. On the other hand, logical scheduling based on the features of the dynamic loading for external operations of the EVs can also lower operational costs.

Recent work has focused increasing attention from the academic and industry communities on improving the BMS performance and ESS structure for EVs in a sustainable way (Mehrjerdi & Hemmati, 2020; Zhang et al., 2021). To demonstrate the significance of managing energy strategy for the optimization of electric and hybrid vehicles, Buccoliero et al. (2019) analyzed the energy management strategy in the hybrid and electric vehicle power trains for the internal management of energy of the EVs.

Zhang et al. (2020) describe a framework for a plug-in hybrid electric bus (HEB) component matching that uses genetic algorithms and dynamic programming in two layers. A hybrid energy storage system (HESS) is recommended as an efficient way to increase battery life because it combines the functions of batteries and super capacitors (SCs) (Iqbal et al., 2021). The batteries in such system have a higher power density, whereas the SCs have a large power density and quick charging and discharging times (Chen et al., 2019; Liu et al., 2021). The HESS optimization, which entails simultaneously optimizing the design and mode of operation of the ESS, has been demonstrated to be an essential strategy for obtaining high overall effectiveness, cost savings, and efficiency improvements.

The on-board control of the energy storage, in addition to potential improvements in LiB system design and material, can help to satisfy the desired performance, reliability, cost and safety requirements. The provision of battery state estimates is a crucial function of BMSs (Wang & Yujie et al., 2019). For example, knowing the state of health of a battery's life is essential for maximizing its use, which results in cost effectiveness and longevity (Zhang et al., 2021). The condition of the battery is also important in terms of the future market (Singh et al., 2022) for used EVs and the subsequent use of EV batteries. The BMS performs a wide range of tasks, including the state of charge or SoC (Aung et al., 2019) and state of health or SoH (Cui & Inwhee, 2021) estimations which are supported by a reliable battery model.

Based on the same operating voltage, the SoH estimate model using a probability density function (PDF) approach has improved accuracy. The SoH will greatly increase the system's ability to store energy. The capacity of lithium-ion cells is frequently used as the basis for conventional SoH estimation. In the age of Big Data, it is now possible to use it to realize the online battery estimation of SoH. One of the most important functions of the BMS in electric and hybrid vehicles is battery state of power (SoP) estimation. One of the most important elements in addressing an EV power battery's main problem with monitoring and safety concerns is a SoC estimate. The SoC is a crucial BMS metric for LiB. The SoC of an EV shows how much charge is left in the battery, much like the measuring device in combustion-engine vehicles. The reliability, dependability, and performance of the battery are greatly influenced by an accurate understanding of SoC.

The equivalent circuit models (ECMs), which use ideal resistors, voltage sources and capacitors to characterize voltage properties of batteries, are the most often used battery models. Because ECMs are so simple, they can be used on board with little computing effort (Kalogiannis et al., 2019). The BMSs may employ various parameters, such as internal resistance (Hu et al., 2020), voltage (Pawar & Mudige, 2020), capacity (Wei et al., 2020), capability to receive a charge, self-discharge and a variety of charge and discharge cycles, based on the purpose of the battery and availability of direct measuring instruments.

18.2 REVIEW OBJECTIVES

This chapter is structured as follows:

- Section 18.3 reveals sources of the research.
- Section 18.4 discusses the use of LiB technology in electric buses.
- Section 18.5 talks about the advantages of LiBs.
- Sections 18.6–18.8 give the SoH, SoP, and SoC definitions and mathematical equations.
- Section 18.9 explains the general concept of battery state estimation.

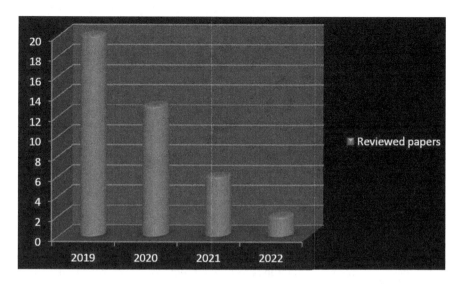

FIGURE 18.1   A 3D line chart showing the reviewed paper distribution from 2019 to 2022.

- Section 18.10 talks about SoH estimation in EBs.
- Section 18.11 discusses SoP estimation in EBs.
- Section 18.12 explains SoC estimation in EBs.
- Section 18.13 evaluates existing methods.
- Section 18.14 presents the future scope and concludes the discussion.

18.3   SELECTION OF SOURCES

Research articles presented in this chapter are obtained from IEEE Xplore, ResearchGate, ScienceDirect, other journal databases, and their respective references, as shown in Figure 18.1.

To determine the future scope and problems, this chapter aims to cover the majority of the significant research findings from 2019 to 2022.

18.4   LITHIUM-ION BATTERY TECHNOLOGY IN ELECTRIC BUSES

Lithium-ion batteries are now part of every aspect of our life from electric bikes, vehicles, and power equipment, to smartphones. There is a rush for greater power and energy. The development of the technology used in LiBs and cells is the primary force behind that competition. Energy is the most important factor for any EV, specifically its kilowatt-hour per kilometer energy consumption, which is primarily related to the weight of the vehicle. Therefore, there is a great competition in the EB category to minimize the batteries' total weight in order to achieve the best energy density.

Advanced technology of the battery involves LiB, which uses lithium ion as an essential part of electrochemistry. The anode's lithium atoms become ionized and lose their electrons during a discharging process. From the anode, the lithium ions travel through the electrolyte to the cathode, where they rejoin their electrons and

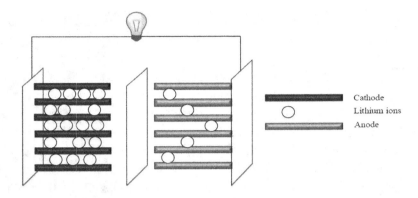

FIGURE 18.2   Diagram of a lithium-ion battery.

become electrically neutral. A micro-permeable separation between the cathode and anode can allow the lithium ions to pass through since they are small enough. Lithium-ion batteries have a charge storage capacity and very high voltage per unit mass and volume, in part due to the small size of lithium. Numerous materials can be used as electrodes in LiBs.

Graphite serves as the anode, and lithium cobalt oxide serves as the cathode in the most typical portable electronic device configuration, which includes laptops and smartphones. Lithium iron phosphate and lithium manganese oxide are two more cathode materials. Both are generally used as an electrolyte in LiBs, as shown in Figures 18.2 and 18.3.

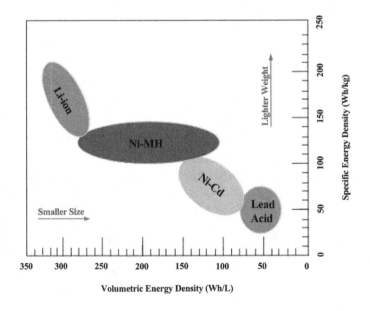

FIGURE 18.3   Comparison of lithium-ion batteries with other battery types.

TABLE 18.1
Lithium-Ion Cell Specification

Item	Specification
Operation voltage range	3–4.3 V
Operation temperature	–10–45°C
Average voltage output	3.8 V
Capacity	8.6 Ah
Dimensions	170 mm × 160 mm × 5.3 mm
Energy density	120 Wh/kg
Power density	2920 W/kg
Weight	233 g

TABLE 18.2
Lithium-Ion Battery Specification

Item	Specification
Operation voltage range	45–64.5 V
Operation temperature	–10–45°C
Average voltage output	57 V
Capacity	155 Ah
Dimensions	240 mm × 330 mm × 1000 mm
Electric energy	8.8 kWh
Lithium-ion cell component	18 series and 15 parallels

TABLE 18.3
Lithium-Ion Battery Module Specification

Item	Specification
Operation voltage range	270–387
Average voltage output	348 V
Capacity	155 Ah
Dimensions	1440 mm × 300 mm × 1000 mm
Electric energy	53 kWh
Lithium-ion battery component	6 series
Weight	480 kg

Tables 18.1–18.3 show the lithium-ion cell, battery, and battery module specifications.

18.5 ADVANTAGES OF LITHIUM-ION BATTERIES

Benefits to using LiB technology are many, leading to a wide range of applications from tiny electrical devices, computers, and smartphones, to automobiles. It is essential to consider the benefits of using a LiB versus another technology, such as a nickel-metal hydride (NiMH) battery.

Due to the benefits of lithium-ion technology, these batteries are finding use in a growing variety of applications. The benefits include a high density of energy, self-discharge, less maintenance, cell voltage, characteristics of load, and various varieties as follows:

- High Density of Energy: Batteries with a significant HED are constantly in demand since electronic devices like smartphones need to operate for long periods of time between charges while still using more power.
- Self-Discharge: Self-discharge is one concern with many battery packs. Compared to other rechargeable batteries, such as nickel-cadmium (NiCd) and NiMH types, lithium-ion cells have a considerably lower rate of self-discharge. In the first 4 h after being charged, it is normally around 5%; but, after that, it decreases to a rate of 1 or 2% per month.
- Less Maintenance: LiBs do not need to be maintained in order to function properly. For NiCd cells, in order to avoid the memory effect, they need to be discharged on a regular basis. Lead acid cells also require attention, like recharging the battery's acid on a regular basis.
- Cell Voltage: Each lithium-ion cell generates roughly 3.6 V of electricity. The voltage of each lithium-ion cell is higher, necessitating lesser cells in many batteries. It is higher than that of an NiCd, NiMH, and even normal alkaline cells at 1.5 V and lead acid at 2 V per cell. For smartphones, only one cell is required, which simplifies management of power.
- Characteristics of Load: An LiB has respectable characteristics of load. Before dropping off when the last charge is expended, they offer 3.6 V per cell in a relatively steady manner.
- Various Varieties: LiBs come in a number of different varieties. This allows for the use of the appropriate technology for a certain application. Some LiB configurations offer a high current density and are perfect for consumer mobile electronics. Others can deliver significantly greater current levels, making them perfect for EVs and power tools.

18.6 STATE OF HEALTH

Electrochemical batteries undergo significant performance loss over the course of their life. As a result, active materials and lithium inventory are lost due to the so-called aging phenomenon. When evaluating battery aging quantitatively in terms of internal resistance and capacity fade, the state of health (SoH) is frequently used. The concept of SoH can be stated mathematically:

$$SoH = \frac{C_A}{C_R} * 100 \tag{18.1}$$

where C_R and C_A represent the rated and actual capacity values.

In automotive applications, a battery is regarded as being at its end-of-life (EOL) if its capacity fades by 20% or its internal resistance rises by 100%. The battery's SoH is a crucial condition that ensures the secure, dependable, and effective performance of battery systems. For battery problem diagnosis, SoC or SoP estimates, and maintenance plans, timely and precise SoH metering during vehicle operations is essential. With current commercially available sensors, neither capacity nor internal resistances are immediately measured. As a result, the key to SOH acquisition is the creation of estimation algorithms that allow for online SOH metering using the inexpensive sensor suite.

18.7 STATE OF POWER

The state of power (SoP) is a crucial component of BMSs since it describes the power that a battery can give to/absorb from the vehicle power train over a period of time (Iqbal et al., 2021).

The threshold current and associated voltage are two factors that can be used to calculate battery SoP, but a number of operating restrictions must be expressly taken into account and observed. A general concept of SoP is given as follows, assuming that the battery power is positive for discharge and negative for charge:

$$SoPCH(t) = max\left(PMINI, V(t + \Delta t).ICHMINI\right) \tag{18.2}$$

$$SoPDCH(t) = max\left(PMAXI, V(t + \Delta t).IDCHMAXI\right) \tag{18.3}$$

where SoPDCH (t) and SoPCH (t) denote the SoP discharging battery and SoP charging battery at the time, t, PMINI and PMAXI are the limitations of the battery power minimum and maximum, Δt denotes the particular future time horizon, $V(t + \Delta t)$ denotes terminal voltage at $(t + \Delta t)$ of the sample time. IDCHMAXI and ICHMINI denote the continuous current of the maximum discharging and continuous current of the minimum charging from t time sampling to $(t + \Delta t)$ time sampling. ICHMINI and IDCHMAXI must be attained while maintaining a number of restrictions.

The current, battery voltage, SoC, and temperature are typically included in these restrictions. Furthermore, if specific physics-based models are applied, important microscopic factors can be restricted. The reference SoP values under the simulation conditions are often produced using a model of the high-fidelity battery that takes into account a variety of limitations. In a lab setting, well-designed pulse tests that take into account some variations of the duration time, applied current rate, etc. can be used to estimate the battery SoP.

18.8 STATE OF CHARGE

The state of charge (SoC) of an electric battery is measured in relation to its rated capacity in percentage points. When discussing a battery's present status while in operation, SoC is typically utilized. When SOC is higher, power consumption is slower; when SOC is lower, power consumption is faster. So, SoC and energy use are tightly connected. The reasons for considering online estimation in EBs is given below:

- Utilizing data from the generator buses, an offline estimating approach is used to estimate the total load power change owing to voltage dependency, and the inertia of the power system is then calculated. Offline estimating is highly precise, but it is challenging to measure, is computationally demanding, is time-consuming, and solves problems slowly.

*   Online estimating is employed to find a solution to the offline estimating problem. Opportunity charging describes the practice of charging buses not only at the terminal but also at stations dispersed throughout the network. There is no requirement for buses to make a fuel stop back at the depot thereby saving time and energy.

18.9 GENERAL CONCEPT OF BATTERY STATE ESTIMATION

Thermal management is the process of observing and regulating temperatures generated by equipment inside electrical enclosures. Technologically sophisticated materials and components with well-known thermodynamic and heat transfer qualities enable control. Temperature estimation enables the actual temperature at different modification levels and locations. The amount of electrical charge in the battery at time t relative to the nominal electrical charge is known as the SoC.

An important metric for evaluating EV battery storage solutions is SoC. Due to the fast-charging, long life cycle, and high energy density (HED) features of LiBs, SoC estimate has received a lot of attention. A battery's SoH is measured against its optimum circumstances. The ratio of peak power to nominal power is known as a battery's SoP.

Based on the state of the battery pack at the time, the peak power is the highest. For the control and optimization of energy in EVs, the SoE of LiBs is a crucial indicator. Due to current or voltage drift of the sensors, the traditional power integral approaches are easily susceptible to cumulative error. Efficiency increases as charge and discharge rates decrease. Figure 18.4 shows the framework for the battery state estimation methodology.

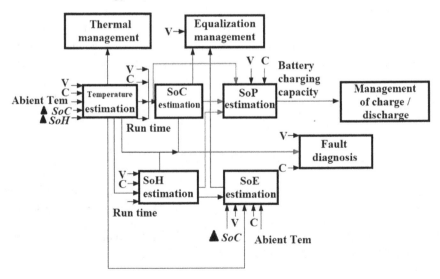

FIGURE 18.4 Framework for the battery state estimation methodology.

18.10   STATE OF HEALTH ESTIMATION IN ELECTRIC BUSES

In a 20–100 kWh energy storage system (ESS) made up of retired bus batteries, Zhang et al. (2021) explained how the battery SoH is determined based on charge voltages data in constant power operation procedures.

The ESS peak shaving and valley filling operation modes are discussed in depth. A comparison is made between incremental capacity analysis (ICA) and probability density function (PDF), two SoH modeling techniques. The findings demonstrate the availability of ICA and PDF under constant power settings for battery SoH modeling.

Based on the same operating voltage, the SoH estimate model using the PDF approach has improved accuracy. A linear positive association exists between the height, H, of the greatest peak on the ICA or PDF curves and the battery SoH, but the ICA model is more precise than the PDF model.

According to the SoH study, replacing some cells with the lower SoH with those of the greater SoH will significantly increase the system's ability to store energy. When a battery's SoH is unknown, the relative age of the battery can be inferred by grading the H value using PDF curves depending on the actual charging voltage information. This is useful for the operation and upkeep of the ESS. In order to maintain an EV, a real-time estimation of the SoH of the LiB is necessary. This chapter investigates an online EV SoH estimation method using iterated extended Gaussian process regression-Kalman filter (GPR-EKF) to combine LiB data at the macro- and the micro-time scale based on daily charge data of EV. This method is based on situations in practical uses such as long EV battery capacity test time, unavailability of regular daily tests, and availability of fully charged battery data of EV and they could be recorded on the required to charge facility Big Data platform.

In order to conduct fitting for data at the macro-time to identify colored measurement noise, Zhou et al. (Zhou et al., 2019) proposed a kernel function GPR integrating a neural network with cycles. In relation, fragment charge data at the micro-time scale is adapted with real-time iterative process to be utilized as the equation of state, effectively addressing issues of real-time SoC calibration and non-linearization.

Actual data is used to validate the relevance, efficacy, and real-time effectiveness of the algorithm in online batteries' SoH estimate. Accurate battery SoH calculation is crucial to ensure the effective, dependable, and safe functioning of the LiB system. A unique data-model fusion battery SoH estimate method was put out by Xiao & Qiu et al. (2019) based on open-circuit voltage (OCV) parametric modeling and taking into account the relationship between capacity degradation and variations in OCV.

In order to accurately represent the aging behavior linked to the progression of cell processes, an OCV model is constructed. Then, a method for estimating battery SoH is created based on the relationship between capacity fading and changes in the parameters of the OCV model.

Additionally, a data-driven methodology is used to determine the suggested battery model's characteristics so that the OCV can be obtained online. The cells that underwent various aging processes have proven the suggested SoH estimate approach. In the age of Big Data, it is now possible to use it to realize the online battery estimation of SoH. Traditional approaches based on theoretical models are unable to account for complex environmental conditions and driving behavior.

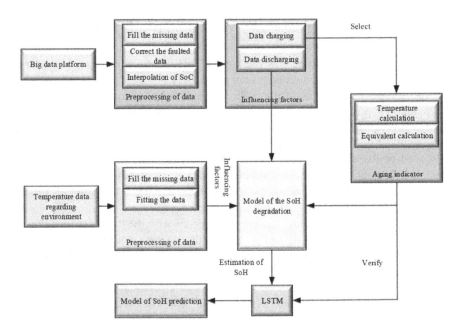

FIGURE 18.5   State of health prediction and estimation flowchart based on actual data.

In this research, Xu et al. (2022) proposes a rough model for SoH deterioration based on actual operational data and environmental temperature data of EVs obtained through a Big Data platform. First, the specific area is taken from the history operating data, and then, using the capacity temperature empirical formula, the capacity offset, and the equivalent capacity at 25°C, the equivalent capacity is determined.

Following that, the operating information and the ambient temperature are combined to calculate the attenuation rate during each charging and discharging procedure. The long short-term memory (LSTM) neural network is then employed to forecast the battery's future decrease pattern and to learn the battery degradation trend, as shown in Figure 18.5.

The SoH in LiBs not only directly affects how quickly EVs accelerate and how far they can travel, but it also represents the batteries' remaining worth. Using Big Data to accomplish online evaluation of battery SoH displays essential significance, particularly with the growth of data collecting and analytical techniques. Song et al. (2020) used an intelligent approach for SoH calculation based on real-world information from EVs that the Big Data platform had gathered.

The health characteristics are derived from historical operational data and are defined by the more easily accessible detection. The deterioration index-driven feed-forward neural network is then used to implement the deep learning (DL) process. The 1-year observation dataset from 700 automobiles with various driving modes serves to verify the prediction model. Table 18.4 gives a detailed evaluation of SoH in an electric bus.

TABLE 18.4

Evaluation of State of Health (SoH) in an Electric Bus

No.	Reference	Technique	Algorithm	Advantages
1.	Zhang et al. (2021)	Methods of SoH modeling ICA and PDF	Locally weighted scatterplot smoothing algorithm	ESS will be improved with higher SoH
2.	Zhou et al. (2019)	SoH using iterated extended GPR-EKF	Gaussian process algorithm	Effective development of battery maintenance standards
3.	Xiao and Qiu et al., (2019)	SoH based on OCV parametric modeling	N/A	Minimum average relative errors
4.	Xu et al. (2022)	SoH degradation based on environmental temperature data and real operating data	Variable sliding window algorithm	Based on partial charging data curves, effective current capacity was determined
5.	Song et al. (2020)	SoH based on real-world data by Big Data analysis	Feed-forward neural network algorithm	Excellent fitting precision

18.11 STATE OF POWER ESTIMATION IN ELECTRIC BUSES

One of the most important functions of the BMS in electric and hybrid vehicles is battery state of power (SoP) estimation. Accurately predicting the SoP for an aging battery is hampered by the inescapable uncertainty in estimates of battery SoC and SoH. In order to address this, the current study by Esfandyari et al. (2019a) seeks to provide a novel strategy for forecasting an aged cell SoP in which no prior understanding of battery SoH is necessary and the estimation method is resistant to errors in SoC estimates. As a result, a modeless control system is used to adjust to various aging states after estimating fresh cell SoP using a combined reference mode of constant level of voltage and current. The closed-loop structure of the control system, which belongs to a class of FLBCs, benefits from a more exact and dependable SoP estimate. The outcomes show how SoP estimation has increased in both accuracy and robustness while ensuring battery safety.

Energy management (EM) is essential to enhancing the fuel efficiency of hybrid commercial vehicles because of their high mileage and heavy load capacities. In this research, Li et al. (2019a) described how the deep deterministic policy gradient (DDPG) method is used to systematically include terrain information into the EM strategy for a power-split HEB. A discrete-continuous hybrid action space, comprising two continuous actions for the engine and four discrete actions for power train mode selections in this study, is a special improvement of this EM system that allows it to search for the best EM strategies.

Additionally, for effective strategy learning with the chosen algorithm, a critic network with dueling architecture and a pretraining stage are coupled. The deep reinforcement learning (DRL)-based EM strategy is trained and tested on various driving cycles and simulated terrains under the assumption that the controller had access to the most recent information on the terrain.

Lithium-ion batteries in EVs and HEVs can operate safely and effectively if the SoP is estimated accurately. Accurate estimate of the SoP is significantly hampered by cell-to-cell variance within a battery pack, especially as the cells age. To precisely estimate the SoP for series connected lithium-ion cells, Esfandyari et al. (2019b) presented a model of the hybrid predictive and fuzzy logic-based control (FLBC) system. The two-step estimation technique begins by calculating the power capacity of a single new cell using the model predictive control algorithm. The second step focuses on choosing a FLBC system without models to account for the concurrent aging state and SoC variations among the cells. Therefore, the current method solely makes use of the real current and cell voltage values along with the new cell's off-line discovered ECM characteristics. It also gains from a closed-loop design that results in a precise and trustworthy SoP estimation.

Recent research has looked into the viability of employing D-FACTS devices in a method known as the PFDD approach to proactively detect high-profile FDI attacks on power grid state estimation. However, the available literature has not comprehensively examined the viability and constraints of such a strategy. The viability and restrictions of using the PFDD approach to prevent FDI attacks on power grid state estimate were discussed by Li et al. (2019a) in this work. It specifically considers single-bus, disorganized multiple-bus, and coordinating numerous FDI operations to carefully investigate the viability of employing PFDD to detect these attacks. It demonstrates that the deployment of distributed flexible AC transmission system (D-FACTS) devices must cover branches that at the very least contain a spanning tree of the grid graph in order for proactive false data detection (PFDD) to be able to identify all three of these forms of false data injection (FDI) attacks directed at buses or superbuses with degrees greater than 1. The minimal efforts needed to activate D-FACTS devices in order to recognize each form of FDI attack are assessed separately, as shown in Figure 18.6.

Planning the necessary infrastructure for charging EB batteries and optimizing the schedules of these vehicles require a thorough understanding of energy use. The bus station arrival times, locations on a map, and a parameter reflecting the travel circumstances are the only easily accessible bus trip parameters used in the model given by Pamuła and Pamuła (2020). For calculating the estimations of energy consumption of bus routes stop-by-stop, a DL network is constructed.

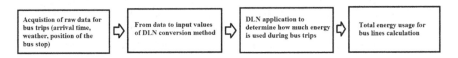

FIGURE 18.6   Energy consumption model for bus lines.

TABLE 18.5

Evaluation of State of Power (SoP) in an Electric Bus

No.	Reference	Technique	Algorithm	Advantages
1.	Esfandyari et al. (2019a)	Using FLBC to estimate aged cell SoP	N/A	Improved SoP estimation accuracy and durability ensure battery functioning inside the safe operating area
2.	Li et al. (2019a)	Electric bus with power split that uses the DRL method	Deep deterministic policy gradient (DDPG)	DRL-based EM technique was enhanced
3.	Esfandyari et al. (2019b)	FLBC and hybrid model predictive method	Model predictive control (MPC)	Power capability of the accurate estimation
4.	Li et al. (2019b)	Estimating the SoP grid using D-FACTS devices	Proactive false data detection (PFDD)	The minimal quantity of effort is necessary to activate D-FACTS devices
5.	Pamuła and Pamuła (2020)	Deep learning and real-world data	N/A	In the case of a uniform fleet of battery EVs, the proposed deep learning network for the assessment of energy usage operates effectively

Deep learning networks are a key component of the major class of Big Data processing techniques. This characteristic enables the approach to be scaled and applied to transport networks of various sizes. The outputs of a regression model based on the gathered data are compared to the estimates of energy consumption. For the set of a few thousand bus journeys, estimation errors do not surpass 7.1%. The study's findings point to areas where there may be power shortages in the network of public transportation, which may be resolved by adding a charging station or adjusting bus schedules as shown in Table 18.5.

18.12 STATE OF CHARGE ESTIMATION IN ELECTRIC BUSES

The Kalman filter method (KFM) is one of the most widely used algorithms to calculate the batteries' state of charge (SoC) due to its reliability and flexibility, among other benefits. This approach still has certain drawbacks, though. The algorithmic Kalman filter approach was created for linear systems and necessitates exact mathematical models. Since LiBs are not linear systems, determining the battery ECM is essential for estimating SoC. An adaptive Kalman filter (AKF) approach and the battery Thevenin equivalent circuit are coupled in this research by Ma & Zeyu et al. (2019) SoC estimation of EV storage stability constantly. Next, the ECM is investigated, and a battery model that may be used to estimate SoC is created. Next, the

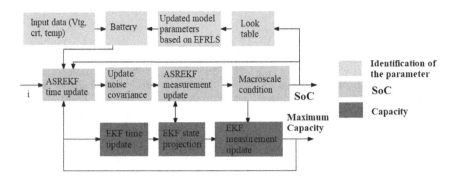

FIGURE 18.7 Schematic of a multiscale framework using an adaptive square root extended Kalman filter (ASREKF) for estimating battery SoC and capacity.

characteristics of the discharge experimental classification models and the related battery charge are designed. Finally, the AKF method is employed to calculate the battery of SoC online, while also applying it to the model in an environment with unknown interference noise. The simulation outcomes demonstrate that the suggested strategy can fix in real-time the SoC estimation inaccuracy brought on by the model fault.

An essential component of how an EV operates is the assessment of the SoC. Even in the event that the vehicle sensors malfunction, the BMS must nevertheless offer reliable information regarding the battery state. Without a battery sensor module, Gruosso et al. (2020) proposed a new methodology for EV SoC estimate that relied on a virtual sensor based on metrics such as voltage of battery, speed, and acceleration pedal location. Using experimental results, the estimator was created using support vector regression (SVR), principal component analysis (PCA), and a dual-polarization battery model (DPBM). It is demonstrated that in the event of the current sensor failing, the resulting model can forecast the battery of SoC with respectable accuracy, as shown in Figure 18.7.

The power battery estimation of SoC largely determines the EV control approach. The power LiB SoC estimate is one of the most crucial difficulties. Jiang et al. (2021) introduced a novel adaptive square root extended Kalman filter (ASREKF) along with Thevenin ECM as an alternative to the extended Kalman filter (EKF) technique that can address the issue of filtering divergence brought on by rounding mistakes in computers. The noise variable is updated using a Sage-Husa adaptive filter, and the covariance matrix is square root decomposed to make sure it is a non-negative constant. The forgetting factor recursive lowest approach is employed for parameter identification, and a multi-scale dual Kalman filter algorithm is used for joint estimate of SoC and capacity. The ternary LiB is subjected to several sorts of dynamic working settings in order to test the algorithm's viability under challenging operating situations, as shown in Figure 18.8.

Using a cubature Kalman filter (CKF) and experimental data to back it, Peng et al. (2019) introduced an improved SoC estimate method of LiB. To compare the estimation accuracy of various models, a first-order resistor and capacitor (RC) model and

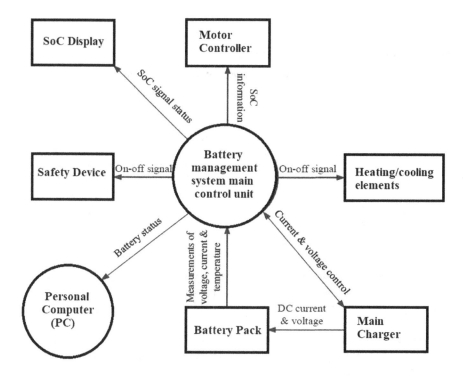

FIGURE 18.8 Diagram of the battery management system.

corresponding fractional order model are first built. Next, a customized hybrid pulse power characteristic (HPPC) experiment based on the square root (SQR) approach is used to determine the model parameters. Then, with no prior knowledge of beginning SoC, a CKF algorithm is applied to estimate the battery SoC for various battery models, as shown in Table 18.6.

The findings demonstrate that the fractional order model can achieve higher accuracy despite using more computational resources than the proposed CKF technique, which has a better estimate robustness than EKF. The CKF algorithms' SoC estimation error is less than 3%. Also, the accuracy of the estimation is checked using a battery management unit in the loop technique, as shown in Figure 18.9.

18.13 EVALUATION OF EXISTING METHODS

Evaluation of the existing methods discussed ways to analyze the performance of the SoC, SoH, and SoP on the ECM for LiB-driven EB. There are many advantages for EB use of LiB technology. The battery SoH is determined based on charge voltages data in constant power operation procedures. The ESSs peak shaving and valley filling operation modes are discussed in depth. A comparison is made between ICA and PDF, which are two SoH modeling techniques. Actual data is used to validate the relevance, efficacy, and real-time effectiveness of the

TABLE 18.6

Evaluation of SoC in an Electric Bus

No.	Reference	Technique	Algorithm	Advantage
1.	Ma & Zeyu et al. (2019)	AKF method	SoC estimation	Real-time correction of the model error-induced estimation of SoC error was made
2.	Gruosso et al. (2020)	Dual polarization ECM method	SVR, nonlinear square root adaptive algorithm	When the current sensor malfunctions, it may accurately forecast the battery of the SoC
3.	Jiang et al. (2021)	ASREKF method	ASREKF	Increased flexibility
4.	Peng et al. (2019)	CKF method	CKF	Fewer estimation errors

algorithm in online batteries' SoH estimate. Based on OCV parametric design and taking into consideration the correlation between capacity degradation and fluctuations in OCV, a novel data model fusion battery SoH estimate method was developed. A rough model for SoH deterioration based on actual operational data and environmental temperature data of EVs was obtained through a Big Data platform. An intelligent approach for SoH calculation based on real-world information from EVs was gathered.

Forecasting an aged cell SoP in which no prior understanding of battery SoH is necessary, and the estimation method is resistant to errors in SoC estimates. Policy gradient method is used to systematically include terrain information into the EM strategy for a power-split HEBs. To precisely estimate the SoP for series connected lithium-ion cells, a model was presented of the hybrid predictive and FLBC system. The viability and restrictions of using the PFDD approach to prevent FDI attacks on power grid state estimate were discussed. An AKF approach and the battery Thevenin equivalent circuit are coupled in this research of SoC estimation of EV storage stability constantly.

Without a battery sensor module, a new methodology was proposed for EV SoC estimate that relied on a virtual sensor based on other metrics, such as voltage of battery, speed, and acceleration pedal location. A novel ASREKF, along with the Thevenin ECM as an alternative to the EKF technique that can address the issue of filtering divergence brought on by rounding mistakes in computers, was discussed. Using a CKF and experimental data to back it, an improved SoC estimate method of LiB was evaluated. The CKF algorithms' SoC estimation error is less than 3%. Futhermore, the accuracy of the estimation is checked using a battery management unit in the loop technique, as shown in Tables 18.7 and 18.8.

18.14 CHALLENGES AND FUTURE SCOPE

Future research will concentrate on the following: optimization of the multi-objective of the fuel cell, super capacitor HESS and battery along with the sizing and best

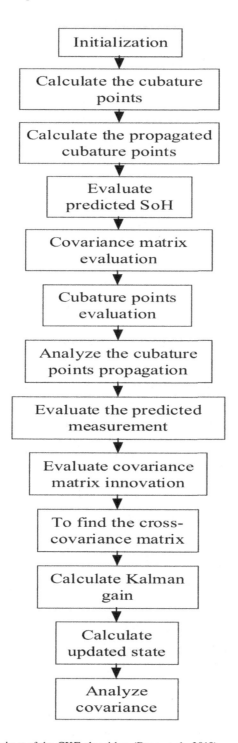

FIGURE 18.9 Flowchart of the CKF algorithm (Peng et al., 2019).

TABLE 18.7
Evaluation of the Existing Methods

No.	Reference	Error	Root Mean Square Error
1.	Zhang et al. (2021)	AEIC = 0.74%; AEPD = 3.58%	N/A
2.	Zhou et al. (2019)	EEC = >8%	N/A
3.	Xiao & Qiu et al. (2019)	ARE = >3%	0.43
4.	Xu et al. (2022)	SoH prediction error = >3%	0.010246
5.	Song et al. (2020)	MAE = 11.57%	0.14
6.	Esfandyari et al. (2019a)	MaAE = 3.77%	N/A
8.	Esfandyari et al. (2019b)	ARE = 0.73%	N/A
10.	Pamuła and Pamuła (2020)	MAPE = 8.2%	0.085
11.	Zeyu & Yang et al. (2019)	MaAE = 3.47%	N/A
12.	Gruosso et al. (2020)	MAE = 0.53%	0.058
13.	Jiang et al. (2021)	MAE = 1.05%	0.0131
14.	Peng et al. (2019)	MAE = 104.09%	0.0618

TABLE 18.8
Comparison between the Parameters of the Existing Methods

No.	Author	Voltage	Capacity	Battery Energy Storage System	Bus Model
1.	Zhang et al. (2021)	Rated voltage = 3.33 V	Rated capacity = 200 Ah	20–100 kWh	BYD K9
2.	Zhou et al. (2019)	Nominal voltage = 537.6 V	Nominal capacity = 540 Ah	N/A	N/A
3.	Xu et al. (2022)	Rated voltage = 598.92 V	Rated capacity = 404 Ah	N/A	North BFC6109GBEV5 model
4.	Song et al. (2020)	N/A	Nominal capacity = 140 Ah and = 26 Ah	N/A	N/A
5.	Esfandyari et al. (2019)	Nominal voltage = 3.2 V	Nominal capacity = 10 Ah	18.4 kWh	CAN
6.	Li et al. (2019b)	Voltage = 657 V	= 37 Ah	N/A	HEB
7.	Esfandyari et al. (2019)	Nominal voltage = 3.2 V	Nominal capacity = 10 Ah	N/A	CAN
8.	Xiao & Qiu et al. (2019)	Nominal voltage = 3.7 V	Nominal capacity = 2200 mAh	37.5 kW	Beijing Bus Dynamic Stress Test
9.	Gruosso et al. (2020)	Maximum voltage = 72 V	Nominal capacity = 150 Ah	N/A	CAN
11.	Peng et al. (2019)	Rated voltage = 3.65 V	Rated capacity = 50 Ah	N/A	Beijing Bus Dynamic Stress Test

Abbreviation: absolute error in incremental capacity, AEIC; absolute error in probability density, AEPD; estimation error control, EEC; average relative error, ARE; mean absolute error, MAE; maximum absolute error, MaAE; mean absolute percentage error, MAPE; state of health, SoH.

configuration, the creation of battery and fuel cell life extension strategies, and the development of the best real-time power splitting strategies. The current research challenges for the balanced and efficient distribution and consumption of power in EVs is to minimize power excesses and loss. When considering the fact that battery systems, particularly those in EV batteries, are extremely nonlinear and uncertain, it will be wise to expand the composite learning technique to batteries for online parameter estimation in a future study (Khang & Shah et al., 2023).

The present study on battery estimates of the SoH carried out in a laboratory setting strongly rely on the stability of the experimental environment because there is currently no proven technology to confirm their application in automobiles. More importantly, there are currently no realistic online predictions for battery SoH in cars made using trustworthy methodologies for SoH estimation. Big Data technology has both benefited and hindered the evaluation of battery health since the advent of the information era. The reliability of battery SoP prediction faces a significant problem because to the inevitability of SoC and SoH estimate inaccuracies. However, the driving range and recharging times of EBs are constrained. Electric buses are also less adaptable than traditional diesel buses since they need specialized charging infrastructure (Khang & Rath et al., 2023).

18.15 CONCLUSION

This review study involved the performance analysis of the SoC, SoH, and SoP existing methods on the ECM for LiB-driven EBs. Planning and deploying large EB fleets and the necessary charging infrastructure now necessitate an evaluation of the energy requirements of buses. Many reducing methods for calculating the energy needs of EBs rely on conventional driving cycles or individual energy demand numbers; however, these do not take into account the specifics of local bus routes (Khang, 2023).

Advantages of LiBs include the high density of energy, low maintenance, load characteristics, self-discharge, and various offered varieties. Evaluation of existing methods, challenges, and future scopes was explained in detail. The existing method does not provide the state of a battery's accurate value, optimal solution and lower in relative error for capacity prediction. Therefore, the shortcomings of the existing approaches will be resolved in the future using improved Remora Optimization Algorithm (Wang S and Rao H et al., 2022) and dual adaptive Kalman filtering algorithm. It can reduce relative error for capacity prediction and provide optimum solutions (Khang & Muthmainnah et al., 2023).

ABBREVIATIONS

Abbreviation	Full Form
AE in IC	Absolute error in incremental capacity
AE in PD	Absolute error in probability density
AKF	Adaptive Kalman filter
APU	Auxiliary power unit
ARE	Average relative error
ASREKF	Adaptive square root extended Kalman filter

BEV	Battery electric vehicles
BM	Battery model
BMS	Battery management system
CKF	Cubature Kalman filter
CTUDC	Chinese typical urban drive cycle
DDPG	Deep deterministic policy gradient
D-FACTS	Distributed flexible ac transmission system
DL	Deep learning
DP	Dual polarization
DP	Dynamic program
DRL	Deep reinforcement learning
EB	Electric buses
ECM	Equivalent circuit modelling
EEC	Estimation error control
EKF	Extended Kalman filter
ESS	Energy storage system
EM	Energy management
EV	Electric vehicles
FLBC	Fuzzy logic-based controller
FDI	False data injection
GBM	Gradient boosting method
GPR	Gaussian process regression
GPR-EKF	Gaussian process regression-Kalman filter
GRA	Grey relational analysis
HEB	Hybrid electric bus
HED	High energy density
HESS	Hybrid energy storage system
HEV	Hybrid electric vehicles
HPPC	Hybrid pulse power characteristic
ICA	Incremental capacity analysis
KFM	Kalman filter method
LiB	Lithium-ion batteries
LSTM	Long short-term memory
MaAE	Maximum absolute error
MAE	Mean absolute error
MAPE	Mean absolute percentage error
MNEDC	Modified new European drive cycle
MPC	Model Predictive Control
NLS	Nonlinear least square
NMH	Nickel metal hydride
OCV	Open circuit voltage
PCA	Principal component analysis
PDF	Probability density function
PEV	Plug in electric vehicles
PFDD	Proactive false data detection
PHEV	Plug-in Hybrid Electric Vehicles

REEB	Range-Extended Electric Bus
RFM	Random Forest Method
RL	Reinforcement Learning
RMSE	Root Mean Square Errors
SC	Super Capacitors
SoC	State of Charge
SoE	State of Energy
SoH	State of Health
SoP	State of Power
SQR	Sequential Quadratic Programming
SVR	Support Vector Regression
WNN	Wavelet Neural Network

REFERENCES

Aung, Htet, Jing Jun Soon, Shu Ting Goh, Jia Min Lew, and Kay-Soon Low. "Battery management system with state-of-charge and opportunistic state-of-health for a miniaturized satellite." IEEE Transactions on Aerospace and Electronic Systems 56, no. 4 (2019): 29782989. https://ieeexplore.ieee.org/abstract/document/8943970/

Buccoliero, Giuseppe, Pier Giuseppe Anselma, Saeed Amirfarhangi Bonab, Giovanni Belingardi, and Ali Emadi. "A new energy management strategy for multimode power-split hybrid electric vehicles." IEEE Transactions on Vehicular Technology 69, no. 1 (2019): 172181. https://ieeexplore.ieee.org/abstract/document/8884742/

Chen, Yuan, Hongyang Li, Mi Tang, Shuming Zhuo, Yanchao Wu, Erjing Wang, Shimin Wang, Chengliang Wang, and Wenping Hu. "Capacitive conjugated ladder polymers for fast-charge and-discharge sodium-ion batteries and hybrid supercapacitors." Journal of Materials Chemistry A 7, no. 36 (2019): 20891–20898. https://pubs.rsc.org/en/content/articlehtml/2019/ta/c9ta07546a

Cui, Shengmin, and Inwhee Joe. "A dynamic spatial-temporal attention-based GRU model with healthy features for state-of-health estimation of lithium-ion batteries." IEEE Access 9 (2021): 27374–27388. https://ieeexplore.ieee.org/abstract/document/9350252/

Dai, Qiongjie, Jicheng Liu, and Qiushuang Wei. "Optimal photovoltaic/battery energy storage/electric vehicle charging station design based on multi-agent particle swarm optimization algorithm." Sustainability 11, no. 7 (2019): 1973. https://www.mdpi.com/2071-1050/11/7/1973

Du, Jiuyu, Feiqiang Li, Jianqiu Li, Xiaogang Wu, Ziyou Song, Yunfei Zou, and Minggao Ouyang. "Evaluating the technological evolution of battery electric buses: China As a case." Energy 176 (2019): 309–319. https://www.sciencedirect.com/science/article/pii/S0360544219304888

Esfandyari, M. J., V. Esfahanian MR, Hairi Yazdi, H. Nehzati, and O. Shekoofa. "A new approach to consider the influence of aging state on lithium-ion battery state of power estimation for hybrid electric vehicle." Energy 176 (2019a): 505–520. https://www.sciencedirect.com/science/article/pii/S0360544219305961

Esfandyari, M. J. MR, Hairi Yazdi, V. Esfahanian, M. Masih-Tehrani, H. Nehzati, and O. Shekoofa. "A hybrid model predictive and fuzzy logic based control method for state of power estimation of series-connected lithium-ion batteries in HEVs." Journal of Energy Storage 24 (2019b): 100758. https://www.sciencedirect.com/science/article/pii/S2352152X19300970

Fan, Likang, Youtong Zhang, Haishi Dou, and Runnan Zou. "Design of an integrated energy management strategy for a plug-in hybrid electric bus." Journal of Power Sources 448 (2020): 227391. https://www.sciencedirect.com/science/article/pii/S0378775319313849

Franke, Thomas, Franziska Bühler, Peter Cocron, Isabel Neumann, and Josef F. Krems. "Enhancing Sustainability of Electric Vehicles: A Field Study Approach to Understanding User Acceptance and Behaviour." In Advances in Traffic Psychology, pp. 295–306. CRC Press, 2019. https://www.taylorfrancis.com/chapters/edit/10.1201/9781315565750-26/enhancing-sustainability-electric-vehicles-field-study-approach-understanding-user-acceptance-behaviour-thomas-franke-franziska-b%C3%BChler-peter-cocron-isabel-neumann-josef-krems

Gruosso, Giambattista, Giancarlo Storti Gajani, Fredy Ruiz, Juan Diego Valladolid, and Diego Patino. "A virtual sensor for electric vehicles' state of charge estimation." Electronics 9, no. 2 (2020): 278. https://www.mdpi.com/2079-9292/9/2/278

Hosseini, Seyedmohsen, and M. D. Sarder. "Development of a Bayesian network model for optimal site selection of electric vehicle charging station." International Journal of Electrical Power & Energy Systems 105 (2019): 110–122. https://www.sciencedirect.com/science/article/pii/S0142061517309936

Hu, Xiaosong, Haifu Jiang, Fei Feng, and Bo Liu. "An enhanced multi-state estimation hierarchy for advanced lithium-ion battery management." Applied Energy 257 (2020): 114019. https://www.sciencedirect.com/science/article/pii/S0306261919317064

Iqbal, Muhammad Zahir, Mian Muhammad Faisal, and Syeda Ramsha Ali. "Integration of supercapacitors and batteries towards high-performance hybrid energy storage devices." International Journal of Energy Research 45, no. 2 (2021): 1449–1479. https://onlinelibrary.wiley.com/doi/abs/10.1002/er.5954

Jiang, Cong, Shunli Wang, Bin Wu, Carlos Fernandez, Xin Xiong, and James CoffieKen. "A state-of-charge estimation method of the power lithium-ion battery in complex conditions based on adaptive square root extended Kalman filter." Energy 219 (2021): 119603. https://www.sciencedirect.com/science/article/pii/S0360544220327109

Kalogiannis, Theodoros Md, Sazzad Hosen, Mohsen Akbarzadeh Sokkeh, Shovon Goutam, Joris Jaguemont, Lu Jin, Geng Qiao, Maitane Berecibar, and Joeri Van Mierlo. "Comparative study on parameter identification methods for dual-polarization lithium-ion equivalent circuit model." Energies 12, no. 21 (2019): 4031. https://www.mdpi.com/1996-1073/12/21/4031

Khang, A., Applications and Principles of Quantum Computing. (1st Ed.) (2023). ISBN: 9798369311684. IGI Global Press. https://doi.org/10.4018/979-8-3693-1168-4

Khang, A., M. Muthmainnah, Prodhan Mahbub Ibna Seraj, Ahmad Al Yakin, Ahmad J. Obaid, and Manas Ranjan Panda. "AI-Aided Teaching Model for the Education 5.0 Ecosystem." AI-Based Technologies and Applications in the Era of the Metaverse. (1st Ed.) (2023). Page (83–104). IGI Global Press. https://doi.org/10.4018/978-1-6684-8851-5.ch004

Khang, A., Kali Charan Rath, Suresh Kumar Satapathy, Amaresh Kumar, Sudhansu Ranjan Das, and Manas Ranjan Panda. "Enabling the Future of Manufacturing: Integration of Robotics and IoT to Smart Factory Infrastructure in Industry 4.0." AI-Based Technologies and Applications in the Era of the Metaverse. (1st Ed.) (2023). Page (25–50). IGI Global Press. https://doi.org/10.4018/978-1-6684-8851-5.ch002

Khang, A., V. Shah, and S. Rani. AI-Based Technologies and Applications in the Era of the Metaverse. (1st Ed.) (2023). IGI Global Press. https://doi.org/10.4018/978-1-6684-8851-5

Li, Yuecheng, Hongwen He, Amir Khajepour, Hong Wang, and Jiankun Peng. "Energy management for a power-split hybrid electric bus via deep reinforcement learning with terrain information." Applied Energy 255 (2019a): 113762. https://www.sciencedirect.com/science/article/pii/S0306261919314497

Li, Beibei, Gaoxi Xiao, Rongxing Lu, Ruilong Deng, and Haiyong Bao. "On feasibility and limitations of detecting false data injection attacks on power grid state estimation using D-FACTS devices." IEEE Transactions on Industrial Informatics 16, no. 2 (2019b): 854–864. https://ieeexplore.ieee.org/abstract/document/8735923/

Liu, Rong, Ao Zhou, Xiaorong Zhang, Jingbo Mu, Hongwei Che, Yanming Wang, TingTing Wang, Zhixiao Zhang, and Zongkui Kou. "Fundamentals, advances and challenges of transition metal compounds-based supercapacitors." Chemical Engineering Journal 412 (2021): 128611. https://www.sciencedirect.com/science/article/pii/ S1385894721002096

Ma, Xiao, Danfeng Qiu, Qing Tao, and Daiyin Zhu. "State of charge estimation of a lithium ion battery based on adaptive Kalman filter method for an equivalent circuit model." Applied Sciences 9, no. 13 (2019): 2765. https://www.mdpi.com/2076-3417/9/13/2765

Ma, Zeyu, Ruixin Yang, and Zhenpo Wang. "A novel data-model fusion state-of-health estimation approach for lithium-ion batteries." Applied Energy 237 (2019): 836–847. https://www.sciencedirect.com/science/article/pii/S0306261918318907

Mehrjerdi, Hasan, and Reza Hemmati. "Stochastic model for electric vehicle charging station integrated with wind energy." Sustainable Energy Technologies and Assessments 37 (2020): 100577. https://www.sciencedirect.com/science/article/pii/ S2213138819304199

Pamuła, Teresa, and Wiesław Pamuła". "Estimation of the energy consumption of battery electric buses for public transport networks using real-world data and deep learning"." Energies 13, no. 9 (2020): 2340. https://www.mdpi.com/1996-1073/13/9/2340

Pawar, Prakash, and TarunKumar Mudige. "An IoT based intelligent smart energy management system with accurate forecasting and load strategy for renewable generation." Measurement 152 (2020): 107187. https://www.sciencedirect.com/science/article/pii/ S026322411931053X

Peng, Jiankun, Jiayi Luo, Hongwen He, and Bing Lu. "An improved state of charge estimation method based on cubature Kalman filter for lithium-ion batteries." Applied Energy 253 (2019): 113520. https://www.sciencedirect.com/science/article/pii/S0306261919311948

Singh, Shikha, Vaibhav More, and Roshan Batheri. "Driving electric vehicles into the future with battery management systems." IEEE Engineering Management Review (2022). https://ieeexplore.ieee.org/abstract/document/9844265/

Song, Lingjun, Keyao Zhang, Tongyi Liang, Xuebing Han, and Yingjie Zhang. "Intelligent state of health estimation for lithium-ion battery pack based on big data analysis." Journal of Energy Storage 32 (2020): 101836. https://www.sciencedirect.com/science/ article/pii/S2352152X2031673X

Tan, Huachun, Hailong Zhang, Jiankun Peng, Zhuxi Jiang, and Yuankai Wu. "Energy management of hybrid electric bus based on deep reinforcement learning in continuous state and action space." Energy Conversion and Management 195 (2019): 548–560. https://www.sciencedirect.com/science/article/pii/S019689041930593X

Tian, Xiang, Yingfeng Cai, Xiaodong Sun, Zhen Zhu, and Yiqiang Xu. "An adaptive ECMS with driving style recognition for energy optimization of parallel hybrid electric buses." Energy 189 (2019): 116151. https://www.sciencedirect.com/science/article/pii/ S0360544219318468

Wang, Bo, Cuo Zhang, and Zhao Yang Dong. "Interval optimization based coordination of demand response and battery energy storage system considering SoC management in a microgrid." IEEE Transactions on Sustainable Energy 11, no. 4 (2020): 2922–2931. https://ieeexplore.ieee.org/abstract/document/9043605/

Wang, Lei, Xiang Wang, and Wenxian Yang. "Optimal design of electric vehicle battery recycling network–From the perspective of electric vehicle manufacturers." Applied Energy 275 (2020): 115328. https://www.sciencedirect.com/science/article/pii/ S0306261920308400

Wang Shikai, Honghua Rao, Changsheng Wen, Heming Jia, Di Wu, Qingxin Liu, and Laith Abualigah. Improved Remora Optimization Algorithm with Mutualistic Strategy for Solving Constrained Engineering Optimization Problems. Processes. 2022; 10(12): 2606. https://doi.org/10.3390/pr10122606

Wang, Yujie, Zhendong Sun, and Zonghai Chen. "Development of energy management system based on a rule-based power distribution strategy for hybrid power sources." Energy 175 (2019): 1055–1066. https://www.sciencedirect.com/science/article/pii/S0360544219305754

Wei, Zhongbao, Difan Zhao, Hongwen He, Wanke Cao, and Guangzhong Dong. "A noise-tolerant model parameterization method for lithium-ion battery management system." Applied Energy 268 (2020): 114932. https://www.sciencedirect.com/science/article/pii/S030626192030444X

Xu, Nan, Yu Xie, Qiao Liu, Fenglai Yue, and Di Zhao. "A data-driven approach to state of health estimation and prediction for a lithium-ion battery pack of electric buses based on real-world data." Sensors 22, no. 15 (2022): 5762.

Zhang, Qichao, Xue Li, Chun Zhou, Yang Zou, Zhichao Du, Mingguang Sun, Yongsheng Ouyang, Dong Yang, and Qiangqiang Liao. "State-of-health estimation of batteries in an energy storage system based on the actual operating parameters." Journal of Power Sources 506 (2021): 230162. https://www.sciencedirect.com/science/article/pii/S0378775321006868

Zhang, Zhendong, Hongwen He, Jinquan Guo, and Ruoyan Han. "Velocity prediction and profile optimization based real-time energy management strategy for plug-in hybrid electric buses." Applied Energy 280 (2020): 116001. https://www.sciencedirect.com/science/article/pii/S030626192031446X

Zhou, Di, Ping Fu, Hongtao Yin, Wei Xie, and Shou Feng". "A study of online state-ofhealth estimation method for in-use electric vehicles based on charge data." IEICE Transactions on Information and Systems 102, no. 7 (2019): 1302–1309. https://search.ieice.org/bin/summary.php?id=e102-d_7_1302

19 Influence of Internal and External Conditions on Floating Solar Photovoltaic Systems with Internet of Things

Dhass A. D., Ganesh Babu L., and Dhiren Patel R.

19.1 INTRODUCTION

It is known that solar photovoltaic (PV) deployment requires a huge amount of contiguous land area, which makes scaling up the project size difficult in many cases. Other options must be researched and established to develop the solar capacity to keep pace with national ambitions. Alternatives like floating solar photovoltaics (FSPVs) have gained traction in recent years and are predicted to continue expanding in the future and to grow rapidly. In 2018, there were 1.314 global warming potential (GWP) of installed capacity, with the total capacity reaching 4.6 GWP in 2022. An FSPV performance characterization currently lacks a widely accepted application case. Further studies in FSPVs is necessary to identify valid use cases and performance measures as shown in Figure 19.1.

According to an early assessment of FSPV designs, energy yields would be about 10% higher than with land-based installations because of the cooling impact of the underlying water body on the temperature of the PV module. The Singapore Tengeh Reservoir test-bed was established in 2016 to host the largest first floating solar installment. The cooling effects were thoroughly examined for eight different commercially available FSPV systems, each with its unique parameters. There was a land-based reference system in place. According to research, air temperatures are normally 2–3°C lower over water than on land, although wind speeds are frequently greater. This results in lower module temperatures of 5–10°C compared to rooftop-mounted modules (Exley et al., 2021a).

It is critical to perform additional studies in this area because FSPVs are one of the most well-known and modern topics in renewable energy (Motahhir et al., 2020). This chapter is structured around the FSPV system, IoT implementation in the analysis of the FSPV, and factors influencing the performance of FSPVs. The main components of the Internet of Things (IoT), internal and external parameters, will be described in detail (Rath et al., 2024).

FIGURE 19.1 Typical floating solar photovoltaic system.

19.2 FLOATING SOLAR PHOTOVOLTAIC SYSTEMS

19.2.1 Need for Floating Solar Photovoltaics

It appears that FSPV has various advantages over conventional PV deployments. By utilizing the water's surface, FSPV avoids the need for extensive land-use modification. First, this benefits countries and regions with limited land resources and high land costs. Second, the cooling effect of the water body holding the FSPV system has been demonstrated to give better performance than ground-based PV. Third, FSPV has been shown to significantly minimize evaporative losses, which could save water in drought-stricken areas. In conjunction with hydroelectric dams, FSPV has been shown in experiments to improve energy efficiency and system dependability (Cagle et al., 2020; Campana et al., 2019; Abid et al., 2019).

Due to the high cost of land-based PV, FSPV is proven to be a competitor that offers several benefits that are helping it gain a commercial advantage. It provides new options for generating power in areas wherever the earth's surface for PV facilities is either in short supply or prohibitively expensive. Additionally, generating power close to urban areas helps lower transmission costs (Kjeldstad et al., 2021). The main components of an FSPV system are like ground-installed PV system, and an FSPV consists of additional components like a floating structure, mooring and anchoring, an inverter (installed at top of the panel), and underwater cables (Khang & Shah et al., 2023).

19.2.2 Floating Solar Photovoltaic System Components

Despite their polymer construction, pontoons are buoyant enough to support big loads in water. An appropriate number of modules can be stacked in series or parallel according to the functional needs and space. These solutions are straightforward and effective based on decades of experience in port and wharf management. In the end, however, the goal of a floating plant is to produce the highest amount of energy

FIGURE 19.2 Floating solar photovoltaic system on a reservoir in one of the Dutch North Sea islands.

at the lowest possible cost while also paying close attention to the plant's robustness (Kumar et al., 2020). Even though pontoons are a well-established technology, they are a versatile and expensive solution, and their goal is not to optimize the FSPV system. There have been many attempts to discover solutions to this problem by employing modular rafts that can be constructed in water to form extended structures that are ideal for mounting PV panels, and most of the methods are depicted in Figure 19.2.

Structural members were made using chopped strand mats (CSMs) on their near surfaces and longitudinally arranged yarn for the pultrusion process (Exley et al., 2021b). The mooring system is a permanent framework that keeps the system in place. Quay, wharves, piers, and jetties are some examples of quay structures (Yoon et al., 2018; Lee et al., 2014; López et al., 2022). Solar panels on a floating system are kept in place by an anchoring mechanism that keeps them from moving around.

Underwater PV cells are used in this PV system. This type's flexibility, lower internal stress, and ability to achieve lower module temperatures make it an attractive alternative to standard PV modules with rigid mounting structures (Solomin et al., 2021; IJSE, 2014; Cazzaniga et al., 2019). In addition to reducing the number of raw materials needed, increasing the system's flexibility also facilitates transportation. However, the technology is still in its infancy, with several uncertainties, such as the long-term dependability of PV modules and the electrical safety in submerged settings (Acharya & Devraj, 2019; Gadzanku et al., 2021; Yousuf et al., 2020). The floating unit maintains the metal framework that supports the PV modules, as shown in Figure 19.3.

19.2.3 Implementation of the Floating Solar Photovoltaic System

In the implementation of the FSPV system in a reservoir, river, or lake area, the following factors need to be considered: (i) reservoir layout, (ii) floating structure, and (iii) PV module orientation angle. The geometry of the model should be considered as most the important. The number of solar PV panels, string connection schemes, distance between each row and column, and proper cable connections (to avoid shadow and mismatch losses) are easy access for extensions.

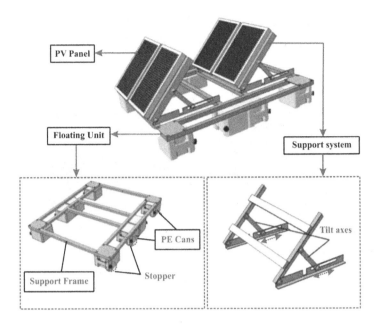

FIGURE 19.3 Schematic representation of a floating solar photovoltaic structure view (El Hammoumi et al., 2021).

19.2.4 Cooling Techniques in Floating Solar Photovoltaic Systems

The performance of an FSPV system is increased by reducing the panel temperature and high solar radiation falling on it. This way, cooling techniques can provide improved performance of a system by considering the water veil cooling and sprinkler cooling system. The water veil cooling technique incorporates a temperature control system that activates when the temperature of the solar panel rises above a predetermined threshold; normally, the solar panel's maximum temperature is 300°C. The water is pumped through the pipes to the top of the panel by a low-pressure submersible water pump. The sprinkler cooling system uses a water-type forced convection system with sprinklers. The temperature of the cells was lowered because the water flowed over the top of the panel.

19.3 INTERNET OF THINGS IN FLOATING SOLAR PHOTOVOLTAIC SYSTEMS

The Internet of Things (IoT) was born when the "Internet, micro-electromechanical systems, wireless technologies, and microservices" were brought together (Exley et al., 2021a; Cagle et al., 2020; Campana et al., 2019; Abid et al., 2019). More simply, the IoT is a system that connects physical and digital objects with single-use identities. It is possible to bridge the gap between information and operational technology with this collaboration without using computer-to-computer or human-to-human communication, as shown in Figure 19.4.

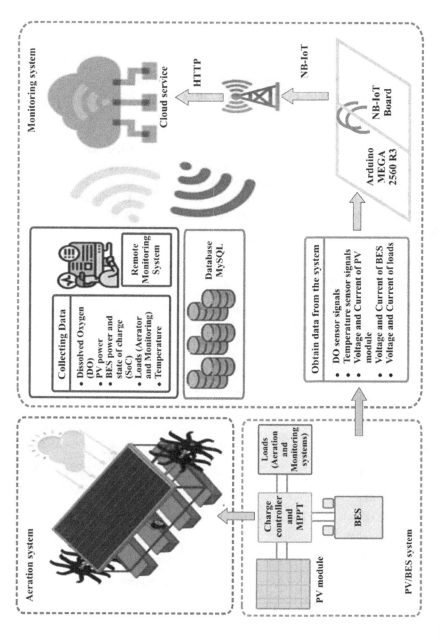

FIGURE 19.4 Internet of Things architecture for remote monitoring of PV systems (Jamroen, 2022).

An Internet router with a firewall is used as a gateway link between the PV system's hardware designs and a website hosted on the Internet. The Arduino server is a key component in combining the web server with ethernet or wireless router modules. There is a microcontroller on an Arduino server for managing and controlling the hardware components of a PV system. This layer, responsible for remote monitoring and control, will receive data from the server (Bellavista et al., 2013; Adhya et al., 2016; Shrihariprasath & Rathinasabapathy, 2016; Tamilselvi et al., 2019).

19.4 FACTORS INFLUENCING FLOATING SOLAR PHOTOVOLTAIC SYSTEM PERFORMANCE

19.4.1 INTERNAL CONDITIONS

Figure 19.5 depicts a conventional solar cell curve with varying (constant) shunt resistance values. During this study, the shunt resistances are referred to as Rsh1 (100 Ω), Rsh2 (200 Ω), Rsh3 (300 Ω), Rsh4 (400 Ω), and Rsh5 (500 Ω).

Typical short-circuit solar cell current and shunt resistance functions are shown in Figure 19.6. All the resistors are between 1 and 10 Ω. Since short circuits have low values, the shunt resistance is very low.

When all losses are considered, the actual energy transferred to the grid at each of the selected locations does not match the expected energy produced by the PV systems for the installed capacity, as shown in Figure 19.7.

The monthly average decrease from the offshore floating photovoltaic (OFPV) system varies from 57 to 104 MWh. Pontoon-based FSPV and general motor (GM)-PV systems send between 46 and 87 MWh less energy to the grid than is generated. High energy yield in the OFPV systems was a result of the high irradiation level

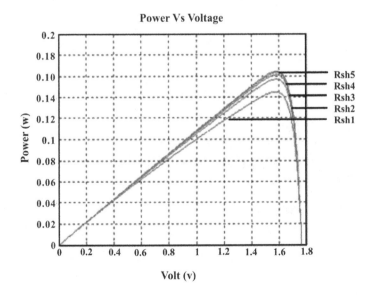

FIGURE 19.5 Power vs. voltage characteristic curve (Dass et al., 2022).

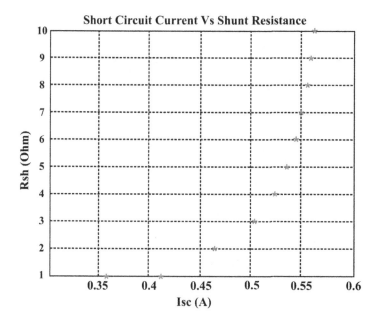

FIGURE 19.6 Typical short-circuit solar cell current and shunt resistance functions (Dass et al., 2022).

in March. In June, there was a noticeable decline in energy production. The peak energy production in the inland FSPV system was also noted in March (Oliveira-Pinto & Stokkermans, 2020).

19.4.2 EXTERNAL CONDITIONS

Any successful floating system's layout of a reservoir, pond, or lake must have a design tailored to the system's specific location, growth, and strategy. Furthermore, the tank wall's 3D geometry and the inside of the tank's 3D geometry are incompatible. As a result, the floating module's geometry must be suitably fitted to the water storage basin's different internal structures. This system was designed with two primary considerations in mind: stability and resiliency.

To prevent water evaporation, the module should first protect as much water as feasible. In addition, the module's dimensions had to be tailored to match those of commercially available PV units. The solar panel's size and angle of inclination, the number of modules to be installed, the space between rows of panels (to reduce shadow effects), and the ease of extension were all evaluated (Khang & Rath et al., 2023).

When the solar panel faces south, the reservoir's main longitudinal axis must be aligned with the base point (Sahu et al., 2016). The most crucial function of a deteriorated PV module is still being carried out. If it is not used extensively, it can still generate electricity from solar energy. It is also possible to have more issues with the degradation that exceeds a certain level (Dass et al., 2022). A solar module may have hot spots where the cells or other components may be damaged by high temperatures

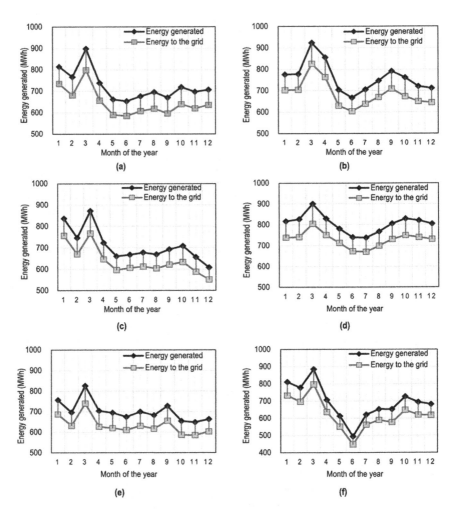

FIGURE 19.7 Power produced by the PV arrays and fed into the grid on a monthly basis: (a) OFPV-1, (b) OFPV-2, (c) OFPV-3, (d) OFPV-4, (e) FPV, and (f) GM-PV system (Ravichandran et al., 2022).

(Sahu et al., 2016; Matthias et al., 2021). A short circuit will cause the voltage to invert and become equal and opposite of the other cells in the series. There is a lot of heat dissipation in these hot locations because of this malfunctioning solar cell, which is a load on the other cells, as shown in Figure 19.8.

The difference between the average temperatures of the FSPV and OFPV modules can be as much as 2.74°C. These results show that heat is transferred from the PV panel's surface to the water basin, acting as the cooling system (Motahhir et al., 2020). An issue with a PV module's color deprivation in the packaging unit, ethylene vinyl acetate (EVA), or the adhesive sandwiched between the solar cells and glass, is the most common source of color variations.

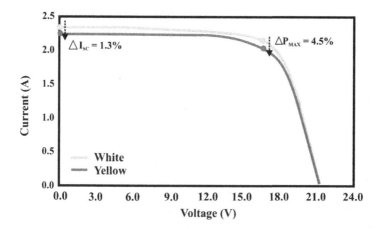

FIGURE 19.8 Current vs. voltage curve properties of photovoltaic solar modules (Kim et al., 2021).

To describe the progression of the discoloration, the EVA starts as a light yellow and then turns dark brown. Changes in the cell color of a solar module reduce the module's overall output power. When the encapsulating polymer loses its adhesion to the solar cell, it is called "delamination." A major issue, because of its dual effects on the equipment housing, is increased exposure to sunlight and water diffusion (Yousuf et al., 2020; Sahu et al., 2016; Ranjbaran et al., 2019).

19.5 PERFORMANCE EVALUATION OF FLOATING SOLAR PHOTOVOLTAICS

More solar energy is needed, even though utility-scale PV system installations take up a lot of land. Land costs and availability may constrain future large-scale initiatives. Because of this, FSPV systems have been developed both on land and in freshwater bodies, and recently off-land. When using high-temperature functioning PV cells, FSPV increases efficiency while reducing environmental impact and biodiversity loss. Hydropower plants and FSPVs have been offered to ensure a steady electricity supply to the grid. Hydraulic energy production may be increased by 65% by installing just 10% of the FSPV plant area in each of the 20 major hydropower reservoirs. Because the wind and waves in these inland waterways are so quiet, the architecture of FSPV systems is identical to that of land-based systems (Khang & Muthmainnah et al., 2023).

Recently, an in-depth assessment of the entire FSPV industry has been completed. As a result, FSPV systems in Korea have an average efficiency that is 11% higher than that of a land-based PV system. In comparison to land-based systems, the number of obstructions that can induce shade loss is reduced, as is the amount of dust. More than half of the world's population resides within 100 km of a maritime shoreline; hence, an off-shore FSPV system may be easily located to supply these places with electricity. Demand for FSPV is increasing in nations like Japan, Singapore, Korea, and the

Philippines, where there is a lack of land for PV installations. In addition to being able to be deployed in a wide variety of waterways, including lakes, rivers, reservoirs, irrigation ponds, wastewater treatment plants, vineyards, fisheries, dams, and canals, FSPV systems can serve multiple purposes (Luo et al., 2021; Tina et al., 2021).

19.6 CONCLUSION

This chapter examined the significance and necessity of installing a FSPV system in a rural area. One of the most exciting areas of PV application is floating PV, which has great market potential. For example, FSPV decarbonizes the energy supply while lowering land-use pressure, provides improved electricity generation efficiency, and minimizes water body evaporation compared to ground-based systems (Khang et al., 2023). But, even though temperature and stratification are crucial drivers of the ecosystem's reaction to FSPV deployment, the impact of FSPV deployment on lake temperature and stratification remains unclear. Photovoltaic system location, indoor and external climatic circumstances, performance system connections, and numerous components all impact FSPV performance. The FSPV system output has been measured with IoT devices and controlled with digital technologies (Khang, 2023).

19.7 FUTURE SCOPE

Studies show that there is significant potential for implementing an FSPV system. In the future, the effects of relative humidity, temperature, and mismatch need to be studied (Khang & Vugar et al., 2024).

REFERENCES

Abid, M., Abid, Z., Sagin, J., Murtaza, R., Sarbassov, D., & Shabbir, M., (2019). Prospects of floating photovoltaic technology and its implementation in Central and South Asian countries. International Journal of Environmental Science and Technology, 16(3), 1755–1762.

Acharya, M., & Devraj, S., (2019). Floating solar photovoltaic (FSPV): A third pillar to the solar PV sector. TERI Discuss. Pap. ETC India Proj. New Delhi Energy Resource Institute, 68. https://www.teriin.org/sites/default/files/2020-02/Floating%20Solar%20 Photovoltaic%20%28FSPV%29%20A%20Third%20Pillar%20to%20Solar%20PV%20 Sector.pdf

Adhya, S., Saha, D., Das, A., Jana, J., & Saha, H., (2016, January). An IoT-based smart solar photovoltaic remote monitoring and control unit. In 2016 2nd international conference on control, instrumentation, energy & communication (CIEC) (pp. 432–436). IEEE. https://ieeexplore.ieee.org/abstract/document/7513793/

Atzori, L., Iera, A., & Morabito, G., (2010). The internet of things: A survey. Computer Networks, 54(15), 2787–2805. https://dergipark.org.tr/en/pub/ijamec/issue/25619/267197

Bellavista, P., Cardone, G., Corradi, A., & Foschini, L., (2013). Convergence of MANET and WSN in IoT urban scenarios. IEEE Sensors Journal, 13(10), 3558–3567. https://ieeexplore.ieee.org/abstract/document/6552998/

Cagle, A.E., Armstrong, A., Exley, G., Grodsky, S.M., Macknick, J., Sherwin, J., & Hernandez, R.R., (2020). The land sparing, water surface use efficiency, and water surface transformation of floating photovoltaic solar energy installations. Sustainability, 12(19). https://www.mdpi.com/2071-1050/12/19/8154

Campana, P.E., Wastage, L., Nookuea, W., Tan, Y.T., & Yan, J.Y., (2019). Optimization and assessment of floating and floating-tracking PV systems integrated in on- and off-grid hybrid energy systems. Solar Energy, 177, 782–795.

Cazzaniga, R., Rosa-Clot, M., Rosa-Clot, P., & Tina, G. M., (2019). Integration of PV floating with hydroelectric power plants. Heliyon, 5(6), e01919. https://www.cell.com/heliyon/pdf/S2405-8440(19)30152-5.pdf

Dass, A. D., Beemkumar, N., Harikrishnan, S., & Ali, H. M. (2022). A review on factors influencing the mismatch losses in solar photovoltaic system. International Journal of Photoenergy, 2022. https://www.hindawi.com/journals/ijp/2022/2986004/

El Hammoumi, A., Chalh, A., Allouhi, A., Motahhir, S., El Ghzizal, A., & Derouich, A., (2021). Design and construction of a test bench to investigate the potential of floating PV systems. Journal of Cleaner Production, 278, 123917.

Exley, G., Armstrong, A., Page, T., & Jones, I. D., (2021a). Floating photovoltaics could mitigate climate change impacts on water body temperature and stratification. Solar Energy, 219, 24–33. https://www.sciencedirect.com/science/article/pii/S0038092X2100116X

Exley, G., Hernandez, R. R., Page, T., Chipps, M., Gambro, S., Hersey, M., & Armstrong, A, (2021b). Scientific and stakeholder evidence-based assessment: Ecosystem response to floating solar photovoltaics and implications for sustainability. Renewable and Sustainable Energy Reviews, 152, 111639. https://www.sciencedirect.com/science/article/pii/S136403212100914X

Gadzanku, S., Beshilas, L., & Grunwald, U. B. (2021). Enabling Floating Solar Photovoltaic (FPV) Deployment: Review of Barriers to FPV Deployment in Southeast Asia. https://www.osti.gov/biblio/1787553

Gudimella, S. V., Thotakura, S., & Kondamudi, S. (2022). Feasibility Study of Floating Solar–Hydro Hybrid System with IoT. In *Smart and Intelligent Systems* (pp. 279–290). Springer, Singapore. https://link.springer.com/chapter/10.1007/978-981-16-2109-3_27

IJSE. International Journal of software engineering and its applications", Vol. 8, No. 1, pp.75–84, 2014.https://www.academia.edu/download/51025568/International_Journal_of_Software_Engine20161222-12297-19y5lz0.pdf

IoT Agenda (2022). Internet of Things (IoT), HTTP://internet of things agenda. Tech target.com/definition/Internet-of-Things-IoT. https://ieeexplore.ieee.org/abstract/document/5501633/

Jamroen, C. (2022). Optimal techno-economic sizing of a standalone floating photovoltaic/battery energy storage system to power an aquaculture aeration and monitoring system. Sustainable Energy Technologies and Assessments, 50, 101862. https://www.sciencedirect.com/science/article/pii/S2213138821008766

Khang, A., *Advanced Technologies and AI-Equipped IoT Applications in High-Tech Agriculture* (1st Ed.) (2023). IGI Global Press. https://doi.org/10.4018/978-1-6684-9231-4

Khang, A., Muthmainnah, M, Seraj, Prodhan Mahbub Ibna, Yakin, Ahmad Al, Obaid, Ahmad J., & Ranjan Panda, Manas. "AI-Aided Teaching Model for the Education 5.0 Ecosystem" *AI-Based Technologies and Applications in the Era of the Metaverse.* (1st Ed.) (2023). Page (83–104). IGI Global Press. https://doi.org/10.4018/978-1-6684-8851-5.ch004

Khang, A., Rath, Kali Charan, Kumar Satapathy, Suresh, Kumar, Amaresh, Ranjan Das, Sudhansu, & Ranjan Panda, Manas. "Enabling the Future of Manufacturing: Integration of Robotics and IoT to Smart Factory Infrastructure in Industry 4.0." *AI-Based Technologies and Applications in the Era of the Metaverse.* (1st Ed.) (2023). Page (25–50). IGI Global Press. https://doi.org/10.4018/978-1-6684-8851-5.ch002

Khang, A., Shah, V., & Rani, S., *AI-Based Technologies and Applications in the Era of the Metaverse.* (1st Ed.) (2023). IGI Global Press. https://doi.org/10.4018/978-1-6684-8851-5

Kim, J., Rabelo, M., Padi, S. P., Yousuf, H., Cho, E. C., & Yi, J., (2021). A review of the degradation of photovoltaic modules for life expectancy. Energies, 14(14), 4278. https://www.mdpi.com/1996-1073/14/14/4278

Kjeldstad, T., Lindholm, D., Marstein, E., & Selj, J., (2021). Cooling of floating photovoltaics and the importance of water temperature. Solar Energy, 218, 544–551. https://www.sciencedirect.com/science/article/pii/S0038092X21002085

Kumar, N. M., Subramaniam, U., Mathew, M., Ajitha, A., & Almakhles, D. J., (2020). Exergy analysis of thin-film solar PV module in ground-mount, floating and submerged installation methods. Case Studies in Thermal Engineering, 21, 100686. https://www.sciencedirect.com/science/article/pii/S2214157X20301064

Lee, Y. G., Joo, H. J., & Yoon, S. J., (2014). Design and installation of floating-type photovoltaic energy generation system using FRP members. Solar Energy, 108, 13–19. https://www.sciencedirect.com/science/article/pii/S0038092X14003326

Littwin, Matthias et al (2021) Performance of New Photovoltaic System Designs Report IEA-PVPS T13-15:2021 April 2021 ISBN 978-3-907281-04-8. https://onlinelibrary.wiley.com/doi/abs/10.1002/solr.202200596

López, M., Soto, F., & Hernández, Z. A. (2022). Assessment of the potential of floating solar photovoltaic panels in bodies of water in mainland Spain. Journal of Cleaner Production, 340, 130752. https://www.sciencedirect.com/science/article/pii/S0959652622003912

Luo, W., Isukapalli, S. N., Vinayagam, L., Ting, S. A., Pravettoni, M., Reindl, T., & Kumar, A., (2021). Performance loss rates of floating photovoltaic installations in the tropics. Solar Energy, 219, 58–64. https://www.sciencedirect.com/science/article/pii/S0038092X20312706

Motahhir, S., Chouder, A., ElHammoumi, A., Benyoucef, A.S., Ghzizal, A. El, Kichou, S., Kara, K., Sanjeevikumar, P., & Silvestre, S., (2020). Optimal energy harvesting from a multi-string PV generator based on an artificial bee colony algorithm. IEEE Systems Journal, 1e8. https://doi.org/10.1109/jsyst.2020.2997744.

Oliveira-Pinto, S., & Stokkermans, J., (2020). Assessment of the potential of different floating solar technologies–overview and analysis of different case studies. Energy Conversion and Management, 211, 112747. https://www.sciencedirect.com/science/article/pii/S0196890420302855

Pveurope, https://www.pveurope.eu/installation/netherlands-floating-pv-system-without-plastic-components, accessed on 5 March, 2022.

Ranjbaran, P., Yousefi, H., Gharehpetian, G. B., & Astaraei, F. R., (2019). A review on floating photovoltaic (FPV) power generation units. Renewable and Sustainable Energy Reviews, 110, 332–347. https://www.sciencedirect.com/science/article/pii/S1364032119303211

Rath, Kali Charan, Khang, A., & Roy, Debanik, "The Role of Internet of Things (IoT) Technology in Industry 4.0," *Advanced IoT Technologies and Applications in the Industry 4.0 Digital Economy* (1 Ed.) (2024). CRC Press. https://doi.org/10.1201/9781003434269-1

Ravichandran, N., Ravichandran, N., & Panneerselvam, B., (2022). Comparative assessment of offshore floating photovoltaic systems using thin film modules for Maldives islands. Sustainable Energy Technologies and Assessments, 53, 102490. https://www.sciencedirect.com/science/article/pii/S2213138822005409

Sahu, A., Yadav, N., & Sudhakar, K., (2016). Floating photovoltaic power plant: A review. Renewable and Sustainable Energy Reviews, 66, 815–824. https://www.sciencedirect.com/science/article/pii/S1364032116304841

Shrihariprasath, B., & Rathinasabapathy, V. (2016, March). A smart IoT system for monitoring solar PV power conditioning units. In 2016 World Conference on Futuristic Trends in Research and Innovation for Social Welfare (Startup Conclave) (pp. 1–5). IEEE. https://ieeexplore.ieee.org/abstract/document/7583930/

Solomin, E., Sirotkin, E., Cuce, E., Selvanathan, S. P., & Kumarasamy, S., (2021). Hybrid floating solar plant designs: A review. Energies, 14(10), 2751. https://www.mdpi.com/1996-1073/14/10/2751

Tamilselvi, K., Jananandhini, E., & Vijayakumar, N., (2019). Design and implementation of IoT enabled smart solar power monitoring system. International Journal of Advanced Research Trends in Engineering and Technology (IJARTET), 6, 14–19.

Tina, G. M., Scavo, F. B., Merlo, L., & Bizzarri, F., (2021). Analysis of water environment on the performances of floating photovoltaic plants. Renewable Energy, 175, 281–295. https://www.sciencedirect.com/science/article/pii/S0960148121006029

Yoon, S. J., Joo, H. J., & Kim, S. H. (2018, June). Structural analysis and design for the development of a floating photovoltaic energy generation system. In IOP Conference Series: Materials Science and Engineering (Vol. 372, No. 1, p. 012021). IOP Publishing. https://iopscience.iop.org/article/10.1088/1757-899X/372/1/012021/meta

Yousuf, H., Khokhar, M. Q., Zahid, M. A., Kim, J., Kim, Y., Cho, E. C., & Yi, J., (2020). A review on floating photovoltaic technology (FPVT). Current Photovoltaic Research, 8(3), 67–78.

Zanella, A., Bui, N., Castellani, A., Vangelista, L., & Zorzi, M., (2014). Internet of things for smart cities. IEEE Internet of Things Journal, 1(1), 22–32. https://doi.org/10.1109/JIOT.2014.2306328

20 Analysis of Internet of Things-Integrated Technology in a Smart Factory

Gurwinder Singh, Priya L., Kumar P., Karthika J., Saikumar Tara, and Nidhya M. S.

20.1 INTRODUCTION

Industry 4.0, frequently known as the fourth modern, it depends on smart production lines to increase yield per laborer and reduce cost. The Internet of Things (IoT), artificial intelligence (AI), and robots are instances of state-of-the-art innovation that are being integrated into customary assembling processes as a feature of Industry 4.0 (Vijayaraghavan & Leevinson, 2019). To help production and effectiveness, smart plants utilize computerized innovations such as IoT, AI, and robots (Garrido-Hidalgo et al., 2019; Arden et al., 2021).

Industry 4.0's smart factories have networked machinery and tools that can share data in real- time and with a centralized control system (Chen et al., 2017). As a result, production facilities may optimize their methods, reduce pollution, and boost adaptability in the face of rapidly changing consumer preferences. As of late, the IoT has been used in smart factories to work with advanced production and assist organizations with running more successfully, efficiently, and economically (Wang et al., 2016). The IoT is a basic innovation empowering the ascent of smart factories (Zhong et al., 2017). For Industry 4.0 to be fully realized, it is necessary to overcome a number of obstacles. Investment in cutting-edge facilities and machinery is a must for a successful Industry 4.0 rollout. This may prove to be quite a challenge for smaller companies or those with less resources. Industry 4.0 requires a skilled labor force familiar with digital tools (Da Silva et al., 2020).

In the age of the smart manufacturing plant and Industry 4.0, sensors are utilized to monitor and record all circumstances and create process boundaries, such as temperature (Kalsoom et al., 2020). In smart plants, IoT sensors can likewise be utilized to track all that data from contributions to yields (Patel et al., 2018). This gives producers quick input on production viability and quality, engaging them to pursue information-driven decisions that improve tasks and outcome (Manavalan & Jayakrishna, 2019). The IoT enables preventive maintenance to be undertaken before equipment faults occur by detecting and predicting when machines will need repair (Dalzochio et al., 2020).

DOI: 10.1201/9781003438137-20

In addition, IoT sensors may be installed in a manufacturing facility to keep an eye out for any security or safety breaches. This may aid in protecting employee safety as well as expensive equipment and assets (Ryalat et al., 2023). Through a system of interconnected sensors, automated systems may exchange information and operate in concert with one another. Through better communication and collaboration, manufacturing times may be cut down considerably, while waste and downtime are reduced (Aceto et al., 2020). Production network the board and stock utilizing the Web of Things (WoT) might assist organizations with upgrading their tasks (Khan & Javaid, 2022). Producers might include IoT in Industry 4.0 to increase productivity, support production, and fix quality control by using energy-saving methods, sensors, and programming (Gupta et al., 2022).

Additionally, by using the abundance of data gathered during analysis with AI and machine learning (ML), plant managers may optimize production operations, decrease downtime, and enhance quality control. Predictive maintenance support is a Web of Things (WoT) use in smart production lines that expects to diminish unscheduled margin time by anticipating when machines and their hardware may be separated from assemblies. Consequently, by examining information from sensors embedded in hardware and foreseeing malfunctions involving IoT in production lines, production line directors might give support timetables and save time (Tucker, 2021).

Stock administration and resource checking are only two of the many purposes of IoT. Internet of Things gadgets in a smart production line lay out an interconnected and robotized climate for continuous cycle observing and examination (Ashima et al., 2021). The convenience of blockchain (Khanh & Khang, 2021) in the smart production process is also investigated to find out how it could be coordinated with future cybersecure enterprises (Fernandez-Carames & Fraga-Lamas, 2019). The IoT and AI in smart assembling (Durana et al., 2021) are explored to foster digital production in organizations. Research into IoT for manufacturing is conducted with the goal of improving the efficiency of smart industrial technology in the manufacture of complex parts (Xu et al., 2020). To develop the IoT-enabled decision-support algorithms for smart factories, researchers are looking at big data analysis for green manufacturing (Kovacova & Lewis, 2021).

The goal of this research is to increase the efficiency of manufacturing facilities by focusing on smart factories in Industry 4.0 (Grabowska, 2020). The objective of exploring Industry 4.0's assembling framework is to find uses for the IoT in cutting-edge processing plants, so that they can work effectively producing individual parts (Kamble et al., 2020). Investigation into a network-based IoT design offers dependable online protection for information representation and observation of the autonomous guided vehicle (AGV) state, thus upgrading navigation and supporting modern productivity (Elsisi & Tran, 2021). The IoT and deep learning technologies are the expected instruments for fostering shortcoming identification and fixing enlistment engines (Tran et al., 2023).

Using the IoT stage and deep learning network methods are explored to propose web-based answers for computer numerical control (CNC) machining processes against cyberattacks (Tran et al., 2022). To further develop yields in tomato development, scientists have looked at utilizing convolutional neural networks (CNNs) for disease recognition and characterization (Sakkarvarthi et al., 2022). The utilization of a Slam Rabbit for exfiltration by the military and police is explored to further develop network protection from cyberattacks (Mohamed et al., 2022). The use of a strong Kalman filter is studied to improve the safety of AGV location estimates in the face of various cyberattacks (Elsisi et al., 2023; Khang & Hahanov et al., 2022).

Soori et al. (2017) recommended virtual machining strategies to survey and further develop CNC machining in recreated settings. Soori & Arezoo (2023) fostered a technique to address layered, mathematical, device redirection, and warm issues in 5-hub CNC machining processes. Soori et al. (2016) offered an outline of current advancements in grinding mix welding techniques to research and improve the adequacy of the course of part production utilizing welding innovations. To diminish lingering pressure and diversion blunder in 5-hub processing of turbine sharp edges, Soori et al. (2016) investigated the utilization of virtual machining innovation. They made use of virtualized machining frameworks to break down and diminish cutting temperature during processing tasks of hard-to-cut parts. They also presented a superior virtual machining way to deal with a further developed surface quality during 5-pivot processing activities of turbine cutting edges.

20.2 PREDICTIVE MAINTENANCE

Predictive maintenance is a significant IoT application in smart plants, since it assists with reducing spontaneous downtime in the assembling system. By estimating when machines and production equipment will need to be repaired using data and analytics, predictive maintenance may reduce downtime and boost productivity in the component manufacturing process. This method may lead to machines and other industrial tools to have longer lives, lower maintenance costs, and more reliable performance. Predictive maintenance is made easier with the help of IoT in smart factories by continually monitoring the state of machinery and equipment, predicting probable breakdowns, and giving a maintenance plan (Khang & Rath et al., 2023).

During the chip-making process, for example, data on temperature, vibration, and energy consumption may be gathered and sent with the help of IoT sensors. In addition, the procedure may be used to optimize maintenance schedules and reduce downtime as part of maintenance improvements. Process observation and control, sensors, AGV applications, and stock administration are essential for the Industry 4.0 IoT 6G-based smart factory System 4.0 framework, as shown in Figure 20.1.

The IoT sensors allow for real-time monitoring of performance and equipment health, which may lead to significant gains in industrial output. Producers can expect breakdowns and plan maintenance early.

The data is analyzed to spot trends and outliers that may be used to predict maintenance needs and plan for them ahead of time (Bhambri et al., 2022). In addition, IoT gadgets may be used to automate tasks such as product assembly and material management. By eliminating the potential for human mistakes during product assembly and material handling, this method may boost productivity. Predictive maintenance and continuous inspection of the production cycle are just two instances of how IoT

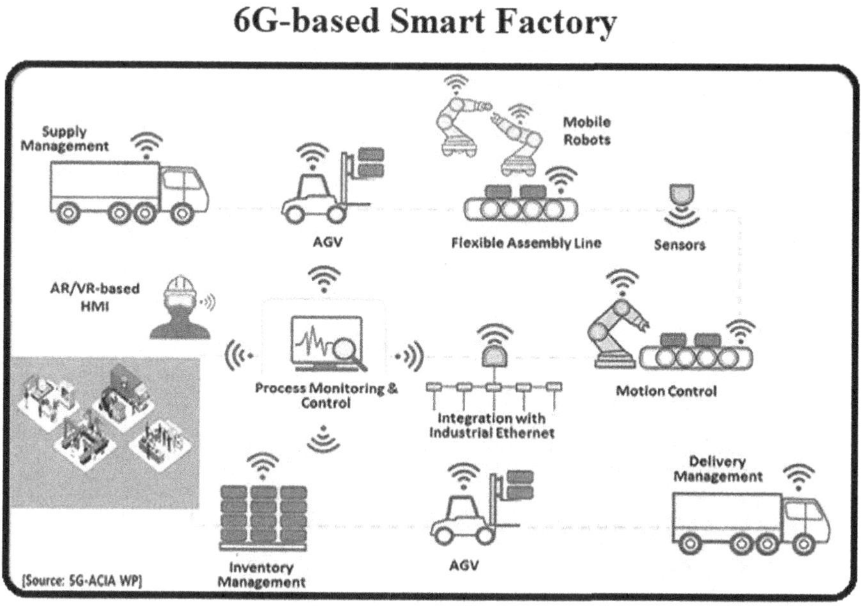

6G-based Smart Factory

FIGURE 20.1   An Industry 4.0 IoT 6G-based smart factory System 4.0.

in smart processing plants is changing the assembling area. This prompts greater efficiency, less downtime, and higher quality, all of which add to more prominent benefits, as shown in Figure 20.2.

20.3 ASSET TRACKING

Asset tracking, in which sensors and other IoT gadgets are used to track the area and status of resources such as hardware, apparatuses, and natural substances during part production, is one example of how IoT may be utilized in Industry 4.0 smart production lines. To further develop production processes, save time, and stretch existing resources, IoT asset tracking gadgets might be used to further develop a smart manufacturing plant's inventory network and production processes by giving precise, constant information on the area and status of resources.

Remote sensors are at the core of IoT-empowered asset tracking (Nica & Stehel, 2021). Sensors and radio frequency identification (RFID) labels permit WoT-empowered GPS frameworks to screen where and how frequently assets are moved. This information is sent to a centralized repository, where it is analyzed and reviewed by AI software. The examination results are relied upon to make better decision regarding the resource's presentation and usage, the assembling system's proficiency, and the machine's predictive maintenance.

Producers can diminish downtime and increase efficiency with the assistance of constant information by instantly recognizing bottlenecks and upgrading production processes. Sensors connected to the IoT may be used by manufacturers to track the

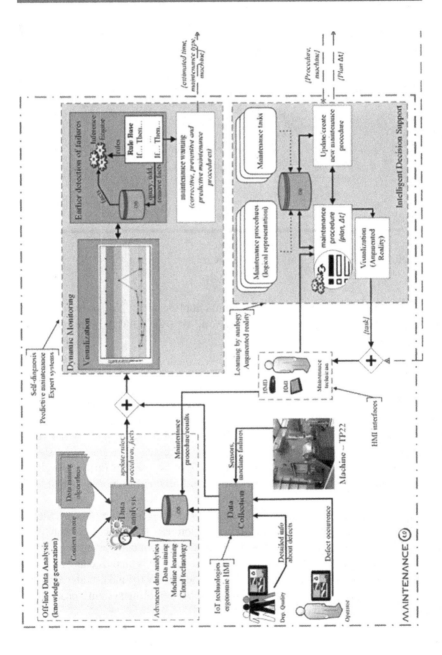

FIGURE 20.2   System architecture of predictive maintenance.

condition of their machinery and determine where parts of it need to be updated. They may employ asset tracking to guarantee that all necessary resources are on hand at all times, which will cut down on downtime and boost output of manufactured parts.

In the food and pharmaceutical sectors, it is crucial to monitor the location and state of goods to guarantee their quality and safety. They may be monitored in real-time with the help of IoT devices. Managers can as a result better plan for maintenance, downtime, and equipment utilization. Inventory management and improved environmental sustainability through increased asset tracking in smart factories are two more benefits for businesses (Khang & Gupta et al., 2023).

By tracking the flow of inputs and outputs, businesses may better manage their stocks and reduce environmental impact associated with manufacturing. This method not only lowers per-part production costs, but also it makes manufacturing more environmentally friendly. When it comes to optimizing the supply chain, IoT-enabled asset tracking is essential in smart manufacturing. In addition to advanced production processes, decreased ecological impact of per-part production, and improved assembling process proficiency, it offers continuous information on the location and state of assets, as shown in Figure 20.3.

In total, the Internet of Things' (Iot's) arrangement in brilliant plants might upgrade item quality by giving production line administrators constant experiences into the assembling system, considering examination and remedial activity in quality assessment and adjustment of fabricated parts as shown in Figure 20.4.

20.4 CONTROLLING THE PRODUCTION PROCESSES

Smart plant tasks depend mostly on IoT-empowered production processes working on improving product quality. Making better use of information gathered from IoT devices and sensors, manufacturing businesses may boost their productivity and profit. Key performance indicators (KPIs) such as production yield, machine usage, and product quality provide real-time data.

Factory managers can promptly address any difficulties that arise in the manufacturing process when they have access to real-time data from KPIs. Production lines, machinery, equipment, and inventories are some of the areas that may benefit from the monitoring and control capabilities of IoT-enabled devices and sensors in the manufacturing process. To guarantee that products are made well, sensors may monitor the factory's temperature, humidity, and other environmental factors. Online condition monitoring of the component manufacturing process is another use for these sensors. Data may be acquired in real-time by linking devices, sensors, and machines to a network, leading to a more streamlined and effective manufacturing procedure (Rani & Bhambri et al., 2023).

Also, IoT sensors can monitor the supply chain for optimal component manufacture and monitoring stock levels. They can track the progression of products through the assembling and store network, revealing helpful information such as stock levels, shipment dates, and more (Manavalan & Jayakrishna, 2019). This method may be used to improve industrial output productivity in terms of parts inventory management. For factories, IoT monitoring and optimization

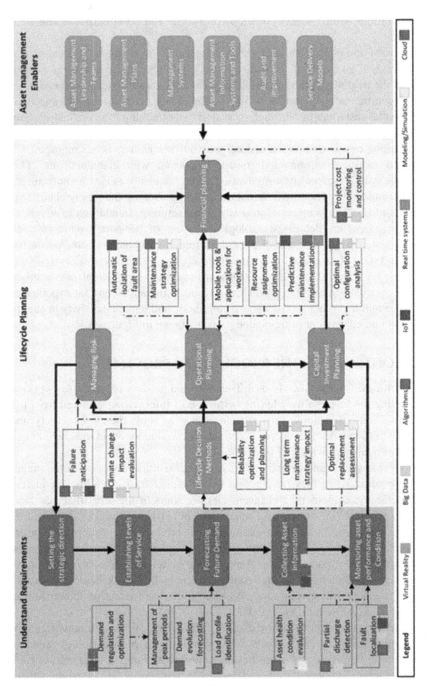

FIGURE 20.3 Asset tracking software and its many areas of application.

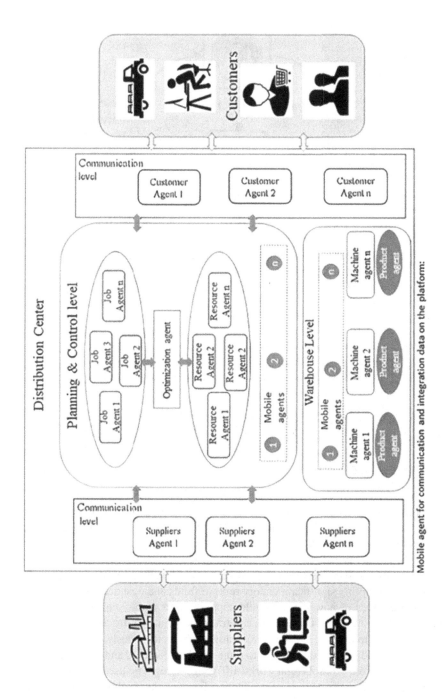

FIGURE 20.4 Inventory management with real-time updates and flexible planning.

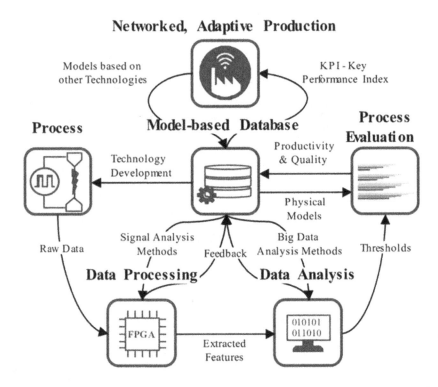

FIGURE 20.5 An IoT-based process checking system in the context of Industry 4.0.

means increased productivity, tighter quality management, and reduced over-head, as shown in Figure 20.5.

20.5 ENERGY EFFICIENCY

Through the use of IoT devices, factories can track their overall energy use and pin-point problem areas. The factory's carbon footprint and operational expenses may both decrease as a result. Devices connected to the IoT can track production energy use in real time and pinpoint sources of waste. The procedure may be used to lessen the burden on the environment and the wallet during the manufacturing of compo-nents. The IoT considers ongoing checking and enhancement of energy use in smart enterprises, prompting significant energy reserve funds and cost decreases.

A few instances of how the IoT could support smart plants' energy proficiency are discussed below. First, IoT sensors can track the plant's entire energy use, from assembling lines to lighting and warming frameworks, continuously. This data might be utilized for additional examination to pinpoint shortcomings and advance cycles. Second, in robotized control frameworks, IoT gadgets might be used to computerize energy use across an assortment of production frameworks. Lighting and warming frameworks, for example, might be customized to answer changes in temperature (Rani & Chauhan et al., 2023).

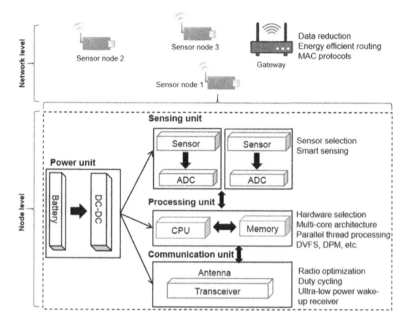

FIGURE 20.6   Smart manufacturing in Industry 4.0 needs energy-efficient wireless sensor networks.

Utilizing IoT, smart production lines might incorporate sustainable power sources such as sun or wind. In addition, the technique may aid in the control of energy usage throughout the manufacturing process, hence decreasing energy expenditures and dependency on fossil fuels. In smart lighting, IoT gadgets can manage factory lights, which may be dimmed in response to the quantity of available natural light, turned off in empty areas, or changed to better suit the activities taking place in a given space.

In heating, ventilation and air conditioning (HVAC) systems, IoT gadgets might be used to screen and improve central air frameworks, for example by adjusting the temperature when a room is empty.

Reducing power consumption in wireless sensor networks in smart manufacturing facilities may decrease carbon footprint, increase productivity, and save money, as shown in Figure 20.6.

20.6   SAFETY MONITORING

Using IoT devices, employers may check if their employees are following safety procedures and immediately identify any dangers. Predictive maintenance of machine and gear is an illustration of IoT-empowered production process checking. Information gathered from sensors on machines and hardware might uncover indications of wear that could prompt a breakdown in the part-producing process. Factory managers may benefit from a more precise maintenance plan thanks to data gleaned from safety monitoring systems, which in turn helps them cut down on downtime and avoid expensive production delays, as shown in Figure 20.7.

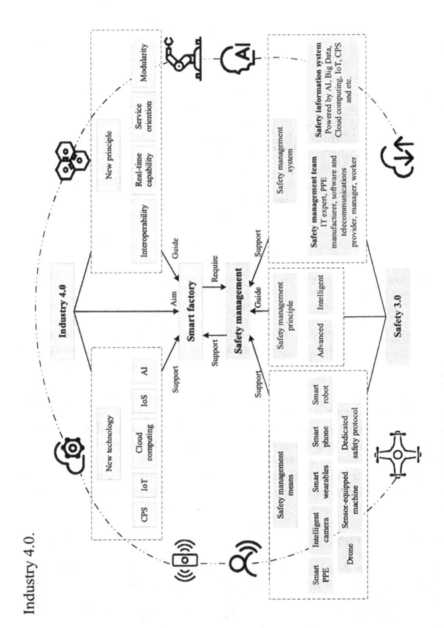

FIGURE 20.7 Combining safety monitoring with Industry 4.0.

Here are a few examples of how IoT might improve factory safety monitoring:

- Observation in Real-Time: Temperature and humidity are only a few variables that might be monitored continuously through IoT. Real-time analysis of this data may help identify risks and provide warnings to employees before an accident happens.
- Predictive Maintenance: With the use of IoT, we can foresee when machines will break down and do preventative maintenance to prevent unsafe situations from occurring.
- Smart Notifications: High concentrations of dangerous gases or unexpected temperature spikes are two examples of situations in which IoT might automatically send out warnings.
- Accessory Electronics: Wearable gadgets enabled by IoT may monitor employees' vitals and notify managers when an employee is feeling stress or weariness.
- Analysis of Risk: IoT data analysis may assist industrial managers discover and address safety issues before they become catastrophic.

20.7   OPTIMIZATION OF THE SUPPLY CHAIN

Use of IoT in supply chain networks and smart production lines leads to increased efficiency. Smart IoT applications include using RFID tags to collect precise information from components and finished goods. Products or other materials may be tagged and their location monitored in real-time (Barari et al., 2021).

Supply chain managers can then optimize stock levels and guarantee timely product delivery thanks to this method of inventory tracking, in addition to predictive maintenance (Cimini et al., 2019). Supply chain logistics may also be improved with the use of IoT, which may be used to monitor deliveries in real-time, giving producers precise data on where their goods are and how they are doing in transit, as shown in Figure 20.8.

Manufacturers may optimize their supply chain and decrease production delays leading to higher productivity and happier customers. Devices connected to the IoT may track the distribution of goods and services, and managers may use this information to streamline logistics, save inventory costs, and speed up shipping times (Oh & Jeong, 2019). To expand store network tasks and increase production effectiveness, manufacturers might profit from IoT-empowered gadgets that give constant information on the location and status of unrefined components and completed items (Ivanov et al., 2018).

Expanded effectiveness, lower costs, increased production, and an overall better production network are some of the various benefits of using IoT in smart processing plants. An ever-increasing number of novel uses of IoT in production networks is expected with future advancement of smart processing plants.

20.8   CONCLUSION

Continuous information is at the core of the smart production line, which expects to reduce waste, augment yield, and decrease any adverse effect on the environment. In order to expand the proficiency with which parts are made, smart manufacturing

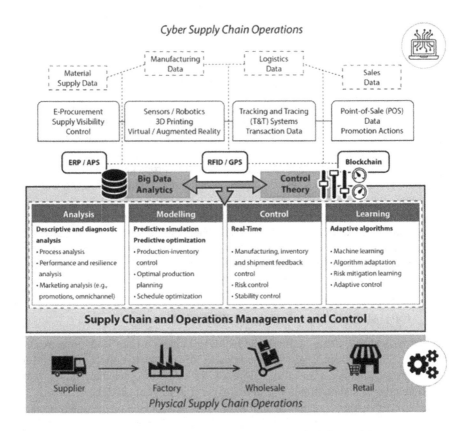

FIGURE 20.8 Digital supply chain and operations control in Industry 4.0.

plants benefit incredibly from IoT-integrated technology. The WoT can possibly modify the modern area by increasing effectiveness, diminishing expenses, and delivery better results. When stock levels get below a desired level, IoT devices may automatically place new orders, eliminating the need for human interaction and guaranteeing that stock is never depleted. Smart factories may increase throughput, productivity, and safety while decreasing waste and downtime in the production of individual components via the networking of machines, devices, and sensors.

With the use of IoT, factory managers can monitor inventory along the way to the consumer. The method may be used to improve supply chain efficiency and cut down on waiting times. The potential of this technology extends well beyond the realm of smart industries. Using IoT sensors, the temperature, humidity, and air quality in a plant may be constantly monitored to ensure employee health and safety. In addition, IoT sensors may be installed on stock goods and strategically distributed throughout the plant to monitor their location and activity. This eliminates the possibility of a product becoming lost or misplaced, since supervisors always know where everything is. Also, IoT sensors can monitor inventories in real-time, allowing factories to better plan for supplies and prevent shortages.

The method may help keep factories stocked with the raw materials they require to keep up with consumer demand and cut down on production delays. Therefore, stockouts and overstocking in the component manufacturing process may be mitigated by optimized inventory levels. With the information gleaned from IoT sensors, manufacturing facility managers can anticipate which products will soon run out of stock and order more in advance (Khang, 2023).

Sensors connected to the IoT may track environmental factors like temperature and humidity to guarantee that stock is kept in ideal conditions. If quality criteria are not satisfied during component manufacture, IoT devices may provide alarms and stop production in real-time. Managers at the plant may then act swiftly to fix the problem and ensure that no flawed goods leave the facility. Machines with IoT connectivity may also be used to automate industrial procedures, which cuts down on wasteful human labor and boosts output. The IoT is revolutionizing smart factory inventory management by streamlining operations and increasing transparency via the provision of real-time data (Khang & Abdullayev et al., 2023).

The use of these technologies allows companies to enhance inventory management practices, cut down on material waste, and boost efficiency in the production of individual parts. The IoT will dramatically alter how automated production facilities function. Factory efficiency may be increased, operations can be optimized, and information can be gathered continuously all due to IoT-empowered gear. Many aspects of IoT in smart industries, however, still need further investigation (Khang & Shah et al., 2023).

REFERENCES

Aceto, G., V. Persico, A. Pescape, Industry 4.0 and health: Internet of things, big data, and cloud computing for healthcare 4.0, J. Ind. Inf. Integr. 18 (2020) 100129. https://www.sciencedirect.com/science/article/pii/S2452414X19300135

Arden, N.S., A.C. Fisher, K. Tyner, X.Y. Lawrence, S.L. Lee, M. Kopcha, Industry 4.0 for pharmaceutical manufacturing: Preparing for the smart factories of the future, Int. J. Pharm. 602 (2021). http://dx.doi.org/10.1109/IVIT55443.2022.10033386

Ashima, R., A. Haleem, S. Bahl, M. Javaid, S.K. Mahla, S. Singh, Automation and manufacturing of smart materials in Additive Manufacturing technologies using Internet of Things towards the adoption of Industry 4.0, Mater. Today: Proc. 45 (2021) 5081–5088. https://www.sciencedirect.com/science/article/pii/S2214785321006751

Barari, A., M. de Sales Guerra Tsuzuki, Y. Cohen, M. Macchi, Intelligent manufacturing systems towards industry 4.0 era, J. Intell. Manuf. 32 (2021) 1793–1796. https://link.springer.com/article/10.1007/s10845-021-01769-0

Bhambri, P., S. Rani, G. Gupta, A. Khang, *Cloud and Fog Computing Platforms for Internet of Things*. (2022). CRC Press. https://doi.org/10.1201/9781003213888

Chen, B., J. Wan, L. Shu, P. Li, M. Mukherjee, B. Yin, Smart factory of industry 4.0: Key technologies, application case, and challenges, IEEE Access 6 (2017) 6505–6519. https://ieeexplore.ieee.org/abstract/document/8207346/

Cimini, C., G. Pezzotta, R. Pinto, S. Cavalieri, Industry 4.0 technologies impacts in the manufacturing And supply chain landscape: An overview, Service Orientation in Holonic and Multi-Agent Manufacturing, Proc. SOHOMA 2018 (2019) 109–120. https://link.springer.com/chapter/10.1007/978-3-030-03003-2_8

Da Silva, V.L., J.L. Kovaleski, R.N. Pagani, J.D.M. Silva, A. Corsi, Implementation of industry 4.0 concept in companies: Empirical evidences, Int. J. Comput. Integrated Manuf. 33 (2020) 325–342. https://www.tandfonline.com/doi/abs/10.1080/0951192X.2019.1699258

Dalzochio, J., R. Kunst, E. Pignaton, A. Binotto, S. Sanyal, J. Favilla, J. Barbosa, Machine learning and reasoning for predictive maintenance in Industry 4.0: Current status and challenges, Comput. Ind. 123 (2020) 103298. https://www.sciencedirect.com/science/article/pii/S0166361520305327

Durana, P., N. Perkins, K. Valaskova, Artificial intelligence data-driven internet of things systems, real-time advanced analytics, and cyber-physical production networks in sustainable smart manufacturing, Econ. Manag. Financ. Mark. 16 (2021) 20–30. https://www.ceeol.com/search/article-detail?id=939239

Elsisi, M., M. Altius, S.-F. Su, C.-L. Su, Robust kalman filter for position estimation of automated guided vehicles under cyberattacks, IEEE Trans. Instrum. Meas. 72 (2023) 1–12. https://ieeexplore.ieee.org/abstract/document/10056247/

Elsisi, M., M.-Q. Tran, Development of an IoT architecture based on a deep neural network against cyber-attacks for automated guided vehicles, Sensors 21 (2021) 8467. https://www.mdpi.com/1424-8220/21/24/8467

Fernandez-Carames, T.M., P. Fraga-Lamas, A review on the application of blockchain to the next generation of cybersecure industry 4.0 smart factories, IEEE Access 7 (2019) 45201–45218. https://ieeexplore.ieee.org/abstract/document/8678753/

Garrido-Hidalgo, C., T. Olivares, F.J. Ramirez, L. Roda-Sanchez, An end-to-end internet of things solution for reverse supply chain management in industry 4.0, Comput. Ind. 112 (2019) 103127. https://www.sciencedirect.com/science/article/pii/S0166361519301915

Grabowska, S., Smart factories in the age of Industry 4.0, Manag. Syst. Prod. Eng. 28 (2020) 90–96. https://sciendo.com/article/10.2478/mspe-2020-0014

Gupta, P., C. Krishna, R. Rajesh, A. Ananthakrishnan, A. Vishnuvardhan, S.S. Patel, C. Kapruan, S. Brahmbhatt, T. Kataray, D. Narayanan, Industrial internet of things in intelligent manufacturing: A review, approaches, opportunities, open challenges, and future directions, Int. J. Interact. Des. Manuf. (2022) 1–23. https://link.springer.com/article/10.1007/s12008-022-01075-w

Ivanov, D., S. Sethi, A. Dolgui, B. Sokolov, A survey on control theory applications to operational systems, supply chain management, and Industry 4.0, Annu. Rev. Control 46 (2018) 134–147. https://www.sciencedirect.com/science/article/pii/S1367578818301238

Kalsoom, T., N. Ramzan, S. Ahmed, M. Ur-Rehman, Advances in sensor technologies in the era of smart factory and industry 4.0, Sensors 20 (2020) 6783. https://www.mdpi.com/1424-8220/20/23/6783

Kamble, S.S., A. Gunasekaran, A. Ghadge, R. Raut, A performance measurement system for industry 4.0 enabled smart manufacturing system in SMMEs - A review and empirical investigation, Int. J. Prod. Econ. 229 (2020) 107853. https://www.sciencedirect.com/science/article/pii/S0925527320302176

Khang, A., *AI and IoT-Based Technologies for Precision Medicine.* (1st Ed.) (2023). ISBN: 9798369308769. IGI Global Press. https://doi.org/10.4018/979-8-3693-0876-9

Khang, A., V. Abdullayev, A.V. Alyar, M. Khalilov, B. Murad, AI-Aided Data Analytics Tools and Applications for the Healthcare Sector, *AI and IoT-Based Technologies for Precision Medicine.* (1st Ed.) (2023). ISBN: 9798369308769. IGI Global Press. https://doi.org/10.4018/979-8-3693-0876-9.ch018

Khang, A., S.K. Gupta, S. Rani, D.A. Karras, *Smart Cities: IoT Technologies, Big Data Solutions, Cloud Platforms, and Cybersecurity Techniques.* (1st Ed.) (2023). CRC Press. https://doi.org/10.1201/9781003376064

Khang, A., V. Hahanov, G.L. Abbas, V.A. Hajimahmud, "Cyber-Physical-Social System and Incident Management," *AI-Centric Smart City Ecosystems: Technologies, Design and Implementation.* (1st Ed.) (2022). CRC Press. https://doi.org/10.1201/9781003252542-2

Khang, A., V.A. Hajimahmud, H. Vladimir, V. Shah, *Advanced IoT Technologies and Applications in the Industry 4.0 Digital Economy*. (1st Ed.) (2024). CRC Press. https://doi.org/10.1201/9781003434269

Khang, A., K.C. Rath, S. Kumar Satapathy, A. Kumar, S. Ranjan Das, M. Ranjan Panda. "Enabling the Future of Manufacturing: Integration of Robotics and IoT to Smart Factory Infrastructure in Industry 4.0," *AI-Based Technologies and Applications in the Era of the Metaverse*. (1st Ed.) (2023). Pages (25–50). IGI Global Press. https://doi.org/10.4018/978-1-6684-8851-5.ch002

Khang, A., V. Shah, S. Rani, *AI-Based Technologies and Applications in the Era of the Metaverse*. (1st Ed.) (2023). IGI Global Press. https://doi.org/10.4018/978-1-6684-8851-5

Khanh, H.H., A. Khang, "The Role of Artificial Intelligence in Blockchain Applications," *Reinventing Manufacturing and Business Processes through Artificial Intelligence*, 2 (20–40). (2021). CRC Press. https://doi.org/10.1201/9781003145011-2

Khan, I.H., M. Javaid, Role of internet of things (IoT) in adoption of Industry 4.0, J. Ind. Integr. Manag. 7 (2022) 515–533. https://www.worldscientific.com/doi/abs/10.1142/S2424862221500068

Kovacova, M., E. Lewis, Smart factory performance, cognitive automation, and industrial big data analytics in sustainable manufacturing internet of things, J. Self Govern. Manag. Econ. 9 (2021) 9–20. https://www.ceeol.com/search/article-detail?id=983521

Manavalan, E., K. Jayakrishna, A review of Internet of Things (IoT) embedded sustainable supply chain for industry 4.0 requirements, Comput. Ind. Eng. 127 (2019) 925–953. https://www.sciencedirect.com/science/article/pii/S0360835218305709

Mohamed, N., S.K. Almazrouei, A. Oubelaid, M. Elsisi, B.M. El Halawany, S.S. Ghoneim, Air-gapped networks: Exfiltration without privilege escalation for military and police units, Wireless Commun. Mobile Comput. 22 (2022) 1–11. https://www.hindawi.com/journals/wcmc/2022/4697494/

Nica, E., V. Stehel, Internet of things sensing networks, artificial intelligence-based decision-making algorithms, and real-time process monitoring in sustainable industry 4.0, J. Self Govern. Manag. Econ. 9 (2021) 35–47. https://www.ceeol.com/search/article-detail?id=983524

Oh, J., B. Jeong, Tactical supply planning in smart manufacturing supply chain, Robot. Comput. Integrated Manuf. 55 (2019) 217–233. https://www.sciencedirect.com/science/article/pii/S0736584517301266

Patel, P., M.I. Ali, A. Sheth, From raw data to smart manufacturing: AI and semantic web of things for industry 4.0, IEEE Intell. Syst. 33 (2018) 79–86. https://ieeexplore.ieee.org/abstract/document/8497012/

Rani, S., P. Bhambri, A. Kataria, A. Khang, A.K. Sivaraman, *Big Data, Cloud Computing and IoT: Tools and Applications* (1st Ed.) (2023). Chapman & Hall/CRC. https://doi.org/10.1201/9781003298335

Rani, S., M. Chauhan, A. Kataria, A. Khang. IoT Equipped Intelligent Distributed Framework for Smart Healthcare Systems. (2023). In: Rishiwal, V., Kumar, P., Tomar, A., Malarvizhi Kumar, P. (eds) *Towards the Integration of IoT, Cloud and Big Data. Studies in Big Data*, vol 137. Springer, Singapore. https://doi.org/10.1007/978-981-99-6034-7_6

Ryalat, M., H. El Moaqet, M. Al Faouri, Design of a smart factory based on cyberphysical systems and internet of things towards industry 4.0, Appl. Sci. 13 (2023) 2156. https://www.mdpi.com/2076-3417/13/4/2156

Sakkarvarthi, G., G.W. Sathianesan, V.S. Murugan, A.J. Reddy, P. Jayagopal, M. Elsisi, Detection and classification of tomato crop disease using convolutional neural network, Electronics 11 (2022) 3618. https://www.mdpi.com/2079-9292/11/21/3618

Soori, M., B. Arezoo, Dimensional, geometrical, thermal and tool deflection errors compensation in 5-axis CNC milling operations, Aust. J. Mech. Eng. (2023) 1–15. https://www.tandfonline.com/doi/abs/10.1080/14484846.2023.2195149

Soori, M., B. Arezoo, M. Habibi, Tool deflection error of three-axis computer numerical control milling machines, monitoring and minimizing by a virtual machining system, J. Manuf. Sci. Eng. 138 (2016). https://asmedigitalcollection.asme.org/manufacturingscience/article-abstract/138/8/081005/376223

Soori, M., B. Arezoo, M. Habibi, Accuracy analysis of tool deflection error modelling in prediction of milled surfaces by a virtual machining system, Int. J. Comput. Appl. Technol. 55 (2017) 308–320. https://www.inderscienceonline.com/doi/abs/10.1504/IJCAT.2017.086015

Tran, M.Q., M. Amer, A.Y. Abdelaziz, H.-J. Dai, M.-K. Liu, M. Elsisi, Robust fault recognition and correction scheme for induction motors using an effective IoT with deep learning approach, Measurement 207 (2023) 112398. https://www.sciencedirect.com/science/article/pii/S0263224122015950

Tran, M.-Q., M. Elsisi, M.-K. Liu, V.Q. Vu, K. Mahmoud, M.M. Darwish, A.Y. Abdelaziz, M. Lehtonen, Reliable deep learning and IoT-based monitoring system for secure computer numerical control machines against cyber-attacks with experimental verification, IEEE Access 10 (2022) 23186–23197. https://ieeexplore.ieee.org/abstract/document/9718276/

Tucker, G., Sustainable product lifecycle management, industrial big data, and internet of things sensing networks in cyber-physical system-based smart factories, J. Self-Govern. Manag. Econ. 9 (2021) 9–19. https://www.ceeol.com/search/article-detail?id=939801

Vijayaraghavan, V., J.R. Leevinson, Internet of things applications and use cases in the era of industry 4.0, the internet of things in the industrial sector: Security and device connectivity, *Smart Environments, and Industry 4.0* (2019) 279–298. https://link.springer.com/chapter/10.1007/978-3-030-24892-5_12

Wang, S., J. Wan, D. Li, C. Zhang, Implementing smart factory of Industry 4.0: An outlook, Int. J. Distributed Sens. Netw. 12 (2016) 3159805. https://journals.sagepub.com/doi/abs/10.1155/2016/3159805

Witkowski, K., Internet of things, big data, industry 4.0–innovative solutions in logistics and supply chains management, Procedia Eng. 182 (2017) 763–769. https://www.sciencedirect.com/science/article/pii/S1877705817313346

Xu, X., M. Han, S.M. Nagarajan, P. Anandhan, Industrial Internet of Things for smart manufacturing applications using hierarchical trustful resource assignment, Comput. Commun. 160 (2020) 423–430. https://www.sciencedirect.com/science/article/pii/S0140366420306563

Zhong, R.Y., X. Xu, E. Klotz, S.T. Newman, Intelligent manufacturing in the context of industry 4.0: A review, Engineering 3 (2017) 616–630. https://www.sciencedirect.com/science/article/pii/S2095809917307130

21 Revolutionizing Manufacturing

The Impact of Internet of Things Technologies in Smart Factories

Hammad Shahab, Muhammad Mohsin Waqas, and Muthmainnah Muthmainnah

21.1 INTRODUCTION

Smart Internet of Things (IoT)-based factories have revolutionized the manufacturing industry by leveraging cloud computing, a transformative model that has reshaped the way organizations and individuals access and utilize computing resources. By integrating cloud computing with IoT technologies, these factories efficiently connect devices and systems, enabling seamless communication and data exchange. This connectivity facilitates the collection and analysis of vast amounts of data generated by manufacturing processes, empowering factories to enhance productivity and streamline operations. With on-demand access to servers, storage, and applications, smart IoT-based factories optimize resource allocation, drive innovation, and respond effectively to changing market demands. The flexibility and scalability offered by cloud computing enable these factories to adapt quickly, improving efficiency, quality, and overall manufacturing performance (Goswami et al., 2022; Qaisar et al., 2023). The integration of information and communication technology (ICT) in production processes has transformed traditional practices and improved organizational management, as shown in Figure 21.1.

The modern transformations from Industry 1.0 to Industry 5.0 have changed assembling by dynamically expanding proficiency and intricacy. Traditional methods have been transformed as a result of the integration of ICT, which has improved organizational management. Industry 1.0 presented motorization, tackling water and steam ability to supplant physical work and lift efficiency. Industry 2.0 brought large-scale manufacturing through electric power, empowering normalized sequential construction systems and quicker production.

Industry 3.0 saw computerization and robotization, with ICT assuming an essential part in coordinating personal computers and computerized frameworks into assembling processes, upgrading effectiveness and control. Real-time data collection, analysis, and decision-making were made possible by cutting-edge technologies

Industry 1.0	Industry 2.0	Industry 3.0	Industry 4.0	Industry 5.0
mechanization, water and steam powers	mass production, electric power, assembly line	computer automated production, electronics	cyber physical systems, IoT, networking, machine learning	human-robot collaboration, cognitive sytems, customization

FIGURE 21.1 Evolution of smart factories.

like the IoT, cloud computing, and artificial intelligence (AI) thanks to Industry 4.0. This joining of brilliant gadgets, interconnected frameworks, and information-driven experiences fundamentally expanded productivity and intricacy, cultivating more agile and responsive production processes.

Now, Industry 5.0 expands on this foundation by emphasizing human–machine collaboration, combining the strengths of human creativity and problem-solving with the machines' precision and efficacy. These industrial revolutions have shaped the manufacturing landscape, increased efficiency, and propelled the industry forward by integrating ICT (Longo et al., 2020). The development of the future factory also emphasizes human-centered design and ethical considerations. Industry 5.0 is value-oriented and ethical technology engineering. It underscores human prosperity, social impact, and capable innovation use, cultivating a joint effort between humans and trend-setting innovations.

The IoT is all about connecting and sharing information between physical objects like devices and appliances. These objects have sensors, software, and connectivity that help them collect data and exchange it with each other and a central system. With the help of the Internet, they can communicate and work together, making our lives easier and more convenient (Shahab et al., 2020; Shahab et al., 2023). Smart factories utilize IoT technology to optimize various aspects of manufacturing operations.

Sensors, cameras, and drones are deployed in these factories to collect data on factors such as temperature, humidity, machine performance, and product quality. This data is then analyzed by a central computer system, which makes informed decisions on how to enhance production processes and improve overall efficiency. By monitoring and controlling these key variables, smart factories can optimize resource allocation, reduce downtime, and ensure consistent product quality (Brown, 2021). The implementation of IoT in smart factories revolutionizes the manufacturing landscape, enabling precise monitoring and decision-making for enhanced productivity and streamlined operations, as shown in Figure 21.2 (Aheleroff et al., 2020; Shi et al., 2020; Ashima et al., 2021).

The IoT applications span across industries, enabling real-time monitoring, optimization, and personalized solutions in many areas, as shown in Table 21.1 which highlights the key areas where IoT is making a significant impact.

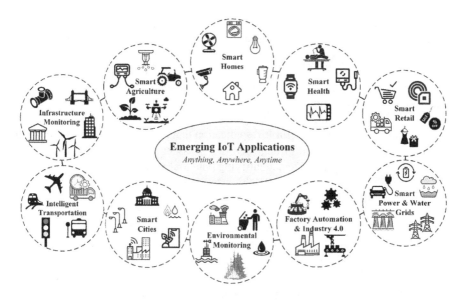

FIGURE 21.2 Application of the Internet of Things in various fields (Swamy & Kota, 2020).

TABLE 21.1

Application of the Internet of Things in Various Industries

Industry	IoT Application
Smart Factories	Real-time monitoring, predictive maintenance, process optimization
Healthcare	Remote patient monitoring, personalized healthcare solutions
Vehicles	Vehicle tracking, diagnostics, autonomous driving capabilities
Retail	Inventory tracking, smart shelves, personalized shopping experiences
Traffic	Traffic pattern monitoring, optimization, real-time updates
Smart Cities	Smart infrastructure, energy management, waste management
Farming	Irrigation management, crop health monitoring, livestock management
Drones	Remote monitoring, data collection, automated tasks
Security	Surveillance, intrusion detection, emergency response
Fitness .	Fitness tracking, vital signs monitoring, personalized fitness plans

Smart IoT-based manufacturing processes have also revolutionized the industry by integrating AI, IoT, and advanced technologies to optimize production practices. Through data analytics, machine learning (ML), and sensor networks, these factories make informed decisions in various aspects, such as resource allocation, quality control, and equipment maintenance.

21.2 ROLE OF IoT IN ENABLING SMART FACTORIES

Internet of Things plays a significant role in empowering smart production lines, changing the assembling business. Data-driven decision-making, seamless connectivity, predictive maintenance, and supply chain optimization are all made possible by it (Fatima et al., 2022). As smart processing plants advance, they now have access to an unparalleled range of tools and services to support their cloud computing needs (Qaisar et al., 2023).

One key aspect of IoT in smart factories is connectivity. It enables devices and systems to communicate and share information, creating a network of interconnected components. With IoT, machines, sensors, and other equipment can work together, enhancing overall operational efficiency (Dolci, 2017). In smart factories, predictive maintenance is yet another useful IoT application that allows continuous monitoring of machinery and equipment through sensors. It assists in predicting when maintenance or repairs are required and identifying potential issues. By minimizing downtime and avoiding costly breakdowns, this strategy ensures uninterrupted production processes (Gupta et al., 2021).

Consolidating IoT advancements in assembling brings a few benefits. First, it makes it possible to control and monitor production processes in real-time, allowing businesses to quickly spot problems and make necessary adjustments. Second, predictive maintenance performed by IoT sensors aids in preventing equipment failures, thereby reducing downtime and costs associated with maintenance (Khang & Misra et al., 2023). Third, IoT improves logistics and inventory management visibility throughout the supply chain. Fourth, IoT-powered data analytics and ML make it possible to make decisions based on data, which improves productivity and optimizes processes. In conclusion, IoT technologies enhance manufacturing resource utilization, quality control, and operational efficiency (Ganesh Babu et al., 2021).

Real-time data collection and exchange are now possible in factories thanks to the integration of IoT devices, sensors, and connectivity. Systems, machines, and devices can communicate and work together seamlessly. Therefore, manufacturing plants become more effective, responsive, and versatile. Process automation, remote control and monitoring, and production operations optimization are all made possible by the transformation. A smart factory's intelligent and connected ecosystem boosts productivity, quality, and competitiveness.

There are numerous advantages of using IoT devices like radio frequency identification (RFID) readers and tags in smart factories. During production processes, smart manufacturing objects (SMOs) can seamlessly interact and communicate with one another due to visibility and traceability in real-time. A 3D real-time visualization model that improves visibility and traceability can be created by using a laser scanner to capture SMO movements. Small and medium-sized (SME) businesses looking to upgrade their manufacturing facilities will find a cost-effective solution in these advancements, which guide production decisions and optimize operations, as shown in Figure 21.3.

Additionally, the usage of cloud-based answers for information advancement in smart plants offers a few advantages. The cloud gives adaptable capacity and handling abilities, taking into consideration the proficient administration and investigation of enormous volumes of assembling information. This enables real-time insights and predictive analytics, which results in enhanced operational efficiency, predictive maintenance, and improved decision-making. The cloud also facilitates seamless data sharing and stakeholder collaboration, which encourages creativity and moves manufacturing processes forward.

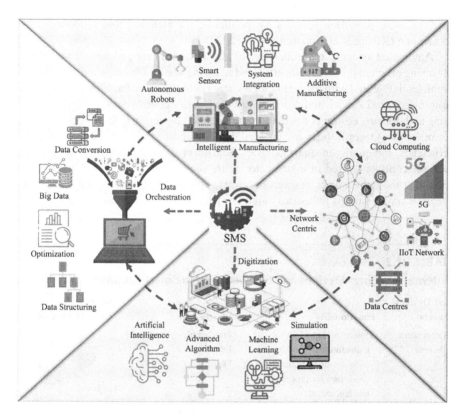

FIGURE 21.3 The application of the Internet of Things in smart factories (Sharma & Villányi, 2022).

21.3 INTERNET OF THINGS DEVICES AND SENSORS IN SMART FACTORIES

Internet of Things devices and sensors play a critical role in the operation of smart factories. These gadgets are implanted in machines, hardware, and items, empowering information assortment, correspondence, and robotization. These IoT devices facilitate connectivity and data exchange within the factory ecosystem, while sensors monitor parameters like temperature, humidity, pressure, and machine performance. They aid in process optimization, predictive maintenance, and improved decision-making by providing real-time data (Santhosh et al., 2020).

Starting from the supply chain, IoT-enabled devices track and monitor the movement of raw materials and components, ensuring timely delivery and efficient inventory management. In the production stage, sensors collect data on machine performance, energy consumption, and product quality, enabling real-time monitoring and control. Finally, in the post-production phase, IoT devices facilitate quality control, track product shipments, and enable customer feedback and data analysis for continuous improvement. There are numerous examples of IoT-enabled devices in smart factories. For instance, connected sensors monitor machine health and performance, providing insights for predictive maintenance and reducing costly downtime (Khang & Hajimahmud et al., 2023).

Automated systems, controlled by IoT devices, optimize production workflows, ensuring efficient resource allocation and reducing waste. Robotics and autonomous vehicles, integrated with IoT technologies, streamline material handling and logistics, improving productivity and reducing errors. Quality control devices, such as cameras and sensors, ensure consistent product quality, detecting defects and deviations in real-time. Overall, these IoT-enabled devices significantly enhance productivity, efficiency, and quality in smart factories (Sharma et al., 2023). Some IoT devices and sensors commonly used in smart factories are shown in Table 21.2. It's important to note that the industry applications may vary, and different devices and sensors can be used across various industries based on specific needs and requirements.

TABLE 21.2

Internet of Things Devices and Sensors Used in Smart Factories

IoT Devices/ Sensors	Functionality	Industry Area	Image of IoT Devices/Sensors
Temperature Sensors	Monitor and regulate temperature in production areas, ensuring optimal conditions for processes and equipment.	Manufacturing, Food and Beverage, Pharmaceuticals	
Pressure Sensors	Measure and control pressure levels in machinery, allowing for real-time monitoring and preventing overpressure situations.	Manufacturing, Oil and Gas, Chemical	
Proximity Sensors	Detect the presence or absence of objects, facilitating automated processes such as conveyor belt control and inventory management.	Manufacturing, Logistics, Warehousing	
Flow Sensors	Monitor and regulate fluid flow rates, ensuring precise control over liquid or gas distribution in manufacturing processes.	Manufacturing, Energy, Water Treatment	

(Continued)

TABLE 21.2 *(Continued)*

Internet of Things Devices and Sensors Used in Smart Factories

IoT Devices/ Sensors	Functionality	Industry Area	Image of IoT Devices/Sensors
Vibration Sensors	Detect and analyze vibrations in equipment to identify abnormalities, enabling predictive maintenance and preventing failures.	Manufacturing, Automotive, Aerospace	
Motion Sensors	Detect motion in specific areas, triggering actions like equipment activation or automated lighting control.	Manufacturing, Warehousing, Security	
Humidity Sensors	Monitor and control humidity levels in production environments, ensuring optimal conditions for sensitive processes or materials.	Manufacturing, Electronics, Agriculture	
Gas Sensors	Detect the presence and measure the concentration of gases, enabling the early detection of leaks or hazardous situations.	Manufacturing, Chemical, Oil and Gas	
Light Sensors	Measure and adjust ambient lighting levels, optimizing energy consumption and providing suitable lighting conditions.	Manufacturing, Warehousing, Energy	
Image Recognition Cameras	Capture visual data for quality control, object identification, and monitoring purposes, enhancing product inspection and security.	Manufacturing, Automotive, Packaging	

21.4   REAL-TIME DATA COLLECTION AND MONITORING IN SMART FACTORIES

Real-time data collection and monitoring in smart factories enables continuous and precise insights into production procedures. Data on machine performance, energy consumption, product quality, and other important parameters are collected in real-time by integrating IoT devices and sensors. This information is then analyzed and used in proactive navigation, predictive maintenance, and cycle streamlining. Smart factories can boost productivity, increase efficiency, and guarantee the smooth operation of manufacturing processes by collecting and monitoring data in real-time (Soori et al., 2023).

Table 21.3 provides an overview of real-time data collection and monitoring in smart factories.

Smart factories' success relies heavily on real-time data collection and analysis. These factories gain valuable insights by capturing and analyzing data in real-time, allowing them to make informed decisions and implement improvements throughout their operations. The capacity to provide immediate visibility into the performance of machines, energy consumption levels, and product quality parameters is what makes real-time data collection so significant. Manufacturers are able to quickly identify bottlenecks, identify anomalies, and adjust optimize their processes with this timely information (Javaid et al., 2022).

Information gathering and observing frameworks through IoT structure the foundation of continuous information assortment in smart plants. Manufacturers can create a comprehensive network of interconnected devices by deploying IoT devices and sensors at various points in their production lines. These gadgets persistently catch and communicate basic information, like temperature, tension, vibration, and quality measurements, to concentrated frameworks. The factory is able to keep a holistic view of its operations due to this real-time data collection, which makes it easier to make proactive decisions and act quickly to fix problems as they arise.

In smart factories, process optimization and predictive maintenance require making use of data analytics. Manufacturers can gain useful insights from the vast amounts of data they collect by making use of cutting-edge analytics methods like AI and ML. With the help of data analytics, patterns, trends, and correlations that would otherwise be difficult to spot can now be found. These experiences can be used to advance production processes, smooth out work processes, and distinguish potential open doors for productivity gains.

Additionally, data analytics enhance predictive maintenance. Manufacturers are able to spot early warning signs of potential failures or performance degradation by analyzing real-time data from machines and equipment. This proactive methodology considers opportune predictive maintenance, lessening spontaneous downtime, and streamlining maintenance plans. Not only does predictive maintenance increase productivity, but it also extends the life of assets, saving money and increasing overall operational efficiency.

A control system architecture that combines hardware and software components to monitor and control industrial processes and operations is referred to as a supervisory control and data acquisition system (SCADA). It gives operators real-time

TABLE 21.3

Real-time Data Collection and Monitoring in Smart Factories

Category	Description	Importance	Real Examples in the Market
Real-Time Data Collection	IoT Sensors: Capture real-time data on machine performance, energy consumption, and product quality	Enables immediate insights	Temperature sensors, vibration sensors, quality sensors
	IoT Gateways: Enable seamless connectivity and data transmission between IoT devices and cloud-based systems	Facilitates real-time monitoring and control	Dell Edge Gateway, Cisco Industrial IoT Gateway, Advantech IoT Gateway
Data Monitoring	SCADA (Supervisory Control and Data Acquisition): Monitor and visualize real-time data from manufacturing processes	Provides real-time visibility	Ignition, Wonderware, Siemens WinCC
	MES (Manufacturing Execution System): Track and monitor manufacturing operations in real-time	Ensures operational efficiency	Rockwell Automation FactoryTalk, SAP Manufacturing Execution, Plex
Predictive Maintenance	Predictive Maintenance Software: Utilize real-time data and analytics for predictive maintenance and equipment optimization	Reduces unplanned downtime	IBM Predictive Maintenance and Quality, SAS Predictive Maintenance, Falkonry
Data Analytics	IoT Platforms: Collect, analyze, and visualize real-time data for enhanced decision-making	Enables data-driven insights	AWS IoT, Microsoft Azure IoT, Google Cloud IoT
	Edge Analytics Software: Perform data processing and analysis at the edge for immediate insights	Enables real-time decision-making	AWS IoT Greengrass, Azure IoT Edge, Google Cloud IoT Edge
Visualization	Dashboard Visualization Tools: Create real-time dashboards for easy monitoring and visualization of data	Enhances data understanding	Grafana, Power BI, Tableau
Connectivity	Edge Gateways: Enable seamless connectivity between IoT devices and cloud-based systems	Facilitates data transmission and connectivity	Dell Edge Gateway, Cisco Industrial IoT Gateway, Advantech IoT Gateway

remote monitoring, supervision, and interaction with a variety of devices, sensors, and equipment. A central host computer or server, human–machine interface (HMI) software, communication infrastructure, and field devices like sensors, actuators, and programmable logic controllers (PLCs) are typically the components of SCADA systems.

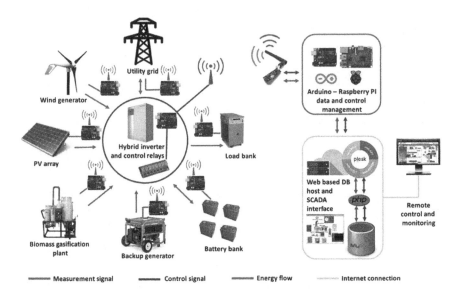

FIGURE 21.4 An IoT-based supervisory control and data acquisition (SCADA) system (Vargas-Salgado et al., 2019).

Smart factories also benefit from the use of SCADA systems that are based on IoT. In smart industries, IoT-based SCADA allows for ongoing observation and control of different assembling processes, bringing about high functional proficiency, diminished margin time, and upgraded efficiency. It enables proactive decision-making, predictive maintenance, and optimal resource allocation by making data collection and analysis from IoT devices and sensors easier, as shown in Figure 21.4.

In the energy area, IoT-based SCADA plays an important role in overseeing and observing complex energy frameworks, such as power matrices, sustainable power age, and dissemination organizations. Operators can monitor energy production, consumption, and distribution with real-time data acquisition and analysis capability, thereby optimizing energy use and grid performance.

SCADA frameworks can accumulate information from IoT gadgets such as brilliant meters and sensors, empowering request reaction systems, and energy proficiency enhancements. By allowing for prompt response and mitigation measures as well as early detection of anomalies, IoT-based SCADA also improves an energy system's overall security and reliability (Vargas-Salgado et al., 2019; Aqeel et al., 2023).

21.5 INTERNET OF THINGS-BASED SUPPLY CHAIN MANAGEMENT AND LOGISTICS

Supply chain management and logistics based on IoT enable data-driven decision-making and optimization. Organizations can gain real-time insight into their inventory, transportation, and distribution processes by incorporating IoT devices and sensors into various stages of the supply chain, as shown in Figure 21.5.

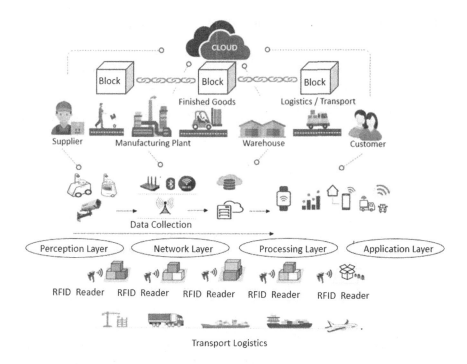

FIGURE 21.5 Manufacturing efficiency and traceability through IoT-based supply chain management and logistics (Pal et al., 2021).

Products are accurately and automatically tracked by IoT devices, such as RFID tags and GPS trackers, which provide real-time information on their location and status. By providing precise inventory data, reducing stockouts, and enhancing demand forecasting, this improves inventory management. Organizations can proactively manage their inventory levels, enhance replenishment procedures, and guarantee the effective allocation of resources with real-time visibility.

The quality, environmental condition, and location of goods during transportation and storage are monitored by IoT-enabled sensors. These sensors, which are able to measure things like temperature and humidity, can ensure that products are kept in the best possible condition and will not get damaged or spoil (Revanth, 2021). The quality and integrity of the goods are safeguarded by real-time monitoring, which enables prompt alerts and proactive responses to any deviations from the desired conditions. It also empowers information-driven independent direction and enhancement.

Advanced analytics and ML methods can be used to analyze the vast amount of real-time data gathered from IoT sensors and devices. This enables businesses to gain valuable insights into the performance of their supply chains, locate bottlenecks and inefficiencies, and make well-informed decisions regarding the improvement of processes. By ensuring timely and accurate deliveries, businesses can increase customer satisfaction, reduce costs, and improve operational efficiency using this data-driven strategy (Thekkoote, 2022).

By staying updated and leveraging technical field knowledge sharing in IoT-enabled supply chain management and logistics, project managers can enhance their effectiveness and drive success in ensuring seamless tracking and monitoring of goods across the entire supply chain (Nawaz et al., 2020). By providing end-to-end visibility, automation, and data-driven optimization in the complex and dynamic supply chain ecosystem, IoT-enabled supply chain management and logistics gives businesses the ability to improve customer service, streamline operations, and gain a competitive advantage in the global market.

21.6 CASE STUDIES OF INTERNET OF THINGS IN MANUFACTURING

The implementation of IoT technology in manufacturing has revolutionized the industry, driving efficiency, productivity, and cost savings. Below are four case studies that highlight successful use of IoT in different areas of manufacturing.

21.6.1 IoT-Enabled Asset Tracking and Optimization in a Smart Factory

For this case study, a smart processing plant conveyed IoT-empowered resource following to further develop tracking and streamline resource use. The plant gained real-time insights into the location, status, and usage of its assets by equipping them with IoT devices and sensors. This empowered effective designation of assets, diminished resource downtime, and improved efficiency.

In addition, data analytics provided useful insights into asset performance and maintenance requirements, facilitating improved decision-making and overall operational efficiency (Khang et al., 2023).

Krishnan & Mendoza Santos (2021) present a system which provides an in-depth analysis of the significance of real-time asset tracking in the manufacturing sector, particularly in the context of smart factories, as shown in Figure 21.6. The

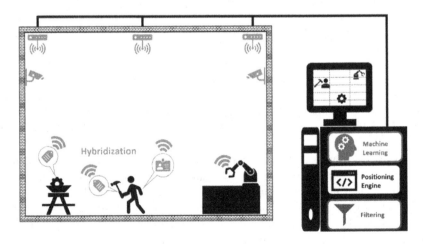

FIGURE 21.6 Real-time asset tracking in smart manufacturing (Krishnan & Mendoza Santos, 2021).

comprehensive discussion of the various technologies and methods for real-time asset tracking gives readers a clear understanding of their options. In addition, they provide useful insights into hardware and software solutions for overcoming the practical difficulties associated with implementing a real-time asset tracking system.

The authors discuss cutting-edge research on a real-time location system (RTLS) for manufacturing, which gives readers a glimpse into the anticipated future developments in the field. They effectively convey the significance of real-time asset tracking in smart manufacturing and provide useful information regarding the techniques, issues, and potential solutions that are currently available.

21.6.2 IoT-Based Quality Control and Defect Detection in Manufacturing Processes

In this case study, a manufacturing company implemented real-time quality control measures by using IoT sensors and vision systems. The sensors observed different parameters during production, guaranteeing consistence with quality standards and recognizing deformities or deviations. Product quality was improved, waste was reduced, and customer satisfaction was raised as a result. An illustration of an IoT-based die-casting system is shown in Figure 21.7.

The study examines how casting parameters affect product quality using data from the IoT system. Korea's die-casting industry, which is primarily made up of SME businesses, has been reluctant to implement smart factory technologies due to financial constraints. In order to encourage the implementation of smart factories, the Korean government is assisting these businesses. However, in order for smart factories to be effective, real-time monitoring is required, and the data that is collected is frequently not utilized.

Consequently, a suitable data analysis and application system for the die-casting environment must be developed. For the purpose of this study, an IoT-based smart

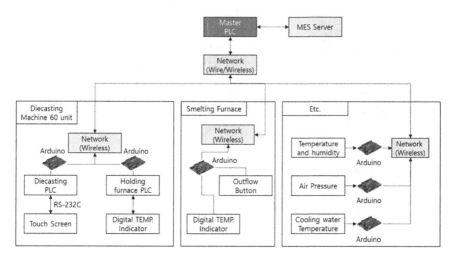

FIGURE 21.7   Die-casting system in a smart factory based on the Internet of Things (Park et al., 2019).

factory was constructed to provide analysis data. To find a connection between the parameters and production quality, data mining techniques were specifically applied to the casting parameter data. The findings of this study are anticipated to be beneficial for the die-casting industry's systematic implementation of smart factories and the creation of a casting parameter management strategy. Algorithms that help identify the best parameters for improved product development and address multicollinearity among casting parameters are also emphasized in the study.

21.6.3 IoT-Enabled Real-Time Inventory Management in a Smart Warehouse

In this case study, a smart warehouse was able to optimize inventory and provide real-time visibility by utilizing IoT devices, such as RFID tags and sensors. The IoT-empowered framework tracked stock levels, giving exact data on stock availability. This enabled effective stock administration, diminished stockouts, and limited conveying costs, as shown in Figure 21.8.

The existing challenges of paper-based operations and limited information sharing between warehouses were solved through the implementation of a cyber–physical

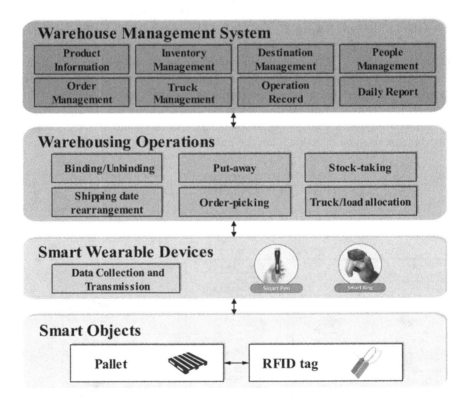

FIGURE 21.8 Real-time inventory management in a smart warehouse based on the Internet of Things (Wu et al., 2020).

system. The system used a combination of technologies for data collection and transmission, along with mobile and desktop applications for operational conduction. The solution resulted in improved efficiency, reduced paper usage, enhanced visibility, and traceability throughout the logistics process. The study also discusses the system architecture, workflow, implementation challenges, and recommendations for further improvement.

The project's significance lies in the development of hardware and software, the potential for paradigm solutions in similar industries, and the demonstration of IoT's transformative impact on logistics operations. This success serves as motivation for other companies to adopt IoT technologies and maintain their competitiveness in the future.

21.6.4 IoT-driven Predictive Maintenance in a Manufacturing Plant

In this case study, a modern assembling plant executed IoT-driven predictive maintenance to recognize and address hardware issues to avoid costly breakdowns. By gathering continuous information from sensors implanted in basic hardware, the plant used predictive maintenance and AI calculations to identify examples and irregularities. This empowered them to foresee machine failures, plan maintenance, and advance support plans.

Accordingly, the plant experienced diminished downtime, further developed hardware quality, and higher reserve funds (Liu et al., 2023). A predictive maintenance system based on ML that was developed for manufacturing environments was presented (Karimanzira & Rauschenbach, 2019). Real-world IoT data from manufacturing systems was used to evaluate the system's effectiveness, with a focus on capturing machinery failure signals in real-time, as shown in Figure 21.9.

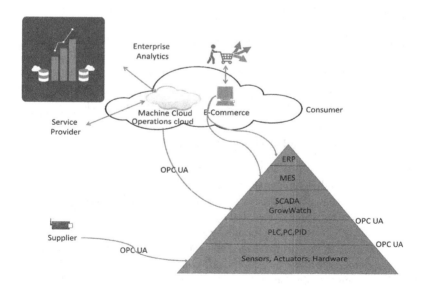

FIGURE 21.9 Predictive analytics based on the Internet of Things for efficient information use (Karimanzira & Rauschenbach, 2019).

Overall, this study adds more insight into the field of predictive maintenance in manufacturing, specifically how ML and IoT data can be used to improve maintenance procedures. The above-mentioned four case studies serve as compelling examples that showcase the wide-ranging applications of IoT in manufacturing, highlighting its remarkable effectiveness in asset tracking, quality control, inventory management, predictive maintenance, and more. These successful implementations illustrate the transformative impact of IoT technologies on operational efficiency, cost reduction, and gaining a competitive advantage in the dynamic manufacturing industry. By harnessing the immense potential of IoT, manufacturers can streamline workflows, optimize processes, and increase overall productivity. These IoT-enabled solutions empower informed decision-making, predictive maintenance, and seamless resource allocation through real-time data insights and automation capabilities.

21.7   CHALLENGES OF IoT FRAMEWORKS

The complex nature of IoT frameworks presents many challenges including data management, scalability and interoperability, integration, training and development, and security and protection.

21.7.1   EFFECTIVE DATA MANAGEMENT

The broad use of heterogeneous IoT gadgets creates a large information volume. These gadgets, coordinated with sensors and actuators, create constant, large information streams with high speed. The detected information is saved on these heterogeneous IoT gadgets, while neighborhood passage/edge and cloud servers are used for constant and future navigation. Dealing with the handling, transmission, accessibility, and capacity of this information is a demanding task that requires a lot of effort.

To address these difficulties, organizational models are prepared to deal with the large volume of crude information created by heterogeneous IoT gadgets. They provide quick information handling, dependable and secure information stockpiling, and proficient information recovery, empowering consistent dynamic cycles and improving the use of IoT innovations (Khang & Shah et al., 2023).

21.7.2   SCALABILITY AND INTEROPERABILITY

In IoT systems, scalability and interoperability pose significant difficulties. The setup of IoT covers different parts including modern machines, mechanical technology, gadgets, sensors, actuators, entryways, edge hubs, edge/cloud information servers, and different networks (wired and remote).

Coordinating between and combining these different innovations is a complicated task. Factors such as synchronization, asset and information sharing, interoperability, and information security further complicate consistent coordination and cooperation. It will take a significant amount of research to develop adaptable and effective methods for collaboration and interoperability in order to overcome these obstacles and guarantee a scalable and interoperable IoT ecosystem in industrial settings.

21.7.3 INTEGRATION WITH EXISTING MANUFACTURING INFRASTRUCTURE

There is a pressing need for robust and adaptable Big Data analytics technologies that take full advantage of the IoT potential in industrial settings and the enormous amount of data generated by IoT devices. This necessitates the use of traditional database management systems that are inefficient at processing and analyzing data. For critical industrial automation operations like predictive maintenance, anomaly detection, and production process optimization, real-time processing of IoT data is essential.

Real-time Big Data analytics technologies should meet the various requirements of IoT applications, such as data rates, latency, and reliability. These advanced analytics solutions support the entire product life cycle, including production, testing, customer feedback, and post-production services, by enabling the processing and visualization of data. Businesses can gain comprehensive insights into their operations by incorporating these technologies, resulting in improved decision-making and overall performance.

21.7.4 WORKFORCE TRAINING AND SKILL DEVELOPMENT

The safety of industrial workers and equipment, timely event detection, alert generation, site localization, and communication with emergency response service providers are essential. Challenges emerge when communication foundations are missing or break down in emergencies, impeding successful coordinated effort and correspondence among IoT gadgets and different frameworks.

To address these difficulties, different organizational models have been proposed utilizing advancements such as UAVs, SDN, edge registering, LTE, and 4G/5G for public wellbeing communication in IoT and smart urban areas. On the other hand, designing disaster-resilient and autonomous architectures that incorporate robust disaster recovery mechanisms for public safety in times of emergency and ensure efficient communication in normal circumstances requires additional research.

21.8 FUTURE TRENDS AND OUTLOOK FOR IoT IN SMART FACTORIES

Consumer acceptance and trust in IoT technologies heavily influence the outlook for IoT in smart factories in the future. The earliest stages of IoT frameworks show difficulties related to security and protection, which have been recognized as central issues.

The security and protection of IoT frameworks directly influence consumer trust, and any shortcomings can deter consumers from embracing IoT frameworks. To guarantee wide reception of IoT frameworks in businesses, compelling consumer trust models should be created and carried out. This features the requirement for additional examination in the field of consumer trust models to advance the acknowledgment and reliability of IoT frameworks in the business (Khang & Rath et al., 2023).

21.9 CONCLUSION

By utilizing real-time data collection, analysis, and connectivity, IoT-based smart factories have revolutionized the manufacturing sector. Execution of IoT in different parts of assembling, including quality control, stock administration, and predictive maintenance, greatly advances functional proficiency. Challenges in interoperability, versatility, security and protection, and consumer trust, for example, should be addressed to understand the capability of IoT in smart processing plants.

With IoT advances, organizations will beat these challenges. The development of IoT-based smart factories, which have the potential to drive significant advancements and reshape the manufacturing industry's future, is ongoing (Khang & Muthmainnah et al., 2023).

REFERENCES

Aheleroff, S. et al., "IoT-Enabled Smart Appliances Under Industry 4.0: A Case Study," Adv. Eng. Informatics, vol. 43, p. 101043, 2020. https://www.sciencedirect.com/science/article/pii/S1474034620300124

Aqeel, M., H. Shahab, M. Naeem, M. S. Shahbaz, F. Qaisar, and M. A. Shahzad, "Intelligent Smart Energy Meter Reading System Using Global System for Mobile Communication," Int. J. Intell. Syst. Appl., vol. 14, no. 1, p. 35, 2023. https://www.mecs-press.org/ijisa/ijisa-v15-n1/IJISA-V15-N1-4.pdf

Ashima, R., A. Haleem, S. Bahl, M. Javaid, S. K. Mahla, and S. Singh, "Automation and Manufacturing of Smart Materials in Additive Manufacturing Technologies Using Internet of Things Towards the Adoption of Industry 4.0," Mater. Today Proc., vol. 45, pp. 5081–5088, 2021. https://www.sciencedirect.com/science/article/pii/S2214785321006751

Brown, M., "Artificial Intelligence Data-Driven Internet of Things Systems, Real-Time Process Monitoring, and Sustainable Industrial Value Creation in Smart Networked Factories," J. Self-Governance Manag. Econ., vol. 9, no. 2, pp. 21–31, 2021. https://www.ceeol.com/search/article-detail?id=965040

Dolci, R., "IoT solutions for precision farming and food manufacturing: artificial intelligence applications in digital food," in 2017 IEEE 41st Annual Computer Software and Applications Conference (COMPSAC), 2017, vol. 2, pp. 384–385. https://ieeexplore.ieee.org/abstract/document/8029960/

Fatima, Z. et al., "Production Plant and Warehouse Automation with IoT and Industry 5.0," Appl. Sci., vol. 12, no. 4, p. 2053, 2022. https://www.mdpi.com/2076-3417/12/4/2053

Ganesh Babu, R., A. Karunakaran, G. Manikandan, S. Kalimuthu Kumar, and R. Selvameena, "IoT in Smart Automation and Robotics with Streaming Analytical Challenges." Emergence of Cyber Physical System and IoT in Smart Automation and Robotics: Computer Engineering in Automation (2021). Page (103–118). Springer. https://link.springer.com/chapter/10.1007/978-3-030-66222-6_7

Goswami, V., P. Jadav, and S. K. Soni, "Review on how IoT has revolutionized greenhouse, manufacturing and medical industries," in Recent Advances in Mechanical Infrastructure: Proceedings of ICRAM 2021, 2022, pp. 179–192. https://link.springer.com/chapter/10.1007/978-981-16-7660-4_16

Gupta, R., P. Srivastava, S. Sharma, and M. Alrasheedi, "Leveraging Big Data to Accelerate Supply Chain Management in Covid-19." The Big Data-Driven Digital Economy: Artificial and Computational Intelligence (2021). Page (1–19). Springer. https://link.springer.com/chapter/10.1007/978-3-030-73057-4_1

Javaid, M., A. Haleem, R. P. Singh, and R. Suman, "Enabling Flexible Manufacturing System (FMS) Through the Applications of Industry 4.0 Technologies," Internet Things Cyber-Physical Syst., vol. 2, pp. 49–62, 2022. https://www.sciencedirect.com/science/article/pii/S2667345222000153

Karimanzira, D., and T. Rauschenbach, "Enhancing Aquaponics Management with IoT-Based Predictive Analytics for Efficient Information Utilization," Inf. Process. Agric., vol. 6, no. 3, pp. 375–385, 2019. https://www.sciencedirect.com/science/article/pii/S2214317318303871

Khang, A., V. A. Hajimahmud, S. K. Gupta, J. Babasaheb, and G. Morris, *AI-Centric Modelling and Analytics: Concepts, Designs, Technologies, and Applications.* (1st Ed.) (2023). CRC Press. https://doi.org/10.1201/9781003400110

Khang, A., A. Misra, S. K. Gupta, and V. Shah, *AI-Aided IoT Technologies and Applications in the Smart Business and Production.* (1st Ed.) (2023). CRC Press. https://doi.org/10.1201/9781003392224

Khang, A., M Muthmainnah, Prodhan Mahbub Ibna Seraj, Ahmad Al Yakin, Ahmad J. Obaid, and Manas Ranjan Panda. "AI-Aided Teaching Model for the Education 5.0 Ecosystem." *AI-Based Technologies and Applications in the Era of the Metaverse.* (1st Ed.) (2023). Page (83–104). IGI Global Press. https://doi.org/10.4018/978-1-6684-8851-5.ch004

Khang, A., Kali Charan Rath, Suresh Kumar Satapathy, Amaresh Kumar, Sudhansu Ranjan Das, and Manas Ranjan Panda. "Enabling the Future of Manufacturing: Integration of Robotics and IoT to Smart Factory Infrastructure in Industry 4.0." *AI-Based Technologies and Applications in the Era of the Metaverse.* (1st Ed.) (2023). Page (25–50). IGI Global Press. https://doi.org/10.4018/978-1-6684-8851-5.ch002

Khang, A., V. Shah, and S. Rani, *AI-Based Technologies and Applications in the Era of the Metaverse.* (1st Ed.) (2023). IGI Global Press. https://doi.org/10.4018/978-1-6684-8851-5

Krishnan, S., and Mendoza Santos R. X., "Real-Time Asset Tracking for Smart Manufacturing," Implement. Ind. 4.0 Model Fact as Key Enabler Futur. Manuf., pp. 25–53, 2021. https://link.springer.com/chapter/10.1007/978-3-030-67270-6_2

Liu, Y., W. Yu, W. Rahayu, and T. Dillon, "An Evaluative Study on IoT Ecosystem for Smart Predictive Maintenance (IoT-SPM) in Manufacturing: Multi-View Requirements and Data Quality," IEEE Internet Things J., 2023. https://ieeexplore.ieee.org/abstract/document/10049619/

Longo, F., A. Padovano, and S. Umbrello, "Value-Oriented and Ethical Technology Engineering in Industry 5.0: A Human-Centric Perspective for the Design of the Factory of the Future," Appl. Sci., vol. 10, no. 12, p. 4182, 2020. https://www.mdpi.com/2076-3417/10/12/4182

Nawaz, J., H. Shahab, M. Ziaullah, and H. Raza, "The Influence of Project manager's Motivation on Project Success Through Developing Trust and Knowledge Sharing," Inf. Manag. Comput. Sci., vol. 3, no. 2, pp. 22–24, 2020. https://www.academia.edu/download/82070649/2imcs2020-22-24.pdf

Pal, K., "Privacy, Security and Policies: a Review of Problems and Solutions With Blockchain-Based Internet of Things Applications in Manufacturing Industry." Procedia Comput. Sci., vol. 191, pp. 176–183, 2021. https://content.iospress.com/articles/semantic-web/sw289

Park, S., K. Changgyun, and S. Youm, "Establishment of an IoT-Based Smart Factory and Data Analysis Model for the Quality Management of SMEs Die-Casting Companies in Korea," Int. J. Distrib. Sens. Networks, vol. 15, no. 10, p. 1550147719879378, 2019.

Qaisar, F., H. Shahab, M. Iqbal, H. M. Sargana, M. Aqeel, and M. A. Qayyum, "Recent Trends in Cloud Computing and IoT Platforms for IT Management and Development: A Review," Pakistan J. Eng. Technol., vol. 6, no. 1, pp. 98–105, 2023. https://hpej.net/journals/pakjet/article/view/2444

Revanth, S., *Intelligent Packaging Solution for Safe and Secured Delivery*. JSS Academy of Technical Education, 2021. https://www.researchgate.net/profile/Prajwal_Nagaraj2/publication/354802887_Intelligent_Packaging_Solution_for_Safe_And_Secured_Delivery_JSS_ACADEMY_OF_TECHNICAL_EDUCATION/links/614d5e4da595d06017e8999c/Intelligent-Packaging-Solution-for-Safe-And-Secured-Delivery-JSS-ACADEMY-OF-TECHNICAL-EDUCATION.pdf

Santhosh, N., M. Srinivsan, and K. Ragupathy, "Internet of Things (IoT) in Smart Manufacturing," in IOP Conference Series: Materials Science and Engineering, 2020, vol. 764, no. 1, p. 12025. https://iopscience.iop.org/article/10.1088/1757-899X/764/1/012025/meta

Shahab, H. et al., "Real-Time Health Monitoring Smart System for Cardiac Patients Using Internet of Things (IoT)," Int. J. Electr. Eng. Emerg. Technol., vol. 6, no. 1, pp. 31–37, 2023. http://ijeeet.com/index.php/ijeeet/article/view/144

Shahab, H., T. Abbas, M. U. Sardar, A. Basit, M. M. Waqas, and H. Raza, "Internet of Things Implications for the Adequate Development of the Smart Agricultural Farming Concepts," Big Data Agric., vol. 3, pp. 12–17, 2020. https://www.academia.edu/download/84250249/bda.01.2021.12.pdf

Sharma, H., R. Garg, H. Sewani, and R. Kashef, "Towards A Sustainable and Ethical Supply Chain Management: The Potential of IoT Solutions," arXiv Prepr. arXiv2303.18135, 2023.

Sharma, R., and B. Villányi, "Evaluation of Corporate Requirements for Smart Manufacturing Systems Using Predictive Analytics," Internet of Things, vol. 19, p. 100554, 2022. https://www.sciencedirect.com/science/article/pii/S254266052200052X

Shi, Z., Y. Xie, W. Xue, Y. Chen, L. Fu, and X. Xu, "Smart Factory in Industry 4.0," Syst. Res. Behav. Sci., vol. 37, no. 4, pp. 607–617, 2020. https://onlinelibrary.wiley.com/doi/abs/10.1002/sres.2704

Soori, M., B. Arezoo, and R. Dastres, "Internet of Things for Smart Factories in Industry 4.0, A Review," Internet Things Cyber-Physical Syst., 2023. https://www.sciencedirect.com/science/article/pii/S2667345223000275

Swamy, S. N., and S. R. Kota, "An Empirical Study on System Level Aspects of Internet of Things (IoT)," IEEE Access, vol. 8, pp. 188082–188134, 2020. https://ieeexplore.ieee.org/abstract/document/9218916/

Thekkoote, R., "Understanding Big Data-Driven Supply Chain and Performance Measures for Customer Satisfaction," Benchmarking An Int. J., vol. 29, no. 8, pp. 2359–2377, 2022. https://www.emerald.com/insight/content/doi/10.1108/BIJ-01-2021-0034/full/html

Vargas-Salgado, C., J. Aguila-Leon, C. Chiñas-Palacios, and E. Hurtado-Perez, "Low-Cost Web-Based Supervisory Control and Data Acquisition System for a Microgrid Testbed: A Case Study in Design and Implementation for Academic and Research Applications," Heliyon, vol. 5, no. 9, 2019. https://www.cell.com/heliyon/pdf/S2405-8440(19)36134-1.pdf

Wu, W., C. Cheung, S. Y. Lo, R. Y. Zhong, and G. Q. Huang, "An IoT-Enabled Real-Time Logistics System for a Third Party Company: A Case Study," Procedia Manuf., vol. 49, pp. 16–23, 2020. https://www.sciencedirect.com/science/article/pii/S2351978920316425

22 Green Intelligent and Sustainable Manufacturing

Key Advancements, Benefits, Challenges, and Applications for Transforming Industry

Alex Khang and Shalom Akhai

22.1 INTRODUCTION

Nowadays, people's awareness of environmental impact is increasingly focused on promoting sustainable practices in various fields (Mensah, 2019; Abbas et al., 2023). Intelligent and sustainable manufacturing, which employs cutting-edge technologies and approaches to develop more effective and environmentally conscious production processes (Vlad & Florin-Alexandru, 2020; Haleem et al., 2023), has emerged as a favored resolution. Over the past few years, sustainable manufacturing has emerged as a significant element of environmental stewardship and corporate social responsibility.

Numerous corporations are allocating resources toward sustainable manufacturing methodologies in an effort to reduce their overall carbon footprint and satisfy consumer demand for eco-friendly products (Amjad et al., 2020; Teixeira et al., 2022). As society progresses toward a more environmentally sustainable future, the significance of sustainable manufacturing will further increase (Quintana-García et al., 2022; Boluk et al., 2019). Thus, we can ensure that industrial production is not only profitable and efficient, but also environmentally responsible and socially beneficial, through the adoption of sustainable practices.

22.1.1 INTELLIGENT MANUFACTURING

Intelligent manufacturing involves the implementation of machine learning (ML) and artificial intelligence (AI) systems to increase production efficiency. As an illustration, by programming robots to execute repetitive tasks with greater speed and precision than human laborers, production times can be accelerated and products of superior quality can be manufactured. In a similar vein, ML algorithms have the capability to forecast product demand (Nahavandi, 2019; Buchmeister et al., 2019),

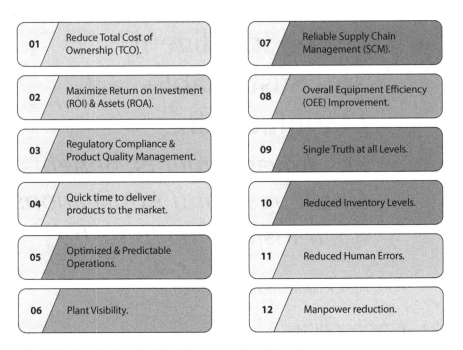

FIGURE 22.1 Key benefits of intelligent manufacturing.

enabling producers to optimize production levels and minimize waste, as shown in Figure 22.1.

22.1.2 SUSTAINABLE MANUFACTURING

Sustainable manufacturing endeavors to reduce the ecological consequences of production by implementing eco-friendly practices and harnessing renewable energy sources. This may encompass the utilization of renewable energy sources such as solar or wind power for energy generation, the adoption of water conservation practices, and the adherence to circular economy tenets for waste reduction and resource optimization (Paul et al., 2014; Nandhini et al., 2022). The fundamental aspects of sustainable manufacturing processes are outlined in Figure 22.2.

Industry-specific production processes and intelligent and sustainable manufacturing necessitate distinct technological approaches and strategic implementations. Nevertheless, the implementation of circular economy principles, advanced robotics and automation, and renewable energy sources are all prevalent methods. Environmental sustainability stands as a primary advantage of intelligent and sustainable manufacturing practices. Manufacturers have the capacity to mitigate their overall environmental impact and aid in the conservation of natural resources through the reduction of pollution and carbon emissions. Furthermore, these practices have the potential to result in enhanced working conditions for

FIGURE 22.2 Sustainable manufacturing processes.

employees, reduced expenses, and increased productivity and efficacy (Javaid et al., 2022; Meng et al., 2018).

Despite the implementation of intelligent and sustainable manufacturing in certain sectors, there remains substantial potential for further advancements and progress. To increase the prevalence of these practices, obstacles including a dearth of awareness among industry professionals and substantial implementation expenses must be overcome. In the face of ongoing environmental challenges, the role of intelligent and sustainable manufacturing in fostering a more sustainable future will grow in significance. Manufacturers have the capacity to pave the way for future generations by adopting environmentally sustainable practices and investing in cutting-edge technologies (Soni & Yadav, 2022; Ng et al., 2022).

22.2 ADVANCEMENTS IN INTELLIGENT AND SUSTAINABLE MANUFACTURING

In the past few years, the manufacturing sector has experienced substantial changes due to the emergence of novel technologies that enhance the efficiency and environmental friendliness of production processes. An example of such a shift is the incorporation of sustainable and intelligent manufacturing methods, which utilize cutting-edge technologies to generate production processes that are both more effective and environmentally conscious.

- **Cutting-Edge Artificial Intelligence** – AI is the most intriguing development in the manufacturing industry. ML can be implemented to forecast consumer demand, analyze data, and optimize production processes. One application of AI is the automation of quality control procedures, which guarantees that each product satisfies rigorous quality criteria. Moreover, AI has the capability to detect inefficiencies within production processes and propose enhancements, resulting in financial savings and increased output (Selvaraj et al., 2021; Duft & Durana, 2020).
- **Machine Learning Systems** – Additionally, ML systems are generating interest in the manufacturing sector. These systems acquire knowledge from data and generate forecasts using that knowledge. They are therefore indispensable for optimization and production planning, as they enable the forecasting of demand and subsequent adjustment of production levels. Additionally, ML systems can be employed to detect latent patterns in data, enabling organizations to identify potential cost reductions and process enhancements (Chou & Tran, 2018; Aldahiri et al., 2021).
- **Advanced Robotics and Automation** – Automation and refined automata are also essential components of intelligent and sustainable manufacturing. Programming robots to execute repetitive tasks with a high degree of consistency and precision results in increased output velocity and product quality. Moreover, the implementation of robotics for hazardous or physically demanding duties mitigates the likelihood of harm to human laborers. Additionally, automation can aid in waste reduction by minimizing errors and optimizing material utilization (Javaid et al., 2021; Buerkle et al., 2023).
- **Novel Renewable Energy Technologies** – Innovative renewable energy technologies are assuming a greater significance in the realm of sustainable manufacturing. In addition to solar-, wind-, and hydro-power, these technologies also consist of biofuels and other alternative energy sources. Manufacturers can mitigate their environmental impact and foster a more sustainable future by utilizing these renewable energy sources (Pandey et al., 2022; Menon et al., 2022).

The progress made in intelligent and sustainable manufacturing can transform the manufacturing sector. Manufacturers can develop environmentally sustainable and advanced production processes through the integration of advanced AI, ML, robotics, and renewable energy technologies (Khang & Ragimova et al., 2024). In the coming years, we can anticipate even more remarkable developments in the field of intelligent and sustainable manufacturing as these technologies continue to improve.

22.3   BENEFITS OF INTELLIGENT AND SUSTAINABLE MANUFACTURING

In our aim for a more environmentally friendly and sustainable future, we must investigate the advantages of intelligent and sustainable manufacturing. It not only contributes to environmental protection but also offers numerous advantages for both enterprises and workers. We shall now explore several of these advantages.

- **Environmental Sustainability** – Sustainability has become the watchword of the 21st century. As climate change emerges as a significant concern, it is imperative that we devise strategies to mitigate carbon emissions such as sustainable manufacturing practices. By reducing waste and using renewable energy sources, businesses can substantially lessen their environmental impact. This contributes to environmental protection and the achievement of corporate social responsibility objectives.
- **Increased Productivity and Efficiency** – AI and ML are examples of intelligent manufacturing technologies that may substantially boost output and efficiency. These systems are capable of analyzing vast quantities of data and delivering insights that can assist organizations in optimizing their operations. Predictive maintenance systems, for instance, can aid in the early detection of equipment malfunctions, thereby decreasing downtime and boosting productivity (Anh et al., 2024).
- **Cost Reduction** – Green manufacturing methods can help organizations save money. Through waste reduction, businesses can reduce disposal expenses. Also, businesses that use renewable energy sources can reduce their energy expenses. Enhanced productivity and efficiency may also result in financial savings.
- **Improved Working Conditions and Supply Chain Transparency** – Intelligent manufacturing technologies can enhance supply chain transparency and working conditions. For instance, hazardous duties can be performed by robotics, thereby reducing the risk of worker injury. Also, supply chains can be made more transparent through the use of blockchain technology, enabling companies to monitor their products from beginning to end.

Intelligent and sustainable manufacturing offers an abundance of advantages. By addressing concerns related to worker welfare and environmental protection, productivity, and efficiency, organizations can transition toward a more sustainable future (Furstenau et al., 2020).

22.4 POTENTIAL APPLICATIONS OF INTELLIGENT AND SUSTAINABLE MANUFACTURING

In an effort to fundamentally transform the manufacturing sector, intelligent and sustainable manufacturing is an innovative approach that integrates cutting-edge technologies with environmentally responsible practices. Its prospective implementations are vast and varied, can revolutionize the sector, and advance sustainability. The ramifications of this methodology are extensive, transcending numerous industries. A number of prospective applications are discussed below.

22.4.1 AUTOMOTIVE MANUFACTURING

Intelligent and sustainable manufacturing is improving efficiency, cost, and environmental impact in the automotive sector. These strategies may eliminate material waste, expedite manufacturing, and increase supply chain transparency. Renewable energy, recycling, and energy conservation may lower production's carbon footprint. Intelligent and sustainable automobile production uses robots and automation to decrease human labor and boost productivity. Composites, aluminum, and carbon fiber reduce vehicle weight, increasing fuel economy and decreasing pollutants. These technologies may be used to produce electric and hybrid automobiles, which need different manufacturing procedures than internal combustion engine vehicles (Khang & Hajimahmud et al., 2024).

Intelligent manufacturing may simplify and reduce the environmental impact for these cars. These technologies may improve efficiency and durability of car components including batteries, engines, and gearboxes. In conclusion, intelligent and sustainable automotive production technologies may improve efficiency, cost, and environmental effect. These solutions can lead the sector to a greener future (Szász et al., 2021; Payalan & Guvensan, 2019).

22.4.2 ELECTRONICS PRODUCTION

Intelligent and sustainable manufacturing processes are growing in the electronics sector to encourage sustainable development. These include AI-driven quality control, automated manufacturing lines, and intelligent energy management. These systems optimize productivity, minimize waste, and increase product quality using ML algorithms. They can also detect equipment problems and arrange maintenance, saving time and money. Renewable energy sources like solar panels and wind turbines minimize carbon footprints and energy expenditures in sustainable manufacturing. Bamboo and other eco-friendly materials are utilized to promote a circular economy (Khang & Hajimahmud et al., 2024).

Blockchain-enabled supply chain transparency guarantees suppliers follow environmental and ethical standards. In conclusion, intelligent and sustainable manufacturing may speed up and improve electronics production. Robotics and automation may boost manufacturing, while renewable energy can lower carbon emissions. Machine learning improves inventory management and lead times. Predictive maintenance and quality control increase product quality and save waste. Finally, manufacturers must adapt to intelligent and sustainable manufacturing which will transform the electronics sector by boosting productivity, lowering prices, and decreasing environmental impact for a better, more sustainable future (Massaoudi et al., 2021).

22.4.3 AEROSPACE ENGINEERING

Aerospace engineering is embracing intelligent and sustainable manufacturing to boost efficiency, productivity, and sustainability. This strategy reduces material waste, which saves resources and money, particularly in businesses with costly and scarce materials. Productivity is another advantage of intelligent and sustainable production. Automating operations and incorporating sophisticated technology may boost production without sacrificing quality, enhancing profits and competitiveness. Robotics and automation may boost production and efficiency. Intelligent and sustainable manufacturing improves labor conditions, supply chain transparency, and environmental sustainability. Manufacturers may improve worker safety, particularly in hazardous situations, by implementing sustainable practices (Khang & Vladimir et al., 2024).

Manufacturing enterprises may lessen their environmental impact by employing renewable energy and recycling trash. Aerospace engineering needs supply chain openness. Since the sector has a complicated worldwide supply chain, blockchain can trace goods and guarantee ethical procurement. Finally, intelligent and sustainable manufacturing may boost aerospace efficiency, production, and sustainability. These technologies have extensive and promising uses, and as the industry confronts rising environmental pressure, they will shape aerospace engineering's future (Brunton et al., 2021; Brevault et al., 2020).

22.4.4 Construction Industry

Sustainable techniques and technology are being used by the construction sector to lessen its environmental impact. Intelligent and sustainable manufacturing technologies may be used to design, build, and assemble buildings. These technologies promote worker safety, efficiency, and environmental sustainability. Material waste minimization is a major advantage of intelligent and sustainable building production. Prefabrication, 3D printing, and modular building decrease construction waste, conserving resources and the environment. Automation and integration of modern technologies, such as Building Information Modeling, may boost production and competitiveness without sacrificing product quality. Intelligent and sustainable manufacturing improves worker safety, productivity, and environmental sustainability (Abioye et al., 2021; Casini, 2021).

Robots and drones can do dangerous jobs, decreasing worker injuries and building company costs. Smart building technologies also improve energy efficiency and performance, saving resources and boosting tenant comfort and well-being. In conclusion, intelligent and sustainable manufacturing may change the construction sector by improving productivity, waste reduction, safety, and sustainability. However, change aversion and the need to spend heavily in new technology and procedures are obstacles. These innovations will influence the construction sector and make buildings more sustainable and efficient (Akhai et al., 2021; Kumar & Akhai, 2022).

22.4.5 Food and Beverage Industry

Intelligent and sustainable manufacturing has emerged from the food and beverage industry's drive toward sustainable practices and innovative technology. This method reduces waste, improves product quality, and boosts industrial efficiency. Automation, sensors, and data analytics can enhance operations and reduce global food waste. Intelligent and sustainable production reduces waste and cuts foodborne illness and recalls by monitoring and controlling food quality and safety in real-time (Khang & Hajimahmud et al., 2024).

Automation and integration of sophisticated technology may boost productivity without lowering quality, allowing producers to adapt swiftly to market needs and consumer preferences. It might also increase supply chain transparency and ethical sourcing, guaranteeing ethical and sustainable raw materials and traceability. Sustainability and customer trust are promoted throughout the supply chain. Finally, intelligent and sustainable manufacturing may assist the food and beverage sector minimize waste and energy consumption, boost productivity, and increase supply chain transparency. New technology and processes need substantial investment, and sustainability must be balanced with customer desire for convenience and cost (Khang, 2024).

Food and beverage manufacturers can minimize waste, increase safety and transparency, and boost market competitiveness by embracing innovative technology and sustainable practices (Cheong et al., 2021; Mahbub, 2020).

22.4.6 PHARMACEUTICAL INDUSTRY

Intelligent and sustainable pharmaceutical manufacturing might transform drug production, testing, and delivery. Innovative technology and sustainable practices may boost pharmaceutical firms' efficiency, waste reduction, and environmental sustainability. Intelligent and sustainable production reduces material waste. Pharmaceutical companies may minimize raw material utilization and environmental impact by streamlining production processes. Automation and robots boost production and quality, speeding medication development. Intelligent and sustainable production promotes product quality.

Monitoring and controlling the production process using automated procedures and modern analytical tools reduces mistakes and inconsistencies. Waste reduction and renewable energy guarantee environmental sustainability. New technology and procedures demand substantial investment, balancing sustainability, regulatory constraints, and patient safety. Using innovative technology and sustainable practices, pharmaceutical businesses may improve production and help the environment (Leng et al., 2020; Mowbray et al., 2022).

22.4.7 TEXTILE INDUSTRY

Intelligent and sustainable production may reduce waste, boost productivity, and reduce environmental impact in the textile sector. Smart materials, digital printing, 3D printing, automation, recycling, upcycling, and renewable energy are examples. Smart materials such as self-cleaning and self-healing fabrics may improve textile quality and usefulness. Digital printing allows accurate printing without dyeing, reducing waste and dangerous chemicals. Complex textile constructions and prototypes may be 3D-printed with minimum waste and material.

Automation reduces labor expenses, boosts productivity, and cuts waste. Recycling and upcycling minimize waste and virgin material consumption. Solar and wind power may lower textile manufacturing's carbon footprint and increase sustainability. In conclusion, intelligent and sustainable manufacturing may assist the textile sector minimize waste, energy use, and environmental impact while improving efficiency and sustainability. Balancing sustainability with consumer desire for affordability and diversity requires major investment in new technology and processes (Manupati et al., 2022).

22.5 FUTURE SCOPE AND CONCLUSION

Intelligent and sustainable manufacturing research might alter industries by enhancing efficiency, productivity, and sustainability. As technology advances and new uses are found, its future appears bright, but difficulties remain. Intelligent and sustainable manufacturing is becoming more advanced and might alter industries and improve sustainability (Khang & Abdullayev et al., 2023).

22.5.1 FUTURE DIRECTIONS AND CHALLENGES

There are various barriers to broad adoption of intelligent manufacturing. These include integrating advanced technologies such as AI, ML, and the Internet of Things (IoT), developing sustainable materials to replace traditional materials, improving data analytics for decision-making, and improving supply chain management for ethical sourcing, waste reduction, and sustainability. These technologies are expensive for smaller enterprises, which hinders their adoption.

Many businesses are used to established manufacturing practices, making change resistance likely. A skills gap in the workforce and a lack of uniform norms and procedures may make it hard for enterprises to meet industry standards. Finally, intelligent and sustainable manufacturing has the potential to revolutionize sectors and improve sustainability. Companies must face important hurdles and impediments to execute these practices. To meet industry requirements, organizations must invest in intelligent and sustainable manufacturing research and development (Arinez et al., 2020; Coalition, 2011).

22.5.2 CONCLUSION

Intelligent and sustainable production may boost efficiency, save costs, and improve sustainability in numerous sectors. Artificial intelligence, machine learning, robotics, automation, and renewable energy have enabled sustainable manufacturing. These practices may enhance supply chain transparency, environmental sustainability, productivity, cost reduction, and working conditions (Khang et al., 2024). They are used in industries such as automotive, electronics, aerospace, construction, food and beverage, pharmaceutical, and textile. However, legislative impediments, skilled-labor shortages, high initial investment costs, and technical restrictions persist. Despite these challenges, there are many possibilities for research and development, and investment and innovation are essential for a sustainable future (Khang, 2023).

REFERENCES

Abbas, A., Ekowati, D., Suhariadi, F., & Fenitra, R. M., (2023). Health implications, leader's societies, and climate change: A global review. *Ecological Footprints of Climate Change: Adaptive Approaches and Sustainability*, 653–675. https://link.springer.com/chapter/10.1007/978-3-031-15501-7_26

Abioye, S. O., Oyedele, L. O., Akanbi, L., Ajayi, A., Delgado, J. M. D., Bilal, M., & Ahmed, A., (2021). Artificial intelligence in the construction industry: A review of present status, opportunities and future challenges. Journal of Building Engineering, 44, 103299. https://www.sciencedirect.com/science/article/pii/S2352710221011578

Akhai, S., Mala, S., & Jerin, A. A., (2021). Understanding whether air filtration from air conditioners reduces the probability of virus transmission in the environment. Journal of Advanced Research, 8. http://medicaljournalshouse.com/index.php/Journal-MedicalSci-MedTechnology/article/view/575

Aldahiri, A., Alrashed, B., & Hussain, W., (2021). Trends in using IoT with machine learning in health prediction system. Forecasting, 3(1), 181–206. https://www.mdpi.com/2571-9394/3/1/12

Amjad, M. S., Rafique, M. Z., Hussain, S., & Khan, M. A., (2020). A new vision of LARG manufacturing—A trail towards Industry 4.0. CIRP Journal of Manufacturing Science and Technology. https://www.sciencedirect.com/science/article/pii/S1755581720300778

Anh, P. T. N., Vladimir, Hahanov, Triwiyanto, Ragimova, Nazila Ali, İsmibeyli, Rashad, Hajimahmud, V. A., & Abuzarova, Vusala Alyar. "AI Models for Disease Diagnosis and Prediction of Heart Disease with Artificial Neural Networks," *Computer Vision and AI-Integrated IoT Technologies in Medical Ecosystem*. (1st Ed.) (2024). CRC Press. https://doi.org/10.1201/9781003429609-9

Arinez, J. F., Chang, Q., Gao, R. X., Xu, C., & Zhang, J., (2020). Artificial intelligence in advanced manufacturing: Current status and future outlook. Journal of Manufacturing Science and Engineering, 142(11). https://asmedigitalcollection.asme.org/manufacturingscience/article-abstract/142/11/110804/1085487

Boluk, K. A., Cavaliere, C. T., & Higgins-Desbiolles, F., (2019). A critical framework for interrogating the United Nations Sustainable Development Goals 2030 Agenda in tourism. Journal of Sustainable Tourism. https://www.tandfonline.com/doi/shareview/10.1080/09669582.2019.1619748

Brevault, L., Balesdent, M., & Morio, J., *Aerospace System Analysis and Optimization in Uncertainty* (2020). Springer International Publishing. https://link.springer.com/content/pdf/10.1007/978-3-030-39126-3.pdf

Brunton, S. L., Nathan Kutz, J., Manohar, K., Aravkin, A. Y., Morgansen, K., Klemisch, J., & McDonald, D., (2021). Data-driven aerospace engineering: Reframing the industry with machine learning. AIAA Journal, 59(8), 2820–2847. https://arc.aiaa.org/doi/abs/10.2514/1.J060131

Buchmeister, B., Palcic, I., & Ojstersek, R., (2019). *Artificial Intelligence in Manufacturing Companies and Broader: An Overview*. DAAAM International Scientific Book, 81–98. https://www.daaam.info/Downloads/Pdfs/science_books_pdfs/2019/Sc_Book_2019-007.pdf

Buerkle, A., Eaton, W., Al-Yacoub, A., Zimmer, M., Kinnell, P., Henshaw, M., & Lohse, N., (2023). Towards industrial robots as a service (IRaaS): Flexibility, usability, safety and business models. Robotics and Computer-Integrated Manufacturing, 81, 102484. https://www.sciencedirect.com/science/article/pii/S0736584522001661

Casini, M., *Construction 4.0: Advanced Technology, Tools and Materials for the Digital Transformation of the Construction Industry* (2021). Woodhead Publishing. https://www.google.com/books?hl=en&lr=&id=GkAyEAAAQBAJ&oi=fnd&pg=PP1

Cheong, Y. S., Seah, C. S., Loh, Y. X., & Loh, L. H., (2021, September). Artificial Intelligence (AI) in the food and beverage industry: improves the customer experience. In 2021 2nd International Conference on Artificial Intelligence and Data Sciences (AiDAS) (pp. 1–6). IEEE. https://ieeexplore.ieee.org/abstract/document/9574261/

Chou, J. S., & Tran, D. S., (2018). Forecasting energy consumption time series using machine learning techniques based on usage patterns of residential households. Energy, 165, 709–726. https://www.sciencedirect.com/science/article/pii/S0360544218319145

Coalition, S. M. L., (2011, June). Implementing 21st century smart manufacturing. In Workshop summary report (pp. 1–36). https://www.academia.edu/download/28748242/smlcpfizer11911presv2.pdf

Duft, G., & Durana, P., (2020). Artificial intelligence-based decision-making algorithms, automated production systems, and big data-driven innovation in sustainable industry 4.0. Economics, Management and Financial Markets, 15(4), 9–18. https://www.ceeol.com/search/article-detail?id=917170

Furstenau, L. B., Sott, M. K., Kipper, L. M., Machado, E. L., Lopez-Robles, J. R., Dohan, M. S., & Imran, M. A., (2020). Link between sustainability and industry 4.0: Trends, challenges and new perspectives. Ieee Access, 8, 140079–140096. https://ieeexplore.ieee.org/abstract/document/9151934/

Haleem, A., Javaid, M., Singh, R. P., Suman, R., & Qadri, M. A., (2023). A pervasive study on green manufacturing towards attaining sustainability. Green Technologies and Sustainability, 100018. https://www.sciencedirect.com/science/article/pii/S2949736123000118

Javaid, M., Haleem, A., Singh, R. P., & Suman, R., (2021). Substantial capabilities of robotics in enhancing industry 4.0 implementation. Cognitive Robotics, 1, 58–75. https://www.sciencedirect.com/science/article/pii/S2667241321000057

Javaid, M., Haleem, A., Singh, R. P., Suman, R., & Gonzalez, E. S., (2022). Understanding the adoption of industry 4.0 technologies in improving environmental sustainability. Sustainable Operations and Computers, 3, 203–217. https://www.sciencedirect.com/science/article/pii/S2666412722000071

Khang, A., *AI and IoT-Based Technologies for Precision Medicine*. (1st Ed.) (2023). ISBN: 9798369308769. IGI Global Press. https://doi.org/10.4018/979-8-3693-0876-9

Khang, A., Abdullayev, V. A., Alyar, Abuzarova Vusala, Khalilov, Matlab, & Murad, Bagirli, AI-Aided Data Analytics Tools and Applications for the Healthcare Sector, "*AI and IoT-Based Technologies for Precision Medicine*". (1st Ed.) (2023). ISBN: 9798369308769. IGI Global Press. https://doi.org/10.4018/979-8-3693-0876-9.ch018

Khang, A., Abdullayev, V., Hrybiuk, O., & Shukla, A.K. (1st Ed.). (2024). *Computer Vision and AI-Integrated IoT Technologies in the Medical Ecosystem* (1st Ed.). CRC Press. https://doi.org/10.1201/9781003429609

Khang, A., Ragimova, Nazila Ali, Bali, Sardarov Yaqub, Hajimahmud, V. A., Bahar, Askarova, & Mehriban, Mammadova, "Using Big Data to Solve Problems in the Field of Medicine," *Computer Vision and AI-Integrated IoT Technologies in Medical Ecosystem*. (1st Ed.) (2024). CRC Press. https://doi.org/10.1201/9781003429609-21

Khang, A, Hajimahmud, V. A., Litvinova, Eugenia, Chumachenko, Svetlana, Abuzarova, Vusala, & Anh, P. T. N., "Application of Computer Vision in the Healthcare Ecosystem," *Computer Vision and AI-Integrated IoT Technologies in Medical Ecosystem*. (1st Ed.) (2024). CRC Press. https://doi.org/10.1201/9781003429609-1

Khang, A, Vladimir, Hahanov, Litvinova, Eugenia, Chumachenko, Svetlana, Zoran, Avromovic, İsmibeyli, Rashad, Ragimova, Nazila Ali, Hajimahmud, V. A., Alyar, Abuzarova Vusala, & Anh, P.T.N. "Medical and BioMedical Signal Processing and Prediction," *Computer Vision and AI-Integrated IoT Technologies in Medical Ecosystem*. (1st Ed.) (2024). CRC Press. https://doi.org/10.1201/9781003429609-7

Khang, A., Vladimir, Hahanov, Litvinova, Eugenia, Chumachenko, Svetlana, Triwiyanto, Ragimova, Nazila Ali, Kadarningsih, Ana, İsmibeyli, Rashad, Hajimahmud, V. A., Alyar, Abuzarova Vusala, Zeynab Mehman, Qaffarova, Bilqeyis Azer, Mammadova, & Anh, P. T. N., "The Era of Digital Healthcare System and Its Impact on Human Psychology," *AI and IoT Technology and Applications for Smart Healthcare Systems*. (2024). CRC Press. https://doi.org/10.1201/9781032686745-1

Kumar, P., & Akhai, S., " Effective energy management in smart buildings using VRV/VRF systems," *Additive Manufacturing in Industry 4.0*. (2022). 27–35. CRC Press. https://doi.org/10.1201/9781003360001-2

Leng, J., Ruan, G., Jiang, P., Xu, K., Liu, Q., Zhou, X., & Liu, C., (2020). Blockchain-empowered sustainable manufacturing and product lifecycle management in industry 4.0: A survey. Renewable and Sustainable Energy Reviews, 132, 110112.

Mahbub, M., (2020). A smart farming concept based on smart embedded electronics, internet of things and wireless sensor network. Internet of Things, 9, 100161. https://www.sciencedirect.com/science/article/pii/S2542660520300044

Manupati, V. K., Putnik, G. D., & Varela, M. L. R. (Eds.). *Smart and Sustainable Manufacturing Systems for Industry 4.0* (2022). CRC Press.

Massaoudi, M., Abu-Rub, H., Refaat, S. S., Chihi, I., & Oueslati, F. S., (2021). Deep learning in smart grid technology: A review of recent advancements and future prospects. IEEE Access, 9, 54558–54578. https://ieeexplore.ieee.org/abstract/document/9395437/

Meng, Y., Yang, Y., Chung, H., Lee, P. H., & Shao, C., (2018). Enhancing sustainability and energy efficiency in smart factories: A review. Sustainability, 10(12), 4779. https://www.mdpi.com/2071-1050/10/12/4779

Menon, A. P., Lahoti, V., Gunreddy, N., Chadha, U., Selvaraj, S. K., Nagalakshmi, R., & Karthikeyan, B., (2022). Quality control tools and digitalization of real-time data in sustainable manufacturing. International Journal on Interactive Design and Manufacturing (IJIDeM), 1–13. https://link.springer.com/article/10.1007/s12008-022-01054-1

Mensah, J., (2019). Sustainable development: Meaning, history, principles, pillars, and implications for human action: Literature review. Cogent Social Sciences, 5(1), 1653531. https://www.tandfonline.com/doi/abs/10.1080/23311886.2019.1653531

Mowbray, M., Vallerio, M., Perez-Galvan, C., Zhang, D., Chanona, A. D. R., & Navarro-Brull, F. J., (2022). Industrial data science–a review of machine learning applications for chemical and process industries. Reaction Chemistry & Engineering, 7, 1471–1509.

Nahavandi, S., (2019). Industry 5.0—A human-centric solution. Sustainability, 11(16), 4371. https://www.mdpi.com/2071-1050/11/16/4371

Nandhini, R., Sivaprakash, B., Rajamohan, N., & Vo, D. V. N., (2022). Carbon-free hydrogen and bioenergy production through integrated carbon capture and storage technology for achieving sustainable and circular economy–A review. Fuel, 342, 126984. https://www.sciencedirect.com/science/article/pii/S001623612203808X

Ng, T. C., Lau, S. Y., Ghobakhloo, M., Fathi, M., & Liang, M. S., (2022). The application of industry 4.0 technological constituents for sustainable manufacturing: A content-centric review. Sustainability, 14(7), 4327. https://www.mdpi.com/2071-1050/14/7/4327

Pandey, M., Gusain, D., & Sharma, S., (2022). Role of Renewable Energy in Attaining Sustainable Development. *Artificial Intelligence for Renewable Energy Systems* (pp. 69–79). Woodhead Publishing. https://www.sciencedirect.com/science/article/pii/B978032390396700002X

Paul, I. D., Bhole, G. P., & Chaudhari, J. R., (2014). A review on green manufacturing: it's important, methodology and its application. Procedia Materials Science, 6, 1644–1649. https://www.sciencedirect.com/science/article/pii/S2211812814005148

Payalan, Y. F., & Guvensan, M. A., (2019). Towards next-generation vehicles featuring the vehicle intelligence. IEEE Transactions on Intelligent Transportation Systems, 21(1), 30–47. https://ieeexplore.ieee.org/abstract/document/8734737/

Quintana-García, C., Marchante-Lara, M., & Benavides-Chicón, C. G., (2022). Towards sustainable development: Environmental innovation, cleaner production performance, and reputation. Corporate Social Responsibility and Environmental Management, 29(5), 1330–1340. https://onlinelibrary.wiley.com/doi/abs/10.1002/csr.2272

Selvaraj, S. K., Raj, A., Dharnidharka, M., Chadha, U., Sachdeva, I., Kapruan, C., & Paramasivam, V., (2021). A cutting-edge survey of tribological behavior evaluation using artificial and computational intelligence models. Advances in Materials Science and Engineering, 2021, 1–17. https://www.hindawi.com/journals/amse/2021/9529199/

Soni, S., & Yadav, U., (2022, November). Sustainable Supply Chain Management: Research Review and its Future. In 2022 International Conference on Computing, Communication, and Intelligent Systems (ICCCIS) (pp. 930–936). IEEE. https://ieeexplore.ieee.org/abstract/document/10037713/

Szász, L., Csíki, O., & Rácz, B. G., (2021). Sustainability management in the global automotive industry: A theoretical model and survey study. International Journal of Production Economics, 235, 108085. https://www.sciencedirect.com/science/article/pii/S092552732100061X

Teixeira, P., Coelho, A., Fontoura, P., Sá, J. C., Silva, F. J., Santos, G., & Ferreira, L. P., (2022). Combining lean and green practices to achieve a superior performance: The contribution for a sustainable development and competitiveness—An empirical study on the Portuguese context. Corporate Social Responsibility and Environmental Management, 29(4), 887–903. https://onlinelibrary.wiley.com/doi/abs/10.1002/csr.2242

Vlad, V. C., & Florin-Alexandru, L. U. C. A., (2020). Delivering sustainability-green marketing evolution. Network Intelligence Studies, (16), 169–179. https://www.ceeol.com/search/article-detail?id=945827

23 Enterprise Resource Planning and Accounting Information Systems
Modeling the Relationship in Manufacturing

*Md Halimuzzaman, Jaideep Sharma,
and Alex Khang*

23.1 INTRODUCTION

An accounting information system (AIS) is a broad structure in an organization that collects, stores, and processes financial and accounting data used by decision-makers. It forms a centralized system where authorized employees store financial information and then distribute that information to various stakeholders in the organization. Important data such as income, purchases, employees, customers, taxes, and more are stored in AIS in a database. This database structure is usually programmed using a query language that allows manipulation of tables and data. Since AIS has many fields that require necessary inputs (either new or old), it is very important that the security is extremely strong to prevent any malicious virus attacks.

An AIS is a discipline that informs theory and practice in accounting and auditing in a way that draws on information systems, broadly defined. At the same time, AIS uses theory and practice from the related fields of MIS and computer science, as well as from accounting, auditing, other business fields including management and marketing, and the fields of economics, psychology, sociology, philosophy, and history.

Enterprise resource planning (ERP) is a way to integrate an organization's data and processes into one single system. These ERP systems typically have many components including hardware and software to achieve integration. ERP refers to the type of software that organizations use to manage day-to-day business activities such as accounting, purchasing, project management, risk and compliance management, and supply chain operations.

This study significantly focuses on the connectivity between ERP and AIS. Here, researchers tried to bridge a model between these two accounting-based tools which will be very impactful for the different organizations and for financial and managerial decision-makers (Khang & Rani et al., 2023).

DOI: 10.1201/9781003438137-23

23.2   STATEMENT OF THE PROBLEM

The purpose of this study is to investigate the impact of implementing an AIS as part of ERP on useful information and successful decision-making. For implementing the accounting or financial data of an organization, it is essential to use the data formulating and accuracy tools. But in developing or under-developed countries, organizations maintain their data manually and do not use ERP, so they face a problem maintaining financial and non-financial data accurately. On the other hand, AISs use data science and are powered by a completely different software. Based on earlier literature, this study has been completed to accelerate the ERP relating to AIS by considering their different parameters. This study also is very meaningful for users of ERP and AIS, researchers, and other personnel.

23.3   RATIONALE OF THE STUDY

ERP is considered the backbone of information systems in a business and supports all parts of business processes by providing information flow between all business functions at all levels. This system offers a competitive advantage, especially when it comes to the value of information. For many users, ERP is a do-it-all system that does everything from entering sales orders to customer service. The ERP software is usually an integrated system that allows a company to standardize its information system to link and automate its core processes. It also provides mechanisms for sharing information within an organization by offering accurate and up-to-date information availability, faster transaction processing, and data quality.

The ERP system allows you to integrate and centralize all your company's information systems into a single one. It provides a common language and database to the members of the organization. On the other hand, an AIS is a technical tool for presenting accounting information. Thus, ERP and AIS are integrated, and all financial data is collected for top management decision-making of various organizations. The researchers conducted the study for modeling between ERP and AIS, which can be useful for users of ERP and AIS software.

23.4   OBJECTIVES OF THE STUDY

Specific objectives of the study are as follows:

- To know the usage of ERP and AIS in different firms.
- To know the cost effectiveness of ERP and AIS.
- To examine the relationship between ERP implementation and fair presentation of AIS.

23.5   LIMITATIONS OF THE STUDY

The main limitations of the study are as follows:

- ERP and AIS are mostly technical terms, so it is difficult for the researcher to explain financial data.

- Accounting data is confidential, so in most cases the researcher fails to collect appropriate data.
- In some cases, a researcher may not be able to fully dedicate themselves to the study due to a time constraint.

23.6   RESEARCH METHOD

The main purpose of this study is to model the relationship between AIS and ERP. Here, the researchers collected relevant data through virtual interviews and structured questionnaires. The questionnaire was also sent to the respondents by e-mail and feedback was collected using the same method. This study was designed to be descriptive, as it primarily uses qualitative, quantitative, and mixed methods. Where necessary, the researchers clarified the research topic and the statements under each variable to avoid ambiguities and/or confusion, thus ensuring that the respondents could fill the questionnaire with confidence from their own perspective. The collected data has been analyzed using the simple tools of SPSS Statistics (Khang & Rath et al., 2023).

23.7   LITERATURE REVIEW

Alzoubi (2012) found that ERP systems facilitate comparison processes of the financial statements of a business organization over time, which enable the decision-makers to better evaluate performance. Also, the use of ERP systems leads to increasing the reliability of AISs through maintaining confidentiality, privacy, and security of information. Finally, the findings of this study highlighted that the use of ERP systems increases the possibility of monitoring all financial and accounting operations to ensure proper implementation.

Odoyo and Ojera (2020) investigated the impact of top management support on the implementation of ERP systems in three universities, as well as the overall impact of AISs on organizational performance. Data was collected through an online questionnaire and analyzed using descriptive and inferential statistics, as well as thematic analysis for qualitative data. The study found that the universities had already adopted and implemented ERP systems, which were primarily being used for financial activities such as managing student finances and payroll. However, the systems had not yet been fully utilized to manage human resources and communication. The study's findings provide valuable insights for institutions that have implemented ERP systems, highlighting the importance of top management support and the potential benefits of fully utilizing such systems. The study also contributes to the broader field of AIS.

Nur and Irfan (2020) explored the user and organizational impact of implementing an ERP-based AIS. Based on data analysis, they implemented a quality AIS to create quality information that users can be satisfied with. Information systems also enhance personal skills as they relate to user experience, satisfaction, and knowledge sharing, which contribute to organizational effectiveness. On the other hand, learning does not affect an individual's skill, and the quality of information does not affect its perceived usefulness. Through this study, organizations can implement a high-quality ERP-based accounting information system that has a positive effect on organizational efficiency.

Belfo and Trigo (2013) showed that current technology comes short when dealing with many of the concerns and challenges of the accounting domain. Technology answers identified in this work can be viewed as the future direction of research in the AIS domain. Although AIS research includes ERP systems, other emerging systems such as the ones identified in this work are also important. Unlike ERP systems, these new systems are not thoroughly studied in the AIS domain, so more research is needed to discover new potentials and benefits that these systems can bring to the organization's management, and how they impact the accounting function.

Halim Al Theebeh et al. (2018) showed the importance of management and planning, followed by the limitations of efficiency and procedures related to institutional operations. This study achieved its goals and determined the relationships between variables. The use of accounting systems and management information is of great importance within organizations in the context of technological developments in the world.

Rahman and Kabir (2020) explained that Cloud ERP systems are a new phenomenon, and that the market is under-developed in some parts of the world, especially in developing countries. Considering Bangladesh's current socio-economic scenario and technological readiness, there is ample opportunity for SMEs in Bangladesh to adopt Cloud ERP.

Azad Chowdhury et al. (2012) explained that many companies have already implemented ERP systems in their businesses. Once organizations understand the benefits of an ERP system, they will use it to energize their business. It is hard to imagine companies without a custom ERP in the distant future. In Bangladesh, some software companies are developing their own ERP systems which are already popular in the domestic market. It is hoped that this sector will become widespread and encourage enterprise organizations to adopt ERP.

Tahura Pervin et al. (2019) showed that ERP implementation negatively impacts the representative validity and verifiability of accounting information. Implementing ERP according to the extended Modified Jones Model, which supports the existing literature, reduces that impact. Research shows that the implementation of ERP contributes to profit management.

Mustafa & Hddas et al. (2014) found that ERP began as a tool to facilitate information flow and exchange information between different business partners. It emerges in response to changing business needs and the obsolescence of existing systems as a result of software development. Today, the use of ERP software has become more common in many companies. The use of sophisticated and comprehensive software allows organizations to control and integrate all business functions and processes with a vast array of innovative technologies.

Emrinaldi and Irfan (2020) showed that when implementing an AIS users should consider the benefits and advantages of the system. They explored the effect of the implementation of an AIS based on ERP on users and the organization. In addition, the information system is related to user skill, satisfaction, and knowledge-sharing that improves personal skills; improved personal skills contribute to better organizational performance. On the other hand, there is no effect of training on personal skills and no effect of information quality on perceived usefulness. Their research gives reasons for an organization to implement a high-quality ERP-based AIS that positively affects performance.

Chowdhury et al. (2021) discussed an IT viewpoint of an ERP project as a large enterprise application in both business and enterprise environments. The project involved execution of many new approaches and their integration with existing programs. Cooperation between industry and IT is expanding between many small businesses and their IT divisions. Achieving this will depend on the quality of cooperation, so certain conditions must be ensured. Enterprise must oversee maturity in ERP, managerial and technical capabilities of their IT division, and the ability of the business and IT to work together.

Khasanah et al. (2021) investigated the effect of the implementation of AISs in the framework of ERP on useful information and successful decision-making, and the accountant's competence in successful decision-making. They also confirmed the influence of the implementation of AISs in the framework of ERP.

The study of Ou et al. (2018) was done for improving the quality of firms' accounting information. First, existing accounting business processes should be re-engineered when a company plans to implement an ERP system and expects effective and efficient use. By thoroughly overhauling these existing processes, ERP implementation will improve accuracy and authenticity and the timeliness of accounting information primarily to support the quality of accounting information.

Second, the findings could provide available guidance for firms to support accounting information quality when implementing ERP across different firms and ownership in transition economies. Companies should pay attention to their own effects of ERP implementation. Small companies should adopt a prudent ERP implementation policy system due to its high cost and complexity. Companies must secure sufficient funds to guarantee ERP systems are successfully launched and assimilated.

Indarto and Endah (2017) tried to create a system design of AIS an ERP. The integrated information system technology is used in improving the performance of an organization dealing with aspects of operation, production, and distribution. Every organization is unique in its ERP implementations. For this, it is necessary to evaluate gradually the needs and capabilities of organizations, including human resources.

The study of Halimuzzaman and Sharma (2022) said that accounting information plays a key role in an ERP enabling environment. An ERP system is responsible for generating accounting information such as financial statements that are used to measure the success of the ERP system implementation, provide financial information to external users, and determine operational performance.

Most studies focus on the impact of ERP systems on financial activities, such as managing student finances and payroll. However, there seems to be a lack of in-depth investigation into how ERP systems can be fully utilized for managing human resources and communication within organizations. Rahman and Kabir (2020) said that Cloud ERP systems are a relatively new phenomenon, and the market for such systems may still be under-developed, particularly in developing countries.

Belfo and Trigo (2013) said that while ERP systems are widely studied in the domain of AIS, there are other emerging systems that have not received as much attention. This suggests a research gap in exploring the potentials and benefits of these alternative systems and their impact on the accounting function.

Tahura Pervin et al. (2019) highlighted in their study that ERP implementation may negatively impact the fair representative validity and verifiability of accounting information, contributing to profit management. This points to a research gap in investigating the specific factors and mechanisms that affect accounting information quality during ERP implementation.

Chowdhury et al. (2021) and Khasanah et al. (2021) touched on the impact of ERP implementation on enterprises. There could be a research gap in investigating the influence of ERP implementation on specific industries, company size, and ownership structure to gain a deeper understanding of the challenges and benefits associated with ERP adoption in different contexts. The study of Ou et al. (2018) emphasized the importance of reengineering business processes during ERP implementation to improve the quality of accounting information. This study is done by focusing on the limitations of the previous studies for improving future research on a related topic.

23.8 ANALYSIS AND RESULTS

23.8.1 PROCESS OF ACCOUNTING INFORMATION SYSTEM

The AIS subsystem processes financial and non-financial transactions that directly affect the processing of financial transactions. For example, customer name and address changes are processed by AIS to keep customer files up-to-date. Although these changes are not technically financial transactions, they provide customers with important information for processing future sales.

Accounting information systems consist of three main subsystems: (1) a transaction processing system (TPS) that supports day-to-day business operations with many messages, documents, and reports to users throughout the organization; (2) general ledger/financial reporting systems (GL/FRS) that generate traditional financial statements such as income statements, balance sheets, cash flow statements, tax returns, and other reports required by law; and (3) a management reporting system (MRS) that provides internal guidance for special financial reports and decision-making information such as budgets, and diversification and debt reports.

23.8.2 TRANSACTION PROCESSING SYSTEM

A TPS is central to the overall function of an information system by translating economic events into financial transactions, recording financial transactions in accounting records (journals and general ledgers), and distributing basic financial information to operations personnel to support their day-to-day operations. It deals with business events that occur frequently. In a given day, the company can process thousands of transactions. To handle such volume efficiently, similar types of transactions are grouped into transaction cycles. A TPS consists of three transaction cycles: revenue cycle, spending cycle, and conversion cycle. Each cycle captures and processes different types of financial transactions.

23.8.3 ENTERPRISE RESOURCE PLANNING CORE APPLICATIONS

The functionality of ERP is divided into two main application categories: core applications and business analytics applications. Core applications are those that support the day-to-day running of your business. When these applications fail, so does the business. Common core applications include sales and distribution, business planning, production planning, shop floor management, and logistics, among others (Khang, 2024b).

Core applications are also referred to as online transaction processing (OLTP) applications. Sales and distribution functions ensure order entry and shipment planning. This includes checking product availability to ensure timely delivery and checking customer credit lines. Unlike the previous example, the customer order is entered into ERP only once. Since all users access a common database, order status can be checked at any time. The customer will then be able to check the order directly via an Internet connection. Such integration reduces manual activities, saves time, and reduces human error.

Business planning consists of demand forecasting, product production planning, and detailed routing information that describes the sequence and stages of the actual production process. Capacity planning and production planning can be very complex; therefore, some ERPs provide simulation tools to help managers decide how to avoid shortages of materials, labor, or production facilities. After the master production plan is completed, the data is fed into the material requirements planning (MRP) module, which provides three key pieces of information: an exception report, material requirements, and inventory requirements.

An exception report identifies potential situations that will lead to production rescheduling, such as late delivery of materials. The material requirements list shows details of supplier shipments and expected receipts of the products and components required for the order. Stock requisitions are used to trigger material purchase orders to suppliers for items that are not in stock. Shop floor management includes detailed production planning, dispatch, and costing activities associated with the actual production process. Finally, the logistics application is responsible for ensuring timely delivery to the customer. This includes inventory and warehouse management and shipping. Most ERPs also include purchasing activities within the logistics function (Hall, 2008).

23.8.4 USE OF ACCOUNTING SOFTWARE

The frequency distribution of accounting software use in firms is shown in Table 23.1. The table also shows that only three out of ten respondents use ERP software, which is 30% of the total respondents.

TABLE 23.1
Use of Accounting Software in Firms

	Frequency	Percent	Cumulative Percent
Yes	3	30.0	30.0
No	7	70.0	100.0
Total	10	100.0	

Source: Field Survey, 2022.

TABLE 23.2
Use of ERP Software in Firms

	Frequency	Percent	Cumulative Percent
Yes	8	80.0	80.0
No	2	23.0	100.0
Total	10	100.0	

Source: Field Survey, 2022.

23.8.5 USE OF ENTERPRISE RESOURCE PLANNING SOFTWARE

The frequency distribution of ERP software use in firms is shown in Table 23.2. This table also shows that only two out of ten respondents do not use ERP software, which is 20% of the total respondents.

23.8.6 COST-EFFECTIVENESS OF ENTERPRISE RESOURCE PLANNING AND ACCOUNTING SOFTWARE

The frequency distribution of cost-effectiveness of ERP vs. accounting software is shown in Table 23.3. This table also shows that only seven of ten respondents agreed that ERP software is cost-effective, while three out of ten respondents agreed that accounting ERP software is cost-effective, where 70% of the total respondents are in favor of ERP software.

23.8.7 ENTERPRISE RESOURCE PLANNING IMPLEMENTATION AND ACCOUNTING INFORMATION

Table 23.4 describes how ERP implementation can fairly represent the accounting information. It shows that eight out of ten respondents think that ERP implementation can fairly represent the accounting information, which is 80% of the total respondents.

TABLE 23.3
Cost-Effectiveness of ERP vs. Accounting Software

	Frequency	Percent	Cumulative Percent
ERP Software	7	70.0	70.0
Accounting Software	3	30.0	100.0
Total	10	100.0	

Source: Field Survey, 2022.

TABLE 23.4

Enterprise Resource Planning Implementation and Representation of Accounting Information

	Frequency	Percent	Cumulative Percent
Yes	8	80.0	80.0
No	2	23.0	100.0
Total	10	100.0	

Source: Field Survey, 2022.

TABLE 23.5

Relationship between AIS and ERP

	Frequency	Percent	Cumulative Percent
Yes	8	80.0	80.0
No	2	23.0	100.0
Total	10	100.0	

Source: Field Survey, 2022.

23.8.8 RELATIONSHIP BETWEEN ACCOUNTING INFORMATION SYSTEMS AND ENTERPRISE RESOURCE PLANNING

The relationship between AIS and ERP is presented in Table 23.5. It shows the frequency distribution of the respondents where eight out of ten agreed that there is a relationship between AIS and ERP, which is 80% of the total respondents.

23.8.9 APPLICATION OF ACCOUNTING INFORMATION SYSTEMS IN AN ENTERPRISE RESOURCE PLANNING ENVIRONMENT

Application of AIS in an ERP environment is shown in Table 23.6. It shows the frequency distribution of the respondents where nine out of ten agreed that AIS is applicable in an ERP environment, which is 90% of the total respondents.

TABLE 23.6

Application of Accounting Information Systems in an Enterprise Resource Planning Environment

	Frequency	Percent	Cumulative Percent
Yes	9	90.0	90.0
No	1	10.0	100.0
Total	10	100.0	

Source: Field Survey, 2022.

TABLE 23.7

Model between Accounting Information Systems and Enterprise Resource Planning

	Frequency	Percent	Cumulative Percent
Yes	8	80.0	80.0
No	2	23.0	100.0
Total	10	100.0	

Source: Field Survey, 2022.

23.8.10 ESTABLISHING A MODEL BETWEEN ACCOUNTING INFORMATION SYSTEMS AND ENTERPRISE RESOURCE PLANNING

A frequency distribution model between AIS and ERP is shown in Table 23.7. The table shows that eight out of ten respondents think that it is possible to establish a model between AIS and ERP, which is 80% of the total respondents.

23.8.11 ENTERPRISE RESOURCE PLANNING IMPLEMENTATION IN MANAGING REVENUE

The implementation of ERP in a firm may help to manage revenue, as shown in Table 23.8. The table shows the frequency distribution where five out of ten respondents think that ERP implementation helps to manage revenue, which is 50% of the total respondents.

23.8.12 EFFECTIVENESS OF ENTERPRISE RESOURCE PLANNING ON USEFULNESS OF ACCOUNTING INFORMATION SYSTEMS FOR FINANCIAL REPORTING

Corporate ERP systems are comprehensive software programs that integrate and automate all the enterprise strategies of an agency. An AIS is a vital part of ERP systems that files and reports financial transactions of an agency. The effectiveness of ERP on the usefulness of AIS for financial reporting to the users of accounting

TABLE 23.8

Enterprise Resource Planning Implementation Helps To Manage Revenue

	Frequency	Percent	Cumulative Percent
Agree	5	50.0	50.0
Disagree	5	50.0	100.0
Total	10	100.0	

Source: Field Survey, 2022.

TABLE 23.9

Effectiveness of Enterprise Resource Planning on the Usefulness of Accounting Information Systems for Financial Reporting

	Frequency	Percent	Cumulative Percent
Yes	7	70.0	50.0
No	3	30.0	100.0
Total	10	100.0	

Source: Field Survey, 2022.

information is an important aspect of any enterprise's financial management, as shown in Table 23.9. The table shows the frequency distribution of the respondents where seven out of ten 7 respondents believe in the effectiveness of ERP on the usefulness of AIS for financial reporting, which is 70% of the total respondents.

23.8.13   A STUDY ON ENTERPRISE RESOURCE PLANNING IMPLEMENTATION IN ACCOUNTING INFORMATION SYSTEMS

Table 23.10 presents the results of a survey that examines the possibility of ERP implementation in relation to AIS. It shows that six out of ten respondents think that ERP implementation is possible in relation with AIS, on a scale from 1 to 10.

23.8.14   A STUDY ON MODELING BETWEEN ENTERPRISE RESOURCE PLANNING AND ACCOUNTING INFORMATION SYSTEMS

Table 23.11 presents the results of a study where respondents were asked to indicate whether they agree or disagree with the statement, "Modeling between ERP and AIS will be economically challenged for the newly established firm in near future."

TABLE 23.10

Possibility of Enterprise Resource Planning Implementation in Accounting Information Systems

	Frequency	Percent	Cumulative Percent
5	1	10.0	10.0
7	6	60.0	70.0
10	3	30.0	100.0
Total	10	100.0	

Source: Field Survey, 2022.

TABLE 23.11

Modeling of Economic Challenge between Enterprise Resource Planning and Accounting Information Systems

	Frequency	Percent	Cumulative Percent
Agree	8	80.0	80.0
Disagree	2	23.0	100.0
Total	10	100.0	

Source: Field Survey, 2022.

The table also shows that eight out of ten respondents agree, which is 80% of the total respondents.

23.9 DISCUSSION

In short, 30% of firms surveyed use accounting software, while 70% do not. Eighty percent of the firms surveyed use ERP software, while 20% do not. Seventy percent of the respondents consider ERP software to be cost-effective, while 30% believe accounting software is cost-effective. Eighty percent of the respondents believe that ERP implementation can fairly represent accounting information, while 20% disagree. Eighty percent of the respondents agree that there is an relation between AIS and ERP, while 20% disagree. Ninety percent of the respondents agree that AIS is applicable in an ERP environment, while 10% disagree. And, finally 80% of the respondents think that it is possible to establish a model between AIS and ERP, while 20% disagree.

Furthermore, 50% of the respondents agree that ERP implementation helps the manager to manage revenue, while the other 50% disagree. Seventy percent of the respondents believe that ERP is effective in enhancing the usefulness of AIS for financial reporting, while 30% disagree. Sixty percent of the respondents rated ERP implementation as a 7 out of 10 in terms of possibility in relation to accounting information, followed by 30% rating it a 10, and 10% rating it a 5. Eighty percent of the respondents agree that modeling between ERP and AIS will be economically challenged for newly established firms in the near future, while 20% disagree.

The majority of firms surveyed are using ERP software, indicating a higher adoption rate compared to traditional accounting software. Respondents generally perceive ERP software to be more cost-effective than accounting software. ERP implementation is considered to fairly represent accounting information by a significant majority of respondents. The relationship between AIS and ERP is acknowledged by most of the respondents, indicating the recognition of the integration and importance of these systems in modern business practices. A vast majority of respondents agree that AIS is applicable in an ERP environment, highlighting the belief in the compatibility and complementarity of the two systems. Although ERP implementation is considered feasible in relation to accounting information, some respondents expressed uncertainty or lower confidence in this aspect. The effectiveness of ERP in enhancing the usefulness of AIS for financial reporting is recognized by a majority, but there is still a portion of respondents who are unsure or disagree. The potential economic challenges of modeling between ERP and AIS for newly established firms are acknowledged by a substantial proportion of respondents (Rath & Khang et al., 2024).

23.10   FINDINGS OF THE STUDY

A transaction processing system (TPS) supports daily business operations by generating reports, documents, and messages for users throughout the organization. It processes financial transactions and non-financial transactions that directly affect the processing of financial transactions.

A general ledger/financial reporting system (GL/FRS) produces traditional financial statements such as the income statement, balance sheet, statement of cash flows, tax returns, and other reports required by law. It is responsible for generating the financial reports that are used by external stakeholders such as investors, creditors, and regulatory authorities.

A management reporting system (MRS) provides internal management with special-purpose financial reports and information needed for decision-making, such as budgets, variance reports, and responsibility reports. It helps you plan, monitor, and evaluate your organization's performance. The application handles two important components of an information system: TPS and core ERP applications (Snehal et al., 2023).

The TPS is responsible for transforming economic events into financial transactions, recording them in accounting records, and providing financial information to support day-to-day operations. The TPS consists of three trading cycles: income, expense, and conversion. On the other hand, the functionality of ERP is divided into two main application groups: basic applications and applications for business analysis. Core applications operationally support the day-to-day activities of the business, such as sales and distribution, business planning, production planning, shop floor control, and logistics. These are also known as OLTP applications. The statement provides examples of how these applications work in a manufacturing firm, including order entry and delivery scheduling, forecasting demand, planning production, inventory management, and shipping. The integration of these applications reduces manual activities, saves time, and decreases human error.

The most of the respondents are using ERP software (80%), while only 30% are using accounting software (Khang et al., 2023). The majority of the respondents (70%) consider ERP software to be cost-effective, while only 30% consider accounting software to be cost-effective. This suggests that ERP software is perceived to be more advantageous in terms of cost compared to accounting software. Moreover, the majority of the respondents (80%) believe that ERP implementation can fairly represent accounting information, and there is an interrelation between AIS and ERP (80%). These findings suggest that the implementation of ERP software can enhance the accuracy of accounting information and streamline business processes. Furthermore, most of the respondents (90%) agreed that AIS is applicable in the

ERP environment, and it is possible to establish a model between AIS and ERP (80%). This implies that the integration of AIS and ERP software can provide a comprehensive and efficient business solution. However, the survey findings also indicate that there is a split in opinion regarding the effectiveness of ERP implementation in managing revenue (50% agree, 50% disagree).

Additionally, only 70% of the respondents believe that ERP software is effective in improving the usefulness of the accounting information system for financial reporting to the users of accounting information. Overall, the survey findings suggest that ERP software is more popular and perceived to be more advantageous than accounting software. The implementation of ERP software can enhance the accuracy of accounting information, streamline business processes, and provide a comprehensive and efficient business solution (Khang & Muthmainnah et al., 2023).

However, opinions are divided on the effectiveness of ERP implementations in revenue management, with only 70% of respondents believing that ERP software effectively improves the effectiveness of accounting information systems for financial reporting.

23.11   RECOMMENDATIONS OF THE STUDY

Based on the results of this study, the following recommendations can be made:

- Further research is needed on the difference of opinion regarding the effectiveness of ERP implementation in revenue management. Understanding the reasons behind this difference in opinion can help organizations address any potential problems or concerns related to ERP implementation.
- It would be beneficial to conduct a cost–benefit analysis to determine the true cost-effectiveness of ERP software compared to accounting software. This can help organizations make more informed decisions about which software to use based on their specific needs and budget.
- Because most respondents believe that AIS is applicable in an ERP environment, it is recommended that organizations explore ways to integrate AIS and ERP software to improve the accuracy and efficiency of their accounting and business processes.
- Organizations should also consider implementing business analytics applications as part of their ERP system to gain insight into their business operations and make data-informed decisions.
- Organizations should prioritize user training and support to ensure that employees are equipped with the necessary skills and knowledge to effectively use ERP software and maximize its benefits.

23.12   CONCLUSION

This study provides an overview of the AIS process and its subsystems. The AIS consists of three main subsystems: TPS, GL/FRS, and MRS. The TPS is responsible for converting economic events into financial transactions, recording financial transactions in accounting records, and distributing basic financial information to support day-to-day operations. It consists of three transaction cycles: revenue cycle, spending cycle, and conversion cycle (Khang, 2024a).

The study also discusses basic applications of ERP systems that operationally support the day-to-day activities of the company. These applications include sales and distribution, business planning, production planning, shop floor management and logistics. ERP systems provide integration that reduces manual activities, saves time, and reduces human error.

Overall, according to the survey, most respondents believe that ERP software is cost-effective, adaptable to an AIS environment, can reliably display accounting information, and enhances the usefulness of AIS for financial reporting. Most respondents also agree that there is a relationship between AIS and ERP and that models can be created between them. However, the survey also highlights that accounting software is rarely used and that respondents rate the effectiveness of ERP in revenue management and financial reporting differently (Khang, 2024c).

REFERENCES

Alzoubi, A., (2012). The effectiveness of the accounting information system under the Enterprise resources planning (ERP). Research Journal of Finance and Accounting, 2(11), 10–19.

Azad Chowdhury, M. S., Toufiqur Rahman, M., Shahabuddin, A. M., & Hassan, M. R., (2012). Implementation of Enterprise resource planning (ERP) in Bangladesh - Opportunities and challenges. International Journal of Business and Management, 16(11), 1–11. https://www.academia.edu/download/70807442/48952.pdf

Belfo, F., & Trigo, A., (2013). Accounting information systems: Tradition and future directions. Procedia Technology, 9, 536–546. https://doi.org/10.1016/j.protcy.2013.12.060

Chowdhury, M. S. A., Rahman, M. T., Shahabuddin, A. M., Hassan, M. R., & Chowdhury, M. S. R. (2021). Implementation of Enterprise resource planning (ERP) in Bangladesh - Opportunities and challenges. International Journal of Business and Management, 16(11), Article 11. https://doi.org/10.5539/ijbm.v16n11p1

Emrinaldi, N., & Irfan, M., (2020). ERP-based accounting information system implementation in organization: A study in Riau, Indonesia. The Journal of Asian Finance, Economics and Business (JAFEB), 7(12), 147–157. https://koreascience.kr/article/JAKO202034651879141.page

Halim Al Theebeh, Z. A., Al-Mubaydeen, T. H., & Fawzi Ismael, M. (2018). The effect of applying the organization Enterprise resource planning system (ERP) in the quality of internal audit: A case of Jordanian commercial banks. International Journal of Economics and Finance, 10(5). https://pdfs.semanticscholar.org/ea56/f1c279392130d-a45b070027177b74b948408.pdf

Halimuzzaman, Md., & Sharma, J. Dr. (2022). Applications of accounting information system (AIS)under Enterprise resource planning (ERP): A comprehensive review. International Journal of Early Childhood Special Education (INT-JECSE), 14(2), 6801–6806. https://doi.org/10.9756/INT-JECSE/V14I2.782

Hall, James A. (2008). Accounting Information Systems (7th Ed.). Cengage Learning. http://lms.aambc.edu.et:8080/xmlui/bitstream/handle/123456789/97/Accounting%20Information%20System-%20JamesHall_2011_AIS_ed7.pdf?sequence=1

Indarto, S. L., & Endah, S. M. D. (2017). The combination of transaction process and design of accounting information system through Enterprise resource planning (ERP). International Journal of Business, Economics and Law, 13, 14–26. https://www.ijbel.com/wp-content/uploads/2017/09/ACC-97.pdf

Khang, A., "Future Directions and Challenges in Designing Workforce Management Systems for Industry 4," *AI-Oriented Competency Framework for Talent Management in the Digital Economy: Models, Technologies, Applications, and Implementation.* (1st Ed.) (2024a). CRC Press. https://doi.org/10.1201/9781003440901-1

Khang, A., "Design and Modelling of AI-Oriented Competency Framework (AIoCF) for Information Technology Sector," *AI-Oriented Competency Framework for Talent Management in the Digital Economy: Models, Technologies, Applications, and Implementation.* (1st Ed.) (2024b). CRC Press. https://doi.org/10.1201/9781003440901-17

Khang, A., "Implementation of AIoCF Model and Tools for Information Technology Sector," *AI-Oriented Competency Framework for Talent Management in the Digital Economy: Models, Technologies, Applications, and Implementation.* (1st Ed.) (2024c. CRC Press. https://doi.org/10.1201/9781003440901-20

Khang, A., Muthmainnah, M, Seraj, Prodhan Mahbub Ibna, Yakin, Ahmad Al, Obaid, Ahmad J., & Ranjan Panda, Manas. "AI-Aided Teaching Model for the Education 5.0 Ecosystem" *AI-Based Technologies and Applications in the Era of the Metaverse.* (1st Ed.) (2023). Page (83–104). IGI Global Press. https://doi.org/10.4018/978-1-6684-8851-5.ch004

Khang, A., Rani, S., Gujrati, R., Uygun, H., & Gupta, S. K., *Designing Workforce Management Systems for Industry 4.0: Data-Centric and AI-Enabled Approaches.* (1st Ed.) (2023). CRC Press. https://doi.org/10.1201/9781003357070

Khang, A., Rath, Kali Charan, Kumar Satapathy, Suresh, Kumar, Amaresh, Ranjan Das, Sudhansu, & Ranjan Panda, Manas. "Enabling the Future of Manufacturing: Integration of Robotics and IoT to Smart Factory Infrastructure in Industry 4.0." *AI-Based Technologies and Applications in the Era of the Metaverse.* (1st Ed.) (2023). Page (25–50). IGI Global Press. https://doi.org/10.4018/978-1-6684-8851-5.ch002

Khang, A., Shah, V., & Rani, S., *AI-Based Technologies and Applications in the Era of the Metaverse.* (1st Ed.) (2023). IGI Global Press. https://doi.org/10.4018/978-1-6684-8851-5

Khasanah, U., Mulyani, S., Akbar, B., & Dahlan, M., (2021). The impact of project management and implementing Enterprise resource planning on decision-making effectiveness: The case of Indonesian state-owned enterprises. Academy of Strategic Management Journal, 20, 1–12.

Mustafa AlBar, A., A. Hddas, M., & Hoque, Md. R., (2014). Enterprise Resource planning (ERP) systems: Emergence, importance and challenges | Atlantis press. The International Technology Management Review, 4(4), 170–175. https://www.atlantis-press.com/journals/itmr/14963

Nur D.P., E., & Irfan, M, (2020). ERP-based accounting information system implementation in organization: A study in Riau, Indonesia. The Journal of Asian Finance, Economics and Business, 7(12), 147–157. https://doi.org/10.13106/JAFEB.2023.VOL7.NO12.147

Odoyo, C., & Ojera, P. (2020). Impact of top management support on accounting information system: A case of Enterprise resource planning (ERP) system. Universal Journal of Management, 8. https://doi.org/10.13189/ujm.2023.080102

Ou, P., Zhao, H., & Zhou, Z., (2018). Does the implementation of ERP improve the quality of accounting information? Evidence from chinese a-share listed manufacturing firms. Journal of Applied Business Research (JABR), 34(1), 43–54. https://www.clutejournals.com/index.php/JABR/article/view/10090

Rahman, I., & Kabir, Md. R., (2020). Benefits and challenges of cloud ERP adoption by SMEs. Journal of Business Administration, 41(1), 23–39. http://iba-du.edu/upload_images/Vol.%2041_No.1_Article_2.pdf

Snehal, M., Babasaheb, J., & Khang, A., "Workforce Management System: Concepts, Definitions, Principles, and Implementation," *Designing Workforce Management Systems for Industry 4.0: Data-Centric and AI-Enabled Approaches*, pp. 1–13. (1st Ed.) (2023). CRC Press. https://doi.org/10.1201/9781003357070-1

Tahura Pervin, Most, Bakul Sarkar, J., & Kumar Bala, S., (2019). Effect of ERP implementations on faithful representation and verifiability of accounting information leading to earnings management: Bangladesh Perspective. DUET Journal, 5(1), 67–75. http://103.133.35.64:8080/jspui/handle/123456789/434

24 Ransomware Resilience Strategies for Manufacturing Systems
Safeguarding the Enterprise Resource Planning and Human Resource Management Data

J. A. Raja, Alex Khang, and R. Vani

24.1 INTRODUCTION

In an era defined by digital transformation, where organizations increasingly rely on technology for their operations, the rise of cyberthreats has paralleled this progress. One such menacing threat is ransomware, an insidious form of malware that can cripple businesses by encrypting critical data and demanding payment in exchange for its release. While ransomware attacks have targeted a broad spectrum of industries, the impact on ERP and HRM systems is particularly alarming. These systems, repositories of sensitive employee information and vital organizational data, have become prime targets for cybercriminals seeking both financial gains and strategic disruption (Garcia-Perez et al., 2023).

24.1.1 RANSOMWARE AS A GROWING THREAT TO ENTERPRISE RESOURCE PLANNING AND HUMAN RESOURCE MANAGEMENT SYSTEMS

Ransomware, often propagated through deceptive e-mail attachments, malicious links, or compromised websites, has evolved from mere nuisance attacks to sophisticated campaigns executed by well-funded cybercrime syndicates. The rationale behind these attacks is clear: by crippling an organization's access to its own data, criminals aim to extract significant ransom payments, often in cryptocurrency, as a condition for data restoration. The impact of a successful ransomware attack on HR systems extends beyond financial loss; it disrupts employee operations, jeopardizes sensitive employee data, erodes organizational reputation, and can lead to legal and regulatory implications (Tsantes & Ransome, 2023).

DOI: 10.1201/9781003438137-24

24.1.2 Ransomware Resilience Strategies

In the face of this escalating threat, organizations cannot afford to be passive bystanders. They must adopt proactive strategies to fortify their defenses, ensure the continuity of operations, and safeguard the confidentiality and integrity of ERP and HRM data. The imperative to protect employee information, financial records, and proprietary data demands a strategic approach that blends technology, employee education, and preparedness (Pyżalski et al., 2022).

24.1.3 Objectives

This chapter is dedicated to understanding the critical nature of ransomware attacks on HR systems and the strategies necessary to build resilience against them. The primary objectives of this chapter are as follows:

1. To provide an in-depth exploration of the ransomware threat landscape as it pertains to ERP and HR systems, shedding light on the evolving tactics employed by cybercriminals to exploit vulnerabilities in these crucial systems.
2. To present a comprehensive framework of ransomware resilience strategies specifically tailored to HR systems. These strategies encompass a spectrum of preventive, detective, and corrective measures aimed at thwarting ransomware attacks and minimizing their impact.
3. To discuss the implications of research findings related to ransomware resilience for HR systems. This includes insights into the effectiveness of various strategies, the role of employee education, and the integration of real-time threat intelligence.
4. To conclude by emphasizing the significance of a proactive approach to ransomware resilience, underscoring the need for ongoing adaptation and preparedness to counter the evolving threat landscape.
5. To identify areas for future research and exploration, examining emerging technologies and methodologies that could further enhance the ability of organizations to safeguard their HR systems and data from ransomware attacks.

As we delve into the subsequent sections of this chapter, we will explore the multifaceted dimensions of ransomware resilience strategies, underscore the importance of a collective defense approach, and equip readers with the knowledge needed to protect their ERP and HR data from the ever-looming ransomware threat (Khang, 2023).

24.2　RELATED WORK

In the dynamic landscape of ERP and HR systems, the constant threat of ransomware demands a strategic and multifaceted approach. This section delves into proactive strategies that organizations can employ to fortify their defenses, mitigate the risk of ransomware infiltrating HR systems, and thwart potential disruptions.

24.2.1 Preventive Measures: Safeguarding Data and Operations

24.2.1.1 Data Backup and Recovery: Immutable Backups for Data Integrity

One of the foundational pillars in ransomware resilience is a robust data backup and recovery strategy. Immutable backups play a pivotal role in ensuring data integrity. Immutable backups prevent unauthorized modifications to backup data, guaranteeing that even in the event of a ransomware attack; organizations possess clean and uncorrupted data for recovery (Sujatha et al., 2022). By keeping multiple versions of backups, organizations can roll back to a point in time before the attack occurred, rendering ransomware's extortion attempts futile.

24.2.1.2 Backup Policies and Procedures: Ensuring Availability and Accessibility

A structured approach to data backup involves establishing well-defined policies and procedures. Backup intervals, retention periods, and secure storage locations should be clearly delineated to ensure the availability of critical data when needed. Regular testing of backup restoration procedures is essential to verify the efficacy of the backup system. Additionally, maintaining backups in secure off-site locations or utilizing cloud-based solutions enhances data availability in the face of localized attacks.

24.2.1.3 User Training and Awareness: Building a Human Firewall

Human error remains a significant vulnerability exploited by ransomware attackers. Educating employees about ransomware risks is a proactive step toward building a human firewall. Tailored training programs empower employees to recognize and respond to threats effectively. Workshops on identifying phishing techniques and distinguishing suspicious e-mails or attachments instill a heightened sense of cybervigilance. By fostering a culture of cyberawareness, organizations can effectively reduce the risk of successful ransomware intrusions (Bandari, 2023).

24.2.1.4 Recognizing Phishing Tactics and Suspicious Activities: Empowering Vigilance

Ransomware often gains a foothold through phishing e-mails, making it crucial for employees to recognize telltale signs of malicious communication. Encouraging employees to scrutinize e-mail senders, verify URLs, and avoid clicking on suspicious links can prevent inadvertent compromise. Prompt reporting of phishing attempts to the IT department facilitates swift response and containment.

24.2.1.5 Endpoint Protection: Advanced Antivirus and Behavior-Based Detection

The endpoint serves as a critical juncture for ransomware entry. Advanced antivirus software equipped with behavior-based detection mechanisms enhances ransomware defense. These systems move beyond traditional signature-based identification, analyzing behaviors to identify potentially malicious activities. Regular updates to antivirus databases are paramount to staying current with emerging threat intelligence. Furthermore, integrating real-time threat intelligence feeds into endpoint protection solutions and enables proactive defense against evolving ransomware variants and tactics (Khang & Vladimir et al., 2024).

24.2.1.6 Regular Updates and Threat Intelligence Integration: Staying Ahead of Threats

Endpoint protection measures are only effective if they are continuously updated. Cybercriminals adapt their tactics rapidly, necessitating a vigilant stance from security teams. Regular updates ensure that the antivirus software can recognize and neutralize the latest ransomware variants. Integrating threat intelligence feeds from reputable sources enhances the software's ability to identify emerging threats, enabling preemptive action to stop ransomware in its tracks (McLaughlin, 2023).

As organizations navigate the intricate landscape of HR systems vulnerability to ransomware, these preventive measures serve as critical safeguards. By prioritizing data integrity, fostering employee awareness, and embracing advanced endpoint protection, organizations can significantly bolster their defenses against ransomware attacks, as shown in Figure 24.1.

24.2.2 DETECTION AND EARLY RESPONSE: UNVEILING RANSOMWARE'S INTRUSION

In the constantly evolving landscape of cyberthreats, ransomware stands out as a particularly insidious adversary. As organizations strive to fortify their defenses, the strategies of detection and early response emerge as pivotal components in their cybersecurity arsenal. This section delves into the multifaceted dimensions of these strategies, shedding light on how they empower organizations to unveil ransomware's

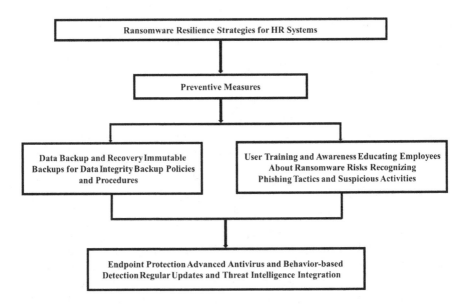

FIGURE 24.1 Bolstering defenses of an organization against ransomware attacks.

intrusion attempts and neutralize them before damage ensues (Khang & Abdullayev et al., 2023).

24.2.2.1 Real-Time Threat Intelligence: Utilizing Threat Feeds for Timely Alerts

The foundation of effective ransomware detection lies in real-time threat intelligence. In an interconnected world, the actions of cybercriminals ripple across borders, demanding swift action to counteract their efforts. Organizations can subscribe to reputable threat intelligence feeds that continuously monitor global cyberthreats. These feeds act as sentinels, vigilantly scanning for indicators of compromise (IoCs) related to emerging ransomware variants. By leveraging these feeds, organizations receive timely alerts, allowing them to react proactively to potential threats before they can materialize into full-blown attacks (Chawki, 2022).

24.2.2.2 Analyzing Emerging Ransomware Threats: Staying One Step Ahead

In the battle against ransomware, staying ahead is imperative. The landscape is in constant flux as cybercriminals adapt and innovate. By dissecting emerging ransomware threats, security experts gain insights into attack methodologies, encryption techniques, and communication channels. Rigorous analysis of malware samples unravels their inner workings, revealing potential vulnerabilities. This intel arms organizations with the knowledge needed to adapt their defenses and fortify weak points, effectively rendering attackers' efforts less effective (Anh et al., 2024).

24.2.2.3 Behavioral Analytics: Monitoring Unusual Patterns and Anomalies

Traditional signature-based approaches to threat detection can falter against the ever-changing ransomware landscape. Behavioral analytics offers a proactive solution by focusing on patterns of behavior. By establishing baselines of normal behavior for systems, applications, and users, security teams can identify deviations that indicate ransomware activities. A sudden surge in file modifications or unauthorized encryption of files triggers alerts, prompting immediate investigation and response. This behavioral approach empowers organizations to detect ransomware in its early stages, mitigating its impact.

24.2.2.4 Leveraging Machine Learning for Behavior Baselines: Enhancing Detection Precision

Machine learning (ML) infuses behavioral analytics with enhanced precision. It learns from historical data to establish dynamic behavior baselines that adapt to shifting conditions. As behaviors change over time, ML identifies and accommodates legitimate deviations while swiftly detecting abnormal activities indicative of ransomware attacks. This self-learning process refines its understanding of normal behavior, minimizing false positives and enabling more accurate detection (Wörmann et al., 2022).

24.2.2.5 Network Segmentation: Micro-Segmentation and Isolation to Prevent Lateral Movement

Network segmentation is a tactical defense mechanism that hampers ransomware's lateral movement within organizations. Micro-segmentation takes this strategy to a granular level by compartmentalizing the network into isolated segments. Each segment houses specific applications and systems, curbing the ability of ransomware to spread. In the unfortunate event of a ransomware intrusion, micro-segmentation contains the threat, preventing it from rapidly traversing the network and causing widespread damage (Khang & Hajimahmud et al., 2024).

The strategies of detection and early response are pivotal in the battle against ransomware. Real-time threat intelligence, combined with the analysis of emerging threats, empowers organizations to anticipate and counteract evolving attack vectors. By harnessing behavioral analytics and ML, abnormal activities are swiftly identified, enabling prompt mitigation. Furthermore, network segmentation, especially micro-segmentation, acts as a formidable barrier against lateral ransomware movement. Embracing these strategies not only safeguards the integrity of HR systems but also reflects a proactive commitment to thwarting the advances of cyber- adversaries, as shown in Figure 24.2.

24.2.3 RECOVERY AND MITIGATION: NAVIGATING THE AFTERMATH

When the storm of a ransomware attack subsides, the journey to recovery and mitigation begins. This phase requires a strategic and coordinated approach to regain

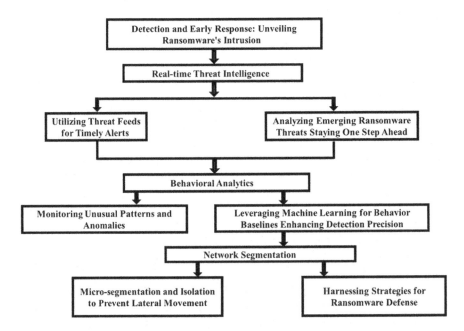

FIGURE 24.2 The integrity of HR systems reflects a proactive commitment to thwarting the advances of cyber-adversaries.

control, minimize damage, and fortify defenses against future threats. This section outlines ten key strategies that organizations can deploy to navigate the aftermath of a ransomware attack effectively.

24.2.3.1 Incident Response Planning: Developing Coordinated Response Protocols

The foundation of effective recovery lies in comprehensive incident response planning. Organizations must have well-defined protocols in place that outline specific steps to be taken when a ransomware attack is detected. These protocols include responsibilities for containment, eradication, communication, and recovery. By establishing a clear chain of command and coordinated action plan, organizations can minimize confusion, streamline decision-making, and respond swiftly to mitigate the impact of the attack.

24.2.3.2 Tabletop Exercises for Simulation and Improvement

Preparedness is sharpened through practice. Tabletop exercises simulate real-life ransomware scenarios, allowing teams to rehearse their response strategies in a controlled environment. These exercises facilitate the identification of gaps in incident response plans and procedures. By conducting these simulations, organizations can fine-tune their response strategies, enhance collaboration between different teams, and ensure that every member understands their role and responsibilities during a real incident (Yamin & Katt, 2022).

24.2.3.3 Forensic Analysis: Decoding the Attack

After an attack, forensic analysis becomes a vital step in understanding the attack's tactics and techniques. By dissecting the ransomware's behavior, entry points, and propagation methods, organizations gain critical insights into the modus operandi of cybercriminals. This understanding is essential for identifying vulnerabilities that were exploited and for uncovering potential weaknesses in the organization's security architecture.

24.2.3.4 Identifying Vulnerabilities for Future Prevention

Post-attack vulnerability assessment is a proactive measure that leverages insights gained from the forensic analysis. Organizations must identify the weaknesses that the attackers exploited and take steps to remediate them. This might involve patching software vulnerabilities, updating security configurations, and enhancing access controls. The goal is to bolster the organization's defenses to prevent similar attacks in the future.

24.2.3.5 Strengthening Access Controls: Limiting Exposure

A ransomware attack often highlights the importance of stringent access controls. Organizations should reassess and tighten user access privileges to critical systems and sensitive data. Implementing the principle of least privilege ensures that users have only the permissions necessary for their roles, reducing the attack surface and minimizing the potential impact of future attacks.

24.2.3.6 Data Recovery and Restoration: Ensuring Business Continuity

The ability to recover encrypted data swiftly is a linchpin of ransomware recovery. Immutable backups created as part of preventive measures become invaluable during this phase. Organizations must ensure that backup restoration processes are well documented, tested, and capable of restoring critical data promptly. This approach empowers organizations to regain normal operations without succumbing to ransom demands.

24.2.3.7 Communication and Stakeholder Management: Transparency and Assurance

Open and transparent communication is essential during the recovery process. Internally, employees should be informed about the incident, the steps being taken for recovery, and any potential impacts on their work. Externally, stakeholders, customers, and regulatory bodies should be kept informed about the incident's impact and the measures being undertaken to safeguard their interests.

24.2.3.8 Legal and Regulatory Compliance: Navigating Legal Implications

Ransomware attacks can have legal and regulatory implications. Organizations must collaborate with legal experts to ensure compliance with relevant laws and regulations. This might involve reporting the incident to regulatory authorities, cooperating with law enforcement, and addressing any obligations related to data breach notifications.

24.2.3.9 Continuous Improvement: Learning from the Experience

Every ransomware incident is an opportunity for improvement. Organizations should conduct post-incident reviews to analyze the effectiveness of response efforts. These reviews inform future adjustments to incident response plans, training programs, and security measures. Continuous improvement ensures that the organization evolves in the face of evolving cyberthreats.

24.2.3.10 Building Resilience: Integrating Lessons Learned

The final phase of recovery involves leveraging the lessons learned to build enduring resilience. Organizations should update incident response plans, enhance security controls, and educate employees based on the insights gained from the attack. By integrating these lessons into the organization's culture, policies, and practices, the organization becomes better prepared to thwart future ransomware threats. By implementing these ten strategies, organizations can effectively navigate the aftermath, minimize damage, and emerge stronger and more resilient against the persistent threat of ransomware, as shown in Figure 24.3.

24.3 RESEARCH IMPLICATIONS OR FINDINGS: ELEVATING RANSOMWARE RESILIENCE

Within the context of ERP and HRM systems, this chapter delves into an exploration of the multifaceted landscape of combating ransomware. As the digital world becomes increasingly interconnected, the implications and findings of this research shed light on the strategies that organizations must employ to elevate ransomware resilience and safeguard their critical data and processes.

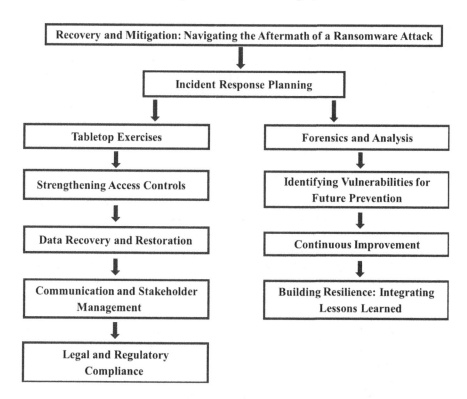

FIGURE 24.3 Multifaceted and strategic approach to defending against the persistent threat of ransomware.

24.3.1 HOLISTIC APPROACH TO RANSOMWARE RESILIENCE

A significant research implication emerges from the understanding that ransomware attacks cannot be effectively mitigated through isolated strategies. The findings underscore the importance of a holistic approach that encompasses a comprehensive range of preventive, detective, and corrective measures. Ransomware, with its continually evolving tactics, demands a multilayered defense that addresses vulnerabilities from various angles. Organizations that adopt this approach bolster their resilience by combining data protection mechanisms, employee training, sophisticated detection technologies, and well-structured incident response plans. This holistic defense mechanism is akin to a fortified castle, where each layer contributes to the overall strength of the defense, making it increasingly challenging for ransomware attackers to breach (Kumar & Mallipeddi, 2022).

24.3.2 ROLE OF EMPLOYEE EDUCATION IN MITIGATING RANSOMWARE

One of the compelling findings of this research pertains to the crucial role of employee education in mitigating ransomware risks. Despite the advancements in cybersecurity technologies, human error remains a potent vulnerability. The research underscores that organizations that prioritize ongoing and engaging employee education programs reap significant benefits. These programs empower employees to recognize and respond to ransomware threats and foster a heightened culture of cyberawareness. Regular training sessions, workshops, and simulations enable employees to understand the nuances of ransomware tactics, particularly those involving phishing and social engineering. Through education, employees become the first line of defense, collectively forming a human firewall that can intercept and thwart ransomware attempts (Khang, 2024).

24.3.3 Significance of Real-Time Threat Intelligence Integration

An essential research finding revolves around the integration of real-time threat intelligence as a pivotal component of ransomware resilience. The digital landscape is dynamic, with new ransomware variants emerging frequently. Real-time threat intelligence, gained through subscription to threat feeds, offers organizations a continuous stream of updated information about emerging threats, attack vectors, and IoCs. The research underscores that this timely information empowers organizations to adapt their defenses swiftly, enhancing their ability to detect and respond to evolving ransomware threats. By integrating real-time threat intelligence, organizations gain a proactive stance, enabling them to anticipate potential attacks, fortify their systems, and update their incident response plans in line with the changing threat landscape (Sun et al., 2023).

Collectively, the implications and findings of this research underline the complexity of ransomware resilience within the domains of ERP and HR systems. The research reinforces that effective defense demands a strategic orchestration of multifaceted strategies. A holistic approach, combined with the power of employee education and the integration of real-time threat intelligence, emerges as a formidable strategy. This integrated defense fortifies organizations against ransomware attacks that target critical HR systems. By embracing these implications and applying the research findings, organizations can cultivate a resilient cybersecurity posture that not only safeguards data and processes but also enhances their ability to thrive in the digital age's evolving threat landscape.

24.4 CONCLUSION

As we conclude this comprehensive exploration into enhancing ransomware resilience within ERP and HRM systems, critical insights emerge that encapsulate the foundational strategies, proactive mindset, and far-reaching implications required to safeguard HRM systems and their data from ransomware attacks.

24.4.1 Recap of Ransomware Resilience Strategies

The chapter delved into ransomware resilience strategies. From the initial steps of preventive measures, such as data backup and user training, to the intricacies of real-time threat intelligence integration and meticulous forensic analysis, every strategy contributes to a multidimensional defense against ransomware. These strategies collectively form a security fabric, wherein each thread reinforces the others. The insights gleaned from this exploration emphasize that a resilient defense is not constructed from a solitary approach but rather many strategies working in concert.

24.4.2 EMPHASIS ON PROACTIVITY OVER REACTIVITY

A paramount finding from this exploration is the importance of adopting a proactive stance in the realm of ransomware defense. Ransomware is not a static adversary; it is a dynamic and evolving threat that thrives on exploiting vulnerabilities. The research underscores the critical significance of organizations that actively invest in education, real-time threat intelligence, and a culture of continuous improvement. By proactively anticipating potential threats, these organizations relegate reactivity to a secondary role. This proactive approach transforms organizations from passive victims awaiting attacks to architects of their own resilience, reshaping the security landscape (Khang & Hajimahmud et al., 2024).

24.4.3 IMPLICATIONS FOR SECURING ENTERPRISE RESOURCE PLANNING AND HUMAN RESOURCE MANAGEMENT SYSTEMS AND DATA

The implications of this research extend far beyond its immediate domain, stretching into the critical realm of HRM systems and their safeguarding. With HRM systems serving as repositories of sensitive employee data, ensuring their protection transcends mere operational necessity; it is a matter of trust. The research underscores that when organizations embrace holistic security strategies and prioritize employee education, they shield valuable data and nurture a sense of security among employees. This, in turn, bolsters their trust in the organization's commitment to safeguarding their personal information, nurturing a foundation of trust between the organization and its workforce (Khang & Rana et al., 2023).

In the broader context, these conclusions are guiding principles for securing the digital landscape against ransomware. As organizations internalize these findings, they forge a path to a future characterized by resilient defenses, fortified systems, and a proactive posture. By embracing a holistic security approach, organizations fortify their critical HRM systems against the multifaceted nature of ransomware attacks. With a proactive mindset, they transcend reactive vulnerabilities, seizing control of the narrative in the face of evolving threats.

In this rapidly evolving digital era, the conclusions drawn from this exploration are not mere final words but seeds of transformative action. As organizations weave the insights of this chapter into their security fabric, they cultivate an environment where ransomware resilience is not a goal but a perpetual journey. By integrating these strategies, adopting a proactive stance, and recognizing the implications for securing HRM systems and data, organizations fortify their defenses and champion a safer digital landscape for themselves, their employees, and the interconnected world. In the pursuit of resilience, the journey continues, fortified by knowledge, driven by proactivity, and steadfast in the commitment to safeguard what matters most.

24.5 FUTURE WORK

24.5.1 CHARTING NEW FRONTIERS IN RANSOMWARE DEFENSE

As we cast our gaze forward, beyond the present landscape of ransomware defense within ERP and HRM systems, a world of unexplored possibilities and emerging challenges comes into view. This section explores future work, outlining intriguing avenues for research and innovation that promise to reshape the ransomware resilience landscape and further fortify the protection of critical HRM systems and ERP data (Khang & Ragimova et al., 2024).

24.5.2 EXPLORING ARTIFICIAL INTELLIGENCE AND MACHINE LEARNING IN RANSOMWARE DEFENSE

The dawn of AI and ML presents an exhilarating opportunity to revolutionize ransomware defense. Future research could delve into harnessing AI and ML algorithms to predict, detect, and mitigate ransomware attacks with unprecedented accuracy. By analyzing vast amounts of data, these technologies can uncover patterns indicative of ransomware activities, enabling organizations to thwart attacks at an early stage. Moreover, AI-driven incident response systems can autonomously orchestrate defensive measures, mitigating damage while minimizing human response time. Such research could redefine ransomware resilience by creating dynamic, self-adapting defense mechanisms that evolve alongside the threat landscape.

24.5.3 INVESTIGATING REGULATORY IMPACT ON RANSOMWARE RESILIENCE

In an era marked by increasing data privacy regulations and compliance mandates, a critical future research avenue lies in understanding the interplay between regulatory frameworks and ransomware resilience. As governments globally enact stringent data protection laws, researchers could delve into the alignment of ransomware defense strategies with regulatory requirements. Investigating the impact of compliance obligations on incident response, data breach notification, and recovery processes could provide organizations with insights into building resilient systems that not only withstand ransomware attacks but also align with legal obligations.

24.5.4 ADVANCING THREAT-HUNTING TECHNIQUES FOR HUMAN RESOURCE MANAGEMENT SYSTEMS

The landscape of threat hunting is ripe for advancement, particularly in the context of HRM systems. Future research can delve into the development of specialized threat hunting methodologies tailored to the unique challenges posed by ransomware attacks on HRM data. By combining traditional threat hunting practices with domain-specific knowledge, researchers can uncover ransomware indicators hidden within the intricacies of HRM processes. This proactive approach allows organizations to identify and neutralize threats before they inflict damage, bolstering ransomware resilience through targeted detection and swift response (Khang, Hajimahmud & Triwiyanto et al., 2024).

24.5.5 ASSESSING BLOCKCHAIN'S ROLE IN DATA INTEGRITY AGAINST RANSOMWARE

Blockchain technology's potential to enhance data integrity and security offers a promising avenue for future exploration. Research could focus on integrating blockchain into HRM systems to create tamper-proof records of employee data and transactions. By adopting a blockchain-based approach, organizations can ensure the immutability of critical HRM data, making it resistant to ransomware attacks aimed at data manipulation or destruction. Furthermore, blockchain's decentralized nature reduces single points of failure, thereby enhancing the overall resilience of HRM systems against ransomware threats.

As we stand on the cusp of the future, these research directions beckon us to embark on a journey of innovation and inquiry. Through the exploration of AI and ML, investigations into the regulatory landscape, advancements in threat hunting techniques, and assessments of blockchain's potential, the ransomware defense arena is poised for transformation. These future avenues promise to enhance the resilience of HRM systems against ransomware, and they contribute to the broader cybersecurity landscape by fostering innovation and adapting to the evolving threat landscape.

This chapter is not an endpoint but a stepping stone into uncharted territory. By embracing these future research directions, organizations, researchers, and innovators have the opportunity to shape the future of ransomware defense. As the digital landscape evolves, our strategies must also evolve. Technology, regulation, and foresight will empower us to create a future where ransomware's impact is diminished, where HRM systems stand resilient in the face of adversity, and where data remains secure and accessible, even in the shadow of the most persistent threats (Khang & Rath et al., 2024).

REFERENCES

Anh, P. T. N. et al. "AI Models for Disease Diagnosis and Prediction of Heart Disease with Artificial Neural Networks," *Computer Vision and AI-Integrated IoT Technologies in the Medical Ecosystem.* (1st Ed.) (2024). CRC Press. https://doi.org/10.1201/9781003429609-9

Bandari, V., (2023). Enterprise Data security measures: A comparative review of effectiveness and risks across different industries and organization types. *International Journal of Business Intelligence and Big Data Analytics*, 6(1), 1–11.

Chawki, M. (2022). Cybercrime and the Regulation of Cryptocurrencies. In: Arai, K. (eds) *Advances in Information and Communication. FICC 2022. Lecture Notes in Networks and Systems*, vol 439. Springer, Cham. https://doi.org/10.1007/978-3-030-98015-3_48

Garcia-Perez, A., Cegarra-Navarro, J. G., Sallos, M. P., Martinez-Caro, E., & Chinnaswamy, A, (2023). Resilience in healthcare systems: Cyber security and digital transformation. *Technovation*, 121(102583), 102583. https://doi.org/10.1016/j.technovation.2022.102583

Khang, A., *AI and IoT-Based Technologies for Precision Medicine.* (1st Ed.) (2023). IGI Global Press. https://doi.org/10.4018/979-8-3693-0876-9

Khang, A., *Medical Robotics and AI-Assisted Diagnostics for a High-Tech Healthcare Industry.* (1st Ed.) (2024). IGI Global Press. https://doi.org/10.4018/979-8-3693-2105-8

Khang, A, Hahanov V., Eugenia L., Svetlana C., Avromovic Z., Ragimova R., Ali N., Hajimahmud, V. A., Alyar, A. V., & Anh, P.T.N. "Medical and BioMedical Signal Processing and Prediction," *Computer Vision and AI-Integrated IoT Technologies in Medical Ecosystem.* (1st Ed.) (2024). CRC Press. https://doi.org/10.1201/9781003429609-7

Khang, A., Hajimahmud, V. A., Alyar, Abuzarova Vusala, Khalilov, Matlab, & Murad, Bagirli, AI-Aided Data Analytics Tools and Applications for the Healthcare Sector, *"AI and IoT-Based Technologies for Precision Medicine"*. (1st Ed.) (2023). ISBN: 9798369308769. IGI Global Press. https://doi.org/10.4018/979-8-3693-0876-9.ch018

Khang, A., Hajimahmud, V. A., Hrybiuk, O., & Shukla, A.K. (1st Ed.). (2024). *Computer Vision and AI-Integrated IoT Technologies in the Medical Ecosystem* (1st Ed.). CRC Press. https://doi.org/10.1201/9781003429609

Khang, A, Hajimahmud, V. A., Litvinova, Eugenia, Chumachenko, Svetlana, Abuzarova, Vusala, & Anh, P. T. N., "Application of Computer Vision in the Healthcare Ecosystem," *Computer Vision and AI-Integrated IoT Technologies in Medical Ecosystem*. (1st Ed.) (2024). CRC Press. https://doi.org/10.1201/9781003429609-1

Khang, A., Hajimahmud, V. A., Triwiyanto, Vusala, A. A., & Ali, R. N., "Cloud Platform and Data Storage Systems in Healthcare Ecosystem," *Medical Robotics and AI-Assisted Diagnostics for a High-Tech Healthcare Industry*. (1st Ed.) (2024). IGI Global Press. https://doi.org/10.4018/979-8-3693-2105-8.ch021

Khang, A., Ragimova, Nazila Ali, Bali, Sardarov Yaqub, Hajimahmud, V. A., Bahar, Askarova, & Mehriban, Mammadova, "Using Big Data to Solve Problems in the Field of Medicine," *Computer Vision and AI-Integrated IoT Technologies in Medical Ecosystem*. (1st Ed.) (2024). CRC Press. https://doi.org/10.1201/9781003429609-23

Khang, A., Rana, G., Tailor, RK, & Hajimahmud, V. A., *Data-Centric AI Solutions and Emerging Technologies in the Healthcare Ecosystem*. (1st Ed.) (2023). CRC Press. https://doi.org/10.1201/9781003356189

Khang, A., Rath, K. C., Anh, P. T. N., Rath, S. K., & Bhattacharya, S., "Quantum-Based Robotics in High-Tech Healthcare Industry: Innovations and Applications," *Medical Robotics and AI-Assisted Diagnostics for a High-Tech Healthcare Industry*. (1st Ed.) (2024). IGI Global Press. https://doi.org/10.4018/979-8-3693-2105-8.ch001

Kumar, S., & Mallipeddi, R. R., (2022). Impact of cybersecurity on operations and supply chain management: Emerging trends and future research directions. *Production and Operations Management, 31*(12), 4488–4500. https://doi.org/10.1111/poms.13859

McLaughlin, K. L., (2023). Defense is the best offense: The evolving role of cybersecurity blue teams and the impact of soar technologies. *EDPACS, 67*(6), 35–41. https://doi.org/10.1080/07366981.2023.2212484

Pyżalski, J., Plichta, P., Szuster, A., & Barlińska, J., (2022). Cyberbullying characteristics and prevention—What can we learn from narratives provided by adolescents and their teachers? *International Journal of Environmental Research and Public Health, 19*(18), 11589. https://doi.org/10.3390/ijerph191811589

Sujatha, R., Prakash, G., & Jhanjhi, N. Z., *Cyber Security Applications for Industry 4.0* (2022). Chapman & Hall/CRC. https://link.springer.com/chapter/10.1007/978-3-319-57870-5_16

Sun, N., Ding, M., Jiang, J., Xu, W., Mo, X., Tai, Y., & Zhang, J, (2023). Cyber threat intelligence mining for proactive cybersecurity defense: A survey and new perspectives. *IEEE Communications Surveys & Tutorials, 25*(3), 1748–1774. https://doi.org/10.1109/comst.2023.3273282

Tsantes, G. K., & Ransome, J., *Cybertax: Managing the Risks and Results* (2023). CRC Press. *Cybertax: Managing the Risks and Results*. CRC Press

Wörmann, J. et al. (2022). *Knowledge augmented machine learning with applications in autonomous driving: A survey*. Computer Science, Machine Learning. https://arxiv.org/abs/2205.04712

Yamin, M. M., & Katt, B., (2022). Modeling and executing cyber security exercise scenarios in cyber ranges. *Computers & Security, 116*(102635), 102635. https://doi.org/10.1016/j.cose.2022.102635

25 Breaking Barriers
Empowering Women in Manufacturing with Machine Vision and Industrial Robotics

Prashasti Pritiprada, Ipseeta Satpathy,
Alex Khang, and B.C.M. Patnaik

25.1 INTRODUCTION

Newsday, India country is becoming more and more connected to and a part of the global economy in the use of raw materials and chemical emissions. The implications of this model for India and other regions of the world in terms of opportunities and threats are unknown. A significant portion of the Indian population's well-being will thus rely on the timely realization of the required investments in sustainability, healthcare, and education. Strong and visionary government policy is an essential component when it comes to using India's land, water, and energy resources.

The International Labour Organization (ILO) reports that as the service sector has grown, so too has women's participation in the workforce. Employers are said to favor young, unmarried women with good education (ILO, 2023). Due to the quick casualization and informalization of the labor market, there has been a widespread belief that labor in India has become more female-dominated in the post-liberalization era. The feminization of labor refers to the rise in formal and informal market opportunities for women brought about by the global expansion of trade, capital flow, and technology. The shift in employment from manufacturing to services in developed countries and from agriculture to manufacturing and services in developing countries has coincided with the trend of labor feminization (Khang & Rath et al., 2023a).

Research is essential for economists, sociologists, development workers, activists, and anyone else who is interested in the social and economic conditions facing women globally in light of the continuous fight for women's rights, the world's rapid urbanization, and efforts to combat poverty. Women are now contributing significantly to economic progress. Through their active participation in industry, services, and agriculture, they make a major contribution to the gross domestic product (GDP). However, female workers, compared to their male counterparts, continue to fall behind in obtaining job opportunities.

DOI: 10.1201/9781003438137-25

Research indicates that women's engagement in the workforce has decreased recently, although the ratio of females to males in the workforce has grown in India. In contrast to the northern parts of India, the developed southern states have a higher percentage of women working due to being more highly educated and having the freedom to make decisions.

The chapter focuses on manufacturing vision advances that have the potential to enhance product quality, dependability, and enable new production processes through technology. Additionally included are the essential elements of a machine vision system's architecture and applications. These factors may be broadly divided into six categories: machine vision justification, picture pre-processing, image processing, scene restrictions, image acquisition, and systematic factors. Here, every facet of these procedures is explained, along with the necessary requirements for an ideal design.

The majority of tasks in the manufacturing facility of future generations will be performed by self-driving machines that depend on sensory input to navigate the workspace, avoid challenges, collaborate with humans, locate and identify functioning parts, get data from different sensors to increase positioning accuracy, among other tasks. Today, many imaging methods are used extensively in manufacturing for inspecting and production control procedures, as well as for robot navigation. These methods include photogrammetry, or stereoscopic perception, structural light, time of flight, and optical triangulation, among others. The components that require to be examined or found will determine the kind of vision system to utilize. Therefore, a comparative analysis of several machine vision approaches for robot guiding is presented in Khang & Hajimahmud et al., (2023).

25.2 WOMEN IN MANUFACTURING

The manufacturing industry has decreased in percentage of overall exports of goods and has made minimal contribution to income growth. Few new jobs have been created by manufacturing goods, and the majority of the employment growth in manufacturing over the past decade has taken place in the unorganized sector, where workers are not protected by retirement or social security plans. The manufacturing sector has poor productivity in part because it is challenging to take advantage of economies of scale due to the generally small size of manufacturing enterprises. The manufacturing industry in India has remarkable financial resources and is skill-intensive, while having a large pool of inexpensive, low-skilled labor (Khang & Rani et al., 2023).

Moreover, businesses have little motivation to expand when remaining small allows them to evade taxes and labor laws. Land acquisition moves slowly, businesses frequently have power shortages, and the transportation infrastructure is inadequate. In India, where males predominate, women are expected to be financially and culturally reliant on their male counterparts. Numerous issues faced by female entrepreneurs include low education, societal and legal impediments, bureaucratic procedures, high cost of production, a culture centered around men, insufficient management skills, lack of self-assuredness, etc. There are several push-pull elements that affect female entrepreneurs. India has prosperous and prominent women in business. The national government implements a number of initiatives to support female entrepreneurs for 5 years. Women possess the ability and will to establish, maintain, and oversee their own business; with the right guidance and support of government agencies, family, and society, these women may become successful entrepreneurs (Khang & Muthmainnah et al., 2023).

Indian women's lives have changed significantly as a result of the country's consistent strong economic development since the early 1990s; nevertheless, female employment has remained below 30%, according to current labor surveys. Five diagnostic facts regarding female employment in India were gleaned from country-wide household surveys, which aid in identifying barriers to greater involvement.

First, women who are not working now have a high need for work. Second, it is challenging to link willing females who are not currently employed. Third, women who have received vocational instruction are more likely to be employed. Fourth, women are far more inclined to have jobs in fields with bigger disparities in salaries and unexplainable income gaps—which are frequently linked to prejudice. Fifth, there is a correlation between more female involvement in a few critical areas and regulations that are advantageous to women, such as mandates. Policies regarding female employment limitations, federal programs, and factories ought to be more effectively looked into and utilized to boost women's revenue.

25.3 INTERSECTION OF TECHNOLOGY: MACHINE VISION AND INDUSTRIAL ROBOTICS

Manufacturing is currently experiencing Industry 4.0, often known as the 4th Industrial Revolution. The manufacturing process is built on computerized physical structures, which communicate with people or machinery in real-time (device-to-device interaction) to track mechanical operations, make autonomous decisions, and initiate operations. The procedures used in fabrication, technology, resource utilization, logistics, and management of life cycles may all be improved using this fresh approach. The idea of "adaptive production," or the capacity to use sensors and control systems, among others to create a proactive system that adjusts to any changes, is promoted by Industry 4.0. But, this type of manufacturing is seldom mechanized, thus interaction with humans is necessary. Robotics ought to have automated and sophisticated abilities to adjust to changing targets and unpredictable settings in order to shorten the distance to reach an objective (Khang & Rath et al., 2023b).

The suggested work demonstrates the methods and approaches used to create a genuine independent industrialized robotics unit that can choose elements coming on a conveyor used for jewelry-making and connect them onto a specially designed frame. At present, skilled human laborers physically complete this kind of job, which is an intermediary stage in arranging the components for the next phase of manufacturing. The suggested job pipeline—selecting the goods and fastening those to a frame—is typical in multiple sectors with a variety of uses, including packing and warehousing.

The main obstacle to the extensive use of additive manufacturing (AM) techniques in industrial environments is variation in the quality of the goods manufactured. In an effort to overcome this obstacle, new information is now available due to the widespread observation of AM operations, as well as the measurement of AM ingredients and parts. This recently discovered information is a useful tool for learning more about AM procedures and making decisions. Gaining such knowledge is made possible by algorithmic learning, which (1) learns the basics of AM operations and (2) finds forecasts and useful suggestions to improve process design and component quality. A survey on machine learning (ML) using AM is provided here.

An additional era of technical progress is already underway with the emergence of Industry 4.0, a novel electronic technology for manufacturing driven by nine key advances in technology. Detectors, devices, components, and information technology systems will all be integrated in this change. Such networked devices, referred to as cyber–physical structures, may communicate with each other via common Internet-based interfaces and use data analysis to self-configure, anticipate failing, and react to change. This enables quicker, more adaptable, and better-performing procedures to manufacture items of greater quality at lower prices by facilitating the collection and analysis of information among equipment.

The fields of science and technology should function on merit-based as well as universalist values, in which the outcomes gathered and the person's contributions solely matter. Researchers, technology professionals, and creative minds have come to recognize feminine involvement in these fields for advancement and development. Challenges concerning the accessibility of women, involvement, development, and reward are gradually gaining traction in the fields of technological development, creativity, and business ownership, which have historically been either male-dominated or gender-insensitive.

25.4 EMPOWERING WOMEN THROUGH SKILL DEVELOPMENT

India's economy is among the most swiftly expanding of the major economies, while its youthful labor population is also rapidly expanding. In 2020, the nation's median age reached 29 years. Attention must be on promoting industrial expansion and being able to handle the increasing population of workers, particularly the unskilled and less skilled. As a result, government initiatives such as "Made in India," "Skill India," and "The Digital India" are geared to generate hundreds of millions jobs.

With such ambitious initiatives, India is now considered an "international production center" and employment is higher because of the economic growth. In an effort to capitalize on this momentum, investors have focused on closing the widening gap in skills in a range of industry domains within the framework of a shifting business climate shaped by cutting-edge technology.

Our daily lives revolve around innovation. The marketplace for information technology (IT) employment is growing, so there are an increasing number of positions that require qualified candidates. Students are pursuing degrees in technological disciplines such as computer engineering, information management systems, or IT as they become aware of the broad job prospects that a profession in technology may provide. However, the proportion of female students majoring in engineering fields is still rather low.

25.5 INTEGRATING MACHINE VISION AND INDUSTRIAL ROBOTICS FOR EFFICIENCY

The designer working in the field of machine vision must identify certain factors before developing an instrument that meets the demands of its intended application. The necessary optical components and the illumination output of dynamic imagery make up the physical components of this module. For this, a variety of illuminating strategies, including organized illumination, may be applied. The visual acquisition phase of the optical systems procedure is when image information participation, visual monitoring, and visual digitalization are completed. The next step to get an accurate representation out of a lit environment is vision detection. The following phase in the procedure of recording and displaying images is digitalization.

The advent of Industry 4.0 brought an innovative development in several domains, such as robotics, 3D printing, artificial intelligence (AI), quantum technology, nanotechnology, biological sciences, and the Internet of Things (IOT). It also brought the revolution of digital technology into the realm of reality. Advances in algorithmic learning, which enable systems to gain knowledge, develop, or act and execute a given activity via information not having to be manually programmed, have led to an important period in the AI sector. Learning from machines may be applied to machining processes in order to improve model and workflow variables, evaluate equipment wellness, or increase efficiency and quality of products. It is referred to as "smart machining," an unusual model for manufacturing in which the equipment is completely networked by a system that is both cyber and physical.

25.6 THE CATALYST: SELF-HELP GROUPS

Self-help groups (SHGs) are tiny, non-profit, unofficial groups founded in 1992 with the intention of allowing participants, usually women, to profit monetarily from cooperation, camaraderie, and shared responsibilities. The advancement of group business strategies and the mobilization of financial resources and savings are among the advantages. The poor may build up money through modest savings thanks to the collaborative strategy, which also makes it easier for individuals to get official funding. Through shared accountability, these groups help the impoverished get beyond the financial risk and escape the grasp of creditors.

Self-help groups have become an essential part of transforming the lives of impoverished women in nearly every nation that is developing, including India. These women collectives—known by many names—play a significant role in female liberation and self-determination.

Self-help groups are seen as an efficient means of reducing hardship and an instrument for promoting rural growth. The improvement in rural India's social and economic standing has been greatly aided by SHGs.

25.7 CHALLENGES AND SOLUTIONS

In the manufacturing sector, an automated assembly line manages a significant number of tasks including categorization, creating artwork, welding, wrapping, and many additional duties. The complicated nature of production has increased, making such machines more susceptible to errors. Here, assembling gets monitored and improved through the application of the digital twin (DT) idea. In mechanical assembly, a multisource based on a model's digital replica network is used. The model has three elements: (1) A machine arm for lifting and grasping things, detectors, and information they are connected with make up the physical environment. (2) A server that hosts a multisource approach and a holographic presentation and control unit make up the virtual space. (3) A means of communication gateway provides accurate information flow between both environments.

Workforce planning is a crucial component of factory operation, as it optimizes the utilization of resources to minimize operational time as well as enhance productivity. Defects and abnormalities may render the method of planning ineffective for real-world scenarios.

Big Data and digital twins are essential components of smart manufacturing, from managing the product lifecycle to repair and maintenance. A number of studies that were mentioned earlier emphasized the value of technology collaboration in the context of smart manufacturing. The idea of using a range of metrics and combining it with technologies, such as augmented reality, IoT, as well as data analytics leads to improved precision surveillance, prompt detection and forecasting of assembling or defects in production, and general production procedure improvement and optimization.

25.8 PROPOSED SOLUTIONS AND STRATEGIES FOR OVERCOMING OBSTACLES

The workforce's response to robots is generally favorable, according to several studies regarding the further development of these types of technology. Digital production innovations release laborers in monotonous and repetitive jobs so they may concentrate on more exciting or fulfilling work. Lower levels of fatigue, stress, boredom, anxiety, physical burden, safety issues, and illnesses related to work are other advantages that improve the health of employees.

The sustainability of the workforce is tied to individual creativity, being deeply engaged with a job, and mental health, among others. The emergence of intelligent machines brought along methods to achieve worker preservation, wellness, and health include encouraging more engagement among workers, acknowledging efforts, motivating everyone to collaborate, constructing talent through instruction and learning possibilities, minimizing stress, as well as promoting confidence.

25.9 FUTURE PROSPECTS: TOWARD A MORE INCLUSIVE MANUFACTURING SECTOR

The application of Big Data, AI, and sophisticated robotic technological advances, as well as their collaboration, to improve production efficiency and optimize vitality or labor requirements is known as smart manufacturing. The structure of smart manufacturing is defined, discussed, and its present level of implementation is stated.

Some research also analyzes the distinctions among the present production structure and what is expected from it, as well as the corresponding innovations and the ways they contribute to smart manufacturing techniques. In order to fully comprehend this quickly evolving technology, a study on the most recent advancements in the industry was conducted, and the results were assessed and displayed alongside the prospects, difficulties in execution, and potential directions for smart manufacturing systems.

The financial success of every nation depends on its agricultural sector. Meeting the nutritional needs of the present-day population is becoming more difficult due to the increasing numbers of people, climate fluctuations, and inadequate resources. Intelligent farming, which is another name for the practice of precision agriculture, has become a cutting-edge instrument to solve the problems facing food security today. The latest technology in this field is powered by the use of ML. It allows a gadget to acquire knowledge despite the need for particular programming.

The future shift in farming will mostly consist of AI- and IoT-equipped farm gear. This provides a thorough analysis of using ML in the agricultural sector. A method based on linear-programming called data envelopment analysis is widely used for effective assessment procedures in a variety of industrial and service-based domains. In the agricultural sector, this has proven to be effective in examining the most efficient resource utilization for environmentally friendly consumption. Previous studies have used a standard two-step procedure where this is used in conjunction with using a regression framework to clarify the influence of outside variables on performance (Khang & Shah et al., 2023).

25.10   ETHICAL CONSIDERATIONS AND SOCIAL IMPACT

One way to support innovative developments in information and communication technology (ICT) is through diversified leaders. The process of digitizing and corporate change are mostly driven by innovation in technology. To be able to accomplish a sustainable future, this approach necessitates people change in addition to corporate reform.

Developing a collaborative mentality, ensuring multiculturalism, or altering cultural norms has been difficult, but these are considered essential components of leaving a legacy that calls for comprehensive technological governance. In society, to keep up with the rapid advancements in technology in education, the workforce, culture, and government, radical reforms must be made. There is a lot of promise in the age of technology to close "the gender management gap" and possibly enhance inclusivity in every company, particularly in the information technology and architecture sectors.

Because the evaluation of sustainable development is multifaceted, knowledge involves researchers in multiple fields (geographical studies, management and business, finance and statistical analysis, technology, environmental and social research, etc.), using a range of strategies and techniques. Biodiversity is frequently evaluated at the corporate and regulatory sectors using metrics that are able to determine, juxtapose, interact, and track advancements made achieving a certain objective (Khang & AIoCF, 2024).

India's economy has rapidly changed over the past 20 years due to businesses concentrating in new markets. The modern job field is the result of generational, ethnic, or geographic transformations. There are significant differences in perspectives on careers and personal life, and a healthy balance between them due to the diversity of employees and the circumstances of employment. Various research examines equilibrium between work and personal life, and regulations in evolving organizational environments. It additionally looks for discrepancies across standards and regulations as well as causes and effects.

25.11 RECOMMENDATIONS FOR INDUSTRY AND POLICY

The conversation about AI has been ongoing for many years. This is frequently portrayed as clever computers one day ruling the globe and reducing humans to menial laborers as a means to uphold a new technological system. Although this image presents ML in a slightly caricatured manner, the truth is that AI is now developed, and a lot of people use gadgets based on this technology on an everyday basis. Artificial Intelligence is not just the domain of forecasters; rather, it is becoming a crucial part of many organizations' operating models and a major critical component of future plans for several businesses, administrations, and healthcare fields worldwide.

Due to AI's transformative power, there exists a notable surge in scholarly research concerning the field. The latest research focuses on the effects and ramifications of the AI discipline instead of its efficacy. Machine learning came out of nowhere through esoteric conversations in academic laboratories and bigger events and legislative forums worldwide.

The argument for AI and ML seems to be met with a great deal of panic all over the world, especially in the European continent, as demonstrated by the European parliament's inquiry into constitutional regulations for robots. Innumerable training sessions, educational events, and meetings are attended by self-described "gurus" who express worries regarding automated machines replacing humans as obsolete or ineffective remnants of previous generations, upending interpersonal relationships, stealing livelihoods, influencing society as a whole, and eventually ruling across the entire globe.

25.12 CONCLUSION

Taking into account factors like representation, accessibility, and the wider influence of technology on gender identities and roles, women's positions in technology have changed over time. Numerous studies advance our knowledge of how gender relations both influence and are influenced by science and technology. The term "gendered technoscience" refers to the recognition that science and technology are social constructs that are influenced by society and that they both actively support and mirror prevailing gender norms and hierarchies. Few studies critically evaluate the gendered aspects of technological progress, illuminating the ways in which scientific and technological breakthroughs interact with and impact gender dynamics in society.

In investigating the many possibilities and problems that women encounter in the manufacturing sector, taking into account both context-specific elements and more general worldwide trends, the researchers probably dig into the global and local aspects of women's empowerment. Given the focus on the manufacturing sector, it is suggested that women's responsibilities in this area be examined, along with concerns related to economic participation, career options, and measures for empowerment. A number of research probably challenge popular ideas about empowerment, acknowledging that real empowerment involves social, political, and cultural aspects in addition to economic progress. It could provide light on how technology might promote inclusive development and act as a catalyst for good change by upending conventional gender norms.

A few companies in India have done a good job at maintaining a healthy gender and geographical diversity. Yet, this is still insufficient. A significant portion of the population, including those with special needs or who belong to the LGBTQ community, is yet unexplored as prospective workers. Bringing these workers aboard might not just provide exposure to a wealth of expertise but also contribute to the development of a workplace centered on "attention" and "reciprocated regard." Another topic of research is the growth of the skills of exceptionally talented female leaders. Because of the need for these women, peer-to-peer contacts have expanded apprenticeships and have the potential to influence standards in various sectors outside of tourism.

By using industrial robots and machine vision, women are able to acquire technical abilities that further develop their skills. Self-help groups are a support community for women that offers a forum for problem-solving, emotional support, and skill development. In addition to advancing women's participation in manufacturing, the symbiotic link between technical growth and community involvement also represents a strong paradigm where social support and technology merge for holistic empowerment (Khang, 2023).

REFERENCES

ILO (2023), ILOSTAT. The leading source of labour statistics, The ILO Department of Statistics. https://ilostat.ilo.org/resources/concepts-and-definitions/ilo-modelled-estimates/

Khang, A., *AI and IoT-Based Technologies for Precision Medicine*. (1st Ed.) (2023). ISBN: 9798369308769. IGI Global Press. https://doi.org/10.4018/979-8-3693-0876-9

Khang, A. and AIoCF, *AI-Oriented Competency Framework for Talent Management in the Digital Economy: Models, Technologies, Applications, and Implementation*. (1st Ed.) (2024). ISBN: 9781032576053. CRC Press. https://doi.org/10.1201/9781003440901

Khang, A., Hajimahmud, V. A., Alyar, Abuzarova Vusala, Khalilov, Matlab, & Murad, Bagirli, AI-Aided Data Analytics Tools and Applications for the Healthcare Sector, *"AI and IoT-Based Technologies for Precision Medicine"*. (1st Ed.) (2023). IGI Global Press. https://doi.org/10.4018/979-8-3693-0876-9.ch018

Khang, A., Muthmainnah, M, Seraj, Prodhan Mahbub Ibna, Yakin, Ahmad Al, Obaid, Ahmad J., & Ranjan Panda, Manas. "AI-Aided Teaching Model for the Education 5.0 Ecosystem" *AI-Based Technologies and Applications in the Era of the Metaverse*. (1st Ed.) (2023). Page (83–104). IGI Global Press. https://doi.org/10.4018/978-1-6684-8851-5.ch004

Khang, A., Rani, S., Gujrati, R., Uygun, H., & Gupta, S. K., *Designing Workforce Management Systems for Industry 4.0: Data-Centric and AI-Enabled Approaches*. (1st Ed.) (2023). CRC Press. https://doi.org/10.1201/9781003357070

Khang, A., Rath, K.C., Kumar Satapathy, Suresh, Kumar, Amaresh, Ranjan Das, Sudhansu, & Ranjan Panda, Manas. "Enabling the Future of Manufacturing: Integration of Robotics and IoT to Smart Factory Infrastructure in Industry 4.0." *AI-Based Technologies and Applications in the Era of the Metaverse.* (1st Ed.) (2023a). Page (25–50). IGI Global Press. https://doi.org/10.4018/978-1-6684-8851-5.ch002

Khang, A., Rath, K.C., Panda, Surabhika, Sree, Pokkuluri Kiran, & Kumar Panda, Santosh. "Revolutionizing Agriculture: Exploring Advanced Technologies for Plant Protection in the Agriculture Sector," *Handbook of Research on AI-Equipped IoT Applications in High-Tech Agriculture.* (1st Ed.) (2023b). Page: 1–22. https://doi.org/10.4018/978-1-6684-9231-4.ch001

Khang, A., Shah, V., & Rani, S., *AI-Based Technologies and Applications in the Era of the Metaverse.* (1st Ed.) (2023). IGI Global Press. https://doi.org/10.4018/978-1-6684-8851-5

26 Optimization of Data-Transfer Machines and Cloud Data Platforms Integration in Industrial Robotics

Tarun Kumar Vashishth, Vikas Sharma, Bhupendra Kumar, and Kewal Krishan Sharma

26.1 INTRODUCTION

In industry revolution 4.0 (IR), industrial robotics has emerged as a linchpin in modern manufacturing. These sophisticated robotic systems have the potential to revolutionize production processes, bringing speed, precision, and consistency to industries ranging from automotive manufacturing to electronics assembly. Yet, to unlock their full potential, these robotic systems require mechanical prowess and the ability to harness and analyze data. This is where the integration of data-transfer machines with cloud data platforms plays a pivotal role. This integration represents a paradigm shift in industrial manufacturing. It is a transformational approach that holds the promise of enhanced manufacturing efficiency, better decision-making, reduced downtime, and ultimately, a competitive edge in the marketplace. This chapter explores this topic, delving into the technical intricacies, challenges, and optimal strategies to maximize the potential of this integration.

As we delve deeper into this subject, we will uncover the fundamental concepts that underpin data integration in the context of industrial robotics. From understanding the sources and formats of data, to examining the critical decision of where data processing should occur—at the edge or in the cloud—we lay the groundwork for a robust integration strategy. Yet, as with any transformative endeavor, challenges abound. Data security emerges as a paramount concern in handling sensitive manufacturing data. Scalability becomes an imperative, given the exponential growth in data volume as manufacturing operations expand. Data quality must be rigorously maintained to ensure that insights derived from integrated data are reliable.

Furthermore, minimizing latency in data transfer is crucial for real-time decision-making, making optimization of network configurations and processing pipelines essential. With a comprehensive understanding of the technical considerations and challenges, we then transition into optimization strategies. Here, we explore the various strategies that manufacturers can employ to fine-tune their data integration

DOI: 10.1201/9781003438137-26

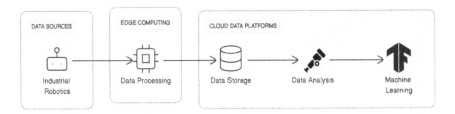

FIGURE 26.1   The integration of data-transfer machines with cloud data platforms.

efforts. Robust data architectures are essential for seamless data flow, while edge computing offers a solution to reduce latency and offload processing tasks from the cloud. Advanced analytics and machine learning (ML) algorithms enable the extraction of actionable insights, from predictive maintenance models to process optimization algorithms. Lastly, we emphasize the importance of continuous improvement, as data integration is an evolving process as shown in Figure 26.1.

Throughout this journey, we will illuminate our exploration with real-world case studies, showcasing how organizations across industries have successfully harnessed data-transfer machine and cloud data platform integration to enhance their manufacturing efficiency. These cases will provide tangible examples of the transformative potential of this approach, offering inspiration and guidance to those seeking to embark on a similar journey. In summary, the integration of data-transfer machines and cloud data platforms is a dynamic and transformative approach that holds the promise of revolutionizing industrial manufacturing. This chapter will provide readers the knowledge and insights needed to navigate the complexities, challenges, and opportunities of this integration, ultimately enabling them to enhance their manufacturing efficiency and secure their position in the competitive landscape of modern industry.

26.2   LITERATURE REVIEW

Shakya (2020) conducted a survey on cloud-based robotic architecture, covering the forces driving the integration of robotics with the cloud, its applications, and the key challenges and concerns associated with this integration. Wang & Zhang et al. (2017) introduced a cloud-based solution designed to facilitate inter-layer interaction and inter-robot negotiation within smart factories. Vick & Vonásek et al. (2015) present a novel concept for flexible motion planning and control of industrial robots, advocating for an open service-based framework rather than a closed monolithic architecture.

Doriya & Chakraborty et al. (2012) introduced the integration of robotic services into service-oriented architecture (SOA) and cloud computing. Their paper highlights the availability of robotic services in the cloud, such as navigation and object recognition, and the support of MapReduce computing clusters for processing substantial data related to cloud robotic services. Mohanarajah & Hunziker et al. (2014) detail the design and deployment of Rapyuta, an open-source cloud robotics platform. Rapyuta empowers robots to delegate resource-intensive computations to secure and adaptable cloud computing environments (Khang & Shah et al., 2023).

Hu & Tay et al. (2012) assessed communication protocols and diverse elastic computing models tailored for various applications within the field of cloud robotics. They delved into the technical hurdles encompassing computation, communication, and security, while elucidating the prospective advantages of cloud robotics across multiple application domains. Jordan & Haidegger et al. (2013) presented a structured and systematic review, encompassing various definitions, concepts, and technologies related to cloud robotics, as well as broader cloud technologies. Shu & Arnarson et al. (2022) introduced a system-independent remote control interface for industrial robots using Industry 4.0 cloud computing technology, with minimal client device requirements.

Horn & Krüger (2016) highlighted the challenge of lacking standard interfaces between machinery, robots, production systems, and cloud infrastructures, limiting the broad implementation of cloud platforms in production environments. Givehchi & Trsek et al. (2013) offered an up-to-date overview of cloud computing technology concepts in industrial automation, categorizing existing research according to automation system levels and discussing research gaps based on their findings. Hegazy & Hefeeda (2014) introduce a novel cloud service, called industrial automation, encompassing various functionalities ranging from feedback control and telemetry to plant optimization and enterprise management. In their survey article, Soni & Kumar (2022) present a comprehensive summary and structured layout of the extensive research on ML techniques in the emerging cloud computing paradigm.

Panicucci & Nikolakis et al. (2020) proposed approach has been successfully implemented into a prototype and rigorously tested in an industrial use case involving the maintenance of a robotic arm. The results obtained demonstrate the methodology's effectiveness and efficiency in supporting predictive analytics within the context of Industry 4.0. In their paper, Lins & Givigi (2021) comprehensively discuss the opportunities and challenges associated with the new paradigm of cloud robotics in the industrial context (Khang & Hajimahmud et al., 2024b).

26.3 TECHNICAL CONSIDERATIONS

Before embarking on the journey of optimizing data-transfer machine and cloud data platform integration in industrial robotics, it is imperative to discuss the technical intricacies that form the foundation of this transformative endeavor as shown in Figure 26.2.

In this section, we explore the essential technical considerations that lay the groundwork for a successful integration strategy.

26.3.1 DATA SOURCES

Understanding the origins of the data is fundamental to effective integration. In industrial robotics, data can emanate from a multitude of sources, as discussed below.

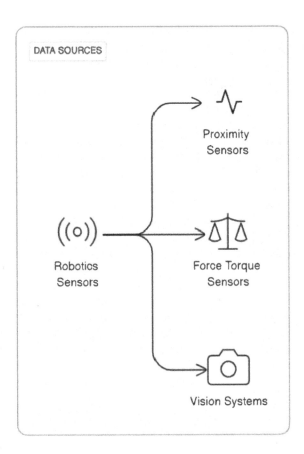

FIGURE 26.2   Origins of data sensors.

26.3.2   ROBOTICS SENSORS

Robotics sensors are essential for gathering real-time data about the robot's surroundings and actions. Here's how different types of robotics sensors are used:

- **Vision Systems:** Vision sensors, such as cameras, LiDAR, and depth sensors, provide visual information about the robot's environment. This data is crucial for tasks such as object recognition, navigation, quality control, and safety monitoring.
- **Force/Torque Sensors:** These sensors measure the forces and torques exerted by the robot. This data is vital for tasks that include delicate object handling, ensuring safety when interacting with humans, and detecting abnormalities in the robot's operation.
- **Proximity Sensors:** Proximity sensors detect the presence or absence of objects within a certain range. They are used for collision avoidance, object detection, and positioning, ensuring the robot operates safely and accurately.

By integrating data from these sensors, manufacturers can optimize robot performance, reduce errors, and enhance safety within their operations.

26.3.3 Production Equipment

Manufacturing machinery and equipment generate a wealth of data related to their operation. This data includes:

- **Performance Data:** Information about machine speed, uptime, downtime, and cycle times.
- **Condition Monitoring:** Data on equipment temperature, vibrations, and other health metrics to predict maintenance needs.
- **Output Metrics:** Production rates, defect rates, and product quality data.

Analyzing this data can help manufacturers identify bottlenecks, predict maintenance issues to prevent downtime, and optimize production schedules for increased efficiency.

26.3.4 Human-Machine Interfaces

Human-machine interfaces (HMIs) are interfaces through which operators and technicians interact with robotic systems. By capturing interaction data, such as button presses, settings adjustments, and decision-making processes, manufacturers can do the following:

- **Improve Training**: Understand how operators use the system and enhance training programs.
- **Identify Usability Issues:** Spot areas where the interface may need improvements.
- **Track Efficiency:** Measure operator performance and identify areas for improvement, as shown in Figure 26.3.

By recording user interactions, manufacturers can enhance training, identify usability issues, and measure operator efficiency, improving overall system performance and usability.

26.3.4.1 Internet of Things Devices

Internet of Things (IoT) devices embedded in manufacturing components can provide a wide range of data, as shown in Figure 26.4, including:

- **Conveyor Belts:** Monitoring conveyor speed, product flow, and potential jams.
- **Robotic Arms:** Collecting data on the robot's movements, load handling, and tool wear.
- **Inventory Management Systems:** Tracking inventory levels, reorder points, and product movement.

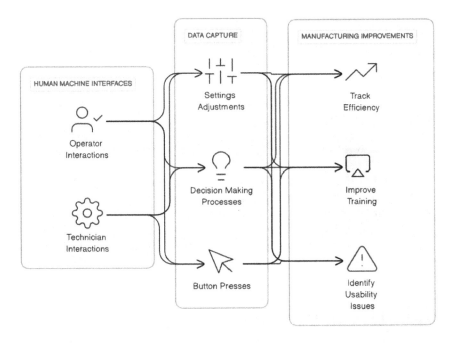

FIGURE 26.3   Human-machine interfaces.

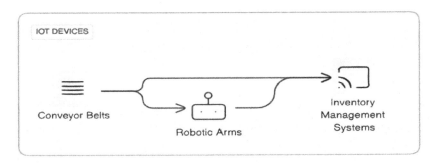

FIGURE 26.4   Internet of Things devices.

Integrating IoT data allows manufacturers to optimize supply chain logistics, reduce waste, and enhance overall efficiency.

26.3.4.2   External Data Sources

External data sources, such as weather data or market demand forecasts, can impact manufacturing processes.

- **Weather Data:** Weather conditions can affect energy consumption, transportation logistics, and production scheduling.

- **Market Demand Forecasts:** Accurate demand forecasts help manufacturers adjust production volumes, reducing overstock or shortages.

Integrating external data sources into the manufacturing ecosystem allows for more agile and responsive production planning.

26.3.4.3 Data Formats and Protocols

Data in industrial settings often comes in a variety of formats and is communicated using diverse protocols. To ensure seamless integration, it is essential to standardize data formats and communication protocols.

26.3.4.4 Standardization

Standardization is the practice of adopting uniform data formats and communication protocols to ensure compatibility and interoperability among various systems and devices. Here's how it works:

- **Data Formats:** Common data formats such as JSON (JavaScript Object Notation), XML (eXtensible Markup Language), or CSV (Comma-Separated Values) provide structured ways to represent data. Using these formats allows different systems to understand and process data consistently.
- **Communication Protocols:** Communication protocols such as MQTT (Message Queuing Telemetry Transport), OPC UA (Open Platform Communications Unified Architecture), or RESTful APIs (Representational State Transfer) define rules for exchanging data between systems. Adhering to widely accepted protocols ensures seamless data exchange.

Standardization facilitates integration by reducing the complexity of mapping and translating data between incompatible formats. It also makes it easier to add new systems or devices to the network without significant reconfiguration, as shown in Figure 26.5.

26.3.4.5 Data Transformation

In complex integration scenarios, data from various sources may not be in a format that is directly compatible with the target system. Data transformation is the process of converting data from one format or protocol to another. Key points to consider are as follows:

- **Middleware Solutions:** Middleware, such as enterprise service buses (ESBs) or integration platforms as a service (iPaaS), can serve as intermediaries that perform data transformations. They can translate between different data structures, ensuring data flows smoothly from source to destination.
- **Data Mapping:** Mapping rules need to be defined to specify how data elements in one format correspond to those in another format. These mappings are essential for accurate data transformation.

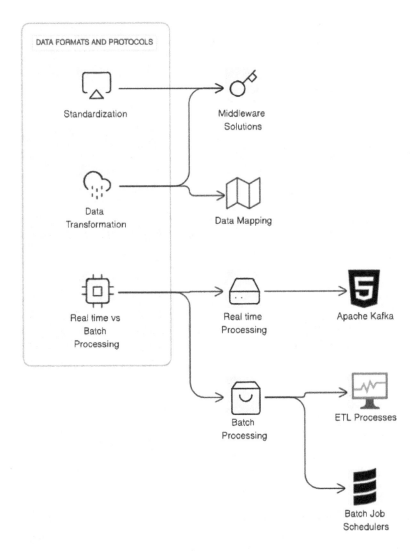

FIGURE 26.5 Data formats and protocols.

Data transformation is critical when integrating legacy systems with modern ones or when connecting devices that use proprietary data formats.

26.3.4.6 Real-Time vs. Batch Processing

The choice between real-time and batch processing depends on the specific integration requirements and the nature of the data being handled:

- **Real-Time Processing:** In real-time integration, data is processed and acted upon as it is generated. This approach is suitable for applications where low latency is crucial, such as real-time monitoring, control systems, or instant alerts. Technologies such as message queues and streaming platforms (e.g., Apache Kafka) are often used for real-time data processing.

- **Batch Processing:** In batch processing, data is collected over a period (e.g., hourly, daily) and processed in chunks. Batch processing is commonly used for data analysis, reporting, and historical data storage. Technologies like ETL (extract, transform, and load) processes and batch job schedulers are used in this approach.

The choice between real-time and batch processing impacts the design of the integration architecture and the selection of appropriate technology stacks. It also depends on factors such as the criticality of real-time data, system scalability, and resource availability.

26.3.4.7 Edge vs. Cloud Computing

Determining where data processing should occur—at the edge (on the robots or machines) or in the cloud—has significant implications for latency, data volume, and cloud capabilities.

26.3.4.8 Latency

Latency refers to the delay between the generation of data and the moment it is processed or acted upon. In the context of edge computing, minimizing latency is often a primary concern. Here's how it works:

- **Real-Time Decision-making:** In scenarios where real-time decision-making is critical, such as autonomous vehicles, industrial robots, or remote surgery, processing data at the edge is essential. Edge devices have the capability to analyze data locally and make instantaneous decisions without relying on a distant cloud server. This reduces the risk of communication delays that could lead to accidents or failures.
- **Low-Latency Applications:** Edge computing is suitable for applications that require low latency, such as video analytics for security systems, where immediate response to detected events is crucial.

Edge devices are equipped with sufficient processing power and artificial intelligence (AI) capabilities to handle these tasks, ensuring rapid response times.

26.3.4.9 Data Volume

Edge devices often have limited storage and processing resources compared to cloud servers. Deciding what data to process locally and what to transmit to the cloud is a critical consideration:

- **Local Data Processing:** Edge devices should preprocess data locally when the volume is manageable and when immediate action is required. For example, in a manufacturing plant, edge devices on robotic arms might process sensor data locally to adjust their movements in real-time.

- **Data Transmission:** Less time-sensitive or voluminous data may be transmitted to the cloud for further analysis and long-term storage. This data can be used for historical analytics, predictive maintenance, or ML model training.

The choice depends on factors such as the capacity of edge devices, the network bandwidth, and the specific use case requirements.

26.3.4.10   Cloud Capabilities

Cloud platforms offer extensive computational power, storage capacity, and scalability, as shown in Figure 26.6. They are suitable for tasks that require complex analytics, ML, or long-term data storage:

- **Complex Analytics:** The cloud can perform deep analysis of historical data, generating insights that might not be feasible at the edge. For example, analyzing years of production data to optimize manufacturing processes.
- **Machine Learning:** Cloud-based ML models can be trained on vast datasets and then deployed to edge devices for real-time inference, enabling advanced AI capabilities.
- **Data Storage:** Cloud platforms provide secure and scalable storage solutions, allowing organizations to retain large volumes of data for compliance, auditing, and historical analysis.

26.3.4.11   Hybrid Approaches

In some scenarios, a hybrid approach combines the strengths of both edge and cloud processing:

- **Edge Processing for Speed:** Data is preprocessed locally at the edge for immediate action. For instance, a security camera detects an intruder and raises an alarm locally.
- **Cloud Processing for Analysis:** Simultaneously, data is sent to the cloud for more in-depth analysis. The cloud can provide contextual analysis, compare data across multiple edge devices, and store historical records.

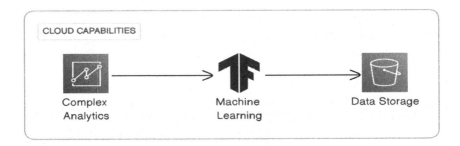

FIGURE 26.6   Cloud capabilities for solving complex tasks.

Hybrid approaches are beneficial when the use case requires a balance between low latency and advanced analysis, or when edge devices have limited resources.

26.3.4.12 Connectivity

Robust and reliable connectivity is the lifeblood of data integration in industrial robotics. Without seamless communication, the entire system can falter. Key considerations are discussed below.

26.3.4.12.1 Wired vs. Wireless

When it comes to connectivity solutions in manufacturing, the choice between wired and wireless depends on several critical factors:

- **Data Volume:** Wired connections, such as Ethernet, can handle higher data volumes with low latency compared to wireless options. If your manufacturing process generates large amounts of data that need to be transmitted quickly and reliably, wired connections may be preferable.
- **Reliability:** Wired connections are generally more reliable than wireless connections because they are less susceptible to interference or signal degradation. In manufacturing environments where downtime can be costly, a wired network might be the preferred choice for mission-critical applications.
- **Distance:** Wireless connections, like Wi-Fi and cellular, are more suitable when devices are spread over a large area or need mobility. They eliminate the need for physical cables, making them more versatile for certain applications.
- **Flexibility:** Industrial IoT protocols, such as LoRa and Zigbee, are suitable for connecting low-power, low-data-rate devices over long distances. They are ideal for remote sensor monitoring or asset tracking applications.

The choice between wired and wireless should be made based on a careful assessment of these factors and the specific requirements of your manufacturing processes.

26.3.4.12.2 Redundancy

Redundancy in network configurations is crucial for ensuring uninterrupted data flow in manufacturing environments. Redundancy can be implemented as follows:

- **Redundant Connections:** Implement redundant connections to critical devices or systems. This means having a backup connection, typically on a separate network or path, ready to take over in case the primary connection fails. Redundant connections prevent costly downtime due to network failures.
- **Failover Mechanisms:** Configure automatic failover mechanisms that seamlessly switch to the backup connection when a failure is detected. This ensures minimal disruption and uninterrupted operations.
- **Load Balancing:** Load balancing can distribute network traffic evenly across multiple connections, optimizing network performance and further enhancing reliability.

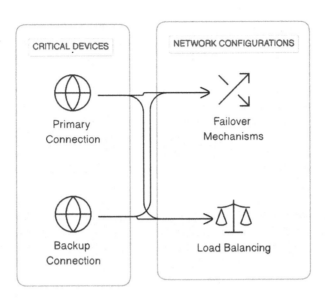

FIGURE 26.7   Redundancy in network configurations.

Redundancy is particularly important in manufacturing where system failures can lead to production delays, quality issues, or safety risks, as shown in Figure 26.7.

26.3.4.12.3 Data Encryption

Manufacturing data often contains sensitive information, and ensuring its security during transmission is paramount. Data encryption is essential to protect against unauthorized access and data breaches. It can be implemented as follows:

- **Transport Layer Security (TLS)/Secure Sockets Layer (SSL):** These encryption protocols provide secure communication over the Internet. They are commonly used to encrypt data transmitted between devices and servers in manufacturing systems.
- **End-to-End Encryption:** Implement end-to-end encryption for critical data flows, ensuring that data remains encrypted from the source to the destination, preventing interception or tampering.
- **Key Management:** Establish robust key management practices to safeguard encryption keys. Proper key management is essential for maintaining the security of encrypted data.

Data encryption should be a non-negotiable aspect of a manufacturing network security strategy, especially when transmitting sensitive production data or complying with industry regulations.

These technical considerations lay the foundation for a successful data-transfer machine and cloud data platform integration strategy. Addressing these elements comprehensively is essential to creating a robust and efficient data ecosystem in industrial robotics.

26.4   CHALLENGES IN DATA INTEGRATION

Let us discuss the challenges associated with data integration in industrial robotics in more detail below.

26.4.1   SECURITY

Handling sensitive manufacturing data, which can include proprietary designs, production processes, and quality control information, necessitates a robust security framework, as shown in Figure 26.8. Here are some key considerations:

- **Encryption:** Data transmitted between machines and cloud platforms must be encrypted to prevent unauthorized access. Protocols such as SSL or TLS are commonly used to establish secure connections.

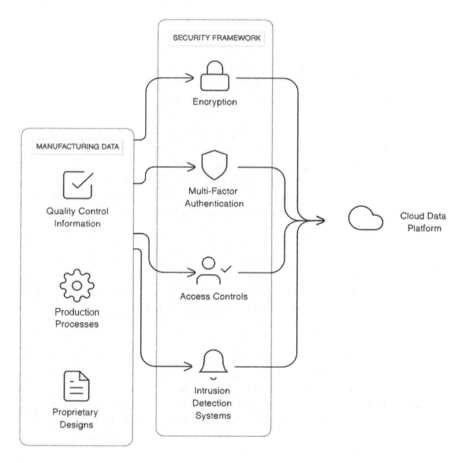

FIGURE 26.8   Security to handle sensitive manufacturing data (Khang & Hajimahmud et al., 2024a).

- **Multi-Factor Authentication (MFA):** Implement MFA for user access to the cloud data platform. This adds an extra layer of security by requiring users to provide multiple forms of verification, such as a password and a temporary code sent to their mobile device.
- **Access Controls:** Define and enforce access controls and permissions to ensure that only authorized individuals can access specific datasets or perform certain actions. Role-based access control (RBAC) can be effective in managing access.
- **Intrusion Detection Systems (IDS):** Deploy IDS to monitor network traffic and system behavior for signs of unauthorized access or suspicious activities. IDS can trigger alerts or take predefined actions when anomalies are detected.

26.4.2 SCALABILITY

The exponential growth in data volume as manufacturing operations expand poses a significant challenge. A failure to address scalability can lead to performance bottlenecks and system downtime. Consider the following strategies:

- **Cloud-Based Scalability:** Use cloud-based services that offer auto-scaling capabilities. This means that as data volume grows, the cloud infrastructure can automatically allocate additional resources to handle the increased load.
- **Load Balancing:** Implement load balancers in your infrastructure to evenly distribute incoming data traffic across multiple servers or instances. This helps prevent overloading of individual components.
- **Horizontal Scaling:** Design your data architecture to support horizontal scaling, where additional servers or resources can be added to the system as needed. This allows you to expand capacity without overhauling the entire infrastructure.

26.4.3 DATA QUALITY

The famous saying "garbage in, garbage out" holds true in data integration. Poor data quality can lead to incorrect decisions and inefficiencies. Below are tips on how to maintain data quality:

- **Data Cleansing:** Develop processes and algorithms to cleanse data of errors, inconsistencies, and duplicates. This may involve removing outliers, correcting typos, and filling in missing values.
- **Data Validation:** Implement validation checks to ensure that incoming data meets predefined criteria. Validation rules can include range checks, format checks, and cross-referencing with known data standards.
- **Monitoring and Auditing:** Continuously monitor data for anomalies or discrepancies. Set up regular audits to review data quality, identify patterns of inconsistency, and take corrective actions.

26.4.4 LATENCY

In industrial robotics, real-time decision-making is often critical, making low latency a priority. Reducing latency in data transfer and processing is essential for timely responses. Consider the following latency tactics:

• **Optimized Network Configurations:** Configure your network infrastructure to minimize data transfer times. This may involve choosing the right network protocols, optimizing router settings, and reducing packet loss.
• **Data Compression:** Compress data before transmission to reduce the amount of data that needs to be transferred. Compression algorithms such as gzip or Brotli can significantly decrease data size without sacrificing information.
• **Local Processing:** As mentioned earlier, leverage edge computing to perform local data processing. This approach reduces the need for data to travel back and forth to the cloud, thereby minimizing latency.

26.4.5 COMPATIBILITY

In a diverse industrial environment, data can originate from various sources and utilize different formats and protocols. Addressing compatibility issues is crucial for seamless integration:

• **Middleware Solutions:** Implement middleware or integration platforms that can act as data translators. These middleware solutions can convert data from one format or protocol to another, ensuring that disparate systems can communicate effectively.
• **Standardization:** Where possible, encourage the use of standardized data formats and communication protocols among different components of the manufacturing process. This simplifies integration efforts and reduces compatibility challenges.

By acknowledging and proactively addressing these challenges, organizations can lay a solid foundation for the optimization of data-transfer machine and cloud data platform integration in industrial robotics. Effective management of security, scalability, data quality, latency, and compatibility issues is essential for achieving the full potential of data-driven manufacturing processes (Khang & Akhai, 2024).

26.5 OPTIMIZATION STRATEGIES

Now, let's explore strategies for optimizing data-transfer machine and cloud data platform integration.

26.5.1 ROBUST DATA ARCHITECTURE

Developing a robust data architecture is at the core of optimizing data integration. This architecture should encompass all aspects of data management, from ingestion to storage, processing, and retrieval. Below are steps on how to achieve it:

- **Data Ingestion:** Implement efficient mechanisms to collect data from various sources, ensuring that data arrives reliably and is properly time-stamped. Use standardized data formats and protocols to simplify ingestion.
- **Data Storage:** Choose appropriate data storage solutions, which may include relational databases, NoSQL databases, or cloud-based data warehouses. Prioritize scalability and redundancy to accommodate the growing volume of manufacturing data.
- **Data Processing:** Implement data processing pipelines that can transform and enrich incoming data in real-time. These pipelines may include data validation, cleansing, and feature engineering steps.
- **High Availability and Redundancy:** Leverage cloud-native services and technologies to ensure high availability and redundancy. Cloud platforms offer features such as automatic failover, data replication, and load balancing that enhance data architecture robustness.

26.5.2 EDGE COMPUTING

Edge computing plays a pivotal role in reducing latency, enhancing real-time decision-making, and offloading processing tasks from the cloud, as shown in Figure 26.9. Here's how to leverage it effectively:

- **Local Data Processing:** Edge devices installed on robots and production machines should preprocess data locally. This can involve basic tasks such as data filtering, aggregation, or even running lightweight ML models for immediate insights.

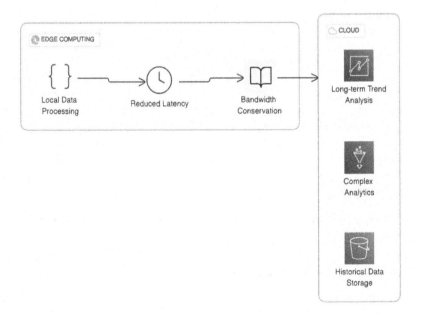

FIGURE 26.9 Edge computing.

- **Reduced Latency:** By processing data at the edge, you reduce the time it takes for critical decisions to be made. This is particularly crucial for tasks such as collision avoidance, where even milliseconds matter.
- **Bandwidth Conservation:** Offloading some processing tasks to the edge helps conserve bandwidth as less data needs to be transmitted to the cloud. This can be cost-effective, especially in scenarios with limited or expensive data connectivity.
- **Edge-Cloud Synergy:** Create a symbiotic relationship between edge devices and the cloud. While edge devices handle real-time tasks, the cloud can manage historical data storage, complex analytics, and long-term trend analysis.

26.5.3 Advanced Analytics

Advanced analytics, including ML and AI, can unlock the full potential of integrated data. Below are tips on how to harness the power of these technologies:

- **Predictive Maintenance:** Develop predictive maintenance models that use historical data to anticipate equipment failures. This proactive approach reduces downtime and extends the lifespan of machinery.
- **Anomaly Detection:** Implement anomaly detection algorithms to identify unusual patterns or deviations in data. This can be crucial for early detection of quality issues or process abnormalities.
- **Optimization Algorithms:** Utilize optimization algorithms to fine-tune manufacturing processes. These algorithms can help optimize production schedules, resource allocation, and energy consumption for improved efficiency.
- **Real-time Decision Support**: Integrate AI-powered decision support systems that assist human operators by providing real-time recommendations based on data analysis. These systems enhance decision-making accuracy and speed.

26.5.4 Continuous Improvement

Data integration is not a one-time effort but an ongoing process that requires continuous monitoring and refinement. Below are steps on how to ensure that your integrated systems remain at their best:

- **Monitoring and Alerts:** Implement robust monitoring tools that track the health and performance of integrated systems. Set up alerts to notify relevant personnel when issues arise, ensuring quick responses.
- **Regular Audits:** Conduct regular audits of integrated data to ensure data quality and integrity. Identify areas for improvement and establish corrective action plans.
- **Embrace Emerging Technologies:** Stay current with emerging technologies and industry best practices. The field of data integration is dynamic, with new tools and techniques continually emerging. Embrace these innovations to maintain a competitive edge.

- **Feedback Loops:** Establish feedback loops that involve end-users and operators. Their insights and feedback can inform improvements in data integration processes and lead to better-tailored solutions.

In conclusion, optimizing data-transfer machine and cloud data platform integration in industrial robotics is a multifaceted endeavor that involves creating a robust data architecture, leveraging edge computing, harnessing advanced analytics, and embracing continuous improvement. By adopting these strategies, organizations can harness the full potential of their integrated data systems, drive manufacturing efficiency, and remain agile in a rapidly evolving industrial landscape.

26.6   CASE STUDIES

Let's discuss some case studies in detail to understand how organizations have successfully applied optimization strategies for data integration in industrial robotics.

26.6.1   CASE STUDY 1: AUTOMOTIVE MANUFACTURING

26.6.1.1   Background

A prominent automotive manufacturer with a focus on quality and efficiency sought to enhance their robotic welding process. The challenge was to reduce defects, optimize welding parameters, and improve overall production efficiency.

26.6.1.2   Optimization Strategies Applied

- **Robust Data Architecture:** The manufacturer implemented a comprehensive data architecture that included data ingestion from welding robots, sensors, and quality control systems. This architecture allowed for real-time data processing and analysis.
- **Advanced Analytics:** Advanced analytics, including ML algorithms, were employed to analyze data from welding robots and sensors. Predictive maintenance models were developed to identify potential welding issues before they led to defects.
- **Continuous Improvement:** A culture of continuous improvement was fostered within the manufacturing team. Regular audits and feedback loops ensured that data quality and integration processes were continuously refined.

26.6.1.3   Results

The implementation of these strategies led to significant improvements discussed below and as shown in Figure 26.10:

- **Reduction in Defects:** The predictive maintenance models identified welding issues early, enabling timely adjustments and reducing defects by 15%.

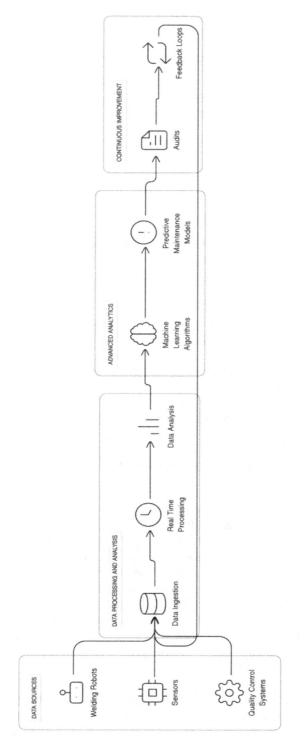

FIGURE 26.10 Automotive manufacturer with a focus on quality and efficiency.

- **Increase in Production Efficiency:** By optimizing welding parameters based on data analysis, the manufacturer achieved a 10% increase in overall production efficiency.
- **Cost Savings:** Reduced defects and improved efficiency resulted in substantial cost savings, making the manufacturing process more competitive.

26.6.2 CASE STUDY 2: ELECTRONICS ASSEMBLY

26.6.2.1 Background

A consumer electronics company specializing in assembly line production faced challenges related to production line efficiency. Their goal was to improve efficiency and product quality while reducing downtime.

26.6.2.2 Optimization Strategies Applied

- **Edge Computing:** The company implemented edge computing devices on their robotic assembly systems. These devices performed real-time data preprocessing, including quality checks, component placement verification, and error detection.
- **Cloud-Based Data Analytics:** Data from the edge devices was transmitted to a cloud-based data analytics platform. This platform performed in-depth analysis of assembly line data, identifying patterns, bottlenecks, and opportunities for improvement.
- **Continuous Improvement:** Regular performance monitoring and data-driven decision-making became integral to the company's operations. Feedback from the assembly line operators was incorporated into the continuous improvement process.

26.6.2.3 Results

The strategies employed yielded impressive results as follows:

- **Increased Efficiency:** The combination of edge computing for real-time monitoring and cloud-based data analytics for in-depth analysis resulted in a 20% increase in production line efficiency.
- **Quality Improvement:** Real-time quality checks reduced defects, improving product quality and reducing rework and warranty costs.
- **Downtime Reduction:** The ability to predict and prevent equipment failures through data analysis significantly reduced downtime, enhancing overall operational reliability.
- **Data-Driven Decision-Making:** By embracing data-driven decision-making, the company established a culture of continuous improvement and innovation, enabling them to stay competitive in the consumer electronics market, as shown in Figure 26.11.

The above case studies demonstrate the tangible benefits of optimizing data-transfer machine and cloud data platform integration in industrial robotics. By applying the right strategies and technologies, organizations can achieve remarkable

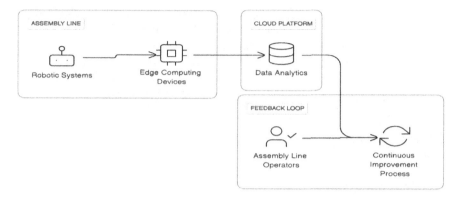

FIGURE 26.11 Challenges in assembly line production.

improvements in efficiency, product quality, and competitiveness. The success stories of the automotive manufacturer and consumer electronics company highlight the transformative potential of data integration in modern manufacturing (Khang & Rath et al., 2024).

26.7 FUTURE DIRECTIONS

Future directions and considerations for the integration of data-transfer machines and cloud data platforms in industrial robotics are discussed in detail below.

26.7.1 OVERCOMING DATA SILOS

26.7.1.1 Strategies for Breaking Down Data Silos within Organizations

Breaking down data silos within organizations is essential to harness the full potential of data integration, as shown in Figure 26.12. Here are strategies for achieving this:

- **Data Governance:** Implement robust data governance frameworks to standardize data definitions, access policies, and ownership. This ensures that data is treated as a valuable enterprise asset rather than being confined within individual departments.
- **Data Integration Platforms:** Invest in data integration platforms that allow data to flow seamlessly across various systems and departments. These platforms facilitate data-sharing while maintaining data quality and security.

FIGURE 26.12 Breaking down data silos within organizations.

- **Cross-Functional Teams:** Create cross-functional teams that comprise members from different departments, including IT, operations, and analytics. These teams can collaborate to identify data silos and devise strategies for data-sharing.
- **Data Culture:** Foster a data-driven culture within the organization. Encourage employees at all levels to use data for decision-making and problem-solving, promoting a mindset of collaboration and knowledge-sharing.

26.7.1.2 Interoperability Standards and Protocols

To ensure seamless data integration, organizations should adhere to interoperability standards and protocols:

- **Industry Standards:** Embrace industry-specific standards like OPC UA for industrial automation or HL7 for healthcare. These standards define common data formats and communication protocols, making integration more straightforward.
- **Application Programming Interfaces and Middleware:** Leverage APIs and middleware solutions to bridge disparate systems. These tools enable data exchange between legacy systems and modern platforms, promoting interoperability.

26.7.2 SECURITY AND COMPLIANCE

26.7.2.1 Evolving Cybersecurity Threats and Mitigation Measures

As data integration in industrial robotics advances, cybersecurity threats increase. Mitigating such threats is done following the below steps:

- **Cybersecurity Awareness:** Educate employees about cybersecurity best practices, including recognizing phishing attempts and maintaining strong passwords. Regular training and awareness programs are essential.
- **Endpoint Security:** Implement robust endpoint security solutions to protect devices and sensors connected to the network. This includes antivirus software, intrusion detection systems, and firmware updates.
- **Zero Trust Architecture:** Adopt a zero trust security model that assumes no trust, even within the organization's network. This model verifies every user and device attempting to access resources, enhancing security.
- **Incident Response Plans:** Develop comprehensive incident response plans that outline steps to take in case of a cybersecurity breach. A well-prepared response can minimize the impact of an attack.

26.7.2.2 Regulatory Developments and Industry Standards

Staying up-to-date on evolving regulations and industry standards in data security and compliance is important and can be done as follows:

- **Data Protection Regulations:** Comply with data protection regulations such as GDPR (General Data Protection Regulation) and CCPA (California Consumer Privacy Act) to ensure that sensitive data is handled lawfully and responsibly.

- **Industry Standards:** Adhere to industry-specific cybersecurity standards and certifications. For example, ISO 27001 certification validates that an organization's information security management system is robust.

26.7.3   Autonomous Robotics and Artificial Intelligence

26.7.3.1   Potential for Autonomous Decision-Making in Industrial Robotics

The integration of AI and autonomous decision-making capabilities into industrial robotics opens up the following possibilities:

- **Predictive Maintenance:** AI algorithms can predict when equipment is likely to fail, enabling proactive maintenance. This minimizes downtime and reduces maintenance costs.
- **Dynamic Process Optimization:** Autonomous robots equipped with AI can adapt to changing production demands and optimize processes in real-time. This flexibility enhances efficiency and resource utilization.
- **Cognitive Robots:** Cognitive robots with natural language processing (NLP) capabilities can interact with human operators more effectively. They can understand and respond to spoken instructions, making human–robot collaboration more intuitive.

26.7.3.2 Ethical Considerations and Human-Machine Collaboration

As robotics and AI become more autonomous, ethical considerations come to the forefront. Below are some ethics to keep in mind:

- **Ethical Frameworks:** Develop ethical frameworks that guide the behavior of autonomous robots. These frameworks should consider issues such as safety, transparency, accountability, and fairness in decision-making.
- **Human Oversight:** Ensure that there is human oversight of autonomous systems, especially in critical industries. Human operators should have the capability to intervene when necessary and override autonomous decisions.
- **Data Ethics:** Consider the ethical implications of the data collected and used by autonomous systems. Respect privacy rights and data protection principles when handling sensitive information.

The future of data-transfer machine and cloud data platform integration in industrial robotics is filled with exciting possibilities and complex challenges. Overcoming data silos, addressing cybersecurity threats, embracing autonomous capabilities, and navigating ethical considerations will be pivotal in realizing the full potential of these technologies. Organizations that adapt to these future directions will be well positioned to enhance manufacturing efficiency, competitiveness, and innovation in the dynamic landscape of industrial robotics (Khang & Rath et al., 2023).

26.8 CONCLUSION

The integration of industrial robotics with cloud-based data platforms and IoT technologies offers manufacturers an unprecedented opportunity to enhance manufacturing efficiency. Through case studies and a comprehensive literature review, we have demonstrated the substantial benefits of this integration, including improved quality, reduced costs, and enhanced competitiveness. However, it is crucial to address challenges related to data security, compliance, and data silos to fully realize these benefits. As technology continues to evolve, the future of industrial robotics promises even greater advances in efficiency and productivity, ultimately reshaping the landscape of modern manufacturing (Khang & Muthmainnah et al., 2023).

REFERENCES

Doriya, R., Chakraborty, P., & Nandi, G. C. (2012, December). Robotic services in cloud computing paradigm. In 2012 International Symposium on Cloud and Services Computing (pp. 80–83). IEEE. DOI: 10.1109/ISCOS.2012.24

Givehchi, O., Trsek, H., & Jasperneite, J. (2013, September). Cloud computing for industrial automation systems—A comprehensive overview. In 2013 IEEE 18th Conference on Emerging Technologies & Factory Automation (ETFA) (pp. 1–4). IEEE. DOI: 10.1109/ETFA.2013.6648080

Hegazy, T., & Hefeeda, M., (2014). Industrial automation as a cloud service. IEEE Transactions on Parallel and Distributed Systems, 26(10), 2750–2763. doi: 10.1109/TPDS.2014.2359894

Horn, C., & Krüger, J. (2016, September). Feasibility of connecting machinery and robots to industrial control services in the cloud. In 2016 IEEE 21st International Conference on Emerging Technologies and Factory Automation (ETFA) (pp. 1–4). IEEE. DOI: 10.1109/ETFA.2016.7733661

Hu, G., Tay, W. P., & Wen, Y., (2012). Cloud robotics: Architecture, challenges and applications. IEEE Network, 26(3), 21–28. doi: 10.1109/MNET.2012.6201212

Jordan, S., Haidegger, T., Kovács, L., Felde, I., & Rudas, I. (2013, July). The rising prospects of cloud robotic applications. In 2013 IEEE 9th International Conference on Computational Cybernetics (ICCC) (pp. 327–332). IEEE. DOI: 10.1109/ICCCyb.2013.6617612

Khang, A, & Akhai, S., "Green Intelligent and Sustainable Manufacturing: Key Advancements, Benefits, Challenges, and Applications for Transforming Industry," Machine Vision and Industrial Robotics in Manufacturing: Approaches, Technologies, and Applications. (1st Ed.) (2024). CRC Press. https://doi.org/10.1201/9781003438137-22

Khang, A., Hajimahmud, V. A., Ali, R. N., Hahanov, V., Avramovic, Z., & Triwiyanto, "The Role of Machine Vision in Manufacturing and Industrial Revolution 4.0," Machine Vision and Industrial Robotics in Manufacturing: Approaches, Technologies, and Applications. (1st Ed.) (2024a). CRC Press. https://doi.org/10.1201/9781003438137-1

Khang, A., Hajimahmud, V. A., Alyar, A. V., Etibar, M. K., Soltanaga, V. A., & Niu, Y., "Application of Industrial Robotics in Manufacturing," Machine Vision and Industrial Robotics in Manufacturing: Approaches, Technologies, and Applications. (1st Ed.) (2024b). CRC Press. https://doi.org/10.1201/9781003438137-5

Khang, A., Muthmainnah, M, Seraj, Prodhan Mahbub Ibna, Yakin, Ahmad Al, Obaid, Ahmad J., & Panda, Manas Ranjan. "AI-Aided Teaching Model for the Education 5.0 Ecosystem," AI-Based Technologies and Applications in the Era of the Metaverse. (1st Ed.) (2023). Page (83–104). IGI Global Press. https://doi.org/10.4018/978-1-6684-8851-5.ch004

Khang, A., Rath, K. C., Satapathy, S. K., Kumar, A., Das, S. R., & Panda, M. R. "Enabling the Future of Manufacturing: Integration of Robotics and IoT to Smart Factory Infrastructure in Industry 4.0," *AI-Based Technologies and Applications in the Era of the Metaverse*. (1st Ed.) (2023). Page (25–50). IGI Global Press. https://doi.org/ 10.4018/978-1-6684-8851-5.ch002

Khang, A., Rath, K. C., Satapathy, S. K., Kumar, A., & Kar, S., "Robotic Process Automation (RPA) Applications and Tools for Manufacturing Sector," *Machine Vision and Industrial Robotics in Manufacturing: Approaches, Technologies, and Applications*. (1st Ed.) (2024). CRC Press. https://doi.org/10.1201/9781003438137-14

Khang, A., Shah, V., & Rani, S., *AI-Based Technologies and Applications in the Era of the Metaverse*. (1st Ed.) (2023). IGI Global Press. https://doi.org/10.4018/978-1-6684-8851-5

Lins, R. G., & Givigi, S. N., (2021). Cooperative robotics and machine learning for smart manufacturing: Platform design and trends within the context of industrial internet of things. IEEE Access, 9, 95444–95455. doi: 10.1109/ACCESS.2021.3094374

Mohanarajah, G., Hunziker, D., D'Andrea, R., & Waibel, M., (2014). Rapyuta: A cloud robotics platform. IEEE Transactions on Automation Science and Engineering, 12(2), 481–493. doi: 10.1109/TASE.2014.2329556

Panicucci, S., Nikolakis, N., Cerquitelli, T., Ventura, F., Proto, S., Macii, E., & Andolina, S., (2020). A cloud-to-edge approach to support predictive analytics in robotics industry. Electronics, 9(3), 492. https://doi.org/10.3390/electronics9030492

Shakya, D. S., (2020). Survey on cloud based robotics architecture, challenges and applications. Journal of Ubiquitous Computing and Communication Technologies, 2(1), 10–18. https://doi.org/10.36548/jucct.2020.1.002

Shu, B., Arnarson, H., Solvang, B., Kaarlela, T., & Pieskä, S., (2022, January). Platform independent interface for programming of industrial robots. In 2022 IEEE/SICE International Symposium on System Integration (SII) (pp. 797–802). IEEE. DOI: 10.1109/SII52469.2022.9708905

Soni, D., & Kumar, N., (2022). Machine learning techniques in emerging cloud computing integrated paradigms: A survey and taxonomy. Journal of Network and Computer Applications, 205, 103419. https://doi.org/10.1016/j.jnca.2022.103419

Vick, A., Vonásek, V., Pěnička, R., & Krüger, J. (2015, July). Robot control as a service— towards cloud-based motion planning and control for industrial robots. In 2015 10th International Workshop on Robot Motion and Control (RoMoCo) (pp. 33–39). IEEE. DOI: 10.1109/RoMoCo.2015.7219710

Wang, S., Zhang, C., Liu, C., Li, D., & Tang, H., (2017). Cloud-assisted interaction and negotiation of industrial robots for the smart factory. Computers & Electrical Engineering, 63, 66–78. https://doi.org/10.1016/j.compeleceng.2017.05.025

Index

Printed in the United States
by Baker & Taylor Publisher Services